SAFETY SYMBOLS	HAZARD	EXAMPLES	PRECAUTION	REMEDY
DISPOSAL 	Special disposal procedures need to be followed.	certain chemicals, living organisms	Do not dispose of these materials in the sink or trash can.	Dispose of wastes as directed by your teacher.
BIOLOGICAL 	Organisms or other biological materials that might be harmful to humans	bacteria, fungi, blood, unpreserved tissues, plant materials	Avoid skin contact with these materials. Wear mask or gloves.	Notify your teacher if you suspect contact with material. Wash hands thoroughly.
EXTREME TEMPERATURE 	Objects that can burn skin by being too cold or too hot	boiling liquids, hot plates, dry ice, liquid nitrogen	Use proper protection when handling.	Go to your teacher for first aid.
SHARP OBJECT 	Use of tools or glassware that can easily puncture or slice skin	razor blades, pins, scalpels, pointed tools, dissecting probes, broken glass	Practice common-sense behavior and follow guidelines for use of the tool.	Go to your teacher for first aid.
FUME 	Possible danger to respiratory tract from fumes	ammonia, acetone, nail polish remover, heated sulfur, moth balls	Make sure there is good ventilation. Never smell fumes directly. Wear a mask.	Leave foul area and notify your teacher immediately.
ELECTRICAL 	Possible danger from electrical shock or burn	improper grounding, liquid spills, short circuits, exposed wires	Double-check setup with teacher. Check condition of wires and apparatus.	Do not attempt to fix electrical problems. Notify your teacher immediately.
IRRITANT 	Substances that can irritate the skin or mucous membranes of the respiratory tract	pollen, moth balls, steel wool, fiberglass, potassium permanganate	Wear dust mask and gloves. Practice extra care when handling these materials.	Go to your teacher for first aid.
CHEMICAL 	Chemicals that can react with and destroy tissue and other materials	bleaches such as hydrogen peroxide; acids such as sulfuric acid, hydrochloric acid; bases such as ammonia, sodium hydroxide	Wear goggles, gloves, and an apron.	Immediately flush the affected area with water and notify your teacher.
TOXIC 	Substance may be poisonous if touched, inhaled, or swallowed	mercury, many metal compounds, iodine, poinsettia plant parts	Follow your teacher's instructions.	Always wash hands thoroughly after use. Go to your teacher for first aid.
OPEN FLAME 	Open flame may ignite flammable chemicals, loose clothing, or hair	alcohol, kerosene, potassium permanganate, hair, clothing	Tie back hair. Avoid wearing loose clothing. Avoid open flames when using flammable chemicals. Be aware of locations of fire safety equipment.	Notify your teacher immediately. Use fire safety equipment if applicable.

Eye Safety
Proper eye protection should be worn at all times by anyone performing or observing science activities.

Clothing Protection
This symbol appears when substances could stain or burn clothing.

Animal Safety
This symbol appears when safety of animals and students must be ensured.

Radioactivity
This symbol appears when radioactive materials are used.

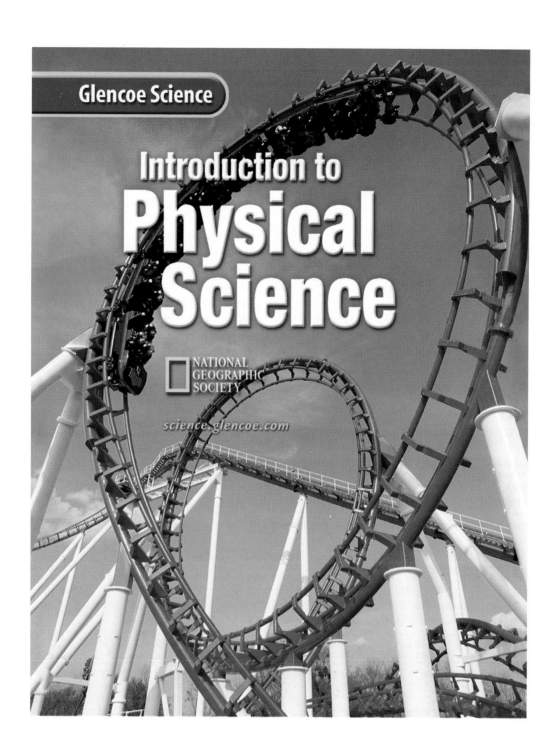

Glencoe Science

Introduction to Physical Science

NATIONAL GEOGRAPHIC SOCIETY

science.glencoe.com

New York, New York   Columbus, Ohio   Woodland Hills, California   Peoria, Illinois

Glencoe Science

Introduction to Physical Science

Student Edition
Teacher Wraparound Edition
Interactive Teacher Edition CD-ROM
Interactive Lesson Planner CD-ROM
Lesson Plans
Content Outline for Teaching
Dinah Zike's Teaching Science with Foldables
Directed Reading for Content Mastery
Foldables: Reading and Study Skills
Assessment
- *Chapter Review*
- *Chapter Tests*
- *ExamView Pro Test Bank Software*
- *Assessment Transparencies*
- *Performance Assessment in the Science Classroom*
- *The Princeton Review Standardized Test Practice Booklet*

Directed Reading for Content Mastery in Spanish
Spanish Resources
English/Spanish Guided Reading Audio Program
Reinforcement
Enrichment
Activity Worksheets
Section Focus Transparencies
Teaching Transparencies
Laboratory Activities
Science Inquiry Labs
Critical Thinking/Problem Solving
Reading and Writing Skill Activities
Mathematics Skill Activities
Cultural Diversity
Laboratory Management and Safety in the Science Classroom
MindJogger Videoquizzes and Teacher Guide
Interactive CD-ROM with Presentation Builder
Vocabulary PuzzleMaker Software
Cooperative Learning in the Science Classroom
Environmental Issues in the Science Classroom
Home and Community Involvement
Using the Internet in the Science Classroom

"Study Tip," "Test-Taking Tip," and "Test Practice" features in this book were written by The Princeton Review, the nation's leader in test preparation. Through its association with McGraw-Hill, The Princeton Review offers the best way to help students excel on standardized assessments.

The Princeton Review is not affiliated with Princeton University or Educational Testing Service.

Glencoe/McGraw-Hill

A Division of The ***McGraw-Hill*** *Companies*

Cover Images: A ride on this roller coaster lasts for about one minute and 20 seconds and reaches a speed of more than 80 km/h.

Send all inquiries to:
Glencoe/McGraw-Hill
8787 Orion Place
Columbus, OH 43240

ISBN 0-07-826880-X
Printed in the United States of America.
7 8 9 10 071/043 06

Authors

National Geographic Society
Education Department
Washington, DC

Cathy Ezrailson
Science Department Head
Academy for Science and Health Professions
Conroe, Texas

Nicolas Hainen
Chemistry/Physics Teacher, retired
Worthington City Schools
Worthington, Ohio

Patricia Horton
Mathematics and Science Teacher
Summit Intermediate School
Etiwanda, California

Deborah Lillie
Math and Science Writer
Sudbury, Massachusetts

Thomas McCarthy, PhD
Science Department Chair
St. Edward's School
Vero Beach, Florida

Dinah Zike
Educational Consultant
Dinah-Might Activities, Inc.
San Antonio, Texas

Eric Werwa, PhD
Department of Physics and Astronomy
Otterbein College
Westerville, Ohio

Margaret K. Zorn
Science Writer
Yorktown, Virginia

Series Reading Consultants

Elizabeth Babich
Special Education Teacher
Mashpee Public Schools
Mashpee, Connecticut

Barry Barto
Special Education Teacher
John F. Kennedy Elementary
Manistee, Michigan

Carol A. Senf
Associate Professor of English
Georgia Institute of Technology
Atlanta, Georgia

Rachel Swaters
Science Teacher
Rolla Middle School
Rolla, Missouri

Nancy Woodson, PhD
Professor of English
Otterbein College
Westerville, Ohio

Series Math Consultants

Michael Hopper, DEng
Manager of Aircraft Certification
Raytheon Company
Greenville, Texas

Teri Willard, EdD
Department of Mathematics
Montana State University
Belgrade, Montana

Content Consultants

Alan Bross, PhD
High-Energy Physicist
Fermilab
Batavia, Illinois

Jack Cooper
Adjunct Faculty Math and Science
Navarro College
Corsicana, Texas

Lisa McGaw
Science Teacher
Hereford High School
Hereford, Texas

Madelaine Meek
Physics Consultant
Editor
Lebanon, Ohio

Carl Zorn, PhD
Staff Scientist
Jefferson Laboratory
Newport News, Virginia

Series Safety Consultants

Malcolm Cheney, PhD
OSHA Chemical Safety Officer
Hall High School
West Hartford, Connecticut

Aileen Duc, PhD
Science II Teacher
Hendrick Middle School
Plano, Texas

Sandra West, PhD
Associate Professor of Biology
Southwest Texas State University
San Marcos, Texas

Series Activity Testers

José Luis Alvarez, PhD
Math and Science Mentor Teacher
El Paso, Texas

Nerma Coats Henderson
Teacher
Pickerington Jr. High School
Pickerington, Ohio

Mary Helen Mariscal-Cholka
Science Teacher
William D. Slider Middle School
El Paso, Texas

José Alberto Marquez
TEKS for Leaders Trainer
El Paso, Texas

Science Kit and Boreal Laboratories
Tonawanda, New York

Reviewers

Desiree Bishop
Baker High School
Mobile, Alabama

Nora M. Prestinari Burchett
Saint Luke School
McLean, Virginia

Anthony DiSipio
Octorana Middle School
Atglen, Pennsylvania

Sandra Everhart
Honeysuckle Middle School
Dothan, Alabama

George Gabb
Great Bridge Middle School
Chesapeake, Virginia

Maria Kelly
St. Leo School
Fairfax, Virginia

Eddie K. Lindsay
Vansant Middle School
Grundy, Virginia

H. Keith Lucas
Stewart Middle School
Fort Defiance, Virginia

Linda Melcher
Woodmont Middle School
Piedmont, South Carolina

Annette Parrott
Lakeside High School
Atlanta, Georgia

Pam Starnes
North Richland Middle School
Fort Worth, Texas

Clabe Webb
Sterling City High School
Sterling City, Texas

Contents in Brief

UNIT 1 The Nature of Science—2

CHAPTER 1 The Nature of Science—4

CHAPTER 2 Measurement—40

UNIT 2 Matter—70

Atoms, Elements, and the Periodic Table—72

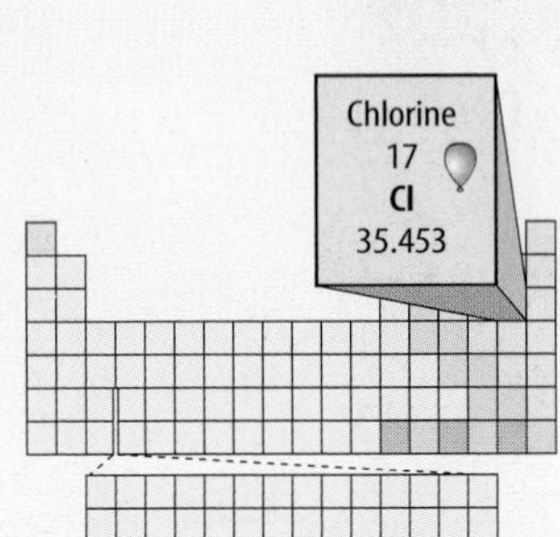

States of Matter—102

Properties and Changes of Matter—134

UNIT 3 Motion and Forces—162

CHAPTER 6 Motion and Momentum—164

CHAPTER 7 Force and Newton's Laws—192

UNIT 4 Energy—224

CHAPTER 10

Thermal Energy—284

UNIT 5

Waves, Sound, and Light—312

CHAPTER 11

Waves—314

UNIT 6 Electricity and Magnetism—436

CHAPTER 15 Electricity—438

CHAPTER 16 Magnetism—468

Interdisciplinary Connections

NATIONAL GEOGRAPHIC Unit Openers

NATIONAL GEOGRAPHIC VISUALIZING

TIME SCIENCE AND Society

TIME SCIENCE AND HISTORY

Oops! Accidents in SCIENCE

Science Stats

Activities

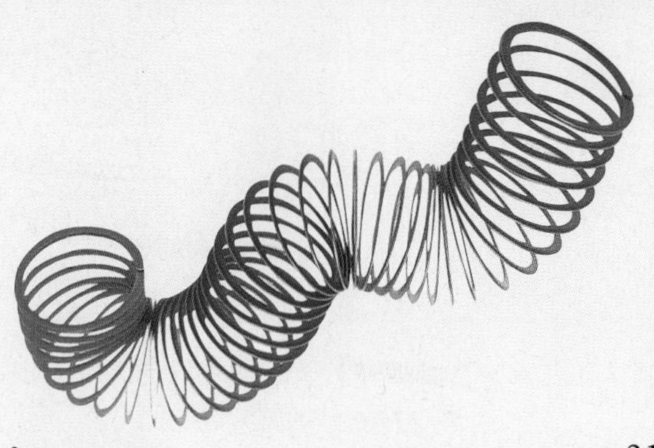

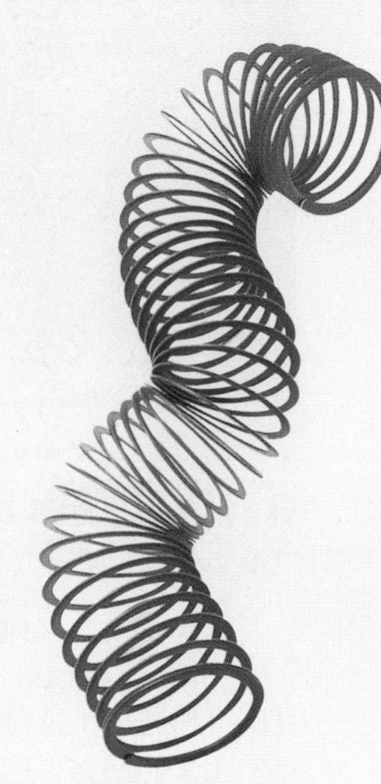

Full Period Labs

Mini
LAB

Activities

Explore Activity

Problem-Solving Activities

Math Skills Activities

Skill Builder Activities

Science

Activities

Math

Technology

Science INTEGRATION

SCIENCE *Online*

THE PRINCETON REVIEW

UNIT 1

The Nature of Science

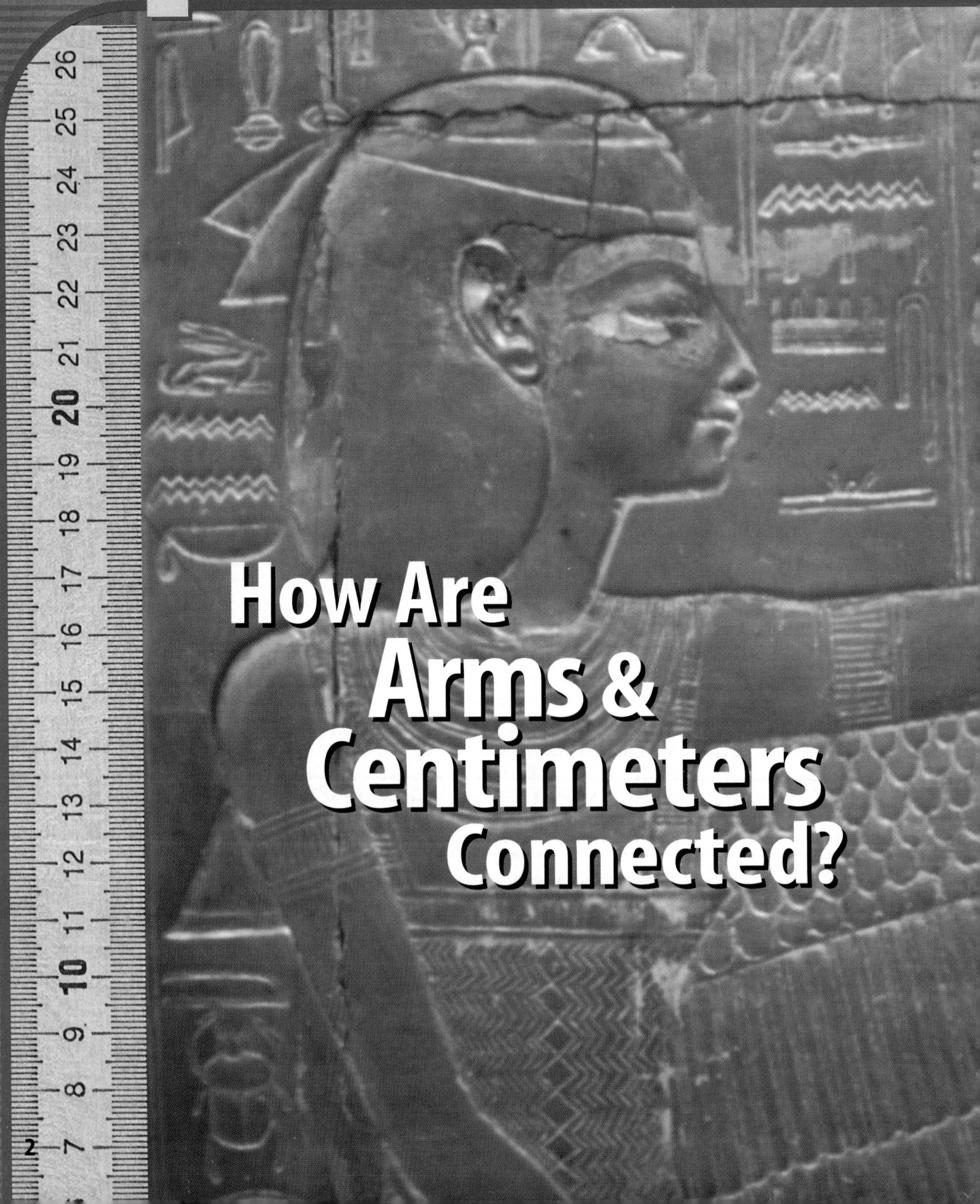

How Are Arms & Centimeters Connected?

About 5,000 years ago, the Egyptians developed one of the earliest recorded units of measurement—the cubit, which was based on the length of the arm from elbow to fingertip. The Egyptian measurement system probably influenced later systems, many of which also were based on body parts such as arms and feet. Such systems, however, could be problematic, since arms and feet vary in length from one person to another. Moreover, each country had its own system, which made it hard for people from different countries to share information. The need for a precise, universal measurement system eventually led to the adoption of the meter as the basic international unit of length. A meter is defined as the distance that light travels in a vacuum in a certain fraction of a second—a distance that never varies. Meters are divided into smaller units called centimeters, which are seen on the rulers here.

SCIENCE CONNECTION

MEASUREMENT SYSTEMS Ancient systems of measurement had their flaws, but they paved the way for the more exact and uniform systems used today. Devise your own measurement system based on parts of your body (for example, the length of your hand or the width of your shoulders) or common objects in your classroom or home. Give names to your units of measurement. Then calculate the width and height of a doorway using one or more of your units.

CHAPTER 1

The Nature of Science

An important part of science is asking questions. Over time, scientists observed an unusual behavior among humpback whales and wondered why they did it. Through scientific investigations, they learned that the humpbacks work together to get food. They swim in circles and blow bubbles. This makes a bubble net that traps small fish and krill—tiny shrimplike animals. Then the whales can swoop up mouthfuls of food.

What do you think?

Science Journal Look at the picture below with a classmate. Discuss what you think this is. Here's a hint: *Dinner is served.* Write your answer or best guess in your Science Journal.

Gravity is a familiar natural force. It keeps you anchored on Earth, but how does it work? Scientists learn about gravity and other concepts by making observations. Noticing things is how scientists start any study of nature. Do the activity below to see how gravity affects objects.

Observe how gravity accelerates objects

1. Collect three identical, unsharpened pencils.
2. Tape two of the pencils together.
3. Hold all the pencils at the same height, as high as you can. Drop them together and observe what happens as they fall.

Observe

Did the single pencil fall faster or slower than the pair? Predict in your Science Journal what would happen if you taped 30 pencils together and dropped them at the same time as you dropped a single pencil.

Before You Read

Making a Know-Want-Learn Study Fold **Make the following Foldable to help you identify what you already know and what you want to know about science.**

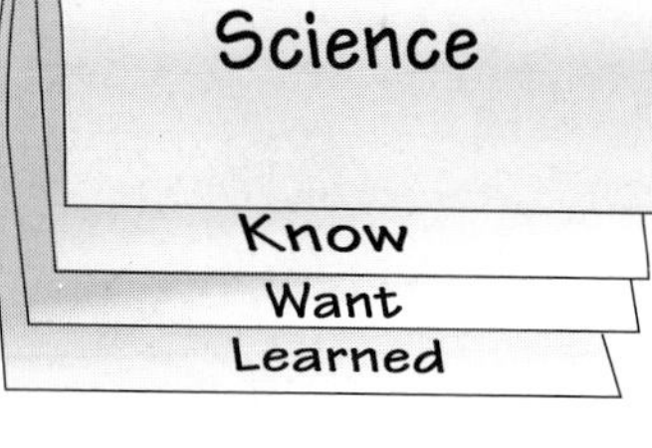

1. Stack two sheets of paper in front of you so the short side of both sheets is at the top.
2. Slide the top sheet up so that about 4 cm of the bottom sheet show.
3. Fold both sheets top to bottom to form four tabs and staple along the topfold, as shown.
4. Label the top flap *Science.* Then, label the other flaps *Know, Want,* and *Learned,* as shown. Before you read the chapter, write what you know about science on the *Know* tab and what you want to know on the *Want* tab.
5. As you read the chapter, list the things you learn about science on the *Learned* tab.

SECTION

What is science?

As You Read

What You'll Learn

- **Define** science and identify questions that science cannot answer.
- **Compare and contrast** theories and laws.
- **Identify** a system and its components.
- **Identify** the three main branches of science.

Vocabulary

science
scientific theory
scientific law
system
life science
Earth science
physical science
technology

Why It's Important

Science can be used to learn more about the world you live in.

Learning About the World

When you think of a scientist, do you imagine a person in a laboratory surrounded by charts, graphs, glass bottles, and bubbling test tubes? It might surprise you to learn that anyone who tries to learn something about the world is a scientist. **Science** is a way of learning more about the natural world. Scientists want to know why, how, or when something occurred. This learning process usually begins by keeping your eyes open and asking questions about what you see.

Asking Questions Scientists ask many questions, too. How do things work? What do things look like? What are they made of? Why does something take place? Science can attempt to answer many questions about the natural world, but some questions cannot be answered by science. Look at the situations in **Figure 1.** Who should you vote for? What does this poem mean? Who is your best friend? Questions about art, politics, personal preference, or morality can't be answered by science. Science can't tell you what is right, wrong, good, or bad.

Figure 1
Some questions about topics such as politics, literature, and art cannot be answered by science.

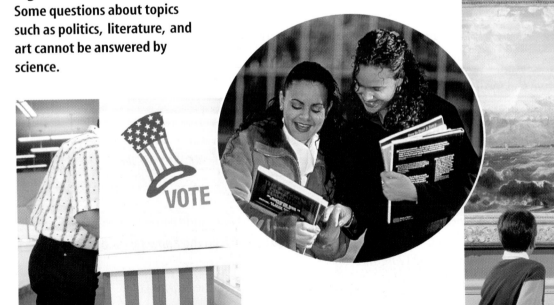

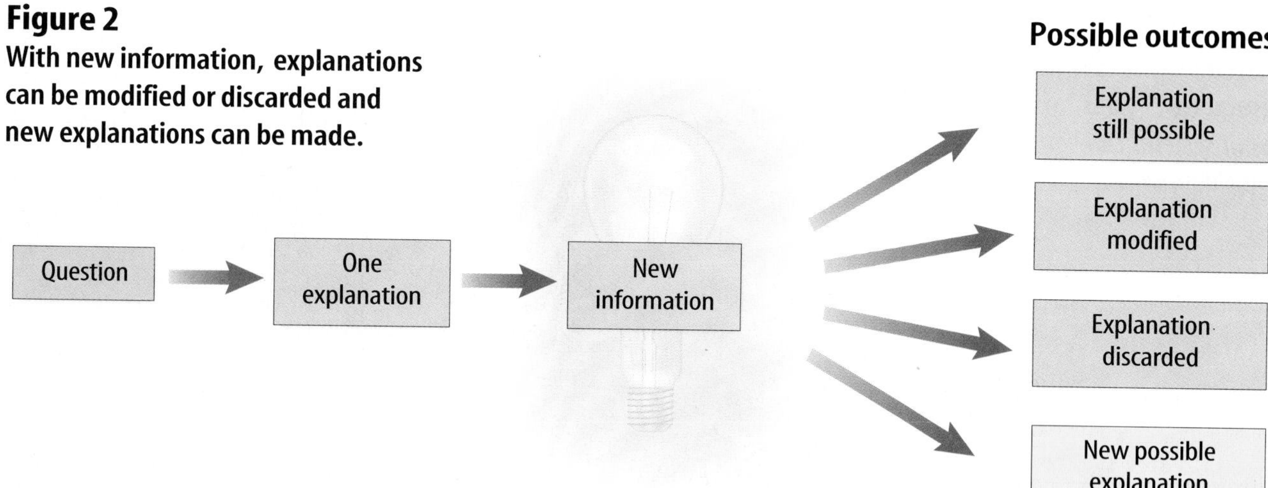

Figure 2
With new information, explanations can be modified or discarded and new explanations can be made.

Possible Explanations If learning about your world begins with asking questions, can science provide answers to these questions? Science can answer a question only with the information available at the time. Any answer is uncertain because people will never know everything about the world around them. With new knowledge, they might realize that some of the old explanations no longer fit the new information. As shown in **Figure 2,** some observations might force scientists to look at old ideas and think of new explanations. Science can only provide possible explanations.

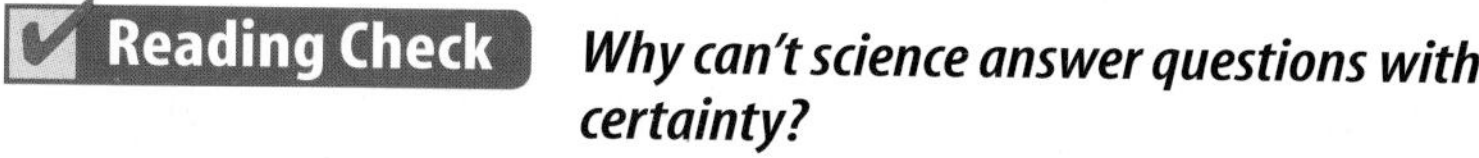
Reading Check *Why can't science answer questions with certainty?*

Scientific Theories An attempt to explain a pattern observed repeatedly in the natural world is called a **scientific theory.** Theories are not simply guesses or someone's opinions, nor are theories only vague ideas. Theories in science must be supported by observations and results from many investigations. They are the best explanations that have been found so far. However, theories can change. As new data become available, scientists evaluate how the new data fit the theory. If enough new data do not support the theory, the theory can be changed to fit the new observations better.

Scientific Laws A rule that describes a pattern in nature is a **scientific law.** For an observation to become a scientific law, it must be observed repeatedly. The law then stands until someone makes observations that do not follow the law. A law helps you predict that an apple dropped from arm's length will always fall to Earth. The law, however, does not explain why gravity exists or how it works. A law, unlike a theory, does not attempt to explain why something happens. It simply describes a pattern.

Figure 3
Systems are a collection of structures, cycles, and processes.
What systems can you identify in this classroom?

Systems in Science

Scientists can study many different things in nature. Some might study how the human body works or how planets move around the Sun. Others might study the energy carried in a lightning bolt. What do all of these things have in common? All of them are systems. A **system** is a collection of structures, cycles, and processes that relate to and interact with each other. The structures, cycles, and processes are the parts of a system, just like your stomach is one of the structures of your digestive system.

Reading Check *What is a system?*

Systems are not found just in science. Your school is a system with structures such as the school building, the tables and chairs, you, your teacher, the school bell, your pencil, and many other things. **Figure 3** shows some of these structures. Your school day also has cycles. Your daily class schedule and the calendar of holidays are examples of cycles. Many processes are at work during the school day. When you take a test, your teacher has a process. You might be asked to put your books and papers away and get out a pencil before the test is distributed. When the time is over, you are told to put your pencil down and pass your test to the front of the room.

Parts of a System Interact In a system, structures, cycles, and processes interact. Your daily schedule influences where you go and what time you go. The clock shows the teacher when the test is complete, and you couldn't complete the test without a pencil.

Classify Parts of a System

Procedure

Think about how your school's cafeteria is run. Consider the physical structure of the cafeteria. How many people run it? Where does the food come from? How is it prepared? Where does it go? What other parts of the cafeteria system are necessary?

Analysis

Classify the parts of your school cafeteria's system as structures, cycles, or processes.

Parts of a Whole All systems are made up of other systems. For example, you are part of your school. The human body is a system—within your body are other systems. Your school is part of a system—district, state, and national. You have your regional school district. Your district is part of a statewide school system. Scientists often break down problems by studying just one part of a system. A scientist might want to learn about how construction of buildings affects the ecosystem. Because an ecosystem has many parts, one scientist might study a particular animal, and another might study the effect of construction on plant life.

SCIENCE Online

Research Visit the Glencoe Science Web site at **science.glencoe.com** for information on Dian Fossey's studies. Write a summary of your research in your Science Journal.

The Branches of Science

Science often is divided into three main categories, or branches—life science, Earth science, and physical science. Each branch asks questions about different kinds of systems.

Life Science The study of living systems and the ways in which they interact is called **life science.** Life scientists attempt to answer questions like "How do whales navigate the ocean?" and "How do vaccines prevent disease?" Life scientists can study living organisms, where they live, and how they interact. Dian Fossey, **Figure 4,** was a life scientist who studied gorillas, their habitat, and their behaviors.

People who work in the health field know a lot about the life sciences. Physicians, nurses, physical therapists, dietitians, medical researchers, and others focus on the systems of the human body. Some other examples of careers that use life science include biologists, zookeepers, botanists, farmers, and beekeepers.

Figure 4
Over a span of 18 years, life scientist Dian Fossey spent much of her time observing mountain gorillas in Rwanda, Africa. She was able to interact with them as she learned about their behavior.

Figure 5
Scientists study a wide range of subjects.

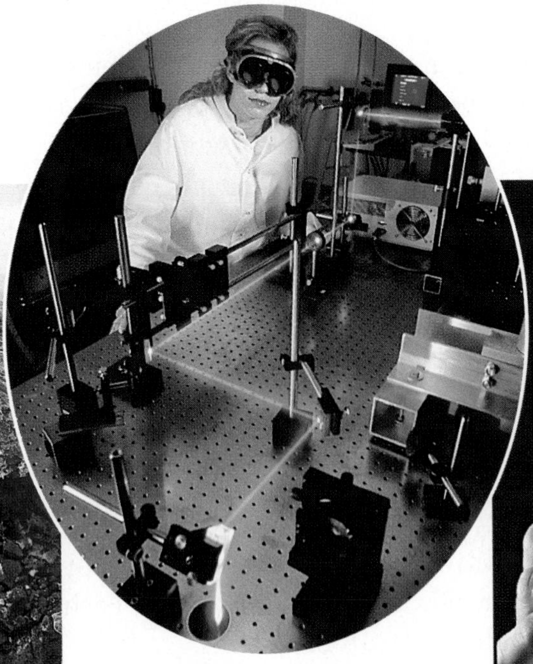

A These volcanologists are studying the temperature of the lava flowing from a volcano.

B This chemist is studying the light emitted by certain compounds.

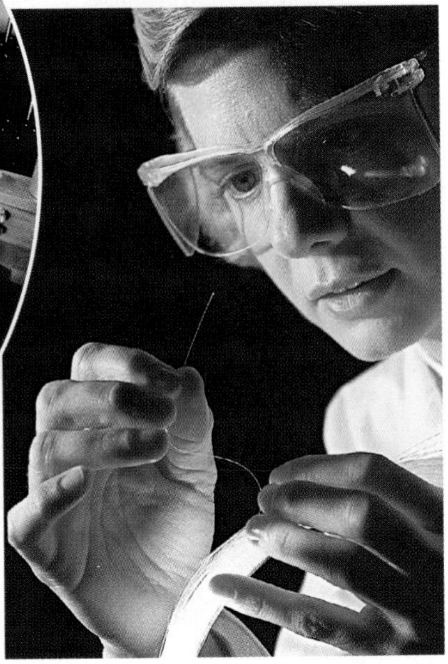

C This physicist is studying light as it travels through optical fibers.

Earth Science The study of Earth systems and the systems in space is **Earth science.** It includes the study of nonliving things such as rocks, soil, clouds, rivers, oceans, planets, stars, meteors, and black holes. Earth science also covers the weather and climate systems that affect Earth. Earth scientists ask questions like "How can an earthquake be detected?" or "Is water found on other planets?" They make maps and investigate how geologic features formed on land and in the oceans. They also use their knowledge to search for fuels and minerals. Meteorologists study weather and climate. Geologists study rocks and geologic features. **Figure 5A** shows a volcanologist—a person who studies volcanoes—measuring the temperature of lava.

Reading Check *What do Earth scientists study?*

Physical Science The study of matter and energy is **physical science.** Matter is anything that takes up space and has mass. The ability to cause change in matter is energy. Living and nonliving systems are made of matter. Examples include plants, animals, rocks, the atmosphere, and the water in oceans, lakes, and rivers. Physical science can be divided into two general fields—chemistry and physics. Chemistry is the study of matter and the interactions of matter. Physics is the study of energy and its ability to change matter. **Figures 5B** and **5C** show physical scientists at work.

Careers Chemists ask questions such as "How can I make plastic stronger?" or "What can I do to make aspirin more effective?" Physicists might ask other types of questions, such as "How does light travel through glass fibers?" or "How can humans harness the energy of sunlight for their energy needs?"

Many careers are based on the physical sciences. Physicists and chemists are some obvious careers. Ultrasound and X-ray technicians working in the medical field study physical science because they study the energy in ultrasound or X rays and how it affects a living system.

Science and Technology Although learning the answers to scientific questions is important, these answers do not help people directly unless they can be applied in some way. **Technology** is the practical use of science, or applied science, as illustrated in **Figure 6.** Engineers apply science to develop technology. The study of how to use the energy of sunlight is science. Using this knowledge to create solar panels is technology. The study of the behavior of light as it travels through thin, glass, fiber-optic wires is science. The use of optical fibers to transmit information is technology. A scientist uses science to study how the skin of a shark repels water. The application of this knowledge to create a material that helps swimmers slip through the water faster is technology.

Figure 6
Solar-powered cars and the swimsuits worn in the Olympics are examples of technology—the application of science.

Section  Assessment

1. What is science?
2. Compare scientific theory and scientific law. Explain how a scientific theory can change.
3. What are the components of a system?
4. Name the three main branches of science.
5. **Think Critically** List two questions that can be answered by science and one that can't be answered by science. Explain.

Skill Builder Activities

6. **Comparing and Contrasting** Compare and contrast life science and physical science. **For more help, refer to the Science Skill Handbook.**
7. **Communicating** In your Science Journal, describe how science and technology are related. **For more help, refer to the Science Skill Handbook.**

Science in Action

As You Read

What You'll Learn

- **Identify** some skills scientists use.
- **Define** hypothesis.
- **Recognize** the difference between observation and inference.

Vocabulary

hypothesis
infer
controlled experiment
variable
constant

Why It's Important

Science can be used to learn more about the world you live in.

Science Skills

You know that science involves asking questions, but how does asking questions lead to learning? Because no single way to gain knowledge exists, a scientist doesn't start with step one, then go to step two, and so on. Instead, scientists have a huge collection of skills from which to choose. Some of these skills include thinking, observing, predicting, investigating, researching, modeling, measuring, analyzing, and inferring. Science also can advance with luck and creativity.

Science Methods Investigations often follow a general pattern. As illustrated in **Figure 7,** most investigations begin by seeing something and then asking a question about what was observed. Scientists often research by talking with other scientists. They read books and scientific magazines to learn as much as they can about what is already known about their question. Usually, scientists state a possible explanation for their observation. To collect more information, scientists almost always make more observations. They might build a model of what they study or they might perform investigations. Often, they do both. How might you combine some of these skills in an investigation?

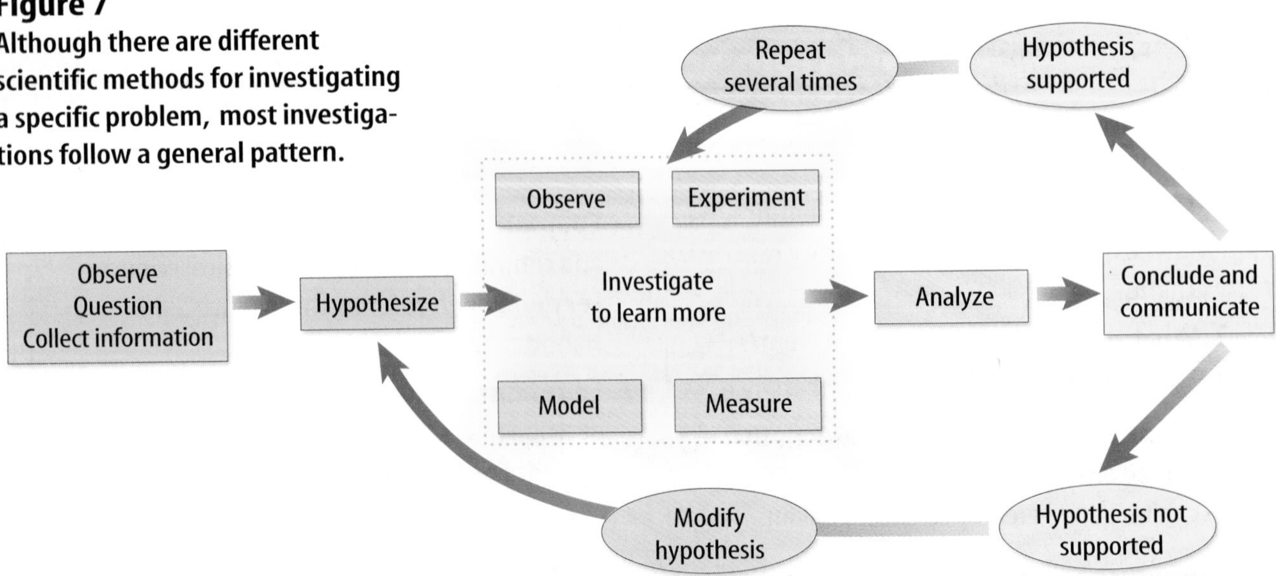

Figure 7
Although there are different scientific methods for investigating a specific problem, most investigations follow a general pattern.

Figure 8
Investigations often begin by making observations and asking questions.

Questioning and Observing Ms. Clark placed a sealed shoe box on the table at the front of the laboratory. Everyone in the class noticed the box. Within seconds the questions flew. "What's in the box?" "Why is it there?"

Ms. Clark said she would like the class to see how they used some science skills without even realizing it.

"I think that she wants us to find out what's in it," Isabelle said to Marcus.

"Can we touch it?" asked Marcus.

"It's up to you," Ms. Clark said.

Marcus picked up the box and turned it over a few times.

"It's not heavy," Marcus observed. "Whatever is inside slides around." He handed the box to Isabelle.

Isabelle shook the box. The class heard the object strike the sides of the box. With every few shakes, the class heard a metallic sound. The box was passed around for each student to make observations and write them in his or her Science Journal. Some observations are shown in **Figure 8.**

Taking a Guess "I think it's a pair of scissors," said Marcus.

"Aren't scissors lighter than this?" asked Isabelle, while shaking the box. "I think it's a stapler."

"What makes you think so?" asked Ms. Clark.

"Well, staplers are small enough to fit inside a shoe box, and it seems to weigh about the same," said Isabelle.

"We can hear metal when we shake it," said Enrique.

"So, you are guessing that a stapler is in the box?"

"Yes," they agreed.

"You just stated a hypothesis," exclaimed Ms. Clark.

"A what?" asked Marcus.

Life Science INTEGRATION

Some naturalists study the living world, using mostly their observational skills. They observe animals and plants in their natural environment, taking care not to disturb the organisms they are studying. Make observations of organisms in a nearby park or backyard. Record your observations in your Science Journal.

Forming a Hypothesis

Procedure

1. Fill a large **pot** with **water.** Drop an unopened **can of diet soda** and an unopened **can of regular soda** into the pot of water and observe what each can does.
2. In your Science Journal, make a list of the possible explanations for your observation. Select the best explanation and write a hypothesis.
3. Read the nutritional facts on the back of each can and compare their ingredients.
4. Revise your hypothesis based on this new information.

Analysis

1. What did you observe when you placed the cans in the water?
2. How did the nutritional information on the cans change your hypothesis?
3. Infer why the two cans behaved differently in the water.

The Hypothesis "A **hypothesis** is a reasonable and educated possible answer based on what you know and what you observe."

"We know that a stapler is small, it can be heavy, and it is made of metal," said Isabelle.

"We observed that what is in the box is small, heavier than a pair of scissors, and made of metal," continued Marcus.

Analyzing Hypotheses "What other possible explanations fit with what you observed?" asked Ms. Clark.

"Well, it has to be a stapler," said Enrique.

"What if it isn't?" asked Ms. Clark. "Maybe you're overlooking explanations because your minds are made up. A good scientist keeps an open mind to every idea and explanation. What if you learn new information that doesn't fit with your original hypothesis? What new information could you gather to verify or disprove your hypothesis?"

"Do you mean a test or something?" asked Marcus.

"I know," said Enrique, "We could get an empty shoe box that is the same size as the mystery box and put a stapler in it. Then we could shake it and see whether it feels and sounds the same." Enrique's test is shown in **Figure 9.**

Making a Prediction "If your hypothesis is correct, what would you expect to happen?" asked Ms. Clark.

"Well, it would be about the same weight and it would slide around a little, just like the other box," said Enrique.

"It would have that same metallic sound when we shake it," said Marcus.

"So, you predict that the test box will feel and sound the same as your mystery box. Go ahead and try it," said Ms. Clark.

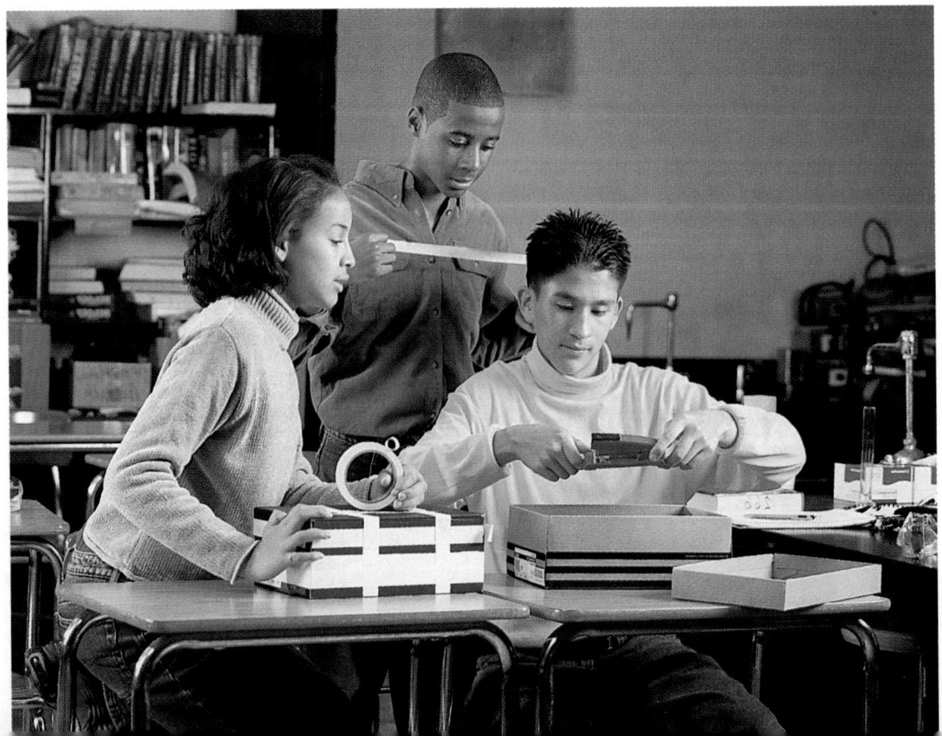

Figure 9
Comparing the known information with the unknown information can be valuable even though you cannot see what is inside the closed box.

Testing the Hypothesis Ms. Clark gave the class an empty shoe box that appeared to be identical to the mystery box. Isabelle found a metal stapler. Enrique put the stapler in the box and taped the box closed. Marcus shook the box.

"The stapler does slide around but it feels just a little heavier than what's inside the mystery box," said Marcus. "What do you think?" he asked Isabelle as he handed her the box.

"It is heavier," said Isabelle "and as hard as I shake it, I can't get a metallic sound. What if we find the mass of both boxes? Then we'll know the exact mass difference between the two."

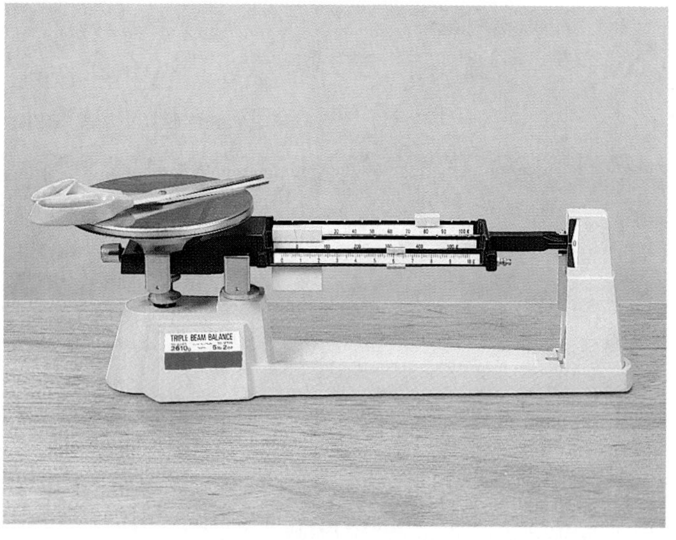

Figure 10
Laboratory balances are used to find the mass of objects.

Using a balance, as shown in **Figure 10,** the class found that the test box had a mass of 410 g, and the mystery box had a mass of 270 g.

Organizing Your Findings "Okay. Now you have some new information," said Ms. Clark. "But before you draw any conclusions, let's organize what we know. Then we'll we have a summary of our observations and can refer back to them when we are drawing our conclusions."

"We could make a chart of our observations in our Science Journals," said Marcus.

"We could compare the observations of the mystery box with the observations of the test box," said Isabelle. The chart that the class made is shown in **Table 1.**

Table 1 Observation Chart

Questions	Mystery Box	Our Box
Does it roll or slide?	It slides and appears to be flat.	It slides and appears to be flat.
Does it make any sounds?	It makes a metallic sound when it strikes the sides of the box.	The stapler makes a thudding sound when it strikes the sides of the box.
Is the mass evenly distributed in the box?	No. The object doesn't completely fill the box.	No. The mass of the stapler is unevenly distributed.
What is the mass of the box?	270 g	410 g

Drawing Conclusions

"What have you learned from your investigation so far?" asked Ms. Clark.

"The first thing that we learned was that our hypothesis wasn't correct," answered Marcus.

"Would you say that your hypothesis was entirely wrong?" asked Ms. Clark.

"The boxes don't weigh the same, and the box with the stapler doesn't make the same sound as the mystery box. But there could be a difference in the kind of stapler in the box. It could be a different size or made of different materials."

"So you infer that the object in the mystery box is not exactly the same type of stapler, right?" asked Ms. Clark.

"What does *infer* mean?" asked Isabelle.

"To **infer** something means to draw a conclusion based on what you observe," answered Ms. Clark.

"So we inferred that the things in the boxes had to be different because our observations of the two boxes are different," said Marcus.

"I guess we're back to where we started," said Enrique. "We still don't know what's in the mystery box."

"Do you know more than you did before you started?" asked Ms. Clark.

"We eliminated one possibility," Isabelle added.

"Yes. We inferred that it's not a stapler, at least not like the one in the test box," said Marcus.

"So even if your observations don't support your hypothesis, you know more than you did when you started," said Ms. Clark.

Figure 11
Observations can be used to draw inferences. *Looking at both of these photos, what do you infer has taken place?*

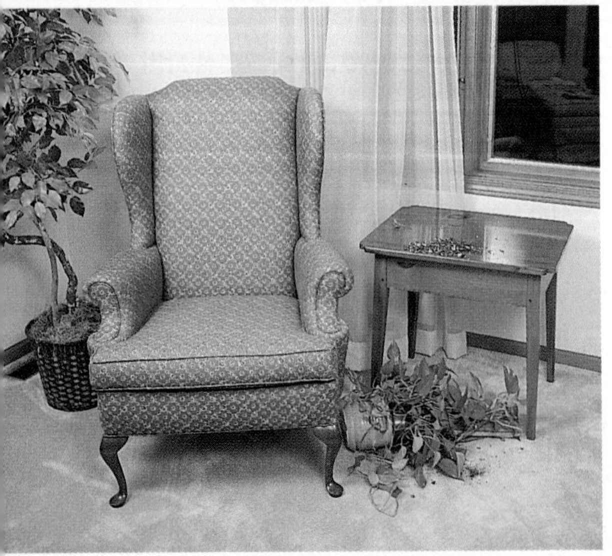

Continuing to Learn "So when do we get to open the box and see what it is?" asked Marcus.

"Let me ask you this," said Ms. Clark. "Do you think scientists always get a chance to look inside to see if they are right?"

"If they are studying something too big or too small to see, I guess they can't," replied Isabelle. "What do they do in those cases?"

"As you learned, your first hypothesis might not be supported by your investigation. Instead of giving up, you continue to gather information by making more observations, making new hypotheses, and by investigating further. Some scientists have spent lifetimes researching their questions. Science takes patience and persistence," said Ms. Clark.

Communicating Your Findings A big part of science is communicating your findings. It is not unusual for one scientist to continue the work of another or to try to duplicate the work of another scientist. It is important for scientists to communicate to others not only the results of the investigation, but also the methods by which the investigation was done. Scientists often publish reports in journals, books, and on the Internet to show other scientists the work that was completed. They also might attend meetings where they make speeches about their work. Scientists from around the world learn from each other, and it is important for them to exchange information freely.

Like the science-fair student in **Figure 12** demonstrates, an important part of doing science is the ability to communicate methods and results to others.

 *Why do scientists share information?*

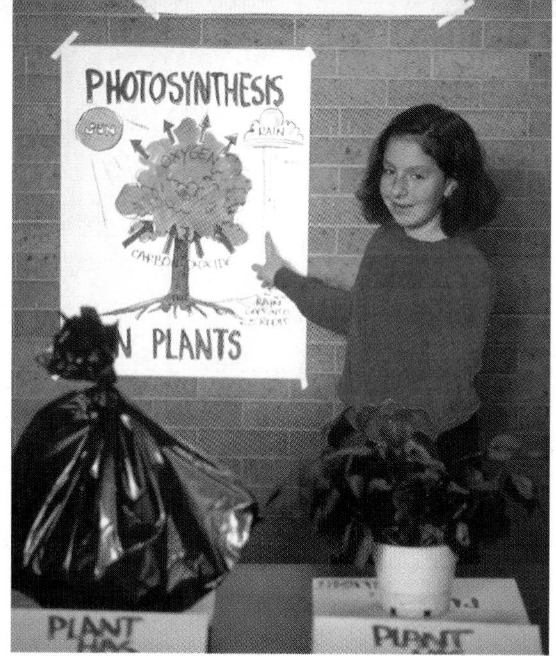

Figure 12
Books, presentations, and meetings are some of the many ways people in science communicate their findings.

Problem-Solving Activity

How can you use a data table to analyze and present data?

Suppose you were given the average temperatures in a city for the four seasons in 1997, 1998, and 1999: spring 1997 was 11°C; summer 1997 was 25°C; fall 1997 was 5°C; winter 1997 was −5°C; spring 1998 was 9°C; summer 1998 was 36°C; fall 1998 was 10°C; winter 1998 was −3°C; spring 1999 was 10°C; summer 1999 was 30°C; fall 1999 was 9°C; and winter 1999 was −2°C. How can you tell in which of the years each season had its coldest average?

Seasonal Temperatures (°C)

	1997	1998	1999
Spring			
Summer			
Fall			
Winter			

Identifying the Problem

The information that is given is not in a format that is easy to see at a glance. It would be more helpful to put it in a table that allows you to compare the data.

Solving the Problem

1. Create a table with rows for seasons and columns for the years. Now insert the values you were given. You should be able to see that the four coldest seasons were spring 1998, summer 1997, fall 1997, and winter 1997.
2. Use your new table to find out which season had the greatest difference in temperatures over the three years from 1997 through 1999.
3. What other observations or comparisons can you make from the table you've created on seasonal temperatures?

Research Visit the Glencoe Science Web site at **science.glencoe.com** for information on variables and constants. Make a poster showing the differences between these two parts of a reliable investigation.

Experiments

Different types of questions call for different types of investigations. Ms. Clark's class made many observations about their mystery box and about their test box. They wanted to know what was inside. To answer their question, building a model—the test box—was an effective way to learn more about the mystery box. Some questions ask about the effects of one factor on another. One way to investigate these kinds of questions is by doing a controlled experiment. A **controlled experiment** involves changing one factor and observing its effect on another while keeping all other factors constant.

Variables and Constants Imagine a race in which the lengths of the lanes vary. Some lanes are 102 m long, some are 98 m long, and a few are 100 m long. When the first runner crosses the finish line, is he or she the fastest? Not necessarily. The lanes in the race have different lengths.

Variables are factors that can be changed in an experiment. Reliable experiments, like the race shown in **Figure 13,** attempt to change one variable and observe the effect of this change on another variable. The variable that is changed in an experiment is called the independent variable. The dependent variable changes as a result of a change in the independent variable. It usually is the dependent variable that is observed in an experiment. Scientists attempt to keep all other variables constant—or unchanged.

The variables that are not changed in an experiment are called **constants.** Examples of constants in the race include track material, wind speed, and distance. This way it is easier to determine exactly which variable is responsible for the runners' finish times. In this race, the runners' abilities were varied. The runners' finish times were observed.

Figure 13
The 400-m race is an example of a controlled experiment. The distance, track material, and wind speed are constants. The runners' abilities and their finish times are varied.

Figure 14
Safety is the most important aspect of any investigation.

Laboratory Safety

In your science class, you will perform many types of investigations. However, performing scientific investigations involves more than just following specific steps. You also must learn how to keep yourself and those around you safe by obeying the safety symbol warnings, shown in **Figure 15.**

In a Laboratory When scientists work in a laboratory, as shown in **Figure 14,** they take many safety precautions.

The most important safety advice in a science lab is to think before you act. Always check with your teacher several times in the planning stage of any investigation. Also make sure you know the location of safety equipment in the laboratory room and how to use this equipment, including the eyewashes, thermal mitts, and fire extinguisher.

Good safety habits include the following suggestions. Before conducting any investigation, find and follow all safety symbols listed in your investigation. You always should wear an apron and goggles to protect yourself from chemicals, flames, and pointed objects. Keep goggles on until activity, cleanup, and handwashing are complete. Always slant test tubes away from yourself and others when heating them. Never eat, drink, or apply makeup in the lab. Report all accidents and injuries to your teacher and always wash your hands after working with lab materials.

In the Field Investigations also take place outside the lab, in streams, farm fields, and other places. Scientists must follow safety regulations there, as well, such as wearing eye goggles and any other special safety equipment that is needed. Never reach into holes or under rocks. Always wash your hands after you've finished your field work.

Eye Safety
Clothing Protection
Disposal
Biological
Extreme Temperature
Sharp Object
Fume
Irritant
Toxic
Animal Safety
Open Flame

Figure 15
Safety symbols are present on nearly every investigation you will do this year. *What safety symbols are on the lab the student is preparing to do in* ***Figure 14?***

Figure 16
Accidents are not planned. Safety precautions must be followed to prevent injury.

Why have safety rules? Doing science in the class laboratory or in the field can be much more interesting than reading about it. However, safety rules must be strictly followed, so that the possibility of an accident greatly decreases. However, you can't predict when something will go wrong.

Think of a person taking a trip in a car. Most of the time when someone drives somewhere in a vehicle, an accident, like the one shown in **Figure 16,** does not occur. But to be safe, drivers and passengers always should wear safety belts. Likewise, you always should wear and use appropriate safety gear in the lab—whether you are conducting an investigation or just observing. The most important aspect of any investigation is to conduct it safely.

Section  Assessment

1. What are four steps scientific investigations often follow?
2. Is a hypothesis as firm as a theory? Explain.
3. What is the difference between an inference and an observation?
4. Why is it important always to use the proper safety equipment?
5. **Think Critically** You are going to use bleach in an investigation. Bleach can irritate your skin, damage your eyes, and stain your clothes. What safety symbols should be listed with this investigation? Explain.

Skill Builder Activities

6. **Drawing Conclusions** While waiting outside your classroom door, the bell rings for school to start. According to your watch, you still have 3 min to get to your classroom. Based on these observations, what can you conclude about your watch? **For more help, refer to the** Science Skill Handbook.
7. **Using a Word Processor** Describe the different types of safety equipment you should use if you are working with a flammable liquid in the lab. **For more help, refer to the** Technology Skill Handbook.

Models in Science

Why are models necessary?

Just as you can take many different paths in an investigation, you can test a hypothesis in many different ways. Ms. Clark's class tested their hypothesis by building a model of the mystery box. A model is one way to test a hypothesis. In science, a **model** is any representation of an object or an event used as a tool for understanding the natural world.

Models can help you visualize, or picture in your mind, something that is difficult to see or understand. Ms. Clark's class made a model because they couldn't see the item inside the box. Models can be of things that are too small or too big to see. They also can be of things that can't be seen because they don't exist anymore or they haven't been created yet. Models also can show events that occur too slowly or too quickly to see. **Figure 17** shows different kinds of models.

As You Read

What You'll Learn

- **Describe** various types of models.
- **Discuss** limitations of models.

Vocabulary
model

Why It's Important
Models can be used to help understand difficult concepts.

Figure 17
Models help scientists visualize and study complex things and things that can't be seen.

Solar system model

Prototype model

Cell model

Dinosaur model

Types of Models

Most models fall into three basic types—physical models, computer models, and idea models. Depending on the reason that a model is needed, scientists can choose to use one or more than one type of model.

Physical Models Models that you can see and touch are called physical models. Examples include things such as a tabletop solar system, a globe of Earth, a replica of the inside of a cell, or a gumdrop-toothpick model of a chemical compound. Models show how parts relate to one another. They also can be used to show how things appear when they change position or how they react when an outside force acts on them.

Earth Science INTEGRATION

A basic type of map used to represent an area of land is the topographic map. It shows the natural features of the land, in addition to artificial features such as political boundaries. Draw a topographic map of your classroom in your Science Journal. Indicate the various heights of chairs, desks, and cabinets, with different colors.

Computer Models Computer models are built using computer software. You can't touch them, but you can view them on a computer screen. Some computer models can model events that take a long time or take place too quickly to see. For example, a computer can model the movement of large plates in the Earth and might help predict earthquakes.

Computers also can model motions and positions of things that would take hours or days to calculate by hand or even using a calculator. They can also predict the effect of different systems or forces. **Figure 18** shows how computer models are used by scientists to help predict the weather based on the motion of air currents in the atmosphere.

Reading Check *What can computer models do?*

Figure 18
A weather map is a computer model showing weather patterns over large areas. Scientists can use this information to predict the weather and to alert people to potentially dangerous weather on the way.

Figure 19
Models can be created using various types of tools.

Idea Models Some models are ideas or concepts that describe how someone thinks about something in the natural world. Albert Einstein is famous for his theory of relativity, which involves the relationship between matter and energy. One of the most famous models Einstein used for this theory is the mathematical equation $E = mc^2$. This explains that mass, m, can be changed into energy, E. Einstein's idea models never could be built as physical models, because they are basically ideas.

Making Models

The process of making a model is something like a sketch artist at work, as shown in **Figure 19.** The sketch artist attempts to draw a picture from the description given by someone. The more detailed the description is, the better the picture will be. Like a scientist who studies data from many sources, the sketch artist can make a sketch based on more than one person's observation. The final sketch isn't a photograph, but if the information is accurate, the sketch should look realistic. Scientific models are made much the same way. The more information a scientist gathers, the more accurate the model will be. The process of constructing a model of King Tutankhamun, who lived more than 3,000 years ago, is shown in **Figure 20.**

Reading Check *How are sketches like scientific models?*

Using Models

When you think of a model, you might think of a model airplane or a model of a building. Not all models are for scientific purposes. You use models, and you might not realize it. Drawings, maps, recipes, and globes are all examples of models.

Thinking Like a Scientist

Procedure

1. Pour 15 mL of **water** into a **test tube.**
2. Slowly pour 5 mL of **vegetable oil** into the test tube.
3. Add two drops of **food coloring** and observe the liquid for 5 min.

Analysis

1. Record your observations of the test tube's contents before and after the oil and the food coloring were added to it.
2. Infer a scientific explanation for your observations.

NATIONAL GEOGRAPHIC

VISUALIZING THE MODELING OF KING TUT

Figure 20

More than 3,000 years ago, King Tutankhamun ruled over Egypt. His reign was a short one, and he died when he was just 18. In 1922, his mummified body was discovered, and in 1983 scientists recreated the face of this most famous of Egyptian kings. Some of the steps in building the model are shown here.

This is the most familiar image of the face of King Tut—the gold funerary mask that was found covering his skeletal face.

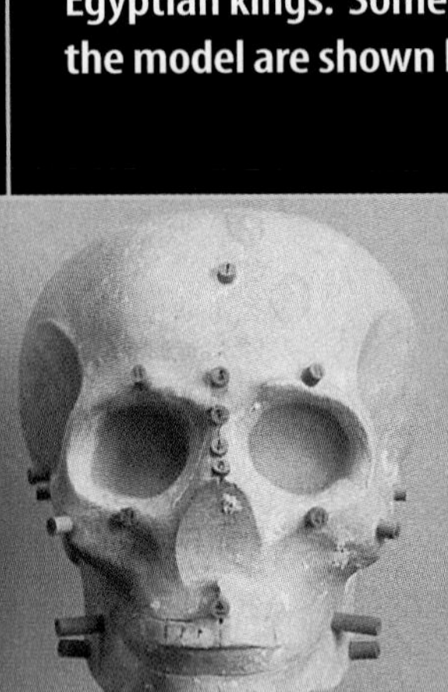

A First, a scientist used measurements and X rays to create a cast of the young king's skull. Depth markers (in red) were then glued onto the skull to indicate the likely thickness of muscle and other tissue.

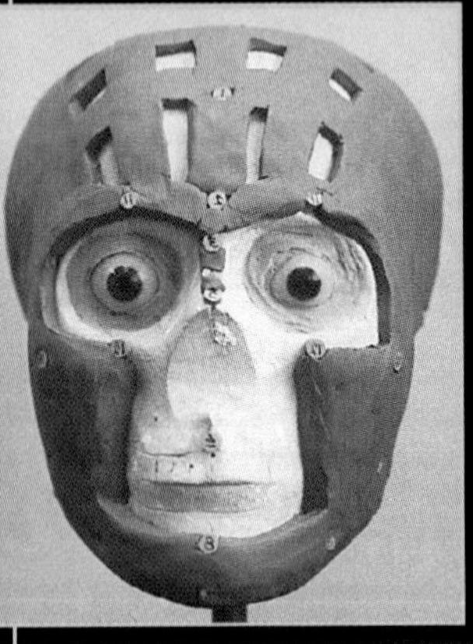

B Clay was applied to fill in the area between the markers.

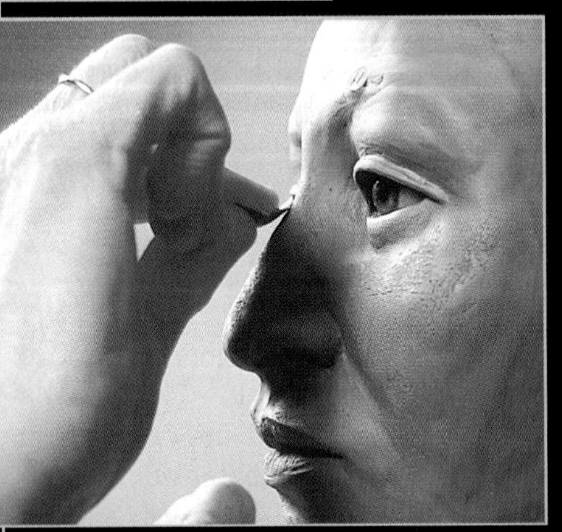

C Next, the features were sculpted. Here, eyelids are fashioned over inlaid prosthetic, or artificial, eyes.

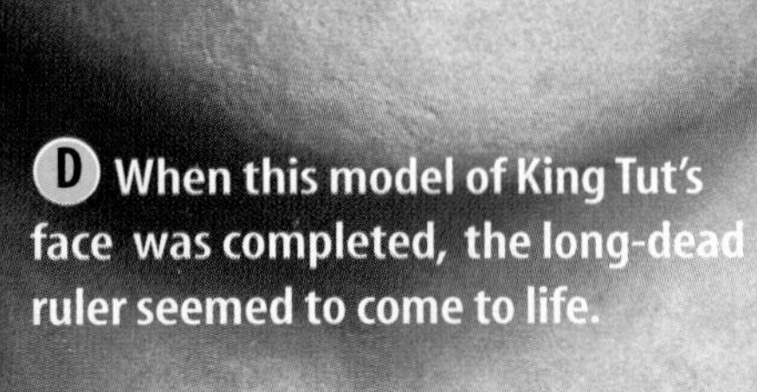

D When this model of King Tut's face was completed, the long-dead ruler seemed to come to life.

Models Communicate Some models are used to communicate observations and ideas to other people. Often, it is easier to communicate ideas you have by making a model instead of writing your ideas in words. This way others can visualize them, too.

Models Test Predictions Some models are used to test predictions. Ms. Clark's class predicted that a box with a stapler in it would have characteristics similar to their mystery box. To test this prediction, the class made a model. Automobile and airplane engineers use wind tunnels to test predictions about how air will interact with their products.

Models Save Time, Money, and Lives Other models are used because working with and testing a model can be safer and less expensive than using the real thing. Some of these models are shown in **Figure 21.** For example, crash-test dummies are used in place of people when testing the effects of automobile crashes. To help train astronaunts in the conditions they will encounter in space, NASA has built a special airplane. This airplane flies in an arc that creates the condition of weightlessness for 20 to 25 s. Making several trips in the airplane is easier, safer, and less expensive than making a trip into space.

Figure 21
Models are a safe and relatively inexpensive way to test ideas.

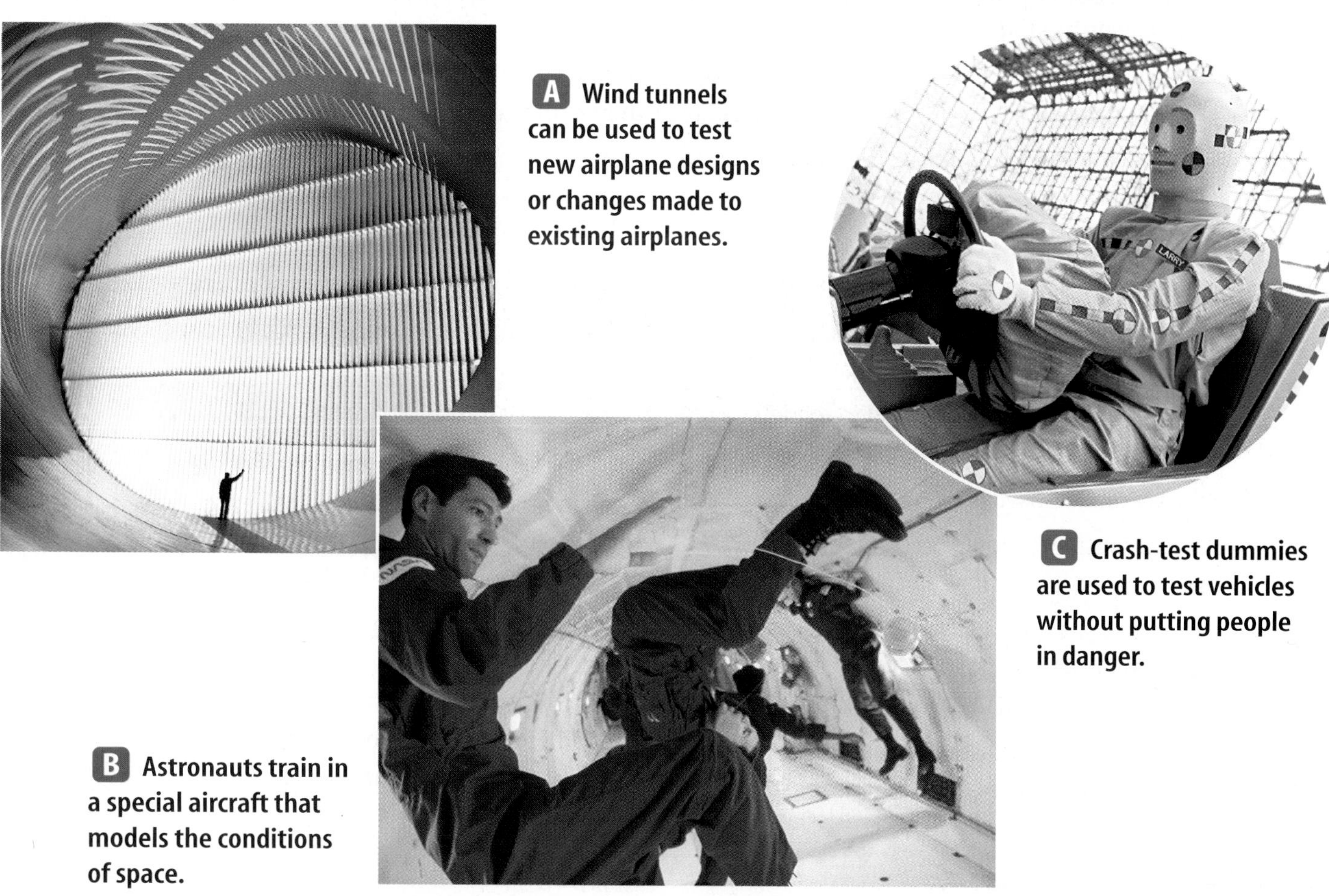

A Wind tunnels can be used to test new airplane designs or changes made to existing airplanes.

B Astronauts train in a special aircraft that models the conditions of space.

C Crash-test dummies are used to test vehicles without putting people in danger.

Figure 22
The model of Earth's solar system changed as new information was gathered.

A **An early model of the solar system had Earth in the center with everything revolving around it.**

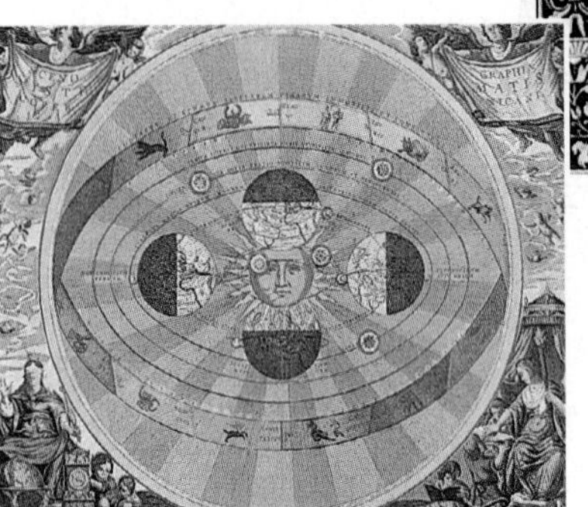

B **Later on, a new model had the Sun in the center with everything revolving around it.**

Limitations of Models

The solar system is too large to be viewed all at once, so models are made to understand it. Many years ago, scientists thought that Earth was the center of the universe and the sky was a blanket that covered the planet.

Later, through observation, it was discovered that the objects you see in the sky are the Sun, the Moon, stars, and other planets. This new model explained the solar system differently. Earth was still the center, but everything else orbited it.

Models Change Still later, through more observation, it was discovered that the Sun is the center of the solar system. Earth, along with the other planets, orbits the Sun. In addition, it was discovered that other planets also have moons that orbit them. A new model, shown in **Figure 22B,** was developed to show this.

Earlier models of the solar system were not meant to be misleading. Scientists made the best models they could with the information they had. More importantly, their models gave future scientists information to build upon. Models are not necessarily perfect, but they provide a visual tool to learn from.

Section  Assessment

1. What type of models can be used to model weather? How are they used?
2. How are models used in science?
3. How do consumer product testing services use models to ensure the safety of the final products produced?
4. Make a table describing three types of models, their advantages and limitations.
5. **Think Critically** Explain how some models are better than others for certain situations.

Skill Builder Activities

6. **Concept Mapping** Develop a concept map to explain models and their uses in science. How is this concept map a model? **For more help, refer to the Science Skill Handbook.**
7. **Using Proportions** On a map of a state, the scale shows that 1cm is approximately 5km. If the distance between two cities is 1.7cm on the map, how many kilometers separate them? **For more help, refer to the Math Skill Handbook.**

SECTION 4 Evaluating Scientific Explanation

Believe it or not?

Look at the photo in **Figure 23.** Do you believe what you see? Do you believe everything you read or hear? Think of something that someone told you that you didn't believe. Why didn't you believe it? Chances are you looked at the facts you were given and decided that there wasn't enough proof to make you believe it. What you did was evaluate, or judge the reliability of what you heard. When you hear a statement, you ask the question "How do you know?" If you decide that what you are told is reliable, then you believe it. If it seems unreliable, then you don't believe it.

Critical Thinking When you evaluate something, you use critical thinking. **Critical thinking** means combining what you already know with the new facts that you are given to decide if you should agree with something. You can evaluate a scientific explanation by breaking it down into two parts. First you can look at and evaluate the observations made during the scientific investigation. Do you agree with what the scientists saw? Then you can evaluate the inferences—or conclusions made about the observations. Do you agree with what the scientists think their observations mean?

As You Read

***What* You'll Learn**

- **Evaluate** scientific explanations.
- **Evaluate** promotional claims.

Vocabulary
critical thinking

***Why* It's Important**

Evaluating scientific claims can help you make better decisions.

Figure 23
In science, observations and inferences are not always agreed upon by everyone. *Do you see the same things your classmates see in this photo?*

Table 2 Favorite Foods

People's Preference	Tally	Frequency
pepperoni pizza	~~||||~~ ~~||||~~ ~~||||~~ ~~||||~~ ~~||||~~ ~~||||~~ ~~||||~~ ||	37
hamburgers with ketchup	~~||||~~ ~~||||~~ ~~||||~~ ~~||||~~ ~~||||~~ |||	28

Evaluating the Data

A scientific investigation always contains observations—often called data. These might be descriptions, tables, graphs, or drawings. When evaluating a scientific claim, you might first look to see whether any data are given. You should be cautious about believing any claim that is not supported by data.

Are the data specific? The data given to back up a claim should be specific. That means they need to be exact. What if your friend tells you that many people like pizza more than they like hamburgers? What else do you need to know before you agree with your friend? You might want to hear about a specific number of people rather than unspecific words like *many* and *more.* You might want to know how many people like pizza more than hamburgers. How many people were asked about which kind of food they liked more? When you are given specific data, a statement is more reliable and you are more likely to believe it. An example of data in the form of a frequency table is shown in **Table 2.** A frequency table shows how many times types of data occur. Scientists must back up their scientific statements with specific data.

Figure 24
These scientists are writing down their observations during their investigation rather than waiting until they are back on land. *Do you think this will increase or decrease the reliability of their data?*

Take Good Notes Scientists must take thorough notes at the time of an investigation, as the scientists shown in **Figure 24** are doing. Important details can be forgotten if you wait several hours or days before you write down your observations. It is also important for you to write down every observation, including ones that you don't expect. Often, great discoveries are made when something unexpected happens in an investigation.

Your Science Journal During this course, you will be keeping a science journal. You will write down what you do and see during your investigations. Your observations should be detailed enough that another person could read what you wrote and repeat the investigation exactly as you performed it. Instead of writing "the stuff changed color," you might say "the clear liquid turned to bright red when I added a drop of food coloring." Detailed observations written down during an investigation are more reliable than sketchy observations written from memory. Practice your observation skills by describing what you see in **Figure 25.**

Can the data be repeated? If your friend told you he could hit a baseball 100 m, but couldn't do it when you were around, you probably wouldn't believe him. Scientists also require repeatable evidence. When a scientist describes an investigation, as shown in **Figure 26,** other scientists should be able to do the investigation and get the same results. The results must be repeatable. When evaluating scientific data, look to see whether other scientists have repeated the data. If not, the data might not be reliable.

Figure 25
Detailed observations are important in order to get reliable data.
Write down at least five sentences describing what you see in this photo.

Evaluating the Conclusions

When you think about a conclusion that someone has made, you can ask yourself two questions. First, does the conclusion make sense? Second, are there any other possible explanations? Suppose you hear on the radio that your school will be running on a two-hour delay in the morning because of snow. You look outside. The roads are clear of snow. Does the conclusion that snow is the cause for the delay make sense? What else could cause the delay? Maybe it is too foggy or icy for the buses to run. Maybe there is a problem with the school building. The original conclusion is not reliable unless the other possible explanations are proven unlikely.

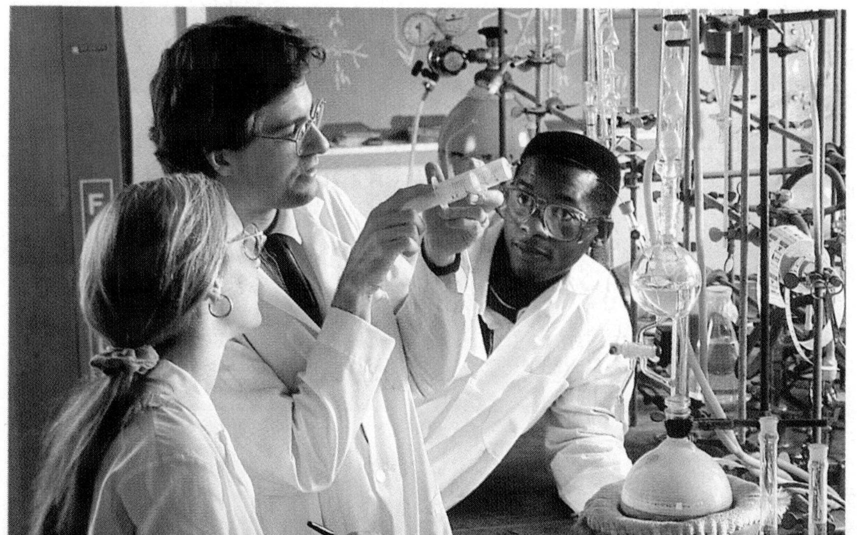

Figure 26
Working together is an important part of science. Several scientists must repeat an experiment and obtain the same results before data are considered reliable.

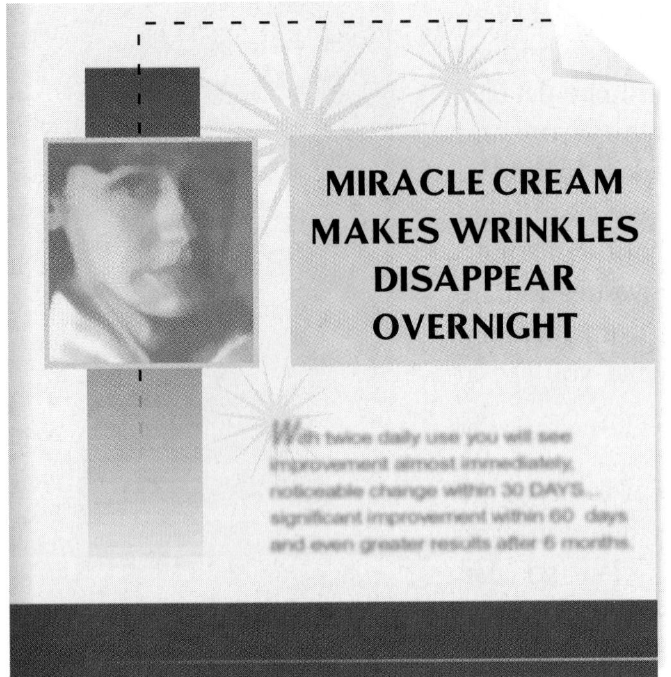

Figure 27
All material should be read with an analytical mind. *What does this advertisement mean?*

Evaluating Promotional Materials

Scientific processes are not used only in the laboratory. Suppose you saw an advertisement in the newspaper like the one in **Figure 27.** What would you think? First, you might ask, "Does this make sense?" It seems unbelievable. You would probably want to hear some of the scientific data supporting the claim before you would believe it. How was this claim tested? How is the amount of wrinkling in skin measured? You might also want to know if an independent laboratory repeated the results. An independent laboratory is one that is not hired by or related in any way to the company that is selling the product or service. It has nothing to gain from the sales of the product. Results from an independent laboratory usually are more reliable than results from a laboratory paid by the selling company. Advertising materials are designed to get you to buy a product or service. It is important that you carefully evaluate advertising claims and the data that support them before making a quick decision to spend your money.

Section  Assessment

1. Explain what is meant by critical thinking and give an example.
2. What types of scientific claims should be verified?
3. Name two parts of a scientific explanation. Give examples of ways to evaluate the reliability of each part.
4. How can vague claims in advertising be misleading?
5. **Think Critically** An advertisement on a food package claims it contains Glistain, a safe, taste enhancer. Make a list of at least ten questions you would ask when evaluating the claim.

Skill Builder Activities

6. **Classifying** Watch three television commercials and read three magazine advertisements. In your Science Journal, record the claims that each advertisement made. Classify each claim as being vague, misleading, reliable, and/or scientific. **For more help, refer to the Science Skill Handbook.**
7. **Researching Information** Visit your school library and choose an article from a news magazine. Pick one that deals with a scientific claim. Learn more about the claim and evaluate it using the scientific process. **For more help, refer to the Science Skill Handbook.**

Activity

What is the right answer?

Scientists sometimes develop more than one explanation for observations. Can more than one explanation be correct? Do scientific explanations depend on judgment?

What You'll Investigate

Can more than one explanation apply to the same observation?

Materials

cardboard mailing tubes
*empty shoe boxes
length of rope
scissors

*Alternate Materials

Goals

- **Make a hypothesis** to explain an observation.
- **Construct** a model to support your hypothesis.
- **Refine** your model based on testing.

Safety Precautions  

WARNING: *Be careful when punching holes with sharp tools.*

Procedure

1. You will be shown a cardboard tube with four ropes coming out of it, one longer than the others. Your teacher will show you that when any of the three short ropes—A, C, or D—is pulled, the longer rope, B, gets shorter. Pulling on rope B returns the other ropes to their original lengths.
2. Make a hypothesis as to how the teacher's model works.
3. **Sketch** a model of a tube with ropes based on your hypothesis. Check your sketch to be sure that your model will do what you expect. Revise your sketch if necessary.

4. Using a cardboard tube and two lengths of rope, build a model according to your design. Test your model by pulling each of the ropes. If it does not perform as planned, modify your hypothesis and your model to make it work like your teacher's model.

Conclude and Apply

1. **Compare** your model with those made by others in your class.
2. Can more than one design give the same result? Can more than one explanation apply to the same observation? Explain.
3. Without opening the tube, can you tell which model is exactly like your teacher's?

Communicating Your Data

Make a display of your working model. Include sketches of your designs. **For more help, refer to the Science Skill Handbook.**

Activity

Identifying Parts of an Investigation

Science investigations contain many parts. How can you identify the various parts of an investigation? In addition to variables and constants, many experiments contain a control. A control is one test, or trial, where everything is held constant. A scientist compares the control trial to the other trials.

What You'll Investigate

What are the various parts of an experiment to test which fertilizer helps a plant grow best?

Materials

description of fertilizer experiment

Goals

- **Identify** parts of an experiment.
- **Identify** constants, variables, and controls in the experiment.
- **Graph** the results of the experiment and draw appropriate conclusions.

Procedure

1. **Read** the description of the fertilizer experiment.
2. **List** factors that remained constant in the experiment.
3. **Identify** any variables in the experiment.
4. **Identify** the control in the experiment.
5. **Identify** one possible hypothesis that the gardener could have tested in her investigation.
6. **Describe** how the gardener went about testing her hypothesis using different types of fertilizers.
7. **Graph** the data that the gardener collected in a line graph.

A gardener was interested in helping her plants grow faster. When she went to the nursery, she found three fertilizers available for her plants. One of those fertilizers, fertilizer A, was recommended to her. However, she decided to conduct a test to determine which of the three fertilizers, if any, helped her plants grow fastest. The gardener planted four seeds, each in a separate pot. She used the same type of pot and the same type of soil in each pot. She fertilized one seed with fertilizer A, one with fertilizer B, and one with fertilizer C. She did not fertilize the fourth seed. She placed the four pots near one another in her garden. She made sure to give each plant the same amount of water each day. She measured the height of the plants each week and recorded her data. After eight weeks of careful observation and record keeping, she had the following table of data.

Plant Height (cm)

Week	Fertilizer A	Fertilizer B	Fertilizer C	No Fertilizer
1	0	0	0	0
2	2	4	1	1
3	5	8	5	4
4	9	13	8	7
5	14	18	12	10
6	20	24	15	13
7	27	31	19	16
8	35	39	22	20

Conclude and Apply

1. **Describe** the results indicated by your graph. What part of an investigation have you just done?
2. Based on the results in the table and your graph, which fertilizer do you think the gardener should use if she wants her plants to grow the fastest? What part of an investigation have you just done?
3. Suppose the gardener told a friend who also grows these plants about her results. What is this an example of?
4. Suppose fertilizer B is much more expensive than fertilizers A and C. Would this affect which fertilizer you think the gardener should buy? Why or why not?
5. Does every researcher need the same hypothesis for an experiment? What is a second possible hypothesis for this experiment (different from the one you wrote in step 5 in the Procedure section)?
6. Did the gardener conduct an adequate test of her hypothesis? Explain why or why not.

Compare your conclusions with those of other students in your class. **For more help, refer to the** Science Skill Handbook.

Women in Science

Nobel prizes are given every year in many areas of science.

Is your family doctor a man or a woman? To your great-grandparents, such a question would likely have seemed odd. Why? Because 100 years ago, there were only a handful of women in scientific fields such as medicine. Women then weren't encouraged to study science as they are today. But that does not mean that there were no female scientists back in your great-grandparents' day. Many women managed to overcome great barriers and, like the more recent Nobel prizewinners featured in this article, made discoveries that changed the world.

Maria Goeppert Mayer

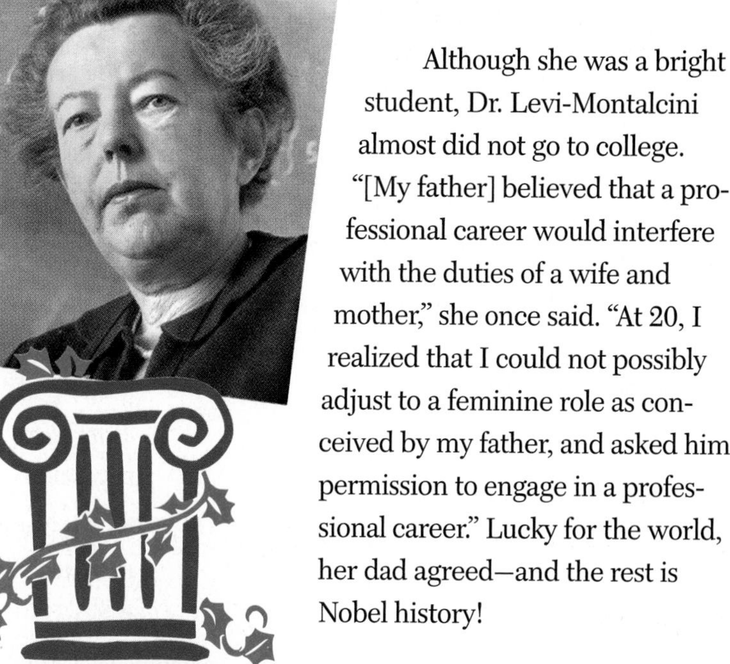

Dr. Maria Goeppert Mayer won the Nobel Prize in Physics in 1963 for her work on the structure of an atom. An atom is made up of protons, neutrons, and electrons. The protons and neutrons exist in the nucleus, or center, of the atom. The electrons orbit the nucleus in shells. Mayer proposed a similar shell model for the protons and neutrons inside the nucleus. This model greatly increased human understanding of atoms, which make up all forms of matter. About the Nobel prize, she said, "To my surprise, winning the prize wasn't half as exciting as doing the work itself. That was the fun—seeing it work out."

Rita Levi-Montalcini

In 1986, the Nobel Prize in Medicine went to Dr. Rita Levi-Montalcini, a biologist from Italy, for her discovery of growth factors. Growth factors regulate the growth of cells and organs in the body. Because of her work, doctors are better able to understand why tumors form and wounds heal.

Although she was a bright student, Dr. Levi-Montalcini almost did not go to college. "[My father] believed that a professional career would interfere with the duties of a wife and mother," she once said. "At 20, I realized that I could not possibly adjust to a feminine role as conceived by my father, and asked him permission to engage in a professional career." Lucky for the world, her dad agreed—and the rest is Nobel history!

Rosalyn Sussman Yalow

In 1977, Dr. Rosalyn Sussman Yalow, a nuclear physicist, was awarded the Nobel Prize in Medicine for discovering a way to measure substances in the blood that are present in tiny amounts, such as hormones and drugs.

The discovery made it possible for doctors to diagnose problems that they could not detect before. Upon winning the prize, Yalow spoke out against discrimination of women. She said, "The world cannot afford the loss of the talents of half its people if we are to solve the many problems which beset us."

CONNECTIONS Research **Write short biographies about recent Nobel prizewinners in physics, chemistry, and medicine. In addition to facts about their lives, explain why the scientists were awarded the prize. How did their discoveries impact their scientific fields or people in general?**

SCIENCE *Online*
For more information, visit science.glencoe.com

Chapter 1 Study Guide

Reviewing Main Ideas

Section 1 What is science?

1. Science is a way of learning more about the natural world. It can provide only possible explanations for questions.
2. A scientific law describes a pattern in nature.
3. A scientific theory attempts to explain patterns in nature.
4. Systems are a collection of structures, cycles, and processes that interact. *Can you identify structures, cycles, and processes in this system?*

5. Science can be divided into three branches—life science, Earth science, and physical science.
6. Technology is the application of science.

Section 2 Science in Action

1. Science involves using a collection of skills.
2. A hypothesis is a reasonable guess based on what you know and observe.
3. An inference is a conclusion based on observation.
4. Controlled experiments involve changing one variable while keeping others constant.
5. You should always obey laboratory safety symbols. You should also wear and use appropriate gear in the laboratory.

Section 3 Models in Science

1. A model is any representation of an object or an event used as a tool for understanding the natural world.
2. There are physical, computer, and idea models.
3. Models can communicate ideas; test predictions; and save time, money, and lives. *How is this model used?*

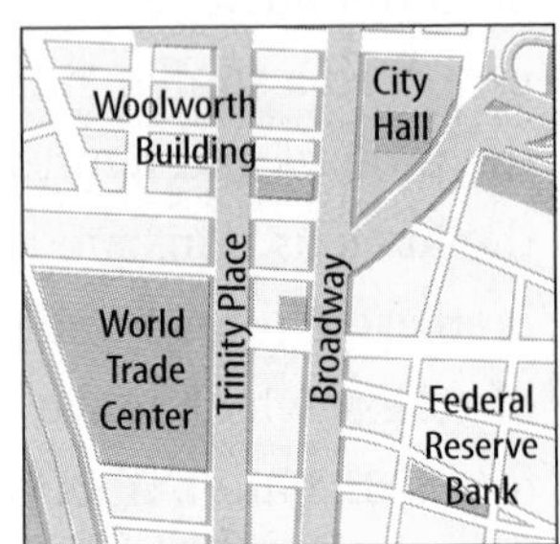

4. Models change as more information is learned.

Section 4 Evaluating Scientific Explanations

1. An explanation can be evaluated by looking at the observations and the conclusions in an experiment.
2. Reliable data are specific and repeatable by other scientists.
3. Detailed notes must be taken *during* an investigation.
4. To be reliable, a conclusion must make sense and be the most likely explanation.

After You Read

FOLDABLES Reading & Study Skills

Without looking at the chapter or at your Foldable, write what you learned about science on the *Learned* fold of your Know-Want-Learn Study Fold.

Chapter 1 Study Guide

Visualizing Main Ideas

Complete the following concept map.

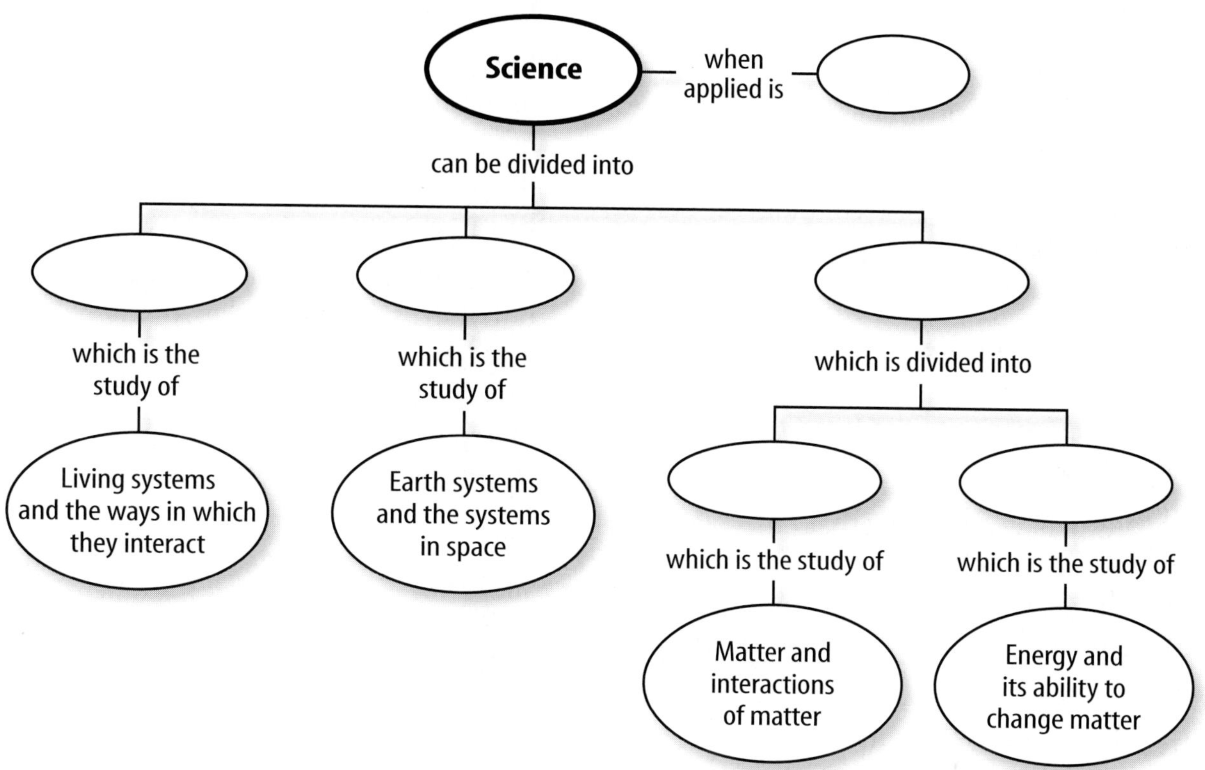

Vocabulary Review

Vocabulary Words

a. constant
b. controlled experiment
c. critical thinking
d. Earth science
e. hypothesis
f. infer
g. life science
h. model
i. physical science
j. science
k. scientific law
l. scientific theory
m. system
n. technology
o. variable

Study Tip

Make a note of anything you don't understand so that you'll remember to ask your teacher about it.

Using Vocabulary

Explain the relationship between the words in the following sets.

1. hypothesis, scientific theory
2. constant, variable
3. science, technology
4. science, system
5. Earth science, physical science
6. critical thinking, infer
7. scientific law, observation
8. model, system
9. controlled experiment, variable
10. scientific theory, scientific law

Chapter 1 Assessment

Checking Concepts

Choose the word or phrase that best answers the question.

1. What does infer mean?
   A) make observations
   B) draw a conclusion
   C) replace
   D) test

2. Which is an example of technology?
   A) a squirt bottle
   B) a poem
   C) a cat
   D) physical science

3. Which branch of science includes the study of weather?
   A) life science
   B) Earth science
   C) physical science
   D) engineering

4. What explains something that takes place in the natural world?
   A) scientific law
   B) technology
   C) scientific theory
   D) experiments

5. Which of the following cannot protect you from splashing acid?
   A) goggles
   B) apron
   C) fire extinguisher
   D) gloves

6. If the results from your investigation do not support your hypothesis, what should you do?
   A) Do nothing.
   B) You should repeat the investigation until it agrees with the hypothesis.
   C) Modify your hypothesis.
   D) Change your data to fit your hypothesis.

7. Which of the following is NOT an example of a scientific hypothesis?
   A) Earthquakes happen because of stresses along continental plates.
   B) Some animals can detect ultrasound frequencies caused by earthquakes.
   C) Paintings are prettier than sculptures.
   D) Lava takes different forms depending on how it cools.

8. An airplane model is an example of what type of model?
   A) physical
   B) computer
   C) idea
   D) mental

9. Using a computer to make a three-dimensional picture of a building is a type of which of the following?
   A) model
   B) hypothesis
   C) constant
   D) variable

10. Which of the following increases the reliability of a scientific explanation?
    A) vague statements
    B) notes taken after an investigation
    C) repeatable data
    D) several likely explanations

Thinking Critically

11. Is evaluating a play in English class science? Explain.

12. Why is it a good idea to repeat an experiment a few times and compare results? Explain.

13. How is using a rock hammer an example of technology? Explain.

14. Why is it important to record and measure data accurately during an experiment?

15. What type of model would most likely be used in classrooms to help young children learn science? Explain.

Developing Skills

16. **Comparing and Contrasting** How are scientific theories and laws similar? How are they different?

17. Drawing Conclusions When scientists study how well new medicines work, one group of patients receives the medicine. A second group does not. Why?

18. Forming Hypotheses Make a hypothesis about the quickest way to get to school in the morning. How could you test your hypothesis?

19. Making Operational Definitions How does a scientific law differ from a state law? Give examples of both types of laws.

20. Making and Using Tables Mohs hardness scale measures how easily an object can be scratched. The higher the number is, the harder the material is. Use the table below to identify which material is the hardest and which is the softest.

Hardness

Object	Mohs Scale
copper	3.5
diamond	10
fingernail	2.5
glass	5.5
quartz	7
steel file	6.5

Performance Assessment

21. Write a Story Write a story illustrating what science is and how it is used to investigate problems.

Technology

Go to the Glencoe Science Web site at **science.glencoe.com** or use the **Glencoe Science CD-ROM** for additional chapter assessment.

Test Practice

Sally and Rafael have just learned about the parts of the solar system in science class. They decided to build a large model to better understand it.

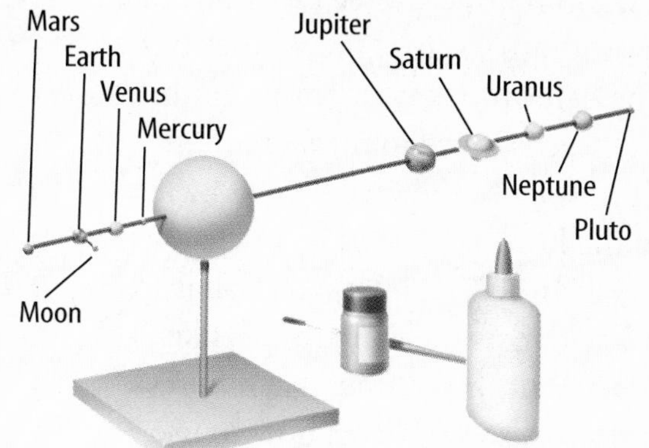

Study the diagram and answer the following questions.

1. According to this information, Rafael and Sally's model of the solar system best represents which kind of scientific model?

A) idea
B) computer
C) physical
D) realistic

2. According to this model, all of the following are represented EXCEPT ___________.

F) the Sun
G) the Moon
H) planets
J) stars

CHAPTER 2

Measurement

Does the expression "winning by a nose" mean anything to you? If you have ever "won by a nose," that means the race was close. Sometimes horse races, such as this one, are so close the winner has to be determined by a photograph. But there is more to measure than just how close the race was. How fast did the horse run? Did he break a record? In this chapter, you will learn how scientists measure things like distance, time, volume, and temperature. You also will learn how to use illustrations, pictures, and graphs to communicate measurements.

What do you think?

Science Journal Look at the picture below with a classmate. Discuss what you think this might be. Here's a hint: *How fast did you come up with an answer?* Write your answer or best guess in your Science Journal.

You make measurements every day. If you want to communicate those measurements to others, how can you be sure that they will understand exactly what you mean? Using vague words without units won't work. Do the Explore Activity below to see the confusion that can result from using measurements that aren't standard.

Measure length

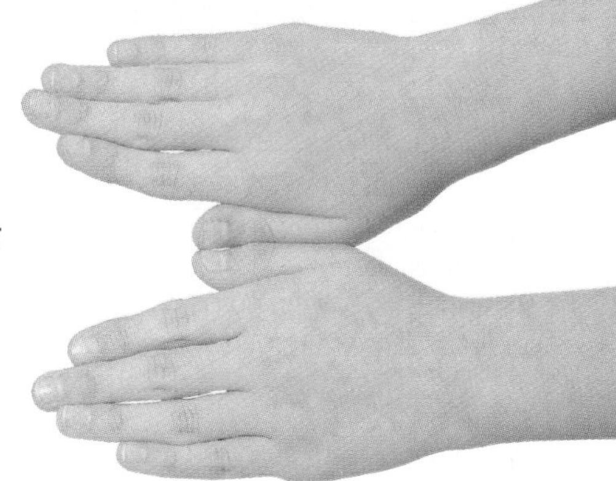

1. As a class, choose six objects to measure in your classroom.
2. Measure each object using the width of your hand and write your measurements in your Science Journal.
3. Compare your measurements to those of your classmates.

Observe

Is your hand the same width as your classmates' hands? Discuss in your Science Journal why it is better to switch from using hands to using units of measurement that are the same all the time.

Before You Read

Making an Organizational Study Fold **When information is grouped into clear categories, it is easier to understand what you are learning. Before you begin reading, make the following Foldable to help you organize your thoughts about measurements.**

1. Place a sheet of paper in front of you so the short side is at the top. Fold the paper in half from the left side to the right side two times. Unfold all the folds.
2. Fold the paper from top to bottom in equal thirds and then in half. Unfold all the folds.
3. Trace over all the fold lines and label the table you created. Label the columns: *Estimate It, Measure It,* and *Round It,* as shown. Label the rows: *Length of* ______, *Volume of* ______, *Mass of* ______, *Temperature of* ______, and *Rate of* ______, as shown.
4. Before you read the chapter, select objects to measure and estimate their measurements. As you read the chapter, complete the *Measure It* column.

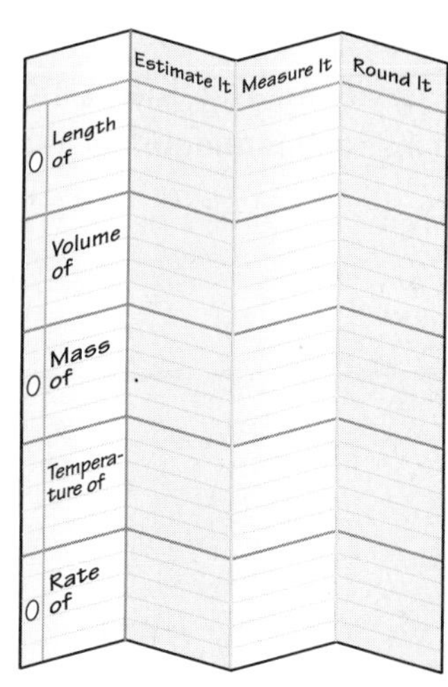

SECTION 1

Description and Measurement

As You Read

What You'll Learn

- **Determine** how reasonable a measurement is by estimating.
- **Identify** and use the rules for rounding a number.
- **Distinguish** between precision and accuracy in measurements.

Vocabulary

measurement
estimation
precision
accuracy

Why It's Important

Measurement helps you communicate information and ideas.

Measurement

How would you describe what you are wearing today? You might start with the colors of your outfit, and perhaps you would even describe the style. Then you might mention sizes—size 7 shoes, size 14 shirt. Every day you are surrounded by numbers. **Measurement** is a way to describe the world with numbers. It answers questions such as how much, how long, or how far. Measurement can describe the amount of milk in a carton, the cost of a new compact disc, or the distance between your home and your school. It also can describe the volume of water in a swimming pool, the mass of an atom, or how fast a penguin's heart pumps blood.

The circular device in **Figure 1** is designed to measure the performance of an automobile in a crash test. Engineers use this information to design safer vehicles. In scientific endeavors, it is important that scientists rely on measurements instead of the opinions of individuals. You would not know how safe the automobile is if this researcher turned in a report that said, "Vehicle did fairly well in head-on collision when traveling at a moderate speed." What does "fairly well" mean? What is a "moderate speed?"

Figure 1
This device measures the range of motion of a seat-belted mannequin in a simulated accident.

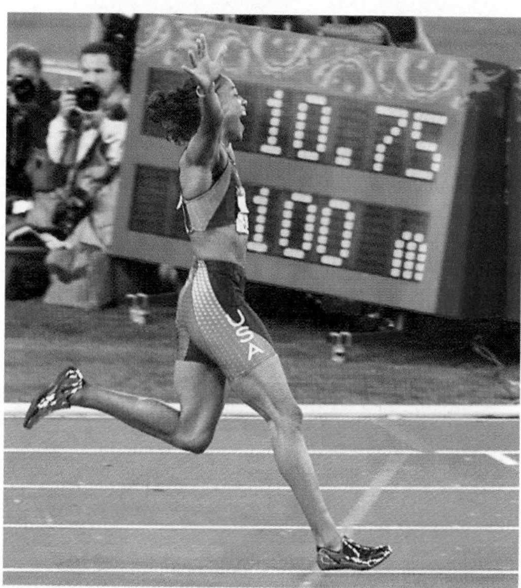

Figure 2
Accurate measurement of distance and time is important for competitive sports like track and field. *Why wouldn't a clock that measured in minutes be precise enough for this race?*

Describing Events Measurement also can describe events such as the one shown in **Figure 2.** In the 1956 summer Olympics, sprinter Betty Cuthbert of Australia came in first in the women's 200-m dash. She ran the race in 23.4 s. In the 2000 summer Olympics, Marion Jones of the United States won the 100-m dash in a time of 10.75 s. In this example, measurements convey information about the year of the race, its length, the finishing order, and the time. Information about who competed and in what event are not measurements but help describe the event completely.

Estimation

What happens when you want to know the size of an object but you can't measure it? Perhaps it is too large to measure or you don't have a ruler handy. **Estimation** can help you make a rough measurement of an object. When you estimate, you can use your knowledge of the size of something familiar to estimate the size of a new object. Estimation is a skill based on previous experience and is useful when you are in a hurry and exact numbers are not required. Estimation is a valuable skill that improves with experience, practice, and understanding.

Reading Check *When should you not estimate a value?*

How practical is the skill of estimation? In many instances, estimation is used on a daily basis. A caterer prepares for each night's crowd based on an estimation of how many will order each entree. A chef makes her prize-winning chili. She doesn't measure the cumin; she adds "just that much." Firefighters estimate how much hose to pull off the truck when they arrive at a burning building.

Chemistry INTEGRATION

A description of matter that does not involve measurement is *qualitative*. For example, water is composed of hydrogen and oxygen. A *quantitative* description uses numbers to describe. For example, one water molecule is composed of one oxygen atom and two hydrogen atoms. Research another compound containing hydrogen and oxygen—hydrogen peroxide. Infer a qualitative and quantitative description of hydrogen peroxide in your Science Journal.

Figure 3
This student is about 1.5 m tall. *Estimate the height of the tree in the photo.*

Using Estimation You can use comparisons to estimate measurements. For example, the tree in **Figure 3** is too tall to measure easily, but because you know the height of the student next to the tree, you can estimate the height of the tree. When you estimate, you often use the word *about.* For example, doorknobs are about 1 m above the floor, a sack of flour has a mass of about 2 kg, and you can walk about 5 km in an hour.

Estimation also is used to check that an answer is reasonable. Suppose you calculate your friend's running speed as 47 m/s. You are familiar with how long a second is and how long a meter is. Think about it. Can your friend really run a 50-m dash in 1 s? Estimation tells you that 47 m/s is unrealistically fast and you need to check your work.

Mini LAB

Measuring Accurately

Procedure

1. Fill a **400-mL beaker** with **crushed ice.** Add enough **cold water** to fill the beaker.
2. Make three measurements of the temperature of the ice water using a **computer temperature probe.** Remove the computer probe and allow it to warm to room temperature between each measurement. Record the measurements in your **Science Journal.**
3. Repeat step two using an **alcohol thermometer.**

Analysis

1. Average each set of measurements.
2. Which measuring device is more precise? Explain. Can you determine which is more accurate? How?

Precision and Accuracy

One way to evaluate measurements is to determine whether they are precise. **Precision** is a description of how close measurements are to each other. Suppose you measure the distance between your home and your school five times with an odometer. Each time, you determine the distance to be 2.7 km. Suppose a friend repeated the measurements and measured 2.7 km on two days, 2.8 km on two days, and 2.6 km on the fifth day. Because your measurements were closer to each other than your friend's measurements, yours were more precise. The term *precision* also is used when discussing the number of decimal places a measuring device can measure. A clock with a second hand is considered more precise than one with only an hour hand.

Degrees of Precision The timing for Olympic events has become more precise over the years. Events that were measured in tenths of a second 100 years ago are measured to the hundredth of a second today. Today's measuring devices are more precise. **Figure 4** shows an example of measurements of time with varying degrees of precision.

Accuracy When you compare a measurement to the real, actual, or accepted value, you are describing **accuracy.** A watch with a second hand is more precise than one with only an hour hand, but if it is not properly set, the readings could be off by an hour or more. Therefore, the watch is not accurate. On the other hand, measurements of 1.03m, 1.04m and 1.06m compared to an actual value of 1.05 m is accurate, but not precise. **Figure 5** illustrates the difference between precision and accuracy.

Reading Check ***What is the difference between precision and accuracy?***

Figure 4
Each of these clocks provides a different level of precision. *Which of the three could you use to be sure to make the 3:35 bus?*

A **Before the invention of clocks, as they are known today, a sundial was used. As the Sun passes through the sky, a shadow moves around the dial.**

B **For centuries, analog clocks—the kind with a face—were the standard.**

C **Digital clocks are now as common as analog ones.**

Figure 5

From golf to gymnastics, many sports require precision and accuracy. Archery—a sport that involves shooting arrows into a target—clearly shows the relationship between these two factors. An archer must be accurate enough to hit the bull's-eye and precise enough to do it repeatedly.

Ⓐ The archer who shot these arrows is neither accurate nor precise—the arrows are scattered all around the target.

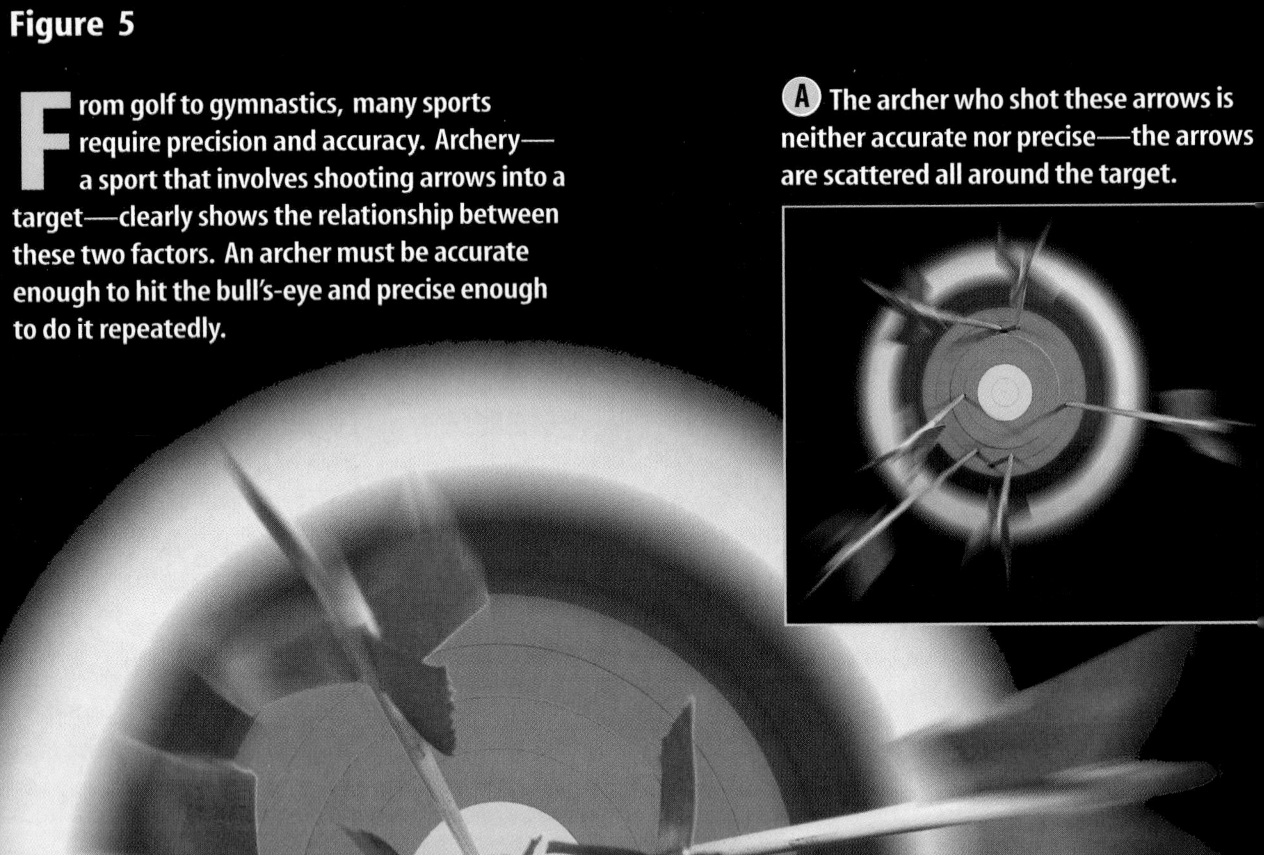

Ⓑ This archer's attempt demonstrates precision but not accuracy—the arrows were shot consistently to the left of the

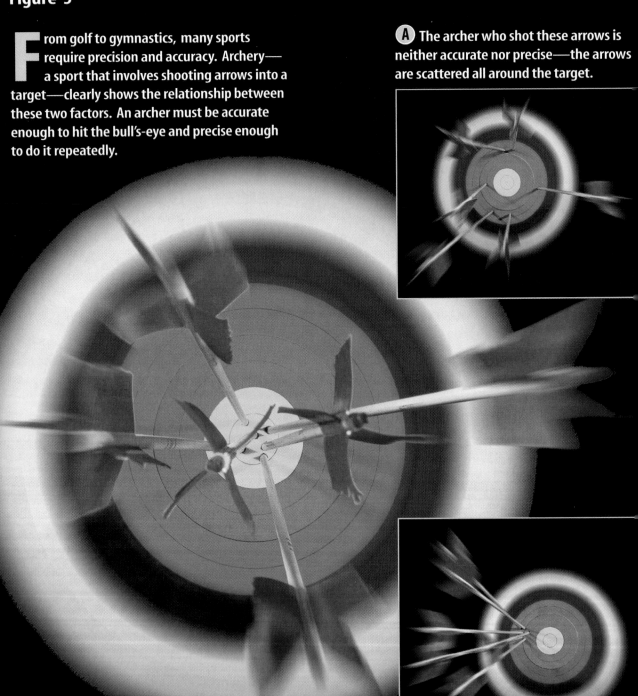

Ⓒ Here we have a winner! All of the arrows have hit the bull's-eye, a result that is both precise and accurate.

Precision and accuracy are important in many medical procedures. One of these procedures is the delivery of radiation in the treatment of cancerous tumors. Because radiation damages cells, it is important to limit the radiation to only the cancerous cells that are to be destroyed. A technique called Stereotactic Radiotherapy (SRT) allows doctors to be accurate and precise in delivering radiation to areas of the brain. The patient makes an impression of his or her teeth on a bite plate that is then attached to the radiation machine. This same bite plate is used for every treatment to position the patient precisely the same way each time. A CAT scan locates the tumor in relation to the bite plate, and the doctors can pinpoint with accuracy and precision where the radiation should go.

Research Visit the Glencoe Science Web site at **science.glencoe.com** for more information about measurement. Communicate to your class what you learn.

Rounding a Measurement Not all measurements have to be made with instruments that measure with great precision like the scale in **Figure 6.** Suppose you need to measure the length of the sidewalk outside your school. You could measure it to the nearest millimeter. However, you probably would need to know the length only to the nearest meter or tenth of a meter. So, if you found that the length was 135.841 m, you could round off that number to the nearest tenth of a meter and still be considered accurate. How would you round this number? To round a given value, follow these steps:

1. Look at the digit to the right of the place being rounded to.
   - If the digit to the right is 0, 1, 2, 3, or 4, the digit being rounded to remains the same.
   - If the digit to the right is 5, 6, 7, 8, or 9, the digit being rounded to increases by one.
2. The digits to the right of the digit being rounded to are deleted if they are also to the right of a decimal. If they are to the left of a decimal, they are changed to zeros.

Look back at the sidewalk example. If you want to round the sidewalk length of 135.841 to the tenths place, you look at the digit to the right of the 8. Because that digit is a 4, you keep the 8 and round it off to 135.8 m. If you want to round to the ones place, you look at the digit to the right of the 5. In this case you have an 8, so you round up, changing the 5 to a 6, and your answer is 136 m.

Figure 6
This laboratory scale measures to the nearest hundredth of a gram.

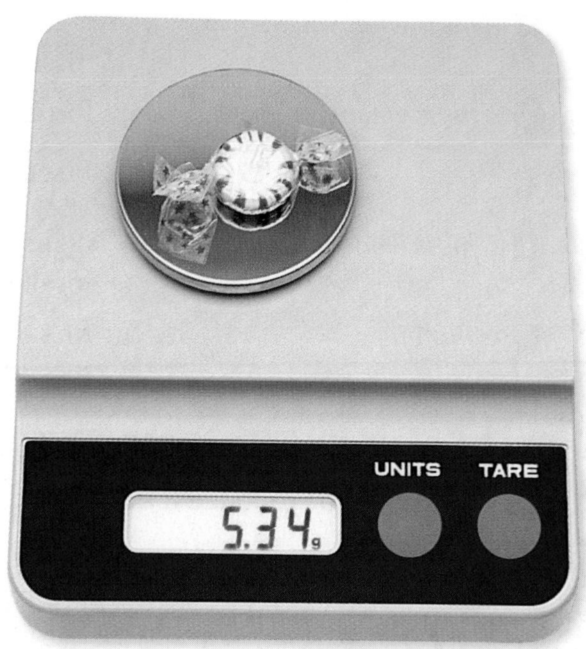

Precision and Number of Digits When might you need to round a number? Suppose you want to divide a 2-L bottle of soft drink equally among seven people. When you divide 2 by 7, your calculator display reads as shown in **Figure 7.** Will you measure exactly 0.285 714 285 L for each person? No. All you need to know is that each person gets about 0.3 L of soft drink.

Using Precision and Significant Digits The number of digits that truly reflect the precision of a number are called the significant digits or significant figures. They are figured as follows:

- Digits other than zero are always significant.
- Final zeros after a decimal point (6.54600 g) are significant.
- Zeros between any other digits (507.0301 g) are significant.
- Zeros before any other digits (0.0002030 g) are NOT significant.
- Zeros in a whole number (1650) may or may not be significant.
- An exact number, such as the number of people in a room or the number of meters in a kilometer, has infinite significant digits.

Math Skills Activity

Rounding

Example Problem

The mass of one object is 6.941 g. The mass of a second object is 20.180 g. You need to know these values only to the nearest whole number to solve a problem. What are the rounded values?

Solution

1. *This is what you know:* mass of first object = 6.941 g
   mass of second object = 20.180 g
2. *This is what you need to know:* the number to the right of the one's place
   first object: 9, second object: 1
3. *This is what you need to use:* digits 0, 1, 2, 3, 4 remain the same
   for digits 5, 6, 7, 8, 9, round up
4. *Solution:* first object: 9 makes the 6 round up = 7
   second object: 1 makes the 0 remain the same = 20

Practice Problem

What are the rounded masses of the objects to the nearest tenth of a unit?

For more help, refer to the Math Skill Handbook.

Following the Rules In the soda example you have an exact number, seven, for the number of people. This number has infinite significant digits. You also have the number two, for how many liters of soda you have. This has only one significant digit.

There are also rules to follow when deciding the number of significant digits in the answer to a calculation. They depend on what kind of calculation you are doing.

- For multiplication and division, you determine the number of significant digits in each number in your problem. The significant digits of your answer are determined by the number with fewer digits.

$$6.14 \times 5.6 = \boxed{34}.384$$

3 digits 2 digits 2 digits

- For addition and subtraction, you determine the place value of each number in your problem. The significant digits of the answer is determined by the number that is least precise.

6.14	to the hundredths
+ 5.6	to the tenths
$\boxed{11.7}$4	to the tenths

Therefore, in the soda example you are dividing and the limiting number of digits is determined by the amount of soda, 2 L. There is one significant digit there; therefore, your answer has one.

Reading Check *What determines the number of significant digits in the answer to an addition problem?*

Figure 7
Sometimes considering the size of each digit will help you realize they are unneeded. In this calculation, the seven ten-thousandths of a liter represents just a few drops of soda.

Section 1 Assessment

1. Estimate the distance between your desk and your teacher's desk. Explain the method you used.
2. Measure the height of your desk to the nearest half centimeter.
3. Sarah's garden is 11.72 m long. Round to the nearest tenth of a meter.
4. John's puppy has chewed on his ruler. Will John's measurements be accurate or precise?
5. **Think Critically** Would the sum of 5.7 and 6.2 need to be rounded? Why or why not? Would the sum of 3.28 and 4.1 need to be rounded? Why or why not?

Skill Builder Activities

6. **Using Precision and Significant Digits** Perform the following calculations and express the answer using the correct number of significant digits: 42.35 + 214; 225/12. **For more help, refer to the Math Skill Handbook.**
7. **Communicating** Describe your backpack in your Science Journal. Include in your description one set of qualities that have no measurements, such as color and texture, and one set of measured quantities, such as width and mass. **For more help, refer to the Science Skill Handbook.**

SI Units

As You Read

What You'll Learn

- **Identify** the purpose of SI.
- **Identify** the SI units of length, volume, mass, temperature, time, and rate.

Vocabulary

SI, meter, mass, kilogram, kelvin, rate

Why It's Important

The SI system is used throughout the world, allowing you to measure quantities in the exact same way as other students around the world.

The International System

Can you imagine how confusing it would be if people in every country used different measuring systems? Sharing data and ideas would be complicated. To avoid confusion, scientists established the International System of Units, or **SI,** in 1960 as the accepted system for measurement. It was designed to provide a worldwide standard of physical measurement for science, industry, and commerce. SI units are shown in **Table 1.**

Reading Check *Why was SI established?*

The SI units are related by multiples of ten. Any SI unit can be converted to a smaller or larger SI unit by multiplying by a power of 10. For example, to rewrite a kilogram measurement in grams, you multiply by 1,000. The new unit is renamed by changing the prefix, as shown in **Table 2.** For example, one millionth of a meter is one *micro*-meter. One thousand grams is one *kilo*gram. **Table 3** shows some common objects and their measurements in SI units.

Table 2 SI Prefixes

Prefix	Multiplier
giga-	1,000,000,000
mega-	1,000,000
kilo-	1,000
hecto-	100
deka-	10
[unit]	1
deci-	0.1
centi-	0.01
milli-	0.001
micro-	0.000 001
nano-	0.000 000 001

Table 1 SI Base Units

Quantity	Unit	Symbol
length	meter	m
mass	kilogram	kg
temperature	kelvin	K
time	second	s
electric current	ampere	A
amount of substance	mole	mol
intensity of light	candela	cd

Length

Length is defined as the distance between two points. Lengths measured with different tools can describe a range of things from the distance from Earth to Mars to the thickness of a human hair. In your laboratory activities, you usually will measure length with a metric ruler or meterstick.

The **meter** (m) is the SI unit of length. One meter is about the length of a baseball bat. The size of a room or the dimensions of a building would be measured in meters. For example, the height of the Washington Monument in Washington, D.C. is 169 m.

Figure 8
These runners have just completed a 10-kilometer race—known as a 10K. *About how many kilometers is the distance between your home and your school?*

Smaller objects can be measured in centimeters (cm) or millimeters (mm). The length of your textbook or pencil would be measured in centimeters. A twenty-dollar bill is 15.5 cm long. You would use millimeters to measure the width of the words on this page. To measure the length of small things such as blood cells, bacteria, or viruses, scientists use micrometers (millionths of a meter) and nanometers (billionths of a meter).

A Long Way Sometimes people need to measure long distances, such as the distance a migrating bird travels or the distance from Earth to the Moon. To measure such lengths, you use kilometers. Kilometers might be most familiar to you as the distance traveled in a car or the measure of a long-distance race, as shown in **Figure 8.** The course of a marathon is measured carefully so that the competitors run 42.2 km. When you drive from New York to Los Angeles, you cover 4,501 km.

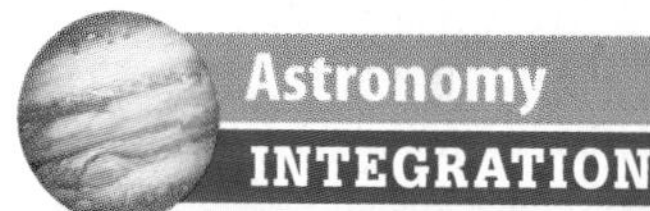

How important are accurate measurements? In 1999, the *Mars Climate Orbiter* disappeared as it was to begin orbiting Mars. NASA later discovered that a unit system error caused the flight path to be incorrect and the orbiter to be lost. Research the error and determine what systems of units were involved. How can using two different systems of units cause errors?

Table 3 Common Objects in SI Measurements

Object	Type of Measurement	Measurement
can of soda	volume	355 cm^3
bag of potatoes	mass	4.5 kg
fluorescent tube	length	1.2 m
refrigerator	temperature	276 K

Figure 9
A cubic meter equals the volume of a cube 1 m by 1 m by 1 m. *How many cubic centimeters are in a cubic meter?*

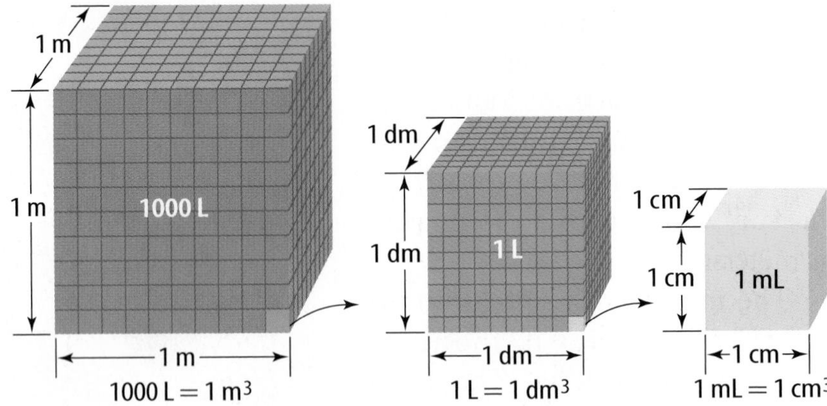

TRY AT HOME

Mini LAB

Measuring Volume

Procedure

1. Fill a plastic or glass **liquid measuring cup** until half full with **water.** Measure the volume.
2. Find an **object,** such as a rock, that will fit in your measuring cup.
3. Carefully lower the object into the water. If it floats, push it just under the surface with a **pencil.**
4. Record in your **Science Journal** the new volume of the water.

Analysis

1. How much space does the object occupy?
2. If 1 mL of water occupies exactly 1 cm^3 of space, what is the volume of the object in cm^3?

Volume

The amount of space an object occupies is its volume. The cubic meter (m^3), shown in **Figure 9,** is the SI unit of volume. You can measure smaller volumes with the cubic centimeter (cm^3 or cc). To find the volume of a square or rectangular object, such as a brick or your textbook, measure its length, width, and height and multiply them together. What is the volume of a compact disc case?

You are probably familiar with a 2-L bottle. A liter is a measurement of liquid volume. A cube 10 cm by 10 cm by 10 cm holds 1 L (1,000 cm^3) of water. A cube 1 cm on a side holds 1 mL (1 cm^3) of water.

Volume by Immersion Not all objects have an even, regular shape. How can you find the volume of something irregular like a rock or a piece of metal?

Have you ever added ice cubes to a nearly full glass of water only to have the water overflow? Why did the water overflow? Did you suddenly have more water? The volume of water did not increase at all, but the water was displaced when the ice cubes were added. Each ice cube takes up space or has volume. The difference in the volume of water before and after the addition of the ice cubes equals the volume of the ice cubes that are under the surface of the water.

The ice cubes took up space and caused the total volume in the glass to increase. When you measure the volume of an irregular object, you do the same thing. You start with a known volume of water and drop in, or immerse, the object. The increase in the volume of water is equal to the volume of the object.

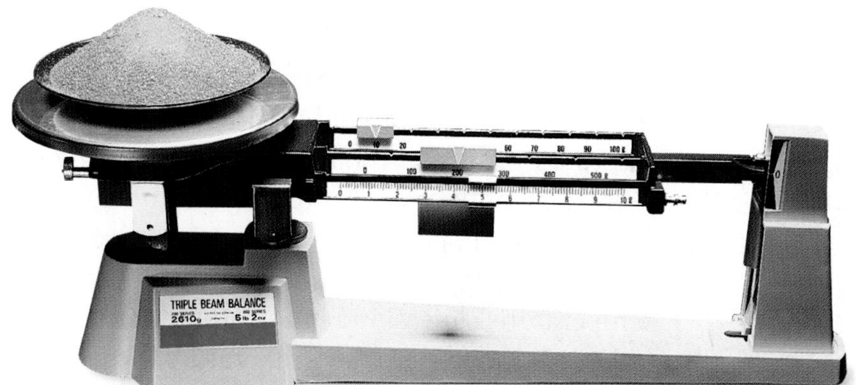

Figure 10
A triple beam balance compares an unknown mass to known masses.

Mass

The **mass** of an object measures the amount of matter in the object. The **kilogram** (kg) is the SI unit for mass. One liter of water has a mass of about 1 kg. Smaller masses are measured in grams (g). One gram is about the mass of a large paper clip.

You can determine mass with a triple beam balance, shown in **Figure 10.** The balance compares an object to a known mass. It is balanced when the known mass of the slides on the balance is equal to the mass of the object on the pan.

Why use the word *mass* instead of *weight?* Weight and mass are not the same. Mass depends only on the amount of matter in an object. If you ride in an elevator in the morning and then ride in the space shuttle later that afternoon, your mass is the same. Mass does not change when only your location changes.

Weight Weight is a measurement of force. The SI unit for weight is the newton (N). Weight depends on gravity, which can change depending on where the object is located. A spring scale measures how a planet's gravitational force pulls on objects. Several spring scales are shown in **Figure 11.**

If you were to travel to other planets, your weight would change, even though you would still be the same size and have the same mass. This is because gravitational force is different on each planet. If you could take your bathroom scale, which uses a spring, to each of the planets in this solar system, you would find that you weigh much less on Mars and much more on Jupiter. A mass of 75 pounds, or 34 kg, on Earth is a weight of 332 N. On Mars, the same mass is 126 N, and on Jupiter it is 782 N.

Reading Check *What does weight measure?*

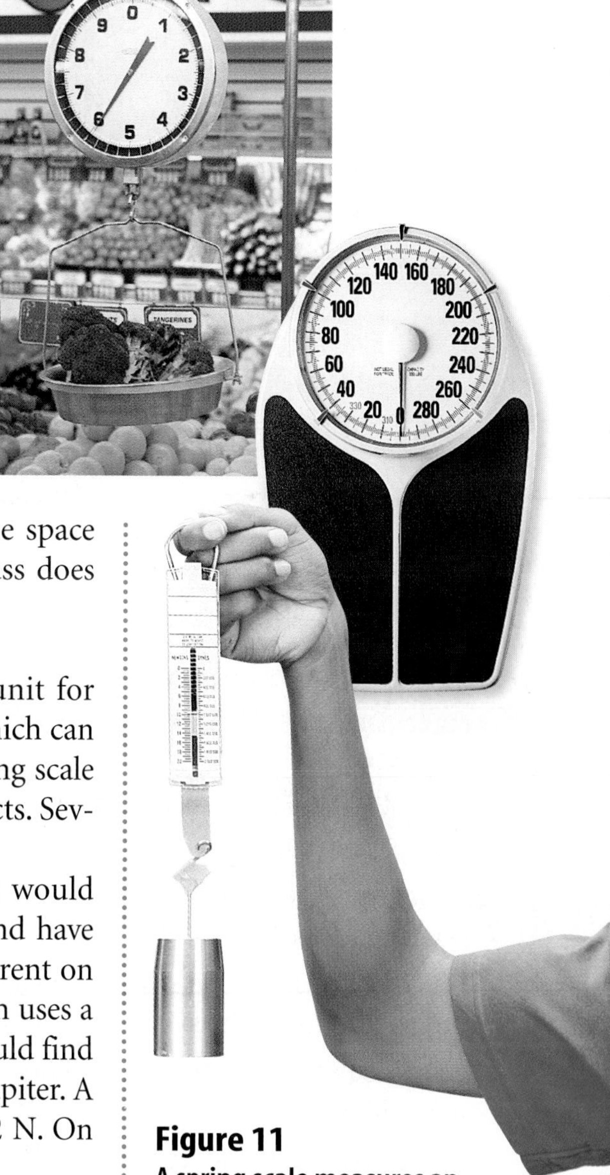

Figure 11
A spring scale measures an object's weight by how much it stretches a spring.

Figure 12
The kelvin scale starts at 0 K. In theory, 0 K is the coldest temperature possible in nature.

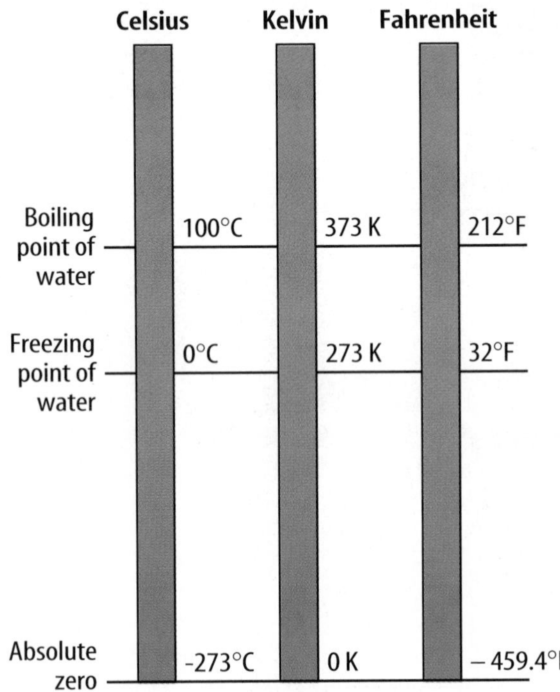

Temperature

The physical property of temperature is related to how hot or cold an object is. Temperature is a measure of the kinetic energy, or energy of motion, of the particles that make up matter.

The Fahrenheit and Celsius temperature scales are two common scales used on thermometers. Temperature is measured in SI with the **kelvin (K)** scale. A 1-K difference in temperature is the same as a 1°C difference in temperature, as shown in **Figure 12.** However, the two scales do not start at zero.

Time and Rates

Time is the interval between two events. The SI unit of time is the second (s). Time also is measured in hours (h). Although the hour is not an SI unit, it is easier to use for long periods of time. Can you imagine hearing that a marathon was run in 7,620 s instead of 2 h and 7 min?

A **rate** is the amount of change of one measurement in a given amount of time. One rate you are familiar with is speed, which is the distance traveled in a given time. Speeds often are measured in kilometers per hour (km/h).

The unit that is changing does not necessarily have to be an SI unit. For example, you can measure the number of cars that pass through an intersection per hour in cars/h. The annual rate of inflation can be measured in percent/year.

Section  Assessment

1. Describe a situation in which different units of measure could cause confusion.
2. What type of quantity does the cubic meter measure?
3. How would you change a measurement in centimeters to kilometers?
4. What SI unit replaces the pound? What does this measure?
5. **Think Critically** You are told to find the mass of a metal cube. How will you do it?

Skill Builder Activities

6. **Measuring in SI** Measure the length, volume, and mass of your textbook in SI units. Describe any tools or calculations you use. **For more help, refer to the** Science Skill Handbook.
7. **Converting Units** A block of wood is 0.2 m by 0.1 m by 0.5 m. Find its dimensions in centimeters. Use these to find its volume in cubic centimeters. Show your work. **For more help, refer to the** Math Skill Handbook.

Activity

Scale Drawing

A scale drawing is used to represent something that is too large or too small to be drawn at its actual size. Blueprints for a house are a good example of a scale drawing.

What You'll Investigate

How can you represent your classroom accurately in a scale drawing?

Materials

1-cm graph paper
pencil
metric ruler
meterstick

Goals

- **Measure** using SI.
- **Make** a data table.
- **Calculate** new measurements.
- **Make** an accurate scale drawing.

Procedure

1. Use your meterstick to measure the length and width of your classroom. Note the locations and sizes of doors and windows.
2. **Record** the lengths of each item in a data table similar to the one below.
3. Use a scale of 2 cm = 1 m to calculate the lengths to be used in the drawing. Record them in your data table.
4. **Draw** the floor plan. Include the scale.

Room Dimensions

Part of Room	Distance in Room (m)	Distance on Drawing (cm)

Conclude and Apply

1. How did you calculate the lengths to be used on your drawing? Did you put a scale on your drawing?
2. What would your scale drawing look like if you chose a different scale?
3. **Sketch** your room at home, estimating the distances. Compare this sketch to your scale drawing of the classroom. When would you use each type of illustration?
4. What measuring tool simplifies this task?

Communicating Your Data

Measure your room at home and compare it to the estimates on your sketch. Explain to someone at home what you did and how well you estimated the measurements. **For more help, refer to the** Science Skill Handbook.

SECTION 3

Drawings, Tables, and Graphs

As You Read

What You'll Learn

- **Describe** how to use pictures and tables to give information.
- **Identify** and use three types of graphs.
- **Distinguish** the correct use of each type of graph.

Vocabulary

table
graph
line graph
bar graph
circle graph

Why It's Important

Illustrations, tables, and graphs help you communicate data about the world around you in an organized and efficient way.

Scientific Illustrations

Most science books include pictures. Photographs and drawings model and illustrate ideas and sometimes make new information more clear than written text can. For example, a drawing of an airplane engine shows how all the parts fit together much better than several pages of text could describe it.

Drawings A drawing is sometimes the best choice to show details. For example, a canyon cut through red rock reveals many rock layers. If the layers are all shades of red, a drawing can show exactly where the lines between the layers are. The drawing can emphasize only the things that are necessary to show.

A drawing also can show things you can't see. You can't see the entire solar system, but drawings show you what it looks like. Also, you can make quick sketches to help model problems. For example, you could draw the outline of two continents to show how they might have fit together at one time.

A drawing can show hidden things, as well. A drawing can show the details of the water cycle, as in **Figure 13.** Architects use drawings to show what the inside of a building will look like. Biologists use drawings to show where the nerves in your arm are found.

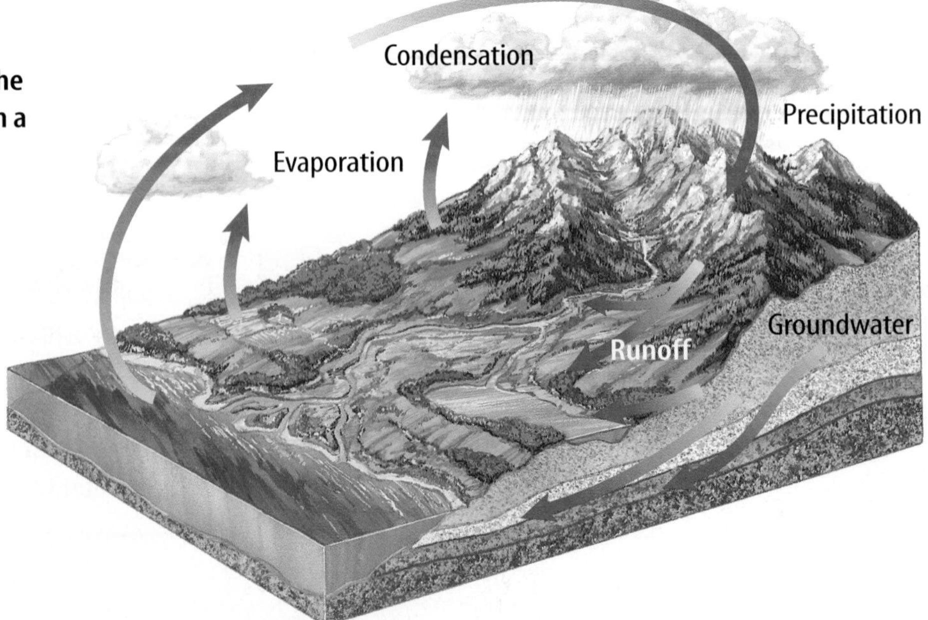

Figure 13
This drawing shows details of the water cycle that can't be seen in a photograph.

Photographs A still photograph shows an object exactly as it is at a single moment in time. Movies show how an object moves and can be slowed down or sped up to show interesting features. In your schoolwork, you might use photographs in a report. For example, you could show the different types of trees in your neighborhood for a report on ecology.

Tables and Graphs

Everyone who deals with numbers and compares measurements needs an organized way to collect and display data. A **table** displays information in rows and columns so that it is easier to read and understand, as seen in **Table 4.** The data in the table could be presented in a paragraph, but it would be harder to pick out the facts or make comparisons.

A **graph** is used to collect, organize, and summarize data in a visual way. The relationships between the data often are seen more clearly when shown in a graph. Three common types of graphs are line, bar, and circle graphs.

Line Graph A **line graph** shows the relationship between two variables. A variable is something that can change, or vary, such as the temperature of a liquid or the number of people in a race. Both variables in a line graph must be numbers. An example of a line graph is shown in **Figure 14.** One variable is shown on the horizontal axis, or *x*-axis, of the graph. The other variable is placed along the vertical axis, or *y*-axis. A line on the graph shows the relationship between the two variables.

Table 4 Endangered Species in the United States

Year	Number of Endangered Species
1980	174
1982	179
1984	192
1986	213
1988	245
1990	263
1992	284
1994	321
1996	324
1998	357

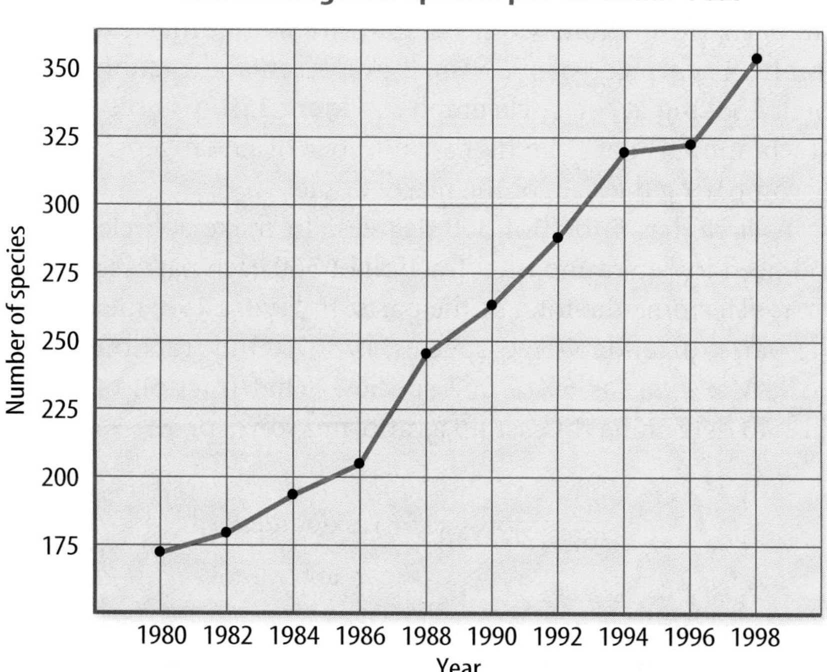

Figure 14
To find the number of endangered animal species in 1988, find that year on the *x*-axis and see what number corresponds to it on the *y*-axis.

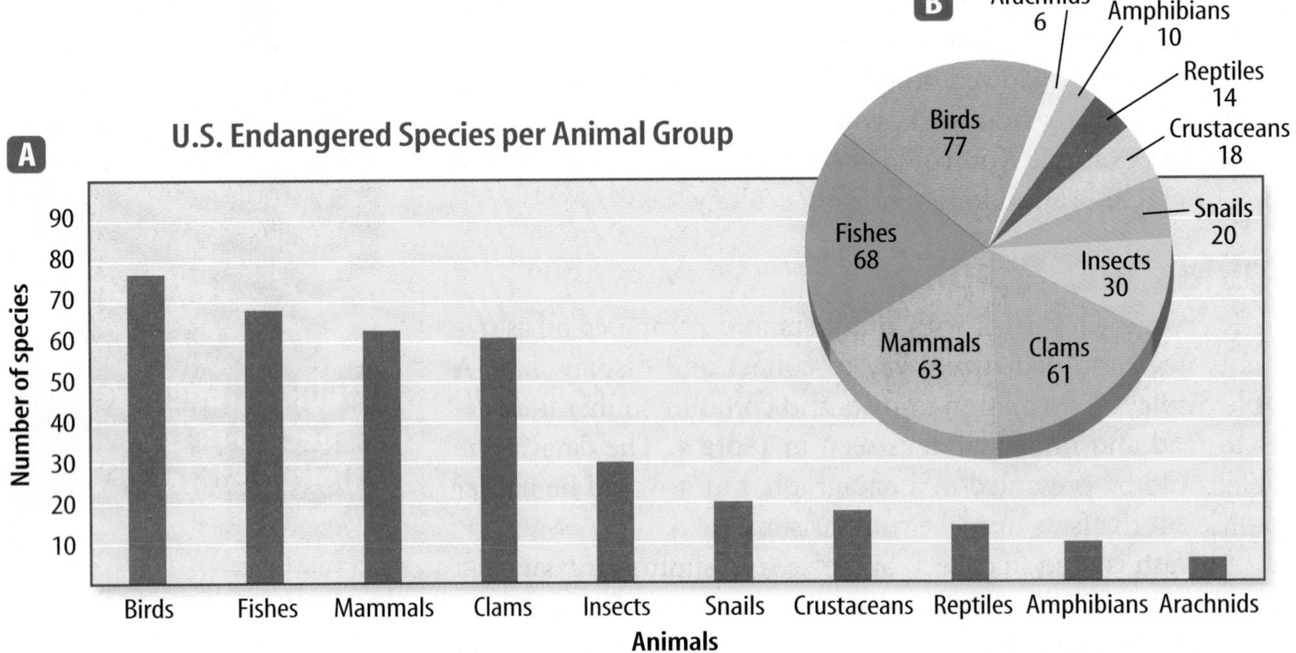

Figure 15
A Bar graphs allow you to picture the results easily. *Which category of animals has the most endangered species?* **B On this circle graph, you can see what part of the whole each animal represents.**

Bar Graph A **bar graph** uses rectangular blocks, or bars, of varying sizes to show the relationships among variables. One variable is divided into parts. It can be numbers, such as the time of day, or a category, such as an animal. The second variable must be a number. The bars show the size of the second variable. For example, if you made a bar graph of the endangered species data from **Figure 14,** the bar for 1990 would represent 263 species. An example of a bar graph is shown in **Figure 15A.**

Circle Graph Suppose you want to show the relationship among the types of endangered species. A **circle graph** shows the parts of a whole. Circle graphs are sometimes called pie graphs. Each piece of pie visually represents a fraction of the total. Looking at the circle graph in **Figure 15B,** you see quickly which animals have the highest number of endangered species by comparing the sizes of the pieces of pie.

A circle has a total of 360 degrees. To make a circle graph, you need to determine what fraction of 360 each part should be. First, determine the total of the parts. In **Figure 15B,** the total of the parts, or endangered species, is 367. One fraction of the total, *Mammals*, is 63 of 367 species. What fraction of 360 is this? To determine this, set up a ratio and solve for x:

$$\frac{63}{367} = \frac{x}{360} \qquad x = 61.8 \text{ degrees}$$

Mammals will have an angle of 61.8 degrees in the graph. The other angles in the circle are determined the same way.

Research Visit the Glencoe Science Web site at **science.glencoe.com** for more information about scientific illustrations. Communicate to your class what you learn.

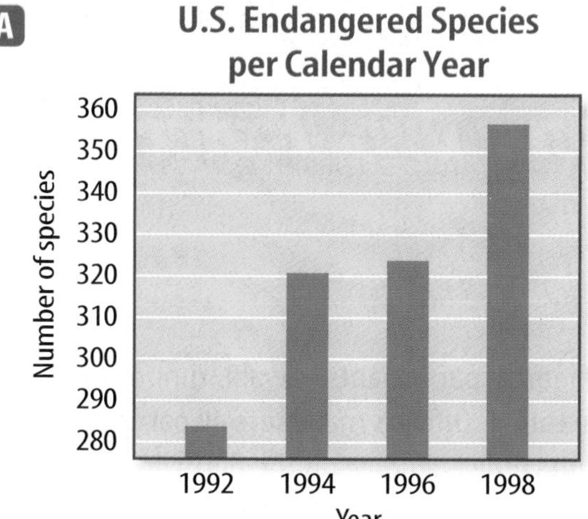

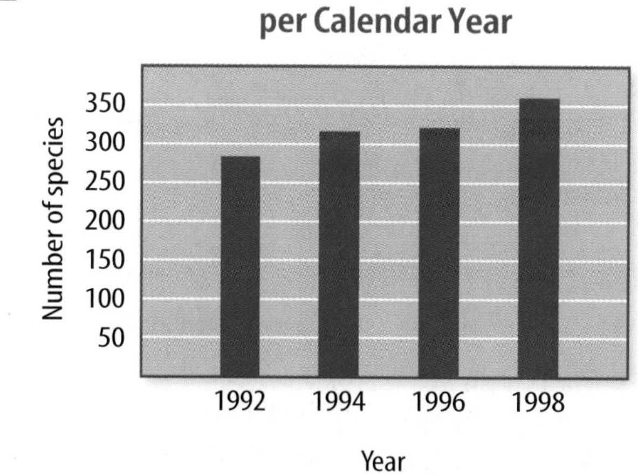

Reading Graphs When you are using or making graphs to display data, be careful—the scale of a graph can be misleading. The way the scale on a graph is marked can create the wrong impression, as seen in **Figure 16A.** Until you see that the *y*-axis doesn't start at zero, it appears that the number of endangered species has quadrupled in just six years.

This is called a broken scale and is used to highlight small but significant changes, just as an inset on a map draws attention to a small area of a larger map. **Figure 16B** shows the same data on a graph that does not have a broken scale. The number of species has only increased 22 percent from 1980 to 1986. Both graphs have correct data, but must be read carefully. Always analyze the measurements and graphs that you come across. If there is a surprising result, look closer at the scale.

Figure 16
Careful reading of graphs is important. A This graph does not start at zero, which makes it appear that the number of species has more than quadrupled from 1980 to 1986. B The actual increase is about 22 percent as you can see from this full graph. The broken scale must be noted in order to interpret the results correctly.

Section  Assessment

1. Describe a time when an illustration would be helpful in everyday activities.
2. Explain how to use **Figure 16** to find the number of endangered species in 1998.
3. Explain the difference between tables and graphs.
4. Suppose your class surveys students about after-school activities. What type of graph would you use to display your data? Explain.
5. **Think Critically** How are line, bar, and circle graphs the same? How are they different?

Skill Builder Activities

6. **Making and Using Graphs** Record the amount of time you spend reading each day for the next week. Then make a graph to display the data. What type of graph will you use? Could more than one kind of graph be used? **For more help, refer to the** Science Skill Handbook.
7. **Using an Electronic Spreadsheet** Use a spreadsheet to display how the total mass of a 500-kg elevator changes as 50-kg passengers are added one at a time. **For more help, refer to the** Technology Skill Handbook.

Activity Design Your Own Experiment

Pace Yourself

Track meets and other competitions require participants to walk, run, or wheel a distance that has been precisely measured. Officials make sure all participants begin at the same time, and each person's time is stopped at the finish line. If you are practicing for a marathon or 10K race, you need to know your speed or pace in order to compare it with those of other participants. How can your performance be measured accurately?

Recognize the Problem

How will you measure the speed of each person in your group? How will you display these data?

Form a Hypothesis

Think about the information you have learned about precision, measurement, and graphing. In your group, make a hypothesis about a technique that will provide you with the most precise measurement of each person's pace.

Goals

- **Design** an experiment that allows you to measure speed for each member of your group accurately.
- **Display** data in a table and a graph.

Possible Materials

meterstick
stopwatch
**watch with a second hand*

**Alternate materials*

Safety Precautions

Work in an area where it is safe to run. Participate only if you are physically able to exercise safely. As you design your plan, make a list of all the specific safety and health precautions you will take as you perform the investigation. Get your teacher's approval of the list before you begin.

Test Your Hypothesis

Plan

1. As a group, decide what materials you will need.
2. How far will you travel? How will you measure that distance? How precise can you be?
3. How will you measure time? How precise can you be?
4. List the steps and materials you will use to test your hypothesis. Be specific. Will you try any part of your test more than once?
5. Before you begin, create a data table. Your group must decide on its design. Be sure to leave enough room to record the results for each person's time. If more than one trial is to be run for each measurement, include room for the additional data.

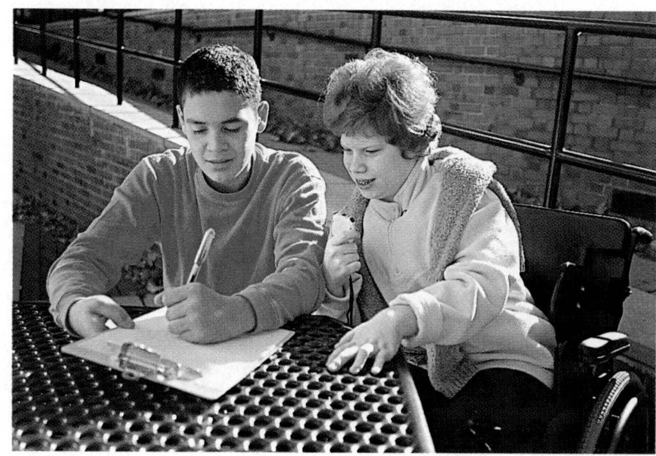

Do

1. Make sure that your teacher approves your plan before you start.
2. Carry out the experiment as planned and approved.
3. Be sure to record your data in the data table as you proceed with the measurements.

Analyze Your Data

1. **Graph** your data. What type of graph would be best?
2. Are your data table and graph easy to understand? Explain.
3. How do you know that your measurements are precise?
4. Do any of your data appear to be out of line with the rest?

Draw Conclusions

1. How is it possible for different members of a group to find different times while measuring the same event?
2. What tools would help you collect more precise data?
3. What other data displays could you use? What are the advantages and disadvantages of each?

Communicating Your Data

Make a larger version of your graph to display in your classroom with the graphs of other groups. **For more help, refer to the Science Skill Handbook.**

Science Stats

Biggest, Tallest, Loudest

Did you know...

... The world's most massive flower belongs to a species called *Rafflesia* (ruh FLEE zhee uh) and has a mass of up to 11 kg. The diameter, or the distance across the flower's petals, can measure up to 1 m.

... The world's tallest building is the Petronus Towers in Kuala Lumpur, Malaysia. It is 452 m tall. The tallest building in the United States is Chicago's Sears Tower, shown here, which measures 442 m.

... The Grand Canyon is so deep— as much as 1,800 m—that it can hold more than four Empire State Buildings stacked on top of one another.

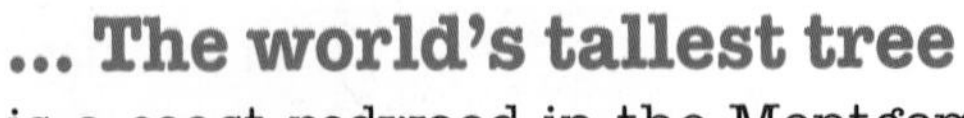

... The world's tallest tree is a coast redwood in the Montgomery Woods State Park in California. The tree stands 112.1 m high.

...The largest animal on Earth is the blue whale. It can grow to be 33.5 m long. If 20 people who are each 1.65 m tall were lying head to toe, it would almost equal this length.

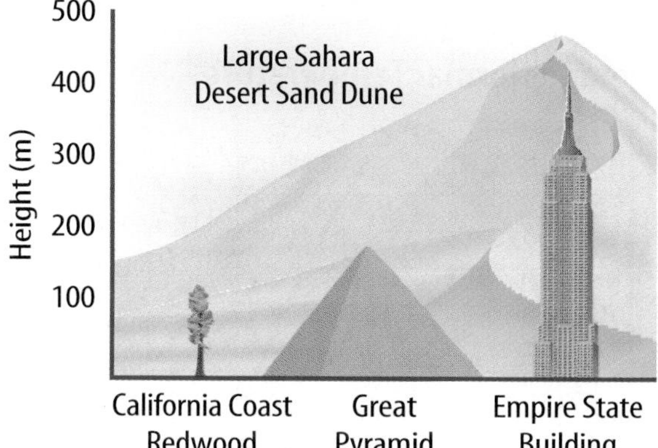

...One of the loudest explosions on Earth was the 1883 eruption of Krakatau (krah kuh TAHEW), an Indonesian volcano. It was heard from more than 3,500 km away.

Do the Math

1. How many of the largest rafflesia petals would you have to place side by side to equal the length of a blue whale?
2. When Krakatau erupted, it ejected 18,000 km^3 of ash and rock. Other large eruptions released the following: Mount Pinatubo—7,000 km^3, Mount Katmai—13,000 km^3, Tambora—30,000 km^3, Vesuvius—5,000 km^3. Make a bar graph to compare the sizes of these eruptions.
3. Use the information provided about the Grand Canyon to calculate how many Sears Towers would have to stand end on end to equal the depth of the canyon.

Go Further

Do research on the Internet at **science.glencoe.com** to find facts that describe some of the shortest, smallest, or fastest things on Earth. Create a class bulletin board with the facts you and your classmates find.

Chapter 2 Study Guide

Reviewing Main Ideas

Section 1 Description and Measurement

1. Measurements such as length, volume, mass, temperature, and rates are used to describe objects and events.
2. Estimation is used to make an educated guess at a measurement.
3. Accuracy describes how close a measurement is to the true value.
4. Precision describes how close measurements are to each other. *Are the shots accurate or precise on the basketball hoop shown?*

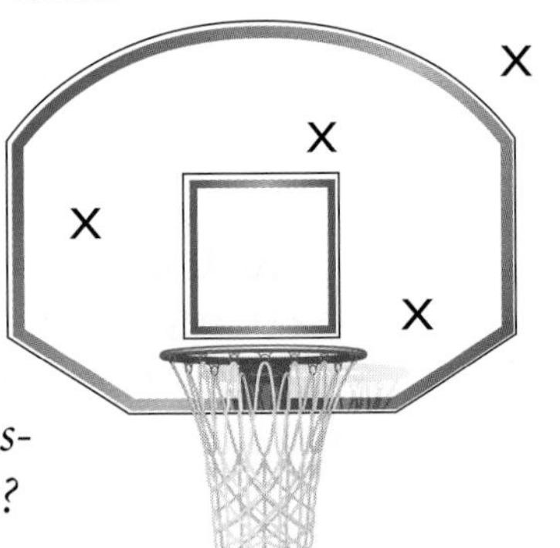

Section 2 SI Units

1. The international system of measurement is called SI. It is used throughout the world for communicating data.
2. The SI unit of length is the meter. Volume—the amount of space an object occupies—can be measured in cubic meters. The mass of an object is measured in kilograms. The SI unit of temperature is the kelvin. *What type of measurement is being made according to the sign shown?*

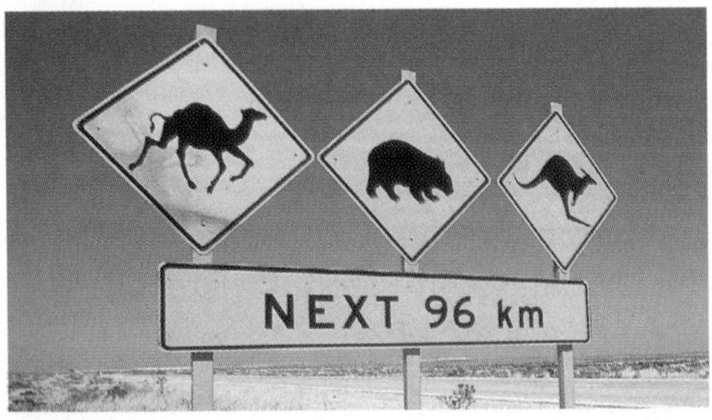

Section 3 Drawings, Tables, and Graphs

1. Tables, photographs, drawings, and graphs can sometimes present data more clearly than explaining everything in words. Scientists use these tools to collect, organize, summarize, and display data in a way that is easy to use and understand.
2. The three common types of graphs are line graphs, bar graphs, and circle graphs. *Which city on the line graph shown is the coldest in the fifth month?*

Average Normal Temperature

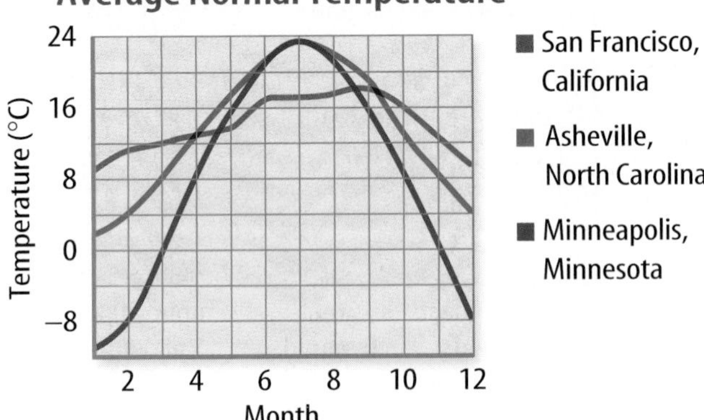

3. Line graphs show the relationship between two variables that are numbers on an *x*-axis and a *y*-axis. Bar graphs divide a variable into parts to show a relationship. Circle graphs show the parts of a whole like pieces of a pie.

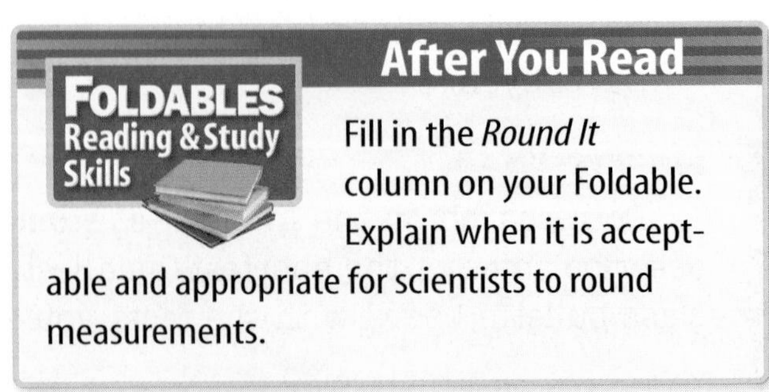

After You Read

Fill in the *Round It* column on your Foldable. Explain when it is acceptable and appropriate for scientists to round measurements.

Visualizing Main Ideas

Complete the following concept map.

SI Measurements

quantities measured | quantities measured

	Mass	Time		Temperature	
Meter			Cubic meter		Newton

SI units used to describe measurements | SI units used to describe measurements

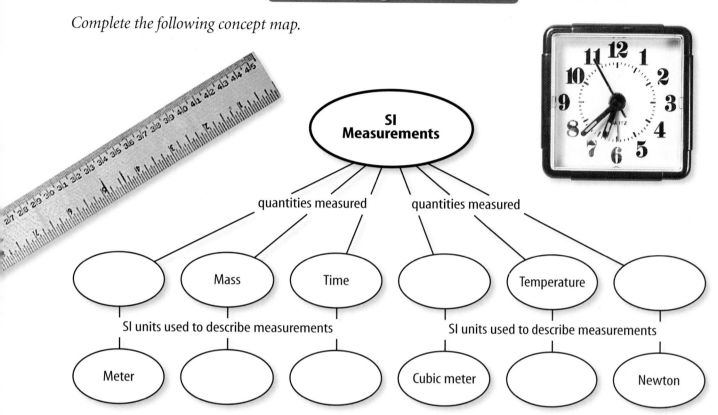

Vocabulary Review

Vocabulary Words

a. accuracy
b. bar graph
c. circle graph
d. estimation
e. graph
f. kelvin
g. kilogram
h. line graph
i. mass
j. measurement
k. meter
l. precision
m. rate
n. SI
o. table

Study Tip

When you encounter new vocabulary, write it down in your Science Journal. This will help you understand and remember them.

Using Vocabulary

Each phrase below describes a vocabulary word. Write the word that matches the phrase describing it.

1. the SI unit for length
2. a description with numbers
3. a method of making a rough measurement
4. the amount of matter in an object
5. a graph that shows parts of a whole
6. a description of how close measurements are to each other
7. the SI unit for temperature
8. an international system of units

Chapter 2 Assessment

Checking Concepts

Choose the word or phrase that best answers the question.

1. The measurement 25.81 g is precise to the nearest what?
   A) gram
   B) kilogram
   C) tenth of a gram
   D) hundredth of a gram
2. What is the SI unit of mass?
   A) kilometer **C)** liter
   B) meter **D)** kilogram
3. What would you use to measure length?
   A) graduated cylinder
   B) balance
   C) meterstick
   D) spring scale
4. The cubic meter is the SI unit of what?
   A) volume **C)** mass
   B) weight **D)** distance
5. Which term describes how close measurements are to each other?
   A) significant digits **C)** accuracy
   B) estimation **D)** precision
6. Which is a temperature scale?
   A) volume **C)** Celsius
   B) mass **D)** mercury
7. Which is used to organize data?
   A) table **C)** precision
   B) rate **D)** meterstick
8. To show the number of wins for each football team in your district, which of the following would you use?
   A) photograph **C)** bar graph
   B) line graph **D)** SI
9. What organizes data in rows and columns?
   A) bar graph **C)** line graph
   B) circle graph **D)** table
10. To show 25 percent on a circle graph, the section must measure what angle?
    A) 25° **C)** 180°
    B) 90° **D)** 360°

Thinking Critically

11. How would you estimate the volume your backpack could hold?
12. Why do scientists in the United States use SI rather than the English system (feet, pounds, pints, etc.) of measurement?
13. List the following in order from smallest to largest: 1 m, 1 mm, 10 km, 100 mm.
14. Describe an instance when you would use a line graph. Can you use a bar graph for the same purpose?
15. Computer graphics artists can specify the color of a point on a monitor by using characters for the intensities of three colors of light. Why was this method of describing color invented?

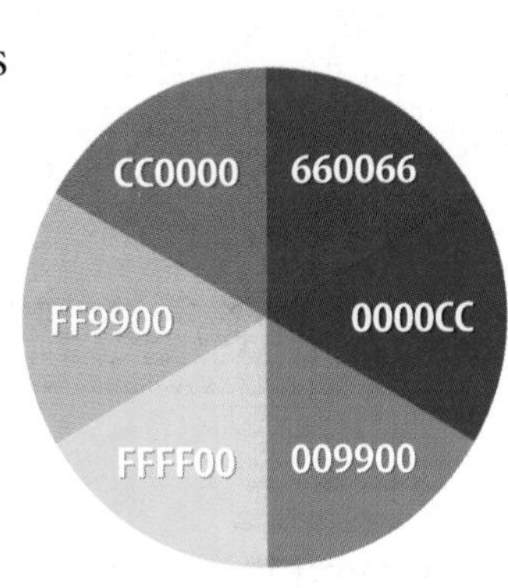

Developing Skills

16. **Measuring in SI** Make a fist. Use a centimeter ruler to measure the height, width, and depth of your fist.
17. **Comparing and Contrasting** How are volume, length, and mass similar? How are they different? Give several examples of units that are used to measure each quantity. Which units are SI?

18. Making and Using Graphs The table shows the area of several bodies of water. Make a bar graph of the data.

Areas of Bodies of Water

Body of Water	Area (km^2)
Currituck Sound (North Carolina)	301
Pocomoke Sound (Maryland/Virginia)	286
Chincoteague Bay (Maryland/Virginia)	272
Core Sound (North Carolina)	229

19. Interpreting Scientific Illustrations What does the figure show? How has this drawing been simplified?

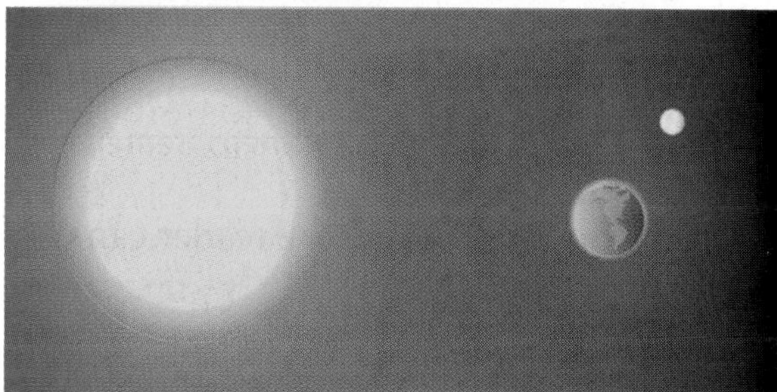

Performance Assessment

20. Poster Make a poster to alert the public about the benefits of using SI units.

21. Newspaper Search Look through a week's worth of newspapers and evaluate any graphs or tables that you find.

Technology

Go to the Glencoe Science Web site at **science.glencoe.com** or use the **Glencoe Science CD-ROM** for additional chapter assessment.

Test Practice

Some students in Mrs. Olsen's science class measured their masses during three consecutive months. They placed their results in the following table. Study the table and answer the following questions.

Student Masses: Sept. – Nov. 1999

Student	September	October	November
Domingo	41.13 kg	40.92 kg	42.27 kg
Latoya	35.21 kg	35.56 kg	36.07 kg
Benjamin	45,330 g	45,680 g	45,530 g
Poloma	31.78 kg	31.55 kg	31.51 kg
Frederick	50,870 g	51,880 g	51,030 g
Fiona	37.62 kg	37.71 kg	37.85 kg

1. According to the table, which shows Frederick's weight in kilograms for the three months?

A) 5.087, 5.118, 5.103
B) 50.87, 51.88, 51.03
C) 508.7, 511.8, 510.3
D) 5,087, 5,118, 5,103

2. According to this information, which lists the students from lightest to heaviest during November?

F) Poloma, Benjamin, Domingo, Frederick
G) Domingo, Latoya, Frederick, Benjamin
H) Fiona, Domingo, Benjamin, Frederick
J) Frederick, Benjamin, Domingo, Poloma

Standardized Test Practice

Reading Comprehension

Read the passage carefully. Then read each question that follows the passage. Decide which is the best answer to each question.

History of Measurement Units

In modern society, units of measurement that have been defined and agreed upon by international scientists are used. In ancient times, people were just beginning to invent and use units of measurement. For example, thousands of years ago, a cabinetmaker would build one cabinet at a time and measure the pieces of wood needed relative to the size of the other pieces of that cabinet. Today, factories manufacture many of the same products. Ancient cabinetmakers rarely made two cabinets that were exactly the same. Eventually, it became obvious that units of measurement had to mean the same thing to everybody.

Measurements, such as the inch, foot, and yard, began many years ago as fairly crude units. For example, the modern-day inch began as "the width of one's thumb." The foot originally was defined as "the length of one's foot." The yard was defined as "the distance from the tip of one's nose to the end of one's arm."

Although using these units of measurement was easier than not using any units of measurement, these ancient units were confusing. Human beings come in many different sizes and shapes, and one person's foot can be much larger than another person's foot. So, whose foot defines a foot? Whose thumb width defines an inch? Ancient civilizations used these kinds of measurements for thousands of years. Over time, these units were redefined and standardized, eventually becoming the exact units of measurement that you know today.

Test-Taking Tip After you read and think about the passage, write one or two sentences that summarize the most important points. Read your sentences out loud.

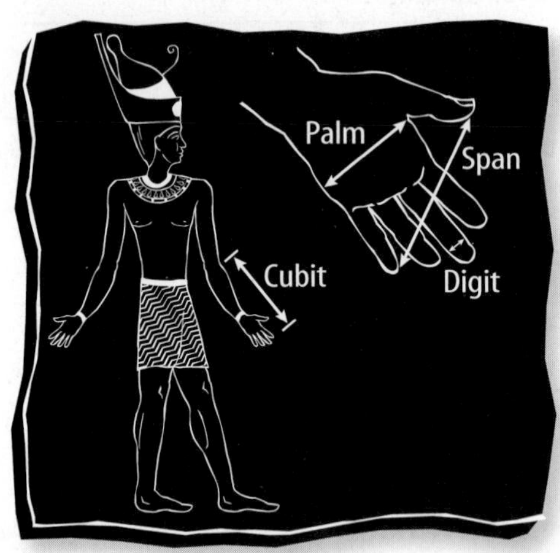

Ancient people created units of measurement.

1. Based on the passage, the reader can conclude that _____.

A) ancient cultures had no concept of measurement

B) standards of measurement developed over a long period of time

C) ancient people were probably good at communicating exacts units of measurement

D) units of measurement are needed only in modern and technologically advanced societies

2. According to the passage, which of these best describes ancient units of measurement?

F) precise

G) incorrect

H) approximate

J) irresponsible

Standardized Test Practice

Reasoning and Skills

Read each question and choose the best answer.

1. All of these are things that can be measured accurately EXCEPT _____.
A) the temperature of a human body
B) the space that a couch takes up in a living room
C) the beauty in a piece of artwork
D) the mass of a rock from the Moon

Test-Taking Tip Think about the reasons why people use measurement and the kinds of things that can and cannot be measured.

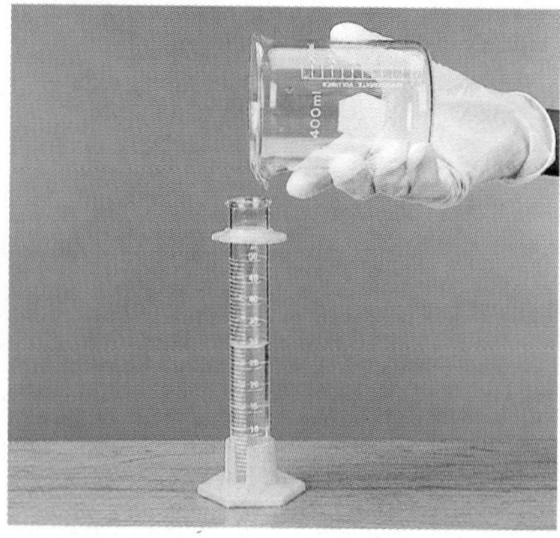

2. Jodie and William are using the graduated cylinder pictured above to measure the volume of liquid in milliliters. What multiple of a liter is a milliliter?
F) 1,000
G) 0.01
H) 0.001
J) 0.000 001

Test-Taking Tip Consider the prefixes used in SI units, as well as the amount of liquid shown.

Group S
• How does this medication work to reduce a fever?
• Why do tides occur?
• What is the melting point of iron?
• What was Earth's climate like in the past?

Group T
• Who would make the best class president?
• Is it right to compliment a friend's new shirt if you don't like the shirt?
• Shouldn't everyone like cauliflower, broccoli, turnips, and spinach?
• Why is a sunset beautiful?

3. The questions in Group S are different from the questions in Group T because only the questions in Group S _____.
A) cannot be answered by science
B) will have answers that are solely opinions
C) can be answered with absolute certainty
D) can be answered by science

Test-Taking Tip Think about the kinds of questions that scientists try to and are able to answer.

Consider this question carefully before writing your answer on a separate sheet of paper.

4. Suppose you decide to investigate this problem: Which brand of fertilizer produces the most tomatoes per plant? Identify the independent and dependent variables. List the constants in your investigation.

Test-Taking Tip Think about the procedures that scientists must go through in order to discover and explain.

UNIT 2 Matter

How Are Refrigerators & Frying Pans Connected?

In the late 1930s, scientists were experimenting with a gas that they hoped would work as a new coolant in refrigerators. They filled several metal canisters with the gas and stored the canisters on dry ice. Later, when they opened the canisters, they were surprised to find that the gas had disappeared and that the inside of each canister was coated with a slick, powdery white solid. The gas had undergone a chemical change. That is, the chemical bonds in its molecules had broken and new bonds had formed, turning one kind of matter into a completely different kind of matter. Strangely, the mysterious white powder proved to be just about the slipperiest substance that anyone had ever encountered. Years later, a creative Frenchman obtained some of the slippery stuff and tried applying it to his fishing tackle to keep the lines from tangling. His wife noticed what he was doing and suggested putting the substance on the inside of a frying pan to keep food from sticking. He did, and nonstick cookware was born!

SCIENCE CONNECTION

PHYSICAL AND CHEMICAL CHANGES Working in teams of 3 or 4, look up and write down the definitions of "physical change" and "chemical change." Then brain-storm to compile a list of 10 physical and 10 chemical changes that you might encounter in everyday life. Make flashcards from your list. On each card, write a description of the change on one side and the type of change on the other side. Pair up with another team and use your flashcards to quiz each other.

CHAPTER 3

Atoms, Elements, and the Periodic Table

The sky is clear and the breeze is light—perfect conditions for a hot-air balloon ride. You lift off and soar above the treetops. During your flight, you look up inside the balloon. What is keeping you airborne? Is it the air, the heat, or the balloon? It has something to do with matter, but how can you tell what is matter and what isn't?

What do you think?

Science Journal Look at the picture below with a classmate. Discuss what this might be. Here's a hint: *It's a small version of the real thing.* Write your answer or best guess in your Science Journal.

You've just finished playing basketball. You're hot and thirsty. You reach for your bottle of water and take a drink. Releasing your grip, you notice that the bottle is nearly empty. Is the bottle really almost empty? According to the dictionary, *empty* means "containing nothing." When you have finished all the water in the bottle, will it be empty or full?

Observe matter

1. Wad up a dry paper towel or tissue and tape it to the inside of a plastic cup as shown.
2. Fill a bowl or sink with water. Turn the cup upside down and slowly push the cup straight down into the water as far as you can.
3. Slowly raise the cup straight up and out of the water. Remove the paper towel or tissue paper and examine it.

Observe

In your Science Journal, describe the activity and its results. Explain what you think happened. Was anything in the cup besides the paper? If so, what was it?

Before You Read

Making a Main Ideas Study Fold **Before you read the chapter, make the following Foldable to help you identify the main ideas about atoms, elements, compounds, and mixtures.**

1. Place a sheet of paper in front of you so the long side is at the top. Fold the paper in half from the left side to the right side and then unfold.
2. Fold each side in to the centerfold line to divide the paper into fourths.
3. Fold the paper in half from top to bottom and unfold again. Label the areas *Atoms, Elements, Compounds* and *Mixtures,* as shown.
4. Through the top thickness of paper, cut along both of the middle fold lines to form four tabs, as shown.
5. As you read the chapter, record information about each on the back of the four tabs.

SECTION

Structure of Matter

As You Read

What You'll Learn

- **Describe** characteristics of matter.
- **Identify** what makes up matter.
- **Identify** the parts of an atom.
- **Compare** the models that are used for atoms.

Vocabulary

matter
atom
law of conservation of matter
electron
nucleus
proton
neutron

Why It's Important

Matter makes up almost everything we see—and much of what we can't see.

What is matter?

Is a glass with some water in it half empty or half full? Actually, neither is correct. The glass is completely full—half full of water and half full of air. What is air? Air is a mixture of several gases, including nitrogen and oxygen, which are kinds of matter. **Matter** is anything that has mass and takes up space. So, even though you can't see it or hold it in your hand, air is matter. What about all the things you can see, taste, smell, and touch? They are made of matter, too. Look at the things in **Figure 1** and determine which of them are matter.

What isn't matter?

You can see the words on this page because of the light from the Sun or from a fixture in the room. Does light have mass or take up space? What about the warmth from the Sun or the heat from the heater in your classroom? Light and heat do not take up space, and they have no mass. Therefore, they are not forms of matter. Emotions, thoughts, and ideas are not matter either. Does this information change your mind about the items in **Figure 1?**

Reading Check *Why is air matter, but light is not?*

Figure 1
A rainbow is formed when light filters through the raindrops, a plant grows from a seed in the ground, and a statue is sculpted from bronze. *Which are matter?*

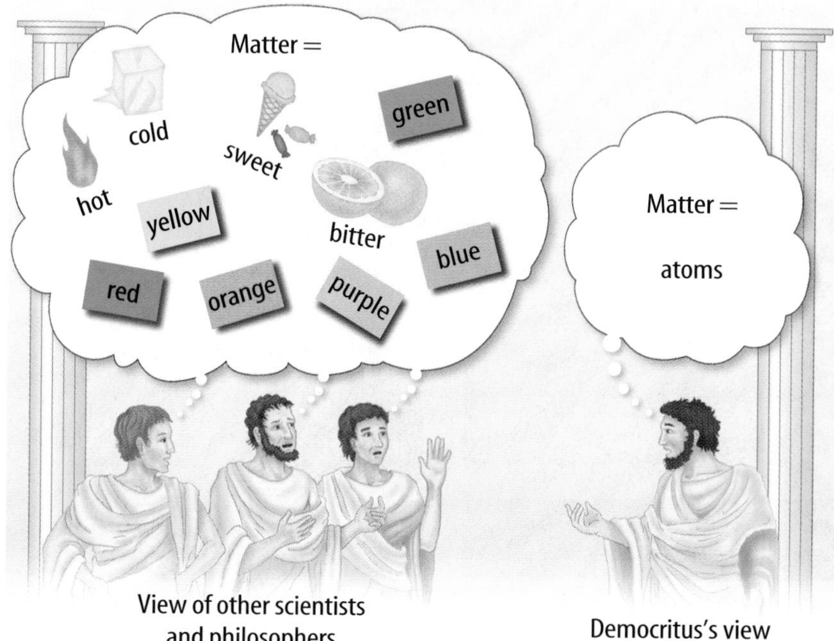

Figure 2
Democritus disagreed with other philosophers who thought that matter could be explained only by descriptive terms. In his view, all of the descriptions of matter were secondary to the identity of the atoms making it up.

What makes up matter?

Suppose you cut a chunk of wood into smaller and smaller pieces. Do the pieces seem to be made of the same matter as the large chunk you started with? If you could cut a small enough piece, would it still have the same properties as the first chunk? Would you reach a point where the last cut resulted in a piece that no longer resembled the first chunk? Is there a limit to how small a piece can be? For centuries, people have asked questions like these and wondered what matter is made of.

An Early Idea Democritus, who lived from about 460 B.C. to 370 B.C., was a Greek philosopher who thought the universe was made of empty space and tiny bits of stuff. He believed that the bits of stuff were so small they could no longer be divided into smaller pieces. He called these tiny pieces atoms. The term *atom* comes from a Greek word that means "cannot be divided." Today an **atom** is defined as a small particle that makes up most types of matter. **Figure 2** shows the difference between Democritus's ideas and those of other scientists and philosophers of the time. Democritus thought that different types of atoms existed for every type of matter and that the atom's identity explained the characteristics of each type of matter. Democritus's ideas about atoms were a first step toward understanding matter. However, his ideas were not accepted for over 2,000 years. It wasn't until the early 1800s that scientists built upon the concept of atoms to form the current atomic theory of matter.

Figure 3
When wood burns, matter is not lost. The total mass of the wood and the oxygen it combines with during a fire equals the total mass of the ash, water vapor, carbon dioxide, and other gases produced. *When you burn wood in a fireplace, what is the source of oxygen?*

Lavoisier's Contribution Lavoisier (la VWAH see ay), a French chemist who lived about 2,000 years after Democritus, also was curious about matter—especially when it changed form. Before Lavoisier, people thought matter could appear and disappear because of the changes they saw as matter burned or rusted. You might have thought that matter can disappear if you've ever watched wood burn in a fireplace or at a bonfire. Lavoisier showed that wood and the oxygen it combines with during burning have the same mass as the ash, water, carbon dioxide, and other gases that are produced, as shown in **Figure 3.** In a similar way, an iron bar, oxygen, and water have the same mass as the rust that forms when they interact. From Lavoisier's work came the **law of conservation of matter,** which states that matter is not created or destroyed—it only changes form.

Making a Model

Procedure
1. Your teacher will give you a **sealed shoe box** that contains **one or more items.**
2. Try to find out how many and what kinds of items are inside the box. You cannot look inside the box. The only observations you can make are by handling the box.

Analysis
1. How many items do you infer are in the box? Sketch the apparent shapes of the items and identify them if you can.
2. Compare your procedure with how scientists perform experiments and make models to find out more about the atom.

Models of the Atom

Models are often used for things that are too small or too large to be observed or that are too difficult to be understood easily. One way to make a model is to make a smaller version of something large. If you wanted to design a new sailboat, would you build a full-sized boat and hope it would float? It would be more effective, less expensive, and safer to build and test a smaller version first. Then, if it didn't float, you could change your design and build another model. You could keep trying until the model works.

In the case of atoms, scientists use large models to explain something that is too small to be looked at. These models of the atom were used to explain data or facts that were gathered experimentally. As a result, these models are also theories.

Dalton's Atomic Model In the early 1800s, an English schoolteacher and chemist named John Dalton studied the experiments of Lavoisier and others. Dalton thought he could design an atomic model that explained the results of those experiments. Dalton's atomic model was a set of ideas—not a physical object. Dalton believed that matter was made of atoms that were too small to be seen by the human eye. He also thought that each type of matter was made of only one kind of atom. For example, gold atoms make up a gold nugget and give a gold ring its shiny appearance. Likewise, iron atoms make up an iron bar and give it unique properties, and so on. Because predictions using Dalton's model were supported by data, the model became known as the Atomic Theory of Matter.

Sizes of Atoms Atoms are so small it would take about 1 million of them lined up in a row to equal the thickness of a human hair. For another example of how small atoms are, look at **Figure 4.** Imagine you are holding an orange in your hand. If you wanted to be able to see the individual atoms on the orange's surface, the size of the orange would have to be increased to the size of Earth. Then, imagine the Earth-sized orange covered with billions and billions of marbles. Each marble would represent one of the atoms on the skin of the orange. No matter what kind of model you use to picture it, the result is the same—an atom is an extremely small particle of matter.

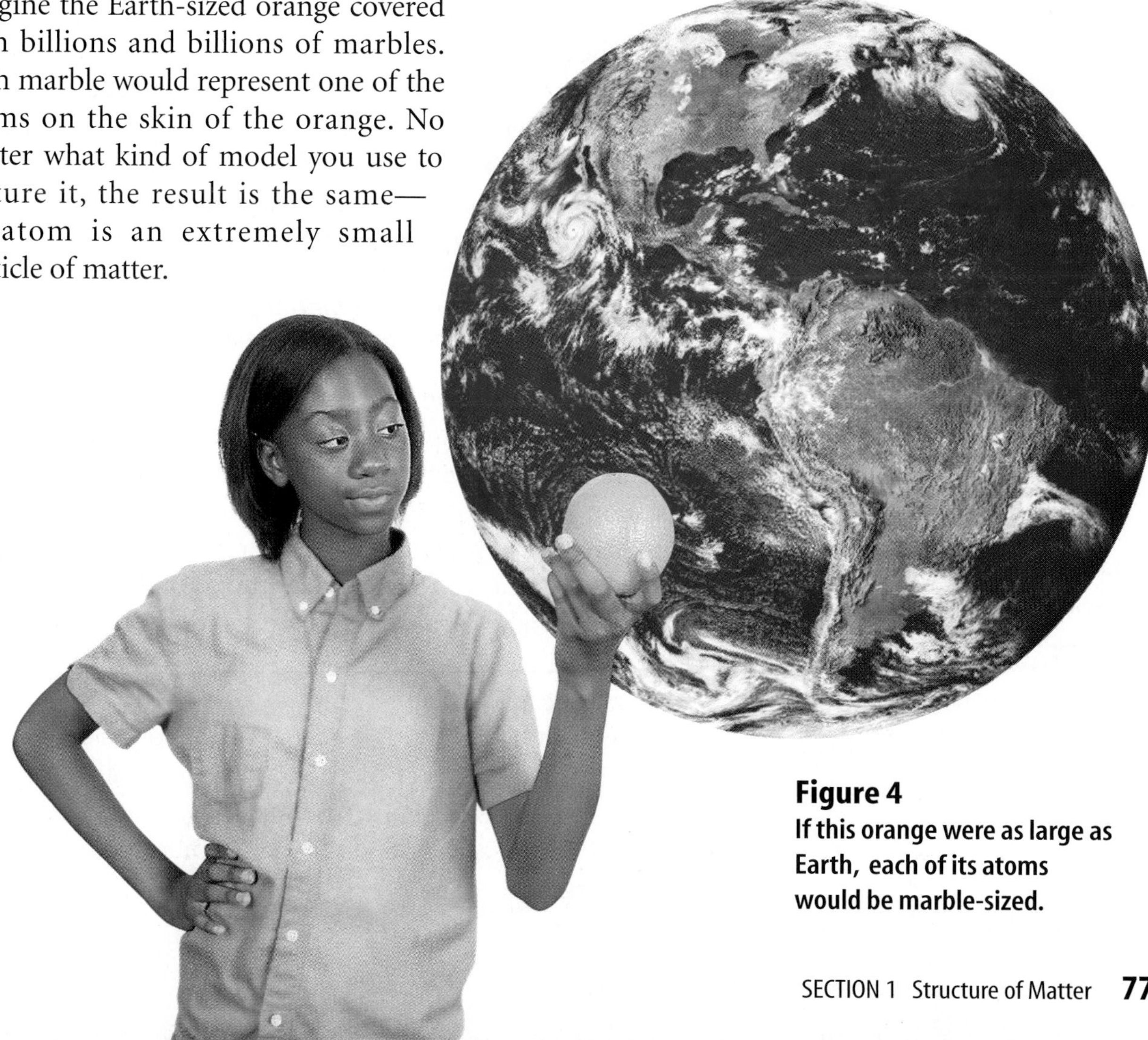

Figure 4
If this orange were as large as Earth, each of its atoms would be marble-sized.

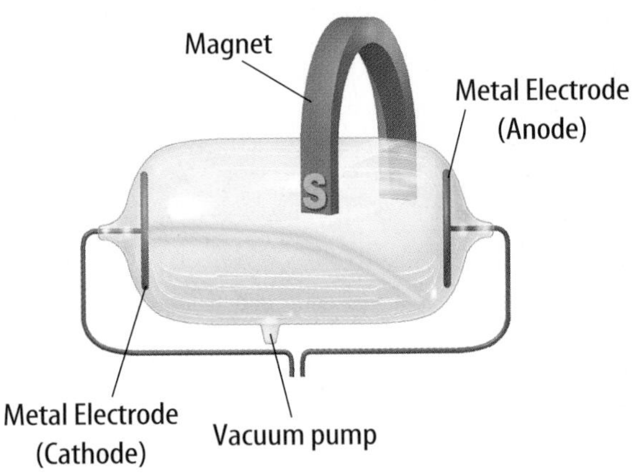

Figure 5
In Thomson's experiment, the magnet caused the cathode rays inside the tube to bend. *What do you think would happen to the cathode rays if the magnet were removed?*

Discovering the Electron One of the many pioneers in the development of today's atomic model was J.J. Thomson, an English scientist. He conducted experiments using a cathode ray tube, which is a glass tube sealed at both ends out of which most of the air has been pumped. Thomson's tube had a metal plate at each end. The plates were connected to a high-voltage electrical source that gave one of the plates—the anode—a positive charge and the other plate—the cathode—a negative charge. During his experiments, Thomson observed rays that traveled from the cathode to the anode. These cathode rays were bent by a magnet, as seen in **Figure 5,** showing that they were made up of particles that had mass and charge. Thomson knew that like charges repel each other and opposite charges attract each other. When he saw that the rays traveled toward a positively charged plate, he concluded that the cathode rays were made up of negatively charged particles. These invisible, negatively charged particles are called **electrons.**

Reading Check *Why were the cathode rays in Thomson's cathode ray tube bent by a magnet?*

Try to imagine Thomson's excitement at this discovery. He had shown that atoms are not too tiny to divide after all. Rather, they are made up of even smaller subatomic particles. Other scientists soon built upon Thomson's results and found that the electron had a small mass. In fact, an electron is 1/1,837 the mass of the lightest atom, the hydrogen atom. In 1906, Thomson received the Nobel Prize in Physics for his work on the discovery of the electron.

Matter that has an equal amount of positive and negative charge is said to be neutral—it has no net charge. Because most matter is neutral, Thomson pictured the atom as a ball of positive charge with electrons embedded in it. It was later determined that neutral atoms contained an equal number of positive and negative charges.

Collect Data Visit the Glencoe Science Web site at **science.glencoe.com** for more information about the particles that make up atoms. Can any of the particles be divided further? Display your data in a table.

Thomson's Model Thomson's model, shown in **Figure 6,** can be compared to chocolate chips spread throughout a ball of cookie dough. However, the model did not provide all the answers to the questions about atoms that puzzled scientists.

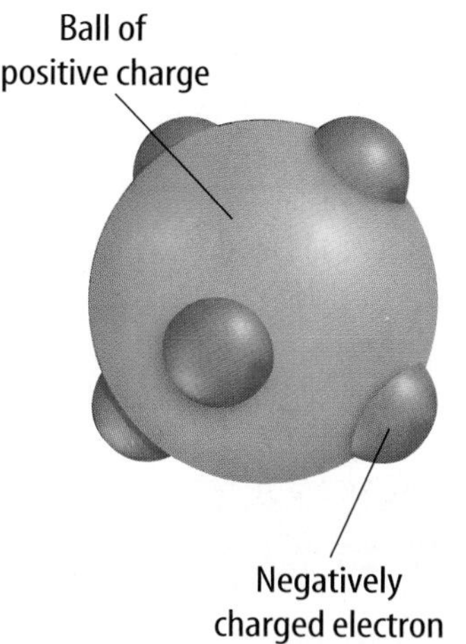

Figure 6
Thomson's model shows the atom as electrons embedded in a ball of positive charge. *How did Thomson know that atoms contain positive and negative charges?*

Rutherford—The Nucleus Scientists still had questions about how the atom was arranged and about the presence of positively charged particles. In 1909, a team of scientists led by Ernest Rutherford began their work on these questions. In their experiment, they bombarded an extremely thin piece of gold foil with alpha particles. Alpha particles are tiny, high-energy, positively charged particles that he predicted would pass through the foil. Most of the particles passed straight through the foil as if it were not there at all. However, other particles changed direction, and some even bounced back. Rutherford thought the result was so remarkable that he later said, "It was almost as incredible as if you had fired a 15-inch shell at a piece of tissue paper, and it came back and hit you."

Positive Center Rutherford concluded that because so many of the alpha particles passed straight through the gold foil, the atoms must be made of mostly empty space. However, because some of the positively charged alpha particles bounced off of something, the gold atoms must contain some positively charged object concentrated in the midst of this empty space. Rutherford called the positively charged, central part of the atom the **nucleus** (NEW klee us). He named the positively charged particles in the nucleus **protons.** He also suggested that electrons were scattered in the mostly empty space around the nucleus, as shown in **Figure 7.**

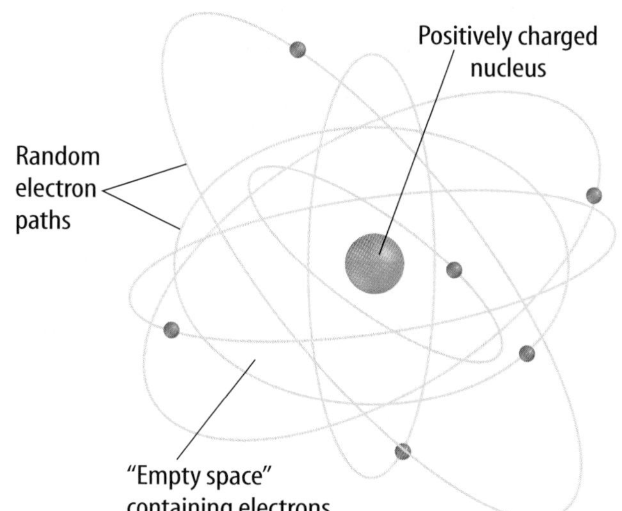

Figure 7
Rutherford concluded that the atom must be mostly empty space in which electrons travel in random paths around the nucleus. He also thought the nucleus of the atom must be small and positively charged. *Where is most of the mass of the atom concentrated?*

Discovering the Neutron Rutherford had been puzzled by one observation from his experiments with alpha particles. After the collisions, the alpha particles seemed to be heavier. Where did this extra mass come from? James Chadwick, a student of Rutherford's, answered this question. The alpha particles themselves were not heavier, but the atoms that had been bombarded had given off new particles. Chadwick experimented with these new particles and found that, unlike electrons, the paths of these particles were not affected by an electric field. To explain his observations, he said that these particles came from the nucleus and had no charge. Chadwick called these uncharged particles **neutrons.** His proton-neutron model of the atomic nucleus is still accepted today.

Physics INTEGRATION

Physicists in the 1920s began to think that electrons—like light—have a wave/particle nature. This is called quantum field theory. Research which two scientists introduced this theory. In your Science Journal, infer how thoughts about atoms changed.

Improving the Atomic Model

Early in the twentieth century, a scientist named Niels Bohr found evidence that electrons in atoms are arranged in energy levels. The lowest energy level is closest to the nucleus and can hold only two electrons. Higher energy levels are farther from the nucleus and can contain more electrons. To explain these energy levels, some scientists thought that the electrons might orbit an atom's nucleus in paths that are specific distances from the nucleus, as shown in **Figure 8.** This is similar to how the planets orbit the Sun.

The Modern Atomic Model As a result of continuing research, scientists now realize that because electrons have characteristics that are similar to waves and particles, their energy levels are not defined, planetlike orbits around the nucleus. Rather, it seems most likely that electrons move in what is called the atom's electron cloud, as shown in **Figure 9.**

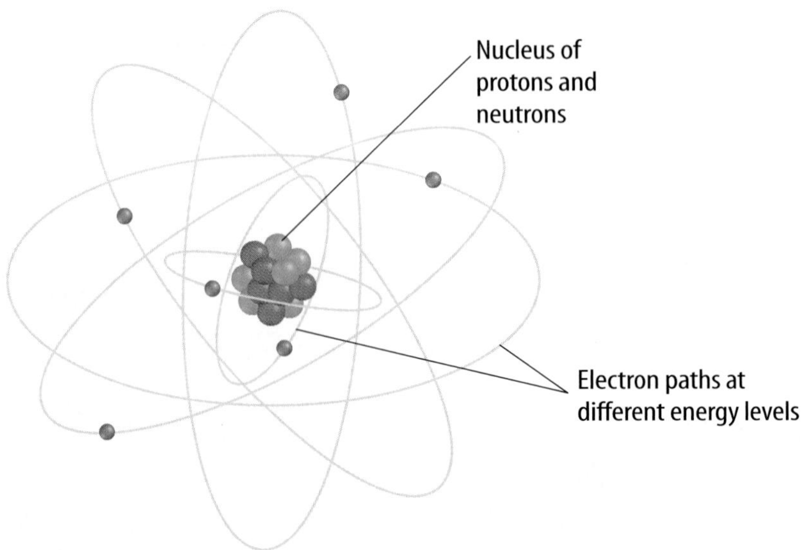

Figure 8
This simplified model shows a nucleus of protons and neutrons and electron paths based on energy levels.

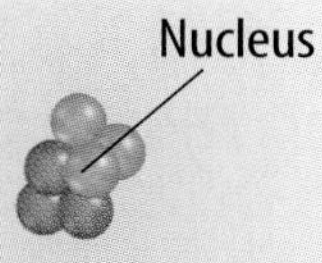

Figure 9
This model of the atom pictures the electrons moving around the nucleus in a region called an electron cloud. The concentration of color represents places where the electron is more likely to be found. *What does the intensity of color near the nucleus suggest?*

The Electron Cloud The electron cloud is a spherical cloud of varying density surrounding the nucleus. The varying density shows where an electron is more or less likely to be. Atoms with electrons in higher energy levels have additional electron clouds of different shapes that also show where those electrons are likely to be.

Further Research Today, scientists called physicists continue to study the basic parts of atoms. They have succeeded in breaking down protons and neutrons into even smaller particles called quarks. These particles can combine to make other kinds of tiny particles, too. The six types of quarks are *up, down, strange, charmed, top,* and *bottom.* Research will continue as new discoveries are made about the structure of matter.

Section 1 Assessment

1. List five examples of matter and five examples that are not matter. Explain your answers.
2. Why was the word *atom* an appropriate term for Democritus's ideas?
3. Name and describe the parts of an atom.
4. List each scientist who contributed to today's understanding of the atom along with his contribution.
5. **Think Critically** When neutrons were discovered, were these neutrons created in the experiment? How does Lavoisier's work help answer this question?

Skill Builder Activities

6. **Classifying** Look at your list from question 4. Classify the information according to the type of discovery each scientist made. Explain why you grouped certain scientists together. **For more help, refer to the** Science Skill Handbook.
7. **Evaluating Others' Data and Conclusions** Analyze, review, and critique the strengths and weaknesses of Thomson's "cookie dough" theory using the results of Rutherford's gold foil experiment. **For more help, refer to the** Science Skill Handbook.

SECTION

The Simplest Matter

As You Read

What You'll Learn

- **Describe** the relationship between elements and the periodic table.
- **Explain** the meaning of atomic mass and atomic number.
- **Identify** what makes an isotope.
- **Contrast** metals, metalloids, and nonmetals.

Vocabulary

element	atomic mass
atomic number	metal
isotope	nonmetal
mass number	metalloid

Why It's Important

Everything on Earth is made of the elements that are listed on the periodic table.

The Elements

Have you watched television today? TV sets are common, yet each one is a complex system. The outer case is made mostly of plastic, and the screen is made of glass. Many of the parts that conduct electricity are metals or combinations of metals. Other parts in the interior of the set contain materials that barely conduct electricity. All of the different materials have one thing in common. They are made up of even simpler materials. In fact, if you had the proper equipment, you could separate the plastics, glass, and metals into these simpler materials.

One Kind of Atom Eventually, though, you would separate the materials into groups of atoms. At that point, you would have a collection of elements. An **element** is matter made of only one kind of atom. More than 115 elements are known and 90 of them occur naturally on Earth. These elements make up gases in the air, minerals in rocks, and liquids such as water. Examples of the 90 naturally occurring elements include the oxygen and nitrogen in the air you breathe and the metals gold, silver, aluminum, and iron. The other 25 elements are known as synthetic elements. These elements have been made by scientists with machines like the one shown in **Figure 10.** Some synthetic elements have important uses in medical testing and are found in smoke detectors and heart pacemaker batteries.

Figure 10
The Tevatron has a circumference of 6.3 km—a distance that allows particles to accelerate to high speeds. These high-speed collisions can create synthetic elements.

Figure 11
When you look for information in the library, a system of organization called the Dewey Decimal Classification System helps you find a book quickly and efficiently.

Dewey Decimal Classification System	
000	Computers, information, and general reference
100	Philosophy and psychology
200	Religion
300	Social sciences
400	Language
500	Science
600	Technology
700	Arts and recreation
800	Literature
900	History and geography

The Periodic Table

Suppose you go to a library, like the one shown in **Figure 11,** to look up information for a school assignment. How would you find the information? You could look randomly on shelves as you walk up and down rows of books, but the chances of finding your book would be slim. Not only that, you also would probably become frustrated in the process. To avoid such haphazard searching, some libraries use the Dewey Decimal Classification System to categorize and organize their volumes and to help you find books quickly and efficiently.

Charting the Elements When scientists need to look up information about an element or select one to use in the laboratory, they need to be quick and efficient, too. Chemists have created a chart called the periodic table of the elements to help them organize and display the elements. **Figure 12** shows how scientists changed their model of the periodic table over time.

On the inside back cover of this book, you will find a modern version of the periodic table. Each element is represented by a chemical symbol that contains one to three letters. The symbols are a form of chemical shorthand that chemists use to save time and space—on the periodic table as well as in written formulas. The symbols are an important part of an international system that is understood by scientists everywhere.

The elements represented by the symbols on the periodic table are placed purposely in their position on the table. There are rows and columns that represent relationships between the elements. The rows in the table are called periods. The elements in a row have the same number of energy levels. The columns are called groups. The elements in each group have similar properties related to their structure. They also tend to form similar bonds.

Data Update For an online update of the number of elements, visit the Glencoe Science Web site at **science.glencoe.com** and select the appropriate chapter.

NATIONAL GEOGRAPHIC VISUALIZING THE PERIODIC TABLE

Figure 12

The familiar periodic table that adorns many science classrooms is based on a number of earlier efforts to identify and classify the elements. In the 1790s, one of the first lists of elements and their compounds was compiled by French chemist Antoine-Laurent Lavoisier, who is shown in the background picture with his wife and assistant, Marie Anne. Three other tables are shown here.

John Dalton (Britain, 1803) used symbols to represent elements. His table also assigned masses to each element.

ELEMENTS

	Wt		Wt
Hydrogen	1	Strontian	46
Azote	5	Barytes	68
Carbon	5½	Iron	50
Oxygen	7	Zinc	56
Phosphorus	9	Copper	56
Sulphur	13	Lead	90
Magnesia	20	Silver	190
Lime	24	Gold	190
Soda	28	Platina	190
Potash	42	Mercury	167

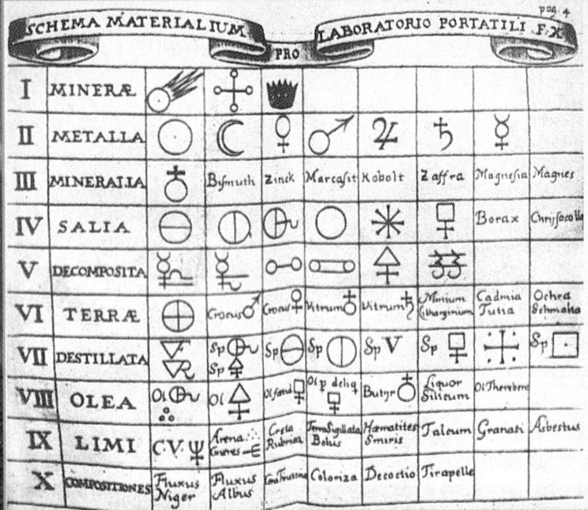

SCHEMA MATERIALIUM PRO LABORATORIO PORTATILI F.X. pag. 4

I MINERÆ								
II METALLA								
III MINERALIA		Bismuth	Zinck	Marcasit	Kobolt	Zaffra	Magnesia	Magnes
IV SALIA							Borax	Chrysocolla
V DECOMPOSITA								
VI TERRÆ		Crocus	Crocus	Vitrum	Vitrum	Minium Lithargirium	Cadmia Tutia	Ochra Schmalta
VII DESTILLATA		Sp	Sp	Sp	Sp V	Sp		Sp
VIII OLEA	Ol	Ol	Ol	Ol p deliq	Butyr	Liquor Silicium	Ol Therebent	
IX LIMI	C.V.	Arena Cineres	Creta Rubrica	Terra Sigillata Bolus	Hæmatites Smiris	Talcum	Granati	Asbestus
X COMPOSITIONES	Fluxus Niger	Fluxus Albus		Coloriza	Decoctio	Tirapelle		

An early alchemist put together this table of elements and compounds. Some of the symbols have their origin in astrology.

Dmitri Mendeleev (Russia, 1869) arranged the 63 elements known to exist at that time into groups based on their chemical properties and atomic weights. He left gaps for elements he predicted were yet to be discovered.

xviii PRINCIPLES OF CHEMISTRY

PERIODIC SYSTEM OF THE ELEMENTS IN GROUPS AND SERIES.

Series	0	I	II	III	IV	V	VI	VII	VIII
1	—	Hydrogen H 1·008	—	—	—	—	—	—	
2	Helium He 4·0	Lithium Li 7·03	Beryllium Be 9·1	Boron B 11·0	Carbon C 12·0	Nitrogen N 14·04	Oxygen O 16·00	Fluorine F 19·0	
3	Neon Ne 19·9	Sodium Na 23·05	Magnesium Mg 24·3	Aluminium Al 27·0	Silicon Si 28·4	Phosphorus P 31·0	Sulphur S 32·06	Chlorine Cl 35·45	
4	Argon Ar 38	Potassium K 39·1	Calcium Ca 40·1	Scandium Sc 44·1	Titanium Ti 48·1	Vanadium V 51·4	Chromium Cr 52·1	Manganese Mn 55·0	Iron Fe 55·9, Cobalt Co 59, Nickel Ni 59 (Cu)
5		Copper Cu 63·6	Zinc Zn 65·4	Gallium Ga 70·0	Germanium Ge 72·3	Arsenic As 75	Selenium Se 79	Bromine Br 79·95	
6	Krypton Kr 81·8	Rubidium Rb 85·4	Strontium Sr 87·6	Yttrium Y 89·0	Zirconium Zr 90·6	Niobium Nb 94·0	Molybdenum Mo 96·0	—	Ruthenium Ru 101·7, Rhodium Rh 103·0, Palladium Pd 106·5 (Ag)
7		Silver Ag 107·9	Cadmium Cd 112·4	Indium In 114·0	Tin Sn 119·0	Antimony Sb 120·0	Tellurium Te 127	Iodine I 127	
8	Xenon Xe 128	Cæsium Cs 132·9	Barium Ba 137·4	Lanthanum La 139	Cerium Ce 140	—	—	—	— — —
9		—	—	—	—	—	—	—	
10	—	—	—	Ytterbium Yb 173	—	Tantalum Ta 183	Tungsten W 184	—	Osmium Os 191, Iridium Ir 193, Platinum Pt 194·9 (Au)
11		Gold Au 197·2	Mercury Hg 200·0	Thallium Tl 204·1	Lead Pb 206·9	Bismuth Bi 208	—	—	
12	—	—	Radium Rd 224	—	Thorium Th 232	—	Uranium U 239		
HIGHER SALINE OXIDES	R	R_2O	RO	R_2O_3	RO_2	R_2O_5	RO_3	R_2O_7	RO_4
HIGHER GASEOUS HYDROGEN COMPOUNDS					RH_4	RH_3	RH_2	RH	

Identifying Characteristics

Each element is different and has unique properties. These differences can be described in part by looking at the relationships between the atomic particles in each element. The periodic table contains numbers that describe these relationships.

Number of Protons and Neutrons Look up the element chlorine on the periodic table found on the inside back cover of your book. Cl is the symbol for chlorine, as shown in **Figure 13,** but what are the two numbers? The top number is the element's **atomic number.** It tells you the number of protons in the nucleus of each atom of that element. Every atom of chlorine, for example, has 17 protons in its nucleus.

Reading Check ***What are the atomic numbers for Cs, Ne, Pb, and U?***

Isotopes Although the number of protons changes from element to element, every atom of the same element has the same number of protons. However, the number of neutrons can vary even for one element. For example, some chlorine atoms have 18 neutrons in their nucleus while others have 20. These two types of chlorine atoms are chlorine-35 and chlorine-37. They are called **isotopes** (I suh tohps), which are atoms of the same element that have different numbers of neutrons.

You can tell someone exactly which isotope you are referring to by using its mass number. An atom's **mass number** is the number of protons plus the number of neutrons it contains. The numbers 35 and 37, which were used to refer to chlorine, are mass numbers. Hydrogen has three isotopes with mass numbers of 1, 2, and 3. They are shown in **Figure 14.** Each hydrogen atom always has one proton, but in each isotope the number of neutrons is different.

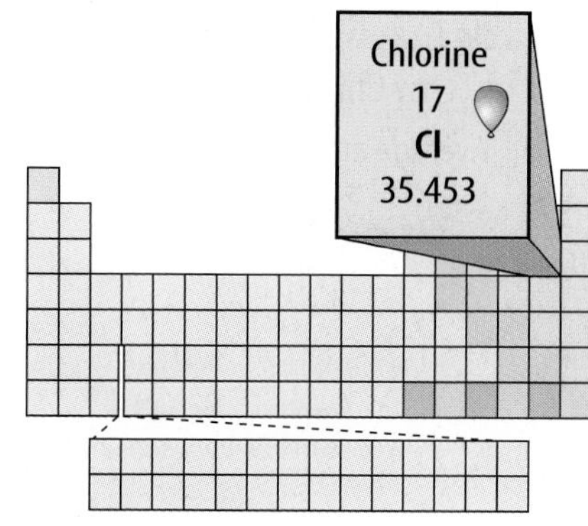

Figure 13
The periodic table block for chlorine shows its symbol, atomic number, and atomic mass. *Are chlorine atoms more or less massive than carbon atoms?*

Figure 14
Three isotopes of hydrogen are known to exist. They have zero, one, and two neutrons in addition to their one proton. Protium, with only the one proton, is the most abundant isotope.

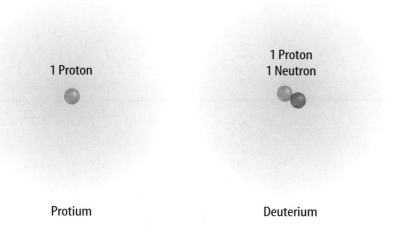

1 Proton

Protium

1 Proton
1 Neutron

Deuterium

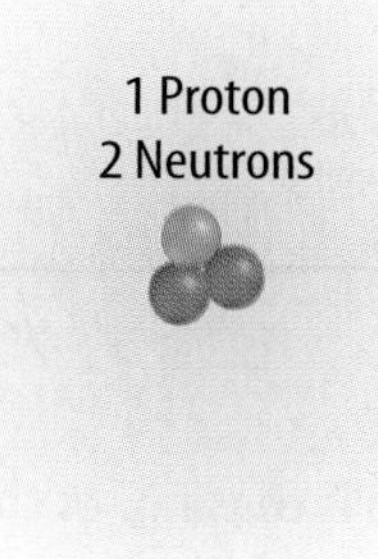

Tritium

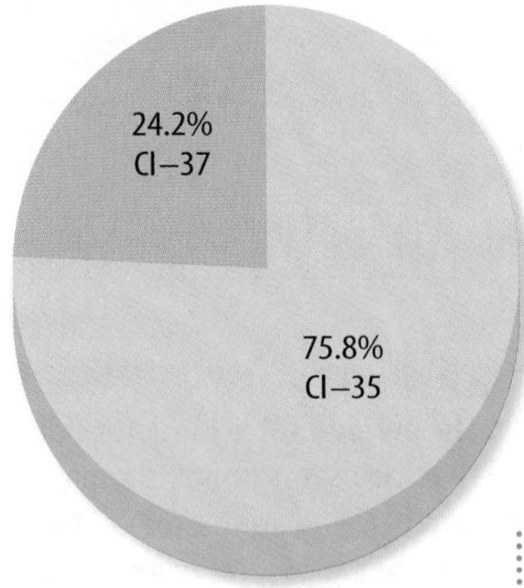

Figure 15
If you have 1,000 atoms of chlorine, about 758 will be chlorine-35 and have a mass of 34.97 u each. About 242 will be chlorine-37 and have a mass of 36.97 u each. The total mass of the 1,000 atoms is 35,454 u, so the average mass of one chlorine atom is about 35.45 u.

Atomic Mass The **atomic mass** is the weighted average mass of the isotopes of an element. The atomic mass is the number found below the element symbol in **Figure 12.** The unit that scientists use for atomic mass is called the atomic mass unit, which is given the symbol u. It is defined as 1/12 the mass of a carbon-12 atom.

The calculation of atomic mass takes into account the different isotopes of the element. Chlorine's atomic mass of 35.45 u could be confusing because there aren't any chlorine atoms that have that exact mass. About 76 percent of chlorine atoms are chlorine-35 and about 24 percent are chlorine-37, as shown in **Figure 15.** The weighted average mass of all chlorine atoms is 35.45 u.

Classification of Elements

Elements fall into three general categories—metals, metalloids (MET ul oydz), and nonmetals. The elements within a category have similar properties.

Metals generally have a shiny or metallic luster and are good conductors of heat and electricity. All metals, except mercury, are solids at room temperature. Metals are malleable (MAL yuh bul), which means they can be bent and pounded into various shapes. The beautiful form of the shell-shaped basin in **Figure 16** is a result of this characteristic. Metals are also ductile, which means they can be drawn into wires without breaking. If you look at the periodic table, you can see that most of the elements are metals.

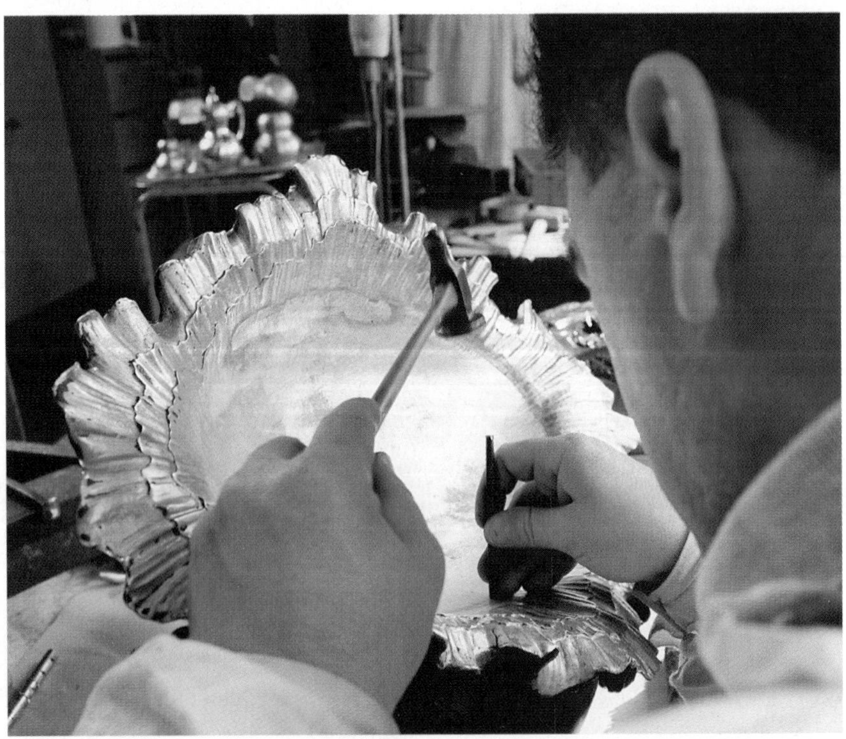

Figure 16
The artisan is chasing, or chiseling, the malleable metal into the desired form.

Other Elements **Nonmetals** are elements that are usually dull in appearance. Most are poor conductors of heat and electricity. Many are gases at room temperature, and bromine is a liquid. The solid nonmetals are generally brittle, meaning they cannot change shape easily without breaking. The nonmetals are essential to the chemicals of life. More than 97 percent of your body is made up of various nonmetals, as shown in **Figure 17.** You can see that, except for hydrogen, the nonmetals are found on the right side of the periodic table.

Metalloids are elements that have characteristics of metals and nonmetals. On the periodic table, metalloids are found between the metals and nonmetals. All metalloids are solids at room temperature. Some metalloids are shiny and many are conductors, but they are not as good at conducting heat and electricity as metals are. Some metalloids, such as silicon, are used to make the electronic circuits in computers, televisions, and other electronic devices.

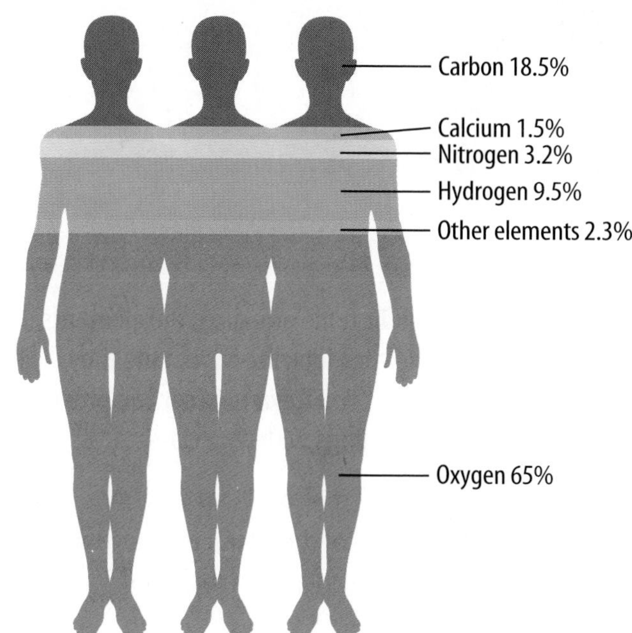

Figure 17
You are made up of mostly nonmetals.

Reading Check *What is a metalloid?*

Section  Assessment

1. What is an element?
2. Describe the difference between atomic number and atomic mass.
3. What are isotopes? How are two isotopes of an element different?
4. Explain some of the uses of metals based on their properties.
5. **Think Critically** Hector is new to your class today. He missed the lesson on how to use the periodic table to find information about the elements. Describe how you would teach Hector to find the atomic number for the element oxygen. Explain what this information tells him about oxygen.

Skill Builder Activities

6. **Interpreting Data** Look up the atomic mass of the element boron in the periodic table inside the back cover of this book. The naturally occurring isotopes of boron are boron-10 and boron-11. Which of the two isotopes is more abundant? Explain your reasoning. **For more help, refer to the** Science Skill Handbook.
7. **Solving One-Step Equations** An atom of niobium has a mass number of 93. How many neutrons are in the nucleus of this atom? An atom of phosphorus has 15 protons and 15 neutrons in its nucleus. What is the mass number of this isotope? **For more help, refer to the** Math Skill Handbook.

Activity

Elements and the Periodic Table

The periodic table organizes the elements, but what do they look like? What are they used for? In this activity, you'll examine some elements and share your findings with your classmates.

What You'll Investigate

What are some of the characteristics and purposes of the chemical elements?

Goals

- **Classify** the chemical elements.
- **Organize** the elements into the groups and periods of the periodic table.

Materials

colored markers	large bulletin board
large index cards	$8^1/_2 \times 14$ inch paper
Merck Index	thumbtacks
encyclopedia	**pushpins*
**other reference materials*	**Alternate materials*

Safety Precaution 

Use care when handling sharp objects.

Procedure

1. Select the assigned number of elements from the list provided by your teacher.
2. **Design** an index card for each of your selected elements. On each card, mark the element's atomic number in the upper left-hand corner and write its symbol and name in the upper right-hand corner.
3. **Research** each of the elements and write several sentences on the card about its appearance, its other properties, and its uses.
4. **Classify** each of your elements as a metal, a metalloid, or a nonmetal based upon its properties.

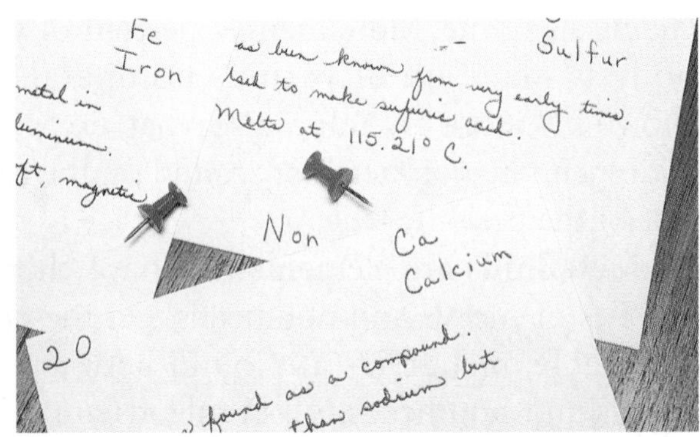

5. **Write** the appropriate classification on each of your cards using the colored marker chosen by your teacher.
6. Work with your classmates to make a large periodic table. Use thumbtacks to attach your cards to a bulletin board in their proper positions on the periodic table.
7. **Draw** your own periodic table. Place the elements' symbols and atomic numbers in the proper locations on your table.

Conclude and Apply

1. **Interpret** the class data and classify the elements into the categories metal, metalloid, and nonmetal. Highlight each category in a different color on your periodic table.
2. **Predict** the properties of a yet-undiscovered element located directly under francium on the periodic table.

Communicating Your Data

Compare and contrast your table with that of a friend. Discuss the differences. **For more help, refer to the** Science Skill Handbook.

Compounds and Mixtures

Substances

Scientists classify matter in several ways that depend on what it is made of and how it behaves. For example, matter that has the same composition and properties throughout is called a **substance.** Elements, such as a bar of gold or a sheet of aluminum, are substances. When different elements combine, other substances are formed.

As You Read

***What* You'll Learn**

- **Identify** the characteristics of a compound.
- **Compare and contrast** different types of mixtures.

Vocabulary
substance
compound
mixture

***Why* It's Important**

The food you eat, the materials you use, and all matter can be classified by these terms.

Compounds What do you call the colorless liquid that flows from the kitchen faucet? You probably call it water, but maybe you've seen it written H_2O. The elements hydrogen and oxygen exist as separate, colorless gases at room temperature. However, these two elements can combine, as shown in **Figure 18,** to form the compound water, which is different from the elements that make it up. A **compound** is a substance whose smallest unit is made up of atoms of more than one element bonded together.

Compounds often have properties that are different from the elements that make them up. Water is distinctly different from the elements that make it up. It is also different from another compound made from the same elements. Have you ever used hydrogen peroxide (H_2O_2) to disinfect a cut? This compound is a different combination of hydrogen and oxygen and has different properties.

Water is a nonirritating liquid that is used for bathing, drinking, cooking, and much more. In contrast, hydrogen peroxide carries warnings on its labels such as *Keep Hydrogen Peroxide Out of the Eyes.* Although it is useful in solutions for cleaning contact lenses, it is not safe for your eyes directly from the bottle.

Figure 18
A space shuttle is powered by the reaction between liquid hydrogen and liquid oxygen. The reaction produces a large amount of energy and the compound water. *Why would a car that burns hydrogen rather than gasoline be friendly to the environment?*

Figure 19
The elements hydrogen and oxygen can form two compounds—water and hydrogen peroxide. Note the differences in their structure.

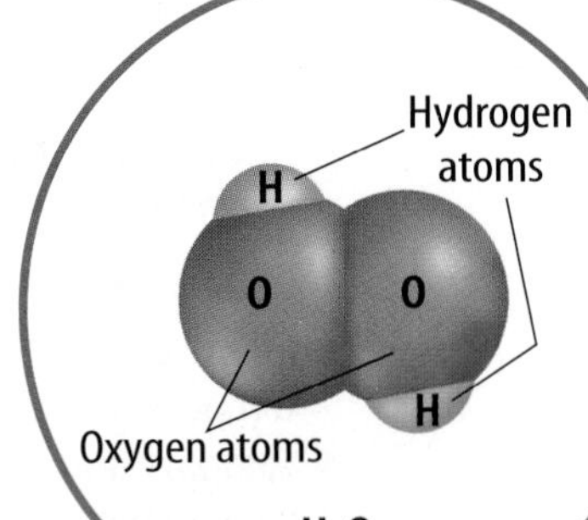

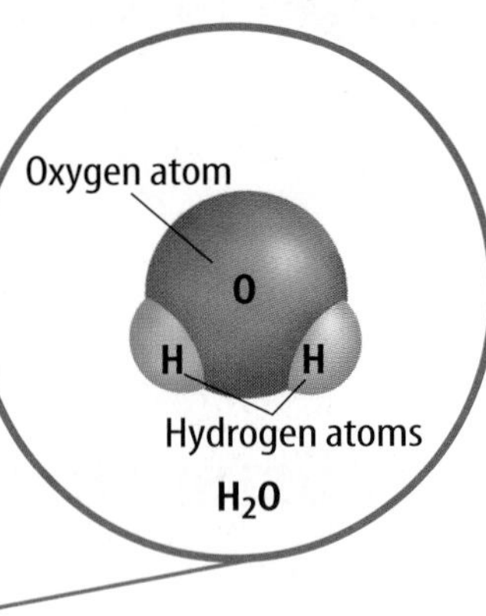

Compounds Have Formulas What's the difference between water and hydrogen peroxide? H_2O is the chemical formula for water, and H_2O_2 is the formula for hydrogen peroxide. The formula tells you which elements make up a compound as well as how many atoms of each element are present. Look at **Figure 19.** The subscript number written below and to the right of each element's symbol tells you how many atoms of that element exist in one unit of that compound. For example, hydrogen peroxide has two atoms of hydrogen and two atoms of oxygen. Water is made up of two atoms of hydrogen and one atom of oxygen.

Carbon dioxide, CO_2, is another common compound. Carbon dioxide is made up of one atom of carbon and two atoms of oxygen. Carbon and oxygen also can form the compound carbon monoxide, CO, which is a gas that is poisonous to all warm-blooded animals. As you can see, no subscript is used when only one atom of an element is present. A given compound always is made of the same elements in the same proportion. For example, water always has two hydrogen atoms for every oxygen atom, no matter what the source of the water is. No matter what quantity of the compound you have, the formula of the compound always remains the same. If you have 12 atoms of hydrogen and six atoms of oxygen, the compound is still written H_2O, but you have six molecules of H_2O ($6\ H_2O$), not $H_{12}O_6$. The formula of a compound communicates its identity and makeup to any scientist in the world.

Reading Check ***Propane has three atoms of carbon and eight atoms of hydrogen. What is propane's chemical formula?***

Comparing Compounds

Procedure

1. Collect the following substances—granular **sugar, rubbing alcohol,** and **salad oil.**
2. Observe the color, appearance, and state of each substance. Note the thickness or texture of each substance.
3. Stir a spoonful of each substance into separate **glasses** of **hot tap water** and observe.

Analysis

1. Compare the different properties of the substances.
2. The formulas of the three substances are made of only carbon, hydrogen, and oxygen. Infer how they can have different properties.

Mixtures

When two or more substances (elements or compounds) come together but don't combine to make a new substance, a **mixture** results. Unlike compounds, the proportions of the substances in a mixture can be changed without changing the identity of the mixture. For example, if you put some sand into a bucket of water, you have a mixture of sand and water. If you add more sand or more water, it's still a mixture of sand and water. Its identity has not changed. Air is another mixture. Air is a mixture of nitrogen, oxygen, and other gases, which can vary at different times and places. Whatever the proportion of gases, it is still air. Even your blood is a mixture that can be separated, as shown in **Figure 20,** by a machine called a centrifuge.

Reading Check *How do the proportions of a mixture relate to its identity?*

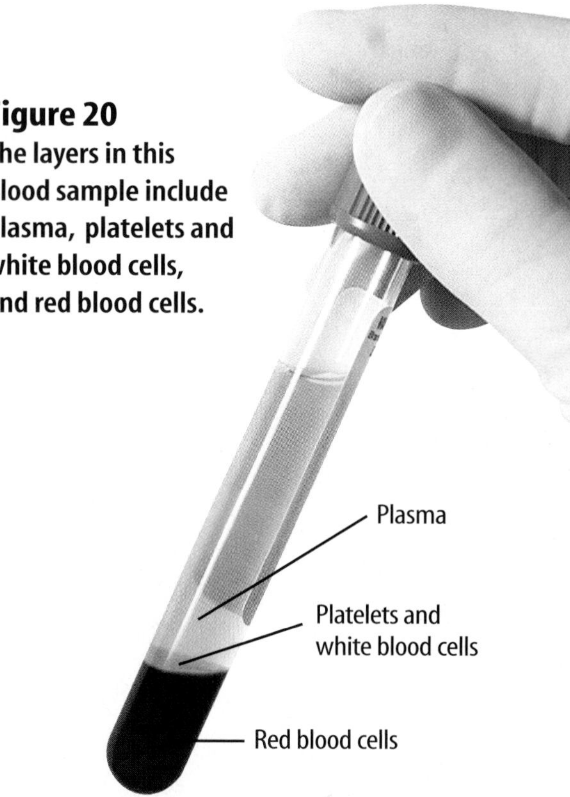

Figure 20
The layers in this blood sample include plasma, platelets and white blood cells, and red blood cells.

Problem-Solving Activity

What's the best way to desalt ocean water?

You can't drink ocean water because it contains salt and other suspended materials. Or can you? In many areas of the world where drinking water is in short supply, methods for getting the salt out of salt water are being used to meet the demand for fresh water. Use your problem solving skills to find the best method to use in a particular area.

Methods for Desalting Ocean Water

Process	Amount of Water a Unit Can Desalt in a Day (m^3)	Special Needs	Number of People Needed to Operate
Distillation	1,000 to 200,000	lots of energy to boil the water	many
Electrodialysis	10 to 4,000	stable source of electricity	1 to 2 persons

Identifying the Problem

The table above compares desalting methods. In distillation, the ocean water is heated. Pure water boils off and is collected, and the salt is left behind. Electrodialysis uses electric current to pull salt particles out of water.

Solving the Problem

1. What method(s) might you use to desalt the water for a large population where energy is plentiful? What method(s) would you chose to use in a single home?

Figure 21
Mixtures are part of your everyday life.

Your blood is a mixture made up of elements and compounds. It contains white blood cells, red blood cells, water, and a number of dissolved substances. The different parts of blood can be separated and used by doctors in different ways. The proportions of the substances in your blood change daily, but the mixture does not change its identity.

Research Visit the Glencoe Science Web site at **science.glencoe.com** for more information about separating mixtures.

Separating Mixtures Sometimes you can use a liquid to separate a mixture of solids. For example, if you add water to a mixture of sugar and sand, only the sugar dissolves in the water. The sand then can be separated from the sugar and water by pouring the mixture through a filter. Heating the remaining solution will separate the water from the sugar.

At other times, separating a mixture of solids of different sizes might be as easy as pouring them through successively smaller sieves or filters. A mixture of marbles, pebbles, and sand could be separated in this way.

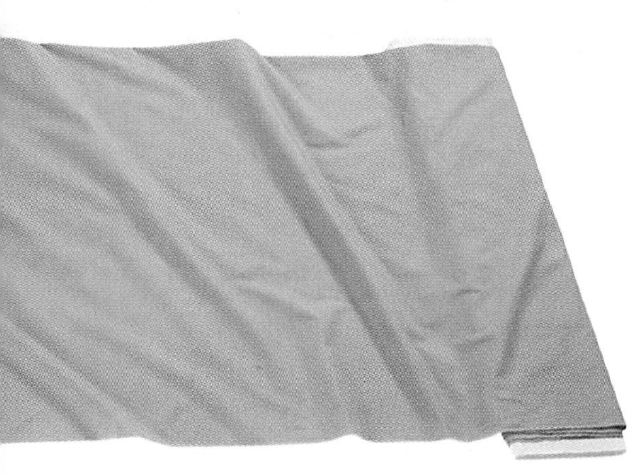

Homogeneous or Heterogeneous Mixtures, such as the ones shown in **Figure 21,** can be classified as homogeneous or heterogeneous. *Homogeneous* means "the same throughout." You can't see the different parts in this type of mixture. In fact, you might not always know that homogeneous mixtures are mixtures because you can't tell by looking. Which mixtures in **Figure 21** are homogeneous? No matter how closely you look, you can't see the individual parts that make up air or the parts of the mixture called brass in the lamp shown. Homogeneous mixtures can be solids, liquids, or gases.

A heterogeneous mixture has larger parts that are different from each other. You can see the different parts of a heterogeneous mixture, such as sand and water. How many heterogeneous mixtures are in the figure? A pepperoni and mushroom pizza is a tasty kind of heterogeneous mixture. Other examples of this kind of mixture include tacos, vegetable soup, a toy box full of toys, or a tool box full of nuts and bolts.

Earth Science INTEGRATION

Scientists called geologists study rocks and minerals. A mineral is composed of a pure substance. Rocks are mixtures and can be described as being homogeneous or heterogeneous. Research to learn more about rocks and minerals and note some examples of homogeneous and heterogeneous rocks in your Science Journal.

Section  Assessment

1. List three examples of compounds and three examples of mixtures. Explain your choices.
2. How can you tell that a substance is a compound by looking at its formula?
3. Which kind of mixture is sometimes difficult to distinguish from a compound? Why?
4. What is the difference between homogeneous and heterogeneous mixtures?
5. **Think Critically** Was your breakfast a compound, a homogeneous mixture, or a heterogeneous mixture? Explain.

Skill Builder Activities

6. **Comparing and Contrasting** Compare and contrast compounds and mixtures based on what you have learned from this section. **For more help, refer to the Science Skill Handbook.**
7. **Using a Database** Use a computerized card catalog or database to find out about one element from the periodic table. Include information about the properties and uses of the mixtures and/or compounds the element is found in. **For more help, refer to the Technology Skill Handbook.**

Activity

Mystery Mixture

You will encounter many compounds that look alike. For example, a laboratory stockroom is filled with white powders. It is important to know what each is. In a kitchen, cornstarch, baking powder, and powdered sugar are compounds that look alike. To avoid mistaking one for another, you can learn how to identify them. Different compounds can be identified by using chemical tests. For example, some compounds react with certain liquids to produce gases. Other combinations produce distinctive colors. Some compounds have high melting points. Others have low melting points.

What You'll Investigate

How can the compounds in an unknown mixture be identified by experimentation?

Goals

- **Test** for the presence of certain compounds.
- **Decide** which of these compounds are present in an unknown mixture.

Materials

test tubes (4)
cornstarch
powdered sugar
baking soda
mystery mixture
small scoops (3)
dropper bottles (2)
iodine solution
white vinegar
hot plate
250-mL beaker
water (125 mL)
test-tube holder
small pie pan

Safety Precautions

WARNING: *Use caution when handling hot objects. Substances could stain or burn clothing. Be sure to point the test tube away from your face and your classmates while heating.*

Procedure

1. Copy the data table into your Science Journal. Record your results for each of the following steps.
2. Place a small scoopful of cornstarch on the pie pan. Do the same for the sugar and baking soda. Add a drop of vinegar to each. Wash and dry the pan after you record your observations.
3. Place a small scoopful of cornstarch, sugar, and baking soda on the pie pan. Add a drop of iodine solution to each one.
4. Place a small scoopful of each compound in a separate test tube. Hold the test tube with the test-tube holder and with an oven mitt. Gently heat the test tube in a beaker of boiling water on a hot plate.
5. Follow steps 2 through 4 to test your mystery mixture for each compound.

Identifying Presence of Compounds

Substance to Be Tested	Fizzes with Vinegar	Turns Blue with Iodine	Melts When Heated
Cornstarch			
Sugar			
Baking soda			
Mystery mix			

Conclude and Apply

1. Use your observations to form a hypothesis about compounds in your mystery mixture. Describe how you arrived at your conclusion.
2. How would you be able to tell if all three compounds were not in your mystery mixture sample?
3. What would you conclude if you tested baking powder from your kitchen and found that it fizzed with vinegar, turned blue with iodine, and did not melt when heated?

Make a different data table to display your results in a new way. **For more help, refer to the** **Science Skill Handbook.**

Ancient Views

air & ether

water

wood, fire, and ash

metal

earth

Two cultures observed the world around them differently

# of Matter

The world's earliest scientists were people who were curious about the world around them and who tried to develop explanations for the things they observed. This type of observation and inquiry flourished in ancient cultures such as those found in India and China. In some cases, their views of the world weren't so different from ours. Matter, for example, is defined today as anything that has mass and takes up space. Read on to see how the ancient Indians and Chinese defined matter.

Indian Ideas

To Indians living about 3,000 years ago, the world was made up of five elements: fire, air, earth, water, and ether, which they thought of as an unseen substance that filled the heavens. Building upon this concept, the early Indian philosopher Kashyapa (kah SHI ah pah) proposed that the five elements could be broken down into smaller units called parmanu (par MAH new). Parmanu were similar to atoms in that they were too small to be seen but still retained the properties of the original element. Kashyapa also believed that each type of parmanu had unique physical and chemical properties.

Parmanu of earth elements, for instance, were heavier than parmanu of air elements. The different properties of the parmanu determined the characteristics of a substance. Kashyapa's ideas about matter are similar to those of the Greek philosopher Democritus, who lived centuries after Kashyapa. Historians are unsure as to whether the two men developed their views separately, or whether trade and communication with India influenced Greek thought.

Chinese Ideas

Ancient Chinese also broke matter down into five elements: fire, wood, metal, earth, and water. Unlike the early Indians, however, the Chinese believed that the elements constantly changed form. For example, wood can be burned and thus changes to fire. Fire eventually dies down and becomes ashes, or earth. Earth gives forth metals from the ground. Dew or water collects on these metals, and the water then nurtures plants that grow into trees, or wood.

This cycle of constant change was explained in the fourth century B.C. by the philosopher Tsou Yen. Yen, who is known as the founder of Chinese scientific thought, wrote that all changes that took place in nature were linked to changes in the five elements. In his writings, Yen also developed a classification system for matter.

CONNECTIONS Research **Write a brief paragraph that compares and contrasts the ancient Indian and Chinese views of matter. How are they different? Similar? Which is closer to the modern view of matter? Explain.**

For more information, visit science.glencoe.com

Chapter 3 Study Guide

Reviewing Main Ideas

Section 1 Structure of Matter

1. Matter is anything that occupies space and has mass. It includes the things that you can see, touch, taste, or smell. Matter does not include light, sound, heat, thoughts, or emotions.
2. Matter is made up of atoms of different kinds.
3. Atoms are made of smaller parts called protons, neutrons, and electrons. *Which particle was discovered using an apparatus like the one pictured?*

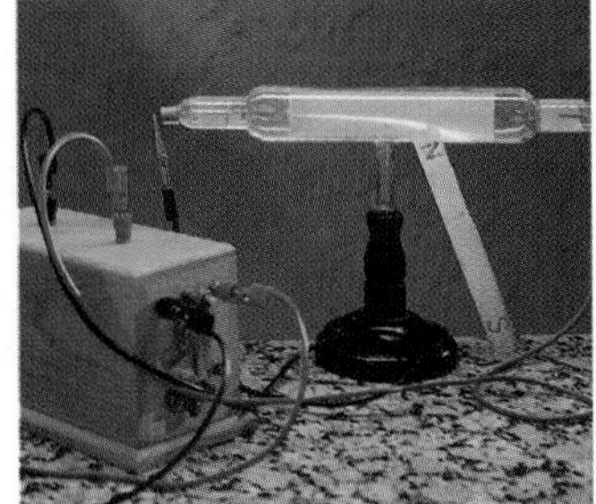

4. Many models of atoms have been created as scientists try to discover and define the atom's internal structure. Today's model has a central nucleus with the protons and neutrons, and an electron cloud surrounding it that contains the electrons.

Section 2 The Simplest Matter

1. Elements are the basic building blocks of matter.
2. An element's atomic number tells how many protons its atoms contain, and its atomic mass tells the average mass of its atoms. The chemical symbol for each element is understood by scientists everywhere. Information about elements is displayed on the periodic table.
3. Isotopes are two or more atoms of the same element that have different numbers of neutrons.
4. Each element has a unique set of properties and is generally classified as a metal, metalloid, or nonmetal. *How would you classify the spool of wire in the picture?*

Section 3 Compounds and Mixtures

1. Compounds are substances that are produced when elements combine. Compounds contain specific proportions of the elements that make them up. A compound's properties are different from those of the elements from which it is formed.
2. Mixtures are combinations of compounds and elements that have not formed new substances. Their proportions can change. Homogeneous mixtures contain individual parts that cannot be seen. However, you can see the individual parts of heterogeneous mixtures. *Is the orange juice pictured a homogeneous or heterogeneous mixture?*

After You Read

FOLDABLES Reading & Study Skills

Under each tab of your Foldable, list several everyday examples of the atoms, elements, compounds and mixtures.

Visualizing Main Ideas

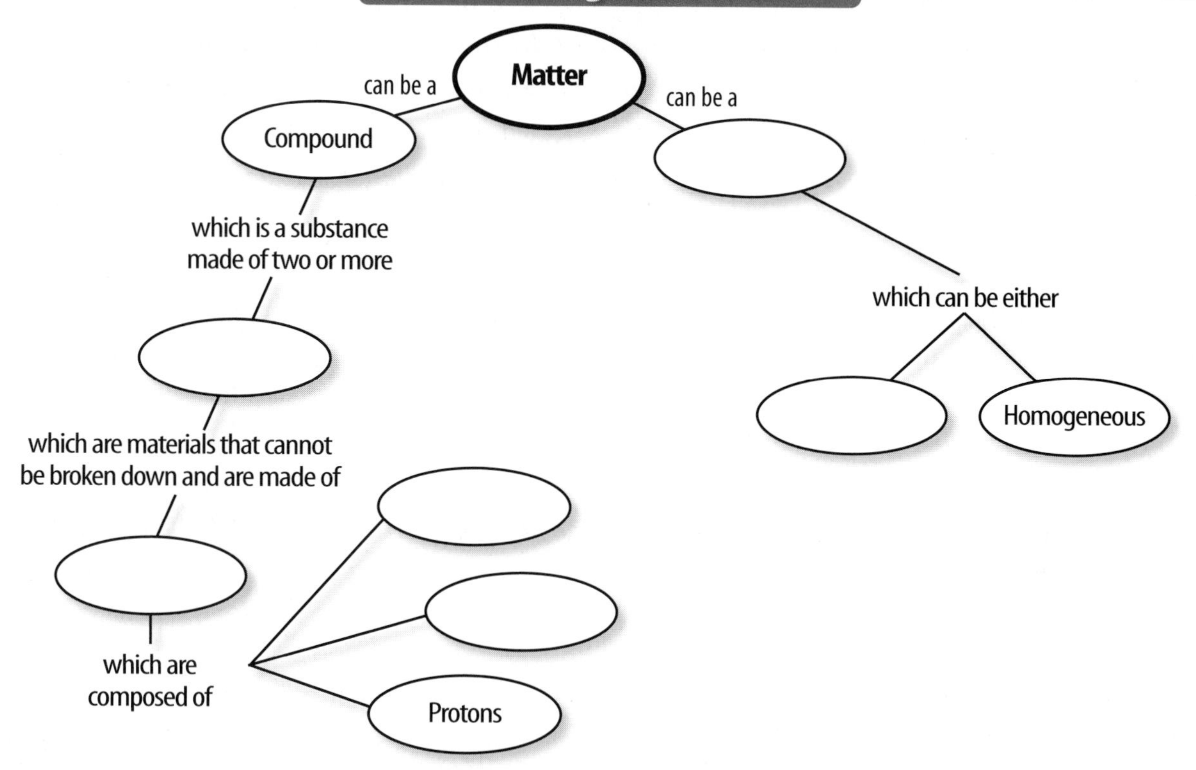

Vocabulary Review

Vocabulary Words

- **a.** atom
- **b.** atomic mass
- **c.** atomic number
- **d.** compound
- **e.** electron
- **f.** element
- **g.** isotope
- **h.** law of conservation of matter
- **i.** mass number
- **j.** matter
- **k.** metal
- **l.** metalloid
- **m.** mixture
- **n.** neutron
- **o.** nonmetal
- **p.** nucleus
- **q.** proton
- **r.** substance

Study Tip

Find out what concepts, objectives, or standards are being tested well before the test. Keep these concepts in mind as you answer the questions.

Using Vocabulary

Replace the underlined word or phrase with the correct vocabulary word.

1. The <u>neutron</u> is the particle in the nucleus of the atom that carries a positive charge and is counted to identify the atomic number.
2. The new substance formed when elements combine chemically is a <u>mixture</u>.
3. Anything that has mass and takes up space is <u>metal</u>.
4. The particles in the atom that account for most of the mass of the atom are protons and <u>electrons</u>.
5. Elements that are shiny, malleable, ductile, good conductors of heat and electricity, and make up most of the periodic table are <u>nonmetals</u>.

Chapter 3 Assessment

Checking Concepts

Choose the word or phrase that best answers the question.

1. What is a solution an example of?
   A) element
   B) heterogeneous mixture
   C) compound
   D) homogeneous mixture

2. The nucleus of one atom contains 12 protons and 12 neutrons, while the nucleus of another atom contains 12 protons and 16 neutrons. What are the atoms?
   A) two different atoms
   B) two different elements
   C) two isotopes of an element
   D) negatively charged

3. What is a compound?
   A) a mixture of chemicals and elements
   B) a combination of two or more elements
   C) anything that has mass and occupies space
   D) the building block of matter

4. What does the atom consist of?
   A) electrons, protons, and alpha particles
   B) neutrons and protons
   C) electrons, protons, and neutrons
   D) elements, protons, and electrons

5. In an atom, where is an electron located?
   A) in the nucleus with the proton
   B) on the periodic table of the elements
   C) with the neutron
   D) in a cloudlike formation surrounding the nucleus

6. How is matter defined?
   A) the negative charge in an atom
   B) anything that has mass and occupies space
   C) the mass of the nucleus
   D) sound, light, and energy

7. What are two atoms that have the same number of protons called?
   A) metals **C)** isotopes
   B) nonmetals **D)** metalloids

8. What are the majority of the elements on the periodic table called?
   A) metals **C)** nonmetals
   B) metalloids **D)** compounds

9. Which element is a metalloid?
   A) bromine **C)** potassium
   B) silicon **D)** iron

10. Which is a heterogeneous mixture?
   A) air **C)** a salad
   B) brass **D)** apple juice

Thinking Critically

11. A chemical formula is written to indicate the makeup of a compound. What is the ratio of sulfur atoms to oxygen atoms in SO_2?

12. An atom contains seven electrons and seven protons. What element is this atom? Explain your answer.

13. What happens to an element when it becomes part of a compound?

14. Cobalt-60 and cobalt-59 are isotopes. How can they be the same element but have different mass numbers?

15. What did Rutherford's gold foil experiment tell scientists about atomic structure?

Developing Skills

16. **Predicting** Suppose Rutherford had bombarded aluminum foil with alpha particles instead of the gold foil he used in his experiment. What observations do you predict Rutherford would have made? Explain your prediction.

17. Comparing and Contrasting Aluminum is close to carbon on the periodic table. Explain the properties that make aluminum a metal and carbon a nonmetal.

18. Drawing Conclusions You are shown a liquid that looks the same throughout. You're told that it contains more than one type of element and that the proportion of each varies throughout the liquid. Is this an element, a compound, or a mixture?

19. Interpreting Scientific Illustrations Look at the two carbon atoms below. Explain whether or not the atoms are isotopes.

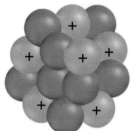

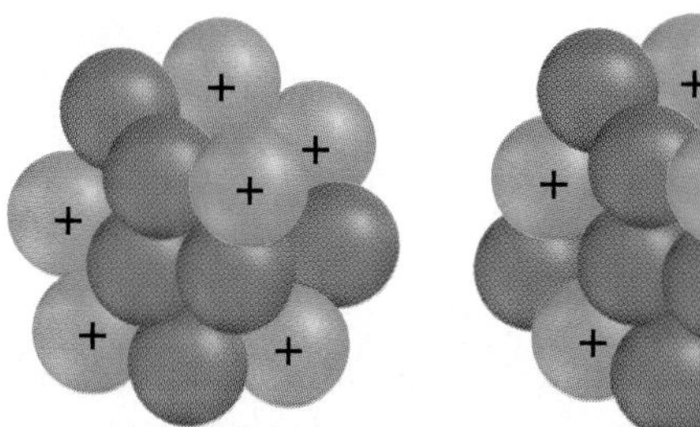

Performance Assessment

20. Newspaper Article Research the source, composition, and properties of asbestos. Why was it used in the past? Why is it a health hazard now? What is being done about it? Write a newspaper article to share your findings.

Technology

Go to the Glencoe Science Web site at **science.glencoe.com** or use the **Glencoe Science CD-ROM** for additional chapter assessment.

Test Practice

A researcher is analyzing four different compounds in the laboratory. The formulas for the compounds are listed below.

H_2O Water	H_2O_2 Hydrogen peroxide
H_2SO_4 Sulfuric acid	SO_2 Sulfur dioxide

Study the formulas and answer the following questions.

1. Which of the compounds contains the most oxygen atoms?
A) water
B) sulfur dioxide
C) sulfuric acid
D) hydrogen peroxide

2. What is the ratio of oxygen to hydrogen in sulfuric acid?
F) 2 to 1
G) 1 to 2
H) 1 to 1
J) 2 to 4

3. What is the ratio of hydrogen to oxygen in a hydrogen peroxide?
A) 2 to 1
B) 4 to 2
C) 1 to 1
D) 2 to 4

CHAPTER 4

States of Matter

Ah-h-h-h, a good hot soak on a cold, snowy day! This Asian monkey called a macaque is experiencing one of the properties of matter—it can transfer thermal energy. In this case, thermal energy is transferred from a warmer object (the hot spring water) to a colder object (the macaque monkey). In this chapter, you will learn about other properties of solids, liquids, gases, and plasma—the four states of matter.

What do you think?

Science Journal Look at the picture below with a classmate. Discuss what you think is happening. Here's a hint: *Several of these bring flowers in May.* Write your answer or best guess in your Science Journal.

In a few short months, the lake that is now the solid surface supporting you on ice skates will be a liquid in which you can swim. Many substances, such as water, change as they become warm or cool.

Experiment with a freezing liquid

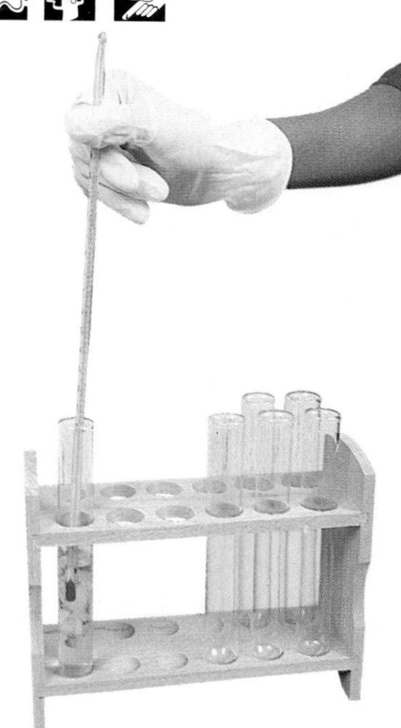

1. Make a table to record temperature and appearance. Obtain a test tube containing an unknown liquid from your teacher. Place the test tube in a rack.
2. Insert a thermometer into the liquid. **WARNING:** *Do not allow the thermometer to touch the bottom of the test tube.* Starting immediately, observe and record the substance's temperature and appearance every 30 s.
3. Continue making measurements and observations until you're told to stop.

Observe

In your Science Journal, describe your investigation and observations. Did anything unusual happen while you were observing? If so, what?

Before You Read

Making an Organizational Study Fold **Make the following Foldable to help you organize your thoughts into clear categories about states of matter.**

1. Place a sheet of paper in front of you so the short side is at the top. Fold the paper in half from the left side to the right side two times. Unfold all the folds.
2. Fold the paper in half from top to bottom. Then fold it in half again. Unfold all the folds and trace over all the fold lines.
3. Label the rows *Liquid Water, Water as a Vapor,* and *Water as a Solid (Ice).* Label the columns *Define States, + Heat,* and *−Heat* as shown. As you read the chapter, define the states of matter listed on your Foldable in the *Define States* column.

	Define States	+ Heat	− Heat
Liquid Water			
Water as a Vapor			
Water as a Solid (Ice)			

Matter

As You Read

What You'll Learn

- **Recognize** that matter is made of particles in constant motion.
- **Relate** the three states of matter to the arrangement of particles within them.

Vocabulary

matter, solid, liquid, gas

Why It's Important

Everything you can see, taste, and touch is matter. Without matter—well, nothing would matter!

What is matter?

Take a look at the beautiful scene in **Figure 1.** What do you see? Perhaps you notice the water and ice. Maybe you are struck by the Sun in the background. All of these images show examples of matter. **Matter** is anything that takes up space and has mass. Matter doesn't have to be visible—even air is matter.

States of Matter All matter is made up of tiny particles, such as atoms, molecules, or ions. Each particle attracts other particles. In other words, each particle pulls other particles toward itself. These particles also are constantly moving. The motion of the particles and the strength of attraction between the particles determine a material's state of matter.

Reading Check *What determines a material's state of matter?*

There are three familiar states of matter—solid, liquid, and gas. The fourth state of matter is plasma. Stars, lightning, and neon lights contain matter in the plasma state. Although plasma is common in the universe, it is not common on Earth. For that reason, this chapter will focus only on the three states of matter that are common on Earth.

Figure 1
Matter exists in all four states in this scene. *Identify the solid, liquid, gas, and plasma in this photograph.*

Solids

What makes a solid a solid? Think about some solids that you are familiar with. Chairs, floors, rocks, and ice cubes are a few examples of matter in the solid state. What properties do all solids share? A **solid** is matter with a definite shape and volume. For example, when you pick up a rock from the ground and place it in a bucket, it doesn't change shape or size. A solid does not take the shape of a container in which it is placed. This is because the particles of a solid are packed closely together, as shown in **Figure 2.**

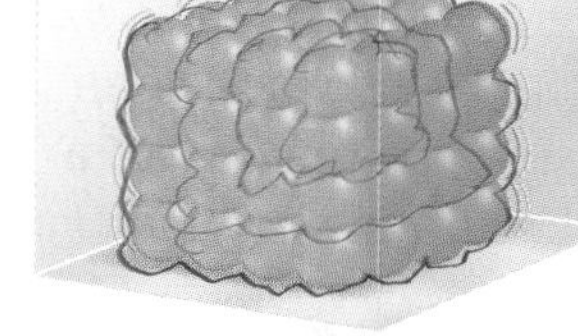

Solid

Figure 2
The particles in a solid vibrate in place, maintaining a constant shape and volume.

Particles in Motion The particles that make up all types of matter are in constant motion. Does this mean that the particles in a solid are moving too? Although you can't see them, a solid's particles are vibrating in place. The particles do not have enough energy to move out of their fixed positions.

Reading Check *What motion do solid particles have?*

Crystalline Solids In some solids, the particles are arranged in a repeating, three-dimensional pattern called a crystal. These solids are called crystalline solids. In **Figure 3** you can see the arrangement of particles in a crystal of sodium chloride, which is table salt. The particles in the crystal are arranged in the shape of a cube. Diamond, another crystalline solid, is made entirely of carbon atoms that form crystals that look more like pyramids. Sugar, sand, and snow are other crystalline solids.

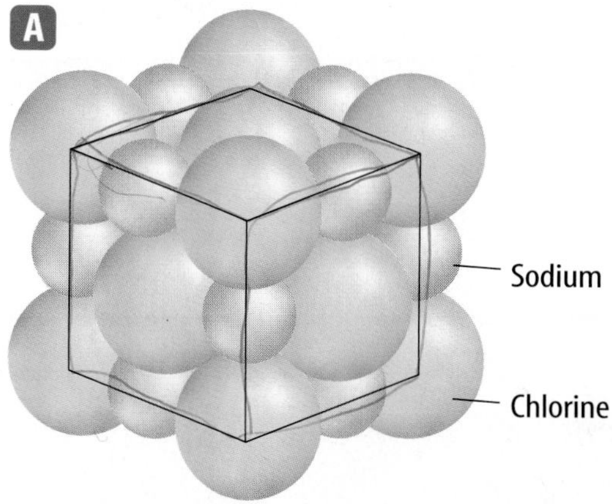

Figure 3
A The particles in a crystal of sodium chloride (NaCl) are arranged in an orderly pattern. B This magnified image shows the cubic shape of sodium chloride crystals.

Amorphous Solids Some solids come together without forming crystal structures. These solids often consist of large particles that are not arranged in a repeating pattern. Instead, the particles are found in a random arrangement. These solids are called amorphous (uh MOR fuhs) solids. Rubber, plastic, and glass are examples of amorphous solids.

Earth Science INTEGRATION

About 74.93 percent of Earth's freshwater is in the form of solid ice. Most of the remaining freshwater, about 25.04 percent, exists as a liquid in lakes, rivers, and in the ground. A small fraction, about 0.03 percent, of Earth's freshwater can be found in the air as water vapor, which is the gas state of water. Create a circle graph showing the states of Earth's freshwater.

Reading Check *How is a crystalline solid different from an amorphous solid?*

Liquids

From the orange juice you drink with breakfast to the water you use to brush your teeth at night, matter in the liquid state is familiar to you. How would you describe the characteristics of a liquid? Is it hard like a solid? Does it keep its shape? A **liquid** is matter that has a definite volume but no definite shape. When you pour a liquid from one container to another, the liquid takes the shape of the container. The volume of a liquid, however, is the same no matter what the shape of the container. If you pour 50 mL of juice from a carton into a pitcher, the pitcher will contain 50 mL of juice. If you then pour that same juice into a glass, its shape will change again but its volume will not.

Free to Move The reason that a liquid can have different shapes is because the particles in a liquid move more freely, as shown in **Figure 4,** than the particles in a solid. The particles in a liquid have enough energy to move out of their fixed positions but not enough energy to move far apart.

Figure 4
The particles in a liquid stay close together, although they are free to move past one another.

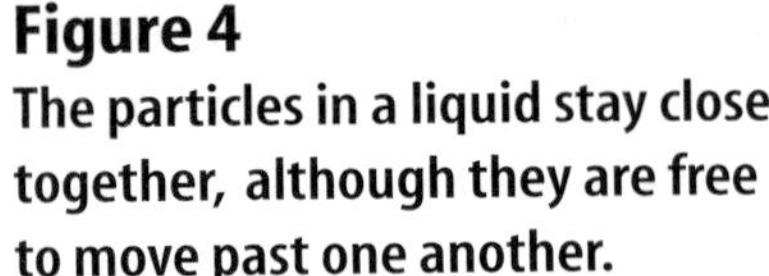

Liquid

Viscosity Do all liquids flow the way water flows? You know that honey flows more slowly than water and you've probably heard the phrase "slow as molasses." Some liquids flow more easily than others. A liquid's resistance to flow is known as the liquid's viscosity. Honey has a high viscosity. Water has a lower viscosity. The slower a liquid flows, the higher its viscosity is. The viscosity results from the strength of the attraction between the particles of the liquid. For many liquids, viscosity increases as the liquid becomes colder.

Surface Tension If you're careful, you can float a needle on the surface of water. This is because attractive forces cause the particles on the surface of a liquid to pull themselves together and resist being pushed apart. You can see in **Figure 5A** that particles beneath the surface of a liquid are pulled in all directions. Particles at the surface of a liquid are pulled toward the center of the liquid and sideways along the surface. No liquid particles are located above to pull on them. The uneven forces acting on the particles on the surface of a liquid are called surface tension. Surface tension causes the liquid to act as if a thin film were stretched across its surface. As a result you can float a needle on the surface of water. For the same reason, the water strider in **Figure 5B** can move around on the surface of a pond or lake. When a liquid is present in small amounts, surface tension causes the liquid to form small droplets, as shown in **Figure 5C.**

SCIENCE *Online*

Research Visit the Glencoe Science Web site at **science.glencoe.com** for more information about the states of matter. How does the fourth state of matter, plasma, differ from the others? Make a poster that describes and gives examples of the four states of matter.

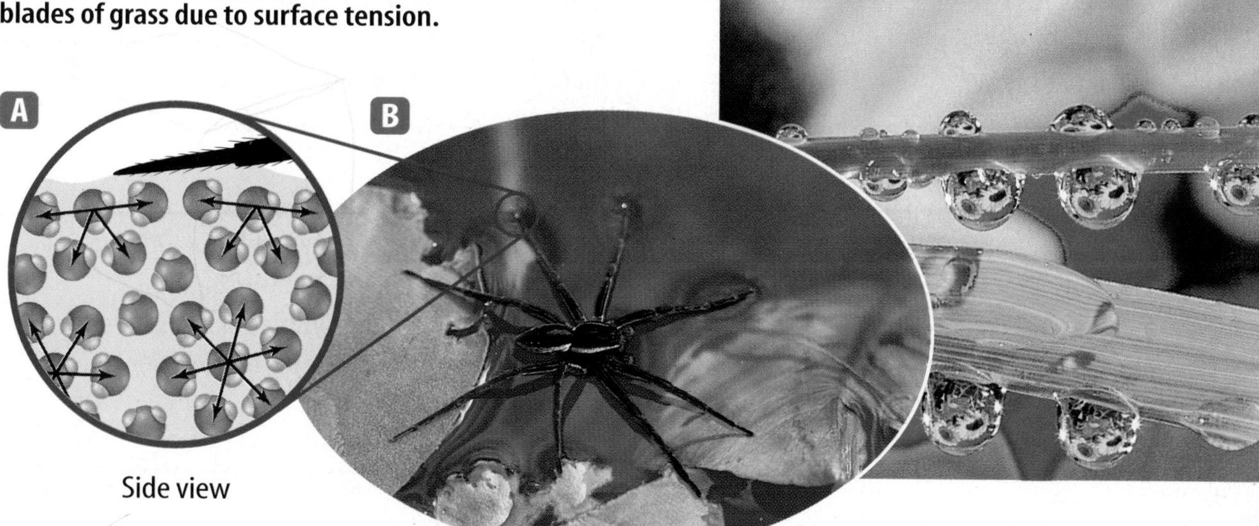

Figure 5
A These arrows show the forces pulling on the particles of a liquid. Surface tension exists because the particles at the surface experience different forces than those at the center of the liquid. B Surface tension allows this strider to float on water as if the water had a thin film. C Water drops form on these blades of grass due to surface tension.

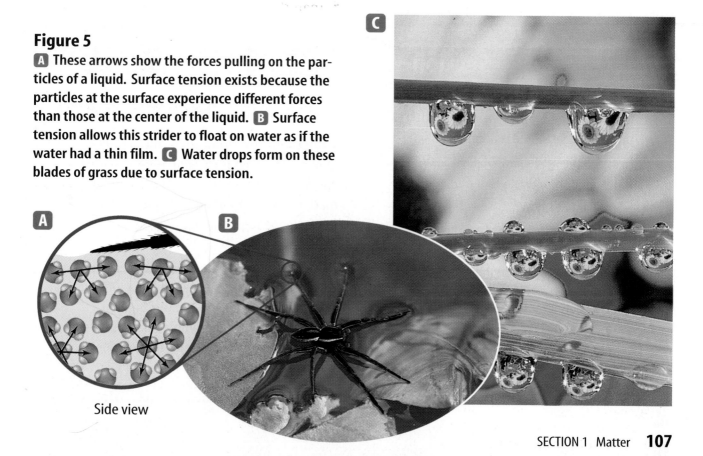

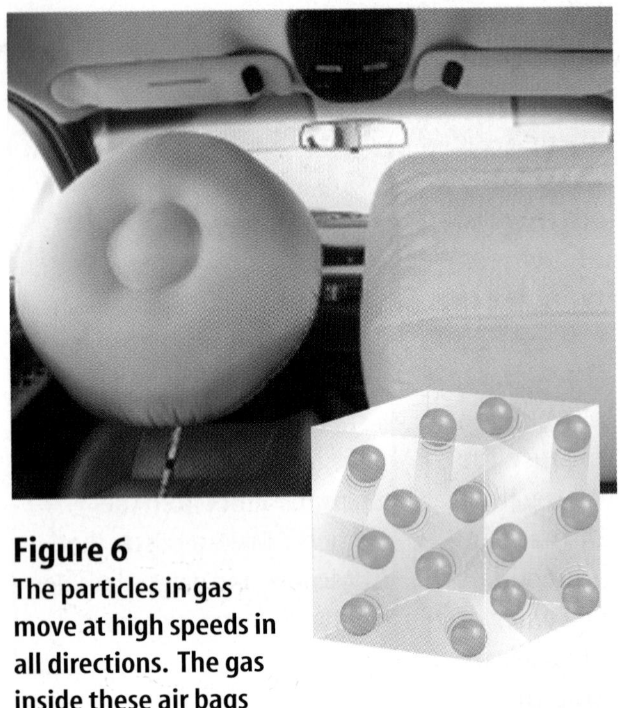

Figure 6
The particles in gas move at high speeds in all directions. The gas inside these air bags spreads out to fill the entire volume of the bag.

Gases

Unlike solids and liquids, most gases are invisible. The air in the air bags in **Figure 6** and the helium in some balloons are examples of gases. **Gas** is matter that does not have a definite shape or volume. The particles in gas are much farther apart than those in a liquid or solid. Gas particles move at high speeds in all directions. They will spread out evenly, as far apart as possible. If you poured a small volume of a liquid into a container, the liquid would stay in the bottom of the container. However, if you poured the same volume of a gas into a container, the gas would fill the container completely. A gas can expand or be compressed. Decreasing the volume of the container squeezes the gas particles closer together.

Reading Check *How will the shape and volume of helium gas change when it escapes from a balloon?*

You sometimes will hear the term *vapor* applied to gases. A vapor is matter that exists in the gas state but is generally a liquid or solid at room temperature. Water, for example, is a liquid at room temperature. Steam, the gas state of water, is called water vapor.

Section 1 Assessment

1. Define matter in your own words and provide at least three examples.
2. Describe the movement of particles within solids, liquids, and gases.
3. Why do liquids flow?
4. A scientist places 25 mL of a yellow substance into a 50-mL container. The substance quickly fills the entire container. In which state of matter is the substance? Why?
5. **Think Critically** Two of the three common states of matter can be grouped together. Which two states share a similar property? Explain your reasoning.

Skill Builder Activities

6. **Venn Diagram** Using what you have read, draw a Venn diagram in your Science Journal and fill in the characteristics of the states of matter. Add information that you've gained from experience. **For more help, refer to the** Science Skill Handbook.
7. **Communicating** You are surrounded by solids, liquids, and gases all the time. In your Science Journal, make a table with three columns. List several examples of each state of matter. **For more help, refer to the** Science Skill Handbook.

Changes of State

Thermal Energy and Heat

Shards of ice fly from the sculptor's chisel. As the crowd looks on, a swan slowly emerges from a massive block of ice. As the day wears on, however, drops of water begin to fall from the sculpture. Drip by drip, the sculpture is transformed into a puddle of liquid water. What makes matter change from one state to another? To answer this question, you need to take another look at the particles that make up matter.

Energy Simply stated, energy is the ability to do work or cause change. The energy of motion is called kinetic energy. Particles within matter are in constant motion. The amount of motion of these particles depends on the kinetic energy they possess. Particles with more kinetic energy move faster and farther apart. Particles with less energy move more slowly and stay closer together.

The total energy of all the particles in a sample of matter is called thermal energy. Thermal energy depends on the number of particles in a substance as well as the amount of energy each particle has. If either the number of particles or the amount of energy each particle in a sample has increases, the thermal energy of the sample increases. The hot water and snow in **Figure 7** have different amounts of energy.

As You Read

What **You'll Learn**

- **Define and Compare** thermal energy and temperature.
- **Relate** changes in thermal energy to changes of state.
- **Explore** energy and temperature changes on a graph.

Vocabulary

temperature
heat
melting
freezing
vaporization
condensation

Why **It's Important**

Matter changes state as it heats up or cools down.

Figure 7
You know how it feels to be hot and cold. This hot spring, for example, feels much hotter than the snow around it. *How is hot matter different from cold matter?*

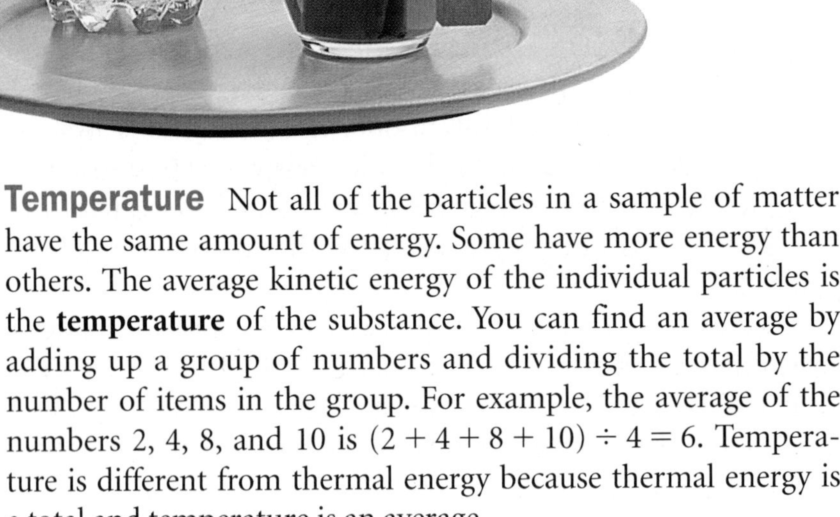

Figure 8
The particles in hot tea move faster than those in iced tea. The temperature of hot tea is higher than the temperature of iced tea.

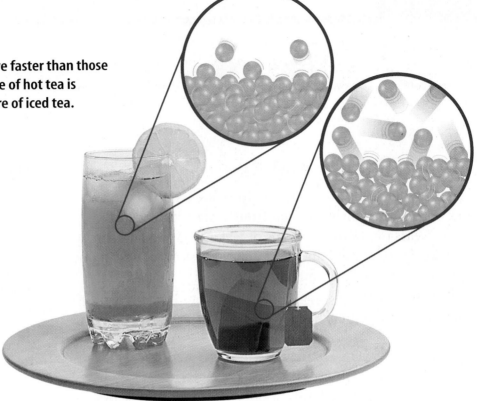

Temperature Not all of the particles in a sample of matter have the same amount of energy. Some have more energy than others. The average kinetic energy of the individual particles is the **temperature** of the substance. You can find an average by adding up a group of numbers and dividing the total by the number of items in the group. For example, the average of the numbers 2, 4, 8, and 10 is $(2 + 4 + 8 + 10) \div 4 = 6$. Temperature is different from thermal energy because thermal energy is a total and temperature is an average.

You know that the iced tea is colder than the hot tea, as shown in **Figure 8.** Stated differently, the temperature of iced tea is lower than the temperature of hot tea. You also could say that the average kinetic energy of the particles in the iced tea is less than the average kinetic energy of the particles in the hot tea.

Thermal energy is one of several different forms of energy. Other forms include the chemical energy in chemical compounds, the electrical energy used in appliances, the electromagnetic energy of light, and the nuclear energy stored in the nucleus of an atom. Make a list of examples of energy that you are familiar with.

Heat When a warm object is brought near a cooler object, thermal energy will be transferred from the warmer object to the cooler one. The movement of thermal energy from a substance at a higher temperature to one at a lower temperature is called **heat.** When a substance is heated, it gains thermal energy. Therefore, its particles move faster and its temperature rises. When a substance is cooled, it loses thermal energy, which causes its particles to move more slowly and its temperature to drop.

How is heat related to temperature?

Specific Heat

If you walk from the grass to the pavement on a hot summer day, you know that the pavement is much hotter than the grass. Both surfaces were heated by the Sun and therefore received the same amount of thermal energy. Why does the temperature of one increase faster than the temperature of the other? The reason is that each surface has a different specific heat. The specific heat of a substance is the amount of heat needed to raise the temperature of 1 g of a substance 1°C.

Substances that have a low specific heat, such as most metals, heat up quickly because they require only small amounts of heat to cause their temperatures to rise. A substance with a high specific heat, such as the water in **Figure 9,** heats up slowly because a much larger quantity of heat is required to cause its temperature to rise by the same amount.

Figure 9
One reason the water in this lake is much colder than the surrounding sand is because the specific heat of water is higher than that of sand.

Changes Between the Solid and Liquid States

Matter can change from one state to another when thermal energy is absorbed or released. A change from one physical state of matter to another is known as change of state. The graph in **Figure 11** shows the changes in temperature and thermal energy that occur as you gradually heat a container of ice.

Melting As the ice in **Figure 11** is heated, it absorbs thermal energy and its temperature rises. At some point, the temperature stops rising and the ice begins to change into liquid water. The change from the solid state to the liquid state is called **melting.** The temperature at which a substance changes from a solid to a liquid is called the melting point. The melting point of water is 0°C.

Amorphous solids, such as rubber and glass, don't melt in the same way as crystalline solids. Because they don't have crystal structures to break down, these solids get softer and softer as they are heated, as you can see in **Figure 10.**

Figure 10
Rather than melting into a liquid, glass gradually softens. Glass blowers use this characteristic to shape glass into beautiful vases while it is hot.

NATIONAL GEOGRAPHIC **VISUALIZING STATES OF MATTER**

Figure 11

Like most substances, water can exist in three distinct states—solid, liquid, or gas. At certain temperatures, water changes from one state to another. This diagram shows what changes occur as water is heated or cooled.

MELTING When ice melts, its temperature remains constant until all the ice turns to water. Continued heating of liquid water causes the molecules to vibrate even faster, steadily raising the temperature.

FREEZING When liquid water freezes, it gives up energy and turns into the solid state, ice.

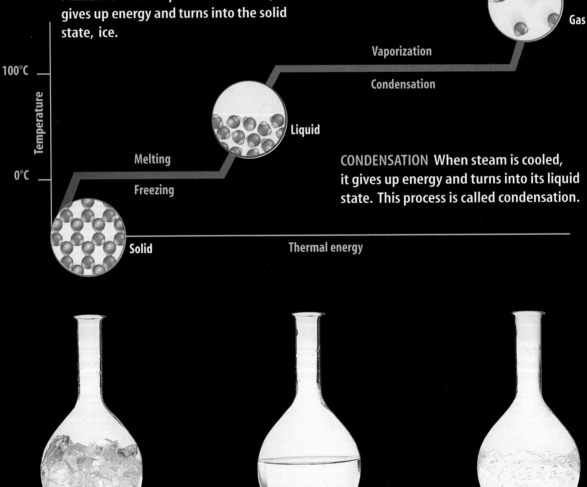

VAPORIZATION When water reaches its boiling point of 100°C, water molecules are vibrating so fast that they break free of the attractions that hold them together in the liquid state. The result is vaporization—the liquid becomes a gas. The temperature of boiling water remains constant until all of the liquid turns to steam.

CONDENSATION When steam is cooled, it gives up energy and turns into its liquid state. This process is called condensation.

Gas
Vaporization
Condensation
100°C
Temperature
Liquid
Melting
0°C
Freezing
Solid
Thermal energy

Solid state: ice

Liquid state: water

Gaseous state: steam

Freezing The process of melting a crystalline solid can be reversed if the liquid is cooled. As the liquid cools, it loses thermal energy. As a result, its particles slow down and come closer together. Attractive forces begin to trap particles, and the crystals of a solid begin to form. The change from the liquid state to the solid state is called **freezing**. As you can see in **Figure 11**, freezing and melting are opposite processes.

The temperature at which a substance changes from the liquid state to the solid state is called the freezing point. The freezing point of the liquid state of a substance is the same temperature as the melting point of the solid state. For example, solid ice melts at 0°C and liquid water freezes at 0°C.

During freezing, the temperature of a substance remains constant while the particles in the liquid form a crystalline solid. Because particles in a liquid have more energy than particles in a solid, energy is released during freezing. This energy is released into the surroundings. After all of the liquid has become a solid, the temperature begins to decrease again.

SCIENCE Online

Research Visit the Glencoe Science Web site at **science.glencoe.com** for more information about freezing. Make a list of several substances and the temperatures at which they freeze. Find out how the freezing point affects how the substance is used. Share your findings with the class.

Problem-Solving Activity

How can ice save oranges?

During the spring, Florida citrus farmers carefully watch the fruit when temperatures drop close to freezing. When the temperatures fall below 0°C, the liquid in the cells of oranges can freeze and expand. This causes the cells to break, making the oranges mushy and the crop useless for sale. To prevent this, farmers spray the oranges with water just before the temperature reaches 0°C. How does spraying oranges with water protect them?

Identifying the Problem

Using the diagram in **Figure 11**, consider what is happening to the water at 0°C. Two things occur. What are they?

Solving the Problem

1. What change of state and what energy changes occur when water freezes?
2. How does the formation of ice on the orange help the orange?

Explaining What You Feel

Procedure

1. Use a **dropper** to place one drop of **rubbing alcohol** on the back of your hand.
2. Describe how your hand feels during the next 2 min.
3. Wash your hands.

Analysis

1. What changes in the appearance of the rubbing alcohol did you notice?
2. What sensation did you feel during the 2 min? How can you explain this sensation?

Changes Between the Liquid and Gas States

After an early morning rain, you and your friends enjoy stomping through the puddles left behind. But later that afternoon when you head out to run through the puddles once more, the puddles are gone. The liquid water in the puddles changed into a gas. Matter changes between the liquid and gas states through vaporization and condensation.

Vaporization As liquid water is heated, its temperature rises until it reaches 100°C. At this point, liquid water changes into water vapor. The change from a liquid to a gas is known as **vaporization** (vay pur uh ZAY shun). You can see in **Figure 11** that the temperature of the substance does not change during vaporization. However, the substance absorbs thermal energy. The additional energy causes the particles to move faster until they have enough energy to escape the liquid as gas particles.

Two forms of vaporization exist. Vaporization that takes place below the surface of a liquid is called boiling. When a liquid boils, bubbles form within the liquid and rise to the surface, as shown in **Figure 12.** The temperature at which a liquid boils is called the boiling point. The boiling point of water is 100°C.

Vaporization that takes place at the surface of a liquid is called evaporation. Evaporation, which occurs at temperatures below the boiling point, explains how puddles dry up. Imagine that you could watch individual water molecules in a puddle. You would notice that the molecules move at different speeds. Although the temperature of the water is constant, remember that temperature is a measure of the average kinetic energy of the molecules. Some of the fastest-moving molecules overcome the attractive forces of other molecules and escape from the surface of the water.

Figure 12
During boiling, liquid changes to gas, forming bubbles in the liquid that rise to the surface.

Figure 13
The drops of water on these glasses and pitcher of lemonade were formed when water vapor in the air lost enough energy to return to the liquid state. This process is called condensation.

Location of Molecules It takes more than speed for water molecules to escape the liquid state. During evaporation, these faster molecules also must be near the surface, heading in the right direction, and they must avoid hitting other water molecules as they leave. With the faster particles evaporating from the surface of a liquid, the particles that remain are the slower, cooler ones. Evaporation cools the liquid and anything near the liquid. You experience this cooling effect when perspiration evaporates from your skin.

Condensation Pour a nice, cold glass of lemonade and place it on the table for a half hour on a warm day. When you come back to take a drink, the outside of the glass will be covered by drops of water, as shown in **Figure 13.** What happened? As a gas cools, its particles slow down. When particles move slowly enough for their attractions to bring them together, droplets of liquid form. This process, which is the opposite of vaporization, is called **condensation.** As a gas condenses to a liquid, it releases the thermal energy it absorbed to become a gas. During this process, the temperature of the substance does not change. The decrease in energy changes the arrangement of particles. After the change of state is complete, the temperature continues to drop, as you saw in **Figure 11.**

Reading Check *What energy change occurs during condensation?*

Condensation formed the droplets of water on the outside of your glass of lemonade. In the same way, water vapor in the atmosphere condenses to form the liquid water droplets in clouds. When the droplets become large enough, they can fall to the ground as rain.

SCIENCE Online

Research Visit the Glencoe Science Web site at **science.glencoe.com** for more information about how condensation is involved in weather. Find out how condensation is affected by the temperature as well as the amount of water in the air.

Figure 14
The solid dry ice at the bottom of this beaker of water is changing directly into gaseous carbon dioxide. This process is called sublimation.

Changes Between the Solid and Gas States

Some substances can change from the solid state to the gas state without ever becoming a liquid. During this process, known as sublimation, the surface particles of the solid gain enough energy to become a gas. One example of a substance that undergoes sublimation is dry ice. Dry ice is the solid form of carbon dioxide. It often is used to keep materials cold and dry. At room temperature and pressure, carbon dioxide does not exist as a liquid. Therefore, as dry ice absorbs thermal energy from the objects around it, it changes directly into a gas. When dry ice becomes a gas, it absorbs thermal energy from water vapor in the air. As a result, the water vapor cools and condenses into liquid water droplets, forming the fog you see in **Figure 14.**

Section  2 Assessment

1. How are thermal energy and temperature similar? How are they different?
2. How does a change in thermal energy cause matter to change from one state to another? Give an example.
3. During which three changes of state is energy absorbed?
4. What are two types of vaporization?
5. **Think Critically** How can the temperature of a substance remain the same even if the substance is absorbing thermal energy?

Skill Builder Activities

6. **Making and Using Graphs** Using the data you collected in the Explore Activity, plot a temperature-time graph. Describe your graph. At what temperature does the graph level off? What was the liquid doing during this time period? **For more help, refer to the Science Skill Handbook.**
7. **Communicating** In your Science Journal, explain why you can step out of the shower into a warm bathroom and begin to shiver. **For more help, refer to the Science Skill Handbook.**

Activity

A Spin Around the Water Cycle

Some of the water in the puddle you stepped in this morning could have rolled down a dinosaur's back millions of years ago because water moves through the environment in a never-ending cycle. Changes in water's physical state enable living things to use this resource.

What You'll Investigate

How does the temperature of water change as it is heated from a solid to a gas?

Materials

hot plate
ice cubes (100 mL)
Celsius thermometer
**electronic temperature probe*
wall clock
**watch with second hand*
stirring rod
250-mL beaker
**Alternate materials*

Goals

- **Measure** the temperature of water as it heats.
- **Observe** what happens as the water changes from one state to another.
- **Graph** the temperature and time data.

Safety Precautions

Procedure

1. Copy the data table shown.
2. Put 150 mL of water and 100 mL of ice into the beaker and place the beaker on the hot plate. Do not touch the hot plate.
3. Put the thermometer into the ice/water mixture. Do not stir with the thermometer or allow it to rest on the bottom of the beaker. After 30 s, read the temperature and record it in your data table.

Characteristics of Water Sample

Time (min)	Temperature (°C)	Physical State
0.0		
0.5		
1.0		
1.5		
2.0		

4. Plug in the hot plate and turn the temperature knob to the medium setting.
5. Every 30 s, read and record the temperature and physical state of the water until it begins to boil. Use the stirring rod to stir the contents of the beaker before making each temperature measurement. Stop recording. Allow the water to cool.
6. Use your data to make a graph plotting time on the *x*-axis and temperature on the *y*-axis. Draw a smooth curve through the data points.

Conclude and Apply

1. How did the temperature of the ice/water mixture change as you heated the beaker?
2. How did the state of water change as you heated the beaker?
3. **Describe** the shape of the graph during any changes of state.

Communicating Your Data

Add captions to your graph. Use the detailed graph to explain to your class how water changes state. **For more help, refer to the** Science Skill Handbook.

SECTION 3 Behavior of Fluids

As You Read

***What* You'll Learn**

- **Explain** why some things float but others sink.
- **Describe** how pressure is transmitted through fluids.

Vocabulary

pressure
buoyant force
Archimedes' principle
density
Pascal's principle

***Why* It's Important**

Pressure enables you to squeeze toothpaste from a tube, and buoyant force helps you float in water.

Pressure

It's a beautiful summer day when you and your friends go outside to play volleyball, much like the kids in **Figure 15.** There's only one problem—the ball is flat. You pump air into the ball until it is firm. The firmness of the ball is the result of the motion of the air particles in the ball. As the air particles in the ball move, they collide with one another and with the inside walls of the ball. As each particle collides with the inside walls, it exerts a force, pushing the surface of the ball outward. A force is a push or a pull. The forces of all the individual particles add together to make up the pressure of the air.

Pressure is equal to the force exerted on a surface divided by the total area over which the force is exerted.

$$(P)\text{ pressure} = (F)\text{ force}/(A)\text{ area}$$

When force is measured in newtons (N) and area is measured in square meters (m^2), pressure is measured in newtons per square meter (N/m^2). This unit of pressure is called a pascal (Pa). A more useful unit when discussing atmospheric pressure is the kilopascal (kPa), which is 1,000 pascals.

Figure 15
Without the pressure of air inside this volleyball, the ball would be flat.

Figure 16
The force of the dancer's weight on pointed toes results in a higher pressure than the same force on flat feet. *Why is the pressure different?*

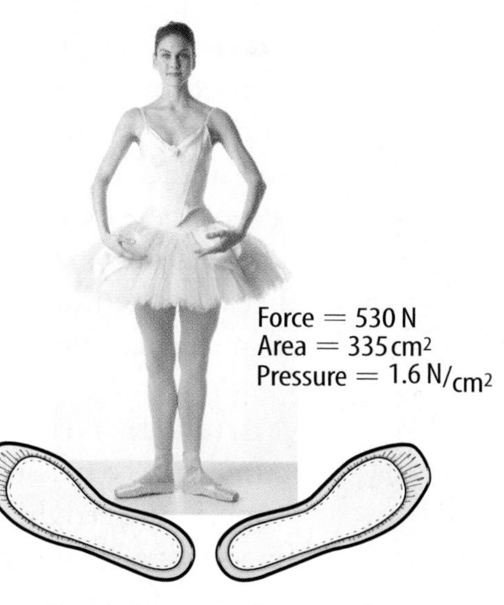

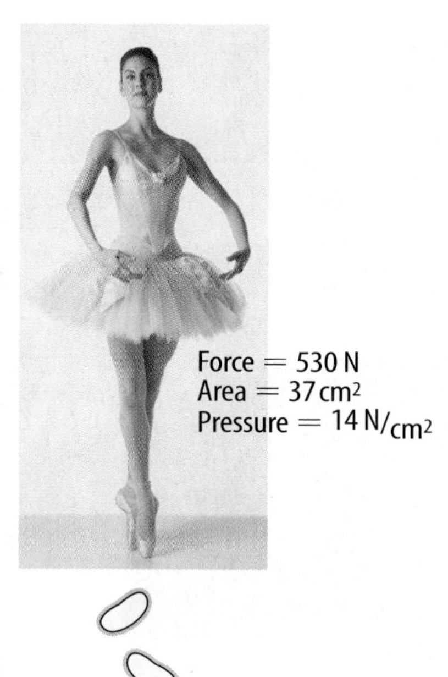

Force and Area You can see from the equation on the opposite page that pressure depends on the quantity of force exerted and the area over which the force is exerted. As the force increases over the same area, pressure increases. If the force decreases, the pressure will decrease. However, if the area changes, the same amount of force can result in different pressure. **Figure 16** shows that if the force of the ballerina's weight is exerted over a smaller area, the pressure increases. If that same force is exerted over a larger area, the pressure will decrease.

Reading Check *What variables does pressure depend on?*

Atmospheric Pressure You can't see it and you usually can't feel it, but the air around you presses on you with tremendous force. The pressure of air also is known as atmospheric pressure because air makes up the atmosphere around Earth. Atmospheric pressure is 101.3 kPa at sea level. This means that air exerts a force of about 101,000 N on every square meter it touches. This is approximately equal to the weight of a large truck.

It might be difficult to think of air as having pressure when you don't notice it. However, you often take advantage of air pressure without even realizing it. Air pressure, for example, enables you to drink from a straw. When you first suck on a straw, you remove the air from it. As you can see in **Figure 17,** air pressure pushing down on the liquid in your glass then forces liquid up into the straw. If you tried to drink through a straw inserted into a sealed, airtight container, you would not have any success because the air would not be able to push down on the surface of the drink.

Figure 17
The downward pressure of air pushes the juice up into the straw.

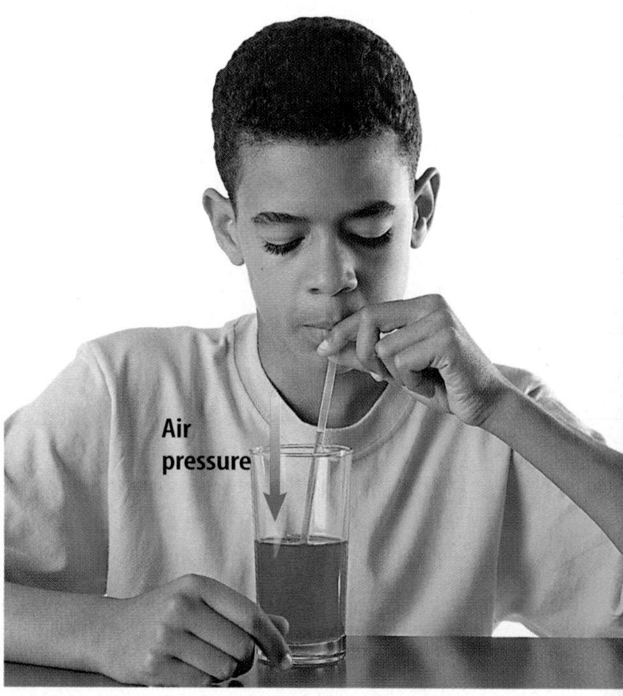

Figure 18
Atmospheric pressure exerts a force on all surfaces of this dancer's body. *Why can't she feel the pressure?*

Balanced Pressure If air is so forceful, why don't you feel it? The reason is that the pressure exerted outward by the fluids in your body balances the pressure exerted by the atmosphere on the surface of your body. Look at **Figure 18.** The atmosphere exerts a pressure on all surfaces of the dancer's body. She is not crushed by this pressure because the fluids in her body exert a pressure that balances atmospheric pressure.

Variations in Atmospheric Pressure Atmospheric pressure changes with altitude. Altitude is the height above sea level. As altitude increases atmospheric pressure decreases. This is because fewer air particles are found in a given volume. Fewer particles have fewer collisions and, therefore, exert less pressure. This idea was tested in the seventeenth century by a French physician named Blaise Pascal. He designed an experiment in which he filled a balloon only partially with air. He then had the balloon carried to the top of a mountain. **Figure 19** shows that as Pascal predicted, the balloon expanded while being carried up the mountain. Although the amount of air inside the balloon stayed the same, the air pressure pushing in on it from the outside decreased. Consequently, the particles of air inside the balloon were able to spread out further.

Figure 19
Notice how the balloon expands as it is carried up the mountain. The reason is because atmospheric pressure decreases with altitude. With less pressure pushing in on the balloon, the gas particles within the balloon are free to expand.

The Pressure in a Moving Fluid

What happens to the pressure in a fluid if the fluid is moving? Try the following experiment. Place an empty soda can on the desktop and blow to the right of the can, as shown in **Figure 20.** How would you expect the can to move?

When you blow to the right of the can, the can moves to the right, toward the moving air. The air pressure exerted on the right side of the can, where the air is moving, is less than the air pressure on the left side of the can, where the air is not moving. As a result, the force exerted by the air pressure on the left side is greater than the force exerted on the right side, and the can is pushed to the right.

Figure 20
By blowing on one side of the can, you decrease the air pressure on that side. Because the air pressure on the opposite side is now greater, the can moves to the side you're blowing on.

Bernoulli's Principle

The surprising behavior of the can is an example of Bernoulli's Principle, which was discovered by the Swiss scientist Daniel Bernoulli in the eighteenth century. According to **Bernoulli's principle,** when the speed of a fluid increases, the pressure exerted by the fluid decreases. When you blew across the side of the can, the pressure exerted by the air on that side of the can decreased because the air was moving faster than on the other side. As a result, the can was pushed toward the side you blew across.

Damage From High Winds You might have seen photographs of people preparing for a hurricane by closing shutters or nailing boards across the outside of windows. In a hurricane, the high winds blowing outside the house cause the pressure outside the house to be less than the pressure inside. This difference in pressure can be large enough to cause windows to be pushed out and shatter.

Hurricanes and other high winds can sometimes blow roofs from houses. When wind blows across the roof of a house, the pressure outside the roof decreases. If the wind outside is blowing fast enough, the outside pressure can become so low that the roof can be pushed off the house by the higher pressure inside.

✔ Reading Check ***How are roofs pulled off of houses during hurricanes?***

Observing Bernoulli's Principle

Procedure

1. Tie a **piece of string** to the handle of a **plastic spoon.**
2. Turn on a **faucet** to make a stream of water.
3. Holding the string, bring the spoon close to the stream of water.

Analysis

Use Bernoulli's principle to explain the motion of the spoon.

Figure 21
The air moving past the chimney causes the pressure above the chimney to be lower than it is inside the house. This forces more smoke up the chimney.

Chimneys and Bernoulli's Principle In a fireplace, the hotter, less dense air above the fire is pushed upward by the cooler air in the room. Wind outside the house can increase the rate at which the smoke rises. Look at **Figure 21.** Air moving across the top of the chimney causes the air pressure above the chimney to decrease, according to Bernoulli's principle. As a result, more smoke is pushed upward by the higher pressure of the air in the room.

Float or Sink

You may have noticed that you feel lighter in water than you do when you climb out of it. While you are under water, you experience water pressure pushing on you in all directions. Just as air pressure increases as you walk down a mountain, water pressure increases as you swim deeper in water. Water pressure increases with depth. As a result, the pressure pushing up on the bottom of an object is greater than the pressure pushing down on it because the bottom of the object is deeper than the top.

The difference in pressure results in an upward force on an object immersed in a fluid, as shown in **Figure 22A.** This force is known as the **buoyant force.** If the buoyant force is equal to the weight of an object, the object will float. If the buoyant force is less than the weight of an object, the object will sink.

Figure 22
A The pressure pushing up on an immersed object is greater than the pressure pushing down on it. This difference results in the buoyant force. B Weight is a force in the downward direction. The buoyant force is in the upward direction. An object will float if the upward force is equal to the downward force.

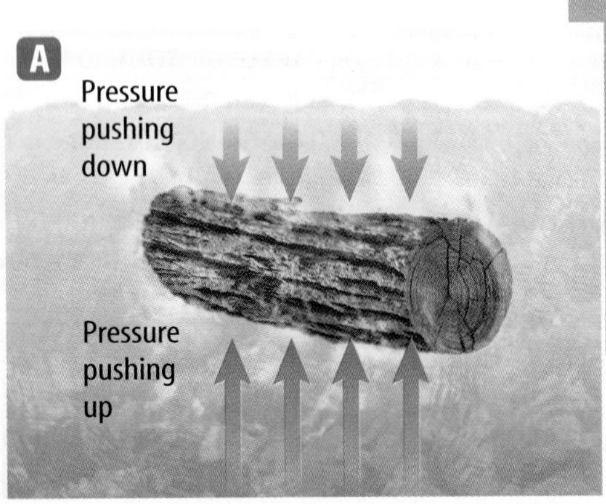

Archimedes' Principle What determines the buoyant force? According to **Archimedes'** (ar kuh MEE deez) **principle,** the buoyant force on an object is equal to the weight of the fluid displaced by the object. In other words, if you place an object in a beaker that already is filled to the brim with water, some water will spill out of the beaker, as in **Figure 23.** If you weigh the spilled water, you will find the buoyant force on the object.

Density Understanding density can help you predict whether an object will float or sink. **Density** is mass divided by volume.

$$\text{density} = \frac{\text{mass}}{\text{volume}}$$

An object will float in a fluid that is more dense than itself and sink in a fluid that is less dense than itself. If an object has the same density as the fluid, the object will neither sink nor float but instead stay at the same level in the fluid. An iceberg floats on water because the density of ice is less than the density of water. A helium balloon rises in air because the density of helium is less than the density of air.

Figure 23
When the golf ball was dropped in the large beaker, it displaced some of the water, which was collected and placed into the smaller beaker. *What do you know about the weight and the volume of the displaced water?*

Math Skills Activity

Calculating Density

Example Problem

You are given a sample of a solid that has a mass of 10.0 g and a volume of 4.60 cm^3. Will it float in liquid water, which has a density of 1.00 g/cm^3?

Solution

1. *This is what you know:* mass = 10.0 g; volume = 4.60 cm^3; density of water = 1.00 g/cm^3

   A sample will float in a substance that is more dense than itself.

2. *This is what you need to find:* the density of the sample
3. *This is the equation you need to use:* density = mass/volume
4. *Substitute the known values:* density = 10.0 g/4.60 cm^3 = 2.17 g/cm^3

   The density of the sample is greater than the density of water. The sample will sink.

Practice Problem

A 7.40-cm^3 sample of mercury has a mass of 102 g. Will it float in water?

For more help, refer to the Math Skill Handbook.

Figure 24
A hydraulic lift utilizes Pascal's principle to help lift this car and this dentist's chair.

Pascal's Principle

What happens if you squeeze a plastic container filled with water? If the container is closed, the water has nowhere to go. As a result, the pressure in the water increases by the same amount everywhere in the container—not just where you squeeze or near the top of the container. When a force is applied to a confined fluid, an increase in pressure is transmitted equally to all parts of the fluid. This relationship is known as **Pascal's principle.**

Hydraulic Systems You witness Pascal's principle when a car is lifted up to have its oil changed or if you are in a dentist's chair as it is raised or lowered, as shown in **Figure 24.** These devices, known as hydraulic (hi DRAW lihk) systems, use Pascal's principle to increase force. Look at the tube in **Figure 25.** The force applied to the piston on the left increases the pressure within the fluid. That increase in pressure is transmitted to the piston on the right. Recall that pressure is equal to force divided by area. You can solve for force by multiplying pressure by area.

$$\text{pressure} = \frac{\text{force}}{\text{area}} \quad \text{or} \quad \text{force} = \text{pressure} \times \text{area}$$

If the two pistons on the tube have the same area, the force will be the same on both pistons. If, however, the piston on the right has a greater surface area than the piston on the left, the resulting force will be greater. The same pressure multiplied by a larger area equals a greater force. Hydraulic systems enable people to lift heavy objects using relatively small forces.

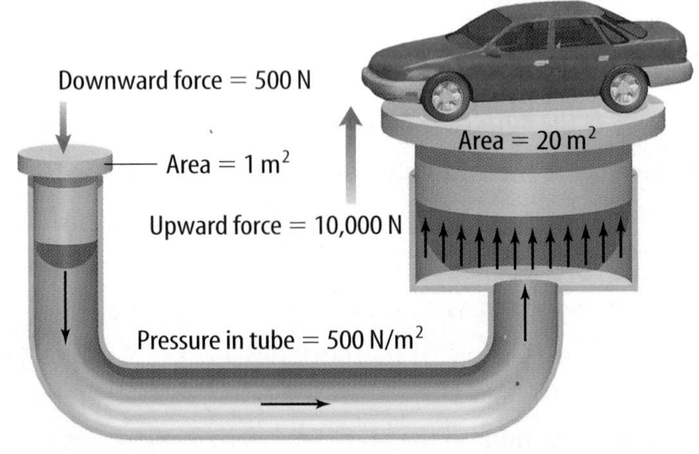

Figure 25
By increasing the area of the piston on the right side of the tube, you can increase the force exerted on the piston. In this way a small force pushing down on the left piston can result in a large force pushing up on the right piston. The force can be great enough to lift a car.

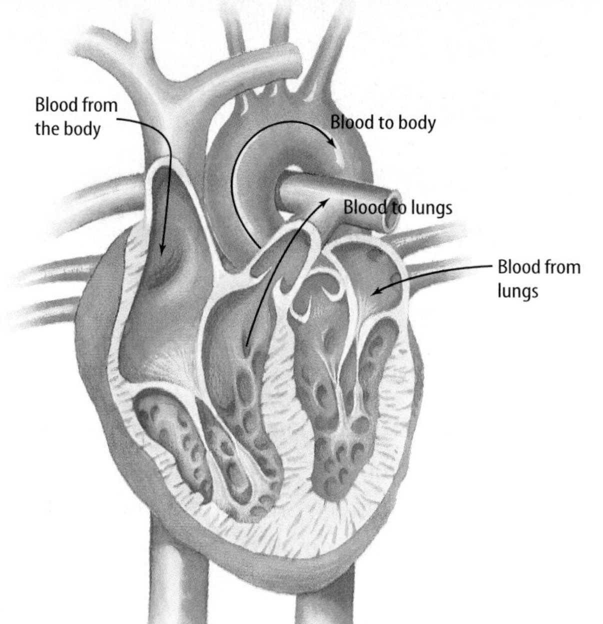

Figure 26
The heart is responsible for moving blood throughout the body. Two force pumps work together to move blood to and from the lungs and to the rest of the body.

Force Pumps If an otherwise closed container has a hole in it, any fluid in the container will be pushed out the opening when you squeeze it. This arrangement, known as a force pump, makes it possible for you to squeeze toothpaste out of a tube or mustard from a plastic container.

Your heart has two force pumps. One pump pushes blood to the lungs, where it picks up oxygen. The other force pump pushes the oxygen-rich blood to the rest of your body. These pumps are shown in **Figure 26.**

SCIENCE Online

Research Visit the Glencoe Science Web site at **science.glencoe.com** for more information about blood pressure. Find out what the term means, how it changes throughout the human body, and why it is unhealthy to have high blood pressure. Communicate to your class what you learn.

Section  Assessment

1. What happens to pressure as the force exerted on a given area increases?
2. How does atmospheric pressure change as altitude increases?
3. State Pascal's principle in your own words.
4. An object floats in a fluid. What do you know about the buoyant force on the object? How does the density of the object compare with the density of the fluid?
5. **Think Critically** All of the air is removed from a sealed metal can. After the air has been removed, the can looks as if it were crushed. Why?

Skill Builder Activities

6. **Recognizing Cause and Effect** A fluid (air or water) flowing quickly past the opening of one end of a hose creates a suction at the other end of the hose. Explain why this happens? **For more help, refer to the Science Skill Handbook.**
7. **Solving One-Step Equations** What pressure is created when 5.0 N of force are applied to an area of 2.0 m^2? How does the pressure change if the force is increased to 10.0 N? What about if instead the area is decreased to 1.0 m^2? **For more help, refer to the Math Skill Handbook.**

Activity Design Your Own Experiment

Design Your Own Ship

Cargo Ship

It is amazing to watch ships that are taller than buildings float easily on water. Passengers and cargo are carried on these ships in addition to the tremendous weight of the ship itself. How can you figure out how much cargo a ship can carry before it sinks? Can you design a ship to hold a specific amount of cargo?

Recognize the Problem

How can you determine the size of a ship needed to keep a certain mass of cargo afloat?

Form a Hypothesis

Think about Archimedes' principle and how it relates to buoyant force. Form a hypothesis about how the volume of water displaced by a ship relates to the mass of cargo the ship can carry.

Possible Materials

balance
small plastic cups (2)
graduated cylinder
metric ruler
scissors
marbles (cupful)
sink
**basin, pan, or bucket*
**Alternate materials*

Safety Precautions

Goals

- **Design** an experiment that uses Archimedes' principle to determine the size of ship needed to carry a given amount of cargo in such a way that the top of the ship is even with the surface of the water.

Test Your Hypothesis

Plan

1. Obtain a set of marbles or other items from your teacher. This is the cargo that your ship must carry. Think about the type of ship you will design. Consider the types of materials you will use. Decide how your group is going to test your hypothesis.
2. **List** the steps you need to follow to test your hypothesis. Include in your plan how you will measure the mass of your ship and cargo, calculate the volume of water your ship must displace in order to float with its cargo, and measure the volume and mass of the displaced water. Also explain how you will design your ship so that it will float with the top of the ship even with the surface of the water.
3. **Prepare** a data table in your Science Journal so that it is ready to use as your group collects data.

Do

1. Make sure your teacher approves your plan before you start.
2. Carry out your experiment as planned. Be sure to follow all proper safety procedures. In particular, clean up any spilled water immediately.
3. While doing the experiment, record your observations carefully and complete the data table in your Science Journal.

Analyze Your Data

1. **Write** your calculations showing how you determined the volume of displaced water needed to make your ship and cargo float.
2. Did your ship float at the water's surface, sink, or float above the water's surface? Draw a diagram of your ship in the water.

Draw Conclusions

1. If your ship sank, how would you change your experiment or calculations to correct the problem? What changes would you make if your ship floated too high in the water?
2. What does the density of a ship's cargo have to do with the volume of cargo the ship can carry? What about the density of the water?

Compare your results with other students' data. Prepare a combined data table or summary showing how the calculations affect the success of the ship. **For more help, refer to the Science Skill Handbook.**

The Incredible

A boric acid and silicone oil mix is sometimes packaged in a plastic egg.

During World War II, when natural resources were scarce and needed for the war effort, the U.S. government asked an engineer to come up with an inexpensive alternative to synthetic rubber. While researching the problem and looking for solutions, the engineer dropped boric acid into silicone oil. The result of these two substances mixing together was—a goo!

Because of its molecular structure, the goo could bounce and stretch in all directions. The engineer also discovered the goo could break into pieces. When strong pressure is applied to the substance, it reacts like a solid and breaks apart. Even though the combination was versatile—and quite amusing, the U.S. government decided the new substance wasn't a good substitute for synthetic rubber.

A serious search turns up a toy

Stretching Goo

A few years later, the recipe for the stretch material fell into the hands of a businessperson, who saw the goo's potential—as a toy. The toymaker paid $147 for rights to the boric acid and silicone oil mixture. And in 1949 it was sold at toy stores for the first time. The material was packaged in a plastic egg and it took the U.S. by storm. Today, the acid and oil mixture comes in a multitude of colors and almost every child has played with it at some time.

The substance can be used for more than child's play. Its sticky consistency makes it good for cleaning computer keyboards and removing small specks of lint from fabrics. People use it to make impressions of newspaper print or comics. Athletes strengthen their grips by grasping it over and over. Astronauts use it to anchor tools on spacecraft in zero gravity. All in all, a most *eggs-cellent* idea!

CONNECTIONS **Research** As a group, examine a sample of the colorful, sticky, stretch toy made of boric acid and silicone oil. Then brainstorm some practical—and impractical—uses for the substance.

SCIENCE *Online*

For more information, visit science.glencoe.com

Reviewing Main Ideas

Section 1 Matter

1. All matter, which includes anything that takes up space and has mass, is composed of tiny particles that are in constant motion.
2. In the solid state, the attractive forces between particles hold them in place to vibrate. Solids have definite shapes and volumes.
3. Particles in the liquid state have defined volumes and are free to move about within the liquid. *What property of liquids is shown in the photo?*

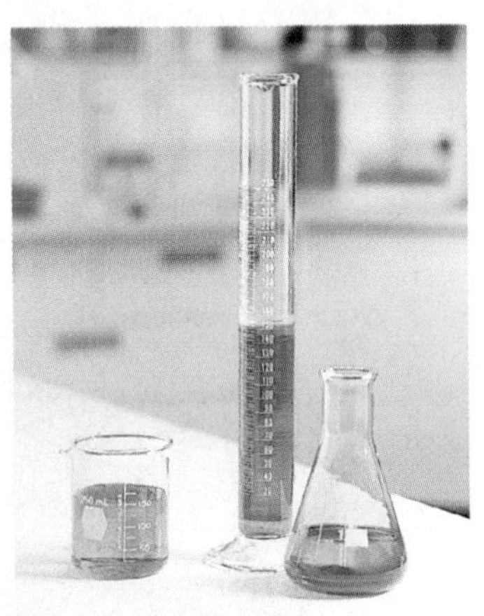

4. Particles in the gas state move about freely and completely fill their containers. Gases have neither definite shapes nor volumes.

Section 2 Changes of State

1. Thermal energy is the total energy of the particles in a sample of matter. The average kinetic energy of the particles is temperature. *At 85°C, which of these samples has a greater amount of thermal energy?*

2. For a change of state to occur, matter must gain or lose thermal energy.
3. An object gains thermal energy during melting when it changes from a solid to a liquid or during vaporization when it changes from a liquid to a gas.
4. An object loses thermal energy during condensation when it changes from a gas into a liquid or during freezing when it changes from a liquid to a solid.

Section 3 Behavior of Fluids

1. Pressure is force divided by area.
2. Fluids exert a buoyant force in the upward direction on objects immersed in them. Archimedes' principle states that the buoyant force on an object is equal to the weight of the fluid displaced by the object.
3. An object will float in a fluid that is more dense than itself. Density is equal to mass divided by volume.
4. Pressure applied to a liquid is transmitted evenly throughout the liquid. This is known as Pascal's principle. *How does Pascal's principle relate to this tube of toothpaste?*

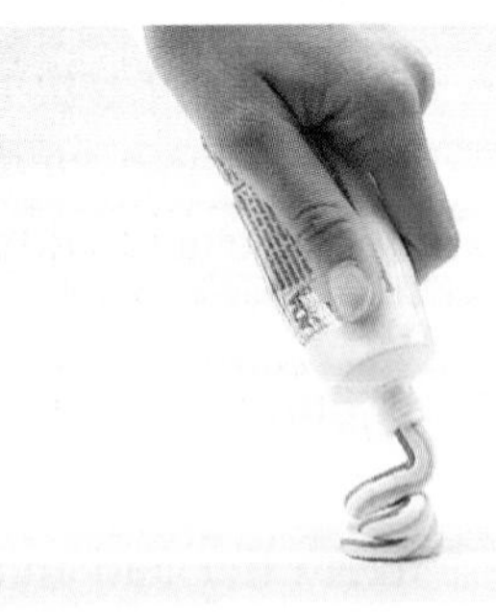

FOLDABLES Reading & Study Skills

After You Read

Use what you learned to write about what happens when heat is added to or lost from the three states of matter on your Organizational Study Fold.

Visualizing Main Ideas

Complete the following concept map on matter.

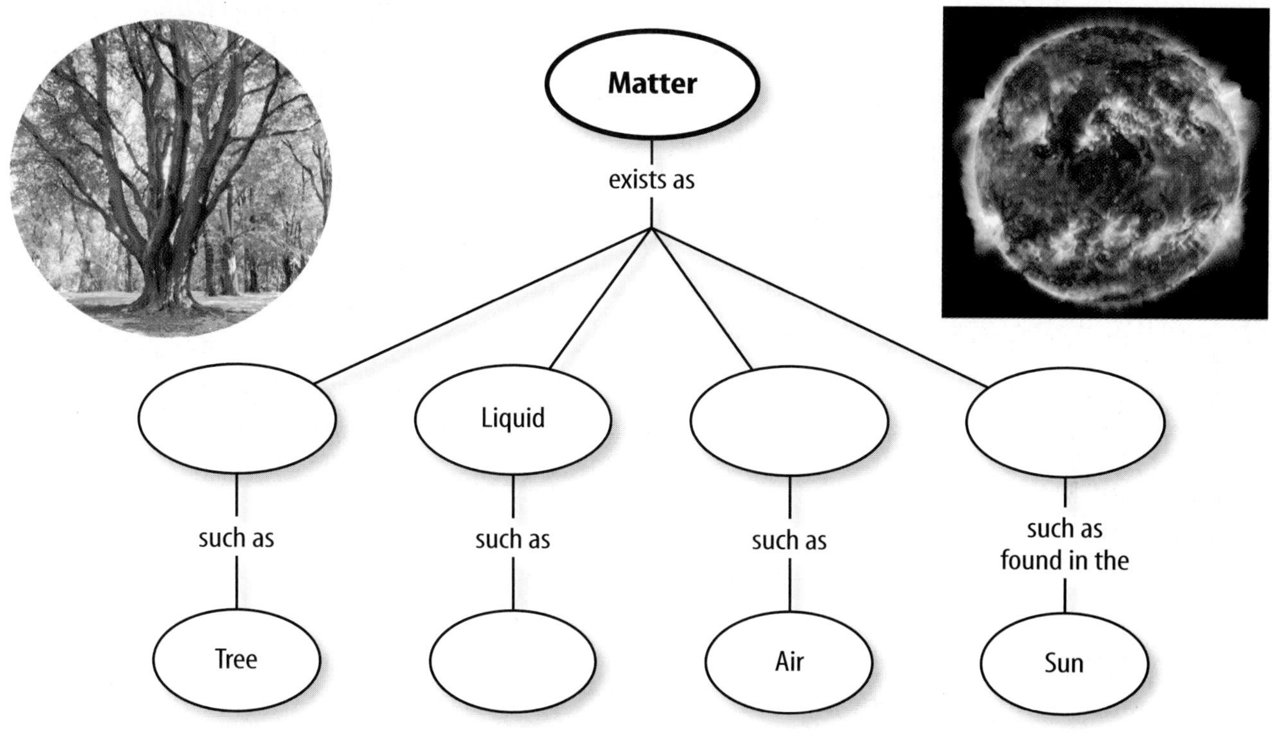

Vocabulary Review

Vocabulary Words

a. Archimedes' principle
b. buoyant force
c. condensation
d. density
e. freezing
f. gas
g. heat
h. liquid
i. matter
j. melting
k. Pascal's principle
l. pressure
m. solid
n. temperature
o. vaporization

Study Tip

Find a quiet place to study, whether at home or school. Turn off the television or radio, and give your full attention to your lessons.

Using Vocabulary

Replace the underlined words with the correct vocabulary words.

1. A <u>liquid</u> can change shape and volume.

2. A <u>solid</u> has a different shape but the same volume in any container.

3. <u>Matter</u> is thermal energy moving from one substance to another.

4. <u>Heat</u> is a measure of the average kinetic energy of the particles of a substance.

5. A substance changes from a gas to a liquid during the process of <u>melting</u>.

6. A liquid becomes a gas during <u>freezing</u>.

7. <u>Pressure</u> is mass divided by volume.

8. <u>Density</u> is force divided by area.

Chapter 4 Assessment

Checking Concepts

Choose the word or phrase that best answers the question.

1. Which description best describes a solid?
A) It has a definite shape and volume.
B) It has a definite shape but not a definite volume.
C) It adjusts to the shape of its container.
D) It can flow.

2. Which of these is a crystalline solid?
A) glass
B) sugar
C) rubber
D) plastic

3. What property enables you to float a needle on water?
A) viscosity
B) temperature
C) surface tension
D) crystal structure

4. What happens to an object as its kinetic energy increases?
A) It holds more tightly to nearby objects.
B) Its mass increases.
C) Its particles move more slowly.
D) Its particles move faster.

5. During which process do particles of matter release energy?
A) melting
B) freezing
C) sublimation
D) boiling

6. How does water vapor in air form clouds?
A) melting
B) evaporation
C) condensation
D) sublimation

7. Which is a unit of pressure?
A) N
B) kg
C) g/cm^3
D) N/m^2

8. What happens to the pressure exerted by a fluid when its speed is increased?
A) The pressure stays the same.
B) The pressure decreases.
C) The pressure increases.
D) The pressure changes direction.

9. In which case will an object float on a fluid?
A) Buoyant force is greater than weight.
B) Buoyant force is less than weight.
C) Buoyant force equals weight.
D) Buoyant force equals zero.

10. Which is equal to the buoyant force on an object?
A) volume of the object
B) weight of the displaced fluid
C) weight of object
D) volume of fluid

Thinking Critically

11. Why does steam cause more severe burns than boiling water?

12. How would this graph change if a greater volume of water were heated? How would it stay the same? Explain.

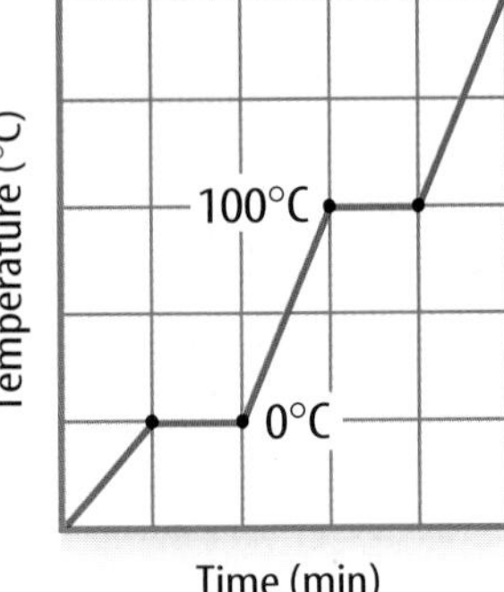

13. Why does the bathroom mirror become fogged while you are taking a shower?

14. The boiling point of a substance decreases as altitude increases. Based on this information, infer the relationship between boiling point and air pressure. Draw a graph.

15. A king's crown has a volume of 110 cm^3 and a mass of 1,800 g. The density of gold is 19.3 g/cm^3. Is the crown pure gold?

Developing Skills

16. Forming Operational Definitions Write operational definitions that explain the properties of and differences among solids, liquids, and gases.

17. **Concept Mapping** Prepare a sequence chart to show the events that occur as a solid changes into a liquid and then into a gas.

18. **Drawing Conclusions** A helium balloon will pop when it reaches a high enough elevation. Explain why this happens.

19. **Calculating** A hydraulic device has two pistons. How much force do you have to apply to the piston with an area of 10 cm^2 to lift an object weighing 2,000 N on a piston with an area of 50 cm^2?

20. **Making and Using Graphs** In January of 2000, Francisco "Pipin" Ferreras of Cuba dove to a depth of 150 m without any scuba equipment. Make a depth-pressure graph for the data below. Based on your graph, how does water pressure vary with depth? Note: The pressure at sea level, 101.3 kPa, is called one atmosphere (atm).

Water Pressure

Depth (m)	Pressure (atm)	Depth (m)	Pressure (atm)
0	1.0	100	11.0
25	3.5	125	13.5
50	6.0	150	16.0
75	8.5	175	18.5

Performance Assessment

21. **Storyboard** Create a visual-aid storyboard to show ice changing to steam. There should be a minimum of five frames.

TECHNOLOGY

Go to the Glencoe Science Web site at **science.glencoe.com** or use the **Glencoe Science CD-ROM** for additional chapter assessment.

Test Practice

Seth is studying the forces exerted on objects in water and has drawn the following illustration of his experiment.

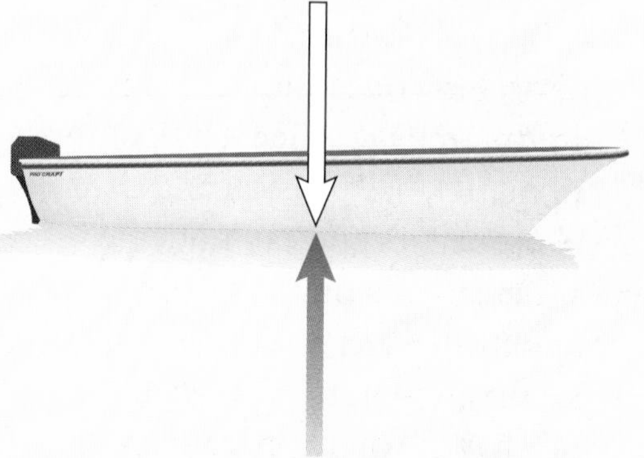

Study the diagram and answer the following questions:

1. The most likely reason the boat is floating rather than sinking is that ______.
   A) the boat's weight is pushing it down
   B) the boat's weight is greater than the buoyant force
   C) the buoyant force is greater than the boat's weight
   D) the boat's weight is equal to the buoyant force

2. Seth wanted to find out how shape affects buoyancy. To compare these two variables, he should ______.
   F) use boats of different sizes
   G) use different-shaped objects of the same weight
   H) use similarly shaped objects of different weights
   J) use objects with different textures

CHAPTER 5

Properties and Changes of Matter

This iceberg once was part of an Antarctic ice shelf. Ice, like all matter, has physical and chemical properties and can undergo changes. Density is a physical property. Ice floats in water because it is less dense than water. It underwent a physical change when it became an iceberg. In this chapter you'll learn about other physical properties and changes and chemical properties and changes.

What do you think?

Science Journal Look at the picture below with a classmate. Discuss what you think might be happening. Here's a hint: *This change makes a tasty snack.* Write your answer or best guess in your Science Journal.

Using your senses to observe characteristics of matter will help you classify, or categorize, it. Classifying different types of matter helps you understand what the types of matter are and can help you identify unknown types of matter. In this activity, you will observe and compare the characteristics of two items that you might be familiar with.

Compare characteristics 

1. Obtain a table-tennis ball and a golf ball from your teacher.
2. How are the two balls similar?
3. Which ball is heavier?
4. Compare the surfaces of the table-tennis ball and the golf ball. How are their surfaces different?
5. Place each ball in water and observe.

Observe

If you were to create a classification system to classify different kinds of balls, which characteristics might you use? Describe your classification system in your Science Journal.

Before You Read

Making a Classify Study Fold **Make the following Foldable to help you organize types of properties and changes into groups based on their common features.**

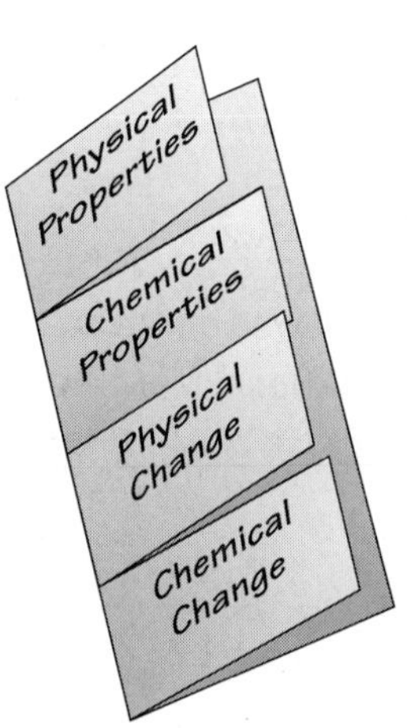

1. Place a sheet of paper in front of you so the short side is at the top. Fold the paper in half from the left side to the right side.
2. Now fold the paper in half from top to bottom. Then fold it in half again top to bottom. Unfold the last two folds.
3. Through the top thickness of paper, cut along each of the fold lines to form four tabs as shown.
4. Label the four sections *Physical Properties, Chemical Properties, Physical Change,* and *Chemical Change* as shown.
5. Before you read the chapter, list examples of each type of property and each type of change.
6. As you read the chapter, add to or correct what you have written under each tab.

SECTION

Physical Properties

As You Read

What You'll Learn

- **Describe** the common physical properties of matter.
- **Explain** how to find the density of a substance.
- **Compare and contrast** the properties of acids and bases.

Vocabulary

physical property
density
state of matter

Why It's Important

When you learn about physical properties, you can better describe the world around you.

Physical Properties

Have you ever been asked by a teacher to describe something that you saw on a field trip? How would you describe the elephant in the exhibit shown in **Figure 1?** What features can you use in your description—color, shape, size, and texture? These features are all properties, or characteristics, of the elephant. Scientists use the term *physical property* to describe a characteristic of matter that you can detect with your senses. A **physical property** is any characteristic of matter that can be observed without changing the identity of the material. All matter, such as the elephant, has physical properties.

Common Physical Properties You probably are familiar with some physical properties, such as color, shape, smell, and taste. You might not be as familiar with others, such as mass, volume, and density. Mass (m) is the amount of matter in an object. A golf ball has more mass than a table-tennis ball. Volume (V) is the amount of space that matter takes up. A swimming pool holds a larger volume of water than a paper cup does. **Density** (D) is the amount of mass in a given volume. A golf ball is more dense than a table-tennis ball. Density is determined by finding the mass of a sample of matter and dividing this mass by the volume of the sample.

$$\text{Density} = \text{mass/volume} \quad \text{or} \quad D = \frac{m}{V}$$

Figure 1
This large gray African elephant is displayed on the main floor of the National Museum of Natural History in Washington, D.C.

Density A table-tennis ball and a golf ball are about the same volume. When you decided which had a higher density, you compared their masses. Because they are about the same volume, the one with more mass had the higher density. Suppose you were asked if all the bowling balls in **Figure 2** were identical. They appear to be the same size, shape, and color, but do they all have the same mass? If you could pick up these bowling balls, you would discover that their masses differ. You also might notice that the heavier balls strike the pins harder. Although the volumes of the balls are nearly identical, the densities of the bowling balls are different because their masses are different.

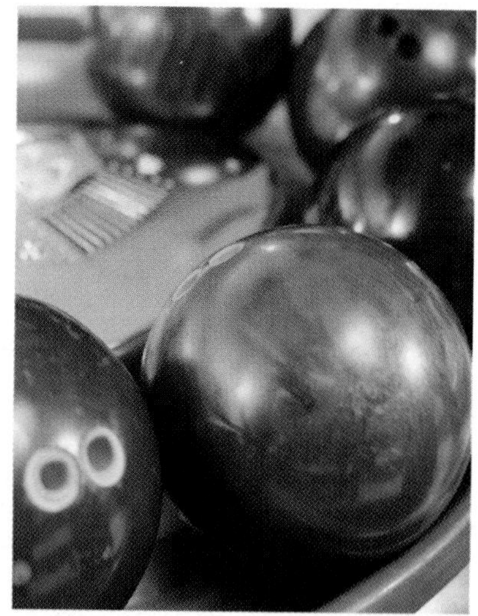

Figure 2
These bowling balls look the same but have different densities.

Identifying Unknown Substances In some cases, density also can be used to identify unknown compounds and elements. The element silver, for example, has a density of 10.5 g/cm^3 at 20°C. Suppose you want to know whether or not a ring is pure silver. You can find the ring's density by dividing the mass of the ring by its volume. If the density of the ring is determined to be 11.3 g/cm^3, then the ring is not pure silver.

Math Skills Activity

Determining the Density of a Material

Example Problem

An antique dealer decided to use density to help determine the material used to make a statue. The volume of the statue is 1,000 cm^3 and the mass is 8,470 g. What is its density?

Solution

1. *This is what you know:* density = mass/volume = m/V; $m = 8{,}470$ g, $V = 1{,}000$ cm^3
2. *This is what you need to find:* density needed: D
3. *This is the equation you need to use:* $D = m/V$
4. *Substitute the known values into the equation:* $D = m/V = 8{,}470 \text{ g}/1{,}000 \text{ cm}^3 = 8.470 \text{ g/cm}^3$

Check your answer by substituting it and the known values back into the original equation.

Practice Problem

If a candlestick has a mass of 8.5 g and a volume of 0.96 cm^3, what is its density?

For more help, refer to the Math Skill Handbook.

Figure 3
All three states of water are present here—solid, liquid, and gas—but you can only see the solid and liquid states. The water vapor in the air is not visible.

State of Matter State of matter is another physical property. The **state of matter** tells you whether a sample of matter is a solid, a liquid, or a gas. This property depends on the temperature and pressure of the matter. The ice in **Figure 3** is water in the solid state. Water in the liquid state can be seen in the ocean and in the clouds. Gaseous water cannot be seen but exists as vapor in the air. In each case, each molecule of water is the same—two hydrogen atoms and one oxygen atom. But water appears to be different because it exists in different states, as shown in **Figure 3.**

Size-Dependent and Size-Independent Properties Some physical properties change when the size of an object changes. These properties are called size-dependent properties. For example, a wooden block might have a volume of 30 cm^3 and a mass of 20 g. A larger block might have a volume of 60 cm^3 and a mass of 40 g. The volume and mass of the block change when the size of the block changes. However, the density of both blocks is 0.67 g/cm^3. Density does not change with a change in size. Density is an example of a size-independent property. Other examples of size-dependent and size-independent properties are shown in **Table 1.**

Mini LAB

Classifying Properties

Procedure

1. Obtain three different-sized **blocks** of the same type of wood.
2. Write all of your observations of each block in your **Science Journal** as you make your measurements.
3. Measure the length, width, height, and mass of each block. Calculate the volume and density of each block.

Analysis

1. Which properties were size-dependent?
2. Which properties were size-independent?

Table 1 Physical Properties

Type of Property	Property
Size-dependent properties	length, width, height, volume, mass
Size-independent properties	density, color, state

Physical Properties of Acids and Bases

One way to describe matter is to classify it as either an acid or a base. The strength of an acid or base can be determined by finding the pH of the sample. The pH scale has a range of below 0 to above 14. Acids have a pH below 7. Bases have a pH above 7. A sample with a pH of exactly 7 is neutral—neither acidic nor basic. Pure water is a substance with a pH of exactly 7.

Figure 4
When you sip a carbonated soft drink, you drink carbonic and phosphoric (faws FOR ihk) acids.

Properties of Acids What do you think of when you hear the word *acid?* Do you picture a dangerous chemical that can burn your skin, make holes in your clothes, and even destroy metal? Some acids, such as concentrated hydrochloric acid, are like that. But some acids are edible. One example is shown in **Figure 4.** Carbonated soft drinks contain acids. Every time you eat a citrus fruit such as an orange or a grapefruit, you eat citric and ascorbic (uh SOR bihk) acids. What properties do these and other acids have in common?

Imagine the sharp smell of a freshly sliced lemon. That scent comes from the citric acid in the fruit. Take a big bite out of the fruit shown in **Figure 5** and you would immediately notice a sour taste. If you then rubbed your molars back and forth, your teeth would squeak. All of these physical properties are common in acids.

Reading Check *What are two examples of foods that contain acids?*

Health INTEGRATION

Vitamin C and alpha-hydroxy acids are found in fruits and are the active ingredient in some anti-aging skin creams. It is believed that these ingredients slow down the aging process. Research safety issues regarding these products as well as how these ingredients work.

Figure 5
All citrus fruits contain citric and ascorbic acids, which is why these fruits taste sour.

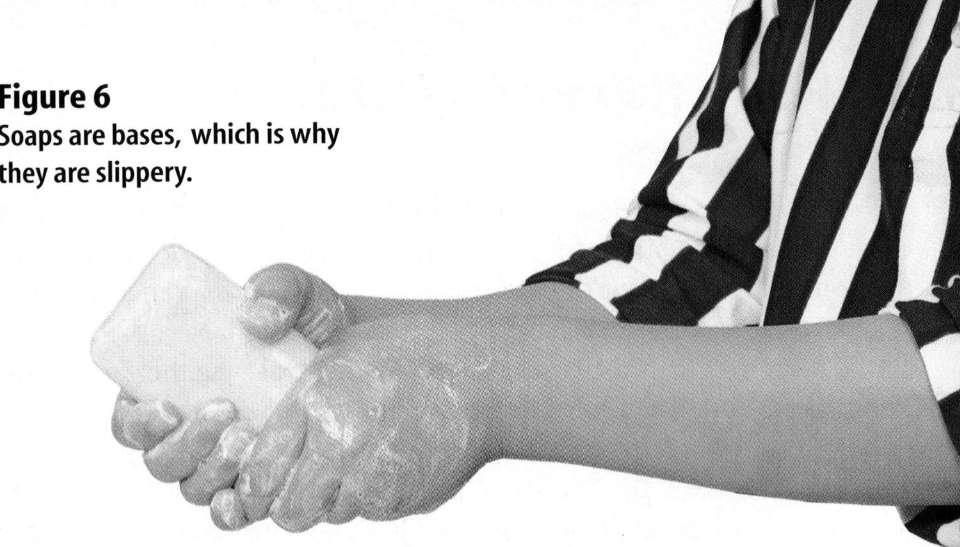

Figure 6
Soaps are bases, which is why they are slippery.

Research Visit the Glencoe Science Web site at **science.glencoe.com** for information about the common and industrial uses of acids and bases. Communicate to your class what you learn.

Physical Properties of Bases Bases have physical properties that are different from acids. A familiar example of a base is ammonia (uh MOH nyuh), often used for household cleaning. If you got a household cleaner that contained ammonia on your fingers and then rubbed your fingers together, they would feel slippery. Another familiar base is soap, shown in **Figure 6,** which also has a slippery feel. You shouldn't taste soap, but if you accidentally did, you'd notice a bitter taste. A bitter taste and a slippery feel are physical properties of bases.

Reading Check *What are two examples of products that contain bases?*

It is important to note that you should never taste, touch, or smell anything in a lab unless your teacher tells you to do so.

Section  Assessment

1. Define the term *physical property* and describe the physical properties of salt.
2. Define the term *density,* describe how it is determined, and explain why it is a size-independent property.
3. What are two physical properties of acids?
4. What are two physical properties of bases?
5. **Think Critically** How could you identify a pure metal if you have a balance, a graduated cylinder, and a table of densities for metals? (1 mL = 1 cm^3)

Skill Builder Activities

6. **Solving One-Step Equations** What is the density of a substance with a mass of 65.7 g and volume of 3.40 cm^3? **For more help, refer to the Math Skill Handbook.**
7. **Making and Using Tables** Make a table and list ten things in your home. On the table, include the following physical properties for each item: *color, state of matter, shape,* and *hardness.* **For more help, refer to the Science Skill Handbook.**

Chemical Properties

A Complete Description

You've observed that the density of a table-tennis ball is less than the density of a golf ball. You also have noticed the state of water in an ice cube and a lake. You've noticed the taste of acid in a lemon and the slippery feel of a base such as ammonia. However, a description of something using only physical properties is not complete. What type of property describes how matter behaves?

Common Chemical Properties If you strike a match on a hard, rough surface, the match probably will start to burn. Phosphorus (FAWS for us) compounds on the match head and the wood in the match combine with oxygen to form new materials. Why does that happen? The phosphorus compounds and the wood have the ability to burn. The ability to burn is a chemical property. A **chemical property** is a characteristic of matter that allows it to change to a different type of matter.

Reading Check *What is a chemical property?*

You see an example of a chemical property when you leave a half-eaten apple on your desk, and the exposed part turns brown. The property you observe is the ability to react with oxygen. Two other chemical properties are shown in **Figure 7.**

As You Read

What You'll Learn

- **Describe** chemical properties of matter.
- **Explain** the chemical properties of acids and bases.
- **Explain** how a salt is formed.

Vocabulary

chemical property
reactivity
salts

Why It's Important

Chemical properties can help you predict how matter will change.

Figure 7
The chemical properties of a material often require a warning about its careful use.

A Gasoline is flammable. Gas pumps warn customers not to get near them with anything that might start the gasoline burning.

B Toxicity (tahk SIH suh tee) indicates how poisonous something is. Workers who use toxic chemicals have to wear protective clothing.

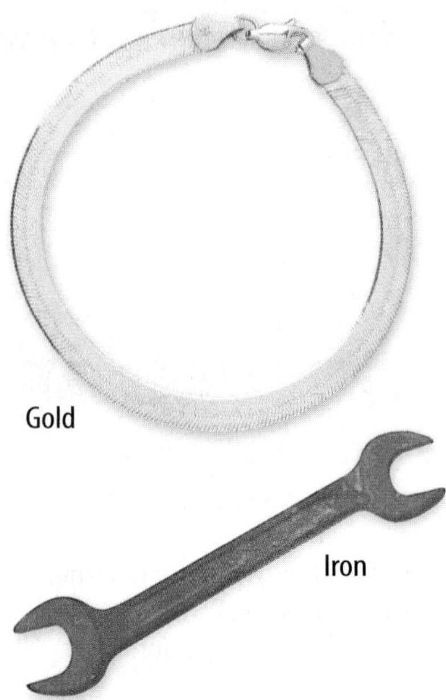

Figure 8
Gold and iron have different chemical properties that make them suitable for different uses.

Choosing Materials Look at **Figure 8.** Would you rather wear a bracelet made of gold or one made of iron? Why? Iron is less attractive and less valuable than gold. It also has an important chemical property that makes it unsuitable for jewelry. Think about what happens to iron when it is left out in moist air. Iron rusts easily because of its high reactivity (ree ak TIH vuh tee) with oxygen and moisture in the air. **Reactivity** is how easily one thing reacts with something else. The low reactivity of silver and gold, in addition to their desirable physical properties, makes those metals good choices for jewelry.

Reading Check *What is reactivity?*

Chemical Properties and Pools The "chlorine" added to swimming pools is actually a compound called hypochlorous acid, which forms when chlorine reacts with water. This acid kills bacteria, insects, algae, and plants. The person in **Figure 9** is testing the pool water to see whether it has the correct amount of chlorine.

Any time you have standing water, mosquitoes and other insects can lay eggs in it. Various plants and algae can turn a sparkling blue pool into a slimy green mess. Bacteria are another problem. When you go swimming, you bring along millions of uninvited guests—the normal bacteria that live on your skin. The chlorine compounds kill the bacteria—as well as insects, algae, and plants that might be in the pool.

Hypochlorous acid can cause problems as well. It combines with nitrogen in the pool to form chloramines. Have your eyes ever burned after swimming in a pool? Chloramines can irritate the skin and eyes of swimmers.

Figure 9
Pool water must be tested to keep the water safe for swimmers.

Chemical Properties of Acids and Bases You have learned that acids and bases have physical properties that make acids taste sour and bases taste bitter and feel slippery. The chemical properties of acids and bases are what make them both useful but sometimes harmful. Several acids and bases are shown in **Table 2.**

Acids Many acids react with, or corrode, certain metals. Have you ever used aluminum foil to cover leftover spaghetti or tomato sauce? **Figure 10** shows what you might see the next day. You might see small holes in the foil where it has come into contact with the tomatoes in the sauce. The acids in tomato sauce, oranges, carbonated soft drinks, and other foods are edible. However, many acids can damage plant and animal tissue. Small amounts of nitric (NITE rihk) acid and sulfuric (sulf YER ihk) acid are found in rain. This rain, called acid rain, harms plant and animal life in areas where acid rain falls. Sulfuric acid that has no water mixed with it is useful in many industries because it removes water from certain materials. However, that same property causes burns on skin that touches sulfuric acid.

Figure 10
Aluminum reacts easily with acids, which is why acidic food, such as tomatoes, should not be cooked or stored in aluminum.

Table 2 Common Acids and Bases

Name of Acid	Formula	Where Found
Acetic acid	$HC_2H_3O_2$	Vinegar
Acetylsalicylic acid	$HC_9H_7O_4$	Aspirin
Ascorbic acid (vitamin C)	$H_2C_6H_6O_6$	Citrus fruits, tomatoes
Carbonic acid	H_2CO_3	Carbonated drinks
Hydrochloric acid	HCl	Gastric juice in stomach
Name of Base		
Aluminum hydroxide	$Al(OH)_3$	Deodorant, antacid
Calcium hydroxide	$Ca(OH)_2$	Leather tanning, manufacture of mortar and plaster
Magnesium hydroxide	$Mg(OH)_2$	Laxative, antacid
Sodium hydroxide	$NaOH$	Drain cleaner, soap making
Ammonia	NH_3	Household cleaners, fertilizer, production of rayon and nylon

Figure 11
These everyday items contain salts.

Bases A strong base is as dangerous as a strong acid. A base, such as sodium hydroxide (hi DRAHK side) can damage living tissue. It is not uncommon for someone who smells strong ammonia to get a bloody nose or to get a burn if a strong base is touched. Ammonia feels slippery to the touch because the base reacts with the proteins in the tissues on your fingertips, which results in damaged tissue.

Salts What happens in reactions between acids and bases? Acids and bases often are studied together because they react with each other to form water and other useful compounds called salts. **Salts** are compounds made of a metal and nonmetal that are formed when acids and bases react. Look at **Figure 11.** That white solid in your salt shaker—table salt—is the most common salt. Table salt, sodium chloride, can be formed by the reaction between the base sodium hydroxide and hydrochloric acid. Other useful salts are calcium carbonate, which is chalk, and ammonium chloride, which is used in some types of batteries.

Section 2 Assessment

1. Define the term *chemical property* and give an example of a chemical property of a substance.
2. Describe at least two chemical properties of an acid.
3. Describe at least two chemical properties of a base.
4. Describe what is formed when an acid and a base react.
5. **Think Critically** Think about safety precautions you take around your home. Which ones are based upon physical properties and which ones are based upon chemical properties? Explain.

Skill Builder Activities

6. **Classifying** Classify each of the following properties as being physical or chemical. **For more help, refer to the Science Skill Handbook.**
   - **a.** Iron will rust when left out in the air.
   - **b.** Lye feels slippery.
   - **c.** Iodine is poisonous.
   - **d.** Solid sulfur shatters when struck.
   - **e.** Gasoline burns.
7. **Communicating** In your Science Journal, write a poem describing the physical and chemical properties of an acid or a base. **For more help, refer to the Science Skill Handbook.**

SECTION 3

Physical and Chemical Changes

As You Read

***What* You'll Learn**

- **Identify** physical and chemical changes.
- **Exemplify** how physical and chemical changes affect the world you live in.

Vocabulary

physical change
chemical change

***Why* It's Important**

Many of the changes around you are chemical changes.

Physical Change

The crowd gathers at a safe distance and the cameras from the news media are rolling. A sense of excitement, fear, and anticipation fills the air. The demolition experts are making their final inspections. Then, in just a few seconds, the old stadium becomes a pile of rubble. The appearance of the stadium changed.

What is physical change? Most matter can undergo physical change. A **physical change** is any change in size, shape, form, or state where the identity of the matter stays the same. Only the physical properties change. The stadium in **Figure 12** underwent a physical change from its original form to a pile of steel and concrete. The materials are the same; they just look different.

Reading Check *What is a physical change?*

Figure 12
This stadium underwent a physical change—its form changed.

Examples of Physical Changes How can you recognize a physical change? Just look to see whether or not the matter has changed size, shape, form, or state. If you cut a watermelon into chunks, the watermelon has changed size and shape. That's a physical change. If you pop one of those chunks into your mouth and bite it, you have changed the watermelon's size and shape again.

Change of State Matter can undergo a physical change in another way, too. It can change from one state to another. Suppose it's a hot day. You and your friends decide to make snow cones. A snow cone is a mixture of water, sugar, food coloring, and flavoring. The water in the snow cone is solid, but in the hot sunshine, it begins to warm. When the temperature of the water reaches its melting point, the solid water begins to melt. The chemical composition of the water—two hydrogens and one oxygen—does not change. However, its form changes. This is an example of a physical change. The solid water becomes a liquid and drips onto the sidewalk. As the drops of liquid sit in the sunshine, the water changes state again, evaporating to become a gas. Water also can change from a solid to liquid by boiling. Other examples of change of state are shown in **Figure 13.**

Figure 13
The four most common changes of state are shown here.

A A solid will melt, becoming a liquid.

B As it cools, this liquid metal will become solid steel.

C Water vapor in the air changes to liquid water when dew forms.

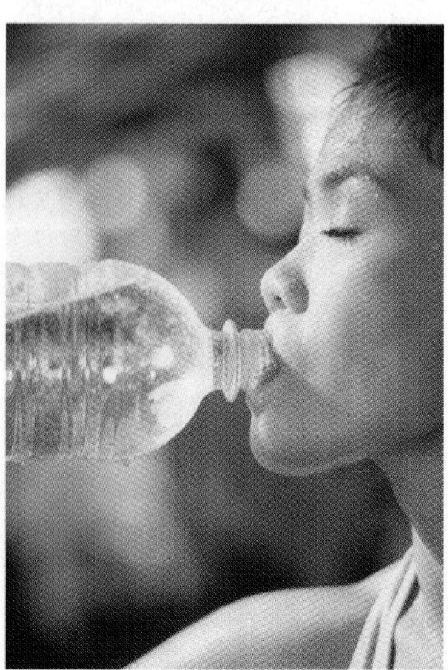

D Liquid water in perspiration changes to a gas when it evaporates from your skin.

Figure 14
Chemical changes occur all around you.

A **This unprotected car fender was exposed to salt and water which caused it to rust.**

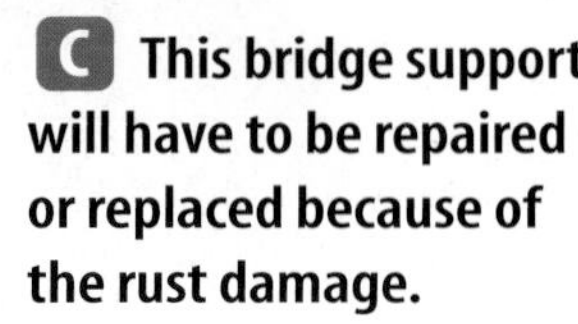

C **This bridge support will have to be repaired or replaced because of the rust damage.**

B **Apples and pennies darken due to chemical changes.**

Chemical Changes

Unprotected cars driven on salted roads and steel structures like the one shown in **Figure 14** can begin to rust after only a few winters. A shiny copper penny becomes dull and dark. An apple left out too long begins to turn brown. What do all these changes have in common? Each of these changes is a chemical change. A **chemical change** occurs when one type of matter changes into a different type of matter with different properties.

Reading Check *What happens during a chemical change?*

Examples of Chemical Change Chemical changes are going on around you—and inside you—every day. Plants use photosynthesis to produce food—the product of chemical changes. When you eat fruits and vegetables produced by photosynthesis, these products must be chemically changed again so that the cells in your body can use them as food. There are many chemical changes occurring outside of your body, too. Silver tarnishing, copper forming a green coating, iron rusting, and petroleum products combusting are all examples of chemical changes that are occurring around you. Although these reactions may be occurring at different rates and producing different products, they are still examples of chemical changes.

Comparing Chemical Changes

Procedure

1. Separate a piece of **fine steel wool** into two halves.
2. Dip one half in **tap water** and the other half in the same amount of **salt water.**
3. Place both pieces of steel wool on a **paper plate** and label them. Observe every day for five days.

Analysis

1. What happened to the steel wool that was dipped in the salt water?
2. What might be a common problem with machinery that is operated near an ocean?

Figure 15
Chemical changes are common when food, such as cake, is cooked.

New Materials Are Formed Ice melts, paper is cut, metal is hammered into sheets, and clay is molded into a vase. Seeing signs of these physical changes is easy—something changes shape, size, form, or state.

The only sure way to know whether a chemical change has occurred is if a new type of matter is formed that is chemically different from the starting matter. A chemical change cannot be reversed easily. For example, when wood burns, you see it change to ash and gases that have properties that are different from the wood and oxygen that burned. You can't put the ash and gases back together to make wood. When the cake shown in **Figure 15** is baked, changes occur that make the cake batter become solid. The chemical change that occurs when baking powder mixes with water results in bubbles that make the cake rise. Raw egg in the batter undergoes changes that make the egg solid. These changes cannot be reversed.

Research Visit the Glencoe Science Web site at **science.glencoe.com** for information about the chemical changes that make glowsticks glow when bent.

How can you be sure that a chemical change has occurred?

Signs of Chemical Change In these examples, you know that a chemical change occurred because you can see that a new substance forms. It's not always easy to tell when new substances are formed. What are other signs of chemical change?

One sign of a chemical change is the release or absorption of energy in the form of light, heat, or sound. Release of energy is obvious when something burns—light and heat are given off. Sometimes an energy change is so small or slow that it is difficult to notice, like when something rusts. Another sign that indicates a chemical change is the formation of a gas or a solid that is not the result of a change of state.

Chemical and Physical Changes in Nature

Often, a color change is evidence of a chemical change, an example of which is shown in **Figure 16.** Leaves can contain yellow pigments that are masked, or hidden, by green chlorophyll. In the fall, chlorophyll stops being produced. A chemical change causes the remaining chlorophyll to break down, revealing these yellow pigments. Different chemical changes produce red pigments.

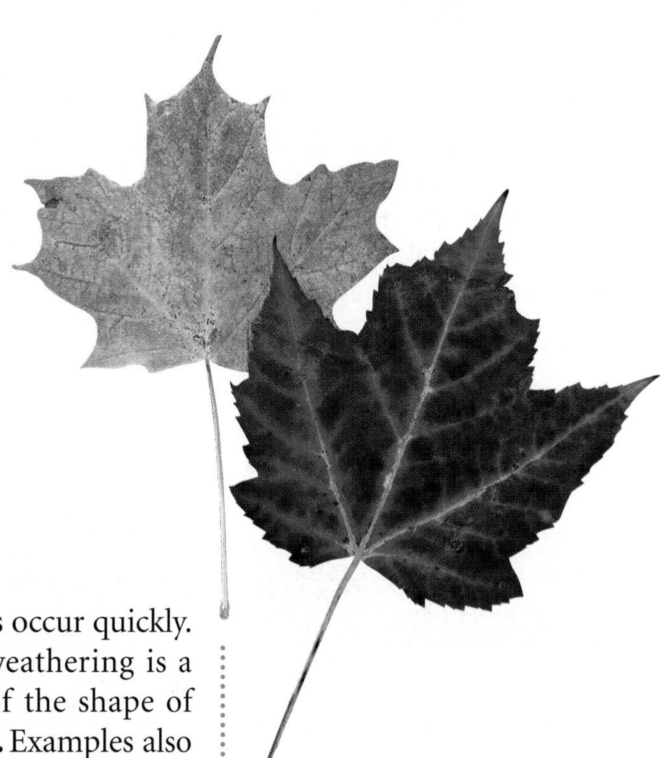

Figure 16
Chemical changes that occur in the fall bring about the color changes in these leaves.

Physical Weathering Some physical changes occur quickly. Others take place over a long time. Physical weathering is a physical change that is responsible for much of the shape of Earth's surface. Examples are shown in **Figure 17.** Examples also can be found in your own school yard. All of the soil that you see comes from physical weathering. Wind and water erode rocks, breaking them into small bits. Water fills cracks in rocks. When it freezes and thaws several times, the rock splits into smaller pieces. No matter how small the pieces of rock are, they are made up of the same things that made up the bigger pieces of rock. The rock simply has undergone a physical change. Gravity, plants, animals, and the movement of land during earthquakes also help cause physical changes on Earth.

Figure 17
You can see dramatic examples of physical weathering caused by water and wind on rocky coastlines.

Figure 18
Over many years, acidic rainwater slowly reacts with layers of limestone rock. It forms caves and collects minerals that it later deposits as cave formations.

Environmental Science
INTEGRATION

Carlsbad Caverns in New Mexico contain cave formations similar to the ones shown here. Stalagmites are cave formations that form on the floor of the cave and grow upward. Inside Carlsbad Caverns you will find a stalagmite called the Giant Dome that is 19 m tall. Research and find out more information about this huge cave.

Chemical Weathering Cave formations like the one in **Figure 18** form by chemical weathering. As drops of water drip through the rocks above this cavern room, minerals become dissolved in the water. These icicle shapes, or stalactites, are formed when the water evaporates leaving the mineral deposits. There are instances of unnatural chemical weathering. For instance, the acid in acid rain can chemically weather marble buildings and statues, and other outdoor objects.

Section  Assessment

1. List five physical changes you can observe in your home. Explain how you decided that each change is physical.
2. When carbon burns, what kind of change occurs? Explain.
3. Describe how physical changes can alter Earth's surface.
4. What are signs that a chemical change has occurred?
5. **Think Critically** Which of the following involves a chemical change: *combining an acid and base, dew forming,* and *souring milk.*

Skill Builder Activities

6. **Drawing Conclusions** When you mixed two substances together, you observed that heat, gas, and light were produced. Is this change likely chemical or physical? Explain. **For more help, refer to the Science Skill Handbook.**
7. **Developing Multimedia Presentations** Prepare a multimedia presentation that shows the steps in mixing, baking, and cutting a cake. Identify each step as a physical or a chemical change. **For more help, refer to the Technology Skill Handbook.**

Activity

Sunset in a Bag

How do you know when a chemical change occurs? You'll see some signs of chemical change in this activity.

What You'll Investigate

What is evidence of a chemical change?

Goals

- **Observe** a chemical change.
- **Identify** some signs of chemical change.

Materials

baking soda
calcium chloride
phenol red solution
warm water
teaspoons (2)
resealable plastic bag
graduated cylinder

Safety Precautions

Procedure

1. Add 20 mL of warm water to the plastic bag. Add a teaspoon of calcium chloride to the water, seal the bag, and slosh the contents to mix the solution. Record your observations.
2. Add 5 mL of phenol red solution to the bag. Seal the bag, slosh the contents, and record your observations.
3. Open the bag and quickly add a teaspoon of baking soda. Seal the bag and slosh the contents to mix the ingredients together. Observe what happens.

Conclude and Apply

1. In which steps did a physical change occur? In which steps did a chemical change occur? How do you know?
2. Does a change in energy always indicate a chemical change? Why or why not?

Communicating Your Data

Compare your conclusions with those of other students in your class. **For more help, refer to the** Science Skill Handbook.

Activity **Design Your Own Experiment**

Homemade pH Scale

The stronger an acid or base is, the more likely it is to be harmful to living organisms. A pH scale is used to measure how strong acids and bases are. A solution with a pH below 7 is acidic, a pH of 7 is neutral, and a pH above 7 is basic. In this activity, you will measure the pH of some things using treated paper. When it is dipped into a solution, this paper changes color. Check the color against the chart below to find the pH of the solution.

Recognize the Problem

How acidic or basic are some common household items?

Form a Hypothesis

Think about the properties of acids and bases. In your group, make a hypothesis about which kinds of solutions you are testing are acids and which kinds are bases.

Goals

- **Design** an experiment that allows you to test solutions to find the pH of each.
- **Classify** a solution as an acid or a base according to its pH.

Possible Materials

vial of pH paper, 1–14
pH color chart
distilled water
fruit juices
vinegar
salt
sugar
soft drinks
household cleaners
soaps and detergents
antacids

Safety Precautions

Never eat, taste, smell, or touch any chemical during a lab.

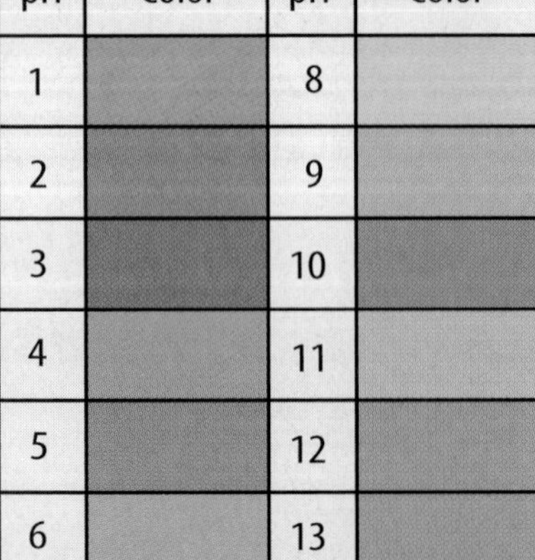

pH	Color	pH	Color
1		8	
2		9	
3		10	
4		11	
5		12	
6		13	
7		14	

pH of Solutions

Solution to Be Tested	pH	Acid, Base, or Neutral

Test Your Hypothesis

Plan

1. As a group, decide which materials you will test. If a material is not a liquid, dissolve it in water so you can test the solution.
2. List the steps and materials that you need to test your hypothesis. Be specific. What parts of the experiment will you repeat, if any?
3. Before you begin, copy a data table like the one shown into your Science Journal. Be sure to leave room to record results for each solution tested. If there is to be more than one trial for each solution, include room for the additional trials.
4. Reread the entire experiment to make sure that all the steps are in logical order.

Do

1. Make sure your teacher approves your plan and data table. Be sure that you have included any suggested changes.
2. Carry out the experiment as planned and approved. Wash your hands when you are done.
3. **Record** the pH value of each solution in the data table as you complete each test. Determine whether each solution is acidic, basic, or neutral.

Analyze Your Data

1. Were any materials neither acids nor bases? How do you know?
2. Using your data table, conclude which types of materials are usually acidic and which are usually basic.
3. At what pH do you think acids become too dangerous to touch? Bases? Explain your answers.
4. What is the pH range of the foods that you tested?

Draw Conclusions

Perhaps you have been told that you can use vinegar to dissolve hard-water deposits because vinegar is an acid. If you run out of vinegar, which of the items you tested could you most likely use instead of vinegar for this purpose?

Compare your findings with those of other student groups. Discuss why any differences in the data might have occurred.

SCIENCE CAN CHANGE THE COURSE OF HISTORY!

Acid rain is eroding some of the world's most famous monuments

CRUMBLING

The Taj Mahal in India, the Acropolis in Greece, and the Colosseum in Italy, have stood for centuries. They've survived wars, souvenir-hunters, and natural weathering from wind and rain. But now, something far worse threatens their existence—acid rain. Over the last few decades, this form of pollution has eaten away at some of history's greatest monuments.

Acid rain leads to health and environmental risks. It also harms human-made structures. Most of these structures are made of sandstone, limestone, and marble. Acid rain causes the calcium in these stones to form calcium sulfate, or gypsum. Gypsum's powdery little blotches are sometimes called "marble cancer." When it rains, the gypsum washes away, along with some of the surface of the monument. In many cases, acidic soot falls into the cracks of monuments. When rainwater seeps into the cracks, acidic water is formed, which further damages the structure.

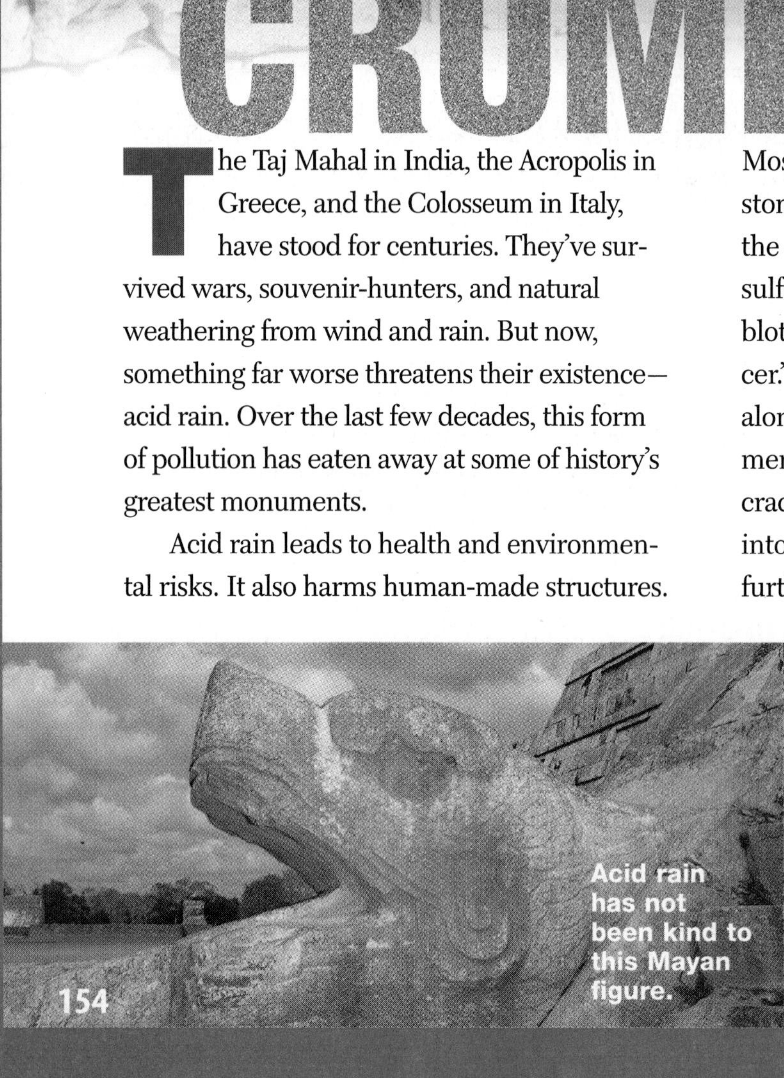

Acid rain has not been kind to this Mayan figure.

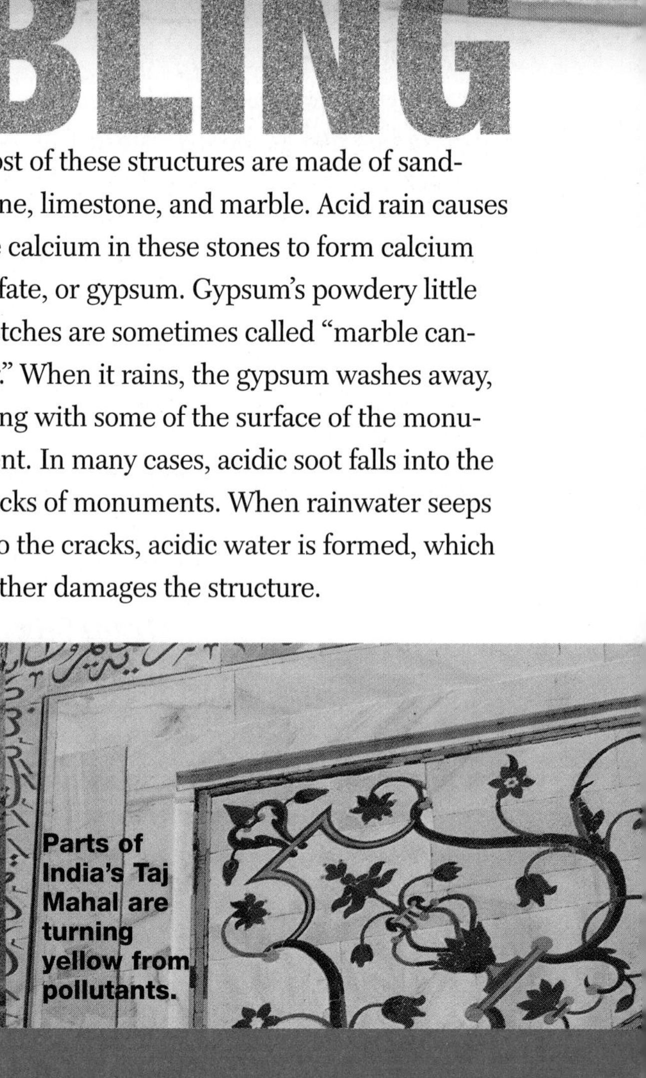

Parts of India's Taj Mahal are turning yellow from pollutants.

Greece's Parthenon is slowly being eaten away by acid rain.

MONUMENTS

In Agra, India, the smooth, white marble mausoleum called the Taj Mahal has stood since the seventeenth century. But acid rain is making the surface of the building yellow and flaky. The pollution is caused by hundreds of factories surrounding Agra that emit damaging chemicals.

What moisture, molds, and the roots of vegetation didn't do in 1,500 years, acid rain is doing in decades. It is destroying the Mayan ruins of Mexico. Acid rain is causing statues to crumble and paintings on walls to flake off.

Acid rain is affecting national monuments and treasures in just about every urban location in the world. These include the Capitol building in Washington, D.C., churches in Germany, and stained-glass windows in Sweden. Because of pollution, many corroding statues displayed outdoors have been brought inside museums. In London, acid rain has forced workers to repair and replace so much of Westminster Abbey that the structure is becoming a mere copy of the original.

Throughout the world, acid rain has weathered many structures more in the last 20 years than in the prior 2,000 years. This is one reason some steps have been taken in Europe and the United States to reduce emissions from the burning of fossil fuels. If these laws don't work, many irreplaceable art treasures could be gone forever.

CONNECTIONS Identify Which monuments and buildings represent the United States? Brainstorm a list with your class. Then choose a monument, and using your school's media center or the Glencoe Science Web site, learn more about it. Is acid rain affecting it in any way?

SCIENCE *Online*

For more information, visit science.glencoe.com

Chapter 5 Study Guide

Reviewing Main Ideas

Section 1 Physical Properties

1. A physical property can be observed without changing the makeup of the material. *What are some physical properties of the pinecone shown here?*

2. Acids and bases have physical properties. Acids have a sharp smell and a sour taste. Bases have a bitter taste and feel slippery.
3. Mass, volume, state of matter, and density are examples of physical properties.

Section 2 Chemical Properties

1. A chemical property is a characteristic of matter that allows it to change to a different type of matter.
2. Acids and bases are in many household products. *In the figure below, which substances are acidic and which are basic?*

3. Acids and bases react with each other to produce water and a salt.

Section 3 Physical and Chemical Changes

1. A physical change is a change in the size, shape, form, or state of matter. The chemical makeup of the matter stays the same.
2. Water undergoes a change of state when it changes from a solid to a liquid or a liquid to a gas. The reverse processes are also physical changes.
3. In chemical changes, new matter is changed to a different type of matter.
4. Evidence that a chemical change might have occurred includes a color or energy change or the formation of a gas or solid. *In the figure below, what evidence indicates that a chemical change might have occurred?*

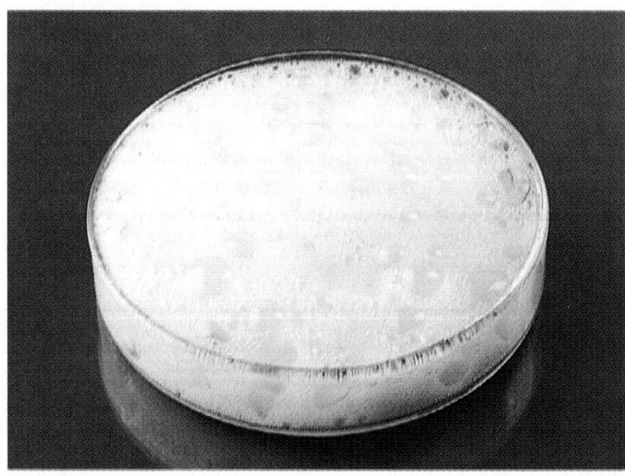

After You Read

FOLDABLES Reading & Study Skills

Under the tabs of your Classify Study Fold, write the definition of both types of properties and both types of changes.

Visualizing Main Ideas

Complete the following concept map about matter.

Matter
has
undergoes
Changes
which can be either
which can be either
Physical
such as
such as
Reactivity
State of Matter
which is identified by a
such as a change in
Shape
Energy change

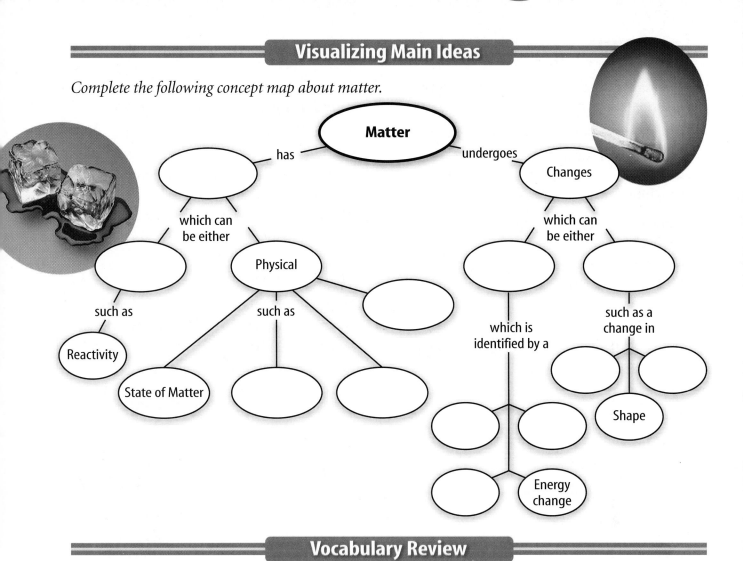

Vocabulary Review

Vocabulary Words

a. chemical change
b. chemical property
c. density
d. physical change
e. physical property
f. reactivity
g. salt
h. state of matter

Study Tip

After you've read a chapter, go back to the beginning and speed-read through what you've just read.

Using Vocabulary

Answer the following questions using complete sentences.

1. Mass divided by volume is the formula for which physical property?
2. Which type of properties include color, shape, size, and state?
3. Snow melting in sunshine is an example of which type of change?
4. Acid rain damaging marble statues is an example of which type of change?
5. Iron rusts in moist air. Which chemical property is this?

Chapter 5 Assessment

Checking Concepts

Choose the word or phrase that best answers the question.

1. Which of the following is a chemical property of a substance?
   A) density, 1.00 g/cm^3 **C)** mass, 5.00 g
   B) white powder **D)** reacts with HCl

2. Which item below is a sign of a chemical change?
   A) change of water vapor to liquid
   B) release of energy
   C) change from a liquid to a solid
   D) change in shape

3. Which type of change listed below results in new compounds being formed?
   A) chemical **C)** seasonal
   B) physical **D)** state

4. Which answer below is another term for solid, liquid, and gas?
   A) physical changes
   B) physical properties of soil
   C) chemical changes
   D) states of matter

5. Salts are formed when which of the following react?
   A) solids and gases **C)** bases and gases
   B) acids and bases **D)** acids and solids

6. Which term below would best describe the change that occurs when a window is broken?
   A) chemical **C)** neutral
   B) weathering **D)** physical

7. Which of the following physical properties does a base have?
   A) cold to touch
   B) gives off gas
   C) slippery and bitter taste
   D) sharp smell and sour taste

8. Which of the following changes when water evaporates?
   A) the physical properties of the water
   B) the chemical properties of the water
   C) the color of the water
   D) the mass of the water

9. Which of the following clearly identifies a chemical change?
   A) cutting the substance into smaller pieces
   B) freezing the substance
   C) boiling the substance
   D) A new substance is formed.

10. Which of the following is NOT a sign that a chemical change occurred when two clear liquids were mixed?
    A) A color change occurred.
    B) Gas was released.
    C) A white solid settled to the bottom.
    D) The volume doubled.

Thinking Critically

11. Think about what you know about density. Could a bag of feathers have more mass than the same size bag of rocks? Explain.

12. Sugar dissolves in water. Is this a physical property or a chemical property of sugar?

13. When butane burns, it combines with oxygen in the air to form carbon dioxide and water. Which two elements must be present in butane?

14. Identify each of the following as either a physical property or a chemical property.
    a. Sulfur shatters when hit.
    b. Copper statues turn green.
    c. Baking soda is a white powder.
    d. Newspaper turns brown when it is exposed to air and light.

15. Identify each of the following as a physical change or a chemical change.
   a. Metal is drawn out into a wire.
   b. Sulfur in eggs tarnishes silver.
   c. Baking powder bubbles when water is added to it.

Developing Skills

16. **Interpreting Scientific Illustrations** Review the pictures below and determine whether each is a chemical change or a physical change.

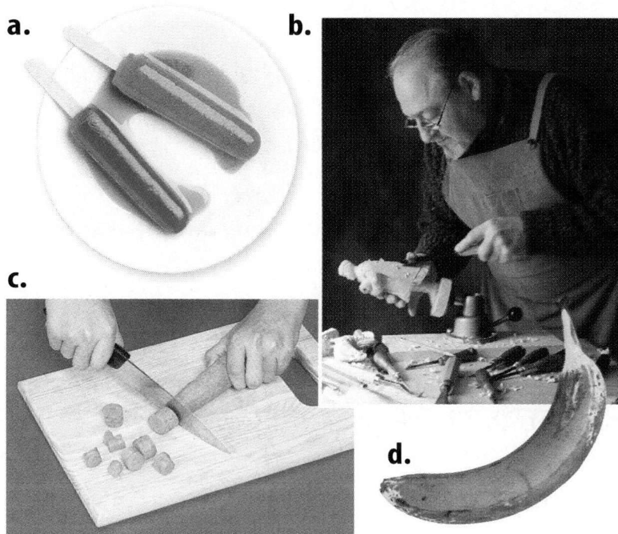

Performance Assessment

17. **Display** Create a display that demonstrates the characteristics of a chemical change. Be sure your display shows release of energy, change of color, and the formation of a solid.

Technology

Go to the Glencoe Science Web site at **science.glencoe.com** or use the **Glencoe Science CD-ROM** for additional chapter assessment.

Test Practice

Russell used a triple-beam balance to determine that the mass of an aluminum cube was 337 g. Then he placed the cube in a beaker of water. His experiment is shown in the diagram below.

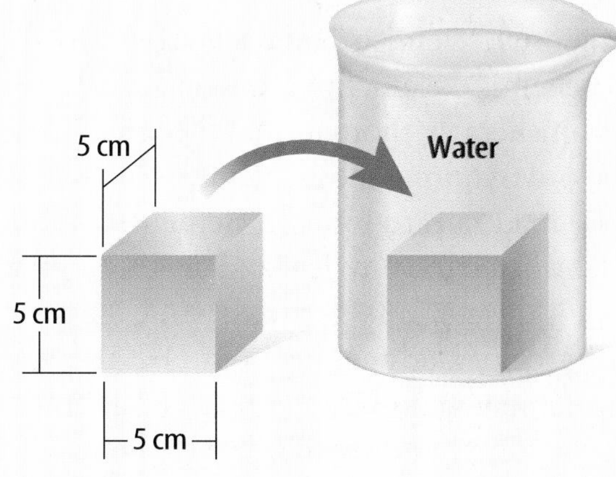

Mass = 337 g
Volume = 125 cm^3

Study the diagram and answer the following questions.

1. Using the information contained in the diagram, what is the density of the cube?
   A) 2.70 g/cm^3
   B) 0.371 g/cm^3
   C) 337 g/cm^3
   D) 125 g/cm^3

2. Cutting the cube into smaller pieces is an example of a _____.
   F) chemical property
   G) physical property
   H) chemical change
   J) physical change

3. According to the diagram, the aluminum cube _____.
   A) is more dense than water
   B) is less dense than water
   C) has more volume than the water
   D) floats in water

Standardized Test Practice

Reading Comprehension

Read the passage. Then read each question that follows the passage. Decide which is the best answer to each question.

Grouping the Elements Using their Properties

By 1860, scientists had discovered a total of 63 chemical elements. Dmitri Mendeleev, a Russian chemist, thought that there had to be some order among the elements.

He made a card for each element. On the card, he listed the physical and chemical properties of the element, such as atomic mass, density, color, and melting point. He also wrote each element's combining power, or its ability to form compounds with other elements.

When he arranged the cards in order of increasing atomic mass, Mendeleev noticed that the elements followed a periodic, or repeating, pattern. After every seven cards, the properties repeated. He placed each group of seven cards in rows, one row under another. He noticed that the columns in his chart formed groups of elements that had similar chemical and physical properties.

In a few places, Mendeleev had to move a card one space to the left or right to maintain the similarities of his groups. This left a few empty spaces. He predicted that they would be filled with elements that were unknown. He even predicted their properties. Fifteen years later, three new elements were discovered and placed in the empty spaces of the periodic table. Their physical and chemical properties agreed with Mendeleev's predictions.

Today there are more than 100 known elements. An extra column has been added for the noble gases, a group of elements that were not yet discovered in Mendeleev's time. Members of this group almost never combine with other elements. As new elements are discovered or are made <u>artificially</u>, scientists can place them in their proper place on the periodic table thanks to Mendeleev.

Test-Taking Tip To answer questions about a sequence of events, make a time line of what happened in each paragraph of the passage.

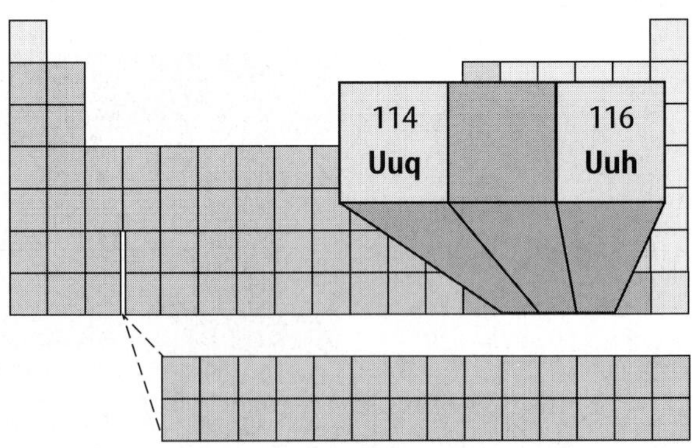

Even the modern periodic table has empty spaces for elements that have not been discovered yet.

1. Which of the following occurred FIRST in the passage?

A) Three new elements were discovered 15 years after Mendeleev developed the periodic table.

B) The noble gases were discovered and added to the periodic table.

C) Mendeleev predicted properties of unknown elements.

D) New elements were made in the laboratory and added to the periodic table.

2. The word <u>artificially</u> in this passage means _____.

F) unnaturally

G) artistically

H) atomically

J) radioactively

Standardized Test Practice

Reasoning and Skills

Read each question and choose the best answer.

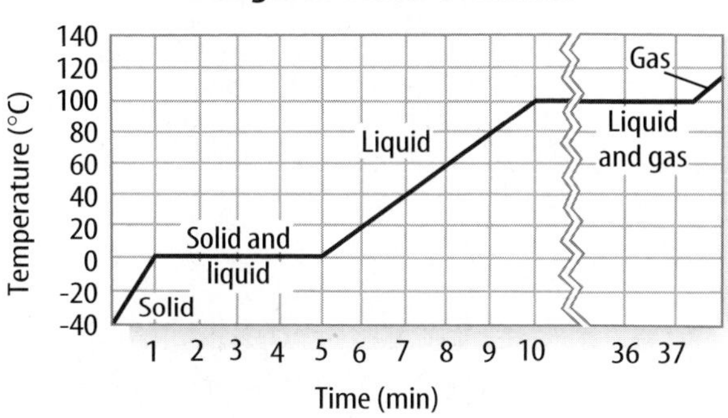

1. The graph shows the change in temperature that occurs as ice changes to water vapor. How much higher than the starting temperature is the boiling point?

A) 40°C
B) 100°C
C) 140°C
D) 180°C

Test-Taking Tip Boiling point is the flat section of the graph where liquid changes to gas.

2. What is being measured in the illustration?

F) boiling point
G) melting point
H) density
J) flammability

Test-Taking Tip Think about what you would measure with a thermometer in a liquid that you are heating.

Properties of Selected Pure Substances

Substance	Melting Point (°C)	Boiling Point (°C)	Color
Aluminum	660.4	2519	silver metallic
Argon	-189.2	-185.7	colorless
Mercury	-38.8	356.6	silver metallic
Water	0	100	colorless

3. Room temperature is about 20°C. In the table, which substance is a solid at room temperature?

A) aluminum
B) argon
C) mercury
D) water

Test-Taking Tip Remember that negative temperatures are below zero.

Read this question carefully before writing your answer on a separate sheet of paper.

4. The density of pure water is 1.00 g/cm^3. Ice floats on water, thus, the density of ice is *less* than that of water. Design an experiment to determine the density of an ice cube. List all the necessary steps.
(Volume = Length × Width × Height; Density = Mass / Volume)

Test-Taking Tip Consider all the information provided in the question.

UNIT 3

Motion and Forces

How Are Waffles & Running Shoes Connected?

For centuries, shoes were made mostly of leather, cloth, or wood. These shoes helped protect feet, but they didn't provide much traction on slippery surfaces. In the early twentieth century, manufacturers began putting rubber on the bottom of canvas shoes, creating the first "sneakers." Sneakers provided good traction, but the rubber soles could be heavy—especially for athletes. One morning in the 1970s, an athletic coach stared into the waffles on the breakfast table and had an idea for a rubber sole that would be lighter in weight but would still provide traction. That's how the first waffle soles were born. Waffle soles soon became a world standard for running shoes.

SCIENCE CONNECTION

FRICTION Treads on tires help increase friction between a wet or snow-covered road surface and the tire by enabling the tire to make contact with the road surface beneath a layer of snow or water. At school or in a tire shop, compare the treads on a snow tire and an all-weather tire. Draw conclusions about how each type of tread helps increase traction on wet or snow-covered roads. Then, create a poster comparing how three different tire treads help increase traction.

CHAPTER 6

Motion and Momentum

Racers, like the ones shown here, want to know who is the fastest. How can you determine who's the fastest? What has to be measured to determine a racer's speed? How can you describe motion when speed is changing? In this chapter you will learn how to describe motion, including motion that is changing. You will also study how motion changes when objects collide.

What do you think?

Science Journal Look at the picture below with a classmate. Discuss what this might be or what is happening. Here's a hint: *You can see these almost everywhere, day or night.* Write your answer or your best guess in your Science Journal.

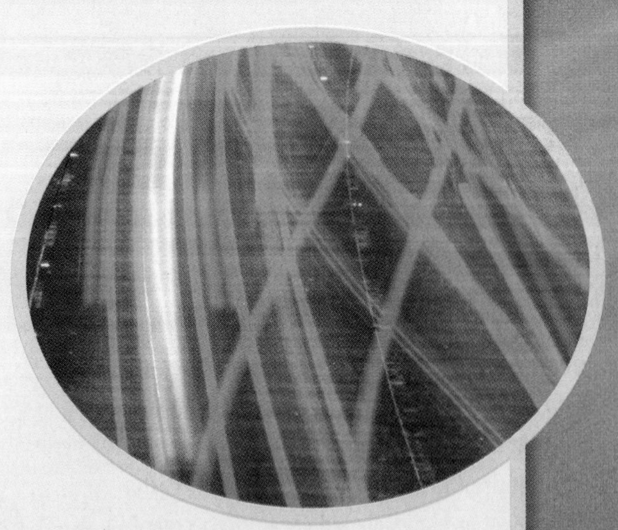

How is it possible for a 70-kg football player to knock down a 110-kg football player? The smaller player usually must be running faster. Mass makes a difference when two objects collide, but the speed of the objects also matters. Explore the behavior of colliding objects during this activity.

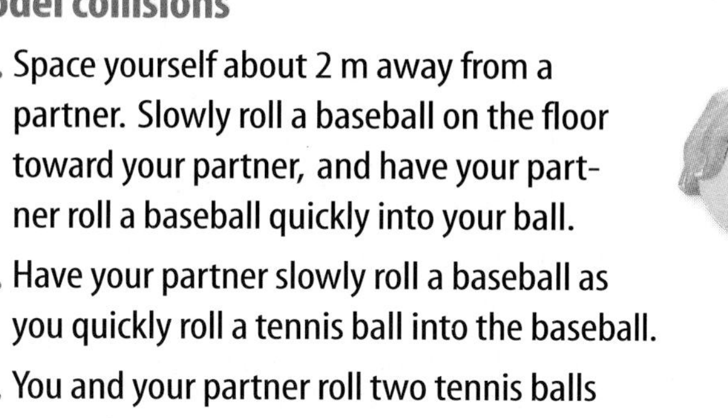

Model collisions

1. Space yourself about 2 m away from a partner. Slowly roll a baseball on the floor toward your partner, and have your partner roll a baseball quickly into your ball.
2. Have your partner slowly roll a baseball as you quickly roll a tennis ball into the baseball.
3. You and your partner roll two tennis balls toward each other at the same speed.

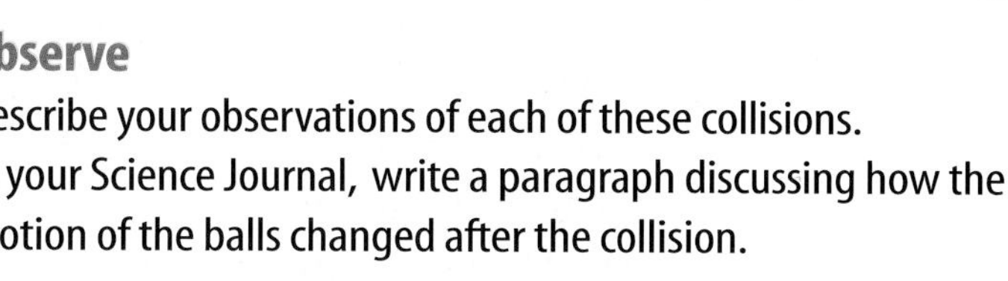

Observe

Describe your observations of each of these collisions. In your Science Journal, write a paragraph discussing how the motion of the balls changed after the collision.

Before You Read

Making a Vocabulary Study Fold **Knowing the definition of vocabulary words is a good way to ensure that you understand the content of the chapter.**

1. Place a sheet of notebook paper in front of you so the short side is at the top and the holes are on the right side. Fold the paper in half from the left side to the right side.
2. Through the top thickness of paper, cut along every third line from the outside edge to the fold, forming tabs.
3. Before you read, write the vocabulary words from each section in this chapter on the front of the tabs. Under each tab, write what you think the word means.
4. As you read the chapter, add to and correct your definitions.

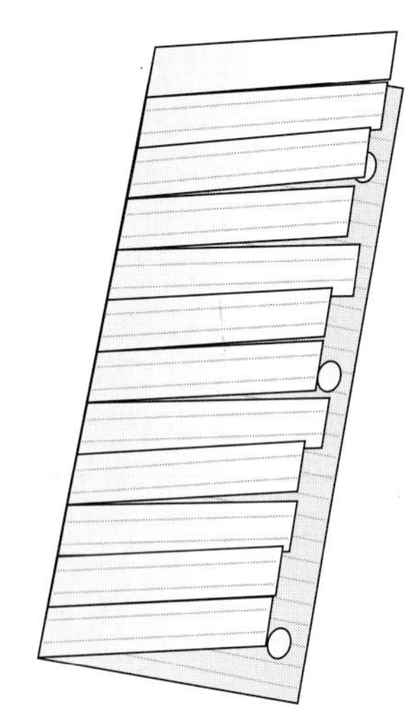

SECTION

What is motion?

As You Read

***What* You'll Learn**

- **Define** distance, speed, and velocity.
- **Graph** motion.

Vocabulary

speed
average speed
instantaneous speed
velocity

***Why* It's Important**

The different motions of objects you see every day can be described in the same way.

SCIENCE *Online*

Research Visit the Glencoe Science Web site at **science.glencoe.com** for more information about early attempts to study motion. Make a table to show what you learn.

Matter and Motion

All matter in the universe is constantly in motion, from the revolution of Earth around the Sun to electrons moving around the nucleus of an atom. Plants grow. Lava flows from a volcano. Bees move from flower to flower as they gather pollen. Blood circulates through your body. These are all examples of matter in motion. How can the motion of these different objects be described?

Changing Position

To describe an object in motion, you must recognize first that the object is in motion. Something is in motion if it is changing position. It could be a fast-moving airplane, a leaf swirling in the wind, or water trickling from a hose. Even your school is moving through space attached to Earth. When an object moves from one location to another, it is changing position. The runners shown in **Figure 1** sprint from the start line to the finish line. Their positions change so they are in motion.

Figure 1
When running a race, you are in motion because your position changes.

Relative Motion Determining whether something changes position requires a point of reference. An object changes position if it moves relative to a reference point. To visualize this, picture yourself competing in a 100-m dash. You begin just behind the start line. When you pass the finish line, you are 100 m from the start line. If the start line is your reference point then your position has changed by 100 m relative to the start line, and motion has occurred. Look at **Figure 2.** How can you determine that the dog has been in motion?

✔ Reading Check *How do you know if an object has changed position?*

Figure 2
Motion occurs when something moves relative to a reference point. ***The dog has moved relative to what object?***

Distance and Displacement Suppose you are to meet your friends at the park in five minutes. Can you get there on time by walking, or should you ride your bike? To help you decide, you need to know the distance you will travel to get to the park. This distance is the length of the route you will travel from your house to the park.

Suppose the distance you traveled from your house to the park was 200 m. When you get to the park, how would you describe your location? You could say that your location was 200 m from your house. To describe your location exactly, you also would have to tell in what direction you traveled. Did you travel 200 m east or 200 m west? Your final position would depend on the distance traveled and the direction. To describe your location, you would specify your displacement. Displacement includes the distance between the starting and stopping points, and the direction in which you travel. **Figure 3** shows the difference between distance and displacement.

Figure 3
Distance is how far you have walked. Displacement is the direction and difference in position between your starting point and your ending point.

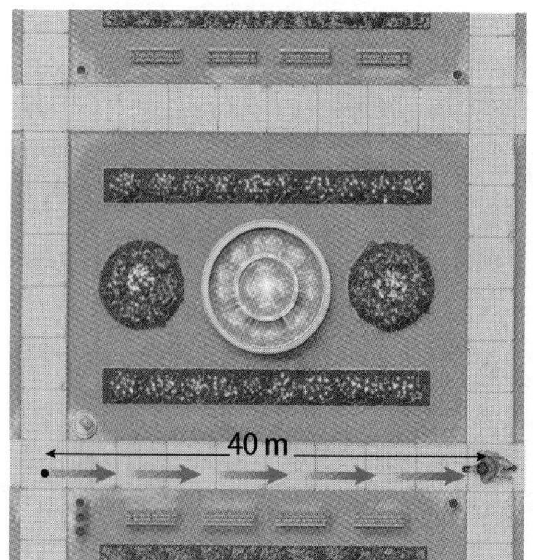

Distance: 40 m
Displacement: 40 m east

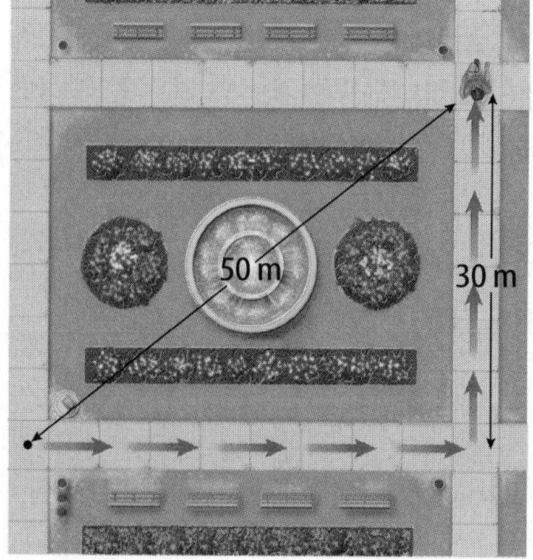

Distance: 70 m
Displacement: 50 m northeast

Distance: 140 m
Displacement: 0 m

Speed

Knowing how fast something is moving can be important. The faster something is moving, the less time it takes to travel a certain distance. **Speed** is the distance traveled divided by the time taken to travel the distance. This definition can be written as the following equation:

$$\text{speed} = \frac{\text{distance}}{\text{time}}$$

For example, the fastest runners can run the 100-m dash in about 10 s. When sprinters run 100 m in 10 s, their speed is as follows:

$$\text{speed} = \frac{\text{distance}}{\text{time}} = \frac{100 \text{ m}}{10 \text{ s}} = 10 \text{ m/s}$$

The units of speed are units of distance divided by units of time. In SI units, the units of speed are meters per second (m/s).

Life Science INTEGRATION

Different animals can move at different top speeds. What are some of the fastest animals? Research the characteristics that help animals run, swim, or fly at high speed.

Math Skills Activity

Calculating Speed

Example Problem

Calculate the speed of a swimmer who swims 100 m in 56 s.

Solution

1. *This is what you know:* distance: 100 m; time: 56 s
2. *This is what you need to know:* speed
3. *This is the equation you need to use:* speed = distance/time
4. *Substitute the known values:* speed = (100 m)/(56 s); speed = 1.8 m/s

Check your answer by multiplying the calculated speed by the time. Did you calculate the distance that was given in the problem?

Practice Problem

A runner completes a 400-m race in 43.9 s. In a 100-m race, he finishes in 10.4 s. In which race was his speed faster?

For more help, refer to the Math Skill Handbook.

Average Speed If a sprinter ran the 100-m dash in 10 s, she probably couldn't have run the entire race with a speed of 10 m/s. Consider that when the race started, the sprinter wasn't moving. Then, as she started running, she moved faster and faster, which increased her speed. During the entire race, the sprinter's speed could have been different from instant to instant. However, the sprinter's motion for the entire race can be described by her average speed, which is 10 m/s. **Average speed** is found by dividing the total distance traveled by the time taken.

✔ Reading Check *How is average speed calculated?*

An object in motion can change speeds many times as it speeds up or slows down. The speed of an object at one instant of time is the object's **instantaneous speed.** To understand the difference between average and instantaneous speeds, think about walking to the library. If it takes you 0.5 h to walk 2 km to the library, your average speed would be as follows:

$$\text{speed} = \frac{\text{distance}}{\text{time}}$$

$$= \frac{2\text{ km}}{0.5\text{ h}} = 4\text{ km/h}$$

However, you might not have been moving at the same speed throughout the trip. At a crosswalk, your instantaneous speed might have been 0 km/h. If you raced across the street, your speed might have been 7 km/h. If you were able to walk at a steady rate of 4 km/h during the entire trip, you would have moved at a constant speed. Average speed, instantaneous speed, and constant speed are illustrated in **Figure 4.**

TRY AT HOME **Mini LAB**

Measuring Average Speed

Procedure

1. Measure the distance between two marks, such as two doorways.
2. Time yourself walking from one mark to the other.
3. Time yourself walking slowly, walking safely and quickly, and walking with a varying speed; for example, slow/fast/slow.

Analysis

1. Calculate your average speed in each case.
2. Predict how long it would take you to walk 100 m slowly, at your normal speed, and quickly.

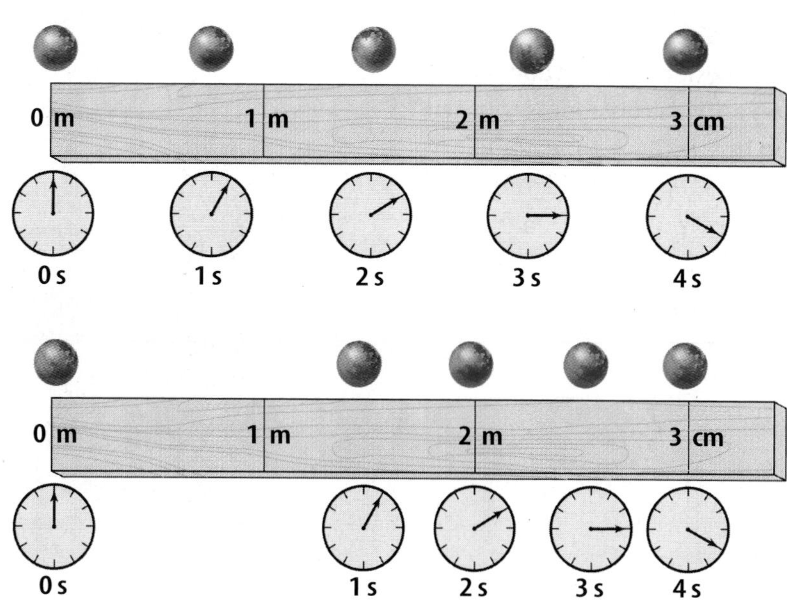

Figure 4
The average speed of each ball is the same from 0 s to 4 s.

A This ball is moving at a constant speed. In each second, the ball moves the same distance.

B This ball has a varying speed. Its instantaneous speed is fast between 0 s and 1 s and slow between 2 s and 3 s.

Graphing Motion

You can represent the motion of an object with a distance-time graph. For this type of graph, time is plotted on the horizontal axis and distance is plotted on the vertical axis. **Figure 5** shows the motion of two students who walked across a classroom, plotted on a distance-time graph.

Research Visit the Glencoe Science Web site at **science.glencoe.com** for information about how the land speed record has changed over the past century. Make a chart showing what you learn.

Distance-Time Graphs and Speed The distance-time graph can be used to compare the speeds of objects. Look at the graph shown in **Figure 5.** According to the graph, after 1 s, student A had traveled 1 m. Her average speed during the first second is as follows:

$$\text{speed} = \frac{\text{distance}}{\text{time}} = \frac{1 \text{ m}}{1 \text{ s}} = 1 \text{ m/s}$$

Student B, however, only traveled 0.5 m in the first second. His average speed is

$$\text{speed} = \frac{\text{distance}}{\text{time}} = \frac{0.5 \text{ m}}{1 \text{ s}} = 0.5 \text{ m/s}$$

So student A traveled faster than student B. Now compare the steepness of the lines on the graph in **Figure 5.** The line representing the motion of student A is steeper than the line of student B. A steeper line on the distance-time graph represents a greater speed. A horizontal line on the distance-time graph means that no change in position occurs. Then the speed, represented by the line on the graph, is zero.

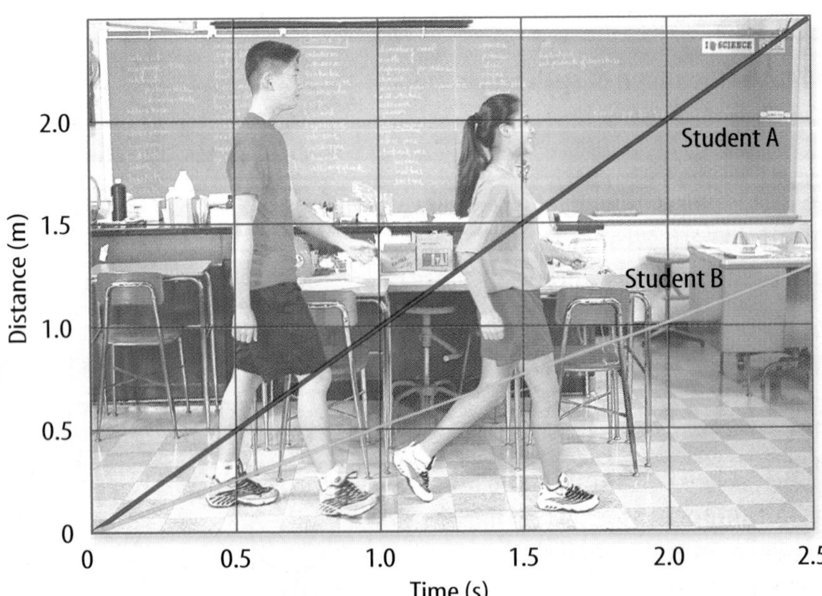

Figure 5
The motion of two students walking across a classroom is plotted on this distance-time graph.
Which student moved faster?

Velocity

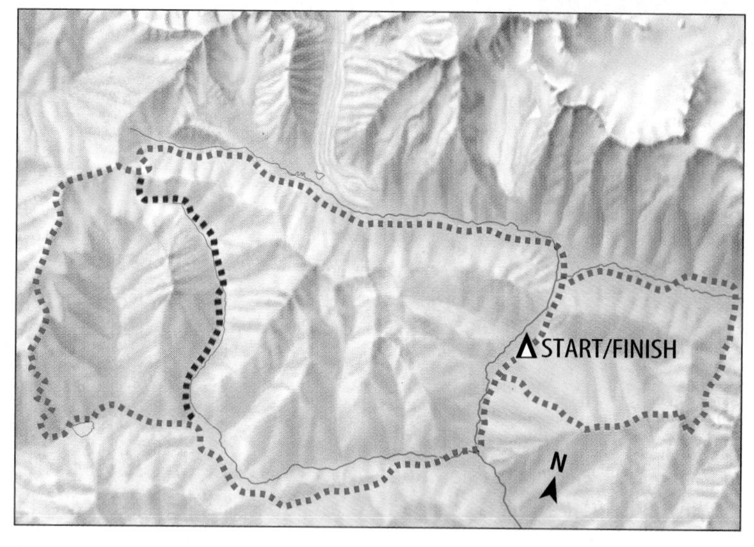

Figure 6
A map helps determine the direction in which you need to travel.

If you are hiking in the woods, it is important to know in which direction you should walk in order to get back to camp. You want to know not only your speed, but also the direction in which you are moving. The **velocity** of an object is the speed of the object and direction of its motion. This is why a compass and a map, like the one shown in **Figure 6,** are useful to hikers. To get back to camp before nightfall, they need to know how far, how fast, and in what direction they need to travel. The map and the compass help the hikers to determine what their velocity must be. Velocity has the same units as speed, but it also includes the direction of motion.

The velocity of an object can change if the object's speed changes, its direction of motion changes, or they both change. For example, suppose a car is traveling at a speed of 60 km/h north and then turns left at an intersection and continues on with a speed of 60 km/h. The speed of the car is constant at 60 km/h, but the velocity changes from 60 km/h north to 60 km/h west. Why can you say the velocity of a car changes as it comes to a stop at an intersection?

Section  Assessment

1. A dancer moves 5 m toward the left of the stage over the course of 15 s. What is her average velocity for this time?
2. If you know an object's velocity, do you know its speed? Explain.
3. An airplane flies a distance of 650 km at an average speed of 300 km/h. How much time did the flight take?
4. **Think Critically** A bee flies 25 m north of the hive, then 10 m east, 5 m west, and 10 m south. How far north and east of the hive is it now? Explain how you calculated your answer.

Skill Builder Activities

5. **Making and Using Graphs** You walk forward at 1.5 m/s for 8 s. Your friend decides to walk faster and starts out at 2.0 m/s for the first 4 s. But then she slows down and walks forward at 1.0 m/s for the next 4 s. Make a distance-time graph of your motion and your friend's motion. Who walked farther? **For more help, refer to the Science Skill Handbook.**
6. **Using a Database** Use a database to research the top speeds of different animals. Convert all data to units of m/s. **For more help, refer to the Technology Skill Handbook.**

Acceleration

As You Read

What You'll Learn

- **Define** acceleration.
- **Predict** what effect acceleration will have on motion.

Vocabulary
acceleration

Why It's Important
Whenever an object changes its motion, it accelerates.

Acceleration and Motion

When you watch the first few seconds of a liftoff, a rocket barely seems to move. With each passing second, however, you can see it move faster until it reaches an enormous speed. How could you describe the change in the rocket's motion? When an object changes its motion, it is accelerating. **Acceleration** is the change in velocity divided by the time it takes for the change to occur.

Like velocity, acceleration has a direction. If an object speeds up, the acceleration is in the direction that the object is moving. If an object slows down, the acceleration is opposite to the direction that the object is moving. What if the direction of the acceleration is at an angle to the direction of motion? Then the direction of motion will turn toward the direction of the acceleration.

Speeding Up You get on a bicycle and begin to pedal. The bike moves slowly at first, then it accelerates because its speed increases. When an object that is already in motion speeds up, it also is accelerating. Imagine that you are biking along a level path and you start pedaling harder. Your speed increases. When its speed is increasing, an object is accelerating.

Suppose a toy car is speeding up, as shown in **Figure 7.** Each second, the car moves at a greater speed and travels a greater distance than it did in the previous second. When the car stops accelerating, it will move in a straight line at the speed it reached when the acceleration stopped.

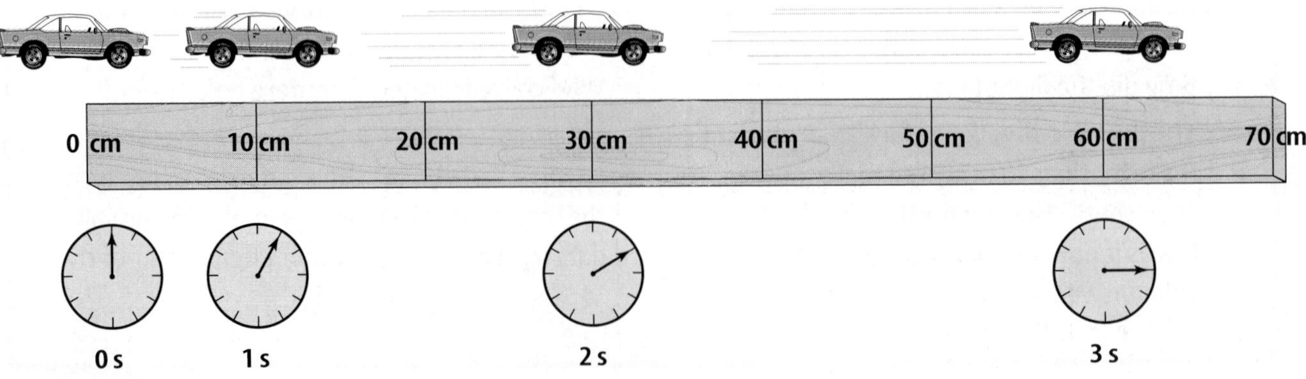

Figure 7
The toy car is accelerating to the right. The speed is increasing.

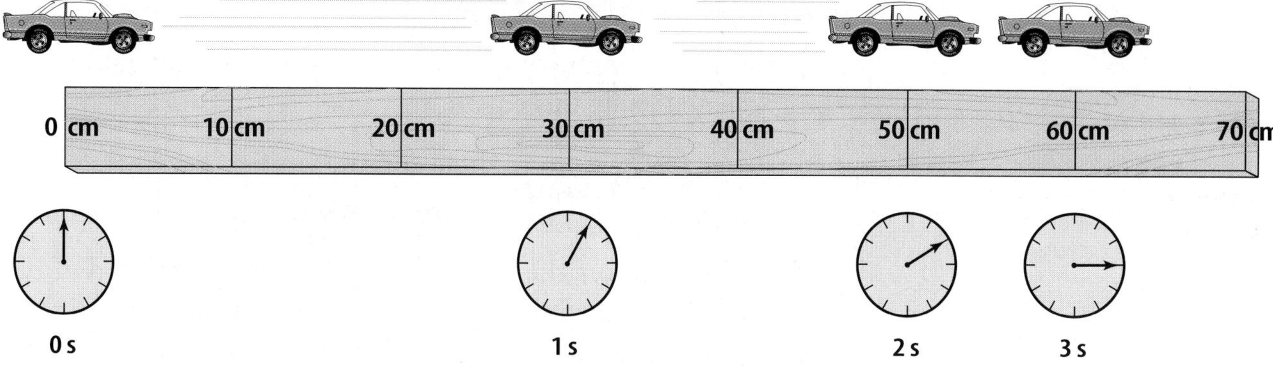

Figure 8
The car is moving to the right but accelerating to the left. In each time interval, it covers less distance and moves more slowly.

Slowing Down Now suppose you are biking at a speed of 4 m/s and you apply the brakes. This causes you to slow down. It might sound odd, but because your speed changes, you have accelerated. Acceleration occurs when an object slows down, as well as when it speeds up. The car in **Figure 8** is slowing down. During each time interval, the car travels a smaller distance, so its speed is decreasing.

In each of these examples, speed is changing, so acceleration is occurring. Because speed is decreasing, the direction of the acceleration is opposite to the direction of motion. Any time an object slows down, its acceleration is in the opposite direction of its motion.

Changing Direction Motion is not always along a straight line. If the acceleration is at an angle to the direction of motion, the object will turn. At the same time, it might speed up, slow down, or have no change in speed.

Picture yourself again riding a bicycle. When you lean to one side and turn the handlebars, the bike turns. Because the direction of the bike's motion has changed, the bike has accelerated. The acceleration is in the direction that the bicycle turned.

Figure 9 shows another example of an object that is accelerating. The ball starts moving upward, but its direction of motion changes as its path turns downward. Here the acceleration is downward. The longer the ball accelerates, the more its path turns toward the direction of acceleration.

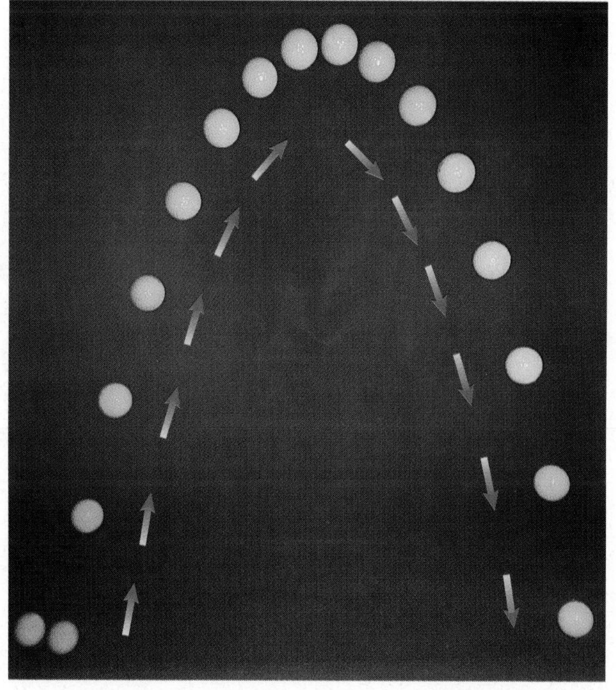

Figure 9
The ball starts out by moving forward and upward, but the acceleration is downward, so the ball's path turns in that direction.

Calculating Acceleration

If an object is moving in a straight line, its acceleration can be calculated using this equation.

$$\text{acceleration} = \frac{\text{final speed} - \text{initial speed}}{\text{time}}$$

In this equation, the final speed is the speed at the end of the time period and the initial speed is the speed at the beginning of the time period. Also, time is the length of time over which the motion changes.

This equation also can be written in a simpler way by using symbols. Let a stand for acceleration and t stand for time. Then let s_f stand for the final speed and s_i stand for the initial speed. Then the above equation can be written as follows.

$$a = \frac{(s_f - s_i)}{t}$$

The unit of acceleration is distance divided by time squared. In SI units, acceleration has units of meters per second squared (m/s^2).

Math Skills Activity

Calculating Acceleration

Example Problem

Calculate the acceleration of a bus whose speed changes from 6 m/s to 12 m/s over a period of 3 s.

1. *This is what you know:* initial speed: $s_i = 6$ m/s
   final speed: $s_f = 12$ m/s
   time: $t = 3$ s
2. *This is what you need to know:* acceleration: a
3. *This is the equation you need to use:* $a = (s_f - s_i)/t$
4. *Substitute the known values:* $a = (12 \text{ m/s} - 6 \text{ m/s})/(3 \text{ s}) = (6 \text{ m/s})/(3 \text{ s})$
   $= 2 \text{ m/s}^2$

Check your answer by multiplying the calculated acceleration by the time. Then add the initial speed. Did you calculate the final speed given in the problem?

Practice Problem

A train's velocity increases from 7 m/s to 18 m/s over a period of 120 s. Calculate its acceleration.

For more help, refer to the Math Skill Handbook.

Figure 10
When skidding to a stop, you are slowing down. This means you have a negative acceleration.

Positive and Negative Acceleration An object is accelerating when it speeds up, and the acceleration is in the same direction as the motion. An object also is accelerating when it slows down, but the acceleration is in the direction opposite the motion, such as the bicycle in **Figure 10.** How else is acceleration different when an object is speeding up and slowing down?

Suppose you were riding your bicycle in a straight line and speeded up from 4 m/s to 6 m/s in 5 s. You could calculate your acceleration from the equation on the previous page.

$$a = \frac{(s_f - s_i)}{t}$$
$$= \frac{(6 \text{ m/s} - 4 \text{ m/s})}{5 \text{ s}} = \frac{+2 \text{ m/s}}{5 \text{ s}}$$
$$= +0.4 \text{ m/s}^2$$

When you speed up, your final speed always will be greater than your initial speed. So subtracting the initial speed from the final speed gives a positive number. As a result, your acceleration is positive when you are speeding up.

Suppose you slow down from a speed of 4 m/s to 2 m/s in 5 s. Now the final speed is less than the initial speed. You could calculate your acceleration as follows:

$$a = \frac{(s_f - s_i)}{t}$$
$$= \frac{(2 \text{ m/s} - 4 \text{ m/s})}{5 \text{ s}} = \frac{-2 \text{ m/s}}{5 \text{ s}}$$
$$= -0.4 \text{ m/s}^2$$

Because your final speed is less than your initial speed, your acceleration is negative when you slow down.

Mini LAB

Modeling Acceleration

Procedure

1. Use **masking tape** to lay a course on the floor. Mark a starting point and place marks along a straight path at 10 cm, 40 cm, 90 cm, 160 cm, and 250 cm from the start.
2. Clap a steady beat. On the first beat, the person walking the course is at the starting point. On the second beat, the walker is on the first mark, and so on.

Analysis

1. Describe what happens to your speed as you move along the course. Infer what would happen if the course were extended farther.
2. Repeat step 2, starting at the other end. Are you still accelerating? Explain.

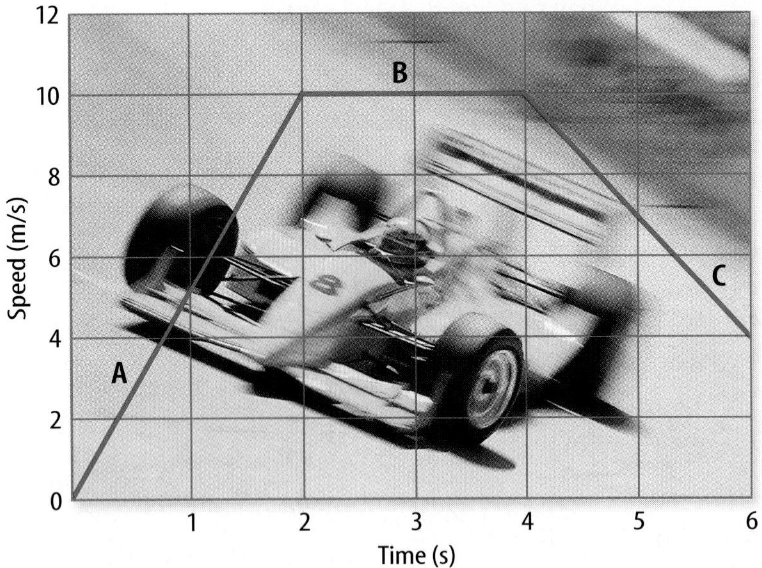

Figure 11
The speed-time graph can be used to find acceleration. When the line rises, the object is speeding up. When it is horizontal, the acceleration is zero. When the line falls, the object is slowing down.

Graphing Accelerated Motion

The motion of an object that is accelerating can be shown with a graph. For this type of graph, speed is plotted on the vertical axis and time on the horizontal axis. Take a look at **Figure 11.** On section A of the graph, the speed changes from 0 m/s to 10 m/s during the first 2 s. The acceleration over this time period is 5 m/s^2. The object is speeding up, so the acceleration is positive. Look at the line in section A. It slopes upward to the right. An object that is speeding up will have a line on a speed-time graph that slopes upward.

Now look at section C. Between 4 s and 6 s the speed changes from 10 m/s to 4 m/s. The acceleration is –3 m/s^2. The object is slowing down, so the acceleration is negative. On the speed-time graph, the line in section C is sloping downward to the right. An object that is slowing down will have a line on a speed-time graph that slopes downward.

On section B, where the line is horizontal, the change in speed is zero. So a horizontal line on the speed-time graph represents an acceleration of zero or constant speed.

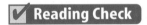

Reading Check *How is an acceleration of zero represented on a speed-time graph?*

Section 2 Assessment

1. A runner accelerates from 0 m/s to 3 m/s in 12 s. What was the acceleration?
2. A speed-time graph shows a line sloping downward. How was the speed changing?
3. In what three ways can acceleration change an object's motion?
4. An object falls with an acceleration of 9.8 m/s^2. What is its speed after 2 s?
5. **Think Critically** You start to roll backward down a hill on your bike, so you use the brakes to stop your motion. In what direction did you accelerate?

Skill Builder Activities

6. **Forming Operational Definitions** Give an operational definition of acceleration. **For more help, refer to the Science Skill Handbook.**
7. **Making and Using Graphs** A sprinter had the following speeds at different times during a race: 0 m/s at 0 s, 4 m/s at 2 s, 7 m/s at 4 s, 10 m/s at 6 s, 12 m/s at 8 s, and 10 m/s at 10 s. Plot these data on a speed-time graph. During what time intervals is the acceleration positive? Negative? Is the acceleration ever zero? **For more help, refer to the Science Skill Handbook.**

Momentum

Mass and Inertia

The world you live in is filled with objects in motion. How can you describe these objects? Objects have many properties such as color, size, and composition. One important property of an object is its mass. The **mass** of an object is the amount of matter in the object. In SI units the unit for mass is the kilogram.

The weight of an object is related to the object's mass. Objects with more mass weigh more than objects that have less mass. A bowling ball has more mass than a pillow, so it weighs more than a pillow. However, the size of an object is not the same as the mass of the object. For example, a pillow is larger than a bowling ball, but the bowling ball has more mass.

Objects with different masses are different in an important way. Think about what happens when you try to stop someone who is rushing toward you. A small child is easy to stop. A large adult is hard to stop. The more mass an object has, the harder it is to slow it down, speed it up, or turn it. This tendency of an object to resist a change in its motion is called **inertia.** Objects with more mass have more inertia, as shown in **Figure 12.** The more mass an object has, the harder it is to change its motion.

As You Read

What You'll Learn

- **Explain** the difference between mass and inertia.
- **Define** momentum.
- **Predict** motion using the law of conservation of momentum.

Vocabulary

mass
inertia
momentum
law of conservation of momentum

Why It's Important

Objects in motion have momentum. The motion of objects after they collide depends on their momentum.

Figure 12
The more mass an object has, the greater its inertia is. A table-tennis ball responds to a gentle hit that would move a tennis ball only slightly.

Momentum

Life Science INTEGRATION

A running animal has momentum. A small animal might be able to turn more quickly than a larger pursuing predator, because the smaller animal has less momentum. The larger an animal is and the faster it runs, the harder it is to turn or stop. Research the sizes of some predators and their usual prey.

You know that the faster a bicycle moves, the harder it is to stop. Just as increasing the mass of an object makes it harder to stop, increasing the speed or velocity of an object also makes it harder to stop. The **momentum** of an object is a measure of how hard it is to stop the object. This depends on the object's mass and velocity. The momentum of an object can be calculated from this equation.

$$\text{momentum} = \text{mass} \times \text{velocity}$$

Momentum is usually symbolized by p. If m stands for mass and v stands for velocity, this equation can be written like this.

$$p = mv$$

According to this equation, the momentum increases if the mass of the object or its velocity increases. Mass is measured in kilograms and velocity has units of meters per second, so momentum has units of kilograms multiplied by meters per second (kg·m/s). Also, because velocity includes a direction, momentum has a direction that is the same direction as its velocity.

Math Skills Activity

Calculating Momentum

Example Problem

Calculate the momentum of a 14 kg bicycle traveling north at 2 m/s.

Solution

1. *This is what you know:* mass: $m = 14$ kg; velocity: $v = 2$ m/s north
2. *This is what you need to find:* momentum: p
3. *This is the equation you need to use:* $p = mv$
4. *Substitute the known values:* $p = 14 \text{ kg} \times 2 \text{ m/s north}$ $= 28 \text{ kg·m/s north}$

Check your answer by dividing your momentum calculation by the mass of the bicycle. Did you calculate the velocity given in the problem?

Practice Problem

A 10,000-kg train is traveling east at 15 m/s. Calculate the momentum of the train.

For more help, refer to the Math Skill Handbook.

Conservation of Momentum

If you've ever played billiards, you know that when the cue ball hits another ball, the motion of both balls changes. The cue ball slows down and may change direction, so its momentum decreases. Meanwhile, the other ball starts moving, so its momentum increases. It seems as if momentum is transferred from the cue ball to the other ball.

In fact, during the collision the momentum lost by the cue ball was gained by the other ball. This means that the total momentum of both balls was the same just before and just after the collision. This is true for any collision, as long as no outside forces such as friction act on the objects and change their speeds after the collision. According to the **law of conservation of momentum,** the total momentum of objects that collide with each other is the same before and after the collision. This is true for the collisions of the billiard balls shown in **Figure 13,** as well as for atoms, cars, football players, or any other matter.

Figure 13
When the cue ball hits the other billiard balls, it slows down because it transfers part of its momentum to the other billiard balls. *What would happen to the speed of the cue ball if all of its momentum were transferred to the other billiard balls?*

Using Momentum Conservation

Outside forces such as gravity and friction are almost always acting on objects that are colliding. However, sometimes the effects of these forces are small enough that they can be ignored. Then the law of conservation of momentum enables you to predict how the motions of objects will change after a collision.

There are many ways that collisions can occur. Sometimes the objects that collide will bounce off of each other, like the bowling ball and bowling pins in **Figure 14A.** In some collisions, objects will stick to each other after the collision, like the two football players in **Figure 14B.** In this type of collision, the law of conservation of momentum enables the speeds of the objects after the collision to be calculated.

Figure 14
In these collisions, the total momentum before the collision equals the total momentum after the collision.

A When the bowling ball hits the pins, some of its momentum is transferred to the pins. The ball slows down and the pins speed up.

B When one player tackles the other, they both change speeds but momentum is conserved.

Figure 15
Momentum is conserved in the collision of the backpack and the student. A Before the student on skates and the backpack collide, she is not moving. B After the collision, the student and the backpack move together at a slower speed than the backpack had before the collision.

Sticking Together Picture yourself standing on a pair of skates when someone throws a backpack to you, as in **Figure 15.** When you catch the backpack, you and the backpack continue to move in the same direction that the backpack was moving before the collision.

The law of conservation of momentum can be used to find your speed or velocity after you catch the backpack. Suppose a backpack with a mass of 2 kg is tossed at a speed of 5 m/s. You have a mass of 48 kg, and initially you are at rest. Then the total momentum before the collision would be

$$\begin{aligned}\text{total momentum} &= \text{momentum of backpack} + \text{your momentum}\\ &= 2\text{ kg} \times 5\text{ m/s} + 48\text{ kg} \times 0\text{ m/s}\\ &= 10\text{ kg}\cdot\text{m/s}\end{aligned}$$

After the collision, the total momentum remains the same and only one object is moving. It has a combined mass of you and the backpack. You can use the equation for momentum to find the new velocity.

$$\begin{aligned}\text{total momentum} &= (\text{mass of backpack} + \text{your mass}) \times \text{velocity}\\ 10\text{ kg}\cdot\text{m/s} &= (2\text{ kg} + 48\text{ kg}) \times \text{velocity}\\ 10\text{ kg}\cdot\text{m/s} &= (50\text{ kg}) \times \text{velocity}\\ 0.2\text{ m/s} &= \text{velocity}\end{aligned}$$

This is your velocity right after you catch the backpack. The final velocity is much less than the initial velocity of the backpack. The velocity decreases because the mass of you and the backpack together is much greater than the mass of the backpack alone.

As you continue to move on your skates, the force of friction between the ground and the skates slows you down. As a result, the momentum of you and the backpack together continually decreases until you come to a stop.

NATIONAL GEOGRAPHIC VISUALIZING CONSERVATION OF MOMENTUM

Figure 16

The law of conservation of momentum can be used to predict the results of collisions between different objects, whether they are subatomic particles smashing into each other at enormous speeds, or the collisions of marbles, as shown on this page. What happens when one marble hits another marble initially at rest? The results of the collisions depend on the masses of the marbles.

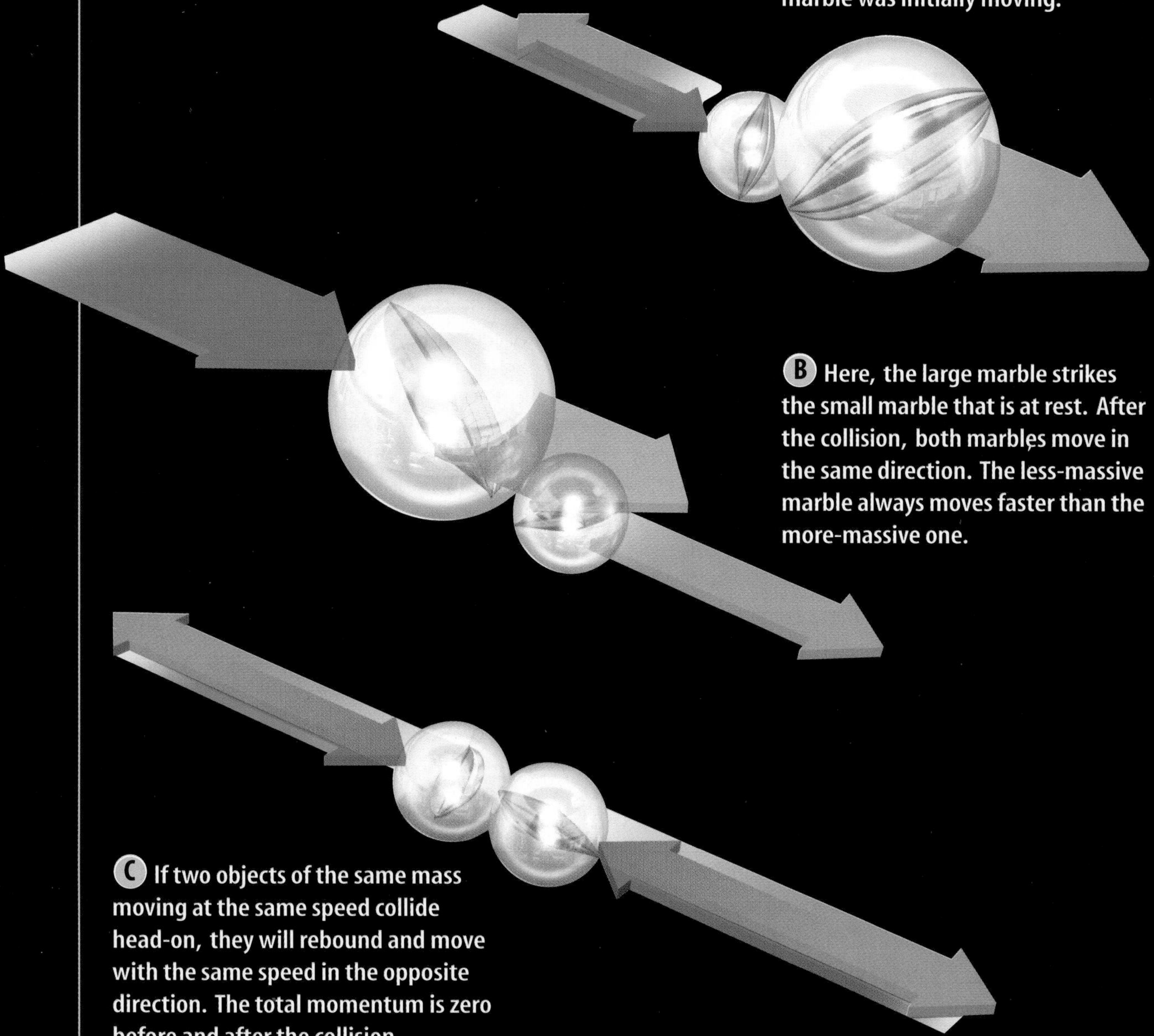

A Here, a less-massive marble strikes a more-massive marble that is at rest. After the collision, the smaller marble bounces off in the opposite direction. The larger marble moves in the same direction that the small marble was initially moving.

B Here, the large marble strikes the small marble that is at rest. After the collision, both marbles move in the same direction. The less-massive marble always moves faster than the more-massive one.

C If two objects of the same mass moving at the same speed collide head-on, they will rebound and move with the same speed in the opposite direction. The total momentum is zero before and after the collision.

Figure 17
When bumper cars collide, they bounce off each other, and momentum is transferred.

Bouncing Off In some types of collisions the objects involved, like the bumper cars in **Figure 17,** bounce off each other when they collide. The law of conservation of momentum can be used to help determine how these objects move after they collide. The results of collisions between two objects of various masses are shown in **Figure 16.**

For example, what happens if two objects of the same mass moving with the same speed collide head on? The objects reverse their direction of motion after the collision but still move with the same speed. What happens when one object directly hits an object at rest and both have the same mass? The first object transfers all of its momentum to the object at rest and comes to a stop.

Section  Assessment

1. When a player uses a golf club to hit a ball, how is momentum transferred?
2. What is the momentum of a 0.1-kg mass moving at 5 m/s?
3. A system of two balls has a momentum of 1 kg·m/s. Ball A has a momentum of −3 kg·m/s. What is the momentum of ball B?
4. **Think Critically** You watch a film in which one billiard ball rolls forward and hits another. After the collision the second billiard ball rolls away and the first one is motionless. Can you tell whether the film is being shown forward or in reverse?

Skill Builder Activities

5. **Predicting** Two balls of the same mass move toward each other with equal speeds and in the opposite direction. Predict how the balls will move after the collision if they collide and then stick together. Explain your answer. **For more help, refer to the** Science Skill Handbook.
6. **Solving One-Step Equations** A 0.2-kg ball is moving left at 3 m/s. It strikes a 0.5-kg ball that is at rest. Immediately after the collision, the 0.2-kg ball comes to a stop. How fast is the 0.5-kg ball moving if the momentum is conserved? **For more help, refer to the** Math Skill Handbook.

Activity

Collisions

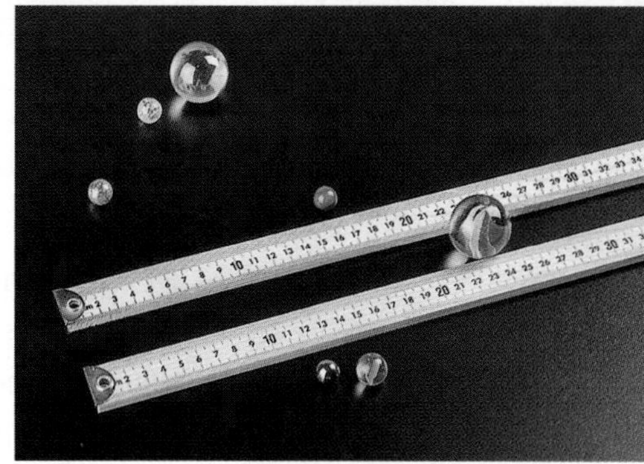

A collision occurs when a baseball bat hits a baseball or a tennis racket hits a tennis ball. What would happen if you hit a baseball with a table-tennis paddle, or a table-tennis ball with a baseball bat? How do the masses of colliding objects change the results of collisions?

What You'll Investigate

How does changing the size and number of marbles in a collision affect the collision?

Materials

small marbles (5)
large marbles (2)
metersticks (2)
tape

Goals

- **Compare and contrast** different collisions.
- **Determine** how the speeds after a collision depend on the masses of the colliding objects.

Safety Precautions

Procedure

1. Tape the metersticks next to each other, slightly farther apart than the width of the large marbles. This limits the motion of the marbles to nearly a straight line.
2. Place a small marble in the center of the track formed by the metersticks. Place another small marble at one end of the track. Shoot this marble toward the small target marble by flicking it with your finger. Describe the collision.
3. Repeat step 2, replacing the two small marbles with the two large marbles.
4. Repeat step 2, replacing the small shooter marble with a large marble.
5. Repeat step 2, replacing the small target marble with a large marble.
6. Repeat step 2, replacing the small target marble with four small marbles that are touching.
7. Place two small marbles at opposite ends of the metersticks. Shoot the marbles toward each other and describe the collision.
8. Place two large marbles at opposite ends of the metersticks. Shoot the marbles toward each other and describe the collision.
9. Place a small marble and a large marble at opposite ends of the metersticks. Shoot the marbles toward each other and describe the collision.

Conclude and Apply

1. **Compare and contrast** the results of the various types of collisions.
2. In which collisions did the shooter marble change direction? How did the mass of the target marble compare with the shooter marble in these collisions?

Communicating Your Data

Make a chart showing your results. You might want to make before-and-after sketches, with short arrows to show slow movement and long arrows to show fast movement. **For more help, refer to the** Science Skill Handbook.

Activity

Design Your Own Experiment

Car Safety Testing

Imagine that you are a car designer. How can you create an attractive, fast car that is safe? When a car crashes, the passengers have inertia that can keep them moving. How can you protect the passengers from stops caused by sudden, head-on impacts?

Recognize the Problem

How can you design a car to win a race and protect the passenger in a head-on crash at the end of the race?

Form a Hypothesis

Develop a hypothesis about how to design a car to deliver a plastic egg quickly and safely through a race course and a crash at the end.

Goals

- **Construct** a fast car.
- **Design** a safe car that will protect a plastic egg from the effects of inertia when the car crashes.

Safety Precautions

Protect your eyes from possible flying objects.

Possible Materials

insulated foam meat trays or fast food trays
insulated foam cups
straws, narrow and wide
straight pins
tape
plastic eggs

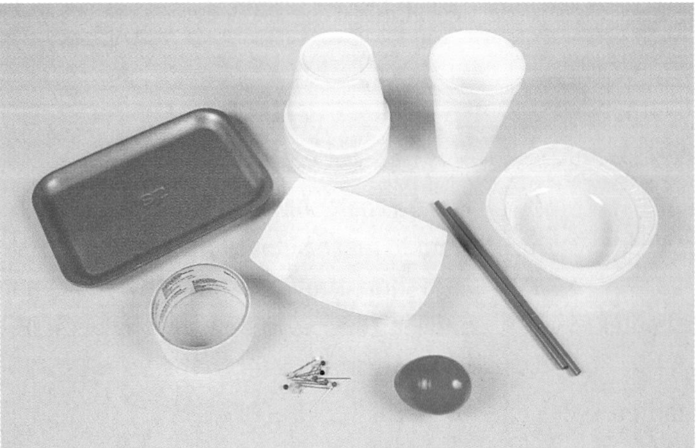

Test Your Hypothesis

Plan

1. Be sure your group has agreed on the hypothesis statement.
2. **Sketch** the design for your car. List the materials you will need. Remember that to make the car move smoothly, narrow straws will have to fit into the wider straws.
3. As a group, make a detailed list of the steps you will take to test your hypothesis.
4. Gather the materials you will need to carry out your experiment.

Do

1. Make sure your teacher approves your plan before you start. Include any changes suggested by your teacher in your plans.
2. Carry out the experiment as planned.
3. **Record** any observations that you made while doing your experiment. Include suggestions for improving your design.

Analyze Your Data

1. **Compare** your car design to the designs of the other groups. What made the fastest car fast? What slowed the slowest car?
2. **Compare** your car's safety features to those of the other cars. What protected the eggs the best? How could you improve the unsuccessful designs?
3. What effect would decreasing the speed of your car have on the safety of the egg?

Draw Conclusions

1. How did the best designs protect the egg?
2. If you were designing cars, what could you do to better protect passengers from sudden stops?

Write a descriptive paragraph on how a car could be designed to protect its passengers effectively. Include a sketch of your designs.

What Goes Around Comes Around

The Story of Boomerangs

Picture this—A group of kids is gathered on the flat, yellow plain near their encampment in the Australian outback. One youth steps forward. With the flick of an arm, the youth flings a long, flat, angled stick that soars and spins into the sky. The stick's path curves until it returns—spinning right back into the thrower's hand. Another thrower steps forward with another stick. The contest goes on all afternoon.

That scene could be from today. Or, it could have taken place 10,000—or more—years ago. The kids were throwing boomerangs—elegantly curved sticks. Because of how boomerangs are shaped and thrown, they always return to the thrower.

Archaeologists in Australia have unearthed boomerangs from 15,000 years ago. The boomerang developed from simple clubs that early people threw to stun and kill prey animals. These people became very good throwers and probably soon discovered that clubs with different shapes had different properties in the air. They gradually refined their designs into a throwing stick resembling today's boomerangs. As boomerangs became more refined, they also might have been used for fun.

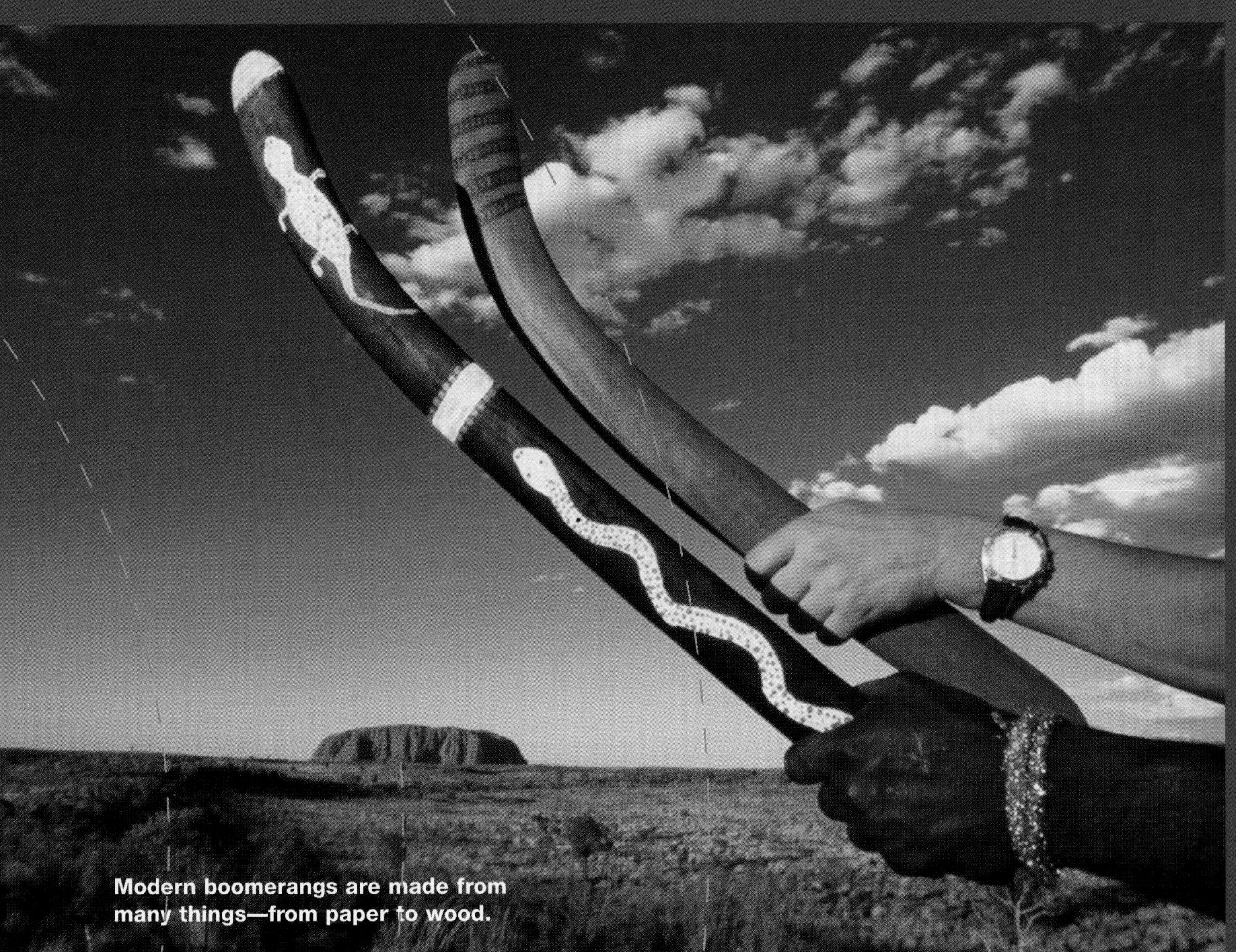

Modern boomerangs are made from many things—from paper to wood.

Making a Comeback

There are many different types of boomerangs, but they have a few things in common, each of which is related to how a boomerang works. First, boomerangs are flat on the bottom and rounded on the top. This shape helps provide lift, just like it does for an airplane wing. When you hold a boomerang to throw it, the flat side is against your palm and your fingers curl around the curved side.

Second, boomerangs are angled. This makes the boomerang spin in the air. When it is thrown correctly, a boomerang spins at right angles to the ground, not horizontally like helicopter blades.

Today, using boomerangs for fun is a popular sport. World-class boomerangers compete at the World Boomerang Championships. Throwers compete in events such as Time Aloft, in which they try to keep the boomerang up in the air as long as possible. In Team Terror, a grueling relay race, throwers perform difficult throws and trick catches, such as behind-the-back or under-the-leg. They use ultra-modern boomerangs—some of which look nothing like the old-style classic boomerang. But they carry on an ancient Australian tradition of competing for the best throw.

CONNECTIONS **Design** **Boomerangs are made from materials ranging from a piece of paper to expensive hardwood. Research at the library to find instructions for making boomerangs. After you and your friends build some boomerangs, have a competition of your own.**

SCIENCE *Online*

For more information, visit science.glencoe.com.

Chapter 6 Study Guide

Reviewing Main Ideas

Section 1 What is motion?

1. An object is in motion if it is changing position.
2. Distance measures the length of the path that an object follows during its motion. Displacement is the change in position between the starting point and the ending point, as well as the direction from the start to end points.
3. Speed is a measure of how quickly the position of an object changes. Velocity includes the speed and direction of motion.
4. Speed can be calculated using the following equation:

$$\text{speed} = \frac{\text{distance}}{\text{time}}$$

5. A distance-time graph can be used to show motion. *Which object is moving the fastest?*

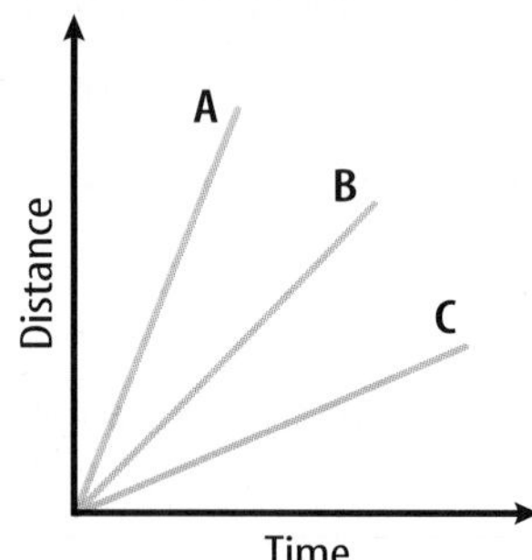

Section 2 Acceleration

1. Acceleration is a measure of how quickly velocity changes. It includes a direction.
2. An object is accelerating when it speeds up, slows down, or turns.
3. When an object speeds up or slows down, its acceleration can be calculated by

$$a = \frac{(s_f - s_i)}{t}$$

4. An object's acceleration can be determined from the speed-time graph. *During what time intervals is the object speeding up? Slowing down? How can you tell?*

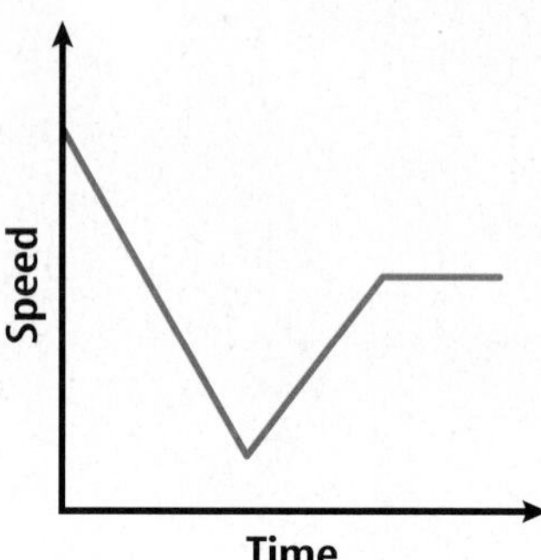

Section 3 Momentum

1. The momentum of an object is a measure of how hard it is to stop the object. Momentum is the product of mass and velocity. It has a direction.
2. Momentum is transferred from one object to another in a collision.
3. According to the law of conservation of momentum, the total amount of momentum of a group of objects does not change unless outside forces act on the objects. *How could you determine the total momentum of these balls? Would it change after they collide? Why or why not?*

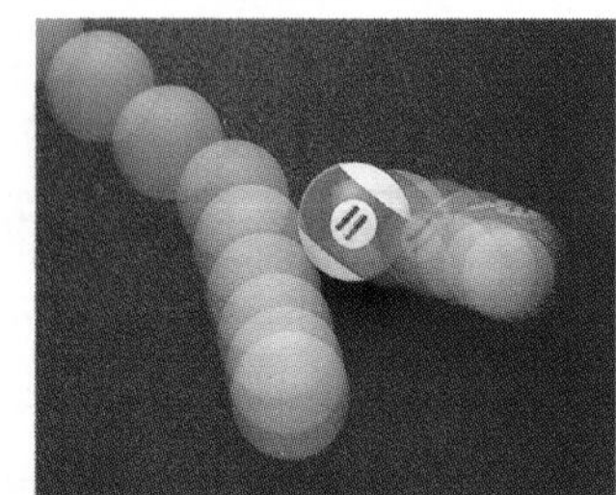

FOLDABLES Reading & Study Skills

After You Read

Use each vocabulary word on your Foldable in a sentence about motion and write it next to the definition of the word.

Chapter 6 Study Guide

Visualizing Main Ideas

Complete the following table comparing different descriptions of motion.

Describing Motion

Quantity	Definition	Direction?
Distance	change in position	no
Displacement	direction and amount of change in position	yes
Speed		no
Velocity	rate of change in position and direction	
Acceleration		
Momentum		yes

Vocabulary Review

Vocabulary Words

a. acceleration
b. average speed
c. inertia
d. instantaneous speed
e. law of conservation of momentum
f. mass
g. momentum
h. speed
i. velocity

Study Tip

Pay attention to the chapter's illustrations. Try to figure out exactly the main point each picture is trying to stress.

Using Vocabulary

Explain the relationship between each pair of words.

1. speed, velocity
2. velocity, acceleration
3. velocity, momentum
4. momentum, law of conservation of momentum
5. mass, momentum
6. mass, inertia
7. momentum, inertia
8. average speed, instantaneous speed

Chapter 6 Assessment

Checking Concepts

Choose the word or phrase that best answers the question.

1. What measures the quantity of matter?
A) speed **C)** acceleration
B) weight **D)** mass

2. A 2-kg ball has a momentum of 10 kg·m/s. What is its speed?
A) 1 m/s **C)** 10 m/s
B) 5 m/s **D)** 20 m/s

3. Which of the following is NOT an example of acceleration?
A) a leaf falling at constant speed
B) a car slowing down
C) a skater spinning
D) a dog running faster and faster

4. Speed is related to change in which of the following?
A) distance **C)** velocity
B) momentum **D)** acceleration

5. A parked car is hit by a moving car, and the two cars stick together. How does the speed of the combined cars compare to the speed of the car before the collision?
A) Combined speed is the same.
B) Combined speed is greater.
C) Combined speed is smaller.
D) Any of these could be true.

6. A car travels for half an hour at 40 km/h. How far does it travel?
A) 10 km **C)** 40 km
B) 20 km **D)** 80 km

7. What is a measure of inertia?
A) weight **C)** momentum
B) gravity **D)** mass

8. What is 18 cm/h north an example of?
A) speed **C)** acceleration
B) velocity **D)** momentum

9. Ball A bumps into ball B. Which of the following is the same before and after the collision?
A) the momentum of ball A
B) the momentum of ball B
C) the sum of the momentums
D) the difference in the momentums

10. What is velocity change divided by time change?
A) speed **C)** momentum
B) displacement **D)** acceleration

Thinking Critically

11. You run 100 m in 25 s. If you later run the same distance in less time, does your average speed increase or decrease? Explain.

12. A car drives from point A to point B. Can its displacement be greater than the total distance that it traveled? Explain.

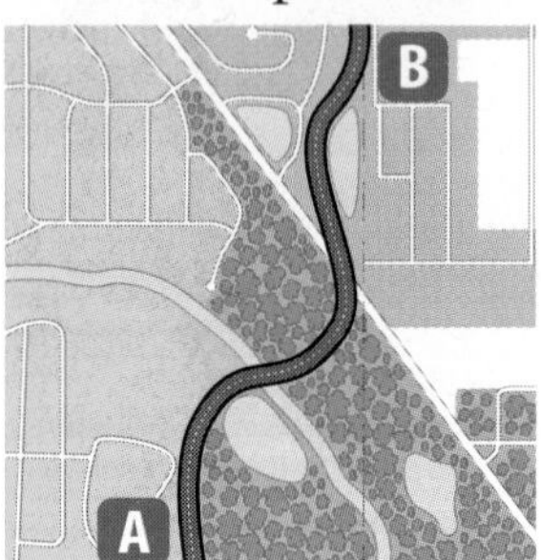

13. The Moon moves around Earth at close to constant speed. Does this mean it is not accelerating? Explain.

14. When a wrecking ball hits a wall, it is not moving fast. How can it have enough momentum to knock down a wall?

Developing Skills

15. Predicting A rocket accelerates at 12 m/s^2 for 8 s. If it starts at rest, what is its final speed?

16. Measuring in SI Measure the width of your desk. Time a pen rolling across the desk, and find the speed of the pen.

17. Making Models The molecules in a gas are modeled as colliding balls. If the molecules all have the same mass, explain what can happen when a fast-moving molecule hits a slow-moving molecule. Include a sketch.

18. Recognizing Cause and Effect Roll one marble into the end of a line of stationary marbles. What do you observe? Why do you think this happened?

19. Making and Using Graphs Use the speed-time graph below. What is the acceleration between $t = 0$ and $t = 3$?

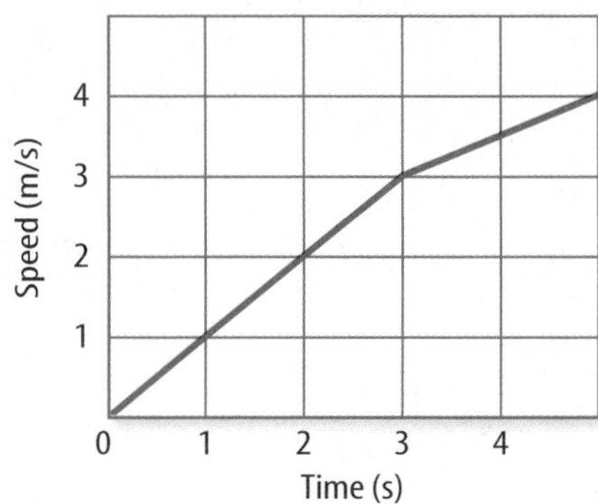

Performance Assessment

20. Demonstration Set up a racetrack and make rules for the type of motion allowed. Demonstrate how to measure distance, measure time, and calculate speed accurately.

21. Poster Make a poster showing how motion graphs represent acceleration and constant speed. Use both speed-time and distance-time graphs.

Technology

Go to the Glencoe Science Web site at **science.glencoe.com** or use the **Glencoe Science CD-ROM** for additional chapter assessment.

Test Practice

Two students are comparing the performance of different electric toy cars by measuring the top speed each car can reach. They also calculate the momentum of each car at its top speed. The table below summarizes their results.

Performance of Toy Cars

Car	Mass (kg)	Velocity (m/s)	Momentum (kg·m/s)
A	1.0	0.2	0.2
B	1.0	0.5	0.5
C	0.5	1.6	0.8
D	3.0	0.2	0.6
E	2.0	0.4	0.8

Study the table and answer the following questions.

1. According to the table, which statement best describes how the students calculated the momentum of the cars?

A) momentum = mass + velocity
B) momentum = mass − velocity
C) momentum = mass × velocity
D) momentum = mass/velocity

2. About how much greater is the momentum of the car with the least mass than that of the car with the greatest mass?

F) 0.2 kg·m/s
G) 0.4 kg·m/s
H) 1.0 kg·m/s
J) 0.5 kg·m/s

CHAPTER 7

Force and Newton's Laws

This train can move! Japan's experimental train, the MLX01, can travel at speeds of more than 500 km/h. It can move this fast because the engineers who built it understood the laws of motion that Isaac Newton first proposed more than 300 years ago. In this chapter, you'll learn about force and Newton's laws of motion. You'll learn why some objects move and why some stay still, and how objects exert forces on each other.

What do you think?

Science Journal Look at the picture below with a classmate. Discuss what this might be or what is happening. Here's a hint: *It's a delicate balancing act.* Write your answer or best guess in your Science Journal.

Imagine being on a bobsled team speeding down an icy run. The force of gravity causes the sled to accelerate as it speeds down the course in a blur. You and your team use your bodies, brakes, and the steering mechanism to exert forces to change the sled's motion, causing it to slow down or turn. The motion of the sled as it speeds up, slows down, and turns can be explained with Newton's laws of motion. These laws tell how forces cause the motion of an object to change.

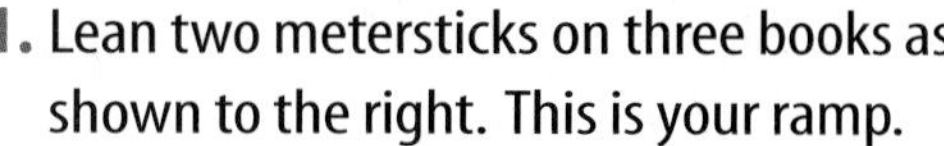

Analyze motion on a ramp

1. Lean two metersticks on three books as shown to the right. This is your ramp.
2. Tap a marble so it rolls up the ramp. Measure how far up the ramp it travels before rolling back.
3. Repeat step 2 using two books, one book, and zero books. The same person should tap with the same force each time.

Observe

Make a table to record the motion of the marble for each ramp height. What would happen if the ramp were perfectly smooth and level?

Before You Read

Making an Organizational Study Fold **When information is grouped into clear categories, it is easier to make sense of what you are learning. Make the following Foldable to help you organize your thoughts about Newton's Three Laws of Motion.**

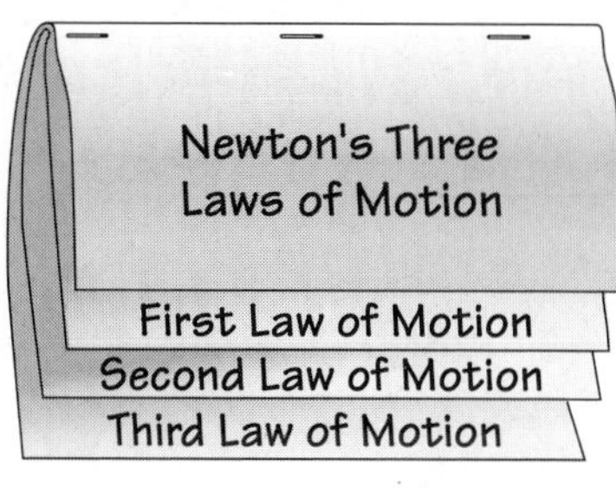

1. Stack two sheets of paper in front of you so the short side of both sheets is at the top.
2. Slide the top sheet up so that about four centimeters of the bottom sheet show.
3. Fold both sheets top to bottom to form four tabs and staple along the topfold as shown.
4. Label each flap *Newton's Three Laws of Motion, First Law of Motion, Second Law of Motion,* and *Third Law of Motion* as shown.
5. As you read the chapter, record what you learn about the laws of motion under the tabs.

SECTION

Newton's First Law

As You Read

What You'll Learn

- **Identify** forces at work.
- **Distinguish** between balanced and net forces.
- **Demonstrate** Newton's first law of motion.
- **Explain** how friction works.

Vocabulary

force
net force
balanced forces
unbalanced forces
Newton's first law of motion
friction

Why It's Important

Newton's first law helps you understand why objects slow down and stop.

Force

A soccer ball sits on the ground, motionless, until you kick it. Your science book sits on the table until you pick it up. If you hold your book above the ground, then let it go, gravity pulls it to the floor. In every one of these cases, the motion of the ball or book was changed by something pushing or pulling on it. An object will speed up, slow down, or turn only if something is pushing or pulling on it.

A **force** is a push or a pull. Examples of forces are shown in **Figure 1.** Think about throwing a ball. Your hand exerts a force on the ball, and the ball accelerates forward until it leaves your hand. After the ball leaves your hand, gravity's force on it causes its path to curve downward. When the ball hits the ground, the ground exerts a force, stopping the ball.

A force can be exerted in different ways. For instance, a paper clip can be moved by the force a magnet exerts, the pull of Earth's gravity, or the force you exert when you pick it up. These are all examples of forces acting on the paper clip.

Figure 1
A force is a push or a pull.

B The magnet on the crane pulls the pieces of scrap metal upward.

A This golf club exerts a force by pushing on the golf ball.

A This door is not moving because the forces exerted on it are equal and in opposite directions.

B The door is closing because the force pushing the door closed is greater than the force pushing it open.

Figure 2
When the forces on an object are balanced, no change in motion occurs, but when the forces on an object are unbalanced, a change in motion does occur.

Combining Forces More than one force can act on an object at the same time. If you hold a paper clip near a magnet, you, the magnet, and gravity all exert forces on the paper clip. The combination of all the forces acting on an object is the **net force.** When more than one force is acting on an object, the net force determines the motion of the object. In this example, the paper clip is not moving, so the net force is zero.

How do forces combine to form the net force? If the forces are in the same direction, they add together to form the net force. If two forces are in opposite directions, then the net force is the difference between the two forces, and it is in the direction of the larger force.

Balanced and Unbalanced Forces A force can act on an object without causing it to accelerate if other forces cancel the push or pull of the force. Look at **Figure 2.** If you and your friend push on a door with the same force in opposite directions, the door does not move. Because you both exert forces of the same size in opposite directions on the door, the two forces cancel each other. Two or more forces exerted on an object are **balanced forces** if their effects cancel each other and they do not cause a change in the object's motion. If the forces on an object are balanced, the net force is zero. If the forces are **unbalanced forces,** their effects don't cancel each other. Any time the forces acting on an object are unbalanced, the net force is not zero and the motion of the object changes.

Whether you run, jump, or sit, forces are being exerted on different parts of your body. Biomechanics is the study of how the body exerts forces and how it is affected by forces acting on it. Research how biomechanics has been used to reduce job-related injuries. Write a paragraph on what you've learned in your Science Journal.

Newton's First Law of Motion

If you stand on a skateboard and someone gives you a push, then you and your skateboard will start moving. You began to move when the force was applied. An object at rest—like you on your skateboard—remains at rest unless an unbalanced force acts on it and causes it to move.

Because a force had to be applied to make you move when you and your skateboard were at rest, you might think that a force has to be applied continually to keep an object moving. Surprisingly, this is not the case. An object can be moving even if the net force acting on it is zero.

Newton's first law of motion describes how an object moves when no net force is acting on it. According to **Newton's first law of motion,** if there is no net force acting on an object the object remains at rest, or if the object is already moving, it continues to move in a straight line with constant speed.

The Italian scientist Galileo Galilei, who lived from 1564 to 1642, was one of the first to understand that a force doesn't need to be constantly applied to an object to keep it moving. Galileo's ideas helped Isaac Newton to better understand the nature of motion. Newton was able to explain the motion of objects in three rules called Newton's laws of motion.

Figure 3
When two objects in contact try to slide past each other, friction keeps them from moving or slows them down.

A Without friction, the rock climber would slide down the rock.

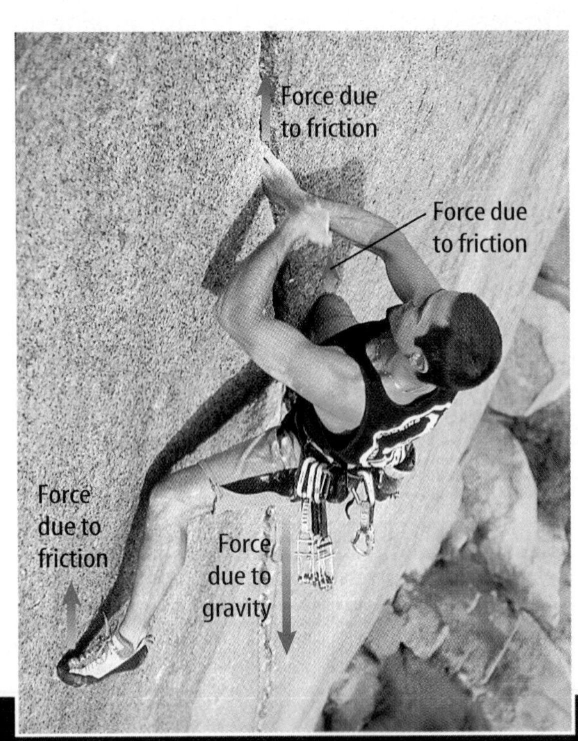

Friction

Galileo realized the motion of an object doesn't change until an unbalanced force acts on it. Every day you see moving objects come to a stop. The force that brings nearly everything to a stop is **friction,** which is the force that acts to resist sliding between two touching surfaces, as shown in **Figure 3.** Friction is why you never see objects moving with constant velocity unless a net force is applied. Friction is the force that eventually brings your skateboard to a stop unless you keep pushing on it. Friction always acts on objects that are sliding or moving through air or water.

B Friction slows down this sliding baseball player.

Opposing Sliding Although several different forms of friction exist, they all have one thing in common. If two objects are in contact, frictional forces always try to prevent one object from sliding on the other object. If you rub your hand against a tabletop, you can feel the friction push against the motion of your hand. If you rub the other way, you can feel the direction of friction change so it is again acting against your hand's motion. Friction always will slow an object down.

Reading Check *What do the different forms of friction have in common?*

Older Ideas About Motion It took a long time for people to understand motion. One reason was that people did not understand the behavior of friction or understand that friction was a force. Because friction causes moving objects to stop, people thought the natural state of an object was to be at rest. For an object to be in motion, something had to be pushing or pulling it continuously. As soon as the force stopped, nature would bring the object to rest.

Galileo understood that an object in constant motion is as natural as an object at rest. It was usually friction that made moving objects slow down and eventually come to a stop. To keep an object moving, a force had to be applied to overcome the effects of friction. If friction could be removed, an object in motion would continue to move in a straight line with constant speed. **Figure 4** shows motion where there is almost no friction.

Research Visit the Glencoe Science Web site at **science.glencoe.com** for more information about the lives of Galileo and Newton. Communicate to your class what you learn.

Figure 4
In an air hockey game, the puck floats on a layer of air, so that friction is almost eliminated. As a result, the puck moves in a straight line with nearly constant speed after it's been hit. *How would the puck move if there was no layer of air?*

Observing Friction

Procedure

1. Lay a **bar of soap,** a **flat eraser,** and a **key** side by side on one end of a **hard-sided notebook.**
2. At a constant rate, slowly lift the end of notebook with objects on it. Note the order in which the objects start sliding.

Analysis

1. For which object was static friction the greatest? For which object was it the smallest? Explain, based on your observations.
2. Which object slid the fastest? Which slid the slowest? Explain why there is a difference in speed.
3. How could you increase and decrease the amount of friction between two materials?

Static Friction If you've ever tried pushing something heavy, like a refrigerator, you might have discovered that nothing happened at first. Then as you push harder and harder, the object suddenly will start to move. When you first start to push, friction between the heavy refrigerator and the floor opposes the force you are exerting and the net force is zero. The type of friction that prevents an object from moving when a force is applied is called static friction.

Static friction is caused by the attraction between the atoms on the two surfaces that are in contact. This causes the surfaces to stick or weld together where they are in contact. Usually, as the surface gets rougher and the object gets heavier, the force of static friction will be larger. To move the object, you have to exert a force large enough to break the bonds holding two surfaces together.

Sliding Friction While static friction keeps an object at rest, sliding friction slows down an object that slides. If you push an object across a room, you notice the sliding friction between the bottom of the object and the floor. You have to keep pushing to overcome the force of sliding friction. Sliding friction is due to the microscopic roughness of two surfaces, as shown in **Figure 5.** A force must be applied to move the rough areas of one surface past the rough areas of the other. The brake pads in a car use sliding friction against the wheels to slow the car. Bicycle brakes, shown in **Figure 6A,** work the same way.

Reading Check ***What is the difference between static friction and sliding friction?***

Figure 5
Microscopic roughness, even on surfaces that seem smooth, such as the tray and metal shelf, causes sliding friction. *What do you think a lubricant does?*

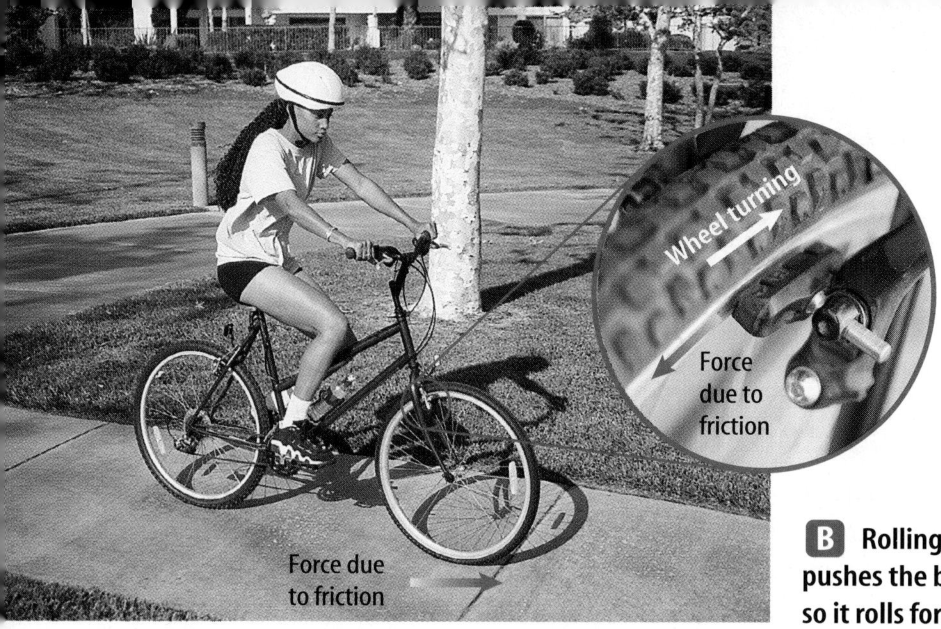

Figure 6
A bicycle uses sliding friction and rolling friction.

A Sliding friction is used to stop this bicycle tire. Friction between the brake pads and the wheel brings the wheel to a stop.

B Rolling friction with the ground pushes the bottom of the bicycle tire, so it rolls forward.

Rolling Friction Another type of friction, rolling friction, is needed to make a wheel or tire turn. Rolling friction occurs between the ground and the part of the tire touching the ground, as shown in **Figure 6B.** Rolling friction keeps the tire from slipping on the ground. If the bicycle tires are rolling forward, rolling friction exerts the force on the tires that pushes the bicycle forward.

It's usually easier to pull a load on a wagon or cart that has wheels rather than to drag the load along the ground. This is because rolling friction between the wheels and the ground is less than the sliding fiction between the load and the ground.

Section  Assessment

1. A car turns to the left at 20 km/h. Is a force acting on the car? Explain.
2. Explain why friction made it difficult to discover Newton's first law of motion.
3. If the net force on an object is zero, are the forces acting on it balanced or unbalanced? Explain.
4. What makes static friction increase?
5. **Think Critically** In the following situations, are the forces balanced or unbalanced? How can you tell?
   a. You push a box until it moves.
   b. You push a box at a constant rate.
   c. You stop pushing a box, and it stops.

Skill Builder Activities

6. **Comparing and Contrasting** Compare and contrast static friction, sliding friction, and rolling friction. **For more help, refer to the Science Skill Handbook.**
7. **Communicating** Most of the meteors that reach Earth's atmosphere burn up on the way down. Friction between the meteor and the atmosphere produces a great deal of heat. Research how the space shuttle is protected from friction when it reenters Earth's atmosphere. Report your findings in your Science Journal. **For more help, refer to the Science Skill Handbook.**

Newton's Second Law

As You Read

***What* You'll Learn**

- **Explain** Newton's second law of motion.
- **Explain** why the direction of force is important.

Vocabulary

Newton's second law of motion
weight

***Why* It's Important**

Newton's second law of motion explains how any object, from a swimmer to a satellite, moves when acted on by forces.

Force and Acceleration

When you go shopping in a grocery store and push a cart, you exert a force to make the cart move. If you want to slow down or change the direction of the cart, a force is required to do this, as well. Would it be easier for you to stop a full or empty grocery cart suddenly, as in **Figure 7?** When the motion of an object changes, the object is accelerating. Acceleration occurs any time an object speeds up, slows down, or changes its direction of motion. Newton's second law describes how forces cause an object's motion to change.

Newton's second law of motion connects force, acceleration, and mass. According to the second law of motion, an object acted upon by a force will accelerate in the direction of the force. The acceleration is given by the following equation

$$\text{acceleration} = \frac{\text{net force}}{\text{mass}}$$

$$a = \frac{F_{net}}{m}$$

In this equation, a is the acceleration, m is the mass, and F_{net} is the net force. If both sides of the above equation are multiplied by the mass, the equation can be written this way:

$$F_{net} = ma$$

Reading Check *What is Newton's second law?*

Figure 7
The force needed to change the motion of an object depends on its mass. *Which grocery cart would be easier to stop suddenly?*

Units of Force Force is measured in newtons, abbreviated N. Because the SI unit for mass is the kilogram (kg) and acceleration has units of meters per second squared (m/s^2), 1 N also is equal to 1 $kg{\cdot}m/s^2$. In other words, to calculate a force in newtons from the equation shown on the prior page, the mass must be given in kg and the acceleration in m/s^2.

Gravity

One force that you are familiar with is gravity. Whether you're coasting down a hill on a bike or a skateboard or jumping into a pool, gravity is at work pulling you downward. Gravity also is the force that causes Earth to orbit the Sun and the Moon to orbit Earth.

A black hole is a star that has collapsed so that all its mass is compressed into a small region that may be less than 10 km in diameter. Near a black hole, the force of gravity is much stronger than the force of gravity near Earth. Research some of the unusual phenomena that occur near black holes.

What is gravity? The force of gravity exists between any two objects that have mass. Gravity always is attractive and pulls objects toward each other. A gravitational attraction exists between you and every object in the universe that has mass. However, the force of gravity depends on the mass of the objects and the distance between them. The gravitational force becomes weaker the farther apart the objects are and also decreases as the masses of the objects involved decrease.

For example, there is a gravitational force between you and the Sun and you and Earth. The Sun is much more massive than Earth, but is so far away that the gravitational force between you and the Sun is too weak to notice. Only Earth has enough mass and is close enough to exert a noticeable gravitational force on you. The force of gravity between you and Earth is about 1,650 times greater than between you and the Sun.

Weight The force of gravity causes all objects near Earth's surface to fall with an acceleration of 9.8 m/s^2. By Newton's second law, the gravitational force on any object near Earth's surface is:

$$F = ma = m \times (9.8\ m/s^2)$$

This gravitational force also is called the weight of the object. Your **weight** on Earth is the gravitational force between you and Earth. Your weight would change if you were standing on a different planet than Earth, as shown in **Table 1**. Your weight on a different planet is the gravitational force between you and the planet.

Table 1 Weight of 60 kg Person on Various Planets

Place	Weight in Newtons If Your Mass Were 60 kg	Percent of Your Weight on Earth
Mars	221	38
Earth	587	100
Jupiter	1,387	236
Pluto	39	0.7

Figure 8
The girl is speeding up because she is being pushed in the same direction that she is moving.

Weight and Mass Weight and mass are different. Weight is a force, just like the push of your hand is a force, and is measured in newtons. When you stand on a bathroom scale, you are measuring the pull of Earth's gravity—a force. However, mass is the amount of matter in an object, and doesn't depend on location. A book with a mass of 1 kg has a mass of 1 kg on Earth or on Mars. However, the weight of the book would be different on Earth and Mars. The two planets would exert a different gravitational force on the book.

Figure 9
The boy is slowing down because the force exerted by his feet is in the opposite direction of his motion.

Using Newton's Second Law

How does Newton's second law determine how an object moves when acted upon by forces? The second law tells how to calculate the acceleration of an object if its mass and the forces acting on it are known. You may remember that the motion of an object can be described by its velocity. The velocity tells how fast an object is moving and in what direction. Acceleration tells how velocity changes. If the acceleration of an object is known, then the change in velocity can be determined.

Speeding Up Think about a soccer ball sitting on the ground. If you kick the ball, it starts moving. You exert a force on the ball, and the ball accelerates only while your foot is in contact with the ball. If you look back at all of the examples of objects speeding up, you'll notice that something is pushing or pulling the object in the direction it is moving, as in **Figure 8.** The direction of the push or pull is the direction of the force. It also is the direction of the acceleration.

Calculating Acceleration Newton's second law of motion can be used to calculate acceleration. For example, suppose you pull a 10-kg sled so that the net force on the sled is 5 N. The acceleration can be found as follows:

$$a = \frac{F_{net}}{m} = \frac{5\text{ N}}{10\text{ kg}} = 0.5\text{ m/s}^2$$

The sled keeps accelerating as long as you keep pulling on it. The acceleration does not depend on how fast the sled is moving. It depends only on the net force and the mass of the sled.

Slowing Down If you wanted to slow down an object, you would have to push or pull it against the direction it is moving. An example is given in **Figure 9.** Here the force is opposite to the velocity or the direction of motion.

Suppose you push a book so it slides across a tabletop. You exert a force on the book when your hand is in contact with it, and the book speeds up. Sliding friction also acts on the book as it starts to move. After the book is no longer in contact with your hand, friction acts in the opposite direction to the book's motion. This causes the book to slow down and come to a stop.

How does acceleration affect how you feel on a roller coaster? To find out more about acceleration and amusement park rides, see the **Amusement Park Rides Field Guide** at the back of the book.

Math Skills Activity

Calculating Force Using Newton's Second Law

Example Problem

A car with a mass of 1,500 kg has an acceleration of 3 m/s^2. Find the force acting on the car.

Solution

1. *This is what you know:* acceleration: $a = 3\text{ m/s}^2$; mass: $m = 1{,}500\text{ kg}$
2. *This what you need to find:* Force: F
3. *This is the equation you need to use:* $F = ma$
4. *Substitute the known values:* $F = (1{,}500\text{ kg}) \times (3\text{ m/s}^2) = 4{,}500\text{ N}$

Check your answer by dividing the force you calculate by the acceleration that was given. Do you calculate the same mass that was given?

Practice Problem

You throw a baseball with a mass of 0.15 kg so it has an acceleration of 40 m/s^2. Find the force you exerted on the baseball.

For more help, refer to the Math Skill Handbook.

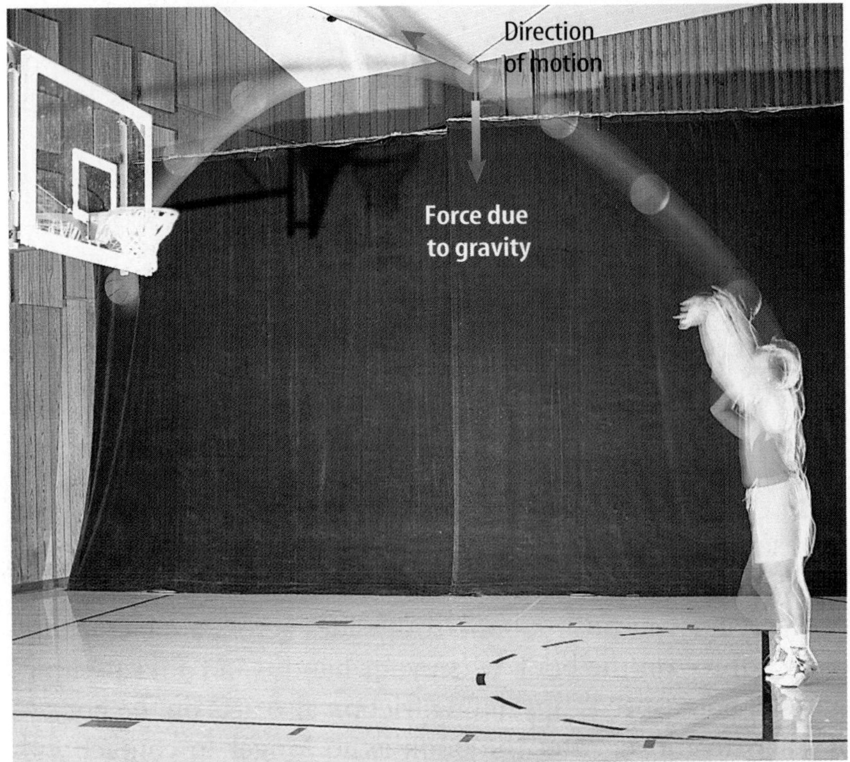

Figure 10
When the ball is thrown, it doesn't keep moving in a straight line. Gravity exerts a force downward that makes it move in a curved path.

Turning Sometimes forces and motion are not in a straight line. If a net force acts at an angle to the direction an object is moving, the object will follow a curved path. The object might be going slower, faster, or at the same speed after it turns.

For example, when you shoot a basketball, the ball doesn't continue to move in a straight line after it leaves your hand. Instead it starts to curve downward, as shown in **Figure 10.** The force of gravity pulls the ball downward. The ball's motion is a combination of its original motion and the downward motion due to gravity. This causes the ball to move in a curved path.

Circular Motion

A rider on a merry-go-round ride moves in a circle. This type of motion is called circular motion. If you are in circular motion, your direction of motion is constantly changing. This means you are constantly accelerating. According to Newton's second law of motion, if you are constantly accelerating, there must be a force acting on you the entire time.

Think about an object on the end of a string whirling in a circle. The force that keeps the object moving in a circle is exerted by the string. The string pulls on the object to keep it moving in a circle. The force exerted by the string is the centripetal force and always points toward the center of the circle. In circular motion the centripetal force is always perpendicular to the motion.

Satellite Motion Objects that orbit Earth are satellites of Earth. Satellites go around Earth in nearly circular orbits, with the centripetal force being gravity. If gravity is pulling satellites toward Earth, why doesn't a satellite fall to Earth like a baseball does? Actually, a satellite is falling to Earth just like a baseball.

Suppose Earth were perfectly smooth with no mountains or hills. Imagine you throw a baseball horizontally. Gravity pulls the baseball downward so it travels in a curved path. If the baseball is thrown faster, its path is less curved, and it travels farther before it hits the ground, as shown in **Figure 11.** If the baseball were traveling fast enough, as it fell, its curved path would follow the curve of Earth's surface. Then the baseball would never hit the ground. Instead, it would continue to fall around Earth.

Figure 11
The faster a ball is thrown, the farther it travels before gravity pulls it to Earth. If the ball is traveling fast enough, Earth's surface curves away from it as fast as it falls downward. Then the ball never hits the ground.

Satellites in orbit are being pulled toward Earth just as baseballs are. The difference is that satellites are moving so fast horizontally that Earth's surface curves downward at the same rate that the satellites are falling downward. The speed at which a object must move to go into orbit near Earth's surface is about 8 km/s, or about 29,000 km/h.

To place a satellite into orbit, a rocket carries the satellite to the desired height. Then the rocket fires again to give the satellite the horizontal speed it needs to stay in orbit.

Air Resistance

Whether you are walking, running, or biking, air is pushing against you. This push is air resistance. Air resistance is a form of friction that acts to slow down any object moving in the air. Air resistance gets larger as an object moves faster.

When an object falls it speeds up as gravity pulls it downward. At the same time, the force of air resistance pushing up on the object is increasing as the object moves faster. Finally, the upward air resistance force becomes large enough to equal the downward force of gravity.

When the air resistance force equals the weight, the net force on the object is zero. By Newton's second law, the object's acceleration then is zero, and its speed no longer increases. The constant speed a falling object reaches when air resistance balances the force of gravity is the terminal velocity.

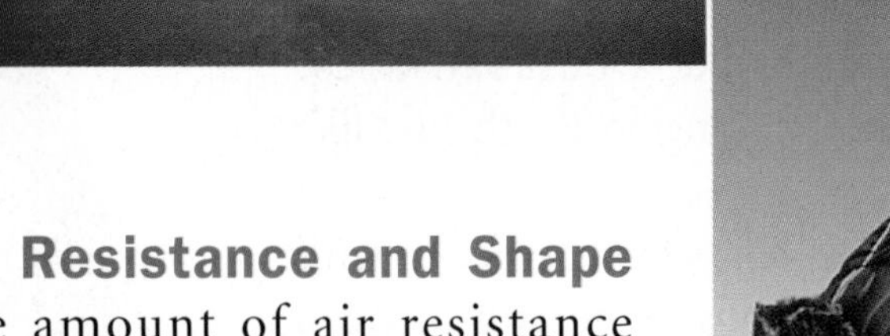

Figure 12
Sky divers can change their air resistance by changing the position of their arms and legs. **A** In a spread-eagle position, the air resistance of the sky diver is greater. **B** With the legs closed and the arms tucked back against the body, the sky diver's shape is narrower and the air resistance is less.

Air Resistance and Shape

The amount of air resistance depends on the object's shape, as well as its speed. Moving at the same speed, the air resistance on a pointed, narrow object is less than on a broad, flat object, such as a leaf or a piece of paper. A falling sky diver in a spread-eagle position, as shown in **Figure 12A,** might reach a terminal velocity of about 200 km/h. But with the arms tucked backward and the legs closed, air resistance is less, and the skydiver might reach a terminal velocity of over 300 km/h. When the skydiver opens the parachute, the force of air resistance on an open parachute is so large that the skydiver's terminal velocity quickly is reduced to about 20 km/h.

Section  Assessment

1. A human cannonball with a mass of 80 kg is fired out of a cannon with a force of 2,400 N. Find the acceleration.
2. A bike rider traveling at 20 km/h on a flat roadway stops pedaling. Make a diagram showing the forces acting on the coasting bike and rider. Using Newton's second law, explain how the bike's motion will change.
3. Suppose you were in a spaceship traveling away from Earth. How would your weight change as you moved farther from Earth?
4. What happens when the air resistance force equals the weight of a falling object?
5. **Think Critically** Explain how you can determine the direction of a force by watching an object's change in motion.

Skill Builder Activities

6. **Drawing Conclusions** Three students are pushing on a box. Two students are pushing on the left side, and one is pushing on the right side. One student on the left pushes with a force of 10 N and the other pushes with a force of 15 N. The student of the right pushes with a force of 20 N. In what direction will the box move? Explain your answer. **For more help, refer to the Science Skill Handbook.**
7. **Solving One-Step Equations** A 1-kg ball is moving at 2 m/s. A force stops the ball in 4 s. Find the acceleration of the ball by dividing the change in speed on the ball by the time needed to stop. Then find the force. **For more help, refer to the Math Skill Handbook.**

Newton's Third Law

Action and Reaction

Newton's first two laws of motion explain how the motion of a single object changes. If the forces acting on the object are balanced, the object will remain at rest or stay in motion with constant velocity. If the forces are unbalanced, the object will accelerate in the direction of the net force. Newton's second law tells how to calculate the acceleration, or change in motion, of an object if the net force acting on it is known.

Newton's third law describes something else that happens when one object exerts a force on another object. Suppose you push on a wall. It may surprise you to learn that if you push on a wall, the wall also pushes on you. According to **Newton's third law of motion,** forces always act in equal but opposite pairs. Another way of saying this is for every action, there is an equal but opposite reaction. This means that when you push on a wall, the wall pushes back on you with a force equal in strength to the force you exerted. When one object exerts a force on another object, the second object exerts the same size force on the first object, as shown in **Figure 13.**

As You Read

What You'll Learn

- **Identify** the relationship between the forces that objects exert on each other.

Vocabulary

Newton's third law of motion

Why It's Important

Newton's third law can help you predict how objects will affect one another.

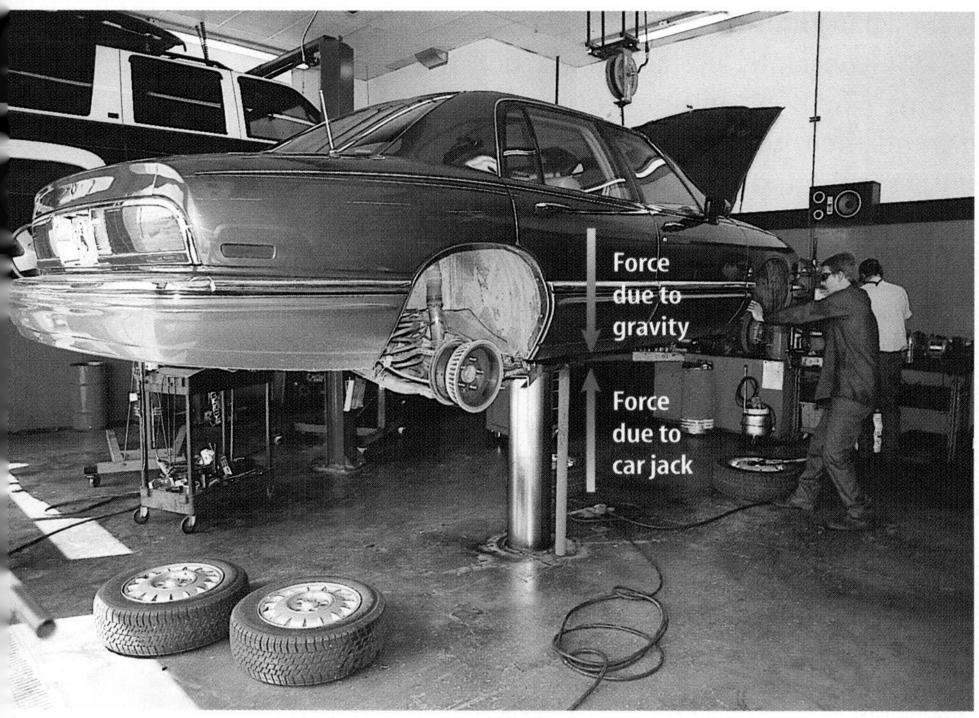

Figure 13
The car jack is pushing up on the car with the same amount of force with which the car is pushing down on the jack.

Figure 14
In this collision, the first car exerts a force on the second. The second exerts the same force in the opposite direction on the first car. *Which car do you think accelerates more?*

Research Visit the Glencoe Science Web site at **science.glencoe.com** for more information about how birds and other animals fly. Communicate to your class what you learn.

Action and Reaction Forces Don't Cancel The forces exerted by two objects on each other are often called an action-reaction force pair. Either force can be considered the action force or the reaction force. You might think that because action-reaction forces are equal and opposite that they cancel. However, action and reaction force pairs don't cancel because they act on different objects. Forces can cancel only if they act on the same object.

For example, imagine you're driving a bumper car and are about to ram a friend in another car, as shown in **Figure 14.** When the two cars collide, your car pushes on the other car. By Newton's third law, that car pushes on your car with the same force, but in the opposite direction. This force causes you to slow down. One force of the action-reaction force pair is exerted on your friend's car, and the other force of the force pair is exerted on your car. Another example of an action-reaction pair is shown in **Figure 15.**

You constantly use action-reaction force pairs as you move about. When you jump, you push down on the ground. The ground then pushes up on you. It is this upward force that pushes you into the air. **Figure 16** shows some examples of how Newton's laws of motion are demonstrated in sporting events.

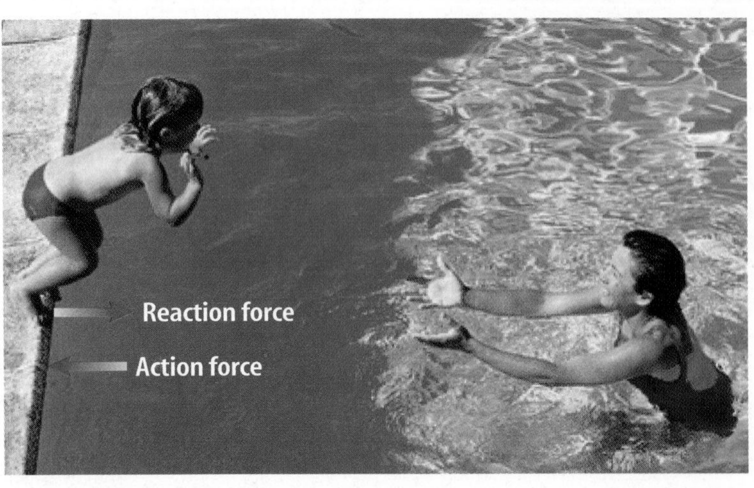

Figure 15
When the child pushes against the wall, the wall pushes against the child.

Birds and other flying creatures also use Newton's third law. When a bird flies, its wings push in a downward and a backward direction. This pushes air downward and backward. By Newton's third law, the air pushes back on the bird in the opposite directions—upward and forward. This force keeps a bird in the air and propels it forward.

NATIONAL GEOGRAPHIC VISUALIZING NEWTON'S LAWS IN SPORTS

Figure 16

Although it is not obvious, Newton's laws of motion are demonstrated in sports activities all the time. According to the first law, if an object is in motion, it moves in a straight line with constant speed unless a net force acts on it. If an object is at rest, it stays at rest unless a net force acts on it. The second law states that a net force acting on an object causes the object to accelerate in the direction of the force. The third law can be understood this way—for every action force, there is an equal and opposite reaction force.

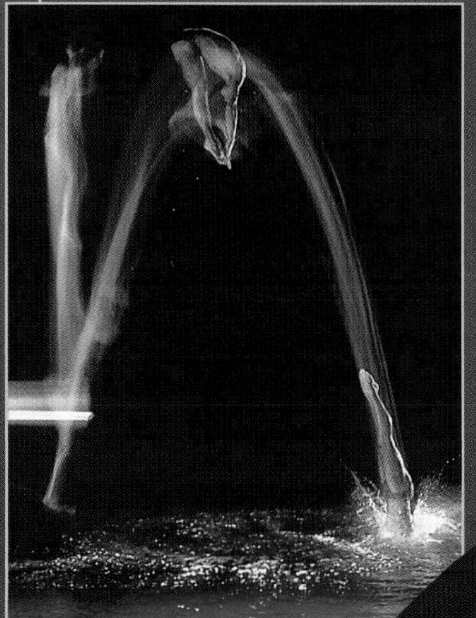

▲ NEWTON'S FIRST LAW According to Newton's first law, the diver does not move in a straight line with constant speed because of the force of gravity.

◀ NEWTON'S SECOND LAW As Tiger Woods hits a golf ball, he applies a force that will drive the ball in the direction of that force—an example of Newton's second law.

▶ NEWTON'S THIRD LAW Newton's third law applies even when objects do not move. Here a gymnast pushes downward on the bars. The bars push back on the gymnast with an equal force.

Figure 17
The force of the ground on your foot is equal and opposite to the force of your foot on the ground. If you push back harder, the ground pushes forward harder.

How do astronauts live under conditions of weightlessness? To find out more about the effects of weightlessness, see the **Living in Space Field Guide** at the end of the book.

Large and Small Objects Sometimes it's easy not to notice an action-reaction pair is because one of the objects is often much more massive and appears to remain motionless when a force acts on it. It has so much inertia, or tendency to remain at rest, that it hardly accelerates. Walking is a good example. When you walk forward, you push backward on the ground. Your shoe pushes Earth backward, and Earth pushes your shoe forward, as shown in **Figure 16.** Earth has so much mass compared to you that it does not move noticeably when you push it. If you step on something that has less mass than you do, like a skateboard, you can see it being pushed back.

A Rocket Launch The launching of a space shuttle is a spectacular example of Newton's third law. Three rocket engines supply the force, called thrust, that lifts the rocket. When the rocket fuel is ignited, a hot gas is produced. As the gas molecules collide with the inside engine walls, the walls exert a force that pushes them out of the bottom of the engine, as shown in **Figure 18.** This downward push is the action force. The reaction force is the upward push on the rocket engine by the gas molecules. This is the thrust that propels the rocket upward.

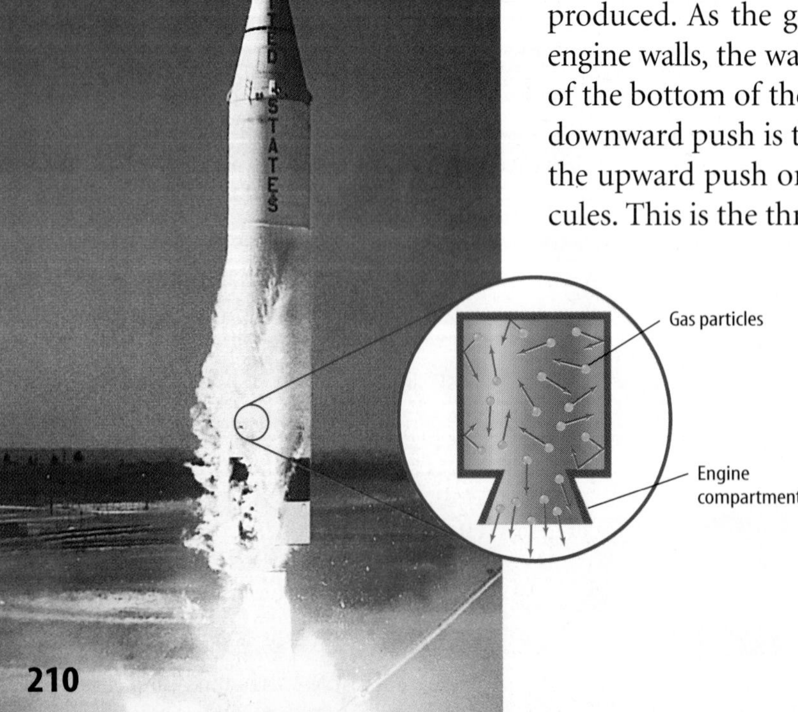

Figure 18
Newton's third law enables a rocket to fly. The rocket pushes the gas molecules downward, and the gas molecules push the rocket upward.

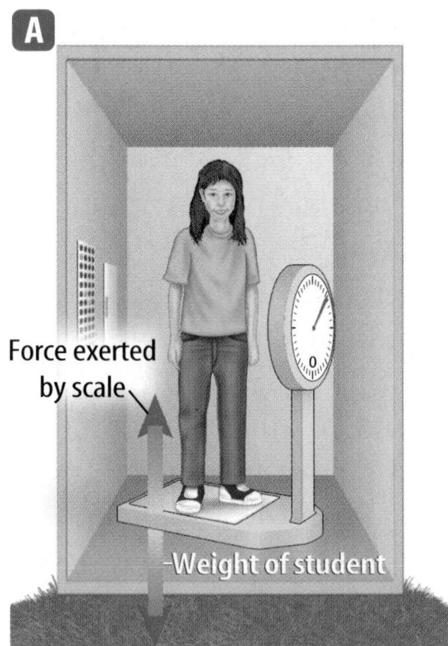

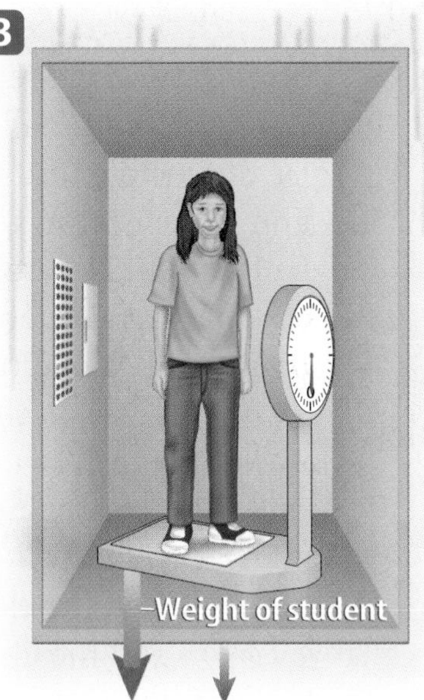

Figure 19
Your weight measured by a scale changes when you are falling. A When you stand on a scale on Earth, the reading on the scale is your weight. B If you were to stand on a scale in a falling elevator, the scale would read zero.

Weightlessness

You may have seen pictures of astronauts floating inside a space shuttle as it orbits Earth. The astronauts are said to be weightless, as if Earth's gravity were no longer pulling on them. Yet the force of gravity on the shuttle is still about 90 percent as large as at Earth's surface. Newton's laws of motion can explain why the astronauts float as if there were no forces acting on them.

Measuring Weight Think about how you measure your weight. When you stand on a scale, your weight pushes down on the scale and causes the springs in the scale to compress. The scale pointer moves from zero and points to your weight. At the same time, by Newton's third law the scale pushes up on you with a force equal to your weight, as shown in **Figure 19A.** This force balances the downward pull of gravity on you.

Free Fall and Weightlessness Now suppose you were standing on a scale in an elevator that is falling, as shown in **Figure 19B.** A falling object is in free fall when the only force acting on the object is gravity. Inside the free-falling elevator, you and the scale are both in free fall. Because the only force acting on you is gravity, the scale no longer is pushing up on you. According to Newton's third law, you no longer push down on the scale. So the scale pointer stays at zero and you seem to be weightless. **Weightlessness** is the condition that occurs in free fall when the weight of an object seems to be zero.

However, you are not really weightless in free fall because Earth is still pulling down on you. With nothing to push up on you, such as your chair, you would have no sensation of weight.

Mini LAB

Measuring Force Pairs

Procedure
1. Work in pairs. Each person needs a **spring scale.**
2. Hook the two scales together. Each person should pull back on a scale. Record the two readings. Pull harder and record the two readings.
3. Continue to pull on both scales, but let the scales move toward one person. Do the readings change?
4. Try to pull in such a way that the two scales have different readings.

Analysis
1. What can you conclude about the pair of forces in each situation?
2. Explain how this experiment demonstrates Newton's third law.

Weightlessness in Orbit To understand how objects move in the orbiting space shuttle, imagine you were holding a ball in the free-falling elevator. If you let the ball go, the position of the ball relative to you and the elevator wouldn't change, because you, the ball, and the elevator are moving at the same speed.

However, suppose you give the ball a gentle push downward. While you are pushing the ball, this downward force adds to the downward force of gravity. According to Newton's second law, the acceleration of the ball increases. So while you are pushing, the acceleration of the ball is greater than the acceleration of both you and the elevator. This causes the ball to speed up relative to you and the elevator. After it speeds up, it continues moving faster than you and the elevator, and it drifts downward until it hits the elevator floor.

Figure 20
These oranges seem to be floating because they are falling around Earth at the same speed as the space shuttle and the astronauts. As a result, they don't seem to be moving relative to the astronauts in the cabin.

When the space shuttle orbits Earth, the shuttle and all the objects in it are in free fall. They are falling in a curved path around Earth, instead of falling straight downward. As a result, objects in the shuttle appear to be weightless, as shown in **Figure 20.** A small push causes an object to drift away, just as a small downward push on the ball in the free-falling elevator caused it to drift to the floor.

Section  Assessment

1. You push a skateboard with a force of 6 N. If your mass is 60 kg, what is the force that the skateboard exerts on you?
2. You jump from a boat to a pier. As you move forward the boat moves backward. Explain.
3. What are the action and reaction forces when a hammer hits a nail?
4. Suppose you and a child that has half your mass are on skates. If the child gives you a push, who will have the greater acceleration? By how much?
5. **Thinking Critically** Suppose you are walking down the aisle of an airliner in flight. Use Newton's third law to describe the effect of your walk on the motion of the airliner.

Skill Builder Activities

6. **Solving One-Step Equations** A person standing on a canoe throws a cement block over the side. The action force on the cement block is 60 N. The reaction force is on the person and canoe. Their total mass is 100 kg. What is their acceleration? **For more help, refer to the** Math Skill Handbook.
7. **Communicating** Some people have trouble understanding Newton's third law. They reason, "If every action has an equal and opposite reaction, nothing ever will move." Explain why objects still can move. (Consider whether the forces act on the same or different objects.) **For more help, refer to the** Science Skill Handbook.

Activity

Balloon Races

A balloon and a rocket lifting off the launch pad have something in common. Both use Newton's third law. In this experiment, you will compare different balloon rocket designs. The balloon rocket is powered by escaping air, and its motion is determined by Newton's first, second, and third laws.

What You'll Investigate

How do Newton's laws explain the motion of different balloon rockets?

Materials

balloons of different sizes and shapes
drinking straws
string
tape
meterstick
stopwatch*
**clock*

**Alternate materials*

Safety Precautions

Goals

- **Measure** the speed of a balloon rocket.
- **Describe** how Newton's laws explain a rocket's motion.

Procedure

1. Run a string across the classroom to make a rocket path. Leave one end loose so you can place the rockets on the string easily.
2. Make a balloon rocket according to the diagram. Don't tie the balloon. Let it run down the track. Measure the distance it travels and the time it takes.
3. Repeat step 2 with different balloons.

Conclude and Apply

1. **Compare and contrast** the distances traveled. Which rocket went the greatest distance?
2. **Calculate** the average speed for each rocket. Compare and contrast them. Which rocket has the greatest average speed?
3. **Infer** which aspects of these rockets made them travel far or fast.
4. **Draw** a diagram showing all the forces acting on a balloon rocket.
5. Use Newton's laws of motion to explain the motion of a balloon rocket from launch until it comes to a stop.

Communicating Your Data

Discuss with classmates which balloon rocket traveled the farthest. Why? **For more help, refer to the** Science Skill Handbook.

Activity

Design Your Own Experiment

Modeling Motion in Two Directions

When you move a computer mouse across a mouse pad, how does the rolling ball tell the computer cursor to move in the direction that you push the mouse? Inside the housing for the mouse's ball are two or more rollers that the ball rubs against as you move the mouse. They measure up-and-down and back-and-forth motions. What happens to the rollers when you move diagonally and at different angles?

Recognize the Problem

Can you move a golf ball from one point to another using forces in only two directions?

Form a Hypothesis

How can you combine forces to move in a straight line, along a diagonal, or around corners? Place a golf ball on something that will slide, such as a plastic lid. The plastic lid is called a skid. Lay out a course to follow on the floor. Write a plan for moving your golf ball along the path without having the golf ball roll away.

Possible Materials

masking tape
stopwatch*
** watch or clock with a second hand*
meterstick*
**metric tape measure*
spring scales marked in newtons (2)
plastic lid
golf ball*
**tennis ball*
**Alternate materials*

Goals

- **Move** the skid across the ground using two forces.
- **Measure** how fast the skid can be moved.
- **Determine** how smoothly the direction can be changed.

Safety Precautions

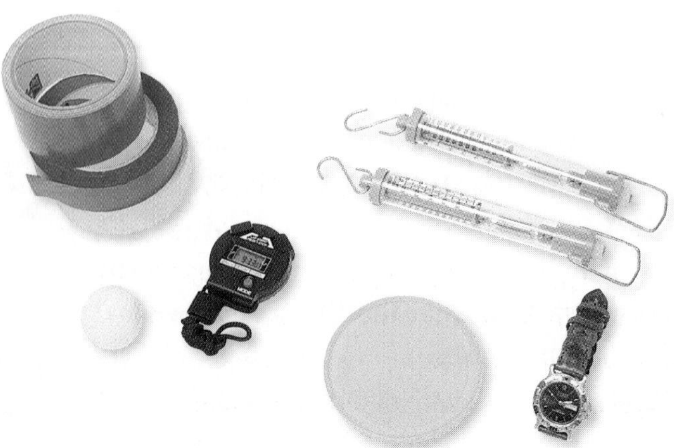

Test Your Hypothesis

Plan

1. Lay out a course that involves two directions, such as always moving forward or left.
2. Attach two spring scales to the skid. One always will pull straight forward. One always will pull to one side. You cannot turn the skid. If one scale is pulling toward the door of your classroom, it always must pull in that direction. (It can pull with zero force if needed, but it can't push.)
3. How will you handle movements along diagonals and turns?
4. How will you measure speed?
5. **Experiment** with your skid. How hard do you have to pull to counteract sliding friction at a given speed? How fast can you accelerate? Can you stop suddenly without spilling the golf ball, or do you need to slow down?
6. **Write** a plan for moving your golf ball along the course by pulling only forward or to one side. Be sure you understand your plan and have considered all the details.

Do

1. Make sure your teacher approves your plan before you start.
2. Move your golf ball along the path.
3. Modify your plan, if needed.
4. **Organize** your data so they can be used to run your course and write them in your Science Journal.
5. **Test** your results with a new route.

Analyze Your Data

1. What was the difference between the two routes? How did this affect the forces you needed to use on the golf ball?
2. How did you separate and control variables in this experiment?
3. Was your hypothesis supported? Explain.

Draw Conclusions

1. What happens when you combine two forces at right angles?
2. If you could pull on all four sides (front, back, left, right) of your skid, could you move anywhere along the floor? Make a hypothesis to explain your answer.

Compare your conclusions with those of other students in your class. **For more help, refer to the** Science Skill Handbook.

Air Bag Safety

After complaints and injuries, air bags in cars are helping all passengers

The car in front of yours stops suddenly. Your mom slams on the brakes, but not fast enough. You hear the crunch of car against car and feel your seat belt grab you. You look up at your mom in the front seat. She's covered with, not blood, thank goodness, but with a big white cloth. You are both okay. Your seat belts and air bags worked perfectly.

Popcorn in the Dash

Air bags have saved more than a thousand lives since 1992. They are like having a giant popcorn kernel in the dashboard that pops and becomes many times its original size. But unlike popcorn, an air bag is triggered by impact, not heat. When the air bag sensor picks up the vibrations of a crash, a chemical reaction is started. The reaction produces a gas that expands in a split second, inflating a balloonlike bag to cushion the driver and possibly the front-seat passenger. The bag deflates just as quickly so it doesn't trap people in the car.

Newton and the Air Bag

When you're traveling in a car, you move with it at whatever speed it is going. According to Newton's first law, you are the object in motion, and you will continue in motion unless acted upon by a force, such as a car crash.

Unfortunately, a crash stops the car, but it doesn't stop you, at least, not right away. You continue moving forward if your car doesn't have air bags or if you haven't buckled your seat belt. You stop when you strike the inside of the car. You hit the dashboard or steering wheel while traveling at the speed of the car. When an air bag inflates, it becomes the force acting on the moving object—you—and it stops you more gently.

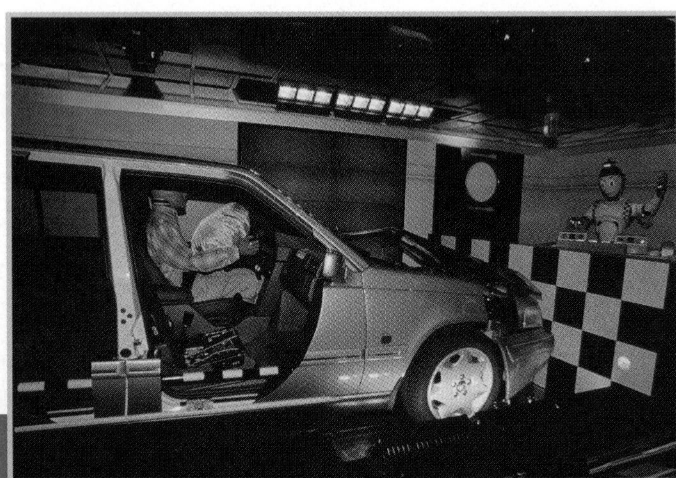

A test measures the speed at which an air bag deploys.

Car manufacturers perform safety tests using dummies and air bags. The dummy is wearing a seat belt to simulate a human driver.

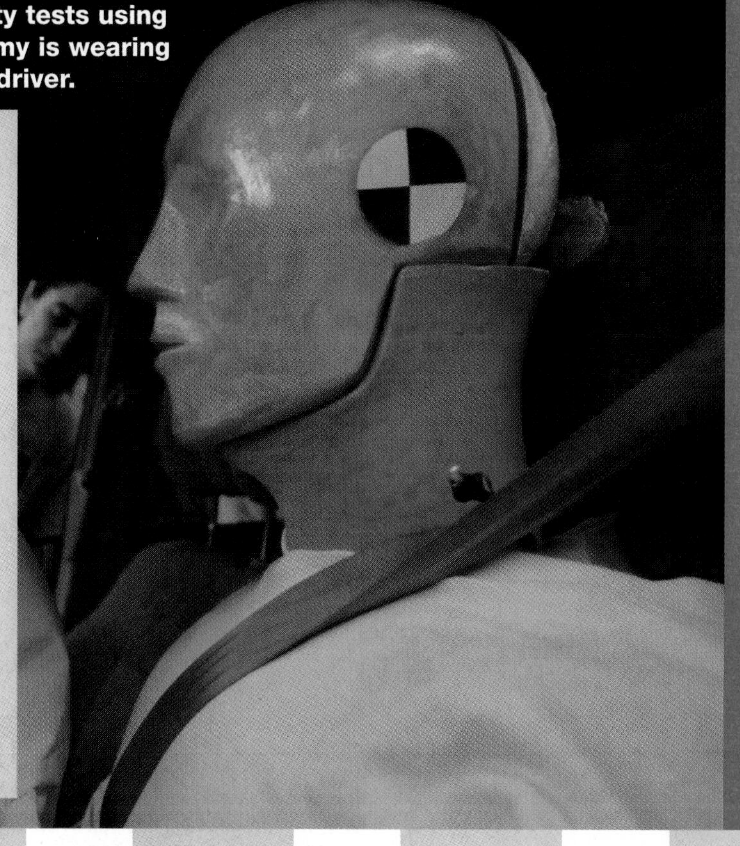

Unexpected Impact

"Our biggest issue was that air bags were not only helpful but dangerous—small children were being harmed by air bags," notes Betsy Ancker-Johnson, a spokesperson for an automobile-maker. She was referring to the fact that air bags pop out with so much force that they have sometimes hurt or killed children and small adults. For this reason, children under the age of 12 should ride in the back seat only, with seat belts buckled. Small adults may have their air bags turned off. Car makers are developing "smart" air bags that will expand just enough to protect a passenger no matter what the size or weight.

CONNECTIONS Measure Draw a steering wheel on a paper plate. Ask classmates to hold it 26 cm in front of them. That's the length drivers should have between the chest and the wheel to make air bags safe. Use a tape measure to check. Inform adult drivers in your family about this safety distance.

SCIENCE *Online*
For more information, visit science.glencoe.com

Chapter 7 Study Guide

Reviewing Main Ideas

Section 1 Newton's First Law

1. A force is a push or a pull.
2. The net force is the combination of all the forces acting on an object.
3. Newton's first law states that objects in motion tend to stay in motion and objects at rest tend to stay at rest unless acted upon by a net force. *Why don't objects in motion on Earth, like a soccer ball, stay in motion forever?*

4. Friction is a force that resists motion between surfaces that are touching each other.

Section 2 Newton's Second Law

1. Newton's second law states that an object acted upon by a net force will accelerate in the direction of this force.
2. The acceleration due to a net force is given by the equation $a = F_{net}/m$. *If a baseball bat hits a bowling ball, why doesn't the bowling ball accelerate as quickly as a baseball that is hit just as hard?*

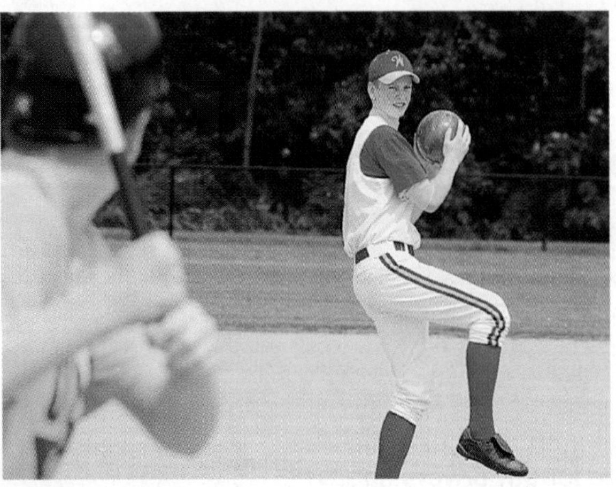

3. The force of gravity between two objects depends on their masses and the distance between them.
4. In circular motion, a force pointing toward the center of the circle acts on an object.

Section 3 Newton's Third Law

1. According to Newton's third law, the forces two objects exert on each other are always equal but in opposite directions. *What are the action and reaction forces acting on the skaters below?*

2. Action and reaction forces don't cancel because they act on different objects.
3. Action and reaction forces are involved in actions such as walking and jumping. Objects in orbit appear to be weightless because they are in free fall around Earth.

After You Read

FOLDABLES Reading & Study Skills

Use the information in your Foldable to help you think of concrete examples for each law of motion. Write them under the tabs.

Chapter 7 Study Guide

Visualizing Main Ideas

Fill in the following concept map on Newtons's laws of motion.

Newton's Laws of Motion

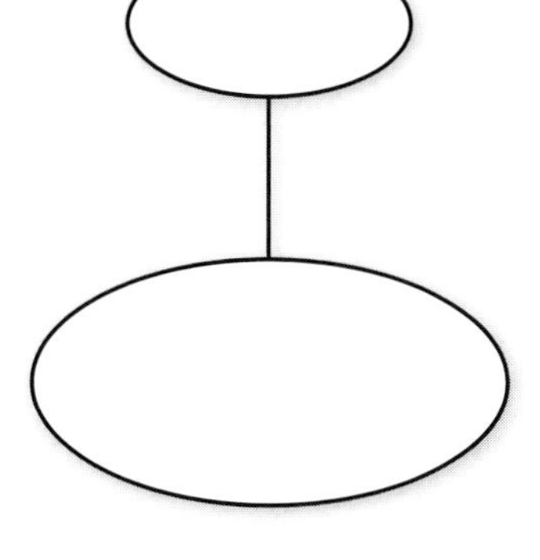

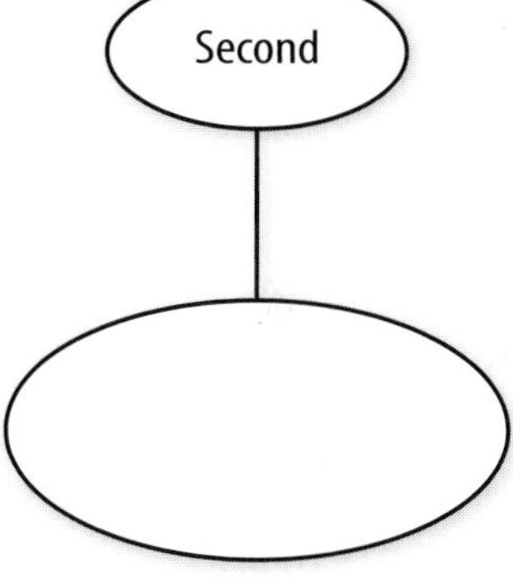

An object at rest will remain at rest until a force is applied

Vocabulary Review

Vocabulary Words

a. balanced forces
b. force
c. friction
d. net force
e. Newton's first law of motion
f. Newton's second law of motion
g. Newton's third law of motion
h. unbalanced forces
i. weight
j. weightlessness

Study Tip

When you read a chapter, make a list of things you find confusing or do not completely understand. Then ask your teacher to explain them.

Using Vocabulary

Explain the differences between the terms in the following sets.

1. force, inertia, weight
2. Newton's first law of motion, Newton's third law of motion
3. friction, force
4. net force, balanced forces
5. weight, weightlessness
6. balanced forces, unbalanced forces
7. friction, weight
8. Newton's first law of motion, Newton's second law of motion
9. friction, unbalanced force
10. net force, Newton's third law of motion

Chapter 7 Assessment

Checking Concepts

Choose the word or phrase that best answers the question.

1. Which of the following changes when an unbalanced force acts on an object?
   A) mass **C)** inertia
   B) motion **D)** weight
2. Which of the following is the force that slows a book sliding on a table?
   A) gravity **C)** sliding friction
   B) static friction **D)** inertia
3. What combination of units is equivalent to the newton?
   A) m/s^2 **C)** $kg \cdot m/s^2$
   B) $kg \cdot m/s$ **D)** kg/m
4. What is a push or pull a definition of?
   A) force **C)** acceleration
   B) momentum **D)** inertia
5. What is the type of friction that is important to walking?
   A) static friction **C)** rolling friction
   B) sliding friction **D)** air resistance
6. An object is accelerated by a net force in which direction?
   A) at an angle to the force
   B) in the direction of the force
   C) in the direction opposite to the force
   D) Any of these is possible.
7. If you exert a net force of 8 N on a 2-kg object, what will its acceleration be?
   A) $4 m/s^2$ **C)** $12 m/s^2$
   B) $6 m/s^2$ **D)** $16 m/s^2$
8. You are riding on a bike. In which of the following situations are the forces acting on the bike balanced?
   A) You pedal to speed up.
   B) You turn at constant speed.
   C) You coast to slow down.
   D) You pedal at constant speed.
9. Which of the following has no direction?
   A) force **C)** weight
   B) acceleration **D)** mass
10. You push against a wall with a force of 5 N. What is the force the wall exerts on your hands?
   A) 0 N **C)** 5 N
   B) 2.5 N **D)** 10 N

Thinking Critically

11. A baseball is pitched east at a speed of 40 km/h. The batter hits it west at a speed of 40 km/h. Did the ball accelerate? Explain.
12. Frequently, the pair of forces acting between two objects are not noticed because one of the objects is Earth. Explain why the force acting on Earth isn't noticed.
13. A car is parked on a hill. The driver starts the car, accelerates until the car is driving at constant speed, drives at constant speed, and then brakes to put the brake pads in contact with the spinning wheels. Explain how static friction, sliding friction, rolling friction, and air resistance are acting on the car.
14. You hit a hockey puck and it slides across the ice at nearly a constant speed. Is a force keeping it in motion? Explain.
15. Newton's third law describes the forces between two colliding objects. Use this connection to explain the forces acting when you kick a soccer ball.

Developing Skills

16. **Recognizing Cause and Effect** Use Newton's third law to explain how a rocket accelerates upon takeoff.

17. Prediciting Two balls of the same size and shape are dropped from a helicopter. One ball has twice the mass of the other ball. On which ball will the force of air resistance be greater when terminal velocity is reached?

18. Interpreting Scientific Illustrations Is the force on the box balanced? Explain.

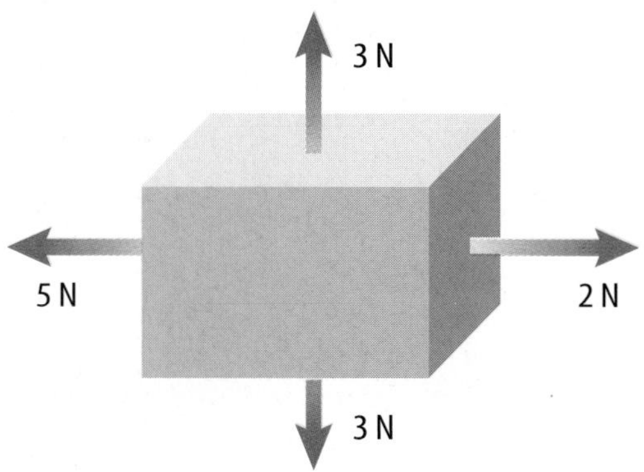

19. Solving One-Step Equations A 0.4-kg object accelerates at 2 m/s^2. Find the force.

Performance Assessment

20. Oral Presentation Research one of Newton's laws of motion and compose an oral presentation. Provide examples of the law. You might want to use a visual aid.

21. Writing in Science Create an experiment that deals with Newton's laws of motion. Document it using the following subject heads: *Title of Experiment, Partners' Names, Hypothesis, Materials, Procedures, Data, Results,* and *Conclusion.*

Technology

Go to the Glencoe Science Web site at **science.glencoe.com** or use the **Glencoe Science CD-ROM** for additional chapter assessment.

Test Practice

The following diagram shows an experiment in which data were collected about falling objects.

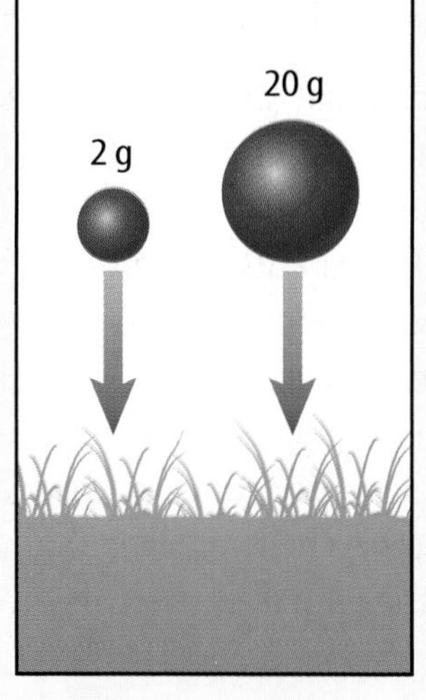

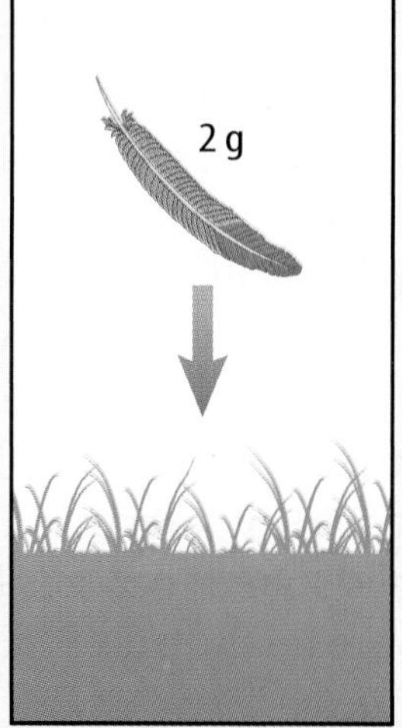

Study the diagram above and then answer the following questions about the experiment.

1. Which of these is the most likely hypothesis for the experiment depicted in the box on the left above?
   - **A)** The more mass an object has, the faster it will travel.
   - **B)** The less mass an object has, the faster it will travel.
   - **C)** Objects with less mass travel faster than objects with more mass.
   - **D)** Objects of different masses can still travel at the same speed.

2. The feather is traveling at a different speed than the balls because the feather _____.
   - **F)** has more gravity acting upon it
   - **G)** has less gravity acting upon it
   - **H)** has more friction acting upon it
   - **J)** has less friction acting upon it

Standardized Test Practice

Reading Comprehension

Read the passage. Then read each question that follows the passage. Decide which is the best answer to each question.

Test-Taking Tip Make a list of the important details in the passage.

Bouncing Back

Have you ever noticed that the balls you use for different sports bounce differently? If you played baseball with a tennis ball, the ball would probably fly into the outfield without much effort when you hit it with your bat. In contrast, if you used a baseball in a tennis match, the ball would not bounce high enough for your opponent to hit it very well. The difference in the way balls bounce depends upon the materials that make up the balls and the way they are constructed.

A ball drops to the floor as a result of gravity. As the ball drops, it gathers speed. When the ball hits the floor, the energy that it has gained goes into deforming the ball, changing it from its round shape. As the ball changes shape, the molecules within it stretch farther apart in some places and squeeze closer together in other places. The strength of the bonds between molecules determines how much they stretch apart and squeeze together. This depends on the chemical composition of the materials in the ball.

Most balls are made of rubber. Rubber is <u>elastic</u>, which means that it returns to its original shape after it's been deformed. Rubber is made of molecules called polymers that are long chains. Normally these chains are coiled up, but when the rubber is stretched, the chains straighten out. Then when the stretching force is removed, the chains coil up again. How high a ball bounces depends on the type of polymer molecules the rubber is made of. Bouncing balls sometimes feel warm because some of the ball's kinetic energy is converted into thermal energy.

A baseball is struck by a bat and flattens. The ball bounces off the bat as it becomes round again.

1. According to information in the passage, it is probably accurate to conclude that _____.

A) all rubber balls bounce the same, no matter what they are made of
B) the way rubber balls bounce depends upon the polymers that they are made of
C) baseballs are better for playing tennis than tennis balls are for playing baseball
D) the higher a ball bounces, the more thermal energy is produced

2. In the context of this passage, the word <u>elastic</u> means _____.

F) able to retain its shape
G) inflexible
H) tightly linked
J) warm

Standardized Test Practice

Reasoning and Skills

Read each question and choose the best answer.

1. Latifah wanted to figure out which race car had the most kinetic energy during a competition. She researched the different race cars to find out their masses. Her experiment could be improved by _____.
   A) writing down a list of observations during the competition
   B) finding out the velocity of each race car during the competition
   C) weighing the cars after the competition
   D) researching motorcycles

Test-Taking Tip Consider the factors that affect an object's kinetic energy.

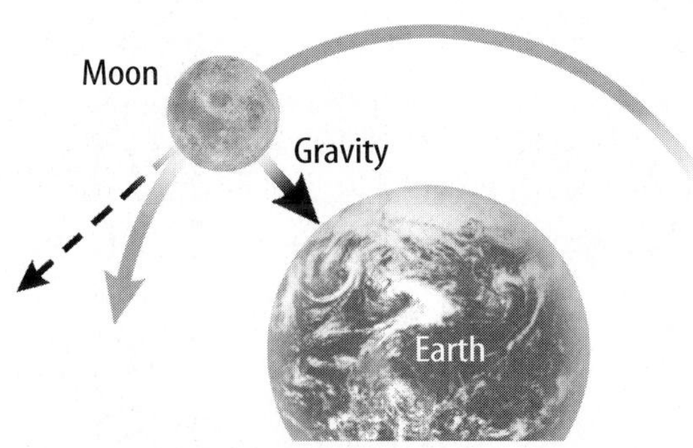

2. Which kind of scientist would most likely use this picture?
   F) biologist
   G) physicist
   H) chemist
   J) zoologist

Test-Taking Tip Review the type of information presented by the picture.

Training Record

End of Month	Maximum Speed (km/h)
1	7.0
2	7.5
3	8.0
4	?

3. These data were collected while an athlete trained for a marathon. If everything remains the same, what will be the maximum speed of the athlete at the end of the fourth month?
   A) 6.5 km/h
   B) 8.0 km/h
   C) 9.0 km/h
   D) 8.5 km/h

Test-Taking Tip Carefully consider the information in both the chart and the question in order to identify the trend.

Consider this question carefully before writing your answer on a separate sheet of paper.

4. As an object's mass increases while its volume stays the same, its density increases. Explain why this statement is true. Use the formula for calculating density to demonstrate how this is true.

Test-Taking Tip Recall the formula for calculating the density of an object.

UNIT 4 Energy

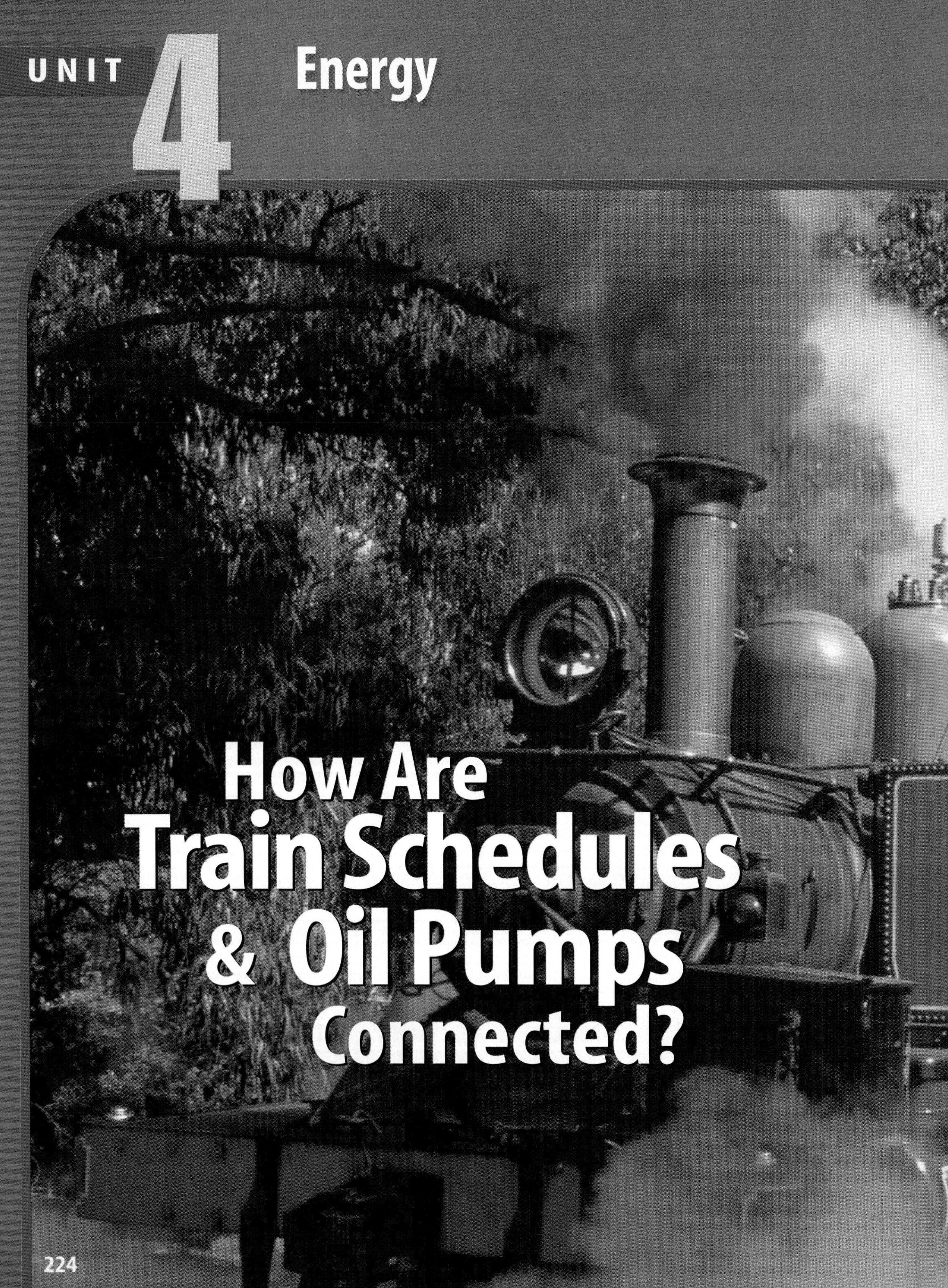

How Are Train Schedules & Oil Pumps Connected?

In the 1800s, trains had to make frequent stops so that their moving parts could be lubricated. Without lubrication, the parts would have worn out due to friction. When the train stopped, a worker had to get out and oil the parts by hand. The process was very time-consuming and made it hard for trains to stay on schedule. Around 1870, an engineer named Elijah McCoy developed the first automatic lubricating device, which oiled the engine while the train was running. (A later version of his automatic lubricator is seen at lower right.) Since then, many kinds of automatic lubricating devices have been developed. Today, automobiles have oil pumps that automatically circulate oil to the moving parts of the engine. When you go for a ride in a car, you can thank Elijah McCoy that you don't have to stop every few miles to oil the engine by hand!

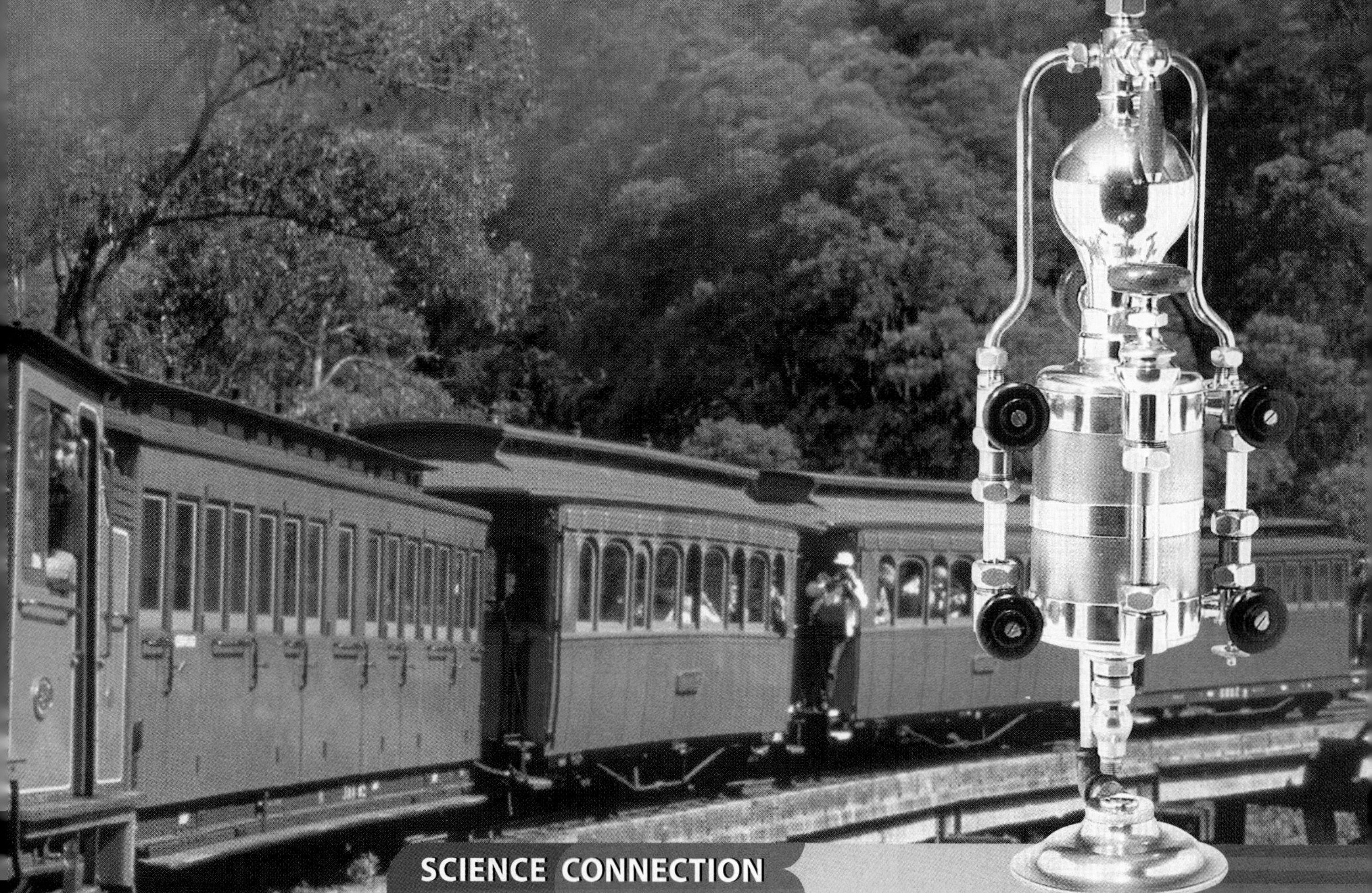

SCIENCE CONNECTION

FRICTION AND LUBRICANTS A lubricant is a substance that reduces friction between surfaces that touch one another. Some of the world's first lubricants were animal and plant products such as lard and vegetable oils. Conduct research to identify a variety of modern-day lubricants. Select one lubricant you learned about and create a poster that shows its source, how it is made or processed, its special properties, and how it is used to reduce friction.

CHAPTER 8

Energy

Volcanoes, earthquakes, lightning, and hurricanes produce some of the most powerful forces in nature. Every one of these phenomena contains a tremendous amount of energy. The river of lava shown in this picture flowing from Mount Etna in Italy has heat energy, light energy, and energy of motion. In this chapter, you will learn about different forms and sources of energy. You also will learn how energy can be transformed from one form into another, and how some forms of energy can be used.

What do you think?

Science Journal Look at the picture below with a classmate. Discuss what is happening. Here's a hint: *Concentrating energy is the key to what is happening here.* Write your answer or best guess in your Science Journal.

A marble and a piece of wood are on a countertop. If nothing disturbs them, they will remain there. However, if you tilt the wood and roll the marble down the slope, the marble acquires a new property—the ability to do something.

Analyze a marble launch 

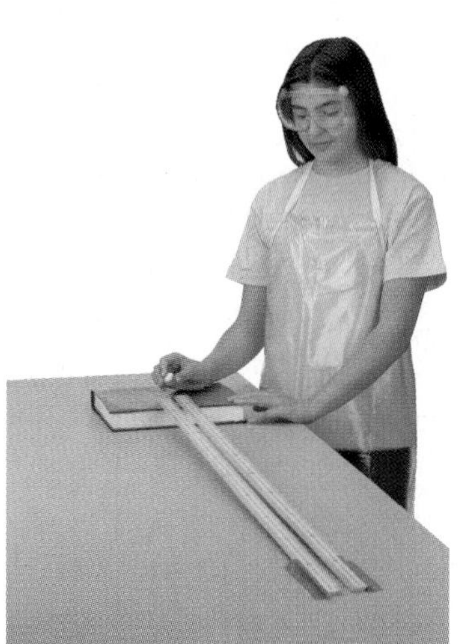

1. Make a track by slightly separating two metersticks placed side by side.
2. On a table, raise one end of the track slightly and measure the height.
3. Roll a marble down the track. Measure the distance from its starting point to where it hits the floor. Repeat. Calculate the average of the two measurements.
4. Repeat steps 2 and 3 for three different heights. Predict what will happen if you use a heavier marble. Test your prediction and record your observations.

Observe

In your Science Journal, describe your experiment and what you discovered. How did the different heights cause the distance to change?

Before You Read

FOLDABLES Reading & Study Skills

Making a Know-Want-Learn Study Fold Make the following Foldable to help identify what you already know and what you want to know about energy.

1. Place a sheet of paper in front of you so the long side is at the top. Fold the paper in half from top to bottom.
2. Fold both sides in. Unfold the paper so three sections show.
3. Through the top thickness of paper, cut along each of the fold lines to the topfold, forming three tabs. Label the tabs *Know*, *Want*, and *Learned*.
4. Before you read the chapter, write what you know and what you want to know under the tabs. As you read the chapter, correct what you have written and add more questions.

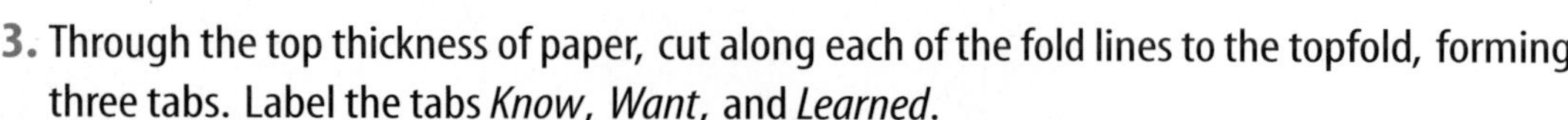

SECTION

What is energy?

As You Read

What You'll Learn

- **Explain** what energy is.
- **Distinguish** between kinetic energy and potential energy.
- **Identify** the various forms of energy.

Vocabulary

energy
kinetic energy
potential energy
thermal energy
chemical energy
radiant energy
electrical energy
nuclear energy

Why It's Important

Energy is the source of all activity.

The Nature of Energy

What comes to mind when you hear the word *energy?* Do you picture running, leaping, and spinning like a dancer or a gymnast? How would you define energy? When an object has energy, it can make things happen. In other words, **energy** is the ability to cause change. What do the items shown in **Figure 1** have in common?

Look around and notice the changes that are occurring—someone walking by or a ray of sunshine that is streaming through the window and warming your desk. Maybe you can see the wind moving the leaves on a tree. What changes are occurring?

Transferring Energy You might not realize it, but you have a large amount of energy. In fact, everything around you has energy, but you notice it only when a change takes place. Anytime a change occurs, energy is transferred from one object to another. You hear a footstep because energy is transferred from a foot hitting the ground to your ears. Leaves are put into motion when energy in the moving wind is transferred to them. The spot on the desktop becomes warmer when energy is transferred to it from the sunlight. In fact, all objects, including leaves and desktops, have energy.

Figure 1
Energy is the ability to cause change. *How can these objects cause change?*

Energy of Motion

Things that move can cause change. A bowling ball rolls down the alley and knocks down some pins, as in **Figure 2A.** Is energy involved? A change occurs when the pins fall over. The bowling ball causes this change, so the bowling ball has energy. The energy in the motion of the bowling ball causes the pins to fall. As the ball moves, it has a form of energy called kinetic energy. **Kinetic energy** is the energy an object has due to its motion. If an object isn't moving, it doesn't have kinetic energy.

Figure 2 The kinetic energy of an object depends on two quantities. *What are those quantities?*

Kinetic Energy and Speed If you roll the bowling ball so it moves faster, what happens when it hits the pins? It might knock down more pins, or it might cause the pins to go flying farther. A faster ball causes more change to occur than a ball that is moving slowly. Look at **Figure 2B.** The professional bowler rolls a fast-moving bowling ball. When her ball hits the pins, pins go flying faster and farther than for a slower-moving ball. All that action signals that her ball has more energy. The faster the ball goes, the more kinetic energy it has. This is true for all moving objects. Kinetic energy increases as an object moves faster.

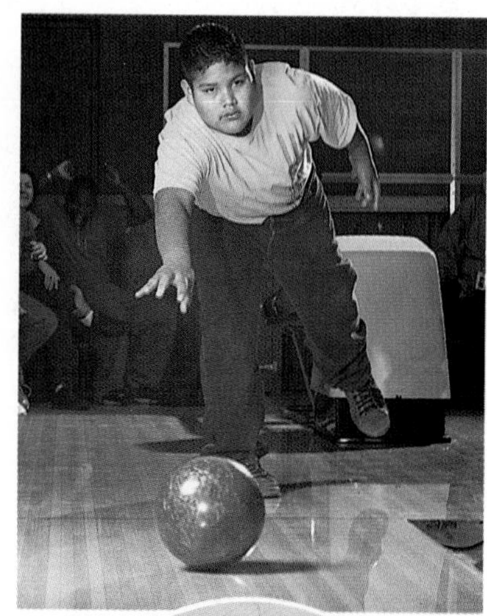

A This ball has kinetic energy because it is rolling down the alley.

B This ball has more kinetic energy because it has more speed.

Kinetic Energy and Mass Suppose, as shown in **Figure 2C,** you roll a volleyball down the alley instead of a bowling ball. If the volleyball travels at the same speed as a bowling ball, do you think it will send pins flying as far? The answer is no. The volleyball might not knock down any pins. Does the volleyball have less energy than the bowling ball even though they are traveling at the same speed? An important difference between the volleyball and the bowling ball is that the volleyball has less mass. Even though the volleyball is moving at the same speed as the bowling ball, the volleyball has less kinetic energy because it has less mass. Kinetic energy also depends on the mass of a moving object. Kinetic energy increases as the mass of the object increases.

C This ball has less kinetic energy because it has less mass.

✓ Reading Check *Why does a volleyball knock over fewer pins than a bowling ball?*

Figure 3
The potential energy of an object depends on its mass and height above the ground.
Which vase has more potential energy, the red one or the blue one?

Energy of Position

An object can have energy even though it is not moving. For example, a glass of water sitting on the kitchen table doesn't have any kinetic energy because it isn't moving. If you accidentally nudge the glass and it falls on the floor, changes occur. Gravity pulls the glass downward, and the glass has energy of motion as it falls. Where did this energy come from?

When the glass was sitting on the table, it had potential (puh TEN chul) energy. **Potential energy** is the energy stored in an object because of its position. In this case, the position is the height of the glass above the floor. The potential energy of the glass changes to kinetic energy as the glass falls. The potential energy of the glass is greater if it is higher above the floor. Potential energy also depends on mass. The more mass an object has, the more potential energy it has. Which object in **Figure 3** has the most potential energy?

Forms of Energy

Food, sunlight, and wind have energy, yet they seem different because they contain different forms of energy. Food and sunlight contain forms of energy different from the kinetic energy in the motion of the wind. The warmth you feel from sunlight is another type of energy that is different from the energy of motion or position.

Thermal Energy The feeling of warmth from sunlight signals that your body is acquiring more thermal energy. All objects have **thermal energy** that increases as its temperature increases. A cup of hot chocolate has more thermal energy than a cup of cold water, as shown in **Figure 4.** Similarly, the cup of water has more thermal energy than a block of ice of the same mass. Your body continually produces thermal energy. Many chemical reactions that take place inside your cells produce thermal energy. Where does this energy come from? Thermal energy released by chemical reactions comes from another form of energy called chemical energy.

Figure 4
The hotter an object is, the more thermal energy it has. A cup of hot chocolate has more thermal energy than a cup of water, which has more thermal energy than a block of ice with the same mass.

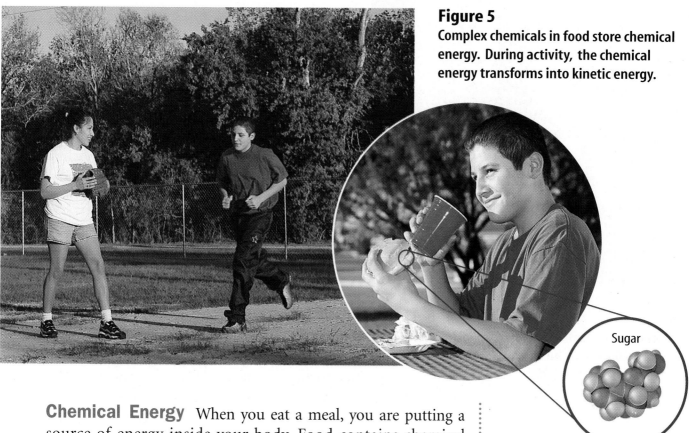

Figure 5
Complex chemicals in food store chemical energy. During activity, the chemical energy transforms into kinetic energy.

Chemical Energy When you eat a meal, you are putting a source of energy inside your body. Food contains chemical energy that your body uses to provide energy for your brain, to power your movements, and to fuel your growth. As in **Figure 5,** food contains chemicals, such as sugar, which can be broken down in your body. These chemicals are made of atoms that are bonded together, and energy is stored in the bonds between atoms. **Chemical energy** is the energy stored in chemical bonds. When chemicals are broken apart and new chemicals are formed, some of this energy is released. The flame of a candle is the result of chemical energy stored in the wax. When the wax burns, chemical energy is transformed into thermal energy and light energy.

Light Energy Light from the candle flame travels through the air at an incredibly fast speed of 300,000 km/s. This is fast enough to circle Earth almost eight times in 1 s. When light strikes something, it can be absorbed, transmitted, or reflected. If the light is absorbed, it will cause the object to warm up. In other words, the thermal energy of the object has increased because light transferred energy to it. The type of energy light carries is called **radiant energy. Figure 6** shows a coil of wire that produces radiant energy when it is heated. To heat the metal, another type of energy can be used—electrical energy.

Reading Check *How do you know that light has energy?*

Figure 6
Electrical energy is transformed into thermal energy in the metal heating coil. As the metal becomes hotter, it emits more radiant energy.

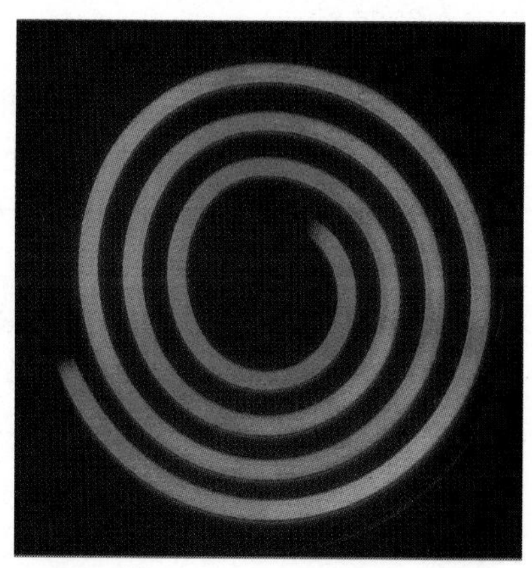

Electrical Energy Electrical lighting is one of the many ways electrical energy is used. Look around at all the devices that use electrical energy. The electric current that comes out of batteries and wall sockets carries **electrical energy.** The amount of electrical energy depends on the voltage. The current out of a 120-V wall socket can carry more energy than the current out of a 1.5-V battery. To produce the enormous quantities of electrical energy consumed each day, large power plants are needed. In the United States, about 20 percent of the electrical energy that is generated comes from nuclear power plants.

Figure 7
Complex power plants are required to obtain useful energy from the nucleus of an atom.

Nuclear Energy Nuclear power plants use the energy stored in the nucleus of an atom to generate electricity. Every atomic nucleus contains energy—**nuclear energy**—that can be transformed into other forms of energy. However, releasing the nuclear energy is a difficult process. It involves the construction of complex power plants, as shown in **Figure 7.** In contrast, all that is needed to release chemical energy from wood is a match.

Section  Assessment

1. How do you know if an object has energy? Do you have energy? Does a rock?
2. Contrast chemical and nuclear energy.
3. How can chemical energy transform into thermal energy? Into light energy?
4. If two vases are side by side on a high shelf, could one have more potential energy than the other? Explain.
5. **Think Critically** A golf ball and a bowling ball have the same kinetic energy. Which one is moving faster? Explain your answer using what you know about kinetic energy. Suppose the golf ball and the bowling ball have the same speed. Which of the two has more kinetic energy?

Skill Builder Activities

6. **Interpreting Data** Review your results from the Explore Activity. Where did the marble have the most kinetic energy? Where did the marble have the most potential energy? Can you infer a relationship between kinetic energy and potential energy based on your observations? **For more help, refer to the** Science Skill Handbook.
7. **Communicating** The term *energy* is used in everyday language. In your Science Journal, record different expressions and ways of using the word *energy.* Decide which ones match the definition of energy presented in this section. **For more help, refer to the** Science Skill Handbook.

SECTION 2

Energy Transformations

Changing Forms of Energy

Chemical, thermal, radiant, and electrical are some of the forms that energy can have. In the world around you, energy is transforming continually between one form and another. You observe some of these transformations by noticing a change in your environment. Forest fires are a dramatic example of an environmental change that can occur naturally as a result of lightning strikes. Another type of change, shown in **Figure 8,** is a mountain biker pedaling to the top of a hill. What energy transformations occur as he moves up the hill?

Tracking Energy Transformations As the mountain biker pedals, many energy transformations are taking place. In his leg muscles, chemical energy is transforming into kinetic energy. The kinetic energy of his leg muscle transforms into kinetic energy of the bicycle. Some of this energy transforms into potential energy as he moves up the hill. Also, some energy is transformed into thermal energy. His body is warmer because chemical energy is being released. Because of friction, the mechanical parts of the bicycle are warmer, too.

As You Read

What You'll Learn

- **Apply** the law of conservation of energy to energy transformations.
- **Identify** how energy changes form.
- **Describe** how electric power plants produce energy.

Vocabulary

law of conservation of energy
generator
turbine

Why It's Important

Many devices you use every day change energy from one form to another.

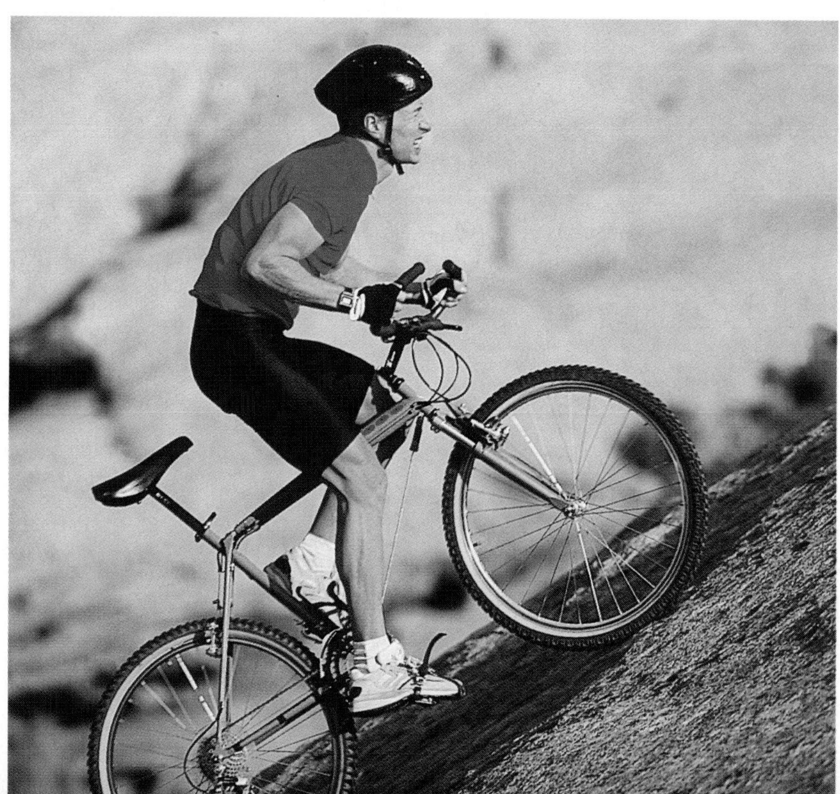

Figure 8
The ability to transform energy allows the biker to climb the hill.
Identify all the forms of energy that are represented in the photograph.

The Law of Conservation of Energy

It can be a challenge to track energy as it moves from object to object. However, one extremely important principle can serve as a guide as you trace the flow of energy. According to the **law of conservation of energy,** energy is never created or destroyed. The only thing that changes is the form in which energy appears. When the biker is resting at the summit, all his original energy is still around. Some of the energy is in the form of potential energy, which he will use as he coasts down the hill. Some of this energy was changed to thermal energy by friction in the bike. Chemical energy was also changed to thermal energy in the biker's muscles, making him feel hot. As he rests, this thermal energy moves from his body to the air around him. No energy is missing—it can all be accounted for.

Reading Check *Can energy ever be lost? Why or why not?*

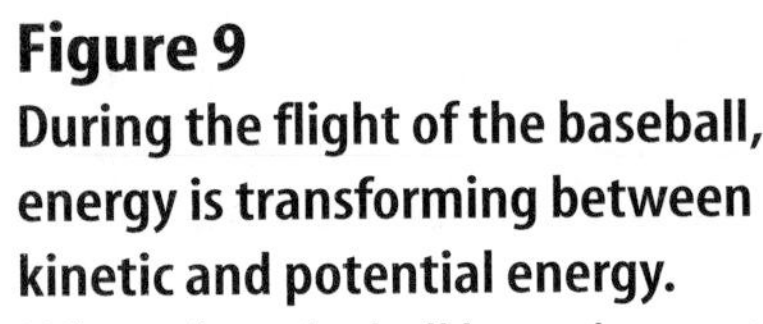

Research Visit the Glencoe Science Web site at **science.glencoe.com** for more information about how energy changes form when it is transformed from one form to another. Use a spreadsheet program to summarize what you've learned.

Changing Kinetic and Potential Energy

The law of conservation of energy can be used to identify the energy changes in a system, especially if the system is not too complicated. For example, tossing a ball into the air and catching it is a simple system. As shown in **Figure 9,** as the ball leaves your hand, most of its energy is kinetic. As the ball rises, it slows and loses kinetic energy. But, the total energy of the ball hasn't changed. The loss of kinetic energy equals the gain of potential energy as the ball flies higher in the air. The total amount of energy always remains constant. Energy moves from place to place and changes form, but it never is created or destroyed.

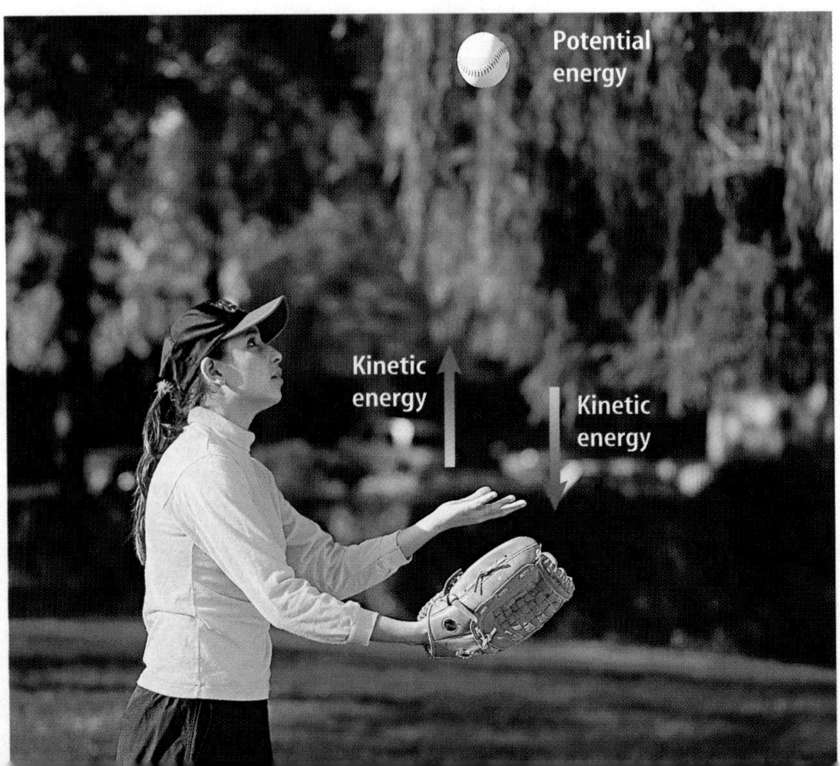

Figure 9
During the flight of the baseball, energy is transforming between kinetic and potential energy.
Where does the ball have the most kinetic energy? Where does the ball have the most total energy?

Hybrid cars that use an electric motor and a gasoline engine for power are now available. These cars get up to 29 km/L. Inventions such as the hybrid car make energy transformations more efficient.

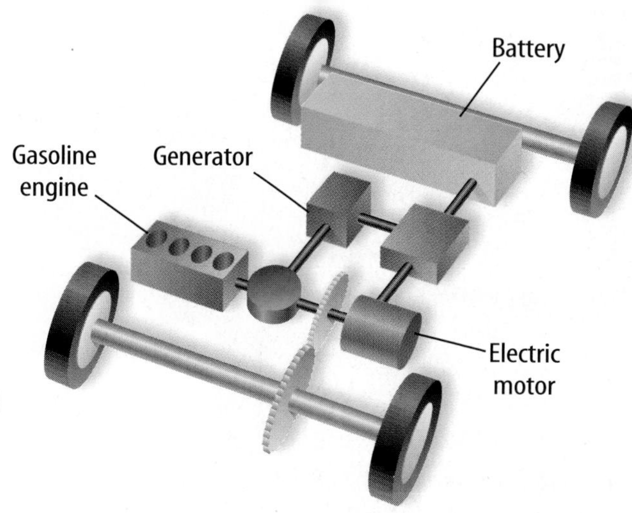

Energy Changes Form

Energy transformations occur constantly all around you. Many machines are devices that transform energy from one form to another. For example, an automobile engine transforms the chemical energy in gasoline into energy of motion. However, not all of the chemical energy is converted into kinetic energy. Instead, some of the chemical energy is converted into thermal energy, and the engine becomes hot. An engine that converts chemical energy into more kinetic energy is a more efficient engine. New types of cars, like the one shown in **Figure 10,** use an electric motor along with a gasoline engine. These engines are more efficient so the car can travel farther on a gallon of gas.

Transforming Chemical Energy

Inside your body, chemical energy also is transformed into kinetic energy. Look at **Figure 11.** The transformation of chemical to kinetic energy occurs in muscle cells. There, chemical reactions take place that cause certain molecules to change shape. Your muscle contracts when many of these changes occur, and a part of your body moves.

The matter contained in living organisms, or biomass, contains chemical energy. When organisms die, chemical compounds in their biomass break down, or decompose. Bacteria, fungi, and other organisms help convert these chemical compounds to simpler chemicals that can be used by other living things.

Thermal energy also is released as these changes occur. For example, a compost pile can contain plant matter, such as grass clippings and leaves. As the compost pile decomposes, chemical energy is converted into thermal energy. This can cause the temperature of a compost pile to reach 60°C.

TRY AT HOME

Mini LAB

Analyzing Energy Transformations

Procedure

1. Place soft **clay** on the floor and smooth out its surface.
2. Hold a **marble** 1.5 m above the clay and drop it. Measure the depth of the crater made by the marble.
3. Repeat this procedure using a **steel ball,** a **rubber ball,** and a **table-tennis ball.**

Analysis

1. Compare the depths of the craters to determine which ball had the most kinetic energy as it hit the clay. Why did this ball have the most kinetic energy?
2. Explain how potential energy was transformed into kinetic energy during your activity.

Figure 11

Paddling a raft, throwing a baseball, playing the violin — your skeletal muscles make these and countless other body movements possible. Muscles work by pulling, or contracting. At the cellular level, muscle contractions are powered by reactions that transform chemical energy into kinetic energy.

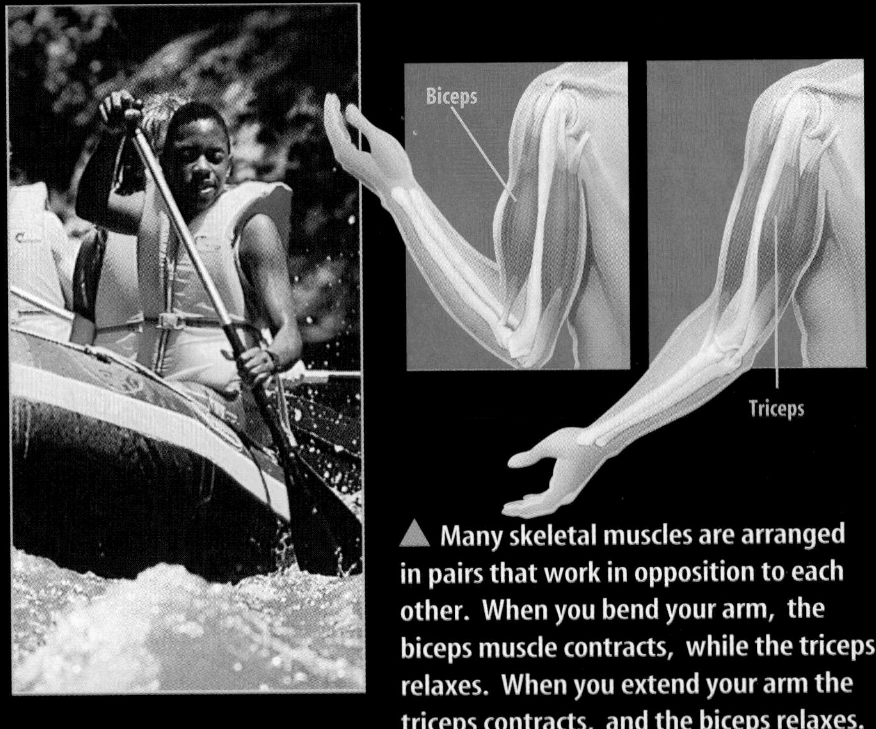

▶ Energy transformations taking place in your muscles provide the power to move.

▲ Many skeletal muscles are arranged in pairs that work in opposition to each other. When you bend your arm, the biceps muscle contracts, while the triceps relaxes. When you extend your arm the triceps contracts, and the biceps relaxes.

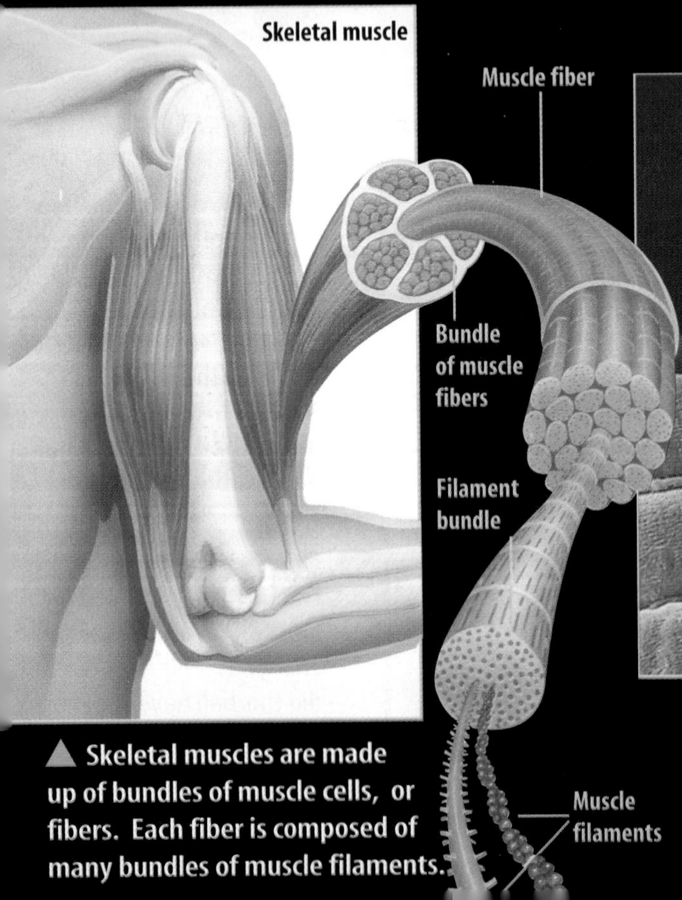

Skeletal muscle

Muscle fiber

Bundle of muscle fibers

Filament bundle

Muscle filaments

Nerve fiber

Muscle fibers

▲ Skeletal muscles are made up of bundles of muscle cells, or fibers. Each fiber is composed of many bundles of muscle filaments.

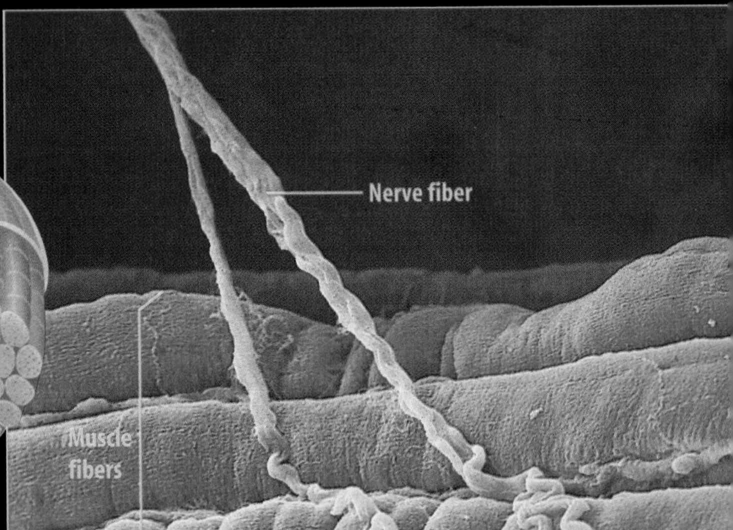

▲ A signal from a nerve fiber starts a chemical reaction in the muscle filament. This causes molecules in the muscle filament to gain energy and move. Many filaments moving together cause the

Figure 12
The simple act of listening to a radio involves many energy transformations. A few are diagrammed here.

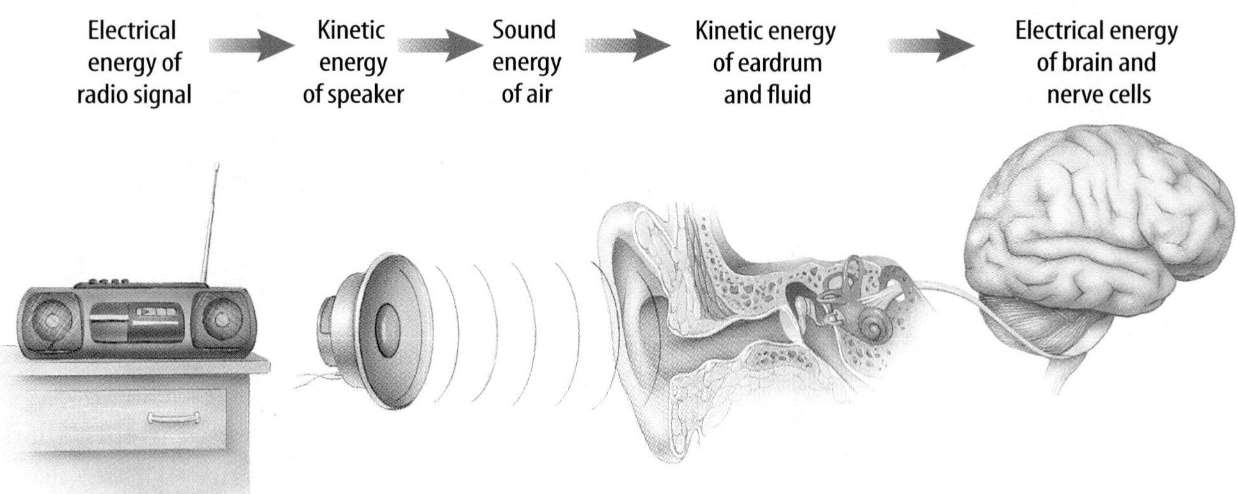

Transforming Electrical Energy Every day you use electrical energy. When you flip a light switch, or turn on a radio or television, or use a hair drier, you are transforming electrical energy to other forms of energy. Every time you plug something into a wall outlet, or use a battery, you are using electrical energy. **Figure 12** shows how electrical energy is transformed into other forms of energy when you listen to a radio. A loudspeaker in the radio converts electrical energy into sound waves that travel to your ear—energy in motion. The energy that is carried by the sound waves causes parts of the ear to move also. This energy of motion is transformed again into chemical and electrical energy in nerve cells, which send the energy to your brain. After your brain interprets this energy as a voice or music, where does the energy go? The energy finally is transformed into thermal energy.

Transforming Thermal Energy Different forms of energy can be transformed into thermal energy. For example, chemical energy changes into thermal energy when something burns. Electrical energy changes into thermal energy when a wire that is carrying an electric current gets hot. Thermal energy can be used to heat buildings and keep you warm. Thermal energy also can be used to heat water. If water is heated to its boiling point, it changes to steam. This steam can be transformed to kinetic energy by steam engines, like the steam locomotives that used to pull trains. Thermal energy also can be transformed into radiant energy. For example, when a bar of metal is heated to a high temperature, it glows and gives off light.

Most organisms have some adaptation for controlling the amount of thermal energy in their bodies. Some living in cooler climates have thick fur coats that help prevent thermal energy from escaping, and some living in desert regions have skin that helps keep thermal energy out. Research some of the adaptations different organisms have for controlling the thermal energy in their bodies.

Figure 13
Thermal energy moves from the hot chocolate to the cooler surroundings. *What happens to the hot chocolate as it loses thermal energy?*

How Thermal Energy Moves Thermal energy can move from one place to another. Look at **Figure 13.** The hot chocolate has thermal energy that moves from the cup to the cooler air around it, and to the cooler spoon. Thermal energy only moves from something at a higher temperature to something at a lower temperature.

Generating Electrical Energy

The enormous amount of electrical energy that is used every day is too large to be stored in batteries. The electrical energy that is available for use at any wall socket must be generated continually by power plants. Every power plant works on the same principle—energy is used to turn a large generator. A **generator** is a device that transforms kinetic energy into electrical energy. In fossil fuel power plants, coal, oil, or natural gas is burned to boil water. As the hot water boils, the steam rushes through a **turbine,** which contains a set of narrowly spaced fan blades. The steam pushes on the blades and turns the turbine, which in turn rotates a shaft in the generator to produce the electrical energy, as shown in **Figure 14.**

Reading Check *What does a generator do?*

Figure 14
A coal-burning power plant transforms the chemical energy in coal into electrical energy. *What are some of the other energy sources that power plants use?*

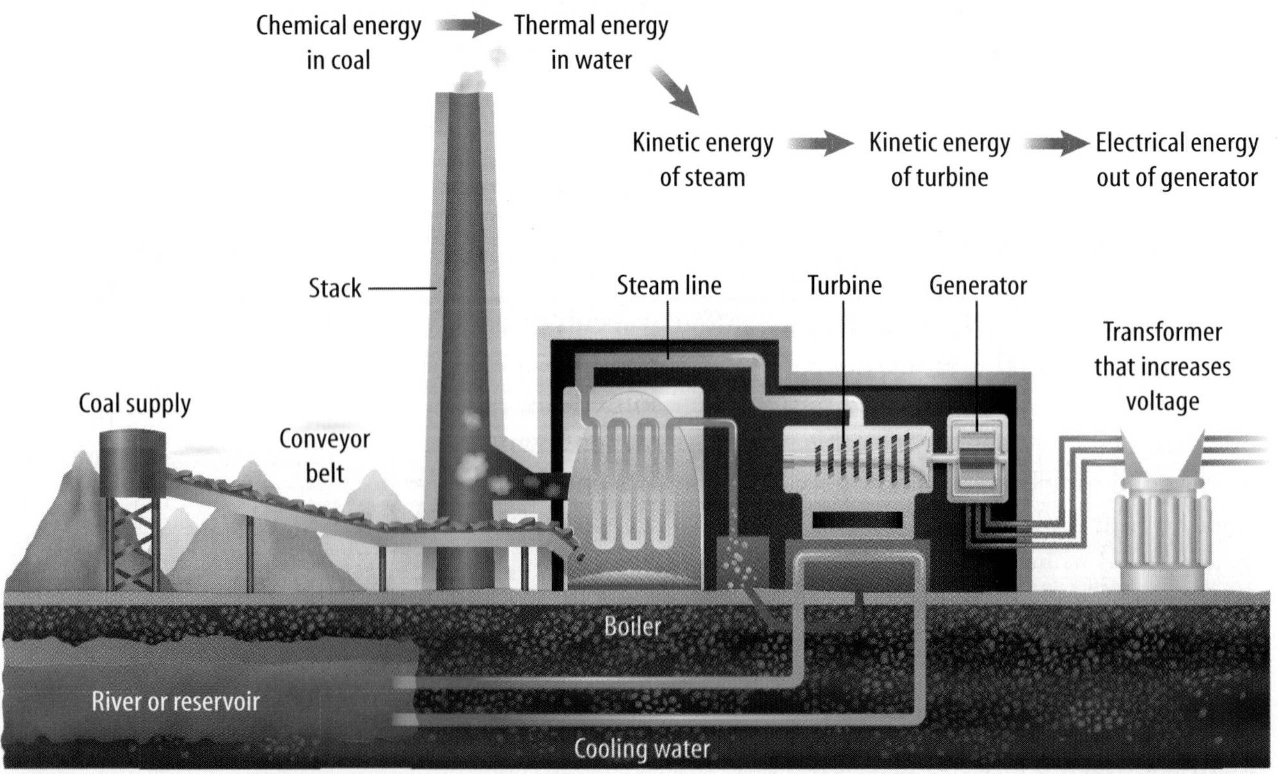

Power Plants Almost 90 percent of the electrical energy generated in the United States is produced by nuclear and fossil fuel power plants, as shown in **Figure 15.** Other types of power plants include hydroelectric (hi droh ih LEK trihk) and wind. Hydroelectric power plants transform the kinetic energy of moving water into electrical energy. Wind power plants transform the kinetic energy of moving air into electrical energy. In these power plants, a generator converts the kinetic energy of moving water or wind to electrical energy.

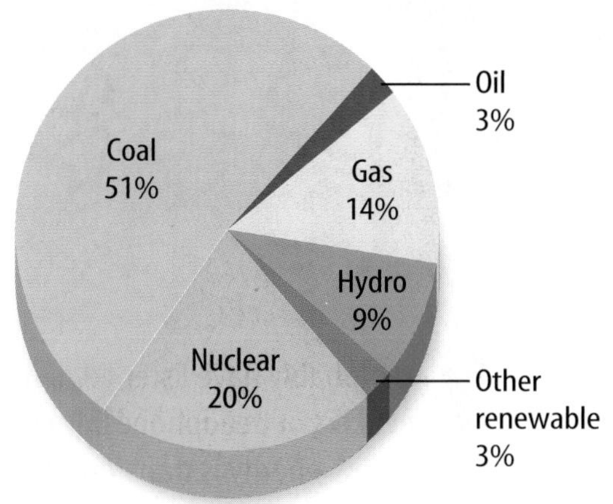

Figure 15
The graph shows sources of electrical energy in the United States. *Which energy source do you think is being used to provide the electricity for the lights overhead?*

To analyze the energy transformations in a power plant, you can diagram the energy changes using arrows. A coal-burning power plant generates electrical energy through the following series of energy transformations.

chemical energy of coal	→	thermal energy of water	→	kinetic energy of steam	→	kinetic energy of turbine	→	electrical energy out of generator

Nuclear power plants use a similar series of transformations. Hydroelectric plants, however, skip the steps that change water into steam because the water strikes the turbine directly.

Section  Assessment

1. What is the law of conservation of energy?
2. If your body temperature is 37°C and you are sitting in a room which has a temperature of 25°C, does your body gain or lose thermal energy? Explain.
3. What are the basic steps involved in generating electricity at a power plant?
4. Diagram the energy transformations that take place at a hydroelectric power plant.
5. **Think Critically** You begin pedaling your bicycle, making it move faster and faster. You notice that at first it is easy to speed up, but then it becomes difficult. You pedal with all your strength, yet you cannot go any faster. Use energy concepts to explain what is happening.

Skill Builder Activities

6. **Testing a Hypothesis** If you drop a rubber ball onto a hard surface, the first bounce will be the highest. How much lower will the second bounce be? If you drop the ball on the top of a shoe box, will it bounce as high? Make a hypothesis. Design and conduct an experiment to test your hypothesis. **For more help, refer to the Science Skill Handbook.**
7. **Using Graphics Software** Use graphics software to diagram all the energy transformations that take place during a conversation. What forms of energy are in the sequence from one person making a sound to a second person hearing that sound? **For more help, refer to the Technology Skill Handbook.**

Activity

Hearing with Your Jaw

You probably have listened to music using speakers or headphones. Have you ever considered how energy is transferred to get the energy from the radio or CD player to your brain? What type of energy is needed to power the radio or CD player? Where does this energy come from? How does that energy become sound? How does the sound get to you? In this activity, the sound from a radio or CD player is going to travel through a motor before entering your body through your jaw instead of your ears.

What You'll Investigate

How can energy be transferred from a radio or CD player to your brain?

Materials

radio or CD player
small electrical motor
headphone jack

Goals

- **Identify** energy transfers and transformations.
- **Explain** your results in terms of transformations of energy and conservation of energy.

Safety Symbols

Procedure

1. Go to one of the places in the room with a motor/radio assembly.
2. Turn on the radio or CD player so that you hear the music.
3. Push the headphone jack into the headphone plug on the radio or CD player.
4. Press the axle of the motor against the side of your jaw.

Conclude and Apply

1. **Describe** what you heard in your Science Journal.
2. What type of energy did you have in the beginning? In the end?
3. **Draw** a diagram to show all of the energy transformations taking place.
4. Did anything get hotter as a result of this activity? Explain.
5. **Explain** your results using the law of conservation of energy.

Compare your conclusions with those of other students in your class. **For more help, refer to the** Science Skill Handbook.

SECTION 3

Sources of Energy

Using Energy

Press a button on the remote control and your favorite program appears on television. Open your refrigerator and pull out something cold to drink. Ride to the mall in a car. For any of these things to occur, a transfer of energy must take place. Radiant energy is transferred to your television, electrical energy is transferred to your refrigerator, and the chemical energy in gasoline is transferred to the engine of the car.

Every day energy is used to provide light and to heat and cool homes, schools, and workplaces. Energy is used to run cars, buses, trucks, trains, and airplanes that transport people and materials from one place to another. Energy also is used to make clothing and other materials and to cook food.

According to the law of conservation of energy, energy can't be created or destroyed. Energy only can change form. If a car or refrigerator can't create the energy they use, then where does this energy come from?

As You Read

***What* You'll Learn**

- **Explain** what renewable, nonrenewable, and alternative resources are.
- **Describe** the advantages and disadvantages of using various energy sources.

Vocabulary

nonrenewable resource
renewable resource
alternative resource
inexhaustible resource
photovoltaic

***Why* It's Important**

Energy is vital for survival and making life comfortable. Developing new energy sources will improve modern standards of living.

Energy Resources

Energy cannot be made, but must come from the natural world. As you can see in **Figure 16,** the surface of Earth receives energy from two sources—the Sun and radioactive atoms in Earth's interior. Of these two energy sources, the energy from the Sun has much more impact on your life. Nearly all the energy you used today can be traced to the Sun, even the gasoline used to power the car or school bus you came to school in.

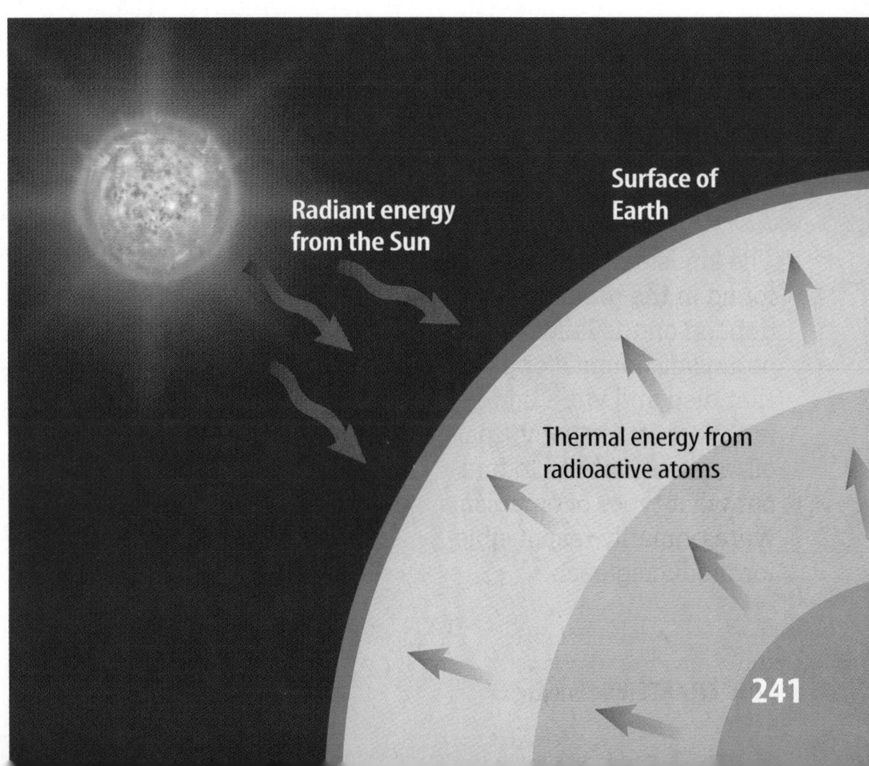

Figure 16
All the energy you use can be traced to one of two sources—the Sun or radioactive atoms in Earth's interior.

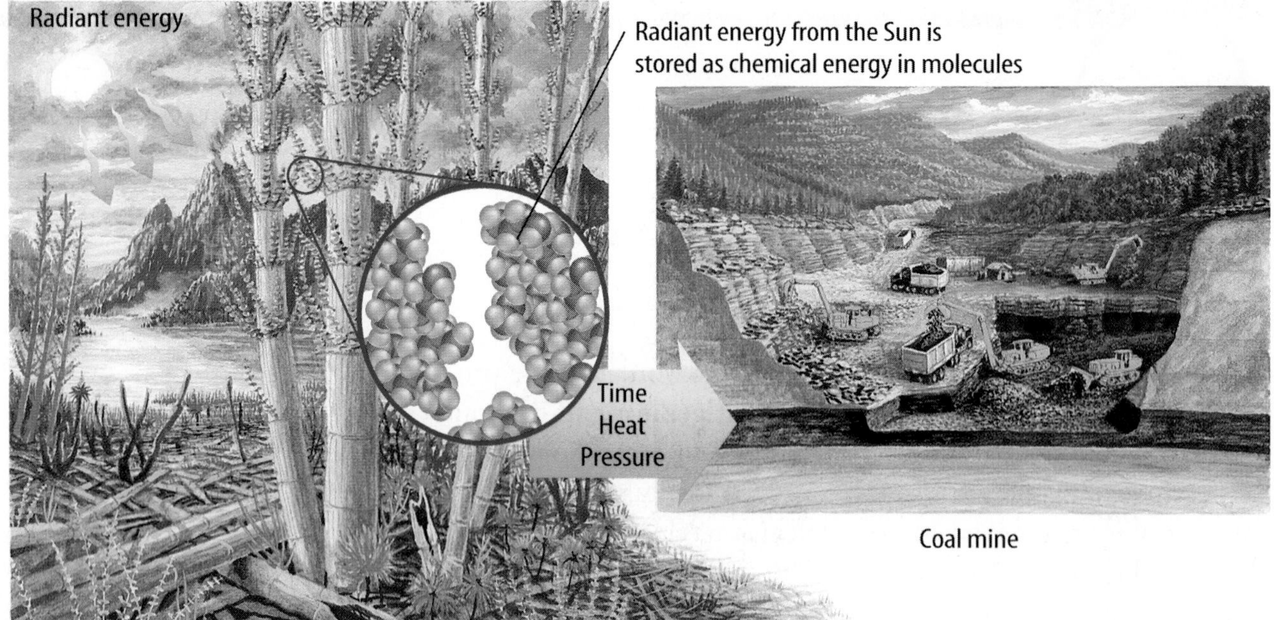

Figure 17
Coal is formed after the molecules in ancient plants are heated under pressure for millions of years. The energy stored by the molecules in coal originally came from the Sun.

Fossil Fuels

Fossil fuels are coal, oil, and natural gas. Oil and natural gas were made from the remains of microscopic organisms that lived in Earth's oceans millions of years ago. Heat and pressure gradually turned these ancient organisms into oil and natural gas. Coal was formed by similar process from the remains of ancient plants that once lived on land, as shown in **Figure 17.**

Through the process of photosynthesis, ancient plants converted the radiant energy in sunlight to chemical energy stored in various types of molecules. Heat and pressure changed these molecules into other types of molecules as fossil fuels formed. Chemical energy stored in these molecules is released when fossil fuels are burned.

Using Fossil Fuels The energy used when you ride in a car, turn on a light, or use an electric appliance usually comes from burning fossil fuels. However, it takes millions of years to replace each drop of gasoline and each lump of coal that is burned. This means that the supply of oil on Earth will continue to decrease as oil is used. An energy source that is used up much faster than it can be replaced is a **nonrenewable resource.** Fossil fuels are nonrenewable resources.

Burning fossil fuels to produce energy also generates chemical compounds that cause pollution. Each year billions of kilograms of air pollutants are produced by burning fossil fuels. These pollutants can cause respiratory illnesses and acid rain. Also, the carbon dioxide gas formed when fossil fuels are burned might cause Earth's climate to warm.

Earth Science INTEGRATION

The kinds of fossil fuels found in the ground depend on the kinds of organisms (animal or plant) that died and were buried in that spot. Research coal, oil, and natural gas to find out what types of organisms were primarily responsible for producing each.

Nuclear Energy

Can you imagine running an automobile on 1 kg of fuel that releases almost 3 million times more energy than 1 L of gas? What could supply so much energy from so little mass? The answer is the nuclei of uranium atoms. Some of these nuclei are unstable and break apart, releasing enormous amounts of energy in the process. This energy can be used to generate electricity by heating water to produce steam that spins an electric generator, as shown in **Figure 18.** Because no fossil fuels are burned, generating electricity using nuclear energy helps make the supply of fossil fuels last longer. Also, unlike fossil fuel power plants, nuclear power plants produce almost no air pollution. In one year, a typical nuclear power plant generates enough energy to supply 600,000 homes with power and produces only 1 m^3 of waste.

Nuclear Wastes Like all energy sources, nuclear energy has its advantages and disadvantages. One disadvantage is the amount of uranium in Earth's crust is nonrenewable. Another is that the waste produced by nuclear power plants is radioactive and can be dangerous to living things. Some of the materials in the nuclear waste will remain radioactive for many thousands of years. As a result the waste must be stored so no radioactivity is released into the environment for a long time. One method is to seal the waste in a ceramic material, place the ceramic in protective containers, and then bury the containers far underground. However, the burial site would have to be chosen carefully so underground water supplies aren't contaminated. Also, the site would have to be safe from earthquakes and other natural disasters that might cause radioactive material to be released.

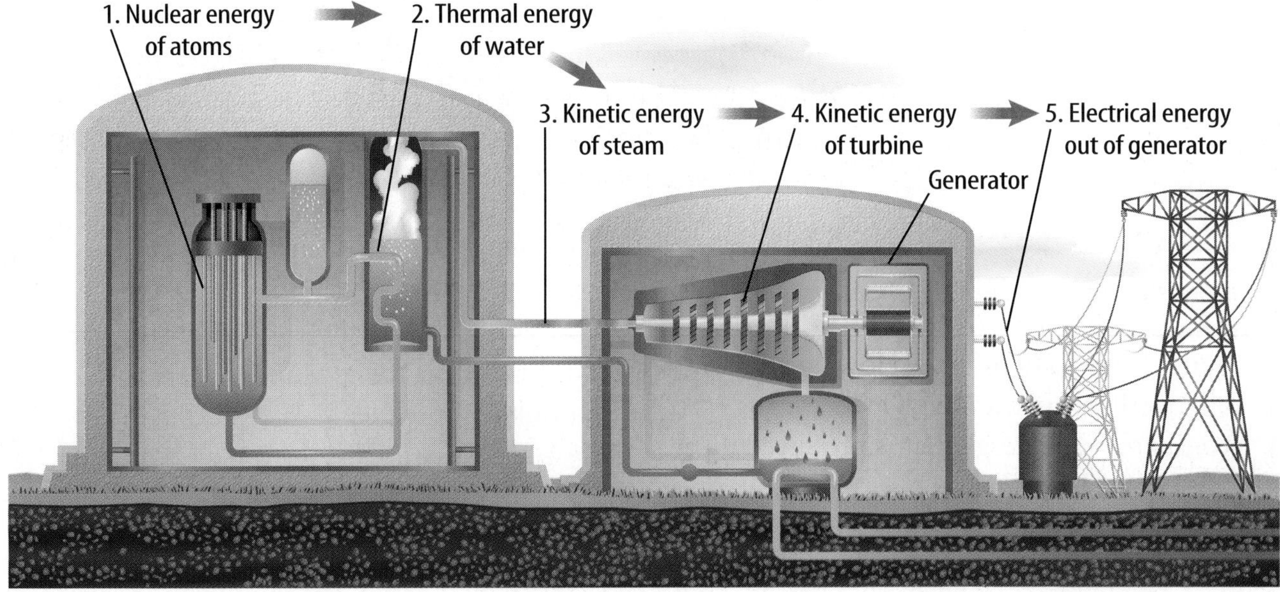

Figure 18
To obtain electrical energy from nuclear energy, a series of energy transformations must occur.

Hydroelectricity

Currently, transforming the potential energy of water that is trapped behind dams supplies the world with almost 20 percent of its electrical energy. Hydroelectricity is the largest renewable source of energy. A **renewable resource** is an energy source that is replenished continually. As long as enough rain and snow fall to keep rivers flowing, hydroelectric power plants can generate electrical energy, as shown in **Figure 19.**

Although production of hydroelectricity is largely pollution free, it has one major problem. It disrupts the life cycle of aquatic animals, especially fish. This is particularly true in the Northwest where salmon spawn and run. Because salmon return to the spot where they were hatched to lay their eggs, the development of dams has hindered a large fraction of salmon from reproducing. This has greatly reduced the salmon population. Efforts to correct the problem have resulted in plans to remove a number of dams. In an attempt to help fish bypass some dams, fish ladders are being installed. Like most energy sources, hydroelectricity has advantages and disadvantages.

SCIENCE *Online*

Data Update Visit the Glencoe Science Web site at **science.glencoe.com** for data about the use of hydroelectricity in various parts of the world. Using a classroom map, present your finds to your class.

Problem-Solving Activity

Is energy consumption outpacing production?

You use energy every day—to get to school, to watch TV, and to heat or cool your home. The amount of energy consumed by an average person has increased over the last 50 years. Consequently, more energy must be produced.

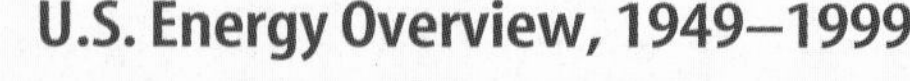

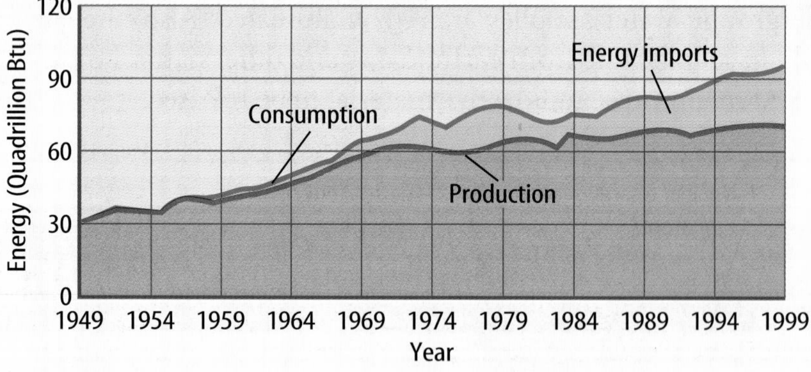

Identifying the Problem

The following graph shows the energy produced and consumed in the United States from 1949 to 1999. How does energy that is consumed by Americans compare with energy that is produced in the United States?

Solving the problem

1. Determine the approximate amount of energy produced in 1949 and in 1999 and how much it has increased in 50 years. Has it doubled or tripled?
2. Do the same for consumption. Has it doubled or tripled?
3. Using your answers for steps 1 and 2 and the graph, where does the additional energy that is needed come from? Give some examples.

1. Potential energy of water
2. Kinetic energy of water
3. Kinetic energy of turbine
4. Electrical energy out of generator
Long-distance power lines

Figure 19
The potential energy of water behind a dam supplies the energy to turn the turbine. *Why is hydroelectric power a renewable energy source?*

Alternative Sources of Energy

Electrical energy can be generated in several ways. However, each has disadvantages that can affect the environment and the quality of life for humans. Research is being done to develop new sources of energy that are safer and cause less harm to the environment. These sources often are called **alternative resources.** These alternative resources include solar energy, wind, and geothermal energy.

Solar Energy

The Sun is the origin of almost all the energy that is used on Earth. Because the Sun will go on producing an enormous amount of energy for billions of years, the Sun is an inexhaustible source of energy. An **inexhaustible resource** is an energy source that can't be used up by humans.

Each day, on average, the amount of solar energy that strikes the United States is more than the total amount of energy used by the entire country in a year. However, less than 0.1 percent of the energy used in the United States comes directly from the Sun. One reason is that solar energy is more expensive to use than fossil fuels. However, as the supply of fossil fuels decreases, the cost of finding and mining these fuels might increase. Then, it may be cheaper to use solar energy or other energy sources to generate electricity and heat buildings than to use fossil fuels.

What is an inexhaustible energy source?

Building a Solar Collector

Procedure

1. Line a **large pot** with **black plastic** and fill with **water.**
2. Stretch **clear-plastic wrap** over the pot and tape it taut.
3. Make a slit in the top and slide a **thermometer** or a **computer probe** into the water.
4. Place your solar collector in direct sunlight and monitor the temperature change every 3 min for 15 min.
5. Repeat your experiment without using any black plastic.

Analysis

1. Graph the temperature changes in both setups.
2. Explain how your solar collector works.

Collecting the Sun's Energy Two types of collectors capture the Sun's rays. If you look around your neighborhood, you might see large, rectangular panels attached to the roofs of buildings or houses. If, as in **Figure 20A,** pipes come out of the panel, it is a thermal collector. Using a black surface, a thermal collector heats water by directly absorbing the Sun's radiant energy. Water circulating in this system can be heated to about 70°C. The hot water can be pumped through the house to provide heat. Also, the hot water can be used for washing and bathing. If the panel has no pipes, it is a photovoltaic (foh toh vol TAY ihk) collector, like the one pictured in **Figure 20B.** A **photovoltaic** is a device that transforms radiant energy directly into electrical energy. Photovoltaics are used to power calculators and satellites, including the *International Space Station.*

Figure 20
Solar energy can be collected and utilized by individuals using A thermal collectors or B photovoltaic collectors.

Reading Check *What does a photovoltaic do?*

Geothermal Energy

Imagine you could take a journey to the center of Earth—down to about 6,400 km below the surface. As you went deeper and deeper, you would find the temperature increasing. In fact, after going only about 3 km, the temperature could have increased enough to boil water. At a depth of 100 km, the temperature could be over 900°C. The heat generated inside Earth is called geothermal energy. Some of this heat is produced when unstable radioactive atoms inside Earth decay, converting nuclear energy to thermal energy.

At some places deep within Earth the temperature is hot enough to melt rock. This molten rock, or magma, can rise up close to the surface through cracks in the crust. During a volcanic eruption, magma reaches the surface. In other places, magma gets close to the surface and heats the rock around it.

Geothermal Reservoirs In some regions where magma is close to the surface, rainwater and water from melted snow can seep down to the hot rock through cracks and other openings in Earth's surface. The water then becomes hot and sometimes can form steam. The hot water and steam can be trapped under high pressure in cracks and pockets called geothermal reservoirs. In some places the hot water and steam are close enough to the surface to form hot springs and geysers.

Geothermal Power Plants In places where the geothermal reservoirs are less than several kilometers deep, wells can be drilled to reach them. The hot water and steam produced by geothermal energy then can be used by geothermal power plants, like the one in **Figure 21,** to generate electricity.

Most geothermal reservoirs contain hot water under high pressure. **Figure 22** shows how these reservoirs can be used to generate electricity. While geothermal power is an inexhaustible source of energy, geothermal power plants can be built only in regions where geothermal reservoirs are close to the surface, such as in the western United States.

Figure 21
This geothermal power plant in Nevada produces enough electricity to power about 50,000 homes.

Heat Pumps Geothermal heat helps keep the temperature of the ground at a depth of several meters at a nearly constant temperature of about 10° to 20°C. This constant temperature can be used to cool and heat buildings by using a heat pump.

A heat pump contains a water-filled loop of pipe that is buried to a depth where the temperature is nearly constant. In summer the air is warmer than this underground temperature. Warm water from the building is pumped through the pipe down into the ground. The water cools and then is pumped back to the house where it absorbs more heat, and the cycle is repeated. During the winter, the air is cooler than the ground below. Then, cool water absorbs heat from the ground and releases it into the house.

Figure 22
The hot water in a geothermal reservoir is used to generate electricity in a geothermal power plant.

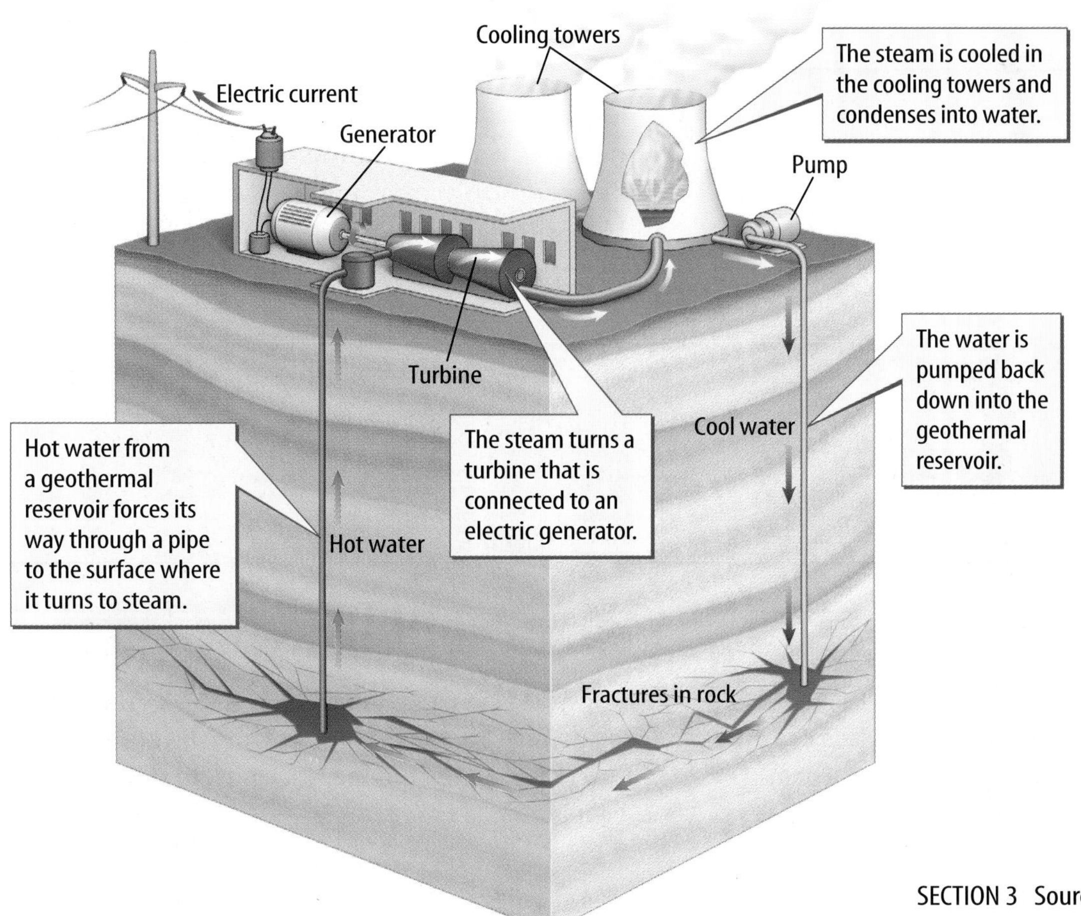
Cooling towers
The steam is cooled in the cooling towers and condenses into water.
Electric current
Generator
Pump
Turbine
The water is pumped back down into the geothermal reservoir.
Cool water
The steam turns a turbine that is connected to an electric generator.
Hot water from a geothermal reservoir forces its way through a pipe to the surface where it turns to steam.
Hot water
Fractures in rock

Energy from the Oceans

The ocean is in constant motion. If you've been to the seashore you've seen waves roll in. You may have seen the level of the ocean rise and fall over a period of about a half day. This rise and fall in the ocean level is called a tide. The constant movement of the ocean is an inexhaustible source of mechanical energy that can be converted into electric energy. While methods are still being developed to convert the motion in ocean waves to electric energy, several electric power plants using tidal motion have been built.

Figure 23
This tidal power plant in Annapolis Royal, Nova Scotia, is the only operating tidal power plant in North America.

Using Tidal Energy A high tide and a low tide each occur about twice a day. In most places the level of the ocean changes by less than a few meters. However, in some places the change is much greater. In the Bay of Fundy in Eastern Canada, the ocean level changes by 16 m between high tide and low tide. Almost 14 trillion kg of water move into or out of the bay between high and low tide.

Figure 23 shows an electric power plant that has been built along the Bay of Fundy. This power plant generates enough electric energy to power about 12,000 homes. The power plant is constructed so that as the tide rises, water flows through a turbine that causes a electric generator to spin, as shown in **Figure 24A**. The water is then trapped behind a dam. When the tide goes out, the trapped water behind the dam is released through the turbine to generate more electricity, as shown in **Figure 24B.** Each day electric power is generated for about ten hours when the tide is rising and falling.

While tidal energy is a nonpolluting, inexhaustible energy source, its use is limited. Only in a few places is the difference between high and low tide large enough to enable a large electric power plant to be built.

Figure 24
A tidal power plant can generate electricity when the tide is coming in and going out.

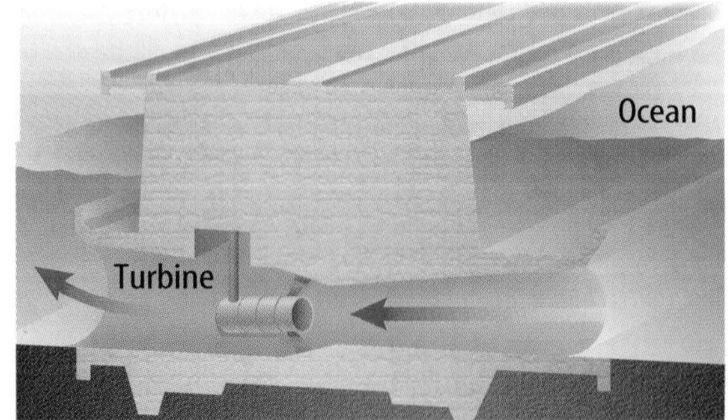

A As the tide comes in, it turns a turbine connected to a generator. When high tide occurs, gates are closed that trap water behind a dam.

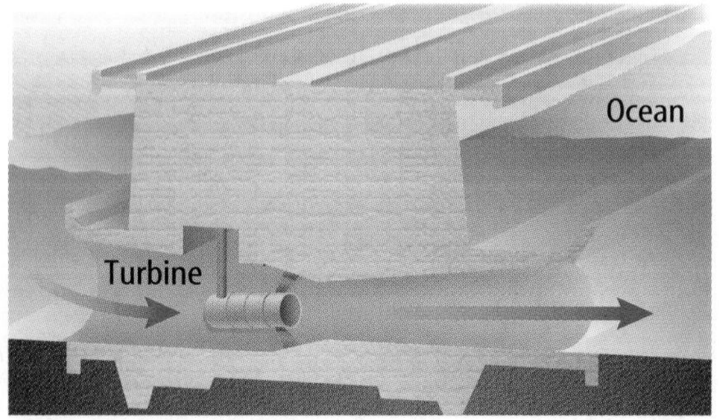

B As the tide goes out and the ocean level drops, the gates are opened and water from behind the dam flows through the turbine, causing it to spin and turn a generator.

Wind

Wind is another inexhaustible supply of energy. Modern windmills, like the ones in **Figure 25,** convert the kinetic energy of the wind to electrical energy. The propeller is connected to a generator so that electrical energy is generated when wind spins the propeller. These windmills produce almost no pollution. Some disadvantages are that windmills produce noise and that large areas of land are needed. Also, studies have shown that birds sometimes are killed by windmills.

Figure 25
Windmills work on the same basic principles as a power plant. Instead of steam turning a turbine, wind turns the rotors. *What are some of the advantages and disadvantages of using windmills?*

Conserving Energy

Fossil fuels are a valuable resource. Not only are they burned to provide energy, but oil and coal also are used to make plastics and other materials. One way to make the supply of fossil fuels last longer is to use less energy. Reducing the use of energy is called conserving energy.

You can conserve energy and also save money by turning off lights and appliances such as televisions when you are not using them. Also keep doors and windows closed tightly when it's cold or hot to keep heat from leaking out of or into your house. Energy could also be conserved if buildings are properly insulated, especially around windows. The use of oil could be reduced if cars were used less and made more efficient, so they went farther on a liter of gas. Recycling materials such as aluminum cans and glass also helps conserve energy.

Section  Assessment

1. What is the ultimate source of most of the energy stored on Earth?
2. What is a renewable resource? Give an example of a renewable and nonrenewable resource and explain the difference.
3. Explain why a heat pump is able to cool a building in the summer and heat the same building in the winter.
4. What are the disadvantages of using hydroelectricity and solar energy?
5. **Thinking Critically** Explain whether or not the following statement is true: All energy on Earth can be traced back to the Sun.

Skill Builder Activities

6. **Using an Electronic Spreadsheet** Use a spreadsheet to compare the effects on the environment of using fossil fuels, nuclear energy, and dams to produce electricity. Include in your spreadsheet the environmental effects of obtaining, transforming, and distributing the energy. **For more help, refer to the Technology Skill Handbook.**
7. **Using Proportions** As you go deeper into Earth, it becomes hotter. Using the information from this section, calculate the increase in temperature at a depth of 200 m below Earth's surface. **For more help, refer to the Math Skill Handbook.**

Energy to Power Your Life

Over the past 100 years, the amount of energy used in the United States and elsewhere has greatly increased. Today, a number of energy sources are available, such as coal, oil, natural gas, nuclear energy, hydroelectric power, wind, and solar energy. Some of these energy sources are being used up and are nonrenewable, but others are replaced as fast as they are used and, therefore, are renewable. Some energy sources are so vast that human usage has almost no effect on the amount available. These energy sources are inexhaustible.

Think about the types of energy you use at home and school every day. In this activity, you will investigate how and where energy is produced, and how it gets to you. You will also investigate alternative ways energy can be produced, and whether these sources are renewable, nonrenewable, or inexhaustible.

Recognize the Problem

What are the sources of the energy you use every day?

Form a Hypothesis

When you wake up in the morning and turn on a light, you use electrical energy. When you ride to school in a car or bus, its engine consumes chemical energy. What other types of energy do you use? Where is that energy produced? Which energy sources are nonrenewable, which are renewable, and which are inexhaustible? What are other sources of energy that you could use instead?

Local Energy Information

Energy Type	
Where is that energy produced?	
How is that energy produced?	
How is that energy delivered to you?	
Is the energy source renewable, nonrenewable, or inexhaustible?	
What type of alternative energy source could you use instead?	

Goals

- **Identify** how energy you use is produced and delivered.
- **Investigate** alternative sources for the energy you use.
- **Outline** a plan for how these alternative sources of energy could be used.

Data Source

SCIENCE*Online* Go to the Glencoe Science Web site at **science.glencoe.com** for more information about sources of energy and for data collected by other students.

Test Your Hypothesis

Plan

1. Think about the activities you do every day and the things you use. When you watch television, listen to the radio, ride in a car, use a hair drier, or turn on the air conditioning, you use energy. Select one activity or appliance that uses energy.
2. **Identify** the type of energy that is used.
3. **Investigate** how that energy is produced and delivered to you.
4. **Determine** if the energy source is renewable, nonrenewable, or inexhaustible.
5. If your energy source is nonrenewable, describe how the energy you use could be produced by renewable sources.

Do

1. Make sure your teacher approves your plan before you start.
2. Organize your findings in a data table, similar to the one that is shown.
3. Go to the Glencoe Science Web site at **science.glencoe.com** to post your data.

Analyze Your Data

1. **Describe** the process for producing and delivering the energy source you researched. How is it created, and how does it get to you?
2. How much of the energy you use every day comes from the energy source you investigated?
3. Is the energy source you researched renewable, nonrenewable, or inexhaustible? Why?
4. What other renewable or inexhaustible energy sources are used, or could be used, to generate electricicty in your area?

Draw Conclusions

1. If the energy source you investigated is nonrenewable, describe how you could reduce your use of this energy source.
2. What alternative sources of energy could you use for everyday energy needs? On the computer, create a plan for using renewable or inexhaustible sources.

Communicating Your Data

Find this *Use the Internet* activity on the Glencoe Science Web site at **science.glencoe.com**. Post your data in the table that is provided. **Compare** your data to those of other students. **Combine** your data with those of other students and make inferences using the combined data.

Chapter 8 Study Guide

Reviewing Main Ideas

Section 1 What is energy?

1. Energy is the ability to cause change. Energy is found in many forms.
2. Moving objects have kinetic energy. The potential energy of an object depends on its height and mass.
3. Potential energy is the energy of position. Radiant energy is the energy of light.
4. Electric current carries electrical energy, and atomic nuclei contain nuclear energy. *What are all the forms of energy that are represented in this picture?*

Section 2 Energy Transformations

1. Energy can be transformed from one form to another. Energy transformations cause changes to occur.
2. All energy transformations obey the law of conservation of energy, which means no energy is ever created or destroyed.
3. Chemical and electrical energy can be converted into other forms of energy such as radiant energy and thermal energy. Thermal energy moves from warm to cool objects.
4. Power plants convert a source of energy into electrical energy. The kinetic energy of steam spins a turbine which causes a generator to spin. The spinning gernerator produces electricity.

Section 3 Sources of Energy

1. Fossil fuels and nuclear energy are nonrenewable energy sources. The use of each of these energy sources produces waste products.
2. Renewable and inexhaustible energy sources include hydroelectric, solar, geothermal, and wind energy. *Why is the energy source used by this hydroelectric plant a renewable source of energy?*
3. Energy shortages might be prevented by conserving energy. Each energy source has advantages and disadvantages. *Look at the two photographs below of the same view of New York but at different times. Explain the difference.*

After You Read

FOLDABLES Reading & Study Skills

Write what you learned about the types, sources and transformation of energy under the Learned tab of your Know-Want-Learn Study Fold.

Chapter 8 Study Guide

Visualizing Main Ideas

Use the following terms and phrases to complete the concept map about energy sources: fossil fuels, hydroelectric, solar, wind, oil, coal, photovoltaic, *and* nonrenewable resources.

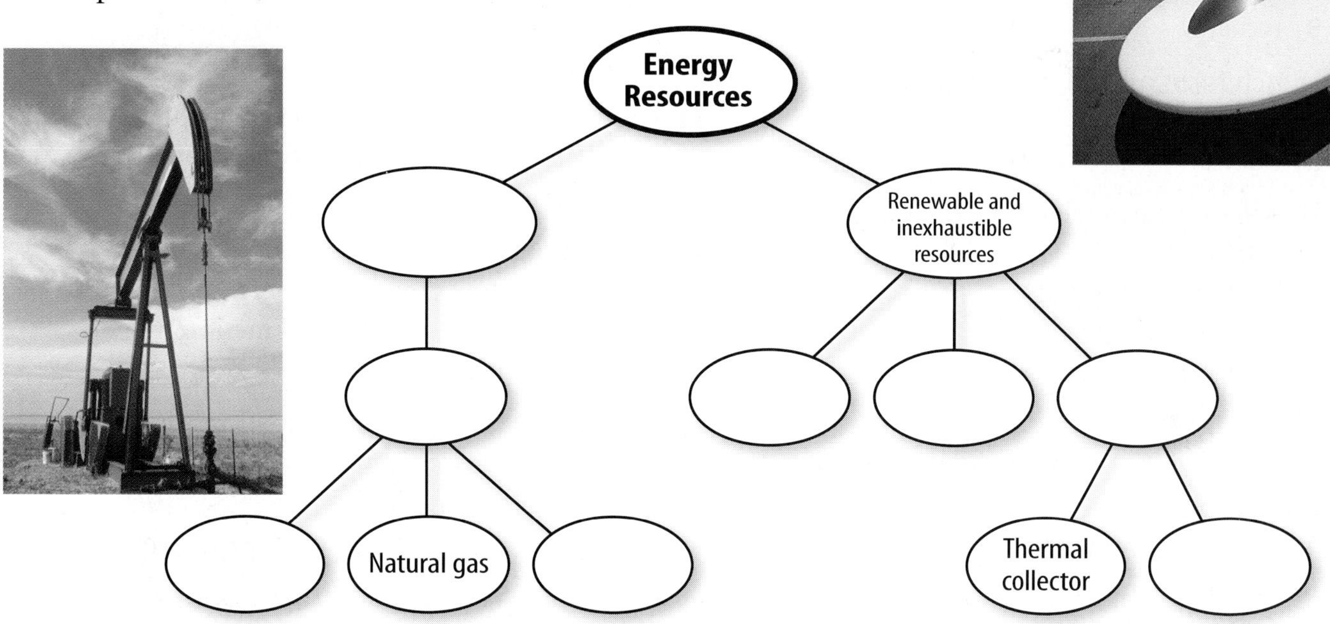

Vocabulary Review

Vocabulary Words

- **a.** alternative resource
- **b.** chemical energy
- **c.** electrical energy
- **d.** energy
- **e.** generator
- **f.** inexhaustible resource
- **g.** kinetic energy
- **h.** law of conservation of energy
- **i.** nonrenewable resource
- **j.** nuclear energy
- **k.** photovoltaic
- **l.** potential energy
- **m.** radiant energy
- **n.** renewable resource
- **o.** thermal energy
- **p.** turbine

Study Tip

Practice reading graphs and charts. Make a table that contains the same information as a graph does.

Using Vocabulary

For each set of terms below, explain the relationship that exists.

1. electrical energy, nuclear energy
2. turbine, generator
3. photovoltaic, radiant energy, electrical energy
4. renewable resource, inexhaustible resource
5. potential energy, kinetic energy
6. kinetic energy, electrical energy, generator
7. thermal energy, radiant energy
8. law of conservation of energy, energy transformations
9. nonrenewable resource, chemical energy

Chapter 8 Assessment

Checking Concepts

1. Objects that are able to fall have what type of energy?
   A) kinetic **C)** potential
   B) radiant **D)** electrical
2. Which form of energy does light have?
   A) electrical **C)** kinetic
   B) nuclear **D)** radiant
3. Muscles perform what type of energy transformation?
   A) kinetic to potential
   B) kinetic to electrical
   C) thermal to radiant
   D) chemical to kinetic
4. Photovoltaics perform what type of energy transformation?
   A) thermal to radiant
   B) kinetic to electrical
   C) radiant to electrical
   D) electrical to thermal
5. Which form of energy does food have?
   A) chemical **C)** radiant
   B) potential **D)** electrical
6. Solar energy, wind, and geothermal are what type of energy resource?
   A) inexhaustible **C)** nonrenewable
   B) inexpensive **D)** chemical
7. Which of the following is a nonrenewable source of energy?
   A) hydroelectricity **C)** wind
   B) nuclear **D)** solar
8. Which of the following does NOT require a generator to generate electricity?
   A) solar **C)** hydroelectric
   B) wind **D)** nuclear
9. Which of the following are fossil fuels?
   A) gas **C)** oil
   B) coal **D)** all of these
10. From where does the surface of Earth acquire most of its energy?
   A) radioactivity **C)** chemicals
   B) Sun **D)** wind

Thinking Critically

11. Explain how the motion of a swing illustrates the transformation between potential and kinetic energy.
12. A skateboard that is coasting along a flat surface will slow down and come to a stop. Explain what happens to the kinetic energy of the skateboard.
13. Describe the energy transformations that occur in the process of toasting a bagel in an electric toaster.
14. In what ways is the formation of coal like the formation of oil and natural gas? How is it different?
15. Explain the difference between the law of conservation of energy and conserving energy. How can conserving energy help prevent energy shortages?

Developing Skills

16. **Researching Information** Find out how spacecraft, such as *Galileo,* obtain the energy they need to operate as they travel through the solar system.

17. Concept Mapping Complete this concept map about energy.

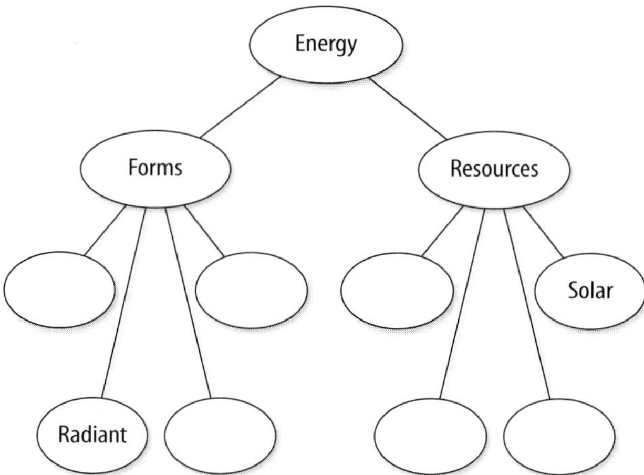

18. Classifying A proposal has been made to use wheat as a source of biomass energy. It can be made into alcohol, which can be burned in engines. How would you classify this source of energy? What are some advantages and disadvantages in using this as a source of energy? Explain.

Performance Assessment

19. Multimedia Presentation Alternative sources of energy that weren't discussed include biomass energy, wave energy, and hydrogen fuel cells. Research an alternative energy source and then prepare a digital slide show about the information you found. Use the concepts you learned from this chapter to inform your classmates about the future prospects of using such an energy source on a large scale.

Technology

Go to the Glencoe Science Web site at **science.glencoe.com** or use the **Glencoe Science CD-ROM** for additional chapter assessment.

Test Practice

Throughout the course of one day, you engage in dozens of energy transformations. The table below gives some examples of different energy transformations.

Types of Energy Transformation

Energy Transformation	Example
Potential ⟶ Kinetic	Ball rolling down a hill
Kinetic ⟶ Potential	A pebble tossed upward
Electrical ⟶ Radiant	A desk lamp
Chemical ⟶ Thermal	Burning fossil fuels
	Music from a radio

1. Which energy transformation occurs when coal is burned in a stove?
   A) potential → kinetic
   B) kinetic → potential
   C) electrical → radiant
   D) chemical → thermal

2. Which of these energy transformations will complete the table?
   F) electrical → radiant
   G) sound → electrical
   H) electrical → sound
   J) electrical → chemical

3. An image displayed on a computer screen most closely matches which example in terms of energy transformation?
   A) ball rolling down a hill
   B) a desk lamp
   C) burning fossil fuels
   D) music from a radio

CHAPTER 9

Work and Simple Machines

Machines enable people to accomplish many different tasks, from eating a meal to building a skyscraper. In this picture, machines such as cranes and trucks are being used to help construct buildings. In this chapter, you will learn about work and what simple machines are. You also will learn how simple machines make doing work easier.

What do you think?

Science Journal Look at the picture below with a classmate. Discuss what you think this might be or what is happening. Here's a hint: *The other six legs are just as hairy.* Write down your answer or best guess in your Science Journal.

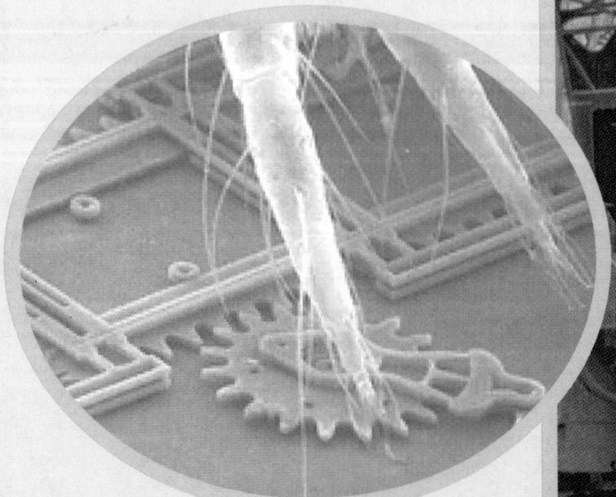

Two of the world's greatest structures were built using different tools. The Great Pyramid at Giza in Egypt was built nearly 5,000 years ago using blocks of limestone moved into place by hand with ramps and levers. In comparison, the Sears Tower in Chicago was built in 1973 using tons of steel that were hoisted into place by gasoline-powered cranes. How do machines such as ramps, levers, and cranes change the forces needed to do a job?

Compare forces

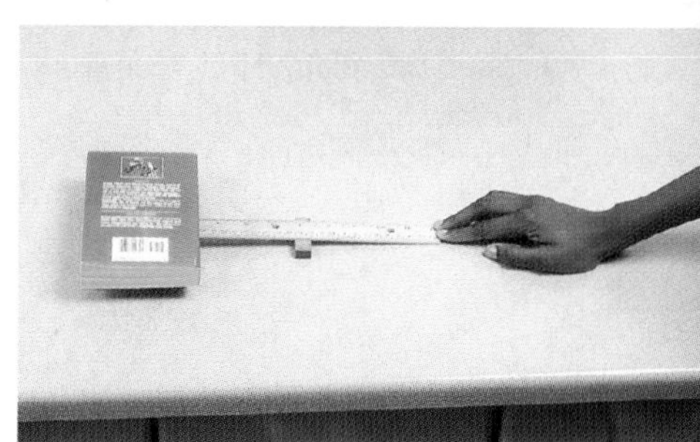

1. Place a ruler on an eraser. Place a book on one end of the ruler.
2. Using one finger, push down on the free end of the ruler to lift the book.
3. Repeat the experiment, placing the eraser in various positions beneath the ruler. Observe how much force is needed in each instance to lift the book.

Observe

In your Science Journal, describe your observations. How did changing the distance between the book and the eraser affect the force needed to lift the book?

Before You Read

Making a Main Ideas Study Fold **Make the following Foldable to help you identify the main ideas or major topics of work and simple machines.**

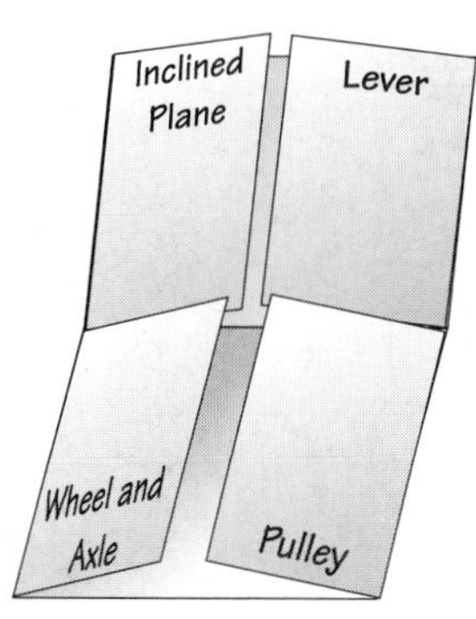

1. Place a sheet of paper in front of you so the long side is at the top. Fold the paper in half from the left side to the right side and then unfold.
2. Fold each side in to the centerfold line to divide the paper into fourths. Fold the paper in half from top to bottom and unfold.
3. Through the top thickness of paper, cut along both of the middle fold lines to form four tabs as shown. Label each tab *Inclined Plane, Wheel and Axle, Lever,* and *Pulley* as shown.
4. Before you read the chapter, fold your Foldable in half to make a book. Title the book *Work* and define work under the title. As you read the chapter, write information under the tabs about the four tools on your Foldable.

SECTION 1

Work and Power

As You Read

***What* You'll Learn**

- **Recognize** when work is done.
- **Calculate** how much work is done.
- **Explain** the relation between work and power.

Vocabulary

work
power

***Why* It's Important**

If you understand work, you can make your work easier.

What is work?

What does the term *work* mean to you? You might think of household chores, a job at an office, a factory, a farm, or the homework you do after school. In science, the definition of work is more specific. **Work** is done when a force causes an object to move in the same direction that the force is applied.

Can you think of a way in which you did work today? Maybe it would help to know that you do work when you lift your books, turn a doorknob, raise window blinds, or write with a pen or pencil. You also do work when you walk up a flight of stairs or open and close your school locker. In what other ways do you do work every day?

Work and Motion Your teacher has asked you to move a box of books to the back of the classroom. Try as you might, though, you just can't budge the box because it is too heavy. Although you exerted a force on the box and you feel tired from it, you have not done any work. In order for you to do work, two things must occur. First, you must apply a force to an object. Second, the object must move in the same direction as your applied force. You do work on an object only when the object moves as a result of the force you exert. The girl in **Figure 1** might think she is working by holding the bags of groceries. However, if she is not moving, she is not doing any work because she is not causing something to move.

Reading Check ***Why don't you do work when you hold a baby?***

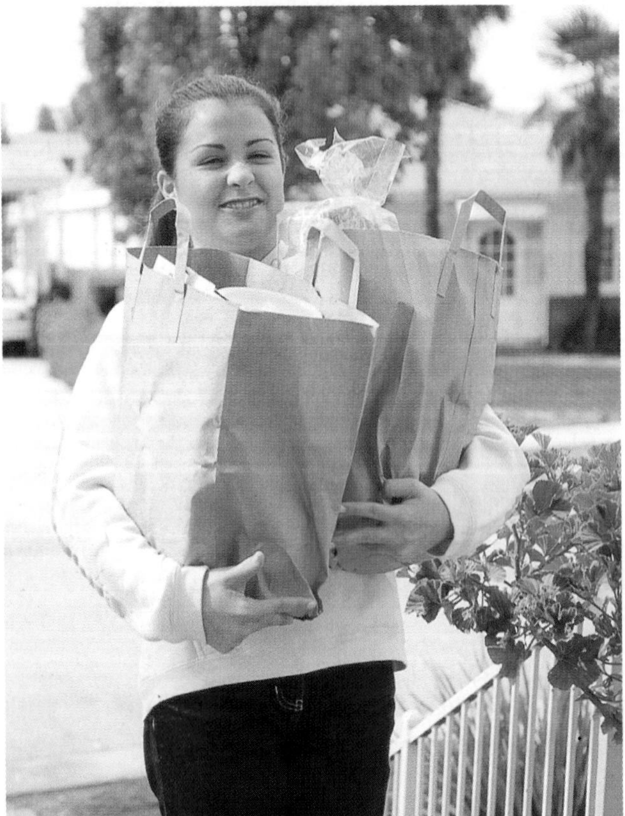

Figure 1
This girl is holding bags of groceries, yet she isn't doing any work. *Why?*

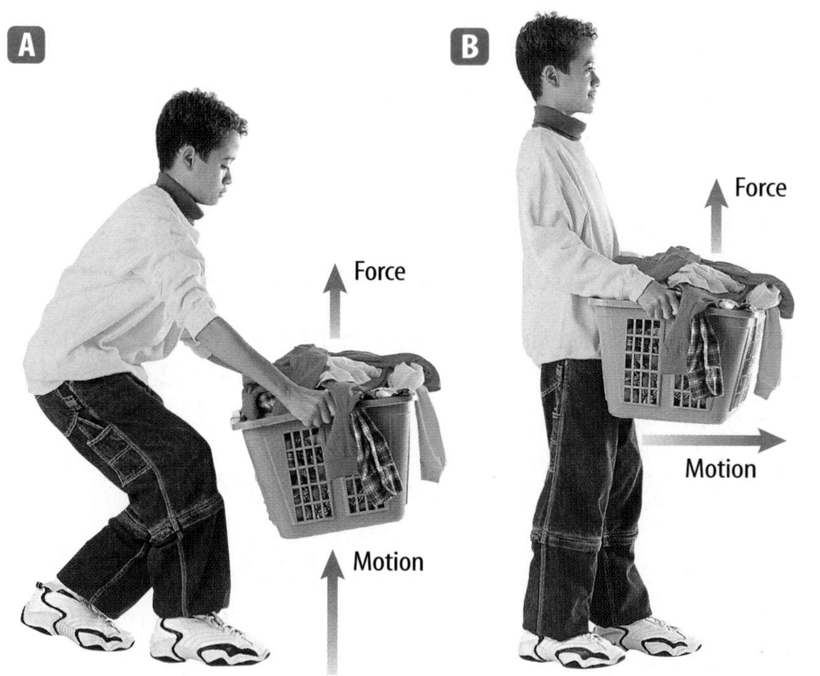

Figure 2
To do work, an object must move in the direction a force is applied. A The boy's arms do work when they exert an upward force on the basket and the basket moves upward. B The boy's arms still exert an upward force on the basket. But when the boy walks forward, no work is done by his arms.

Applying Force and Doing Work Picture yourself lifting the basket of clothes in **Figure 2A.** You can feel your arms exerting a force upward as you lift the basket, and the basket moves upward in the direction of the force your arms applied. Therefore, your arms have done work. Now suppose you carry the basket forward, as in **Figure 2B.** You can still feel your arms applying an upward force on the box to keep it from falling, but now the box is moving forward instead of upward. Because the direction of motion is not in the same direction of the force applied by your arms, no work is done by your arms.

Force in Two Directions Sometimes only part of the force you exert moves an object. Think about what happens when you push a lawn mower. You push at an angle to the ground as shown in **Figure 3.** Part of the force is to the right and part of the force is downward. Only the part of the force that is in the same direction as the motion of the mower—to the right—does work.

Life Science INTEGRATION

You may feel tired after pushing against a wall even though the wall doesn't move. Muscles in your body contract when you push. This contraction is caused by chemical reactions in your muscles that cause molecules to move. As a result, work is done inside your body when you push. Research how a muscle contracts and describe what you learned in your Science Journal.

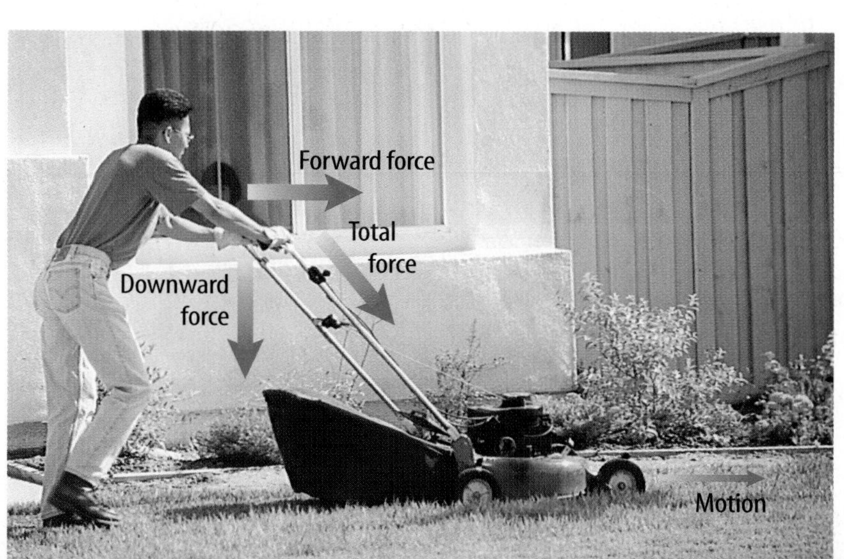

Figure 3
When you exert a force at an angle, only part of your force does work—the part that is in the same direction as the motion of the object.

Calculating Work

Work is done when a force makes an object move. More work is done when the force is increased or the object is moved a greater distance. The work done can be calculated from this equation:

$$\text{Work} = \text{force} \times \text{distance}$$

In SI units, force is measured in newtons and distance is measured in meters. The unit for work is the joule, named in honor of the nineteenth-century scientist James Prescott Joule.

Reading Check *What is the SI unit for work?*

Work and Distance Suppose you give a book a push and it slides across a table. To calculate the work you did, the distance in the above equation is not the distance the book moved. The distance in the work equation is the distance an object moves while the force is being applied. So the distance in the work equation is the distance the book moved while you were pushing.

Math Skills Activity

Calculating Work

Example Problem

A painter lifts a can of paint that weighs 40 N a distance of 2 m. How much work does she do? Hint: to lift a can weighing 40 N, the painter must exert a force of 40 N.

Solution

1. *This is what you know:* force = 40 N; distance = 2 m
2. *This is what you need to know:* work
3. *This is the equation you need to use:* work = force × distance
4. *Substitute the known values into the equation:* work = 40 N × 2 m = 80 J

Check your answer by dividing it by the distance. Did you calculate the same force that was given?

Practice Problem

As you push a lawn mower, the horizontal force is 300 N. If you push the mower a distance of 500 m, how much work do you do?

For more help, refer to the Math Skill Handbook.

What is power?

What does it mean to be powerful? To understand power, imagine two weightlifters lifting the same weight and suppose they lift the weight the same distance. Because they exert the same upward force and move the weight the same distance, each does the same amount of work.

Suppose one weightlifter lifted the weight in 3 s, while the other struggled to lift it in 10 s. You might say that the first weightlifter is stronger, because she lifted the weight in less time. You could also say that she is more powerful. In science, **power** is how quickly work is done. Something has more power or is more powerful if it can do more work in a certain amount of time.

Calculating Power Power can be calculated by dividing the amount of work done by the time needed to do the work. Power can be calculated by this formula:

$$\text{Power} = \frac{\text{work done}}{\text{time needed}}$$

In SI units, the unit of power is the watt, in honor of James Watt, a nineteenth-century British scientist who invented a practical version of the steam engine.

Research Visit the Glencoe Science Web site at **science.glencoe.com** for more information about James Watt and his steam engine. Find out why the unit of power was named after this inventor. Summarize your findings in a brief report.

Math Skills Activity

Calculating Power

Example Problem

You do 200 J of work in 12 s. How much power did you use?

Solution

1. *This is what you know:* work done = 200 J; time needed = 12 s
2. *This is what you need to find:* power
3. *This is the equation you need to use:* power = work done/time needed
4. *Substitute the known values into the equation:* power = 200 J/12 s = 17 watt

Check your answer by dividing it by the work done. Did you calculate the same time that was given?

Practice Problem

In the course of a short race, a car does 500,000 J of work in 7 s. What is the power of the car during the race?

For more help, refer to the Math Skill Handbook.

Measuring Work and Power

Procedure

1. Weigh yourself on a **scale.**
2. Multiply your weight in pounds by 4.45 to convert your weight to newtons.
3. Measure the vertical height of a **ramp or stairway. WARNING:** *Make sure the ramp or stairway is clear of all objects.*
4. Time yourself walking slowly and quickly up the ramp or stairway.

Analysis

1. Calculate and compare the work done and power used in each case.
2. How would the work done and power used change if your weight were twice as large?

Work and Energy If you push a chair and make it move, you do work on the chair. You also change the energy of the chair. Recall that when something is moving it has energy of motion, or kinetic energy. By making the chair move, you increase its kinetic energy.

You also change the energy of an object when you do work and lift it higher. An object has potential energy that increases when it is higher above Earth's surface. By lifting an object, you do work and increase its potential energy.

Power and Energy When you do work on an object you increase the energy of the object. Where does this energy come from? Because energy can never be created or destroyed, if the object gains energy then you must lose energy. When you do work on an object you transfer energy to the object, and your energy decreases. The amount of work done is the amount of energy transferred. So power is also equal to the amount of energy transferred in a certain amount of time.

$$\text{Power} = \frac{\text{energy transferred}}{\text{time needed}}$$

Sometimes energy can be transferred even when no work is done, such as when heat flows from a warm to a cold object. In fact, there are many ways energy can be transferred even if no work is done. Power is always the rate at which energy is transferred, or the amount of energy transferred divided by the time needed.

Section  Assessment

1. What conditions must be met for work to be done?
2. How much work was done to lift a 1,000-kg block to the top of the Great Pyramid, 146 m above the ground?
3. How is power related to work?
4. How much power, in watts, is needed to cut a lawn in 50 min if the work involved is 100,000 J?
5. **Think Critically** Suppose you are pulling a wagon at an angle. How can you make your task easier?

Skill Builder Activities

6. **Comparing and Contrasting** Which example involves more power: 200 J of work done in 20 s or 50 J of work done in 4 s? Explain your answer. **For more help, refer to the** Science Skill Handbook.
7. **Solving One-Step Equations** A 7,460-W engine is used to lift a beam weighing 9,800 N up 145 m. How much work must the motor do to lift this beam at constant speed? How much more work must be done to lift it 290 m? **For more help, refer to the** Math Skill Handbook.

Activity

Building the Pyramids

Imagine moving 2.3 million blocks of limestone, each weighing more than 1,000 kg. That is exactly what the builders of the Great Pyramid at Giza did. Although no one knows for sure exactly how they did it, they probably pulled the blocks most of the way. What could they have done to make their work easier?

What You'll Investigate

How is the force needed to lift a block related to the distance it travels?

Materials

wood block
tape
spring scale
ruler
thin notebooks
meterstick
several books

Goals

- **Compare** the force needed to lift a block with the force needed to pull it up a ramp.

Safety Precautions 

Procedure

1. Stack several books together on a tabletop to model a half-completed pyramid. Measure the height of the books in centimeters. Record the height on the first row of the data table under *Distance.*
2. Use the wood block as a model for a block of stone. Use tape to attach the block to the spring scale.
3. Place the block on the table and lift it straight up the side of the stack of books until the top of the block is even with the top of the books. Record the force shown on the scale in the data table under *Force.*

Work Done Using Different Ramps

Distance (cm)	Force (N)	Work (J)

4. **Arrange** a notebook so that one end is on the stack of books and the other end is on the table. Measure the length of the notebook and record this length as distance in the second row of the data table under *Distance.*
5. **Measure** the force needed to pull the block up the ramp. Record the force in the data table.
6. Repeat steps 4 and 5 using a longer notebook to make the ramp longer.
7. **Calculate** the work done in each row of the data table.

Conclude and Apply

1. How much work did you do in each case?
2. What happened to the force needed as the length of the ramp increased?
3. How could the builders of the pyramids have designed their task to use less force than they would lifting the blocks straight up? Draw a diagram to support your answer.

Communicating Your Data

Add your data to that found by other groups. **For more help, refer to the** Science Skill Handbook.

Using Machines

As You Read

What You'll Learn

- **Explain** how a machine makes work easier.
- **Calculate** the mechanical advantages and efficiency of a machine.
- **Explain** how friction reduces efficiency.

Vocabulary

input force
output force
mechanical advantage
efficiency

Why It's Important

Machines can't change the amount of work you need to do, but they can make doing work easier.

What is a machine?

Did you use a machine today? When you think of a machine you might think of a device, such as a car, with many moving parts powered by an engine or an electric motor. But if you used a pair of scissors or a broom, or cut your food with a knife, you used a machine. A machine is simply a device that makes doing work easier. Even a sloping surface can be a machine.

Mechanical Advantage

Even though machines make work easier, they don't decrease the amount of work you need to do. Instead, a machine changes the way in which you do work. When you use a machine, you exert a force over some distance. For example, you exert a force to move a rake or lift the handles of a wheelbarrow. This force is called the effort force, or the **input force.** The work you do on the machine is equal to the input force times the distance over which your force moves the machine. The work that you do on the machine is the input work.

The machine also does work by exerting a force to move an object over some distance. A rake, for example, exerts a force to move leaves. Sometimes this force is called the resistance force because the machine is trying to overcome some resistance. This force also can be called the **output force.** The work that the machine does is the output work. **Figure 4** shows how a machine transforms input work to output work.

When you use a machine, the output work can never be greater than the input work. So what is the advantage of using a machine? A machine makes work easier by changing the amount of force you need to exert, the distance over which the force is exerted, or the direction in which you exert your force.

Figure 4
No matter what type of machine is used, the output work is never greater than the input work.

Changing Force Work is equal to force times distance. If work stays the same, what happens to force if you exert a force over a longer distance? You can exert a smaller force. Some machines make work easier by allowing you to exert a smaller force over a longer distance.

The mechanical advantage of a machine compares the input force to the output force. **Mechanical advantage** is the number of times the input force is multiplied by a machine.

$$\text{Mechanical advantage} = \frac{\text{output force}}{\text{input force}}$$

For example, suppose that using a pulley system takes you only 300 N to lift a piano that weighs 1,500 N. To lift the piano, the pulley system exerts an upward force of 1,500 N to overcome the downward pull of gravity. This is the output force. The force you exert on the pulley system in the input force, which is 300 N. So the mechanical advantage of the pulley system is five.

What is the mechanical advantage of a machine?

Research Visit the Glencoe Science Web site at **science.glencoe.com** for more information about early types of tools and how they took advantage of simple machines. Design a poster relating several ancient tools to the simple machines you have studied.

Math Skills Activity

Calculating Mechanical Advantage

Example Problem

To pry the lid off a paint can, you apply a force of 50 N to the handle of a screwdriver. What is the mechanical advantage of the screwdriver if it applies a force of 500 N to the lid?

Solution

1. *This is what you know:* output force = 500 N; input force = 50 N
2. *This is what you need to find:* mechanical advantage
3. *This is the equation you need to use:* mechanical advantage = output force/input force
4. *Substitute the known values:* mechanical advantage = (500 N) / (50 N) = 10.

Check your answer by multiplying it by the input force. Do you calculate the same output force that was given?

Practice Problem

To open a bottle, you apply a force of 50 N to a bottle opener. The bottle opener applies a force of 775 N to the bottle cap. What is the mechanical advantage of the bottle opener?

For more help, refer to the Math Skill Handbook.

Figure 5
A When you rake leaves, you move your hands a short distance but the end of the rake moves over a longer distance. B Sometimes it is easier to exert your force in a certain direction. This boy would rather pull down on the rope to lift the flag than to climb to the top of the pole and pull up.

Changing Distance Some machines allow you to exert your force over a shorter distance. In these machines, the output force is less than the input force. The rake in **Figure 5A** is this type of machine. You move your hands a small distance at the top of the handle, but the bottom of the rake moves a greater distance as it moves the leaves. The mechanical advantage of this type of machine is less than one because the output force is less than the input force.

Changing Direction Sometimes it is easier to apply a force in a certain direction. For example, it is easier to pull down on the rope in **Figure 5B** than to pull up on it. Some machines enable you to change the direction of the input force. In these machines neither the force nor the distance is changed. The mechanical advantage of this type of machine is equal to one because the output force is equal to the input force. The three ways machines make doing work easier are summarized in **Figure 6.**

Figure 6
Machines are useful because they can A increase force, B increase distance, or C change the direction in which a force is applied.

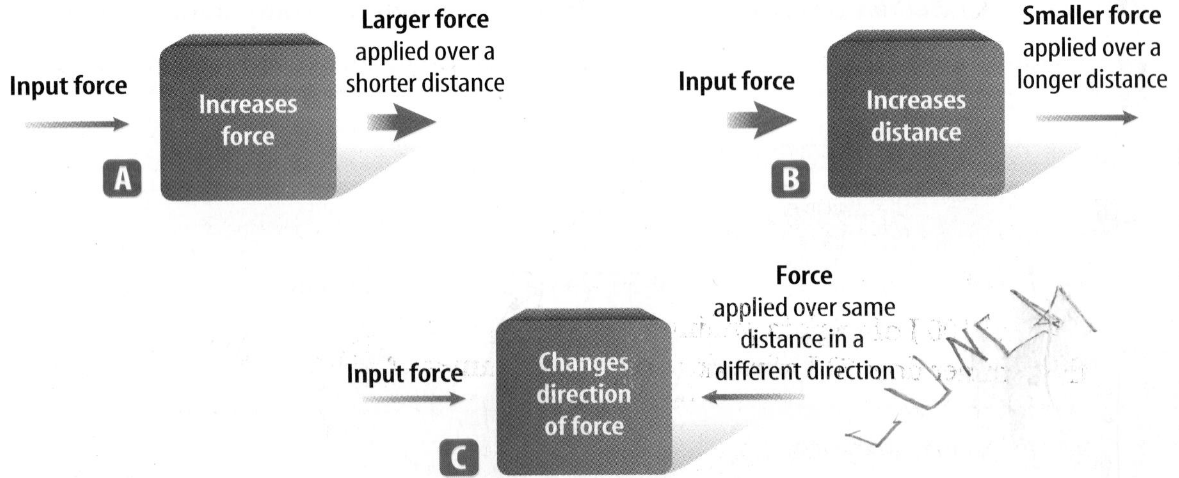

Efficiency

A machine doesn't increase the input work. For a real machine, the output work done by the machine is always less than the input work that you do on the machine. Remember that anytime two surfaces slide past each other, friction resists their motion. In real machines some input work is always used to overcome friction, so the parts of the machine can move.

The ability of a machine to convert the input work to output work is called the machine's **efficiency.** Efficiency is described as a percent.

$$\text{Efficiency} = \frac{\text{output work}}{\text{input work}} \times 100\%$$

An ideal machine has an efficiency of 100 percent. The efficiency of a real machine is always less than 100 percent, because some work is converted into heat by friction. When friction is reduced, the efficiency of a machine increases.

Why is the efficiency of a real machine less than 100 percent?

Life Science INTEGRATION

Chemical reactions that enable your muscles to move also produce heat that helps maintain your body temperature. When you shiver, rapid contraction and relaxation of muscle fibers produces a large amount of heat that helps raise your body temperature. This causes the efficiency of your muscles to decrease as more energy is converted into heat.

Math Skills Activity

Calculating Efficiency

Example Problem

Using a pulley system, a crew does 7,500 J of work to load a box that requires 4,500 J of work. What is the efficiency of the pulley system?

Solution

1. *This is what you know:* work output = 4,500 J; work input = 7,500 J
2. *This is what you need to find:* efficiency
3. *This is the equation you need to use:* efficiency = output work/input work × 100%
4. *Substitute the known values:* efficiency = (4,500 J)/(7,500 J) × 100% = 60%

Check your answer by multiplying it by the work input. Do you calculate the same work output that was given?

Practice Problem

You do 100 J of work in pulling out a nail with a claw hammer. If the hammer does 70 J of work, what is the hammer's efficiency?

For more help, refer to the Math Skill Handbook.

Figure 7
Lubrication can reduce the friction between two surfaces.

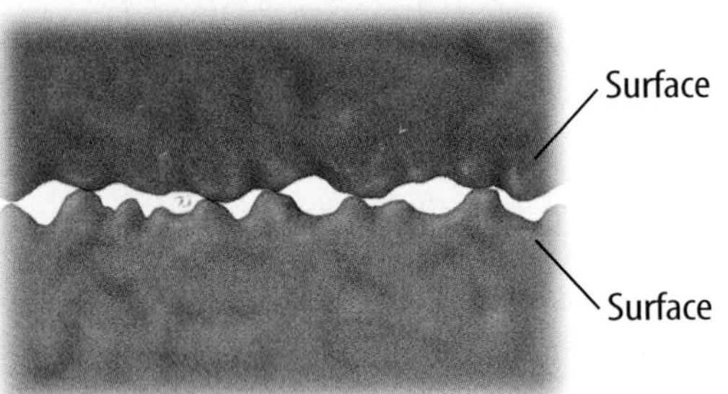

A **Two surfaces in contact can stick together where the high spots on each surface come in contact.**

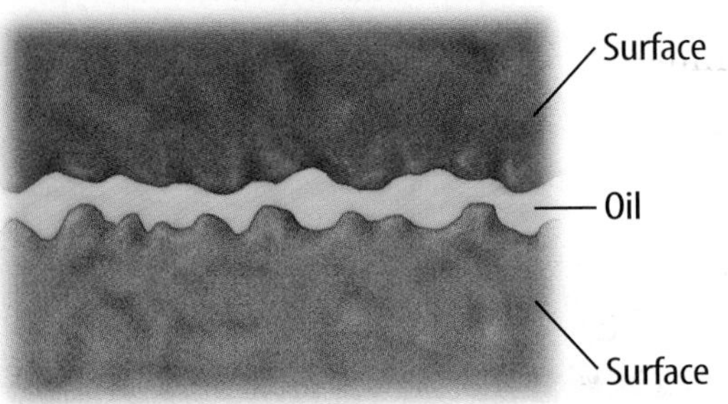

B **Adding oil or another lubricant separates the surface so that fewer high spots make contact.**

Friction To help understand friction, imagine pushing a heavy box up a ramp. As the box begins to move, the bottom surface of the box slides across the top surface of the ramp. Neither surface is perfectly smooth—each has high spots and low spots, as shown in **Figure 7.**

As the two surfaces slide past each other, high spots on the two surfaces come in contact. At these contact points, shown in **Figure 7A,** atoms and molecules can bond together. This makes the contact points stick together. The attractive forces between all the bonds in the contact points added together is the frictional force that tries to keep the two surfaces from sliding past each other.

To keep the box moving, a force must be applied to break the bonds between the contact points. Even after these bonds are broken and the box moves, new bonds form as different parts of the two surfaces come into contact. So as you keep pushing the box, part of the force that you exert is used to break the bonds that keep forming between the contact points.

Friction and Efficiency One way to reduce friction between two surfaces is to add oil. **Figure 7B** shows how oil fills the gaps between the surfaces, and keeps many of the high spots from making contact. Because there are fewer contact points between the surfaces, the force of friction is reduced. More of the input work then is converted to output work by the machine.

Section  Assessment

1. What are three ways in which machines make work easier?
2. How can you find the mechanical advantage of a machine?
3. You do 150 J of work on a machine and the machine does 90 J of work as a result. What is the efficiency of the machine?
4. Explain how friction reduces the efficiency of machines.
5. **Think Critically** Can a machine be useful even if its mechanical advantage is less than one? Explain and give an example.

Skill Builder Activities

6. **Comparing and Contrasting** How does the efficiency of an ideal machine compare with that of a real machine? **For more help, refer to the Science Skill Handbook.**
7. **Using an Electronic Spreadsheet** On a computer, create a spreadsheet that calculates work from force and distance. Input a value for work and then input several different force values. How does the distance change if the work stays the same and the force decreases? **For more help, refer to the Technology Skill Handbook.**

SECTION

Simple Machines

What is a simple machine?

What do you think of when you hear the word *machine?* Many people think of machines as complicated devices such as cars, elevators, or computers. However, some machines are as simple as a hammer, shovel, or ramp. A **simple machine** is a machine that does work with only one movement. The six simple machines are the inclined plane, lever, wheel and axle, screw, wedge, and pulley. A machine made up of a combination of simple machines is called a **compound machine.** A can opener is a compound machine. The bicycle in **Figure 8** is a familiar example of another compound machine.

Inclined Plane

Ramps might have enabled the ancient Egyptians to build their pyramids. To move limestone blocks weighing more than 1,000 kg each, archaeologists hypothesize that the Egyptians built enormous ramps. A ramp is a simple machine known as an inclined plane. An **inclined plane** is a flat, sloped surface. Less force is needed to move an object from one height to another using an inclined plane than is needed to lift the object. As the inclined plane becomes longer, the force needed to move the object becomes smaller.

As You Read

***What* You'll Learn**

- **Distinguish** among the different simple machines.
- **Describe** how to find the mechanical advantage of each simple machine.

Vocabulary

simple machine, compound machine, inclined plane, wedge, screw, lever, wheel and axle, pulley

***Why* It's Important**

Simple machines make up all machines.

Figure 8
Devices that use combinations of simple machines, such as this bicycle, are called compound machines.

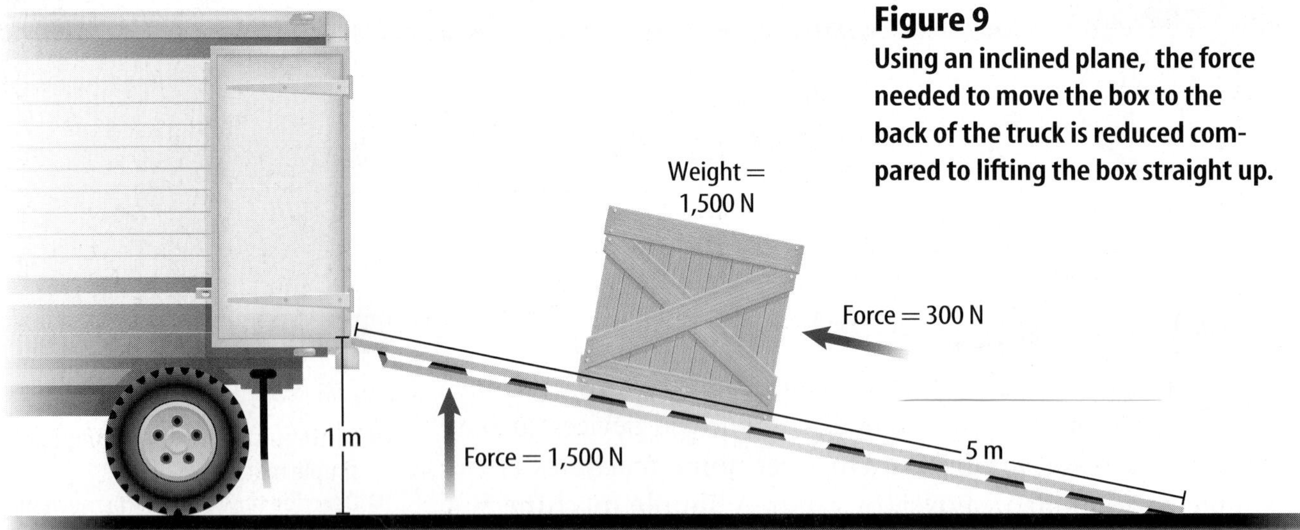

Figure 9
Using an inclined plane, the force needed to move the box to the back of the truck is reduced compared to lifting the box straight up.

Using Inclined Planes Imagine having to lift a box weighing 1,500 N to the back of a truck that is 1 m off the ground. You would have to exert a force of 1,500 N, the weight of the box, over a distance of 1 m, which equals 1,500 J of work. Now suppose that instead you use a 5-m-long ramp, as shown in **Figure 9.** The amount of work you need to do does not change. You still need to do 1,500 J of work. However, the distance over which you exert your force becomes 5 m. You can calculate the force you need to exert by dividing both sides of the equation for work by distance.

$$\text{Force} = \frac{\text{work}}{\text{distance}}$$

If you do 1,500 J of work by exerting a force over 5 m, the force is only 300 N. Because you exert the input force over a distance that is five times as long, you can exert a force that is five times less.

The mechanical advantage of an inclined plane is the length of the inclined plane divided by its height. In this example, the ramp has a mechanical advantage of 5.

Wedge An inclined plane that moves is called a **wedge.** A wedge can have one or two sloping sides. The knife shown in **Figure 10** is an example of a wedge. An axe and certain types of doorstop are also wedges. Just as for an inclined plane, the mechanical advantage of a wedge increases as it becomes longer and thinner.

Figure 10
This chef's knife is a wedge that slices through food.

Figure 11
Wedge-shaped teeth help tear food.

A **Your front teeth help tear an apple apart.**

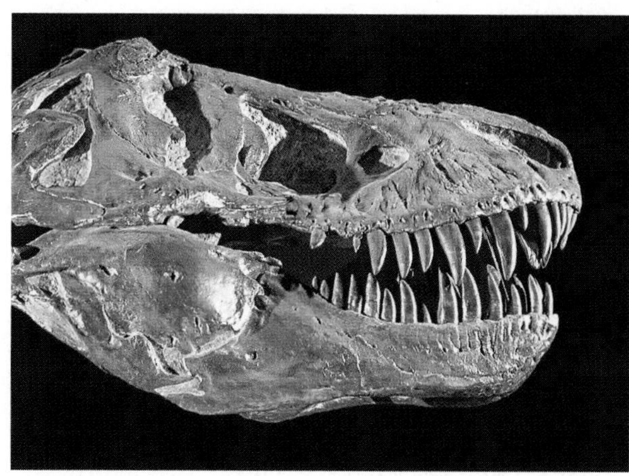

B **The wedge-shaped teeth of this Tyrannosaurus Rex show that it was a carnivore.**

Wedges in Your Body You have wedges in your body. The bite marks on the apple in **Figure 11A** show how your front teeth are wedge shaped. A wedge changes the direction of the applied effort force. As your push your front teeth into the apple, the downward effort force is changed by your teeth into a sideways force that pushes the skin of the apple apart.

The teeth of meat eaters, or carnivores, are more wedge shaped than the teeth of plant eaters, or herbivores. The teeth of carnivores are used to cut and rip meat, while herbivores' teeth are used for grinding plant material. By examining the teeth of ancient animals, such as the dinosaur in **Figure 11B,** scientists can determine what the animal ate when it was living.

The Screw Another form of the inclined plane is a screw. A **screw** is an inclined plane wrapped around a cylinder or post. The inclined plane on a screw forms the screw threads. Just like a wedge changes the direction of the effort force applied to it, a screw also changes the direction of the applied force. When you turn a screw, the force applied is changed by the threads to a force that pulls the screw into the material. Friction between the threads and the material holds the screw tightly in place. The mechanical advantage of the screw is the length of the inclined plane wrapped around the screw divided by the length of the screw. The more tightly wrapped the threads are, the easier it is to turn the screw. Examples of screws are shown in **Figure 12.**

How are screws related to the inclined plane?

Figure 12
The thread around a screw is an inclined plane. Many familiar devices use screws to make work easier.

Figure 13
The mechanical advantage of a lever changes as the position of the fulcrum changes. The mechanical advantage increases as the fulcrum is moved closer to the output force.

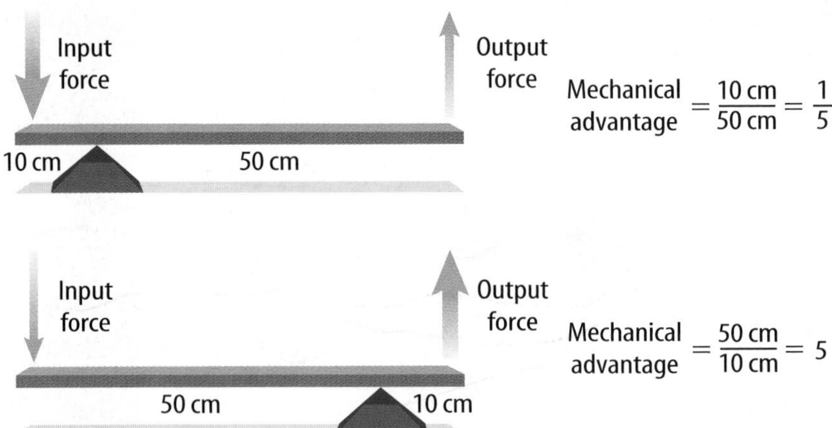

Lever

You step up to the plate. The pitcher throws the ball and you swing your lever to hit the ball? That's right! A baseball bat is a type of simple machine called a lever. A **lever** is any rigid rod or plank that pivots, or rotates, about a point. The point about which the lever pivots is called a fulcrum.

The mechanical advantage of a lever is found by dividing the distance from the fulcrum to the input force by the distance from the fulcrum to the output force, as shown in **Figure 13.** When the fulcrum is closer to the output force than the input force, the mechanical advantage is greater than one.

Levers are divided into three classes according to the position of the fulcrum with respect to the input force and output force. **Figure 15** shows examples of three classes of levers.

Figure 14
A faucet handle is a wheel and axle. A wheel and axle is similar to a circular lever. The center is the fulcrum, and the wheel and axle turn around it. *How can you increase the mechanical advantage of a wheel and axle?*

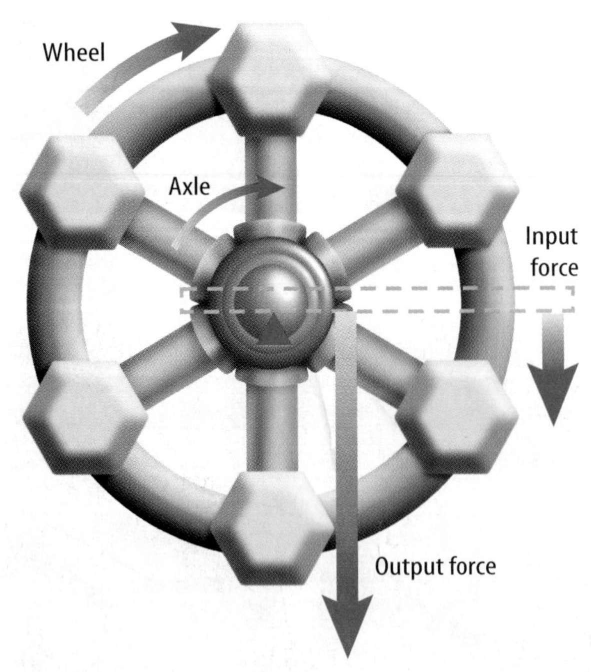

Wheel and Axle

Do you think you could turn a doorknob easily if it were a narrow rod the size of a pencil? It might be possible, but it would be difficult. A doorknob makes it easier for you to open a door because it is a simple machine called a wheel and axle. A **wheel and axle** consists of two circular objects of different sizes that are attached in such a way that they rotate together. As you can see in **Figure 14,** the larger object is the wheel and the smaller object is the axle.

The mechanical advantage of a wheel and axle is usually greater than one. It is found by dividing the radius of the wheel by the radius of the axle. For example, if the radius of the wheel is 12 cm and the radius of the axle is 4 cm, the mechanical advantage is 3.

Figure 15

Levers are among the simplest of machines, and you probably use them often in everyday life without even realizing it. A lever is a bar that pivots around a fixed point called a fulcrum. As shown here, there are three types of levers—first class, second class, and third class. They differ in where two forces—an input force and an output force—are located in relation to the fulcrum.

- ▲ Fulcrum
- ▼ Input force
- ▲ Output force

In a first-class lever, the fulcrum is between the input force and the output force. First-class levers, such as scissors and pliers, multiply force or distance depending on where the fulcrum is placed. They always change the direction of the input force, too.

First-class lever

In a second-class lever, such as a wheelbarrow, the output force is between the input force and the fulcrum. Second-class levers always multiply the input force but don't change its direction.

Second-class lever

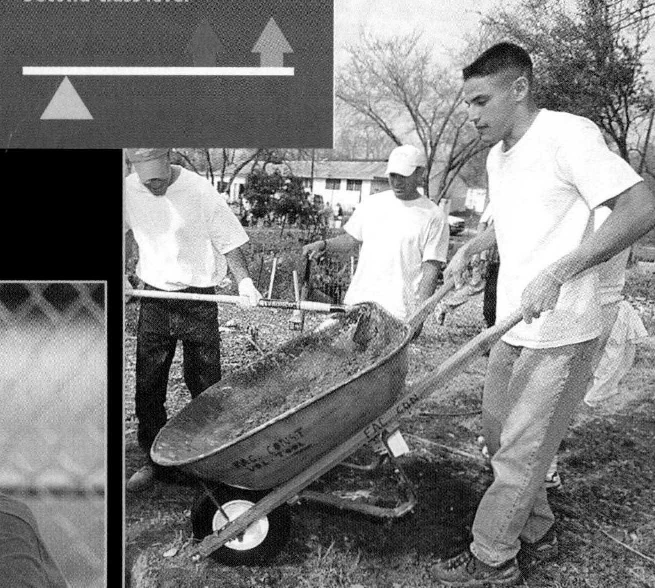

Third-class lever

In a third-class lever, such as a baseball bat, the input force is between the output force and the fulcrum. For a third-class lever, the output force is less than the input force, but is in the same direction

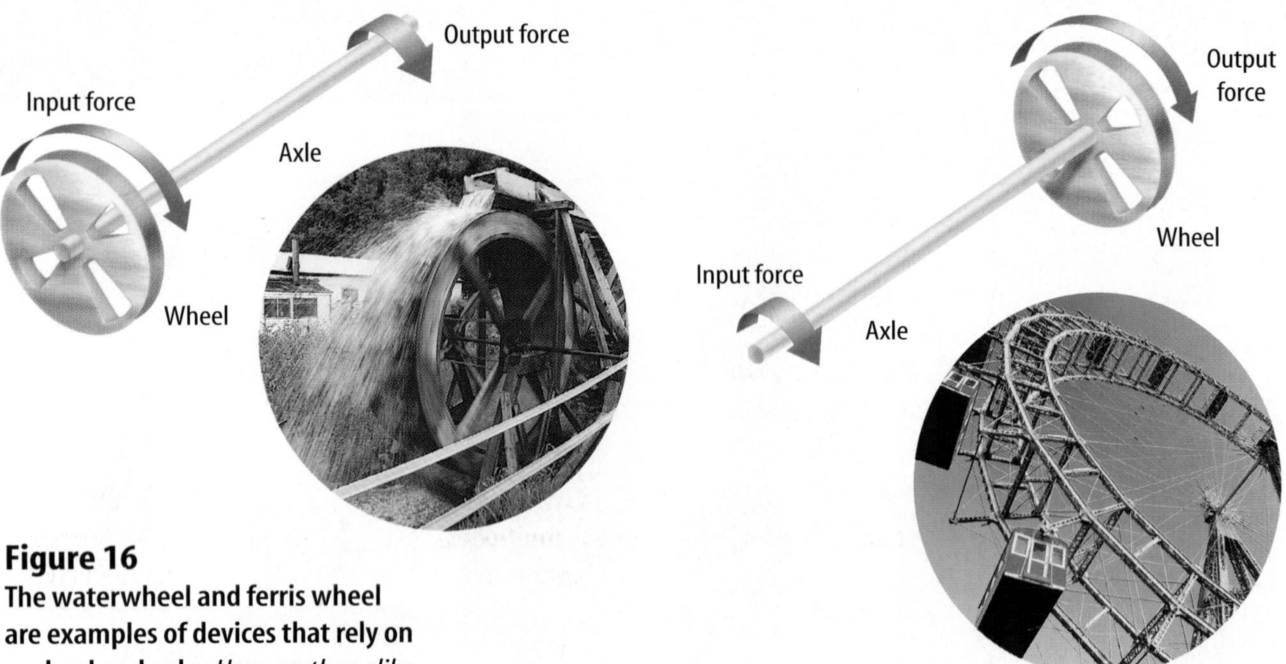

Figure 16
The waterwheel and ferris wheel are examples of devices that rely on a wheel and axle. *How are they alike and how are they different?*

Using Wheels and Axles In some devices, the input force is used to turn the wheel and the output force is exerted by the axle. Because the wheel is larger than the axle, the mechanical advantage is greater than one. So the output force is greater than the input force. A doorknob, a steering wheel, and a screwdriver are examples of this type of wheel and axle.

In other devices, the input force is applied to turn the axle and the output force is exerted by the wheel. Then the mechanical advantage is less than one and the output force is less than the input force. A fan and a ferris wheel are examples of this type of wheel and axle. **Figure 16** shows an example of each type of wheel and axle.

Mini LAB

Observing Pulleys

Procedure

1. Obtain two **broomsticks.** Tie a 3-m-long **rope** to the middle of one stick. Wrap the rope around both sticks four times.
2. Have two students pull the broomsticks apart while a third pulls on the rope.
3. Repeat with two wraps of rope.

Analysis

1. Compare the results.
2. Predict whether it will be easier to pull the broomsticks together with ten wraps of rope.

Pulley

To raise a sail, a sailor pulls down on a rope. The rope uses a simple machine called a pulley to change the direction of the force needed. A **pulley** consists of a grooved wheel with a rope or chain wrapped around it.

Fixed Pulleys Some pulleys, such as the one on a sail, a window blind, or a flagpole, are attached to a structure above your head. When you pull down on the rope, you pull something up. This type of pulley, called a fixed pulley, does not change the force you exert or the distance over which you exert it. Instead, it changes the direction in which you exert your force, as shown in **Figure 17A.** The mechanical advantage of a fixed pulley is 1.

Reading Check *How does a fixed pulley affect the input force?*

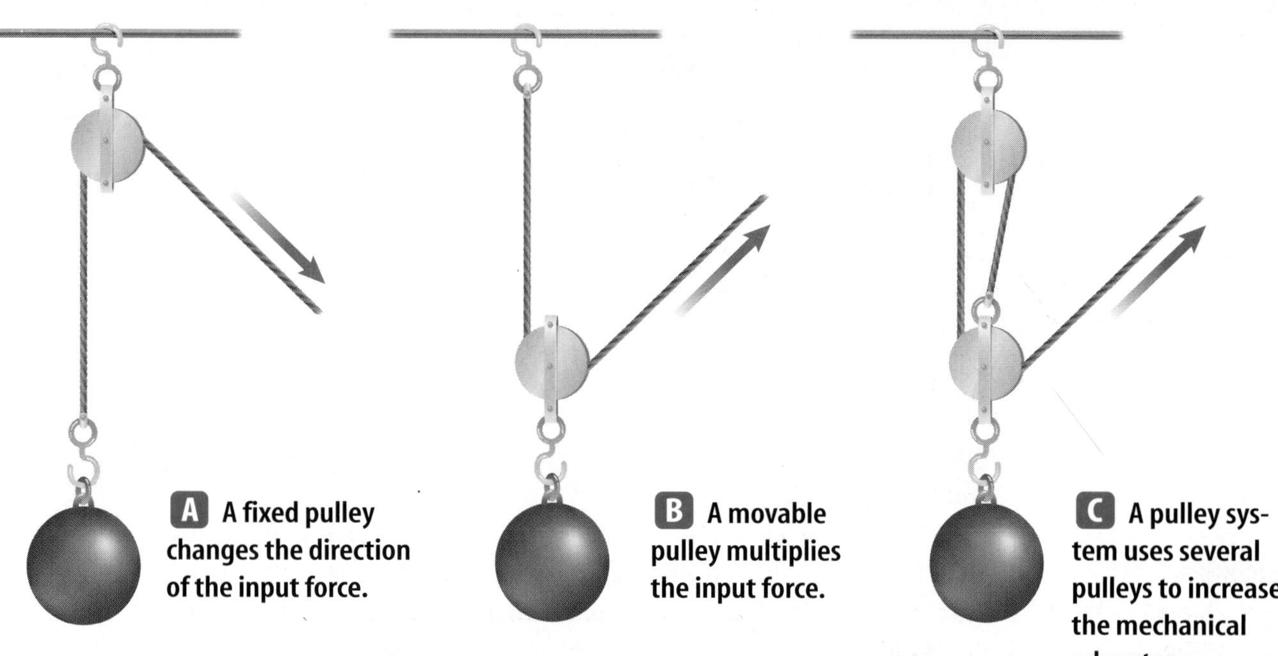

A A fixed pulley changes the direction of the input force.

B A movable pulley multiplies the input force.

C A pulley system uses several pulleys to increase the mechanical advantage.

Figure 17
Pulleys can change force and direction.

Movable Pulleys Another way to use a pulley is to attach it to the object you are lifting, as shown in **Figure 17B.** This type of pulley, called a movable pulley, allows you to exert a smaller force to lift the object. The mechanical advantage of a movable pulley is always 2.

More often you will see combinations of fixed and movable pulleys. Such a combination is called a pulley system. The mechanical advantage of a pulley system is equal to the number of sections of rope pulling up on the object. For the pulley system shown in **Figure 17C** the mechanical advantage is 3.

Section 3 Assessment

1. Define simple and compound machines in your own words.
2. Describe four different simple machines.
3. Why can a machine with a mechanical advantage less than one be useful?
4. How does the mechanical advantage of a wheel and axle change as the size of the wheel increases?
5. **Think Critically** The Great Pyramid is 146 m high. How long would a ramp from the top of the pyramid to the ground need to be to have a mechanical advantage of 4?

Skill Builder Activities

6. **Comparing and Contrasting** How are a lever and a wheel and axle similar? **For more help, refer to the** Science Skill Handbook.
7. **Using Proportions** You are designing a lever to lift an object that weighs 500 N. The lever exerts the output force 1 m from the fulcrum. How far from the fulcrum must an effort force of 250 N be applied to lift the object? Draw a diagram as part of your answer. Label the forces and distances. **For more help, refer to the** Math Skill Handbook.

Activity *Design Your Own Experiment*

Pulley Power

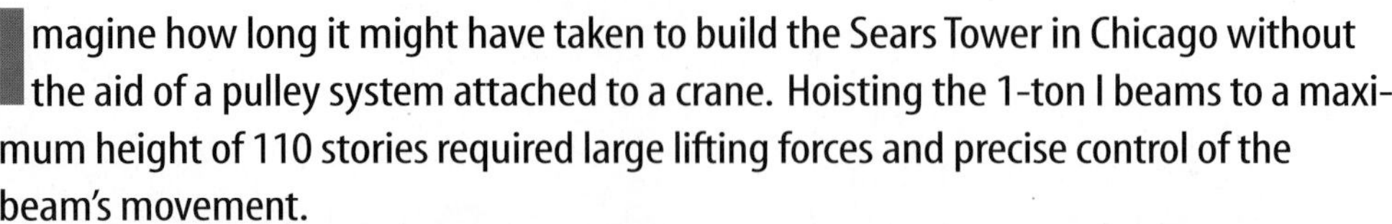

Imagine how long it might have taken to build the Sears Tower in Chicago without the aid of a pulley system attached to a crane. Hoisting the 1-ton I beams to a maximum height of 110 stories required large lifting forces and precise control of the beam's movement.

Construction workers also use smaller pulleys that are not attached to cranes to lift supplies to where they are needed. Pulleys are not limited to construction sites. They also are used to lift automobile engines out of cars, to help load and unload heavy objects on ships, and to lift heavy appliances and furniture.

Recognize the Problem

How can you use a pulley system to reduce the force needed to lift a load?

Form a Hypothesis

Write a hypothesis about how pulleys can be combined to make a system of pulleys to lift a heavy load, such as a brick. Consider the efficiency of your system.

Goals

- **Design** a pulley system.
- **Measure** the mechanical advantage and efficiency of the pulley system.

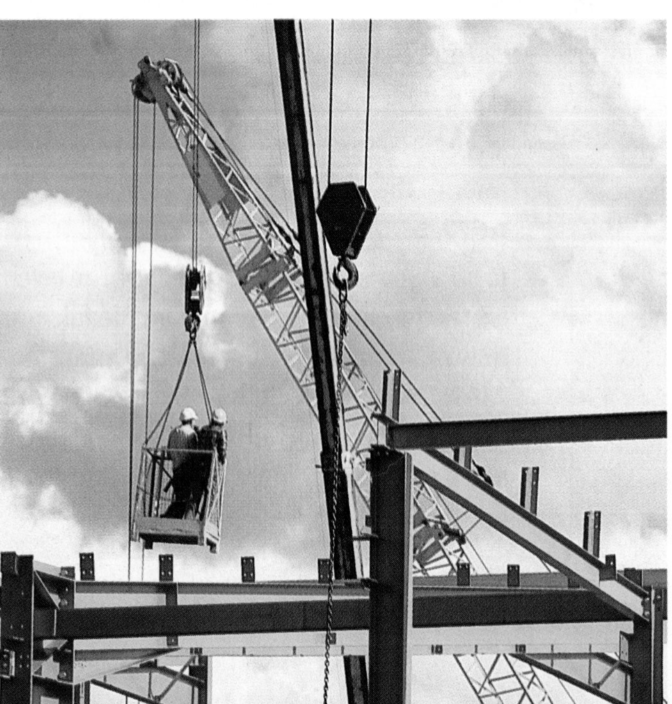

Possible Materials

single- and multiple-pulley systems
nylon rope
steel bar to support the pulley system
meterstick
**metric tape measure*
variety of weights to test pulleys
force spring scale
brick
**heavy book*
balance
**scale*
**Alternate materials*

Safety Precautions

The brick could be dangerous if it falls. Keep your hands and feet clear of it.

Test Your Hypothesis

Plan

1. Decide how you are going to support your pulley system. What materials will you use?
2. How will you measure the effort force and the resistance force? How will you determine the mechanical advantage? How will you measure efficiency?
3. **Experiment** by lifting small weights with a single pulley, double pulley, and so on. How efficient are the pulleys? In what ways can you increase the efficiency of your setup?
4. Use the results of step 3 to design a pulley system to lift the brick. Draw a diagram of your design. Label the different parts of the pulley system and use arrows to indicate the direction of movement for each section of rope.

Do

1. Make sure your teacher approves your plan before you start.
2. Assemble the pulley system you designed. You might want to test it with a smaller weight before attaching the brick.
3. **Measure** the force needed to lift the brick. How much rope must you pull to raise the brick 10 cm?

Analyze Your Data

1. **Calculate** the ideal mechanical advantage of your design.
2. **Calculate** the actual mechanical advantage of the pulley system you built.
3. **Calculate** the efficiency of your pulley system.
4. How did the mechanical advantage of your pulley system compare with those of your classmates?

Draw Conclusions

1. **Explain** how increasing the number of pulleys increases the mechanical advantage.
2. How could you modify the pulley system to lift a weight twice as heavy with the same effort force used here?
3. **Compare** this real machine with an ideal machine.

Communicating Your Data

Show your design diagram to the class. Review the design and point out good and bad characteristics of your pulley system. **For more help, refer to the Science Skill Handbook.**

TIME SCIENCE AND Society

SCIENCE ISSUES THAT AFFECT YOU!

Bionic Pe

People in need of transplants usually receive human organs. But many people's medical problems can only be solved by receiving artificial body parts. These synthetic devices, called prostheses, are used to replace anything from a heart valve to a knee joint. Bionics is the science of creating artificial body parts. A major focus of bionics is the replacement of lost limbs. Through accident, birth defect, or disease, people sometimes lack hands or feet, or even whole arms or legs. For centuries, people have used prostheses to replace limbs. In the past, disabled people used devices like peg legs or artificial arms that ended in a pair of hooks. These protheses didn't do much to replace lost functions of arms and legs.

But today, that's changed, thanks to the work of eighteenth-century scientists Luigi Galvani and Alessandro Volta. Because of their experiments, people began to realize that muscles contract by means of electrical impulses. This knowledge eventually led to an invention called functional neuromuscular stimulation (FNS). Some people are paralyzed because nerves that send electric impulses to certain muscles are destroyed. FNS uses a computer or microprocessor to send electric impulses directly to these muscles. By sending the proper signals, the muscles can be made to move. FNS can allow paralyzed people to walk to a certain extent and to maintain muscle control.

The knowledge that muscles respond to electricity has helped create more effective prostheses. One such prostheses is the myoelectric arm. This battery-powered device connects muscle nerves in an amputated arm to a sensor.

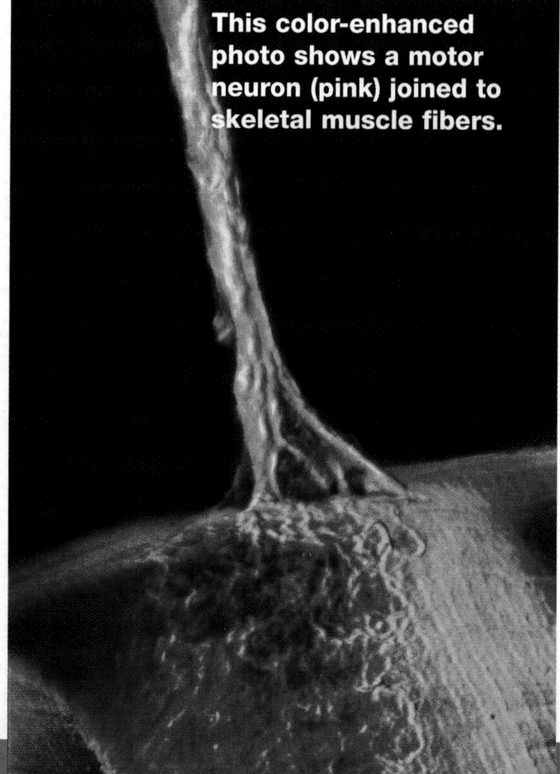
This color-enhanced photo shows a motor neuron (pink) joined to skeletal muscle fibers.

Artificial limbs can help people lead normal lives

ople

The sensor detects when the arm tenses, then transmits the signal to an artificial hand, which opens or closes. New prosthetic hands even give a sense of touch, as well as cold and heat.

Today's leg prostheses are also more sophisticated. The latest models are made of strong, lightweight titanium rods built inside a lifelike plastic covering. They allow users to compete in many sports, even tough ones like the triathlon. In addition, new artificial feet let wearers sense when their weight is on their toes, heels, or the sides of their feet. This gives them better balance.

A recent experiment promises even more amazing bionic technologies. Researchers have trained rats to move a robotic arm by using their brain signals that normally control movement—and without using their muscles at all. One day, this research might produce devices that allow paralyzed people to move artificial limbs just by brain power.

People with leg prostheses can participate in sports.

Myoelectric arms make life easier for people who have them.

CONNECTIONS Research **Use your school's media center to find other aspects of robotics such as walking machines or robots that perform planetary exploration. What are they used for? How do they work? You could take it one step further and learn about cyborgs. Report to the class.**

SCIENCE *Online*
For more information, visit science.glencoe.com

Chapter 9 Study Guide

Reviewing Main Ideas

Section 1 Work and Power

1. Work is done when a force exerted on an object causes the object to move.
2. A force can do work only when it is exerted in the same direction as the object moves. *Is work being done if this car is stuck?*

3. Work is equal to force times distance, and the unit of work is the joule.
4. Power is the rate at which work is done, and the unit of power is the watt.

Section 2 Using Machines

1. A machine changes the size or direction of the input force or the distance over which it is exerted.
2. The mechanical advantage of a machine is its output force divided by its input force. *What is the mechanical advantage of this machine?*

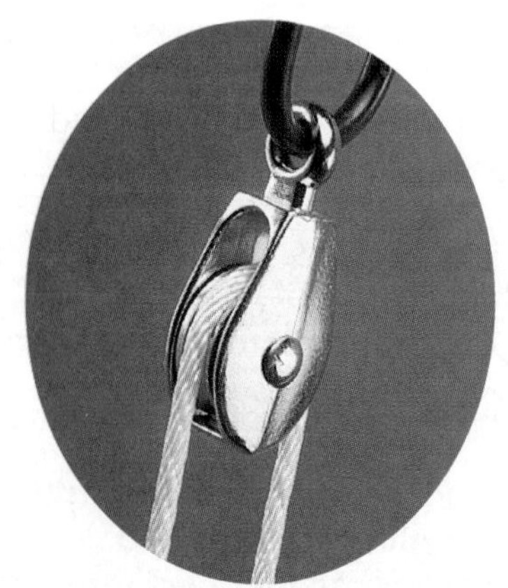

Section 3 Simple Machines

1. A machine that does work with only one movement is a simple machine. A compound machine is a combination of simple machines.
2. Simple machines include the inclined plane, lever, wheel and axle, screw, wedge, and pulley. *What type of simple machine is shown?*

3. Wedges and screws are two types of inclined planes. The mechanical advantage of an inclined plane is its length divided by its height.
4. The mechanical advantage of a lever depends on the location of the fulcrum. The mechanical advantage of a wheel and axle depends on the radius of each circular object.
5. Pulleys can be used to multiply force and change direction. The mechanical advantage of a fixed pulley is one and of a single movable pulley, two.

After You Read

To help you review work and simple machines, use the Foldable you made at the beginning of the chapter.

Visualizing Main Ideas

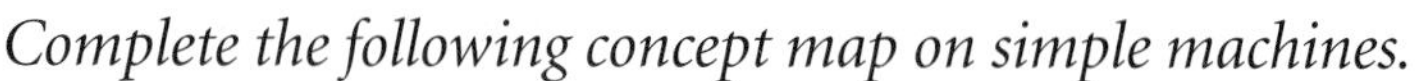

Complete the following concept map on simple machines.

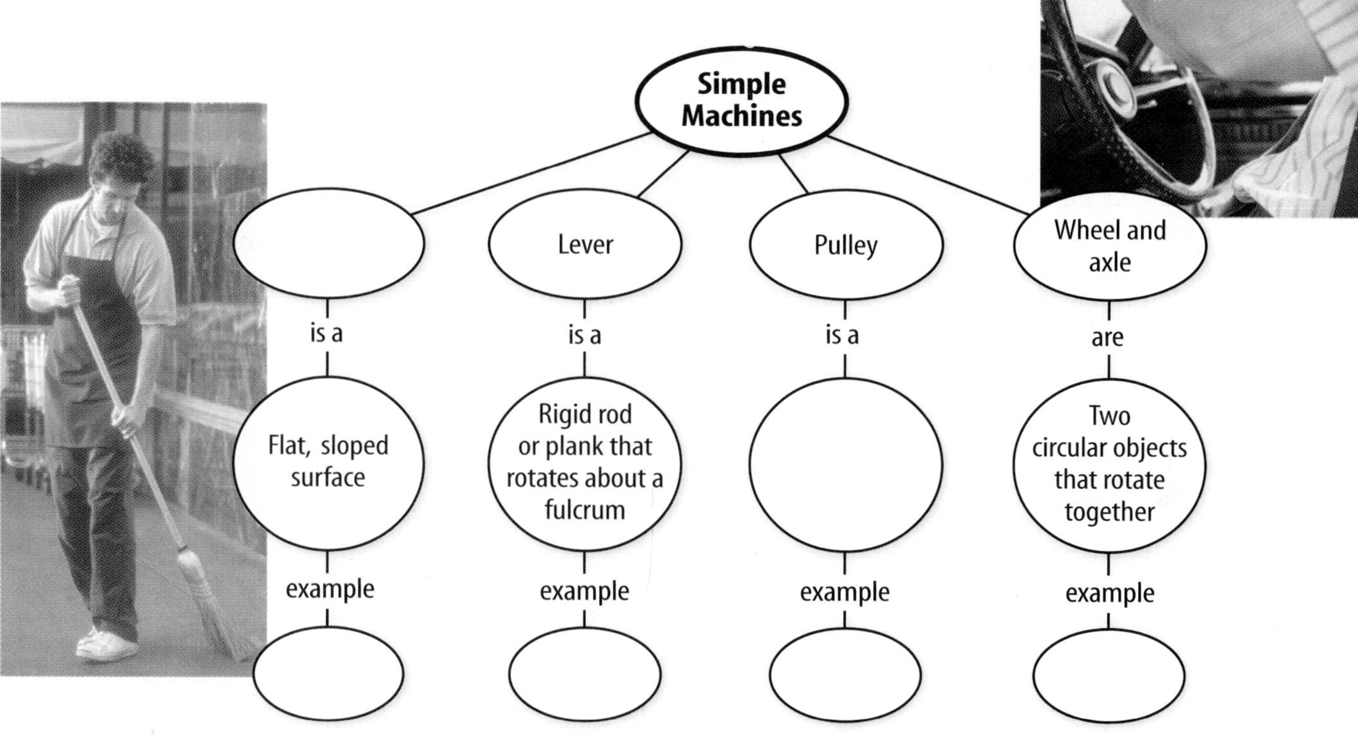

Vocabulary Review

Vocabulary Words

a. compound machine
b. efficiency
c. inclined plane
d. input force
e. lever
f. mechanical advantage
g. output force
h. power
i. pulley
j. screw
k. simple machine
l. wedge
m. wheel and axle
n. work

THE PRINCETON REVIEW **Study Tip**

Without looking back at your textbook, write a summary of each section of the chapter after you've read it. If you write it in your own words, you will better remember it.

Using Vocabulary

Each phrase below describes a vocabulary word. Write the vocabulary word that matches the phrase describing it.

1. percentage of work in to work out
2. force put into a machine
3. force exerted on an object by a machine
4. two rigidly attached wheels
5. output force divided by input force
6. a machine with only one movement
7. an inclined plane that moves
8. a rigid rod that rotates about a fulcrum
9. a flat, sloped surface
10. amount of work divided by time

Chapter 9 Assessment

Checking Concepts

Choose the word or phrase that best answers the question.

1. Which of the following is a requirement for work to be done?
   A) Force is exerted. **C)** Force moves object.
   B) Object is carried. **D)** Machine is used.

2. How much work is done when a force of 30 N moves an object a distance of 3 m?
   A) 3 J **C)** 30 J
   B) 10 J **D)** 90 J

3. How much power is expended when 600 J of work are done in 10 s?
   A) 6 W **C)** 600 W
   B) 60 W **D)** 610 W

4. Which is an example of a simple machine?
   A) baseball bat **C)** can opener
   B) bicycle **D)** car

5. What is mechanical advantage?
   A) input force/output force
   B) output force/input force
   C) input work/output work
   D) output work/input work

6. What is the ideal mechanical advantage of a machine that changes only the direction of the input force?
   A) less than 1 **C)** 1
   B) zero **D)** greater than 1

7. A wheel with a radius of 20 cm is attached to an axle with a radius of 1 cm. What is the output force if the input force on the wheel is 100 N?
   A) 5 N **C)** 500 N
   B) 200 N **D)** 2,000 N

8. Which of the following is a form of the inclined plane?
   A) pulley **C)** wheel and axle
   B) screw **D)** lever

9. A ramp decreases which of the following?
   A) height **C)** input force
   B) output force **D)** input distance

10. If a machine takes in 50 J and puts out 45 J, what is its efficiency?
    A) 0.9 percent **C)** 90 percent
    B) 1.1 percent **D)** 111 percent

Thinking Critically

11. Explain why the output work for any machine can't be greater than the input work.

12. A doorknob is an example of a wheel and axle. Explain why turning the knob is easier than turning the axle.

13. What is the mechanical advantage of a 6-m long ramp that extends from a ground-level sidewalk to a 2-m high porch?

14. How much input force is required to lift an 11,000-N beam using a pulley system with a mechanical advantage of 20?

15. Would a 9 N force applied 2 m from the fulcrum lift the weight? Explain.

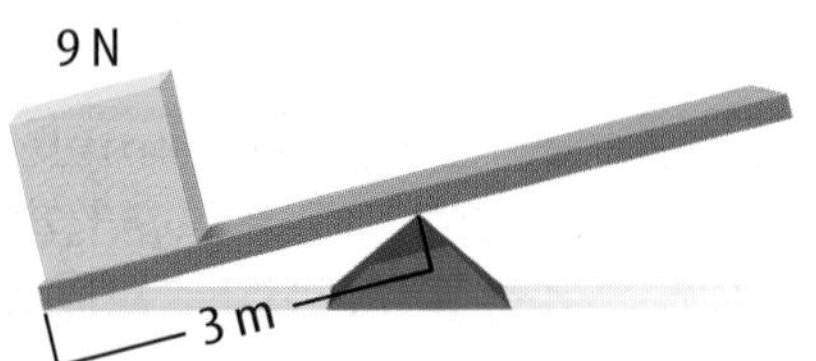

Developing Skills

16. **Measuring in SI** At the 1976 Olympics, Vasili Alexeyev shattered the world record for weight lifting when he lifted 2,500 N from the floor to a point over his head 2 m above the ground. It took him about 5 s to complete the lift. How much work did he do? What was his power?

17. **Predicting** Suppose a lever is in balance. Would this arrangement be in balance on the Moon, where the force of gravity is less? Explain.

18. **Making and Using Graphs** A pulley system has a mechanical advantage of 5. Make a graph of the possible combinations of input force and output force.

19. **Solving One-Step Equations** If you put 8,000 J of work into a machine with an efficiency of 60 percent, what is the work output?

20. **Recognizing Cause and Effect** The diagram below shows a force exerted at an angle to pull a sled. How much work is done if the sled moves 10 m horizontally?

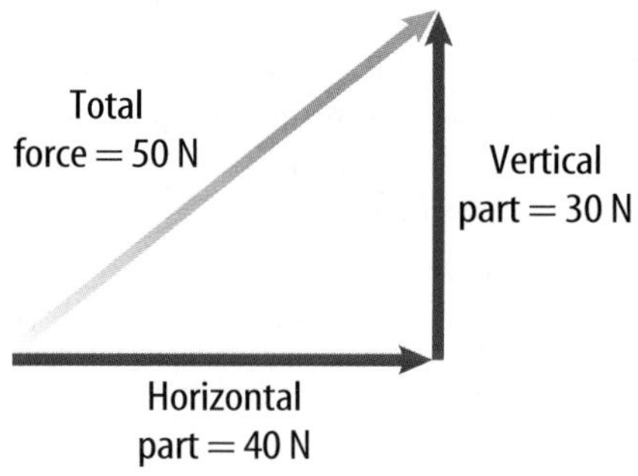

Performance Assessment

21. **Identifying Levers** You have levers in your body. Your muscles and tendons provide the input force. Your joints act as fulcrums. The output force is used to move everything from your head to your hands. Describe and draw any human levers you can identify.

Technology

Go to the Glencoe Science Web site at **science.glencoe.com** or use the **Glencoe Science CD-ROM** for additional chapter assessment.

Test Practice

At state fairs, participants often compete in pulling a 250-pound rock to a 50-meter height by using a simple pulley system. Each participant gets three tries to reach the 50-meter height.

Top Four Competitors

Participant	Bud	Charley	Maxine	Joey
Attempt 1	35 m	18 m	38 m	43 m
Attempt 2	28 m	23 m	35 m	38 m
Attempt 3	42 m	30 m	36 m	21 m

Study the table and answer the following questions.

1. According to this information, which of the participants pulled the 250-pound rock to the highest average height?
   A) Bud
   B) Charley
   C) Maxine
   D) Joey

2. According to the table, the competitor who did the least amount of total work overall was _____.
   F) Bud
   G) Charley
   H) Maxine
   J) Joey

3. According to the table, which of the following is true about the amount of work done by Joey over his three attempts, compared to the other top four competitors?
   A) The range is the smallest
   B) The range is the largest
   C) The average is the lowest
   D) The average is the highest

CHAPTER

10 Thermal Energy

On a sunny day you can feel the energy from the Sun as heat. The dishes shown here collect some of that energy and convert it into other forms of energy. How does heat energy travel through space? And how can heat energy be used to make cars move and refrigerate food? In this chapter you will learn about thermal energy and heat. You also will learn how heat is transferred from place to place and how the flow of heat can be controlled using different materials.

What do you think?

Science Journal Can you guess what this is a picture of? Here's a hint: *The one shown here is old, but you use a modern version of it every day.* In your Science Journal, write what you think it is and how you think it worked.

When you leave a glass of ice water on a kitchen table, the ice gradually melts and the temperature of the water increases. No matter how many times you leave a glass of ice water in a warm room, the water always gets warmer, never colder. What is temperature, and why does the temperature of the water always increase, but never decrease? In this activity you will explore one way of determining temperature.

Test Your Built-in Thermometer

1. Obtain three pans. Fill one pan with lukewarm water. Fill a second pan with cold water and crushed ice. Fill a third pan with very warm tap water. Label each pan.
2. Soak one of your hands in the warm water for a few minutes. Remove your hand from the warm water and put it in the lukewarm water. Does the lukewarm water feel cool or warm?
3. Now soak your hand in the cold water for a few minutes. Remove your hand from the cold water and place it in the lukewarm water. Does the lukewarm water feel cool or warm?

Observe

Write a paragraph in your Science Journal discussing whether your sense of touch would make a useful thermometer.

Before You Read

Making a Main Ideas Study Fold **Make the following Foldable to help you identify the major topics about thermal energy.**

1. Place a sheet of paper in front of you so the short side is at the top. Fold the top third of the paper down and the bottom third up.
2. Open the paper and label the three sections *Temperature, Thermal Energy,* and *Heat.*
3. Before you read the chapter, write what you know about each on your Foldable. As you read the chapter, add to and correct what you have written.

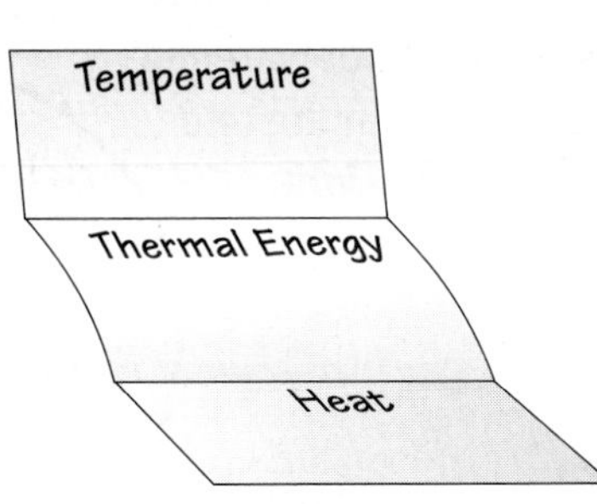

Temperature and Thermal Energy

As You Read

***What* You'll Learn**

- **Explain** how temperature is related to kinetic energy.
- **Describe** three scales used for measuring temperature.
- **Define** thermal energy.

Vocabulary
temperature
thermal energy

***Why* It's Important**
Temperature and thermal energy influence the movement of heat in the environment.

What's Hot? What's Cold?

Imagine it's a hot day and you jump into a swimming pool to cool off. When you first hit the water, you might think it feels cold. Perhaps someone else, who has been swimming for a few minutes, thinks the water feels warm. When you swim in water, touch a hot pan, or swallow a cold drink, your sense of touch tells you whether something is hot or cold. However, the words *cold, warm,* and *hot* can mean different things to different people.

Temperature How hot or cold something feels is related to its temperature. To understand temperature, think of a glass of water sitting on a table. The water might seem perfectly still, but is it? **Figure 1** shows that water is made of molecules that are in constant motion. Because these molecules are always moving, they have energy of motion, or kinetic energy.

However, all water molecules don't move at the same speed. Some are moving faster and some are moving slower. **Temperature** is a measure of the average value of the kinetic energy of the molecules in a substance. The more kinetic energy the molecules have, the higher the temperature. Molecules have more kinetic energy when they are moving faster. So the higher the temperature, the faster the molecules are moving, as shown in **Figure 1.**

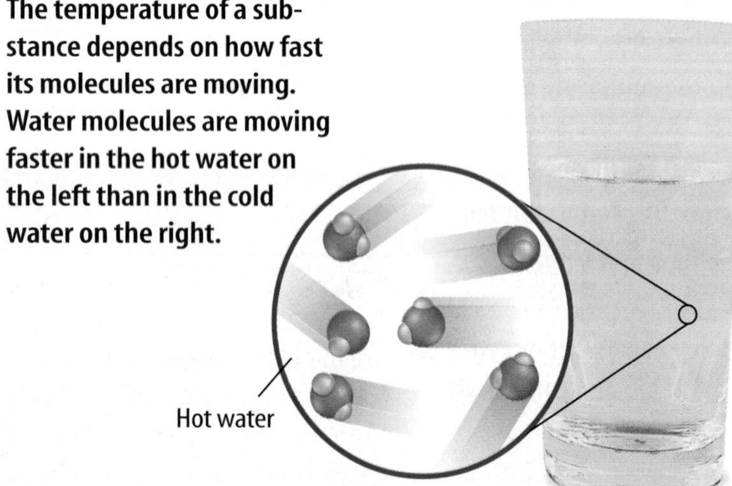

Figure 1
The temperature of a substance depends on how fast its molecules are moving. Water molecules are moving faster in the hot water on the left than in the cold water on the right.

Thermal Expansion It wasn't an earthquake that caused the sidewalk to buckle in **Figure 2.** Hot weather caused the concrete to expand so much that it cracked, and the pieces squeezed each other upward. When the temperature of an object is increased, its molecules speed up and tend to move farther apart. This causes the object to expand. When the object is cooled, its molecules slow down and move closer together. This causes the object to shrink, or contract.

Almost all substances expand when they are heated and contract when they are cooled. The amount of expansion or contraction depends on the type of material and the change in temperature. For example, liquids usually expand more than solids. Also, the greater the change in temperature, the more an object expands or contracts.

Figure 2
Most objects expand as their temperatures increase. Pieces of this concrete sidewalk forced each other upward when the concrete expanded on a hot day.

Why do materials expand when their temperatures increase?

Measuring Temperature

The temperature of an object depends on the average kinetic energy of all the molecules in an object. However, molecules are so small and objects contain so many of them, that it is impossible to measure the kinetic energy of all the individual molecules.

Instead, a practical way to measure temperature is to use a thermometer. Thermometers usually use the expansion and contraction of materials to measure temperature. One common type of thermometer uses a glass tube containing a liquid. When the temperature of the liquid increases, it expands so that the height of the liquid in the tube depends on the temperature.

Temperature Scales To be able to give a number for the temperature, a thermometer has to have a temperature scale. Two common temperature scales are the Fahrenheit and Celsius scales, shown in **Figure 3.**

On the Fahrenheit scale, the freezing point of water is given the temperature 32°F and the boiling point 212°F. The space between the boiling point and the freezing point is divided into 180 equal degrees. The Fahrenheit scale is used mainly in the United States.

On the Celsius temperature scale, the freezing point of water is given the temperature 0°C and the boiling point is given the temperature 100°C. Because there are only 100 Celsius degrees between the boiling and freezing point of water, Celsius degrees are bigger than Fahrenheit degrees. Which is warmer, 50°F or 50°C?

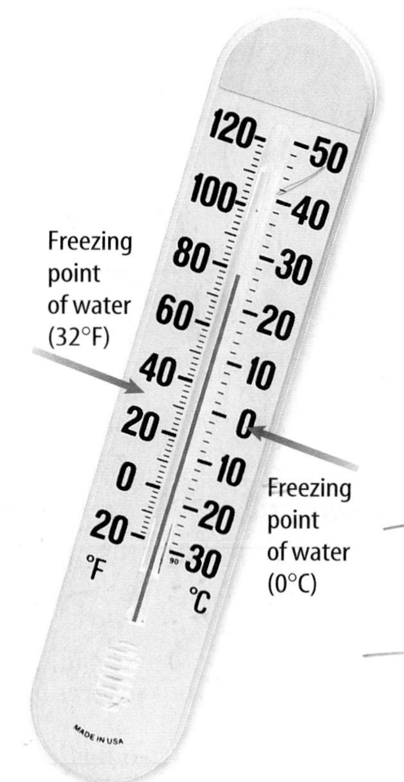

Figure 3
The Fahrenheit and Celsius scales are the most commonly used temperature scales. ***Which has the most degrees between the boiling and freezing points of water?***

Converting Fahrenheit and Celsius Temperatures on the Fahrenheit scale can be converted to Celsius temperatures using this formula.

$$°C = \left(\frac{5}{9}\right)(°F - 32)$$

For example, to convert 68°F to Celsius, first subtract 32, multiply by 5, then divide by 9. The result is 20°C.

The Kelvin Scale Another temperature scale that is sometimes used is the Kelvin Scale. On this scale, 0 K is the lowest temperature an object can have. This temperature is known as absolute zero. The size of a degree on the Kelvin scale is the same as on the Celsius scale. You can change from Kelvin degrees to Celsius degrees by subtracting 273 from the Kelvin temperature.

$$°C = K - 273$$

Math Skills Activity

Converting Fahrenheit to Celsius Temperatures

Example Problem

On a hot summer day, a Fahrenheit thermometer shows the temperature to be 86°F. What is this temperature on the Celsius scale?

Solution

1. *This is what you know:* Fahrenheit temperature: °F = 86
2. *This is what you need to know:* Celsius temperature: °C
3. *This is the equation you need to use:* $°C = \left(\frac{5}{9}\right)(°F - 32)$
4. *Substitute the known values:* $°C = \left(\frac{5}{9}\right)(86 - 32)$

   $= \left(\frac{5}{9}\right)(54) = 30$

Check your answer by multiplying it by $\frac{9}{5}$ *and adding 32.*

Do you calculate the same temperature that was given?

Practice Problem

A person's body temperature is 98.6°F. What is this temperature on the Celsius scale?

For more help, refer to the Math Skill Handbook.

Thermal Energy

The temperature of an object is related to the average kinetic energy of its molecules. But molecules also have potential energy. Potential energy is energy that the molecules have that can be converted into kinetic energy. The sum of the kinetic and potential energy of all the molecules in an object is the **thermal energy** of the object.

The Potential Energy of Molecules When you hold a ball above the ground, it has potential energy. When you drop the ball, its potential energy is converted into kinetic energy as the ball falls toward Earth. It is the attractive force of gravity between Earth and the ball that gives the ball potential energy.

The molecules in a material also exert attractive forces on each other. As a result, the molecules in a material have potential energy. As the molecules get closer together or farther apart, their potential energy changes.

Increasing Thermal Energy Temperature and thermal energy are different. Suppose you have two glasses with the same amount of milk, and at the same temperature. If you pour both glasses of milk into a pitcher, as shown in **Figure 4,** the temperature of the milk won't change. However, because there are more molecules of milk in the pitcher, the thermal energy of the milk in the pitcher is greater. Because the amount of milk doubled, the thermal energy of the milk doubled.

Figure 4
When two substances of equal temperature are combined, the temperature remains the same, but the thermal energy increases.

Section  1 Assessment

1. Explain the difference between temperature and thermal energy.
2. Write a formula for converting from Fahrenheit to Kelvin.
3. How are temperature and kinetic energy related?
4. How does a thermometer use the thermal expansion of a material to measure temperature?
5. **Think Critically** You have two identical bottles of soda. One is placed in the Sun, the other in an ice chest. Which has more thermal energy? Explain.

Skill Builder Activities

6. **Making and Using Tables** Make a table showing the Fahrenheit, Celsius, and Kelvin temperature of the following: *normal body temperature, air temperature on a summer day,* and *air temperature on a winter day.* **For more help, refer to the Science Skill Handbook.**
7. **Solving One-Step Equations** The turkey you're cooking for dinner will be ready when it reaches an internal temperature of 180°F. Convert this temperature to °C and K. **For more help, refer to the Math Skill Handbook.**

SECTION 2

Heat

As You Read

What You'll Learn

- **Explain** the difference between thermal energy and heat.
- **Describe** three ways heat is transferred.
- **Identify** materials that are insulators or conductors.

Vocabulary

heat
conduction
radiation
convection
conductor
specific heat
thermal pollution

Why It's Important

A knowledge of heat and how it is transferred will help you learn to use energy more efficiently.

Heat and Thermal Energy

It's the heat of the day. Heat the oven to 375°F. A heat wave has hit the Midwest. You've often heard the word *heat*, but what is it? Is it something you can see? Can an object have heat? Is heat anything like thermal energy? **Heat** is thermal energy that is transferred from one object to another when the objects are at different temperatures. The amount of heat that is transferred when two objects are brought into contact depends on the difference in temperature between the objects.

For example, no heat is transferred when two pots of boiling water are touching, because the water in both pots is at the same temperature. However, heat is transferred from the pot of hot water in **Figure 5** that is touching a pot of cold water. The hot water cools down and the cold water gets hotter. Heat continues to be transferred until both objects have the same temperature.

Transfer of Heat When heat is transferred, thermal energy always moves from warmer to cooler objects. Heat never flows from a cooler object to a warmer object. The warmer object loses thermal energy and becomes cooler as the cooler object gains thermal energy and becomes warmer. This process of heat transfer can occur in three ways—by conduction, radiation, or convection.

Figure 5
Heat is transferred only when two objects are at different temperatures. Heat always moves from the warmer object to the cooler object.

Conduction When you eat hot pizza, you experience conduction. As the hot pizza touches your mouth, heat moves from the pizza to your mouth. This transfer of heat by direct contact is called **conduction.** Conduction occurs when the particles of one substance collide with the particles of another substance and transfer some kinetic energy.

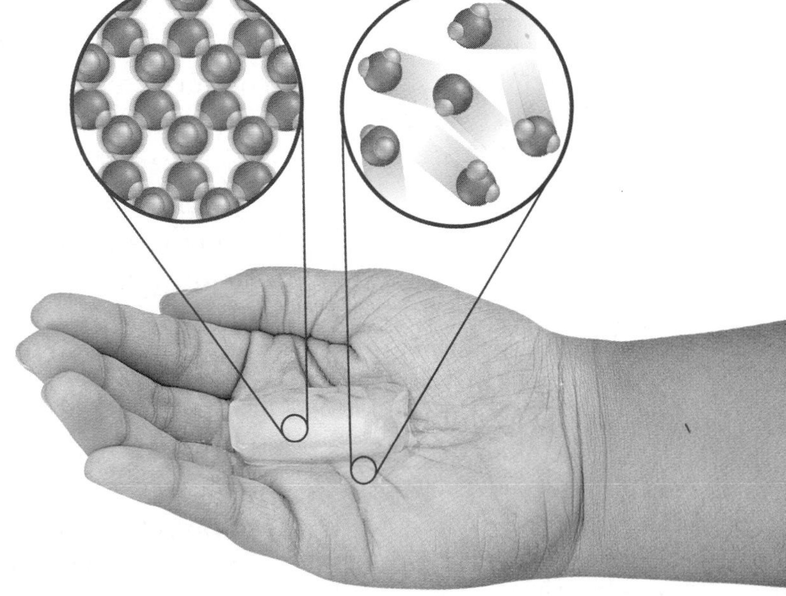

Imagine holding an ice cube in your hand, as in **Figure 6.** The faster-moving molecules in your warm hand bump against the slower-moving molecules in the cold ice. In these collisions, energy is passed from molecule to molecule. Heat flows from your warmer hand to the colder ice, and the slow-moving molecules in the ice move faster. As a result, the ice becomes warmer and its temperature increases. Molecules in your hand move more slowly as they lose thermal energy, and your hand becomes cooler.

Figure 6
An ice cube in your hand melts because of conduction. The solid ice melts, becoming liquid water. Molecules in the water move faster than molecules in the ice. *What is being transferred as the ice cube melts?*

Conduction occurs most easily in solids, where the bonds between atoms and molecules keep them close together. Because they are so close together, atoms and molecules in a solid need to move only a short distance before they bump into one another and transfer energy.

✔ Reading Check *Why does conduction occur easily in solids?*

Radiation On a beautiful, clear day, you walk outside and notice the warmth of the Sun. You know that the Sun heats Earth, but how does this transfer of thermal energy occur? The heat transfer does not occur by conduction, because almost no matter exists between the Sun and Earth. Instead, heat is transferred from the Sun to Earth by radiation. Heat transfer by **radiation** occurs when energy is transferred by electromagnetic waves. These invisible waves carry energy through empty space, as well as through matter. The transfer of thermal energy by radiation can occur in empty space, as well as in solids, liquids, and gases.

The Sun is not the only source of radiation. All objects emit electromagnetic radiation, although warm objects emit more radiation than cool objects. The warmth you feel when you sit next to a fireplace is due to heat transferred by radiation from the fire to your skin.

TRY AT HOME Mini LAB

Comparing Rates of Melting

Procedure

1. Prepare ice water by filling a glass with ice, and then adding water. Let the glass sit until all the ice melts.
2. Place an ice cube in a coffee cup.
3. Place a similar-sized ice cube in another coffee cup and add ice water to a depth of about 1 cm.
4. Time how long it takes both ice cubes to melt.

Analysis

1. Which ice cube melted fastest? Why?
2. Is air or water a better insulator? Explain.

Convection When you heat a pot of water on a stove, heat can be transferred through the water by another process besides conduction and radiation. In a gas or liquid, molecules can move much more easily then they can in a solid. As a result, the more energetic molecules can travel from one place to another, and carry their energy along with them. This transfer of thermal energy by the movement of molecules from one part of a material to another is called **convection.**

Transferring Heat by Convection As a pot of water is heated, heat is transferred by convection. First, thermal energy is transferred to the water molecules at the bottom of the pot from the stove. These water molecules move faster as their thermal energy increases. The faster-moving molecules tend to be farther apart than the slower-moving molecules in the cooler water above. Because the molecules are farther apart in the warm water, this water is less dense than the cooler water. As a result, the warm water rises and is replaced at the bottom of the pot by cooler water. The cooler water is heated, rises, and the cycle is repeated until all the water in the pan is at the same temperature.

Natural Convection Natural convection occurs when a warmer, less dense fluid is pushed away by a cooler, denser fluid. For example, imagine the shore of a lake. During the day, the water is cooler than the land. As shown in **Figure 7,** air above the warm land is heated by conduction. When the air gets hotter, its particles move faster and get farther from each other, making the air less dense. The cooler, denser air from over the lake flows in over the land, pushing the less dense air upward. You feel this movement of incoming cool air as wind. The cooler air then is heated by the land and also begins to rise.

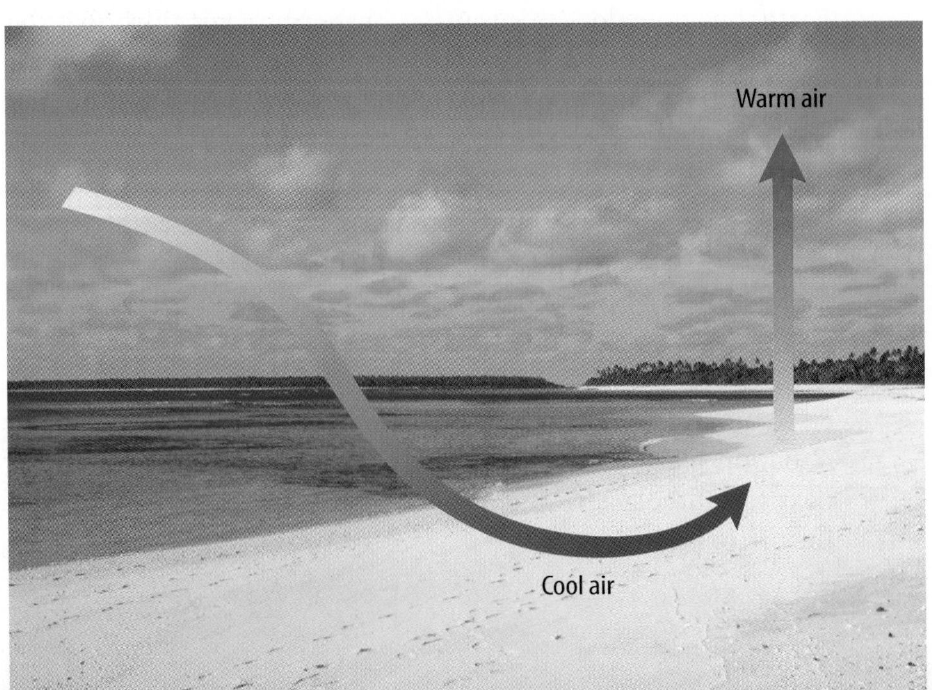

Figure 7
Wind movement near a lake or ocean results from natural convection. Air is heated by the land and becomes less dense. Denser cool air rushes in, pushing the warm air up. The cooler air then is heated by the land and rises and the cycle is repeated.

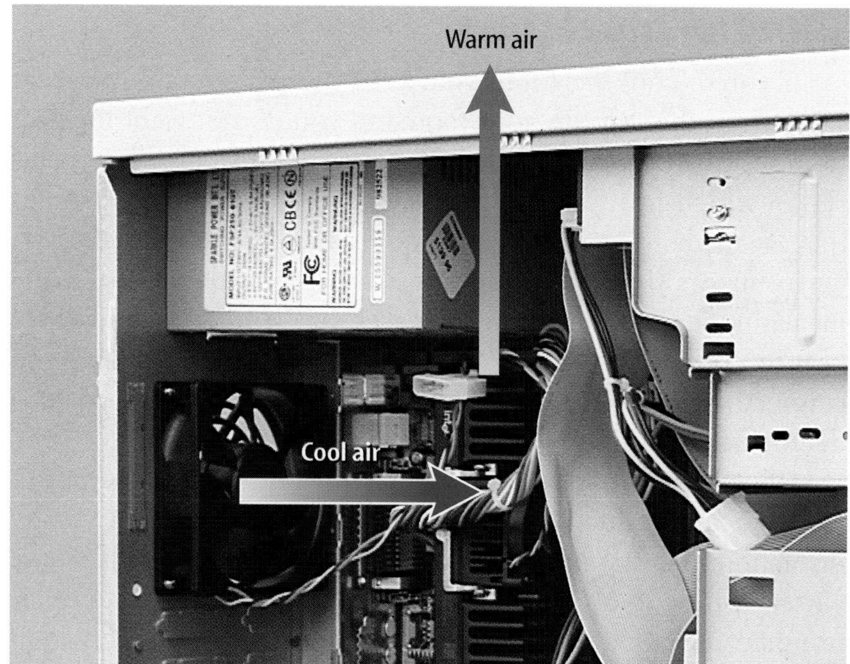

Figure 8
This computer uses forced convection to keep the electronic components surrounded by cooler air.

Forced Convection Sometimes convection can be forced. Forced convection occurs when an outside force pushes a fluid, such as air or water, to make it move and transfer heat. A fan is one type of device that is used to move air. For example, computers use fans to keep their electronic components from getting too hot, which can damage them. The fan blows cool air onto the hot electronic components, as shown in **Figure 8.** Heat from the electronic components is transferred to the air around them by conduction. The warm air is pushed away as cool air rushes in. The hot components then continue to lose heat as the fan blows cool air over them.

Thermal Conductors

Why are cooking pans usually made of metal? Why does the handle of a metal spoon in a bowl of hot soup become warm? The answer to both questions is that metal is a good conductor. A **conductor** is any material that easily transfers heat. Some materials are good conductors because of the types of atoms or chemical compounds they are made up of.

Reading Check *What is a conductor?*

Remember that an atom has a nucleus surrounded by one or more electrons. Certain materials, such as metals, have some electrons that are not held tightly by the nucleus and are freer to move around. These loosely held electrons can bump into other atoms and help transfer thermal energy. The best conductors of heat are metals such as gold and copper.

Observing Convection

Procedure

1. Fill a **250-mL beaker** with room-temperature **water** and let it stand undisturbed for at least 1 min.
2. Using a **hot plate,** heat a small amount of water in a **50-mL beaker** until it is almost boiling.
   WARNING: *Do not touch the heated hot plate.*
3. Carefully drop a **penny** into the hot water and let it stand for about 1 min.
4. Take the penny out of the hot water with **metal tongs** and place it on a table. Immediately place the 250-mL beaker on the penny.
5. Using a **dropper,** gently place one drop of **food coloring** on the bottom of the 250-mL beaker of water.
6. Observe what happens in the beaker for several minutes.

Analysis

1. What happened when you placed the food coloring in the 250-mL beaker? Why?

Life Science INTEGRATION

To survive in its arctic environment, a polar bear needs good insulation against the cold. Underneath its fur, a polar bear has 10 cm of insulating blubber. Research how blubber helps insulate the polar bear from the cold air and write your findings in your Science Journal.

Thermal Insulators

If you're cooking food, you want the pan to conduct heat easily from the stove to your food, but you do not want the heat to move easily to the handle of the pan. An insulator is a material in which heat doesn't flow easily. Most pans have handles that are made from insulators. Liquids and gases are usually better insulators than solids are. Air is a good insulator, and many insulating materials contain air spaces that reduce the transfer of heat by conduction within the material. Materials that are good conductors, such as metals, are poor insulators, and poor conductors are good insulators.

Houses and buildings are made with insulating materials to reduce heat conduction between the inside and outside. Fluffy insulation like that shown in **Figure 9** is put in the walls. Some windows have double layers of glass that sandwich a layer of air or other insulating gas. This reduces the outward flow of heat in the winter and the inward flow of heat in the summer.

Heat Absorption

On a hot day, you can walk barefoot across the lawn, but the asphalt pavement of a street is too hot to walk on. Why is the pavement hotter than the grass? The change in temperature of an object as it absorbs heat depends on the material it is made of.

Figure 9
The insulation in houses and buildings helps stop the transfer of heat between the air inside and air outside.

Specific Heat The amount of heat needed to change the temperature of a substance is related to its specific heat. The **specific heat** of a substance is the amount of heat needed to raise the temperature of 1 kg of that substance by 1°C.

More heat is needed to change the temperature of a material with a high specific heat than one with a low specific heat. For example, the sand on a beach has a lower specific heat than water has. When you're at the beach during the day, the sand feels much warmer than the water does. Radiation from the Sun warms the sand and the water. Because of its lower specific heat, the sand heats up faster than the water. At night, however, the sand feels cool and the water feels warmer. The temperature of the water changes more slowly than the temperature of the sand as they both lose thermal energy to the cooler night air.

Thermal Pollution

Some electric power plants and factories that use water for cooling produce hot water as a by-product. If this hot water is released into an ocean, lake, or river, it will raise the temperature of the water nearby. This increase in the temperature of a body of water caused by adding warmer water is called **thermal pollution.** Rainwater that is heated after it falls on warm roads or parking lots also can cause thermal pollution if it runs off into a river or lake.

Effects of Thermal Pollution Increasing the water temperature causes fish and other aquatic organisms to use more oxygen. Because warmer water contains less dissolved oxygen than cooler water, some organisms can die due to a lack of oxygen. Also, in warmer water, many organisms become more sensitive to chemical pollutants, parasites, and diseases.

Reducing Thermal Pollution Thermal pollution can be reduced by cooling the warm water produced by factories, power plants, and runoff before it is released into a body of water. Cooling towers like the ones shown in **Figure 10** are used to cool the water from some power plants and factories. In some places the warm water is held in cooling ponds where it cools before it is released.

Figure 10
This power plant uses cooling towers to cool its waste water before releasing into the lake.

Section  Assessment

1. Why isn't it correct to say that an object has heat?
2. Describe the three ways that heat can be transferred.
3. Look around your classroom and name some objects that are good insulators and some that are good conductors.
4. In the spring, the temperature of a lake increases more slowly than the temperature of the surrounding land. Explain.
5. **Think Critically** Is it better to have heating vents in your home near the floor or near the ceiling? Why?

Skill Builder Activities

6. **Recognizing Cause and Effect** England and southern Canada are at about the same latitude, and yet they have different climates. Canada usually has cold winters, but England usually has cool winters because of a nearby warm ocean current. Use what you've learned about heat transfer to explain this effect. **For more help, refer to the Science Skill Handbook.**
7. **Communicating** In your Science Journal, describe several examples of heat transfer by conduction in your everyday life. **For more help, refer to the Science Skill Handbook.**

Activity

Heating Up and Cooling Down

Do you remember how long it took for a cup of hot chocolate to cool before you could take a sip? In this activity, investigate how quickly liquids at different temperatures will heat up and cool down.

What You'll Investigate

How does the temperature of a liquid affect how quickly it warms or cools?

Materials

thermometers (5)
400-mL beakers (5)
stopwatch
**watch with second hand*
hotplate
**Alternate materials*

Goals

- Measure the temperature change of water at different temperatures.
- Infer how the rate of heating or cooling depends on the initial water temperature.

Safety Precautions

Do not use mercury thermometers. Use caution when heating with a hot plate. Hot and cold glass appears the same.

Procedure

1. Make a data table to record the temperature of water in five beakers every minute from 0 to 10 min.
2. Fill one beaker with 100 mL of water. Place the beaker on a hotplate and bring the water to a boil. *Safely* remove the hot beaker from the hotplate.

3. Record the water temperature in your data table at minute 0, and then every minute for 10 min.
4. Repeat step 3 starting with hot tap water, cold tap water, refrigerated water, and ice water with the ice removed.

Conclude and Apply

1. **Graph** your data. Plot the lines for all five beakers on one graph. **Label** the lines of your graph.
2. **Calculate** the rate of heating or cooling for the water in each beaker by subtracting the initial temperature of the water from the final temperature and then dividing this answer by 10 min.
3. **Infer** from your results how the difference between room temperature and the initial temperature of the water affected the rate at which it heated up or cooled down.

Communicating Your Data

Share your data and graphs with other classmates and explain any differences among your data.

SECTION 3

Engines and Refrigerators

Heat Engines

Cars have engines. Motorcycles have engines. Lawn mowers have engines. Engines are used everywhere. How do they work? An **engine** is any device that converts thermal energy into mechanical energy. One type of engine burns fuel to produce thermal energy. In an external combustion engine, such as the steam engine shown in **Figure 11,** the fuel is burned outside the engine. The burning fuel converts water into steam that pushes a piston. The moving piston can then do useful work.

Reading Check *What is an engine?*

As You Read

What You'll Learn

- **Identify** what an engine does.
- **Describe** how an internal combustion engine works.
- **Explain** how refrigerators and air conditioners create cool environments.

Vocabulary

engine
internal combustion engine

Why It's Important

Engines help you travel every day, and refrigerators keep your food fresh and cold.

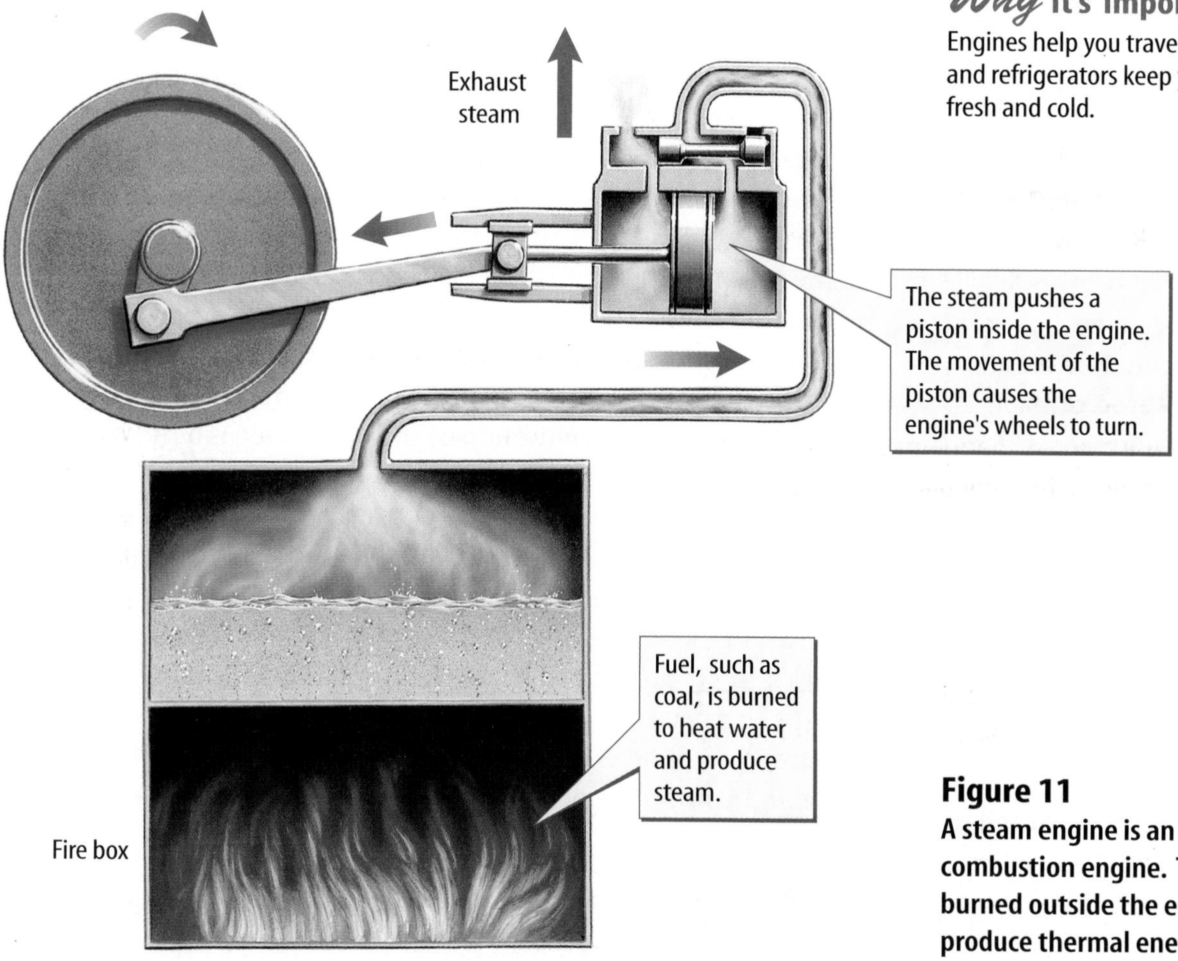

Exhaust steam
The steam pushes a piston inside the engine. The movement of the piston causes the engine's wheels to turn.
Fuel, such as coal, is burned to heat water and produce steam.
Fire box

Figure 11
A steam engine is an external combustion engine. The fuel is burned outside the engine to produce thermal energy.

Figure 12
Internal combustion engines are found in many tools and machines.

Internal Combustion Engines The type of engine you are probably most familiar with is the internal combustion engine. In **internal combustion engines,** the fuel burns in a combustion chamber inside the engine. Many machines, including cars, airplanes, buses, boats, trucks, and lawn mowers, use internal combustion engines, as shown in **Figure 12.**

Most cars have an engine with four or more combustion chambers, or cylinders. Usually the more cylinders an engine has, the more power it can produce. Each cylinder contains a piston that can move up and down. A mixture of fuel and air is injected into a combustion chamber and ignited by a spark. When the fuel mixture is ignited, it burns explosively and pushes the piston down. The up-and-down motion of the pistons turns a rod called a crankshaft, which turns the wheels of the car. **Figure 13** shows how an internal combustion engine converts thermal energy to mechanical energy in a process called the four-stroke cycle.

Several kinds of internal combustion engines have been designed. In diesel engines, the air in the cylinder is compressed to such a high pressure that the highly flammable fuel ignites without the need for a spark plug. Many lawn mowers use a two-stroke gasoline engine. The first stroke is a combination of intake and compression. The second stroke is a combination of power and exhaust.

Research Visit the Glencoe Science Web site at **science.glencoe.com** for more information about advancements in the design of internal combustion engines. Evaluate the advantages and disadvantages of these new designs with your classmates.

How does the burning of fuel mixture cause a piston to move?

NATIONAL GEOGRAPHIC VISUALIZING THE FOUR-STROKE CYCLE

Figure 13

Most modern cars are powered by fuel-injected internal combustion engines that have a four-stroke combustion cycle. Inside the engine, thermal energy is converted into mechanical energy as gasoline is burned under pressure inside chambers known as cylinders. The steps in the four-stroke cycle are shown here.

INTAKE STROKE

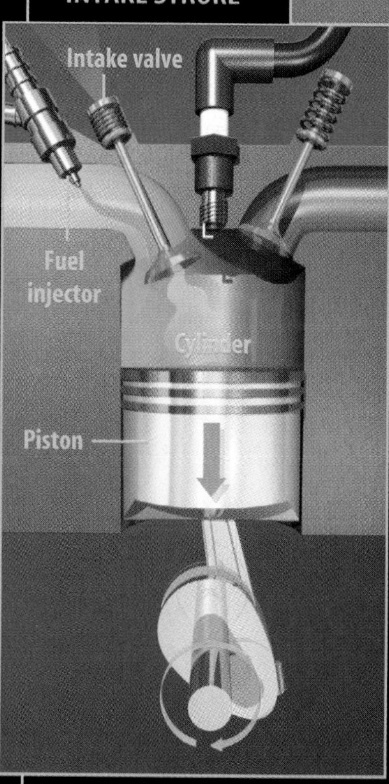

Ⓐ During the intake stroke, the piston inside the cylinder moves downward. As it does, air fills the cylinder through the intake valve, and a mist of fuel is injected into the cylinder.

COMPRESSION STROKE

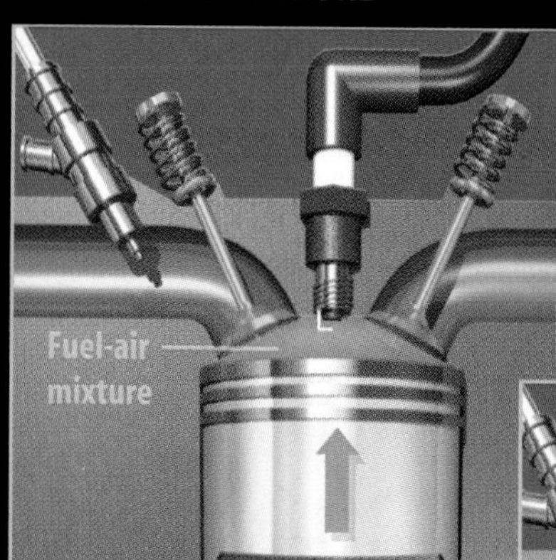

Ⓑ The piston moves up, compressing the fuel-air mixture.

POWER STROKE

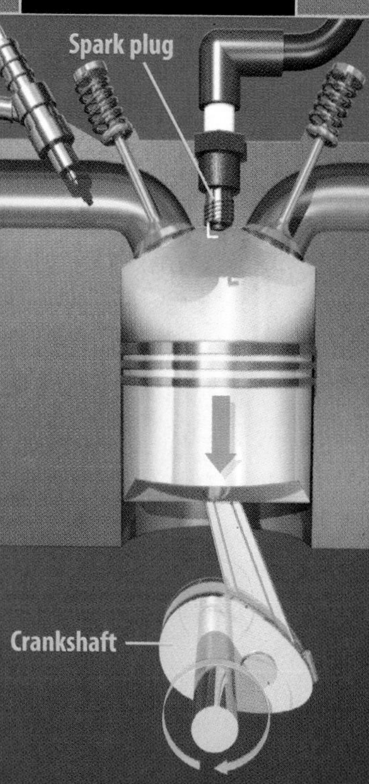

Ⓒ At the top of the compression stroke, a spark ignites the fuel-air mixture. The hot gases that are produced expand, pushing the piston down and turning the crankshaft.

EXHAUST STROKE

Exhaust valve

Exhaust gases

Ⓓ The exhaust valve opens as the piston moves up, pushing the exhaust gases out of the cylinder.

Refrigerators

If thermal energy will only flow from something that is warm to something that is cool, how can a refrigerator be cooler inside than the air in the kitchen? A refrigerator is a heat mover. It absorbs heat from the food and other materials inside the refrigerator. Then it carries the heat to outside the refrigerator, where it is transferred to the surrounding air.

A refrigerator contains a material called a coolant that is pumped through pipes inside and outside the refrigerator. The coolant is the substance that carries heat from the inside to the outside of the refrigerator.

Absorbing Heat **Figure 14** shows how a refrigerator operates. Liquid coolant is forced up a pipe toward the freezer unit. The liquid passes through an expansion valve where it changes into a gas. When it changes into a gas, it becomes cold. The cold gas passes through pipes around the inside of the refrigerator. Because the coolant gas is so cold, it absorbs heat from inside the refrigerator, and becomes warmer.

Releasing Heat However, the gas is still colder than the outside air. So, the heat absorbed by the coolant cannot be transferred to the air. The warm coolant gas then passes through a compressor that compresses the gas. When the gas is compressed, it becomes warmer than room temperature. The gas then flows through the condenser coils, where it transfers heat to the cooler air in the room. As the coolant gas cools, it changes into a liquid. The liquid is pumped through the expansion valve, changes into a gas, and the cycle is repeated.

Figure 14
As refrigerant moves through the coils inside a refrigerator, it absorbs heat and evaporates. The refrigerant is recycled when it cools and condenses in the outside coils and then is brought back to the inside coils.
Where do the transfers of heat in a refrigerator occur?

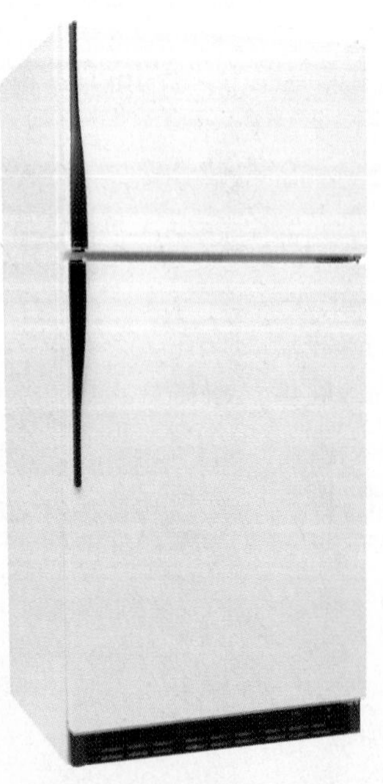

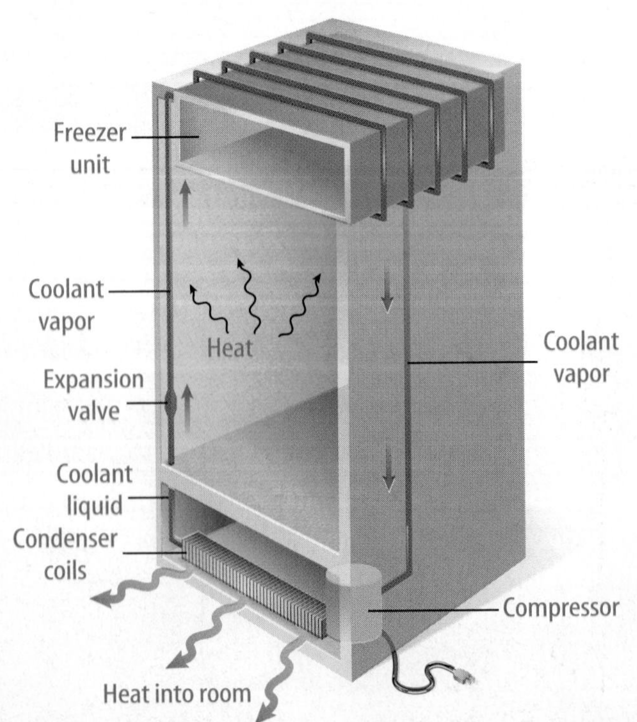

Air Conditioners Most air conditioners cool in the same way that a refrigerator does. You've probably seen air-conditioning units outside of many houses. As in a refrigerator, heat from inside the house is absorbed by the coolant within pipes inside the air conditioner. The coolant then is compressed by a compressor, and becomes warmer. The warmed coolant travels through pipes that are exposed to the outside air. Here the heat is transferred to the outside air.

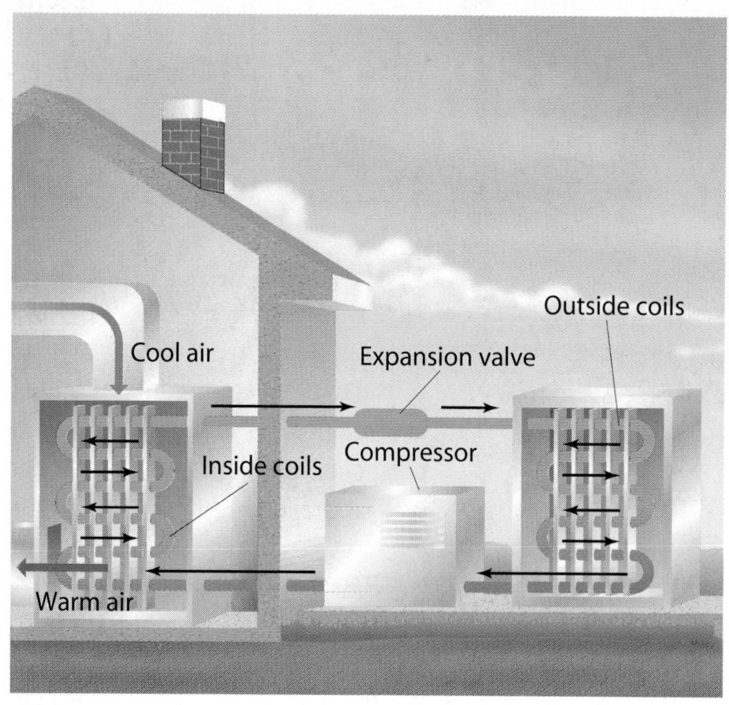

Figure 15
A heat pump can be used to heat and cool a building. In heating mode, the coolant absorbs heat through the outside coils. The coolant is warmed when it is compressed, and transfers heat to the room through the inside coils. In cooling mode, the coolant moves through the system in the opposite direction.

Heat Pumps Some buildings use a heat pump for heating as well as cooling, as shown in **Figure 15.** Like an air conditioner or refrigerator, a heat pump moves heat from one place to another. When a heat pump is used for cooling, it removes thermal energy from the indoor air and transfers it outdoors. When it is used for heating, the heat pump absorbs thermal energy from the outdoor air or some other warm source and transfers this heat inside. The heat pump can reverse itself automatically. It can heat or cool depending on the outside temperature. In summer, the heat pump removes heat from the air inside the building and releases it outside. In winter, it removes heat from the outside ground or air and transfers it inside the house. In areas where the winter temperature is near or below zero, an additional heating coil sometimes is added to provide more heat.

Section  Assessment

1. In an engine, thermal energy is converted into what form of energy?
2. What is the source of thermal energy in an internal combustion engine?
3. Why don't diesel engines use spark plugs?
4. Explain how a refrigerator keeps the food compartment cool.
5. **Think Critically** Why do you think a car has four or more cylinders rather than just one cylinder?

Skill Builder Activities

6. **Concept Mapping** Make an events-chain concept map showing the steps in a four-stroke cycle. **For more help, refer to the Science Skill Handbook.**
7. **Using Graphics Software** Using computer graphics or drawing software, make a diagram that shows a typical refrigeration cycle. **For more help, refer to the Technology Skill Handbook.**

Activity Design Your Own Experiment

Comparing Thermal Insulators

Insulated beverage containers are used to reduce heat transfer. What kinds of containers do you more commonly drink from? Aluminum soda cans? Paper, plastic, or foam cups? Glass containers? In this investigation, compare how well several different containers block heat transfer.

Recognize the Problem

Which types of beverage containers are most effective at blocking heat transfer from a hot drink?

Form a Hypothesis

Predict the temperature change of a hot liquid in several containers made of different materials over a time interval.

Goals

- **Predict** the temperature change of a hot drink in various types of containers over time.
- **Design** an experiment to test the hypothesis and collect data that can be graphed.
- **Interpret** the data.

Possible Materials

hotplate
large beaker
water
graduated cylinder
thermometers
various beverage containers (each about the same size and shape)
material to cover the containers
stopwatch
**watch with a second hand*
tongs
thermal gloves or mitts
**Alternate materials*

Safety Precautions

Use caution when heating liquids. Be sure to use tongs or thermal gloves when handling hot materials. Remember that hot and cold glass appears the same. Treat thermometers with care and keep them away from the edges of tables. Avoid using mercury thermometers.

Test Your Hypothesis

Plan

1. **Decide** what types of containers you will test. Design an experiment to test your hypothesis. This is a group activity, so make certain that everyone gets to contribute to the discussion.
2. **List** the materials you will use in your experiment. Describe exactly how you will use these materials. Which liquid will you test? What temperature will the liquid begin at? How will you cover the hot liquids in the container? What material will you use as a cover?
3. **Identify** the variables and controls in your experiment.
4. **Design** a data table in your Science Journal to record the observations you make.

Do

1. Ask your teacher to examine the steps of your experiment and your data table before you start.
2. To see the pattern of how well various containers retain heat, you will need to graph your data. What kind of graph will you use? Make certain you take enough measurements during the experiment to make your graph.
3. The time intervals between measurements should be the same. Be sure to keep track of time as the experiment goes along. For how long will you measure the temperature?
4. Carry out your investigation and record your observations.

Analyze Your Data

1. **Graph** your data. Use one graph to show the data collected from all your containers. Label each line on your graph.
2. How can you tell by looking at your graphs which containers retain heat best?
3. Did the water temperature change as you had predicted? Use your data and graph to explain your answers.

Draw Conclusions

1. Why did the rate of temperature change vary among the containers? Did the size of the containers affect the rate of cooling?
2. **Conclude** which containers were the best insulators.

Communicating Your Data

Compare your data and graphs with other classmates and explain any differences in your results or conclusions.

The Heat Is...

You may live far from water, but still live on an island—a heat island

Here's a riddle: Rebecca and Julie were crossing a parking lot on a hot summer day. Rebecca had shoes on. Julie did not. They had gone only a short way when one of the girls broke into a run. Who was it and why did she run?

Dark materials, such as asphalt, absorb more heat than light materials. In extreme heat, it's even possible to fry an egg on dark pavement!

If you guess barefoot Julie, you're right. The hot asphalt of the parking lot scorched her feet, and Julie took off like a shot. Paving and building materials such as asphalt and concrete absorb more energy from the Sun and get hotter. Think about all the things that are made of asphalt and concrete in a city.

On

As far as the eye can see, there are buildings and parking lots, sidewalks and streets. The combined effect of these paved surfaces and towering structures can make a city sizzle in the summer. There's even a name for this effect. It's called the heat island effect.

Hot Times

You can think of a city as an island surrounded by an ocean of green trees and other vegetation. In the midst of those green trees, the air can be up to 8°C cooler than it is downtown. During the day in rural areas, the Sun's energy is absorbed by plants and soil. Some of this energy causes water to evaporate, so less energy is available to heat the surroundings. This keeps the temperature lower.

In cities, where there are fewer trees and plants, the buildings, streets, and sidewalks absorb most of the Sun's energy. And as more energy is absorbed, the temperature increases. As the temperature of the streets and buildings rises, they lose heat to cooler objects in their surroundings. The temperature stops rising when heat energy is released at the same rate that energy from the Sun is absorbed.

Higher temperatures aren't the only problems caused by heat islands. People crank up their air conditioners for relief, so the use of energy skyrockets. Also, the added heat speeds up the rates of chemical reactions in the atmosphere. Smog is due to chemical reactions caused by the interaction of sunlight and vehicle emissions. So hotter air means more smog. And more smog means more health problems.

Cool Cures

Several U.S. cities are working with NASA scientists to come up with a cure for the summertime blues. For instance, dark materials absorb heat more efficiently than light materials. So painting buildings, especially roofs, white can reduce heat and save on cooling bills. In Salt Lake City, Utah, where temperatures on dark rooftops can soar to 65°C, the rooftop of a large warehouse was painted white. "I've been up on it plenty of times," says a worker at the warehouse. "It doesn't come up and just drill you with heat like the black ones do."

Planting even small bushes and trees can help cool a city.

CONNECTIONS Design and Research **Go to the Glencoe Science Web site to research NASA's Urban Heat Island Project. What actions are cities taking to reduce the heat-island effect? Design a city area that would help reduce this effect.**

SCIENCE *Online*

For more information, visit science.glencoe.com.

Chapter 10 Study Guide

Reviewing Main Ideas

Section 1 Temperature and Thermal Energy

1. Molecules of matter are moving constantly. Temperature is related to the average value of the kinetic energy of the molecules.
2. Thermometers measure temperature. Three common temperature scales are the Celsius, Fahrenheit, and Kelvin scales.
3. Thermal energy is the total kinetic and potential energy of the particles in matter. *How has thermal energy changed when this iron has melted?*

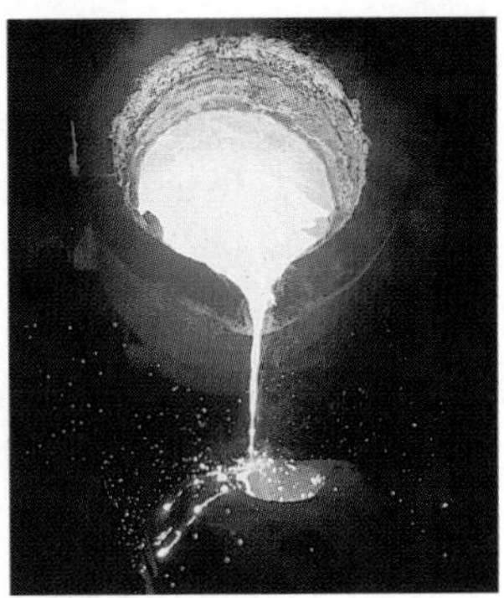

Section 2 Heat

1. Heat is thermal energy that is transferred from a warmer object to a colder object.
2. Heat can be transferred by conduction, convection, and radiation. *Why do you feel warm when you stand in front of a fireplace?*

3. A material that easily transfers heat is called a conductor. A material that resists the flow of heat is an insulator.
4. The specific heat of a substance is the amount of heat needed to change the temperature of 1 kg of the substance 1°C.
5. Thermal pollution occurs when warm water is added to a body of water, such as a river or lake.

Section 3 Engines and Refrigerators

1. A device that converts thermal energy into mechanical energy is an engine.
2. In an internal combustion engine, fuel is burned in combustion chambers inside the engine.
3. Internal combustion engines that are used in cars and airplanes burn fuel to do work, using a four-stroke cycle.
4. Refrigerators and air conditioners use a coolant to move heat from one place to another. *Why is one side of this air conditioner placed outdoors?*

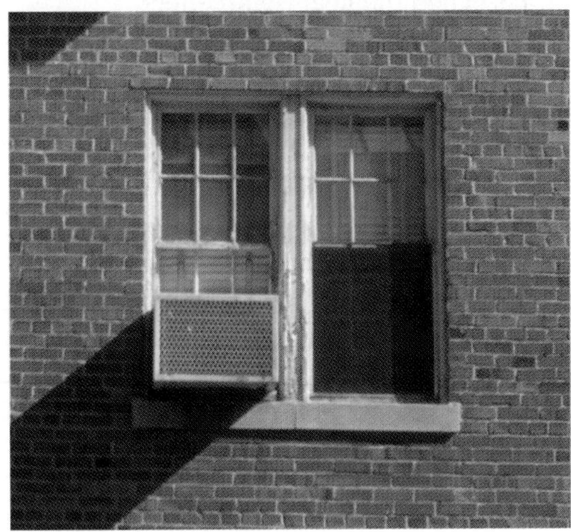

After You Read

FOLDABLES Reading & Study Skills

Write what you learned about the relationship between heat and thermal energy on the back of your Foldable.

Visualizing Main Ideas

Complete the following cycle map about the four-stroke cycle.

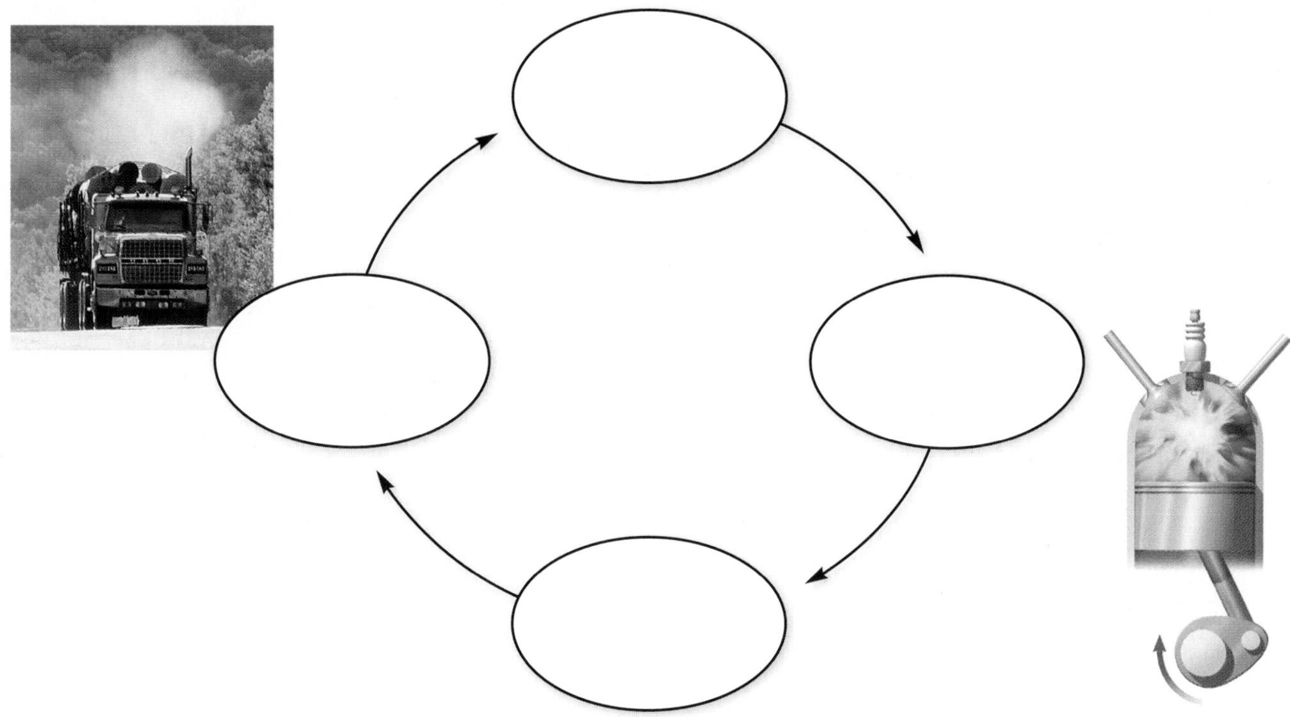

Vocabulary Review

Vocabulary Words

a. conduction
b. conductor
c. convection
d. engine
e. heat
f. internal combustion engine
g. radiation
h. specific heat
i. temperature
j. thermal energy
k. thermal pollution

Study Tip

Practice reading tables. See whether you can devise a graph that shows the same information that a table shows.

Using Vocabulary

Explain the differences in the vocabulary words given below. Then explain how the words are related. Use complete sentences in your answers.

1. internal combustion engine, engine
2. temperature, thermal energy
3. thermal energy, thermal pollution
4. conduction, convection
5. conduction, heat
6. heat, specific heat
7. conduction, radiation
8. convection, radiation
9. conductor, heat

Chapter 10 Assessment

Checking Concepts

Choose the word or phrase that best answers the question.

1. What source of thermal energy does an internal combustion engine use?
   A) steam **C)** burning fuel
   B) hot water **D)** refrigerant

2. What happens to most materials when they become warmer?
   A) They contract. **C)** They vaporize.
   B) They float. **D)** They expand.

3. Which type of heat transfer occurs when two objects at different temperatures are touching?
   A) convection **C)** condensation
   B) radiation **D)** conduction

4. Which of the following describes the thermal energy of particles in a substance?
   A) average value of all kinetic energy
   B) total value of all kinetic energy
   C) total value of all kinetic and potential energy
   D) average value of all kinetic and potential energy

5. Heat being transferred from the Sun to Earth is an example of which process?
   A) convection **C)** radiation
   B) expansion **D)** conduction

6. Many insulating materials contain spaces filled with air because air is what type of material?
   A) conductor **C)** radiator
   B) coolant **D)** insulator

7. What do thermometers measure?
   A) average kinetic energy of particles
   B) heat of particles
   C) evaporation rate
   D) total energy of particles

8. Which of the following is true?
   A) Warm air is less dense than cool air.
   B) Warm air is as dense as cool air.
   C) Warm air has no density.
   D) Warm air is denser than cool air.

9. Which of these is the name for thermal energy that moves from a warmer object to a cooler one?
   A) kinetic energy **C)** heat
   B) specific heat **D)** temperature

10. If the same amounts of heat were added to equal masses of the following objects, which would get hottest?
    A) object with low specific heat
    B) object with medium specific heat
    C) object with high specific heat
    D) object with very high specific heat

Thinking Critically

11. Water is a poor conductor of heat. Yet, when you heat water in a pan, the surface gets hot quickly, even though you are applying heat to the bottom of the water. Explain.

12. List the following temperatures from coldest to warmest: 80° C, 200 K, 50° F.

13. Why do several layers of clothing often keep you warmer than a single layer?

14. The phrase "heat rises" is sometimes used to describe the behavior of heat. For what type of materials is this phrase correct? Explain.

15. In a refrigerator, the coolant absorbs heat from inside the refrigerator and then transfers this heat to the air outside. Describe how the temperature of the coolant is changed as it flows through the refrigerator.

Developing Skills

16. Designing an Experiment Some colors of clothing absorb heat better than other colors. Design an experiment that will test various colors by placing them in the hot Sun for a period of time. Explain your results.

17. Drawing Conclusions Would it be possible to cool a kitchen by leaving the refrigerator door open? Explain.

18. Concept Mapping Complete the following concept map on convection in a liquid.

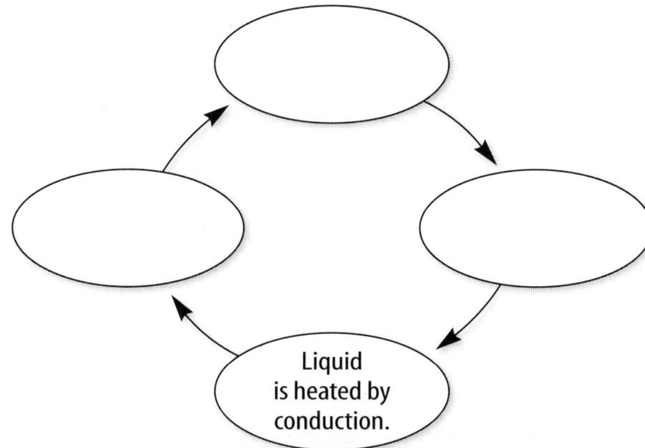

Performance Assessment

19. Poll In the United States, the Fahrenheit temperature scale is used most often. Some people feel that Americans should switch to the Celsius scale. Take a poll of at least 20 people. Find out if they feel the switch to Celsius should be made. Make a list of reasons people give for or against changing.

Technology

Go to the Glencoe Science Web site at **science.glencoe.com** or use the **Glencoe Science CD-ROM** for additional chapter assessment.

Test Practice

Mrs. Keeley's chemistry class is studying how ice changes to water and then to steam as it is heated. They measured the amount of heat added, and the temperature of the ice, water, and steam. The graph below shows their results.

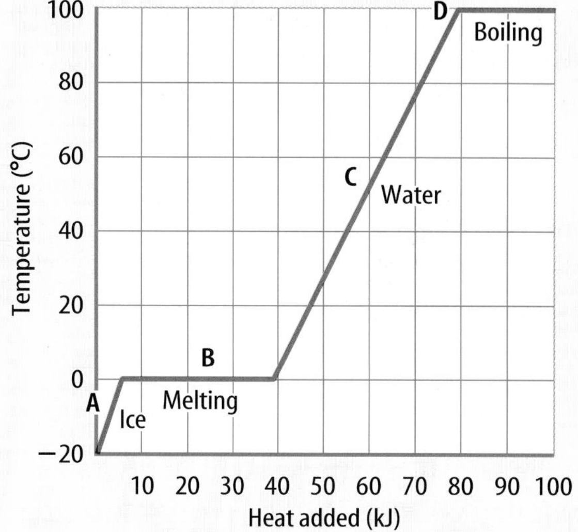

Study the graph and answer the following questions.

1. According to the graph above, at what temperature does ice change to water?

A) 10° C
B) 100° C
C) 0° C
D) −10° C

2. Temperature is a measure of the average kinetic energy of the molecules of a substance. Over what part of the graph does the kinetic energy of the molecules stay the same?

F) A
G) C
H) B
J) Not enough information given

Standardized Test Practice

Reading Comprehension

Read the passage. Then read each question that follows the passage. Decide which is the best answer to each question.

Electric Cars: The Cars of the Future

Have you ever wondered how a car is able to move? In car engines, gasoline is burned to convert chemical energy into thermal energy. The engine then changes some of this thermal energy into kinetic energy that causes the wheels to turn. However, some car manufacturers are also exploring whether cars can be developed that will run on electrical energy rather than gasoline.

Electric cars would use electrical energy to power an electric motor that turns the car's wheels. The electrical energy would be provided by a battery. In a battery chemical reactions occur that convert chemical energy into electrical energy. Eventually, the chemicals in the battery are changed into other chemical compounds and the battery can no longer produce electrical energy. When <u>rechargeable</u> batteries are recharged, the chemical reactions in the battery are reversed. Then the chemicals in the battery that produce electrical energy are restored.

While electric cars would produce no pollution while they are driven, there are potential environmental problems. The rechargeable batteries used by electric cars are heavy, expensive, and contain hazardous materials such as lead. As a result, the manufacture and disposal of these batteries can create environmental problems. Also, the electricity used to charge these batteries usually is generated by power plants that can produce air pollution and other by-products.

Other types of electric cars are being developed that use a hydrogen fuel cell instead of batteries. In this fuel cell hydrogen gas reacts with oxygen to produce electricity. The hydrogen gas can be obtained from water. Although the fuel cell produces almost no pollution, electricity from power plants still is needed to generate the hydrogen gas the fuel cell uses. Research is being done to find other ways to produce hydrogen gas that would result in less pollution.

Several carmakers have developed hybrid cars that combine an internal combustion engine, a battery, and an electric motor. The electric motor assists the internal combustion engine in providing power. During braking, about half of the engine's kinetic energy is used to charge the battery.

Test-Taking Tip Read the passage slowly to make sure you don't miss any important details.

1. From the story, you can infer that <u>rechargeable</u> means _____.

A) brand new
B) reuseable
C) paid by credit card
D) disposable

2. The hydrogen gas used in a hydrogen fuel cell can be obtained from _____.

F) water
G) electric cars
H) power plants
J) hybrid cars

Standardized Test Practice

Reasoning and Skills

Read each question and choose the best answer.

1. Why aren't you doing any work when you push against a solid brick wall?

A) because the wall is much heavier than you are

B) because you can exert only a very small force

C) because only machines can do work

D) because you haven't moved the wall

Test-Taking Tip Recall the definition of work.

2. Which of the following is true about this simple machine?

F) It increases the force needed to lift the object.

G) It decreases the force needed to lift the object.

H) It decreases the work needed to lift the object.

J) It decreases the object's weight.

Test-Taking Tip Consider how the machine works and what you need it to do.

3. Which of the following statements is the best explanation for what likely happened to the sidewalk in the picture above?

A) An animal that lives underground has tunneled under the sidewalk.

B) The sidewalk has expanded because of extremely hot weather.

C) The sidewalk has heaved due to the number of people and other animals that have walked on it.

D) The sidewalk has contracted because of extremely hot weather.

Test-Taking Tip Consider the kind of force needed to cause such a break. How could this force most likely be produced?

Consider the question carefully before writing your answer on a separate sheet of paper.

4. You have 2 L of water at a temperature of 5°C and 1/4 a L of water at a temperature of 5°C. Which volume has more thermal energy? Why?

Test-Taking Tip Think carefully about the definition of thermal energy.

UNIT 5

Waves, Sound, and Light

How Are Radar & Popcorn Connected?

Radar systems—such as the one in this modern air traffic control room—use radio waves to detect objects. In the 1940s, the radio waves used for radar were generated by a device called a magnetron. One day, an engineer working on a radar project was standing near a magnetron when he noticed that the candy bar in his pocket had melted. Intrigued, the engineer got some unpopped popcorn and placed it next to the magnetron. Sure enough, the kernels began to pop. The engineer realized that the magnetron's short radio waves, called microwaves, caused the molecules in the food to move more quickly, increasing the food's temperature. Soon, magnetrons were being used in the first microwave ovens. Today, microwave ovens are used to pop popcorn—and heat many other kinds of food—in kitchens all over the world.

SCIENCE CONNECTION

ELECTROMAGNETIC RADIATION Microwaves and other kinds of radio waves are forms of electromagnetic radiation. So are X rays, gamma rays, infrared radiation, ultraviolet radiation, and visible light. These various forms of electromagnetic radiation differ in the length and frequency of their waves. Find out the wavelengths of the kinds of electromagnetic radiation named above. Then create a diagram that arranges these kinds of radiation in order from longest to shortest.

CHAPTER

11 Waves

On a breezy day in Maui, Hawaii, windsurfers ride the ocean waves. What forces are operating on the windsurfer and his sailboard? The wind catches the sails and helps propel the sailboard, but other forces also are at work—waves. Waves carry energy. You can see the ocean waves in this picture, but there are many kinds of waves you cannot see. Microwaves heat your food, radio waves transmit the music you listen to into your home, and sound waves carry that music from the radio to your ears. In this chapter, you will learn about different types of waves and how they behave.

What do you think?

Science Journal Look at the picture below with a classmate. Discuss what you think this might be. Hint: *Some sunglasses have this kind of lens.* Write your answer or best guess in your Science Journal.

It's a beautiful autumn day. You are sitting by a pond in a park. Music blares from a school marching band practicing for a big game. The music is carried by waves. A fish jumps, making a splash. Waves spread past a leaf that fell from a tree, causing the leaf to move. In the following activity, you'll observe how waves carry energy that can cause objects to move.

Observe wave behavior 

1. Fill a large, clear plastic plate with 1 cm of water.
2. Use a dropper to release a single drop of water onto the water's surface. Repeat.
3. Float a cork or straw on the water.
4. When the water is still, repeat step 2 from a height of 10 cm, then again from 20 cm.

Observe

In your Science Journal, record your observations. How did the motion of the cork depend on the height of the dropper?

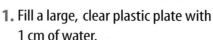

Before You Read

FOLDABLES Reading & Study Skills

Making a Concept Map Study Fold **Make the following Foldable to organize information by diagramming ideas about waves.**

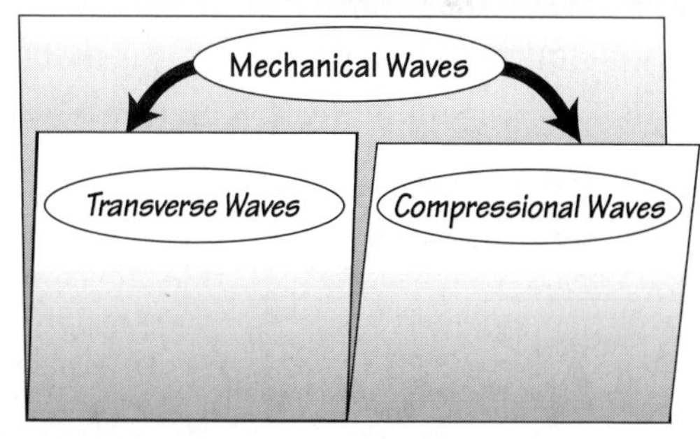

1. Place a sheet of paper in front of you so the long side is at the top. Fold the bottom of the paper to the top, stopping about four centimeters from the top.
2. Draw an oval above the fold. Write *Mechanical Waves* inside the oval.
3. Fold the paper in half from the left side to the right side and then unfold. Through the top thickness of the paper, cut along the fold line to form two tabs.
4. Draw an oval on each tab. Write *Transverse Waves* in one oval and *Compressional Waves* in the other, as shown. Draw arrows from the large oval to the smaller ovals.
5. As you read the chapter, write information about the two types of mechanical waves under the tabs.

SECTION 1

What are waves?

As You Read

What You'll Learn

- **Explain** the relationship among waves, energy, and matter.
- **Describe** the difference between transverse waves and compressional waves.

Vocabulary

wave
mechanical wave
transverse wave
compressional wave
electromagnetic wave

Why It's Important

You can hear music and other sounds because of waves.

What is a wave?

When you are relaxing on an air mattress in a pool and someone does a cannonball dive off the diving board, you suddenly find yourself bobbing up and down. You can make something move by giving it a push or pull, but the person jumping didn't touch your air mattress. How did the energy from the dive travel through the water and move your air mattress? The up-and-down motion was caused by the peaks and valleys of the ripples that moved from where the splash occurred. These peaks and valleys make up water waves.

Waves Carry Energy **Waves** are rhythmic disturbances that carry energy without carrying matter, as shown in **Figure 1A.** You can see the energy of the wave from a speedboat traveling outward, but the water only moves up and down. If you've ever felt a clap of thunder, you know that sound waves can carry large amounts of energy. You also transfer energy when you throw something to a friend, as in **Figure 1B.** However, there is a difference between a moving ball and a wave. A ball is made of matter, and when it is thrown, the matter moves from one place to another. So, unlike the wave, throwing a ball involves the transport of matter as well as energy.

Figure 1
The wave and the thrown ball carry energy in different ways.

A **The waves created by a boat move mostly up and down, but the energy travels outward from the boat.**

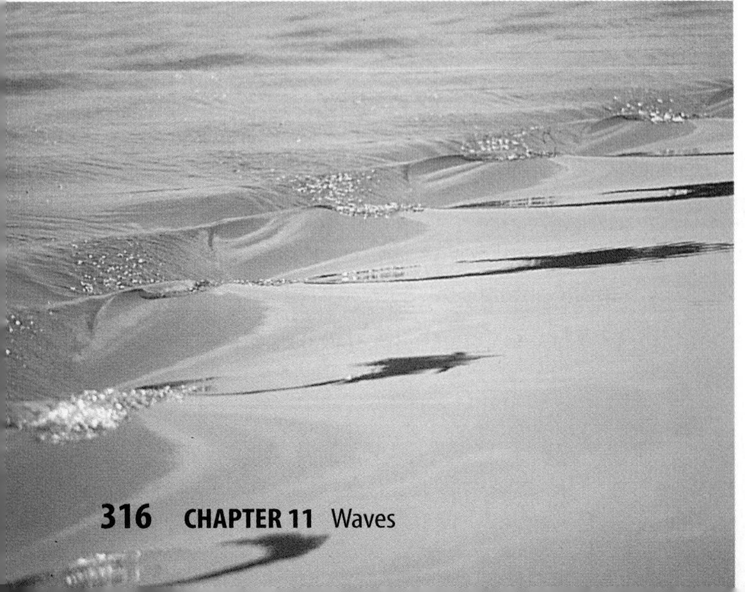

B **When the ball is thrown, the ball carries energy as it moves forward.**

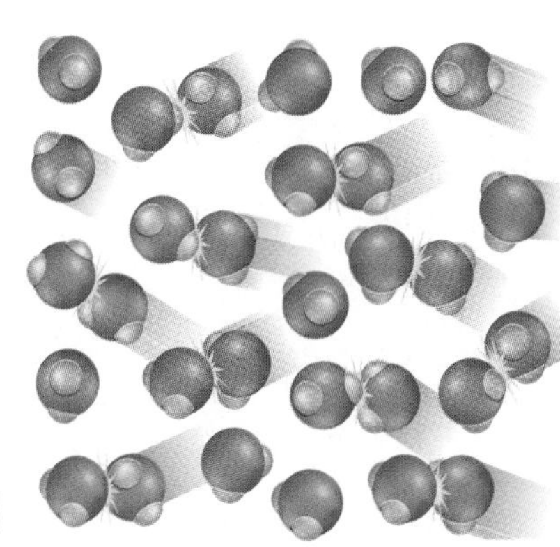

Figure 2

A As the students pass the ball, the students' positions do not change—only the position of the ball changes. B In a water wave, water molecules bump each other and pass energy from molecule to molecule.

A Model for Waves

How does a wave carry energy without transporting matter? Imagine a line of people, as shown in **Figure 2A.** The first person in line passes a ball to the second person, who passes the ball to the next person, and so on. Passing a ball down a line of people is a model for how waves can transport energy without transporting matter. Even though the ball has traveled, the people in line have not moved. In this model, you can think of the ball as representing energy. What do the people in line represent?

Think about the ripples on the surface of a pond. The energy carried by the ripples travels through the water. The water is made up of water molecules. It is the individual molecules of water that pass the wave energy, just as the people in **Figure 2A** pass the ball. The water molecules transport the energy in a water wave by colliding with the molecules around them, as shown in **Figure 2B.**

Reading Check *What is carried by waves?*

Mechanical Waves

In the wave model, the ball could not be transferred if the line of people didn't exist. The energy of a water wave could not be transferred if no water molecules existed. These types of waves, which use matter to transfer energy, are called **mechanical waves.** The matter through which a mechanical wave travels is called a medium. For ripples on a pond, the medium is the water.

A mechanical wave travels as energy is transferred from particle to particle in the medium. For example, a sound wave is a mechanical wave that can travel through air, as well as solids, liquids, and other gases. The sound wave travels through air by transferring energy from gas molecule to gas molecule. Without a medium such as air, you would not hear sounds. In outer space sound waves can't travel because there is no air.

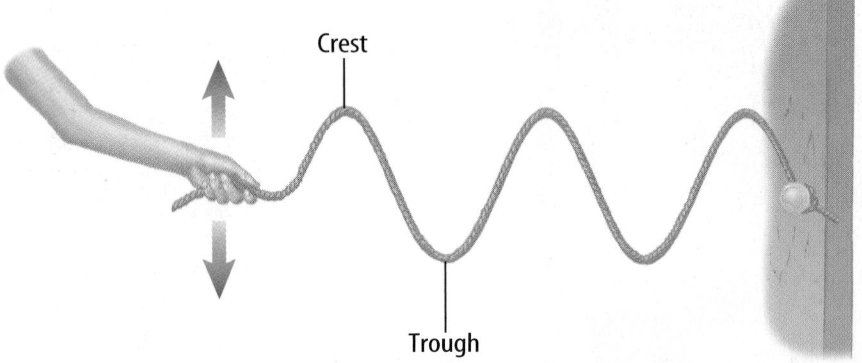

Figure 3
The high points on the wave are called crests and the low points are called troughs.

Transverse Waves In a mechanical **transverse wave,** the wave energy causes the matter in the medium to move up and down or back and forth at right angles to the direction the wave travels. You can make a model of a transverse wave. Stretch a long rope out on the ground. Hold one end in your hand. Now shake the end in your hand back and forth. By adjusting the way you shake the rope, you can create a wave that seems to slide along the rope.

When you first started shaking the rope, it might have appeared that the rope itself was moving away from you. But it was only the wave that was moving away from your hand. The wave energy moves through the rope, but the matter in the rope doesn't travel. You can see that the wave has peaks and valleys at regular intervals. As shown in **Figure 3,** the high points of transverse waves are called crests. The low points are called troughs.

What are the highest points of transverse waves called?

Figure 4
A compressional wave can travel through a coiled spring toy.

A As the wave motion begins, the coils near the string are close together and the other coils are far apart.

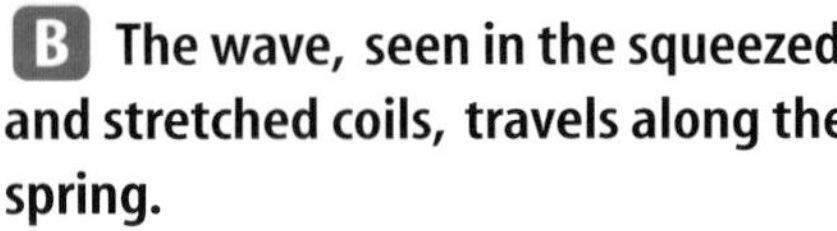

B The wave, seen in the squeezed and stretched coils, travels along the spring.

C The string and coils did not travel with the wave. Each coil moved forward and then back to its original position.

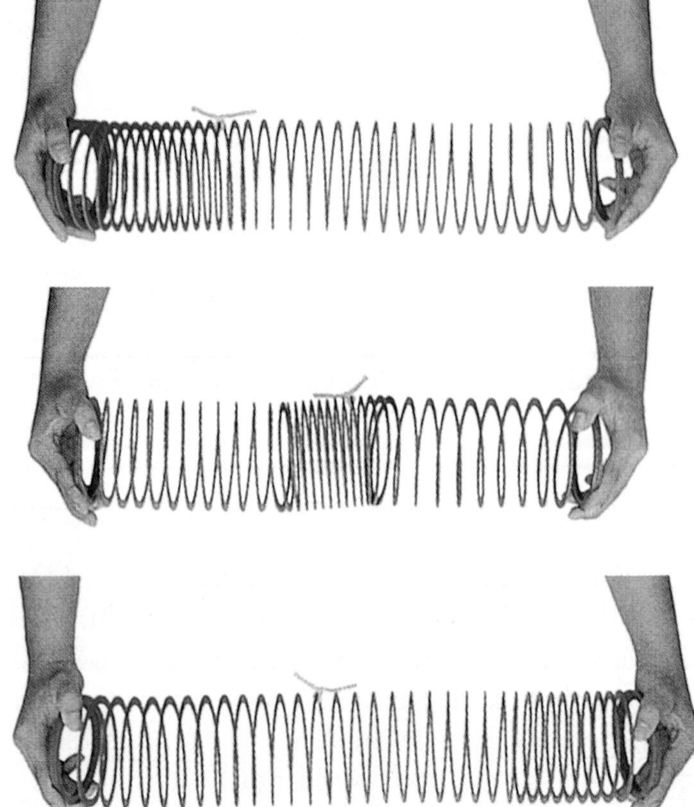

Compressional Waves Mechanical waves can be either transverse or compressional. In a **compressional wave,** matter in the medium moves forward and backward in the same direction that the wave travels. You can make a compressional wave by squeezing together and releasing several coils of a coiled spring toy, as shown in **Figure 4.**

You see that the coils move only as the wave passes. They then return to their original position. So, like transverse waves, compressional waves carry only energy forward along the spring. In this example, the spring is the medium the wave moves through, but the spring does not move along with the wave.

Sound Waves Sound waves are compressional waves. How do you make sound waves when you talk or sing? If you hold your fingers against your throat while you hum, you can feel vibrations. These vibrations are the movements of your vocal cords. If you touch a stereo speaker while it's playing, you can feel it vibrating, too. All waves are produced by something that is vibrating.

Making Sound Waves

How do vibrating objects make sound waves? Look at the drum shown in **Figure 5.** When you hit the drumhead it starts vibrating up and down. As the drumhead moves upward, the molecules next to it are pushed closer together. This group of molecules that are closer together is a compression. As the compression forms, it moves away from the drumhead, just as the squeezed coils move along the coiled spring toy in **Figure 4.**

When the drumhead moves downward, the molecules near it have more room and can spread farther apart. This group of molecules that are farther apart is a rarefaction. The rarefaction also moves away from the drumhead. As the drumhead vibrates up and down, it forms a series of compressions and rarefactions that move away and spread out in all directions. This series of compressions and rarefactions is a sound wave.

Comparing Sounds

Procedure 

1. Hold a **wooden ruler** firmly on the edge of your **desk** so that most of it extends off the edge of the desk.
2. Pluck the free end of the ruler so that it vibrates up and down. Use gentle motion at first, then pluck with more energy.
3. Repeat step 2, moving the ruler about 1 cm further onto the desk each time until only about 5 cm extend off the edge.

Analysis

1. Compare the loudness of the sounds that are made by plucking the ruler in different ways.
2. Describe the differences in the sound as the end of the ruler was extended farther from the desk.

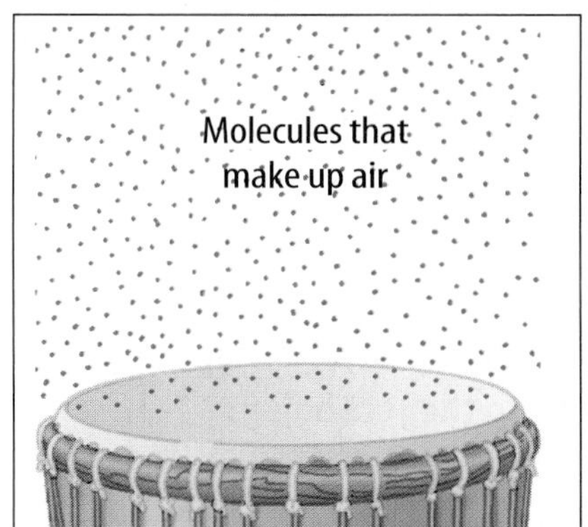

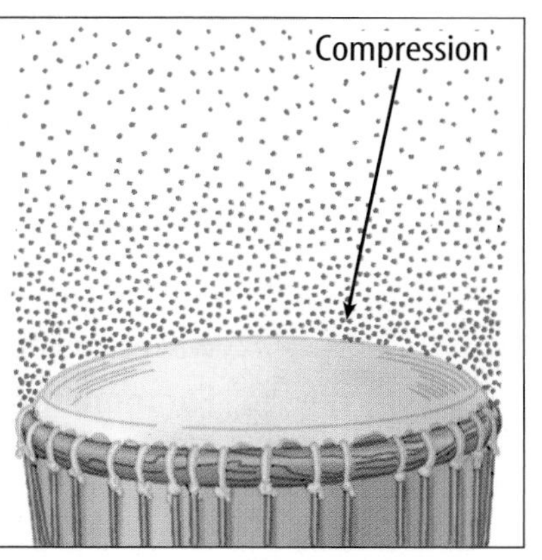

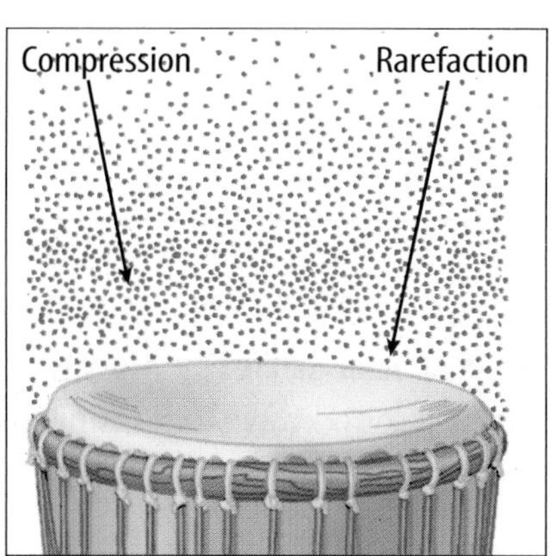

Figure 5
A vibrating drumhead makes compressions and rarefactions in the air. *How are compressions and rarefactions different?*

Electromagnetic Waves

When you listen to the radio, watch TV, or use a microwave oven to cook, you use a different kind of wave—one that doesn't need matter as a medium.

Waves that do not require matter to carry energy are called **electromagnetic waves.** Electromagnetic waves are transverse waves that are produced by the motion of electrically charged particles. Just like mechanical waves, electromagnetic waves also can travel through a medium such as a solid, liquid, or gas. Radio waves are electromagnetic waves that travel through the air from a radio station, and then through the solid walls of your house to reach your radio. However, unlike mechanical waves, electromagnetic waves can travel through outer space or through a vacuum where no matter exists.

Physics INTEGRATION

Maybe you've used a global positioning system (GPS) receiver to determine your location while driving, boating, or hiking. Earth-orbiting satellites send electromagnetic radio waves that transmit their exact locations and times of transmission. The GPS receiver uses information from four of these satellites to determine your location to within about 16 m.

Useful Waves In space, which has no air or any other medium, orbiting satellites beam radio waves to TVs, radios, and cellular phones on Earth's surface. However, radio waves are not the only electromagnetic waves traveling in space. Infrared, visible, and ultraviolet waves travel from the Sun through space before they reach Earth's atmosphere. Infrared waves feel warm when they strike your skin. Without visible light you wouldn't see color or be able to read this page. You use sunscreen to protect yourself from ultraviolet rays. Other useful electromagnetic waves include X rays. X rays are useful not only in medical applications, but also for security checks in airports as luggage is scanned.

Section  Assessment

1. Describe the movement of a floating object on a pond when struck by a wave.
2. Why can't a sound wave travel from a satellite to Earth?
3. Give one example of a transverse wave and one example of a compressional wave. How are they similar and different?
4. What is the difference between a mechanical wave and an electromagnetic wave?
5. **Think Critically** How is it possible for a sound wave to transmit energy but not matter?

Skill Builder Activities

6. **Concept Mapping** Create a concept map that shows the relationships among the following: *waves, mechanical waves, electromagnetic waves, compressional waves,* and *transverse waves.* **For more help, refer to the Science Skill Handbook.**
7. **Using a Word Processor** Use word-processing software to write short descriptions of the waves you encounter during a typical day. **For more help, refer to the Technology Skill Handbook.**

Wave Properties

Amplitude

Can you describe a wave? For a water wave, one way might be to tell how high the wave rises above, or falls below, the normal level. This distance is called the wave's amplitude. The **amplitude** of a transverse wave is one-half the distance between a crest and a trough, as shown in **Figure 6A.** In a compressional wave, the amplitude is greater when the particles of the medium are squeezed closer together in each compression and spread farther apart in each rarefaction.

Amplitude and Energy A wave's amplitude is related to the energy that the wave carries. For example, the electromagnetic waves that make up bright light have greater amplitudes than the waves that make up dim light. Waves of bright light carry more energy than the waves that make up dim light. In a similar way, loud sound waves have greater amplitudes than soft sound waves. Loud sounds carry more energy than soft sounds. If a sound is loud enough, it can carry enough energy to damage your hearing.

As you can see in **Figure 6B,** when a hurricane strikes a coastal area, the resulting water waves can damage almost anything that stands in their path. The large waves caused by a hurricane carry more energy than the small waves or ripples on a pond.

As You Read

What You'll Learn

- **Describe** the relationship between the frequency and wavelength of a wave.
- **Explain** why waves travel at different speeds.

Vocabulary

amplitude
wavelength
frequency

Why It's Important

The energy carried by a wave depends on its amplitude.

Figure 6
A transverse wave has an amplitude.

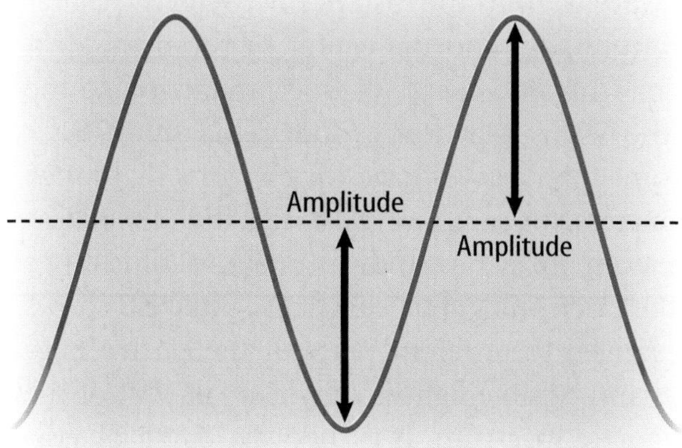

A The amplitude is a measure of how high the crests are or how deep the troughs are.

B A water wave of large amplitude carried the energy that caused this damage.

A **For transverse waves, measure from crest to crest or trough to trough.**

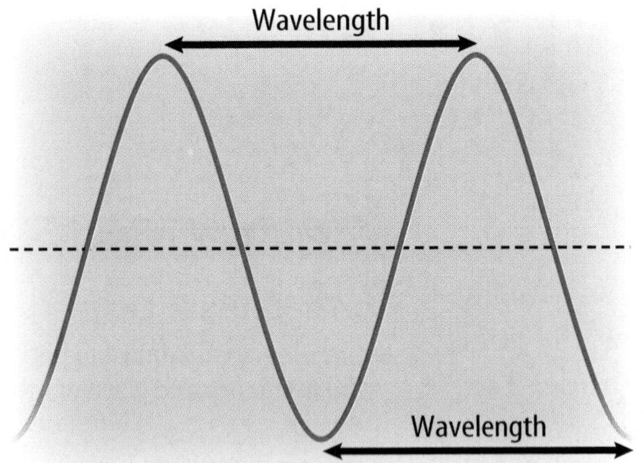

B **For compressional waves, measure from compression to compression or rarefaction to rarefaction.**

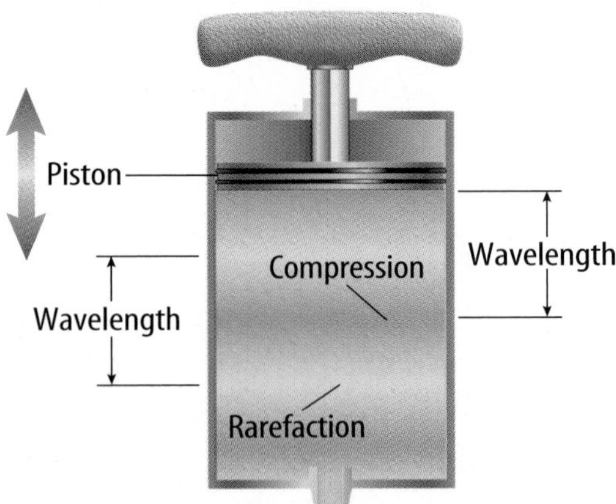

Figure 7
Wavelength is measured differently for transverse and compressional waves.

Figure 8
The wavelengths and frequencies of electromagnetic waves vary.

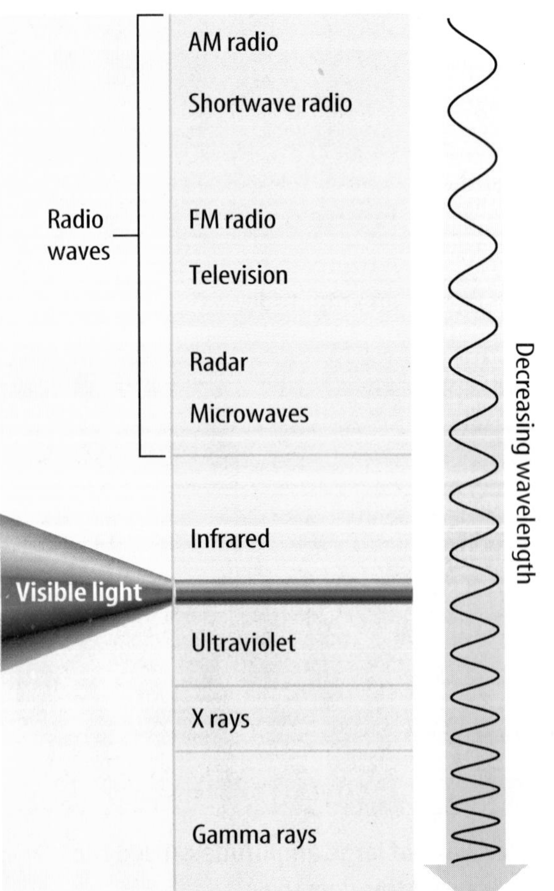

Earth Science INTEGRATION The devastating effect that a wave with large amplitude can have is seen in the aftermath of tsunamis. Tsunamis are huge sea waves that are caused by underwater earthquakes along faults on the seafloor. The movement of the seafloor along the fault produces the wave. As the wave moves toward shallow water and slows down, the amplitude of the wave grows. The tremendous amounts of energy tsunamis carry cause great damage when they move ashore.

Wavelength

Another way to describe a wave is by its wavelength. For a transverse wave, **wavelength** is the distance from the top of one crest to the top of the next crest, or from the bottom of one trough to the bottom of the next trough, as shown in **Figure 7A.** For a compressional wave, the wavelength is the distance between the center of one compression and the center of the next compression, or from the center of one rarefaction to the center of the next rarefaction, as shown in **Figure 7B.**

Electromagnetic waves have wavelengths that range from kilometers, for radio waves, to less than the diameter of an atom, for X rays and gamma rays. This range is called the electromagnetic spectrum. **Figure 8** shows the names given to different parts of the electromagnetic spectrum. Visible light is only a small part of the electromagnetic spectrum. It is the wavelength of visible light waves that determines their color. For example, the wavelength of red light waves is longer than the wavelength of green light waves.

Frequency

The **frequency** of a wave is the number of wavelengths that pass a given point in 1 s. The unit of frequency is the number of wavelengths per second, or hertz (Hz). Recall that waves are produced by something that vibrates. The faster the vibration is, the higher the frequency is of the wave that is produced.

Reading Check *How is the frequency of a wave measured?*

A Sidewalk Model For waves that travel with the same speed, frequency and wavelength are related. To model this relationship, imagine people on two parallel moving sidewalks in an airport, as shown in **Figure 9.** One sidewalk has four travelers spaced 4 m apart. The other sidewalk has 16 travelers spaced 1 m apart.

Now imagine that both sidewalks are moving at the same speed and approaching a pillar between them. On which sidewalk will more people go past the pillar? On the sidewalk with the shorter distance between people, four people will pass the pillar for each one person on the other sidewalk. When four people pass the pillar on the first sidewalk, 16 people pass the pillar on the second sidewalk.

Figure 9
When people are farther apart on a moving sidewalk, fewer people pass the pillar every minute.

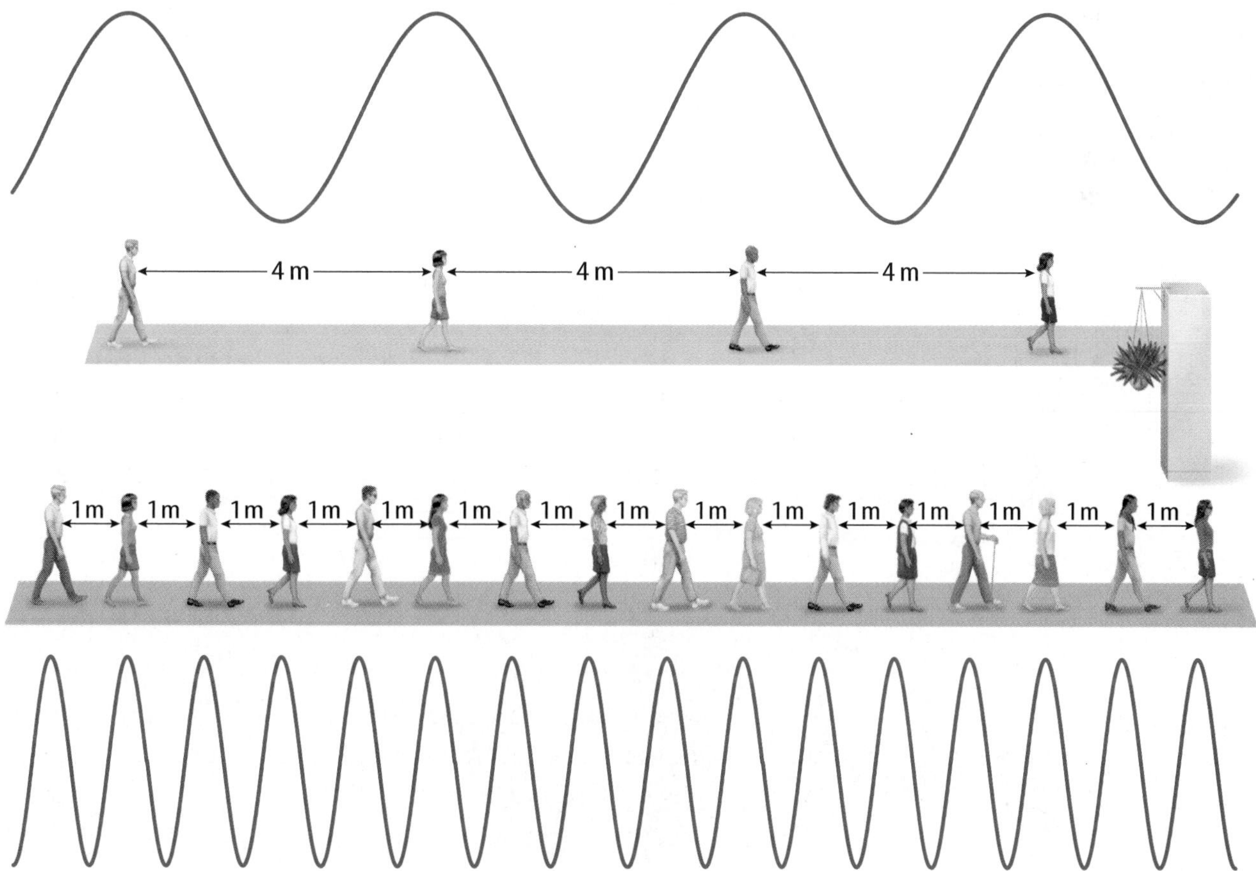

Sound waves with ultra-high frequencies cannot be heard by the human ear, but are used by medical professionals in several ways. They perform echocardiograms of the heart, produce ultrasound images of internal organs, break up blockages in arteries and kill bacteria and sterilize surgical instruments. *How do the wavelengths of these sound waves compare to sound waves you can hear?*

Frequency and Wavelength Suppose that each person in **Figure 9** represents the crest of a wave. Then the movement of people on the first sidewalk is like a wave with a wavelength of 4 m. For the second sidewalk, the wavelength would be 1 m. On the first sidewalk, where the wavelength is longer, the people pass the pillar *less* frequently. Longer wavelengths result in smaller frequencies. On the second sidewalk, where the wavelength is shorter, the people pass the pillar *more* frequently. Higher frequencies result in shorter wavelengths. This is true for all waves that travel at the same speed. As the frequency of a wave increases, its wavelength decreases.

Color and Pitch Because frequency and wavelength are related, either the wavelength or frequency of a light wave determines the color of the light. For example, blue light has a larger frequency and shorter wavelength than red light.

In a sound wave, either the wavelength or frequency determines the pitch. Pitch is the highness or lowness of a sound. A flute makes musical notes with a high pitch and produces sounds of high frequency. A tuba produces notes with a low pitch and a low frequency. When you sing a musical scale, the pitch and frequency increase from note to note. Wavelength and frequency are also related for sound waves traveling in air. As the frequency of sound waves increases, their wavelength decreases. **Figure 10** shows how the frequency and wavelength change for notes on the musical scale.

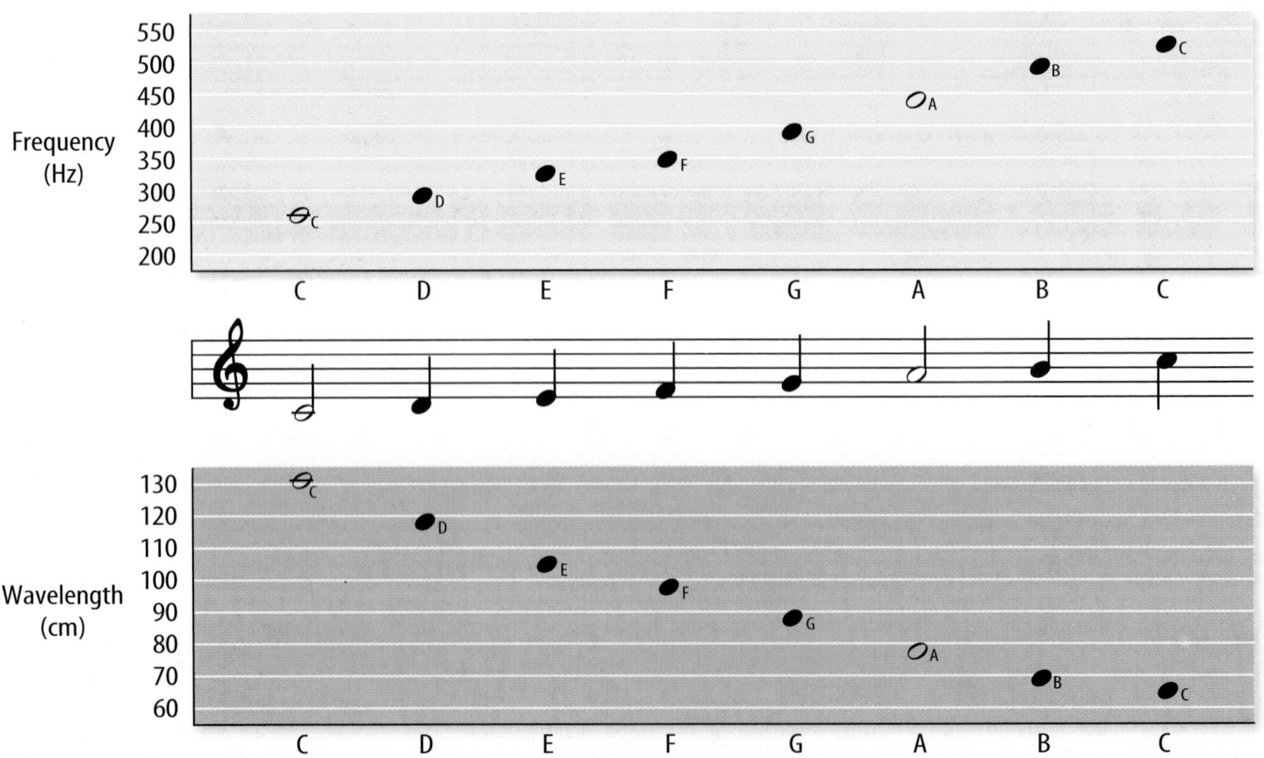

Figure 10
The frequency of the notes on a musical scale increases as the notes get higher in pitch, but the wavelength of the notes decreases.

Wave Speed

You've probably watched a distant thunderstorm approach on a hot summer day. You see a bolt of lightning flash between a dark cloud and the ground. Do the sound waves, or thunder, produced by the lightning bolt reach your ears at the same instant you see the lightning? If the thunderstorm is many kilometers away, several seconds will pass between when you see the lightning and when you hear the thunder. This happens because light travels much faster in air than sound does. Light is an electromagnetic wave that travels through air at about 300 million m/s. On the other hand, sound is a mechanical wave that travels through air at about 340 m/s.

Mechanical waves such as sound usually travel faster in a medium in which the atoms that make up the medium are closer together. Sound travels faster in solids than in liquids and faster in liquids than in gases. This is because atoms are closer to each other in a solid than in a liquid, and closer together in a liquid than in a gas.

Electromagnetic waves such as light behave differently than mechanical waves. Unlike mechanical waves, they travel faster in gases than in solids or liquids. You know that you can get to your next class faster if the hallways are nearly empty than if they are filled with other students. Electromagnetic waves behave the same way. If many atoms are in the medium, electromagnetic waves are slowed down. For example, the speed of light is one and a half times faster in air than it is in glass.

Research Visit the Glencoe Science Web site at **science.glencoe.com** for information about wave speed in different materials. Make a graph to show the differences.

Section  Assessment

1. How does the frequency of a wave change as its wavelength changes?
2. Why is a sound wave with a large amplitude more likely to damage your hearing than one with a small amplitude?
3. What accounts for the time difference in seeing and hearing a fireworks display?
4. Why is the statement "The speed of light is 300 million m/s" not always correct?
5. **Think Critically** Explain the differences between the waves that make up bright, green light and dim, red light.

Skill Builder Activities

6. **Predicting** A biologist studying bison puts her ear next to the ground. By doing this she knows that the herd is coming toward her. Explain. **For more help, refer to the Science Skill Handbook.**
7. **Solving One-Step Equations** The product of the wavelength and the frequency of a wave is the speed of the wave. If a sound wave traveling through water has a speed of 1,470 m/s and a frequency of 2,340 Hz, what is its wavelength? **For more help, refer to the Math Skill Handbook.**

Activity

Waves on a Spring

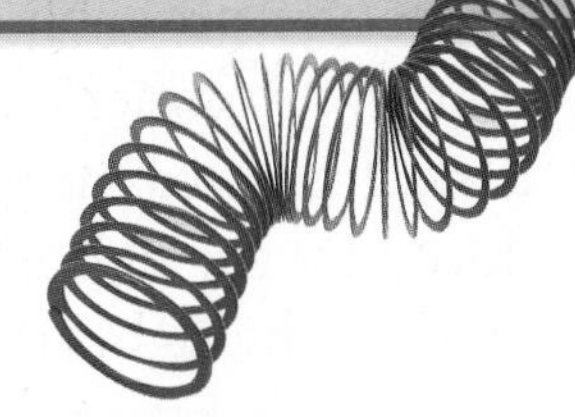

Waves are rhythmic disturbances that carry energy through matter or space. Studying waves can help you understand how the Sun's energy reaches Earth and sounds travel through the air.

What You'll Investigate

What are some of the properties of transverse and compressional waves on a coiled spring?

Materials

long, coiled spring toy
colored yarn (5 cm)
meterstick
stopwatch

Goals

- **Create** transverse and compressional waves on a coiled spring toy.
- **Investigate** wave properties such as speed and amplitude.

Safety Precautions 

WARNING: *Avoid overstretching or tangling the spring to prevent injury or damage.*

Procedure

1. **Prepare** a data table such as the one shown.

Wave Data	
Length of stretched spring toy	
Average time for a wave to travel from end to end—step 4	
Average time for a wave to travel from end to end—step 5	

2. Work in pairs or groups and clear a place on an uncarpeted floor about 6 m × 2 m.
3. Stretch the springs between two people to the length suggested by your teacher. Measure the length.
4. Create a wave with a quick, sideways snap of the wrist. Time several waves as they travel the length of the spring. Record the average time in your data table.
5. Repeat step 4 using waves that have slightly larger amplitudes.
6. Squeeze together about 20 of the coils. Observe what happens to the unsqueezed coils. Release the coils and observe.
7. Quickly push the spring toward your partner, then pull it back.
8. Tie the yarn to a coil near the middle of the spring. Repeat step 7, observing the string.

Conclude and Apply

1. **Classify** the wave pulses you created in each step as compressional or transverse.
2. **Calculate** and compare the speeds of the waves in steps 4 and 5.
3. **Classify** the unsqueezed coils in step 6 as a compression or a rarefaction.
4. **Compare and contrast** the motion of the yarn in step 8 with the motion of the wave.

Communicating Your Data

Write a summary paragraph of how this activity demonstrated any of the vocabulary words from the first two sections of the chapter. **For more help,** refer to the Science Skill Handbook.

SECTION 3

Wave Behavior

Reflection

What causes the echo when you yell across an empty gymnasium or down a long, empty hallway? Why can you see your face when you look in a mirror? The echo of your voice and the face you see in the mirror are caused by wave reflection.

Reflection occurs when a wave strikes an object or surface and bounces off. An echo is reflected sound. Sound reflects from all surfaces. Your echo bounces off the walls, floor, ceiling, furniture, and people. You see your face in a mirror or a still pond, as shown in **Figure 11A,** because of reflection. Light waves produced by a source of light such as the Sun or a lightbulb bounce off your face, strike the mirror, and reflect back to your eyes.

When a surface is smooth and even the reflected image is clear and sharp. However, when light reflects from an uneven or rough surface, you can't see a sharp image because the reflected light scatters in many different directions, as shown in **Figure 11B.**

Reading Check *What causes reflection?*

As You Read

What You'll Learn

- **Explain** how waves can reflect from some surfaces.
- **Explain** how waves change direction when they move from one material into another.
- **Describe** how waves are able to bend around barriers.

Vocabulary

reflection
refraction
diffraction
interference

Why It's Important

The reflection of waves enables you to see objects around you.

A The smooth surface of a still pond enables you to see a sharp, clear image of yourself.

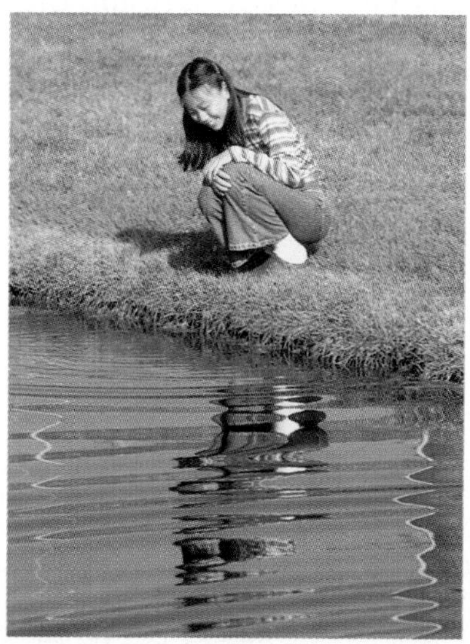

B If the surface of the pond is rough and uneven, your reflected image is no longer clear and sharp.

Figure 11
The image formed by reflection depends on the smoothness of the surface.

Observing How Light Refracts

Procedure

1. Fill a **large, opaque drinking glass or cup** with **water.**
2. Place a **white soda straw** in the water at an angle.
3. Looking directly down into the cup from above, observe the straw where it meets the water.
4. Placing yourself so that the straw angles to your left or right, slowly back away about 1 m. Observe the straw as it appears above, at, and below the surface of the water.

Analysis

1. Describe the straw's appearance from above.
2. Compare the straw's appearance above and below the water's surface in step 4.

Refraction

A wave changes direction when it reflects from a surface. Waves also can change direction in another way. Perhaps you have tried to grab a sinking object when you are in a swimming pool, only to come up empty-handed. Yet you were sure you grabbed right where you saw the object. You missed grabbing the object because the light rays from the object changed direction as they passed from the water into the air. The bending of a wave as it moves from one medium into another is called **refraction.**

Refraction and Wave Speed Remember that the speed of a wave can be different in different materials. For example, light waves travel faster in air than in water. Refraction occurs when the speed of a wave changes as it passes from one substance to another, as shown in **Figure 12.** A line that is perpendicular to the water's surface is called the normal. When a light ray passes from air into water, it slows down and bends toward the normal. When the ray passes from water into air, it speeds up and bends away from the normal. The larger the change in speed of the light wave is, the larger the change in direction is.

You notice refraction when you look down into a fishbowl. Refraction makes the fish appear to be closer to the surface but farther away from you than it is, as shown in **Figure 13.** Light rays reflected from the fish are bent away from the normal as they pass from water to air. Your brain interprets the light that enters your eyes by assuming that light rays always travel in straight lines. As a result, the light rays seem to be coming from a fish that is in a different location.

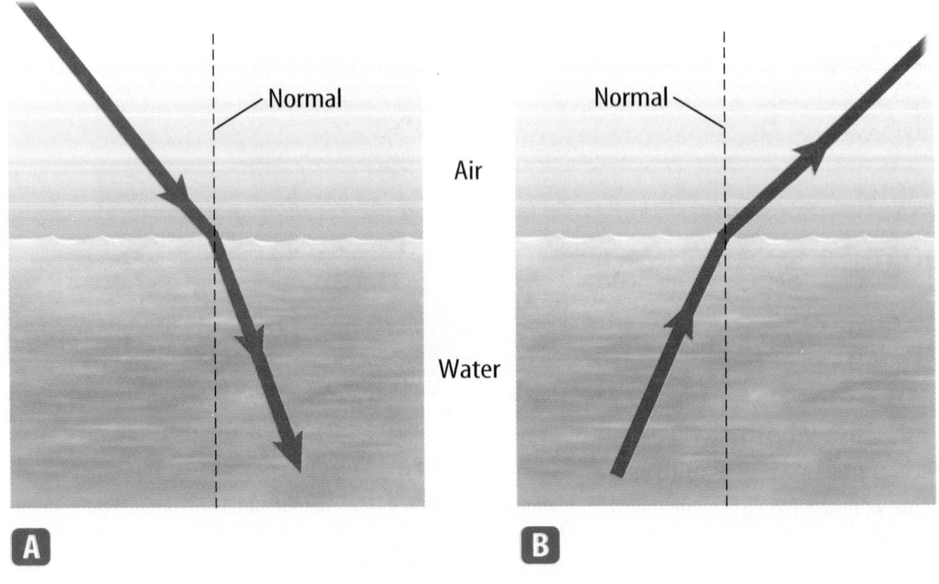

Figure 12
A wave is refracted when it changes speed. **A** As the light ray passes from air to water, it refracts toward the normal. **B** As the light ray passes from water to air, it refracts away from the normal.

Color from Refraction Refraction causes prisms to separate sunlight into many colors and produces rainbows too. **Figure 14** illustrates how refraction and reflection produce a rainbow when light waves from the Sun pass into and out of water droplets in the air.

Reading Check *What produces a rainbow?*

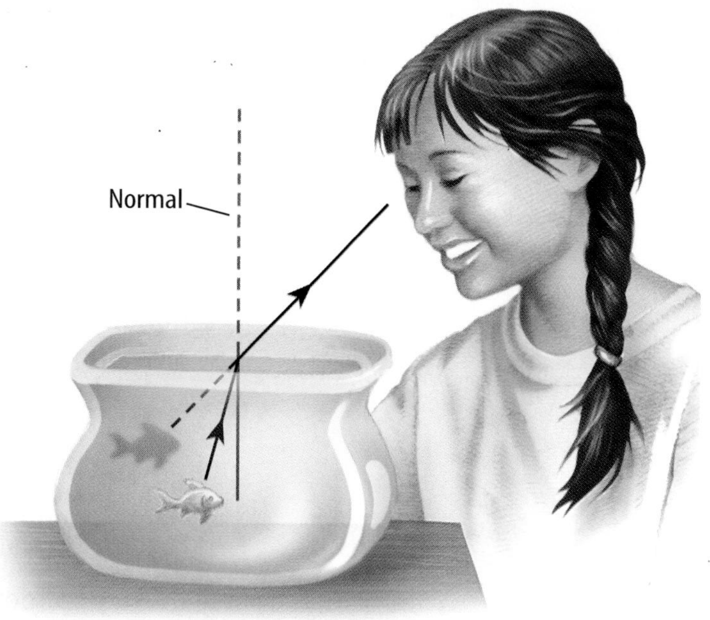

Figure 13
When you look at the goldfish in the water, the fish is in a different position than it appears.

Diffraction

Why can you hear music from the band room when you are down the hall? You can hear the music because the sound waves bend as they pass through an open doorway. This bending isn't caused by refraction. Remember that refraction occurs when waves change speed, but sound waves have the same speed in the band room and in the hallway. Instead, the bending is caused by diffraction. **Diffraction** is the bending of waves around a barrier.

Diffraction of Light Waves Can light waves diffract, too? You can hear your friends in the band room but you can't see them until you reach the open door. Therefore, you know that light waves do not diffract as much as sound waves do.

Are light waves able to diffract at all? Light waves do bend around the edges of an open door. However, for an opening as wide as a door, the amount the light bends is extremely small. As a result, the diffraction of light is far too small to allow you to see around a corner.

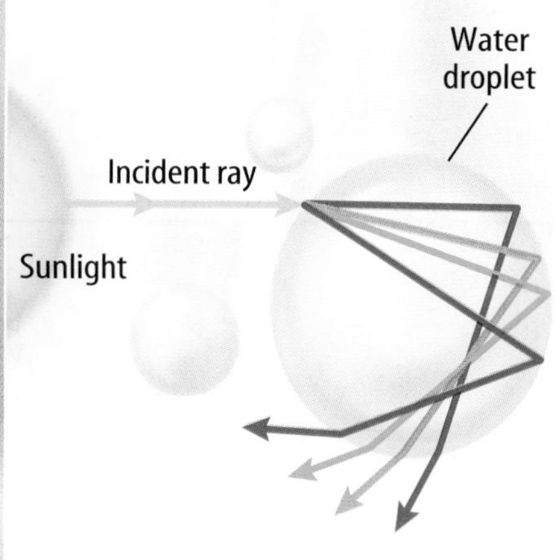

Figure 14
Light rays refract as they enter and leave each water drop. Each color refracts at different angles because of their different wavelengths, so they separate into the colors of the visible spectrum.

Diffraction and Wavelength The reason that light waves don't diffract much when they pass through an open door is that the wavelengths of visible light are much smaller than the width of the door. Light waves have wavelengths between about 400 and 700 billionths of a meter, while the width of doorway is about one meter. Sound waves that you can hear have wavelengths between a few millimeters and about 10 m. They bend more easily around the corners of an open door. A wave is diffracted more when its wavelength is similar in size to the barrier or opening.

Diffraction of Water Waves Perhaps you have noticed water waves bending around barriers. For example, when water waves strike obstacles such as the islands shown in **Figure 15,** they don't stop moving. Here the size and spacing of the islands is not too different from the wavelength of the water waves. So the water waves bend around the islands, and keep on moving. They also spread out after they pass through openings between the islands. If the islands were much larger than the water wavelength, less diffraction would occur.

What happens when waves meet?

Suppose you throw two pebbles into a still pond. Ripples spread from the impact of each pebble and travel toward each other. What happens when two of these ripples meet? Do they collide like billiard balls and change direction? Waves behave differently from billiard balls when they meet. Waves pass right through each other and continue moving as though the other waves never existed.

Figure 15
Water waves bend or diffract around these islands. More diffraction occurs when the object is closer in size to the wavelength.

Wave Interference While two waves overlap a new wave is formed by adding the two waves together. The ability of two waves to combine and form a new wave when they overlap is called **interference.** After they overlap, the individual waves continue to travel on in their original form.

The different ways waves can interfere are shown in **Figure 16** on the next page. Sometimes when the waves meet, the crest of one wave overlaps the crest of another wave. This is called constructive interference. The amplitudes of these combining waves add together to make a larger wave while they overlap. Destructive interference occurs when the crest of one wave overlaps the trough of another wave. Then, the amplitudes of the two waves combine to make a wave with a smaller amplitude. If the two waves have equal amplitudes and meet crest to trough, they cancel each other while the waves overlap.

Science Online

Research Visit the Glencoe Science Web site at **science.glencoe.com** for more information about wave interference.

Waves and Particles Like waves of water, when light travels through a small opening, such as a narrow slit, the light spreads out in all directions on the other side of the slit. If small particles, instead of waves, were sent through the slit, they would continue in a straight line without spreading. The spreading, or diffraction, is only a property of waves. Interference also doesn't occur with particles. If waves meet, they reinforce or cancel each other, then travel on. If particles approach each other, they either collide and scatter or miss each other completely. Interference, like diffraction, is a property of waves, not particles.

Problem-Solving Activity

Can you create destructive interference?

Your brother is vacuuming and you can't hear the television. Is it possible to diminish the sound of the vacuum so you can hear the TV? Can you eliminate unpleasant sounds and keep the sounds you do want to hear?

Identifying the Problem

It is possible to create a frequency that will destructively interfere with the sound of the vacuum and not the television. The graph shows the waves created by the vacuum and the television.

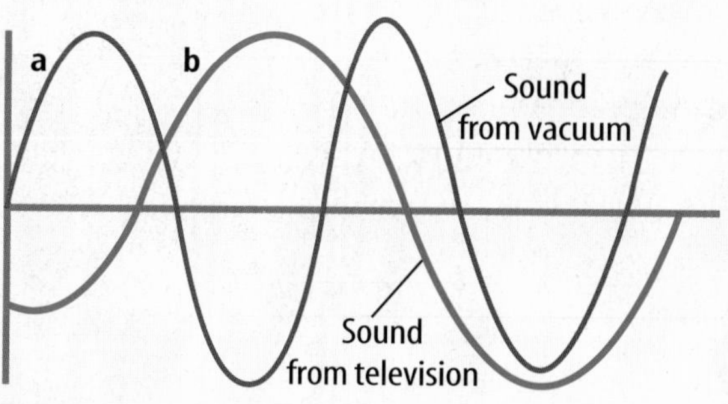

Solving the Problem

1. Can you create the graph of a wave that will eliminate the noise from the vacuum but not the television?
2. Can you create the graph of a wave that would amplify the sound of the television?

VISUALIZING INTERFERENCE

Figure 16

Whether they are ripples on a pond or huge ocean swells, when water waves meet they can combine to form new waves in a process called interference. As shown below, wave interference can be constructive or destructive.

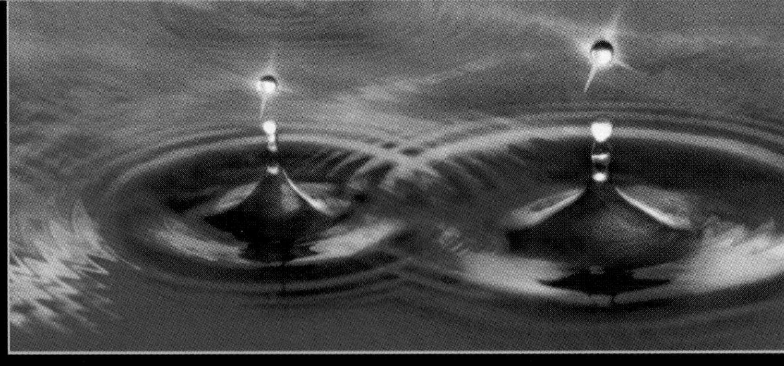

Constructive Interference

In constructive interference, a wave with greater amplitude is formed.

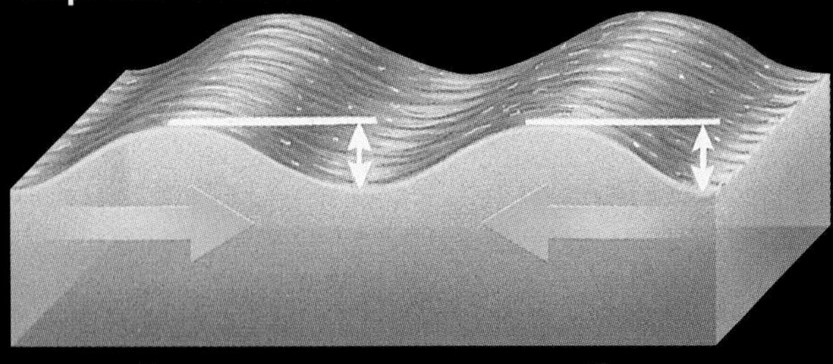

A B

The crests of two waves—A and B—approach each other.

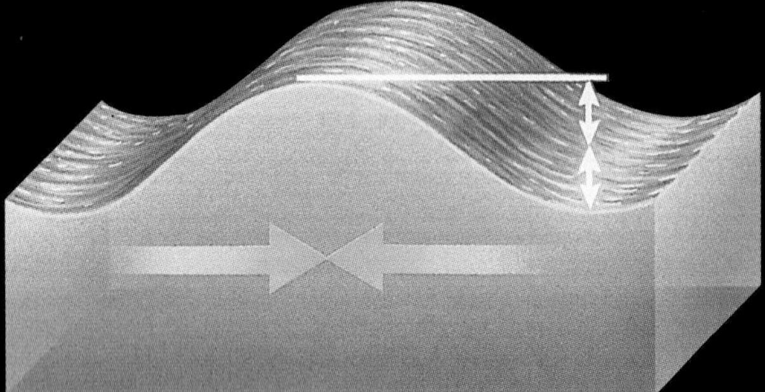

The two waves form a wave with a greater amplitude while the crests of both waves overlap.

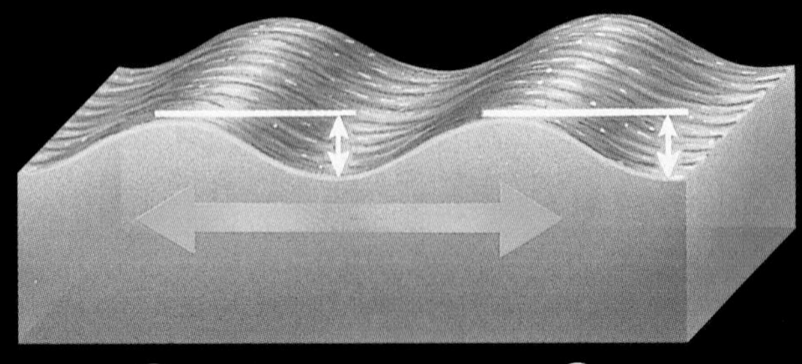

B A

The original waves pass through each other and go on as they started.

Destructive Interference

In destructive interference, a wave with a smaller amplitude is formed.

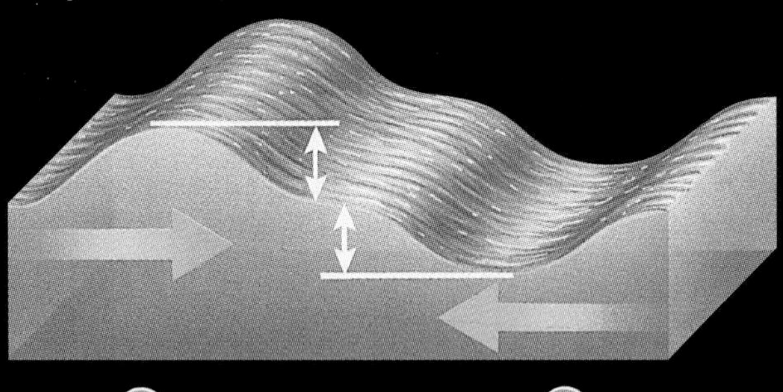

A B

The crest of one wave approaches the trough of another.

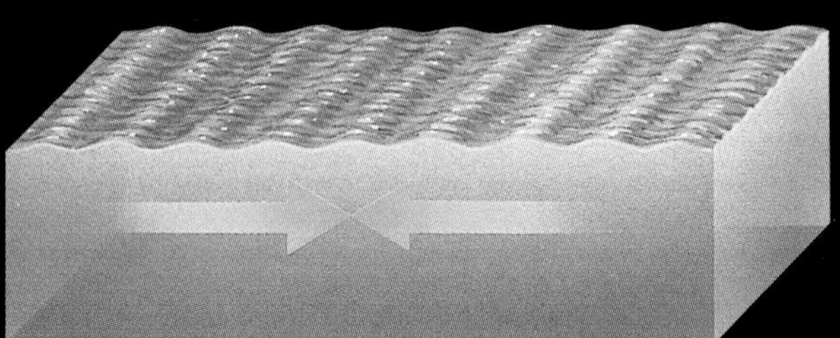

If the two waves have equal amplitude, they momentarily cancel when they meet.

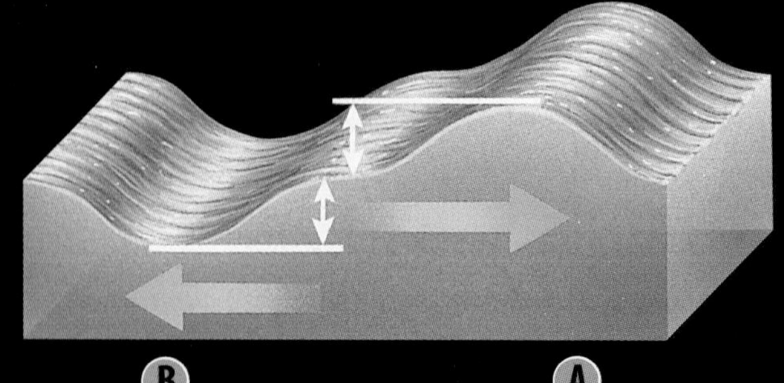

B A

The original waves pass through each other and go on as they started.

Reducing Noise You might have seen someone use a power lawn mower or a chain saw. In the past, many people who performed these tasks damaged their hearing because of the loud noises produced by these machines. Today, specially designed ear protectors absorb the sound from lawn mowers and chain saws. The ear protectors absorb energy and lower the amplitudes of the harmful waves. The waves that reach the ears have smaller amplitudes and won't damage eardrums.

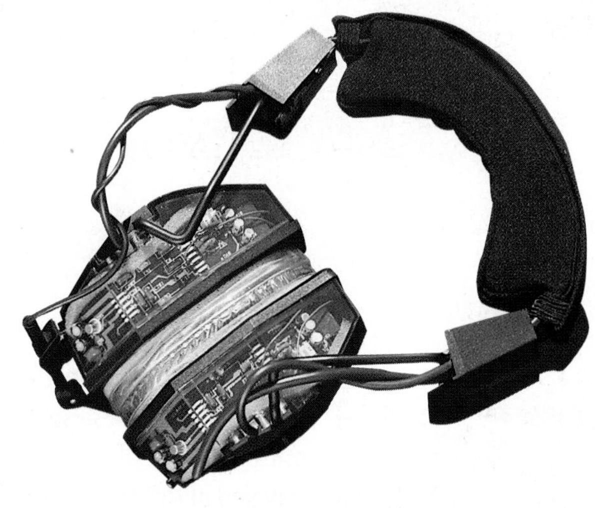

Using Interference Pilots and passengers of small planes have a more complicated problem. They can't use ordinary ear protectors to shut out all the noise of the plane's motor. If they did, the pilots wouldn't be able to hear instructions from air-traffic controllers, and the passengers wouldn't be able to hear each other talk. To solve this problem, engineers invented ear protectors, as shown in **Figure 17,** that have electronic circuits. These circuits detect noise from the aircraft and produce sound frequencies that destructively interfere with the noise. However, the sound frequencies produced do not interfere with human voices, so people can hear and understand normal conversation. In these examples, destructive interference can be a benefit.

Figure 17
Some airplane pilots use special ear protectors that cancel out engine noise but don't block human voices.

Section  Assessment

1. Why don't you see your reflection in a building made of rough, white stone?
2. If you're standing on one side of a building, how are you able to hear the siren of an ambulance on the other side?
3. What behavior of light enables magnifying glasses and contact lenses to bend light rays and help people see more clearly?
4. What is diffraction? How does the amount of diffraction depend on wavelength?
5. **Think Critically** Why don't light rays that stream through an open window into a darkened room spread evenly through the entire room?

Skill Builder Activities

6. **Comparing and Contrasting** When light rays pass from water into a certain type of glass, the rays refract toward the normal. Compare and contrast the speed of light in water and in the glass. **For more help, refer to the Science Skill Handbook.**
7. **Communicating** Watch carefully as you travel home from school or walk down your street. What examples of wave reflection and refraction do you notice? Describe each of these in your Science Journal and explain your reasons. **For more help, refer to the Science Skill Handbook.**

Activity — Design Your Own Experiment

Wave Speed

When an earthquake occurs, it produces waves that are recorded at points all over the world by instruments called seismographs. By comparing the data that they collected from these seismographs, scientists discovered that the interior of Earth must be made of layers of different materials. These data showed that the waves traveled at different speeds as they passed through different parts of Earth's interior.

Recognize the Problem

How can the speed of a wave be measured?

Form a Hypothesis

In some materials, waves travel too fast for their speeds to be measured directly. Think about what you know about the relationship among the frequency, wavelength, and speed of a wave in a medium. Make a hypothesis about how you can use this relationship to measure the speed of a wave within a medium.

Goals

- **Measure** the speed of a wave within a coiled spring toy.
- **Predict** whether the speed you measured will be different in other types of coiled spring toys.

Materials

coiled spring toy
stopwatch
**clock with a second hand*
meterstick
tape

**Alternate materials*

Safety Precautions

Test Your Hypothesis

Plan

1. Make a data table in your Science Journal like the one shown.
2. In your Science Journal, write a detailed description of the coiled spring toy you are going to use. Be sure to include its mass and diameter, the width of a coil, and what it is made of.
3. **Decide** as a group how you will measure the frequency and length of waves in the spring toy. What are your variables? Which variables must be controlled? What variable do you want to measure?
4. Repeat your experiment three times.

Wave Data

	Trial 1	Trial 2	Trial 3
Length spring was stretched (m)			
Number of crests			
Wavelength (m)			
# of vibrations timed			
# of seconds vibrations were timed			
Wave speed (m/s)			

Do

1. Make sure your teacher approves your plan before you start.
2. Carry out the experiment.
3. While you are doing the experiment, record your observations and measurements in your data table.

Analyze Your Data

1. **Calculate** the frequency of the waves by dividing the number of vibrations you timed by the number of seconds you timed them. Record your results in your data table.
2. Use the following formula to calculate the speed of a wave in each trial.

$$\text{wavelength} \times \text{wave frequency} = \text{wave speed}$$

3. Average the wave speeds from your trials to determine the average speed of a wave in your coiled spring toy.

Draw Conclusions

1. Which variables affected the wave speed in spring toys the most? Which variables affected the speed the least? Was your hypothesis supported?
2. What factors caused the wave speed measured in each trial to be different?

Your Data

Post a description of your coiled spring toy and the results of your experiment on a bulletin board in your classroom. **Compare and contrast** your results with other students in your class.

Science Stats

Waves, Waves, and More Waves

Did you know...

. . . You are constantly surrounded by a sea of waves even when you're on dry land! Electromagnetic waves around us are used to cook our food and transmit signals to our radios and televisions. Light itself is an electromagnetic wave.

. . . The highest recorded ocean wave was 34 meters high, which is comparable to the height of a ten-story building. This super wave was seen in the North Pacific Ocean and recorded by the crew of the naval ship *USS Ramapo* in 1933.

. . . Tsunamis—huge ocean waves— can travel at speeds over 900 km/h.

. . . Waves let dolphins see with their ears! A dolphin sends out ultrasonic pulses, or clicks, at rates of 800 pulses per second. These sound waves are reflected back to the dolphin after they hit another object. This process—echolocation—allows dolphins to recognize obstacles and meals.

Connecting To Math

. . . Earthquakes produce a variety of seismic waves— waves that ripple through Earth after subsurface rock breaks suddenly. The fastest are P and S waves. P waves are compressional waves that travel at about 8 km/s. S waves, which move like ocean waves, travel at about 4.8 km/s.

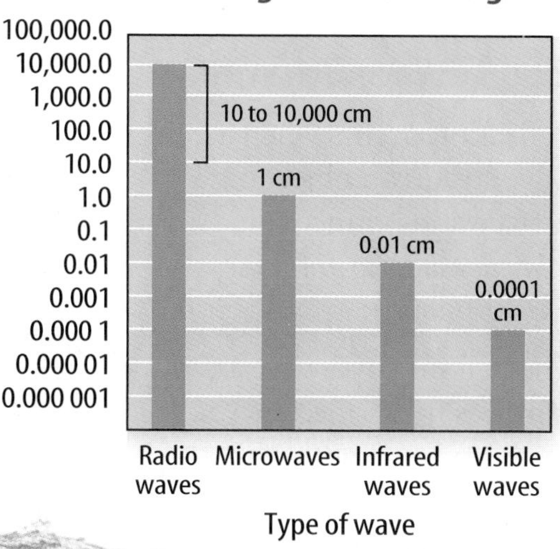

. . . Radio waves from space were discovered in 1932 by Karl G. Jansky, an American engineer. His amazing discovery led to creation of radio astronomy, a field that explores parts of the universe that are hidden by interstellar dust or can't be seen with telescopes.

Do the Math

1. A museum with a dolphin exhibit plays dolphin clicks for its visitors 250 times slower than the rate at which the dolphins emit them. How many clicks do the visitors hear in 10 s?
2. Tsunamis form in the ocean when an earthquake occurs on the ocean floor. How long will it take a tsunami to travel 4,500 km?
3. Make a bar graph to show the speeds of P waves, S waves and tsunamis. Use km/h as your unit of speed.

Go Further

Go to **science.glencoe.com** to learn about discoveries by radio astronomers. Graph the distances of these discoveries from Earth.

Chapter 11 Study Guide

Reviewing Main Ideas

Section 1 What are waves?

1. Waves are rhythmic disturbances that carry energy but not matter.
2. Mechanical waves can travel only through matter. Electromagnetic waves can travel through matter and space.
3. In a mechanical transverse wave, matter in the medium moves back and forth at right angles to the direction the wave travels.
4. In a compressional wave, matter in the medium moves forward and backward in the same direction as the wave. *How does the boat in the picture move as the water wave goes by?*

Section 2 Wave Properties

1. The amplitude of a transverse wave is the distance between the rest position and a crest or a trough.
2. The energy carried by a wave increases as the amplitude increases.
3. Wavelength is the distance between neighboring crests or neighboring troughs.
4. The frequency of a wave is the number of wavelengths that pass a given point in 1 s. *What property of a wave is shown by the figure at the top of the next column?*

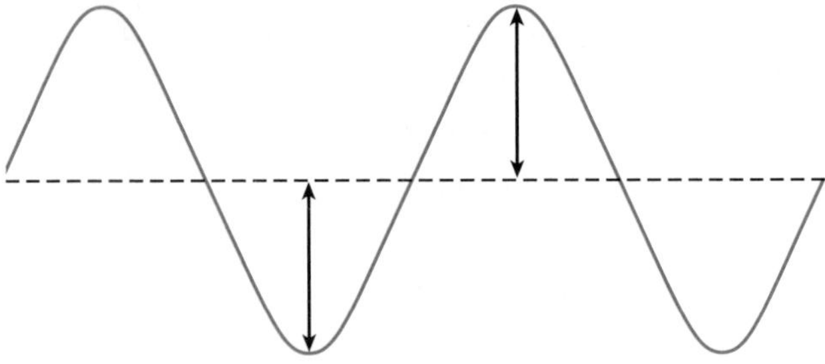

5. Waves travel through different materials at different speeds.

Section 3 Wave Behavior

1. Reflection occurs when a wave strikes an object or surface and bounces off. *Why doesn't the foil show a clear image?*
2. The bending of a wave as it moves from one medium into another is called refraction. A wave changes direction, or refracts, when the speed of the wave changes.
3. The bending of waves around a barrier is called diffraction.
4. Interference occurs when two or more waves combine and form a new wave while they overlap.

After You Read

FOLDABLES Reading & Study Skills

Use your Concept Map Study Fold to compare and contrast transverse and compressional mechanical waves.

Visualizing Main Ideas

Complete the following spider map about waves.

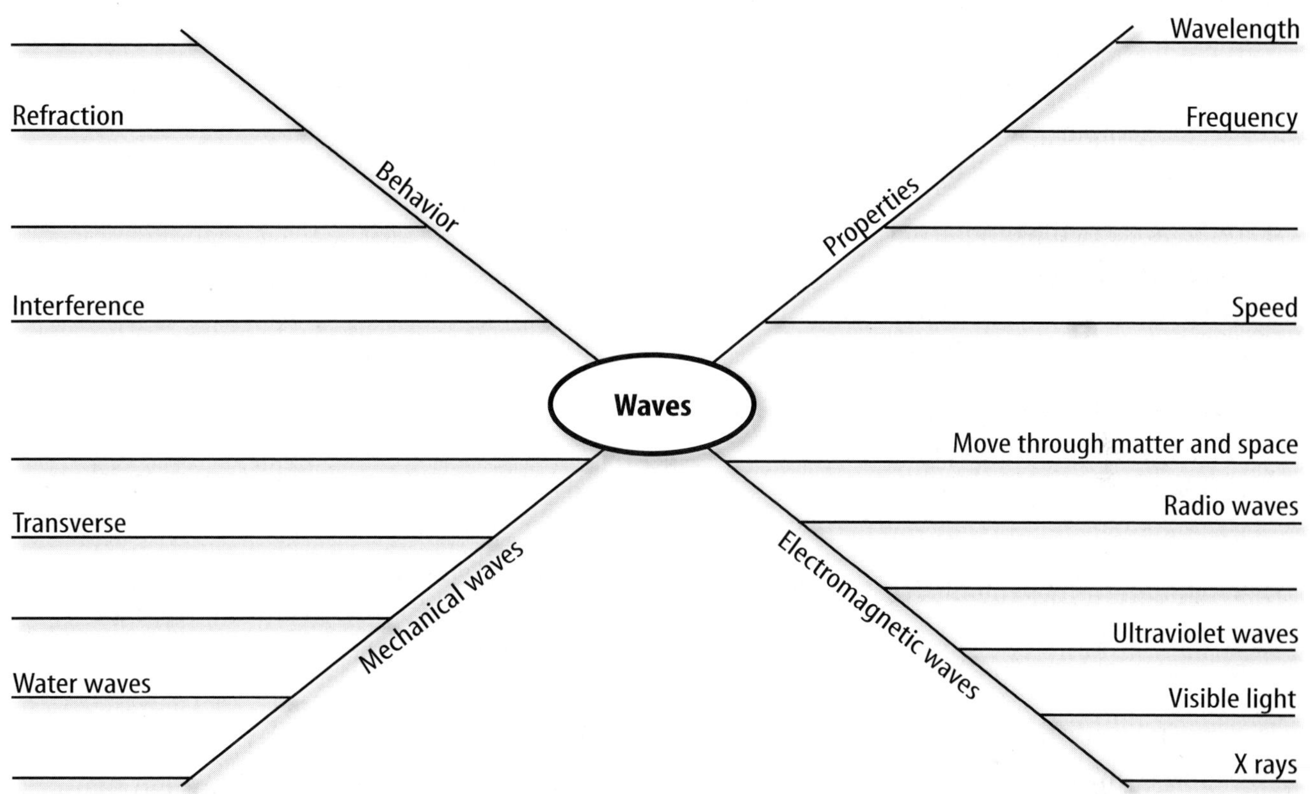

Vocabulary Review

Vocabulary Words

- **a.** amplitude
- **b.** compressional wave
- **c.** diffraction
- **d.** electromagnetic wave
- **e.** frequency
- **f.** interference
- **g.** mechanical wave
- **h.** reflection
- **i.** refraction
- **j.** transverse wave
- **k.** wave
- **l.** wavelength

Study Tip

THE PRINCETON REVIEW

After you've read a chapter, go back to the beginning and speed-read through what you've just read. This will help your memory.

Using Vocabulary

Using the list, replace the underlined words with the correct vocabulary words.

1. Diffraction is the change in direction of a wave going from one medium to another.
2. The type of wave that has rarefactions is a transverse wave.
3. The distance between two adjacent crests of a transverse wave is the frequency.
4. The more energy a wave carries, the greater its wavelength is.
5. A mechanical wave can travel through space without a medium.

Chapter 11 Assessment

Checking Concepts

Choose the word or phrase that best answers the question.

1. What is the material through which mechanical waves travel?
   A) charged particles **C)** a vacuum
   B) space **D)** a medium
2. What is carried from particle to particle in a water wave?
   A) speed **C)** energy
   B) amplitude **D)** matter
3. What are the lowest points on a transverse wave called?
   A) crests **C)** compressions
   B) troughs **D)** rarefactions
4. What determines the pitch of a sound wave?
   A) amplitude **C)** speed
   B) frequency **D)** refraction
5. What is the distance between adjacent wave compressions?
   A) one wavelength **C)** 1 m/s
   B) 1 km **D)** 1 Hz
6. What occurs when a wave strikes an object or surface and bounces off?
   A) diffraction
   B) refraction
   C) a transverse wave
   D) reflection
7. What is the name for a change in the direction of a wave when it passes from one medium into another?
   A) refraction **C)** reflection
   B) interference **D)** diffraction
8. What type of wave is a sound wave?
   A) transverse **C)** compressional
   B) electromagnetic **D)** refracted
9. When two waves overlap and interfere destructively, what does the resulting wave have?
   A) a greater amplitude
   B) more energy
   C) a change in frequency
   D) a lower amplitude
10. What is the difference between blue light and green light?
    A) They have different wavelengths.
    B) One is a transverse wave and the other is not.
    C) They have different pitch.
    D) One is mechanical and the other is not.

Thinking Critically

11. Explain what kind of wave—transverse or compressional—is produced when an engine bumps into a string of coupled railroad cars on a track.
12. Is it possible for an electromagnetic wave to travel through a vacuum? Through matter? Explain your answers.
13. Why does the frequency of a wave decrease as the wavelength increases?
14. Why don't you see your reflected image when you look at a white, rough surface?
15. If a cannon fires at a great distance from you, why do you see the flash before you hear the sound?

Developing Skills

16. **Solving One-Step Equations** An electromagnetic wave travels at the speed of light and has a wavelength of 0.022 m. If the wave speed is equal to the wavelength times the frequency, what is the frequency of the wave?

17. **Forming Hypotheses** Form a hypothesis that can explain this observation. Waves A and B travel away from Earth through Earth's atmosphere. Wave A continues on into space, but wave B does not.

18. **Recognizing Cause and Effect** Explain how the object shown below causes compressions and rarefactions as it vibrates in air.

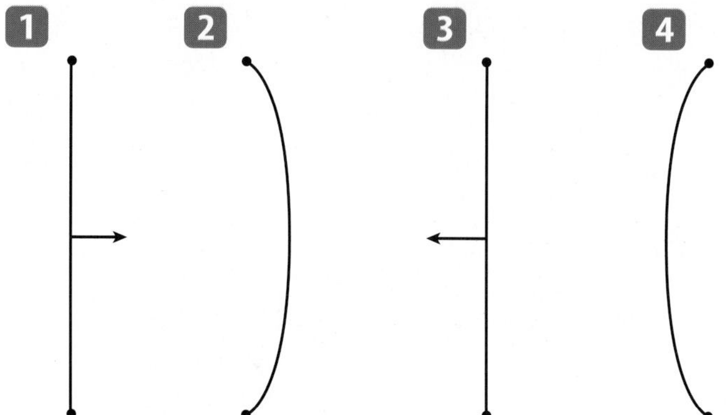

19. **Comparing and Contrasting** AM radio waves have wavelengths between about 200 m and 600 m, and FM radio waves have wavelengths of about 3 m. Why can AM radio signals often be heard behind buildings and mountains but FM radio signals cannot?

Performance Assessment

20. **Making Flashcards** Work with a partner to make flashcards for the bold-faced terms in the chapter. Illustrate each term on the front of the cards. Write the term and its definition on the back of the card. Use the cards to review the terms with another team.

Technology

Go to the Glencoe Science Web site at **science.glencoe.com** or use the **Glencoe Science CD-ROM** for additional chapter assessment.

Test Practice

Kamisha's science teacher told her that her remote control sent signals to the TV and VCR by using infrared waves. She decided to do some research about waves. The information she gathered is shown in the diagram below.

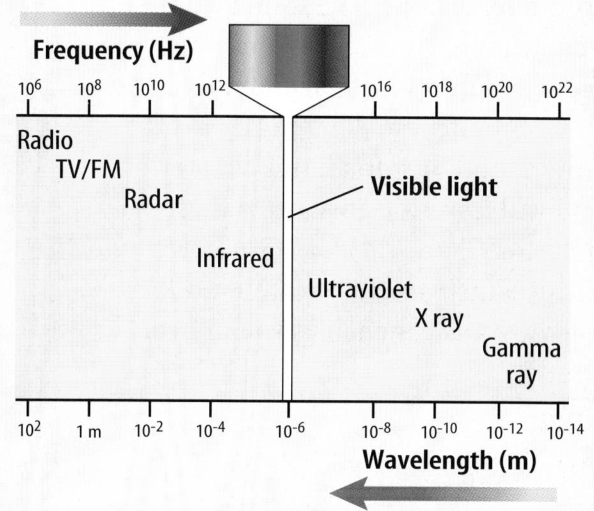

1. According to the diagram, which type of wave has a wavelength greater than 1 m?
   A) radio
   B) infrared
   C) ultraviolet
   D) X ray

2. According to the diagram, which type of wave has the HIGHEST frequency?
   F) radio
   G) ultraviolet
   H) X ray
   J) gamma ray

CHAPTER

12 Sound

Have you ever experienced complete silence? Unless you have stood in a room like this one, you probably have not. This room is lined with materials that absorb sound waves and eliminate sound reflections. The sounds that you hear are created by vibrations. How do vibrations make sounds with different pitches? What makes a sound loud or soft? In this chapter, you will learn the answers to these questions. You will also learn how musical instruments create sound and how the ear enables you to hear sound.

What do you think?

Science Journal Look at the picture below with a classmate. Discuss what might be happening. Here's a hint: *Sound is caused by vibrations.* Write your answer or best guess in your Science Journal.

When you speak or sing, you push air from your lungs past your vocal cords, which are two flaps of tissue inside your throat. When you tighten your vocal cords, you can make the sound have a higher pitch. Do this activity to explore how you change the shape of your throat to vary the pitch of sound.

Observe throat vibrations

1. Hold your fingers against the front of your throat and say *Aaaah.* Notice the vibration against your fingers.
2. Now vary the pitch of this sound from low to high and back again. How do the vibrations in your throat change? Record your observations.
3. Change the sound to an *Ooooh.* What do you notice as you listen? Record your observations.

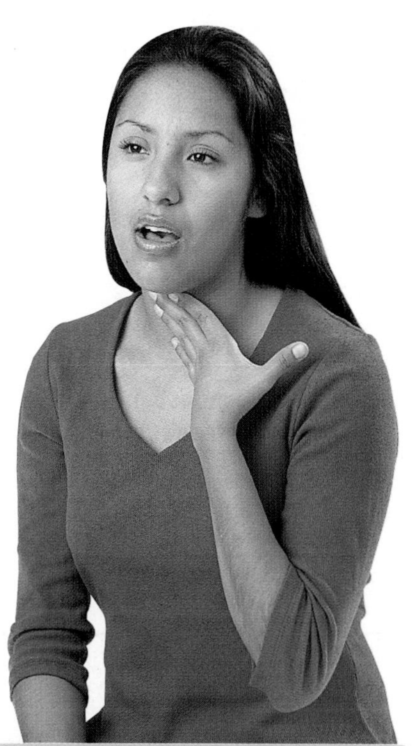

Observe

In your Science Journal, describe how the shape of your throat changed the pitch.

Before You Read

Making a Question Study Fold **Asking yourself questions helps you stay focused so you will better understand sound when you are reading the chapter.**

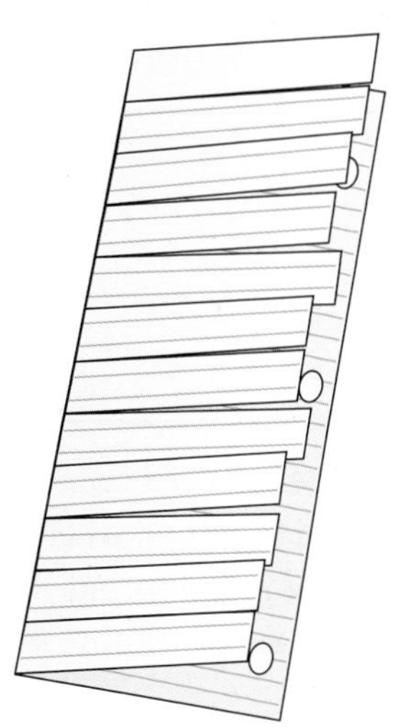

1. Place a sheet of notebook paper in front of you so the short side is at the top and the holes are on the right side. Fold the paper in half from the left side to the right side.
2. Through the top thickness of paper, cut along every third line from the outside edge to the fold, forming tabs.
3. Before you read the chapter, write a question you have about sound on the front of each tab. As you read the chapter, answer your questions and add more information.

SECTION

What is sound?

As You Read

***What* You'll Learn**

- **Identify** the characteristics of sound waves.
- **Explain** how sound travels.
- **Describe** the Doppler effect.

Vocabulary

loudness
pitch
echo
Doppler effect

***Why* It's Important**

Sound gives important information about the world around you.

Sound and Vibration

Think of all the sounds you've heard since you awoke this morning. Did you hear your alarm clock blaring, car horns honking, or locker doors slamming? Every sound has something in common with every other sound. Each is produced by something that vibrates.

Sound Waves

How does an object that is vibrating produce sound? When you speak, the vocal cords in your throat vibrate. These vibrations cause other people to hear your voice. The vibrations produce sound waves that travel to their ears. The other person's ears interpret these sound waves.

A wave carries energy from one place to another without transferring matter. An object that is vibrating in air, such as your vocal cords, produces a sound wave. The vibrating object causes molecules in the air to move back and forth. As these molecules collide with those nearby, they cause other molecules in the air to move back and forth. In this way, energy is transferred from one place to another. A sound wave is a compressional wave, like the wave moving through the coiled spring toy in **Figure 1.** In a compressional wave, particles in the material move back and forth along the direction the wave is moving. In a sound wave, molecules move back and forth along the direction the sound wave is moving.

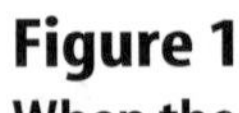

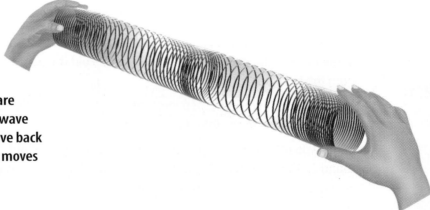

Figure 1
When the coils of a coiled spring toy are squeezed together, a compressional wave moves along the spring. The coils move back and forth as the compressional wave moves past them.

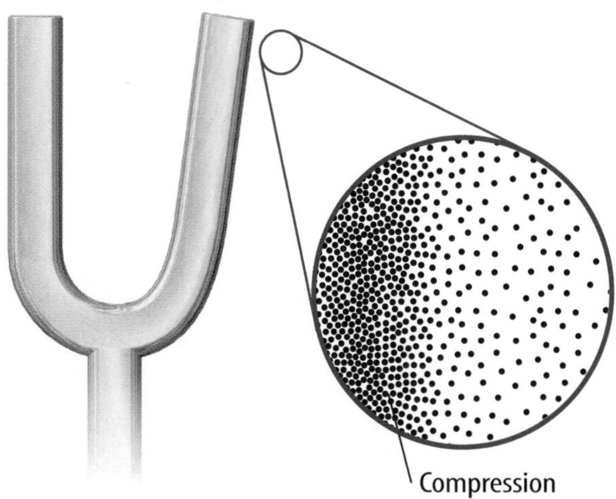

A **When the tuning fork vibrates outward, it forces molecules in the air next to it closer together, creating a region of compression.**

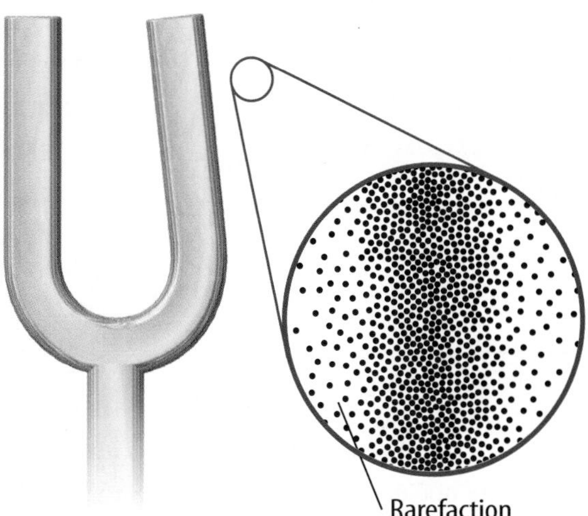

B **When the tuning fork moves back, the molecules in the air next to it spread farther apart, creating a region of rarefaction.**

Making Sound Waves When an object vibrates, it exerts a force on the surrounding air. For example, as the end of the tuning fork moves outward into the air, it pushes the molecules in the air together, as shown in **Figure 2A.** As a result, a region where the molecules are closer together, or more dense, is created. This region of higher density is called a compression. When the end of the tuning fork moves back, it creates a region of lower density called a rarefaction, as shown in **Figure 2B.** As the tuning fork continues to vibrate, a series of compressions and rarefactions is formed. The compressions and rarefactions move away from the tuning fork as molecules in these regions collide with other nearby molecules.

Like other waves, a sound wave can be described by its wavelength and frequency. The wavelength of a sound wave is shown in **Figure 3.** The frequency of a sound wave is the number of compressions or rarefactions that pass by a given point in one second. An object that vibrates faster forms a sound wave with a higher frequency.

Figure 2
A tuning fork makes a sound wave as the ends of the fork vibrate in the air. *Can a sound wave travel in a vacuum?*

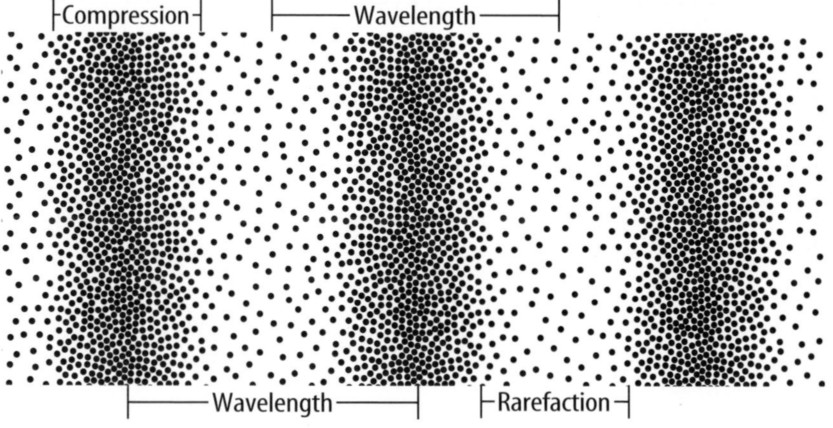

Figure 3
Wavelength is the distance from one compression to another or one rarefaction to another.

TRY AT HOME

Mini LAB

Comparing and Contrasting Sounds

Procedure

1. Shake a set of **keys** and listen to the sound they make in air. Then submerge the keys and one ear in **water.** (A **tub** or a wide, deep **bowl** will work.) Again, shake the keys and listen to the sound. Use a **towel** to dry the keys.
2. Tie a **metal spoon** in the middle of a length of **cotton string.** Strike the spoon on something to hear it ring. Now press the ends of the string against your ears and repeat the experiment. What do you hear?

Analysis

1. Did you hear sounds transmitted through water and through string? Describe the sounds.
2. Compare and contrast the sounds in water and in air.

The Speed of Sound

Sound waves can travel through other materials besides air. In fact, sound waves travel in the same way through different materials as they do in air, although they might travel at different speeds. As a sound wave travels through a material, the particles in the material it is moving through collide with each other. In a solid, molecules are closer together than in liquids or gases, so collisions between molecules occur more rapidly than in liquids or gases. As a result, the speed of sound is usually fastest in solids, where molecules are closest together, and slowest in gases, where molecules are farthest apart. **Table 1** shows the speed of sound through different materials.

The Speed of Sound and Temperature The temperature of the material that sound waves are traveling through also affects the speed of sound. As a substance heats up, its molecules move faster, so they collide more frequently. The more frequent the collisions are, the faster the speed of sound is in the material. For example, the speed of sound in air at 0°C is 331 m/s; at 20°C, it is 343 m/s.

Amplitude and Loudness

What's the difference between loud sounds and quiet sounds? When you play a song at high volume and low volume, you hear the same instruments and voices, but something is different. The difference is that loud sound waves generally carry more energy than soft sound waves do.

Loudness is the human perception of how much energy a sound wave carries. Not all sound waves with the same energy are as loud. Sounds with frequencies between 3,000 Hz and 4,000 Hz sound louder than other sound waves that have the same energy.

Table 1 Speed of Sound in Different Materials

Material	Speed (m/s)
Air	343
Water	1,483
Glass	5,940
Steel	5,640

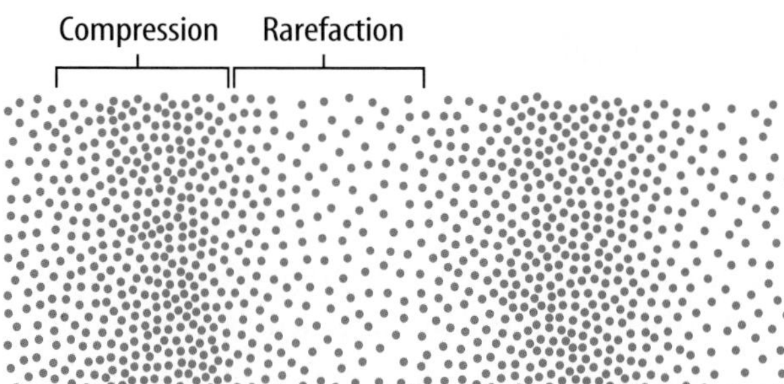

A This sound wave has a lower amplitude.

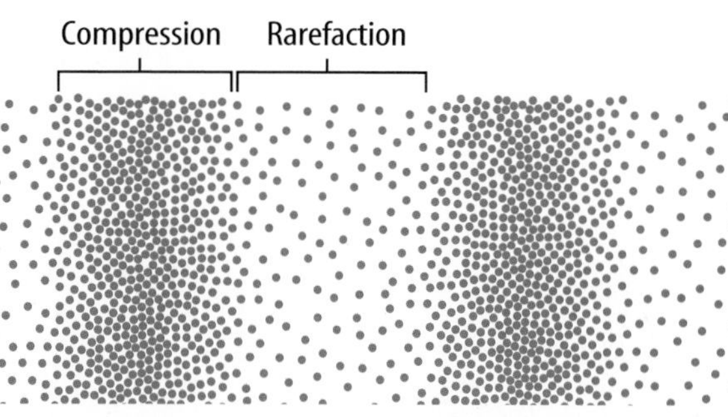

B This sound wave has a higher amplitude. Particles in the material are more compressed in the compressions and more spread out in the rarefactions.

Figure 4
The amplitude of a sound wave depends on how spread out the particles are in the compressions and rarefactions of the wave.

Amplitude and Energy The amount of energy a wave carries depends on its amplitude. For a compressional wave such as a sound wave, the amplitude is related to how spread out the molecules or particles are in the compressions and rarefactions, as **Figure 4** shows. The higher the amplitude of the wave is, the more compressed the particles in the compression are and the more spread out they are in the rarefactions. More energy had to be transferred by the vibrating object that created the wave to force the particles closer together or spread them farther apart. Sound waves with greater amplitude carry more energy and sound louder. Sound waves with smaller amplitude carry less energy and sound quieter.

Reading Check *What determines the loudness of different sounds?*

The Decibel Scale Perhaps an adult has said to you, "Turn down your music, it's too loud! You're going to lose your hearing!" Although the perception of loudness varies from person to person, the energy carried by sound waves can be described by a scale called the decibel (dB) scale. **Figure 5** shows the decibel scale. An increase in the loudness of a sound of 10 dB means that the energy carried by the sound has increased ten times, but an increase of 20 dB means that the sound carries 100 times more energy.

Hearing damage begins to occur at sound levels of about 85 dB. The amount of damage depends on the frequencies of the sound and the length of time a person is exposed to the sound. Some music concerts produce sound levels as high as 120 dB. The energy carried by these sound waves is about 30 billion times greater than the energy carried by sound waves that are made by whispering.

Figure 5
The loudness of sound is measured on the decibel scale.

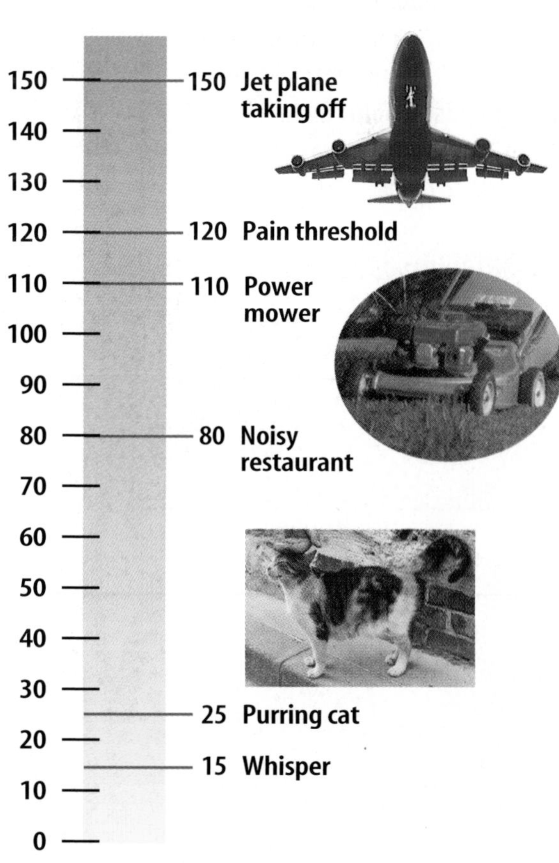

Frequency and Pitch

The **pitch** of a sound is how high or low it sounds. For example, a piccolo produces a high-pitched sound or tone, and a tuba makes a low-pitched sound. Pitch corresponds to the frequency of the sound. The higher the pitch is, the higher the frequency is. A sound wave with a frequency of 440 Hz, for example, has a higher pitch than a sound wave with a frequency of 220 Hz.

The human ear can detect sound waves with frequencies between about 20 Hz and 20,000 Hz. However, some animals can detect even higher and lower frequencies. For example, dogs can hear frequencies up to almost 50,000 Hz. Dolphins and bats can hear frequencies as high as 150,000 Hz, and whales can hear frequencies higher than those heard by humans.

Recall that frequency and wavelength are related. If two sound waves are traveling at the same speed, the wave with the shorter wavelength has a higher frequency. If the wavelength is shorter, then more compressions and rarefactions will go past a given point every second than for a wave with a longer wavelength, as shown in **Figure 6.** Sound waves with a higher pitch have shorter wavelengths than those with a lower pitch.

The Human Voice When you make a sound, you exhale past your vocal cords, causing them to vibrate. The length and thickness of your vocal cords help determine the pitch of your voice. Shorter, thinner vocal cords vibrate at higher frequencies than longer or thicker ones. This explains why children, whose vocal cords are still growing, have higher voices than adults. Muscles in the throat can stretch the vocal cords tighter, letting people vary their pitch within a limited range.

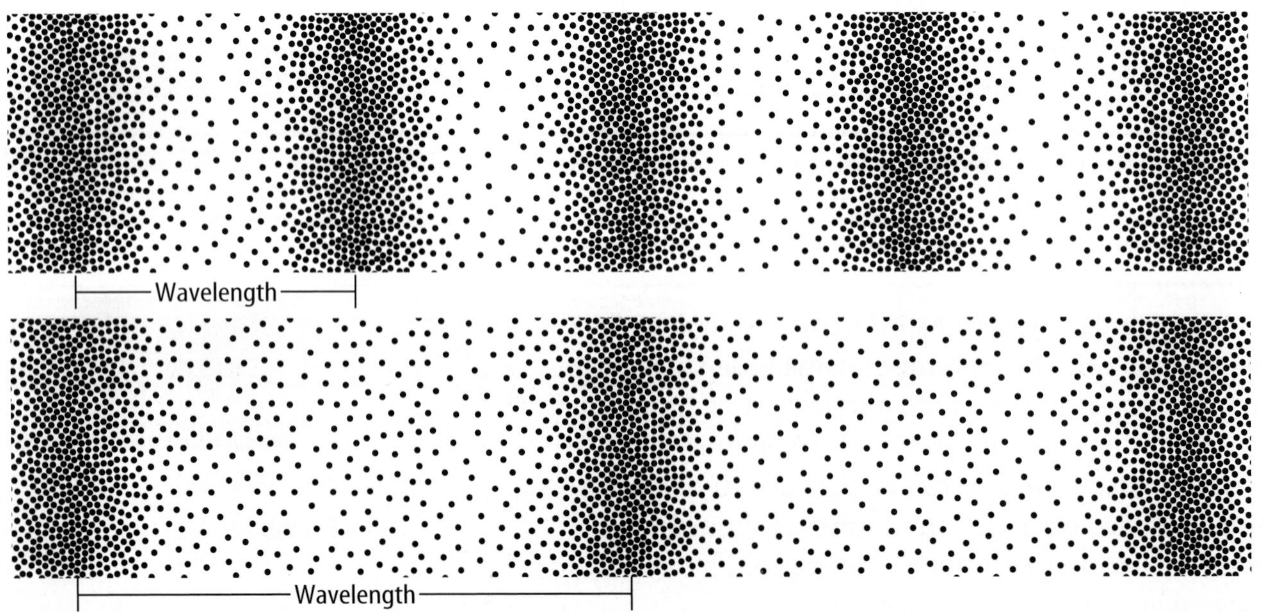

Figure 6
The upper sound wave has a shorter wavelength than the lower wave. If these two sound waves are traveling at the same speed, the upper sound wave has a higher frequency than the lower one. For this wave, more compressions and rarefactions will go past a point every second than for the lower wave. *Which wave has a higher pitch?*

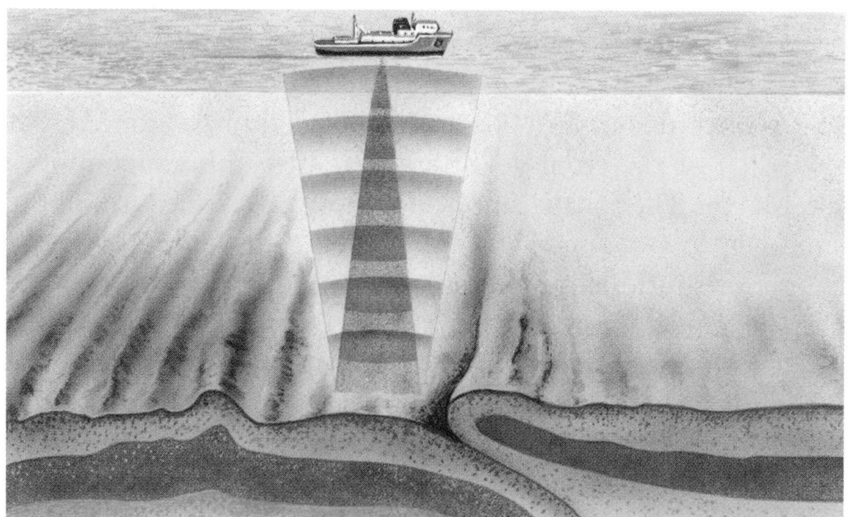

Figure 7
Sonar uses reflected sound waves to determine the location and shape of an object.

Echoes

Sound reflects off of hard surfaces, just like a water wave bounces off the side of a bath tub. A reflected sound wave is called an **echo.** If the distance between you and a reflecting surface is great enough, you might hear the echo of your voice. This is because it might take a few seconds for the sound to travel to the reflecting surface and back to your ears.

Sonar systems use sound waves to map objects underwater, as shown in **Figure 7.** The amount of time it takes an echo to return depends on how far away the reflecting surface is. By measuring the length of time between emitting a pulse of sound and hearing its echo off the ocean floor, the distance to the ocean floor can be measured. Using this method, sonar can map the ocean floor and other undersea features. Sonar also can be used to detect submarines, schools of fish, and other objects.

Research Visit the Glencoe Science Web site at **science.glencoe.com** for more information on how sonar is used to detect objects underwater. Communicate to your class what you learn.

Echolocation Some animals use a method called echolocation to navigate and hunt. Bats, for example, emit high-pitched squeaks and listen for the echoes. The type of echo it hears helps the bat determine exactly where an insect is, as shown in **Figure 8.** Dolphins also use a form of echolocation. Their high-pitched clicks bounce off of objects in the ocean, allowing them to navigate in the same way.

People with visual impairments also have been able to use echolocation. Using their ears, they can interpret echoes to estimate the size and shape of a room, for example.

Figure 8
Bats use echolocation to hunt.
Why is this technique good for hunting at night?

The Doppler Effect

Perhaps you've heard an ambulance siren as the ambulance speeds toward you, then goes past. You might have noticed that the pitch of the siren gets higher as the ambulance moves toward you. Then as the ambulance moves away, the pitch of the siren gets lower. The change in frequency that occurs when a source of sound is moving relative to a listener is called the **Doppler effect. Figure 9** shows why the Doppler effect occurs.

The Doppler effect occurs whether the sound source or the listener is moving. If you drive past a factory as its whistle blows, the whistle will sound higher pitched as you approach. As you move closer you encounter each sound wave a little earlier than you would if you were sitting still, so the whistle has a higher pitch. When you move away from the whistle, each sound wave takes a little longer to reach you. You hear fewer wavelengths per second, which makes the sound lower in pitch.

Radar guns that are used to measure the speed of cars and baseball pitches also use the Doppler effect. Instead of a sound wave, the radar gun sends out a radio wave. When the radio wave is reflected, its frequency changes depending on the speed of the object and whether it is moving toward the gun or away from it. The radar gun uses the change in frequency of the reflected wave to determine the object's speed.

Astronomy INTEGRATION

The frequency of light waves is also changed by the Doppler shift. If a light source is moving away from an observer, the frequencies of the emitted light waves decrease. Research how the Doppler shift is used by astronomers to determine how other objects in the universe are moving relative to Earth.

Problem-Solving Activity

How does Doppler radar work?

Doppler radar is used by the National Weather Service to detect areas of precipitation and to measure the speed at which a storm moves. Because the wind moves the rain, Doppler radar can "see" into a strong storm and expose the winds. Tornadoes that might be forming in the storm then can be identified.

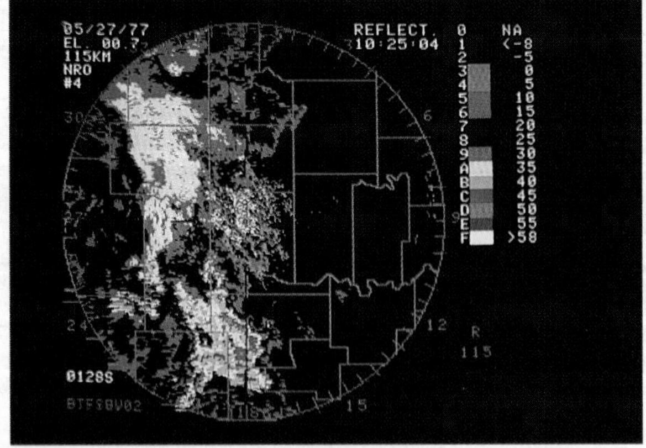

Identify the Problem

An antenna sends out pulses of radio waves as it rotates. The waves bounce off raindrops and return to the antenna at a different frequency, depending on whether the rain is moving toward the antenna or away from it. The change in frequency is due to the Doppler shift.

Solving the Problem

1. If the frequency of the reflected radio waves increases, how is the rain moving relative to the radar station?
2. In a tornado, winds are rotating. How would the radio waves reflected by rotating winds be Doppler-shifted?

NATIONAL GEOGRAPHIC **VISUALIZING THE DOPPLER EFFECT**

Figure 9

You've probably heard the siren of an ambulance as it races through the streets. The sound of the siren seems to be higher in pitch as the ambulance approaches and lower in pitch as it moves away. This is the Doppler effect, which occurs when a listener and a source of sound waves are moving relative to each other.

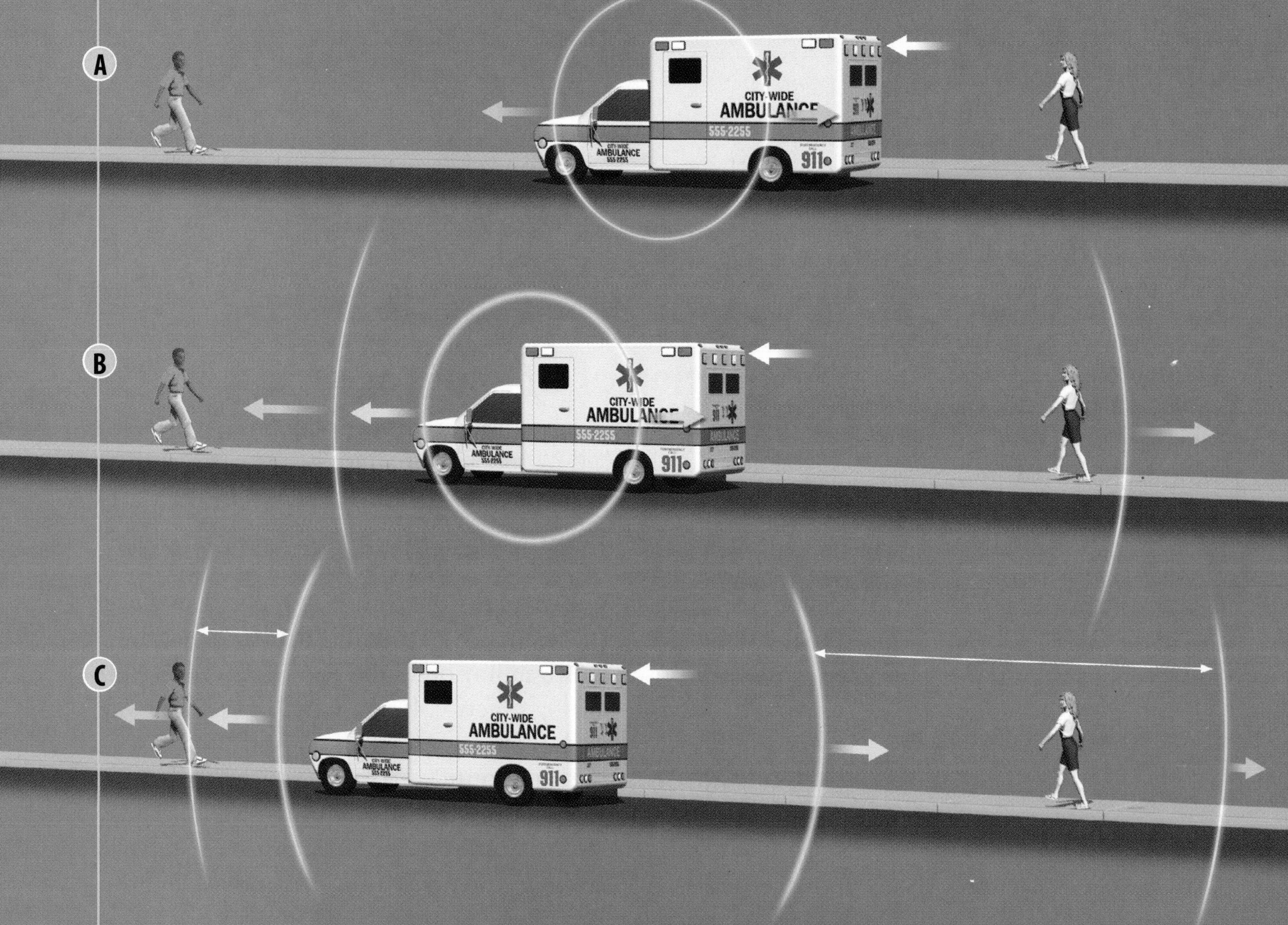

A As the ambulance speeds down the street, its siren emits sound waves. Suppose the siren emits the compression part of a sound wave as it goes past the girl.

B As the ambulance continues moving, it emits another compression. Meanwhile, the first compression spreads out from the point from which it was emitted.

C The waves traveling in the direction that the ambulance is moving have compressions closer together. As a result, the wavelength is shorter and the boy hears a higher frequency sound as the ambulance moves toward him. The waves traveling in the opposite direction have compressions that are farther apart. The wavelength is longer and the girl hears a lower frequency sound as the ambulance moves away from her.

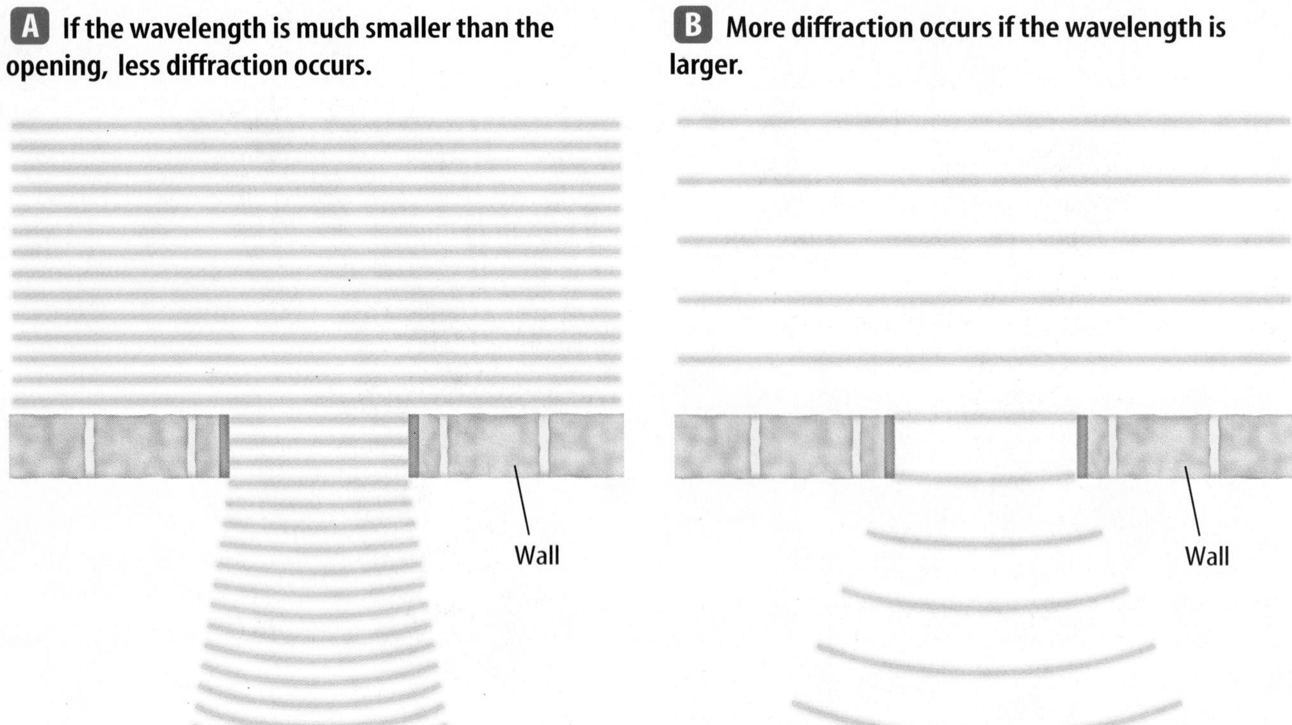

A If the wavelength is much smaller than the opening, less diffraction occurs.
B More diffraction occurs if the wavelength is larger.
Wall
Wall

Figure 10
The spreading of a wave by diffraction depends on the wavelength and the size of the opening.

Diffraction of Sound Waves

Like other waves, sound waves diffract. This means they can bend around obstacles or spread out after passing through narrow openings. The amount of diffraction depends on the wavelength of the sound wave compared to the size of the obstacle or opening. If the wavelength is much smaller than the obstacle, almost no diffraction occurs. As the wavelength becomes closer to the size of the obstacle, the amount of diffraction increases.

You can observe diffraction of sound waves by visiting the school band room during practice. If you stand in the doorway, you will hear the band normally. However, if you stand to one side outside the door or around a corner, you will hear the lower-pitched instruments better. **Figure 10** shows why this happens. The sound waves that are produced by the lower-pitched instruments have lower frequencies and longer wavelengths. These wavelengths are closer to the size of the door opening than the higher-pitched sound waves are. As a result, the longer wavelengths diffract more, and you can hear them even when you're not standing in the doorway.

The diffraction of lower frequencies in the human voice allows you to hear someone talking even when the person is around the corner. This is different from an echo. Echoes occur when sound waves bounce off a reflecting surface. Diffraction occurs when a wave spreads out after passing through an opening, or when a wave bends around an obstacle.

Using Sound Waves

Sound waves can be used to treat certain medical problems. A process called ultrasound uses high-frequency sound waves as an alternative to some surgeries. For example, some people develop small, hard deposits in their kidneys or gallbladders. A doctor can focus ultrasound waves at the kidney or gallbladder. The ultrasound waves cause the deposits to vibrate rapidly until they break apart into small pieces. Then, the body can get rid of them.

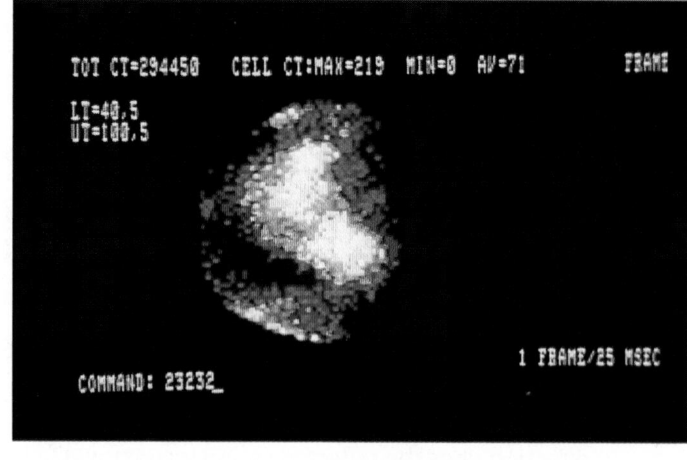

Figure 11
Ultrasound is used to make this image of the heart. *How else is ultrasound used in medicine?*

Ultrasound can be used to make images of the inside of the body, just as sonar is used to map the seafloor. One common use of ultrasound is to examine a developing fetus. Also, ultrasound along with the Doppler effect can be used to examine the functioning of the heart. An ultrasound image of the heart is shown in **Figure 11.** This technique can help determine if the heart valves and heart muscle are functioning properly, and how blood is flowing through the heart.

The Doppler effect can be also used with sonar to determine the speed and direction of a detected object, such as a submarine or a school of fish.

Section  Assessment

1. When the amplitude of a sound wave is increased, what happens to the loudness of the sound? The pitch?
2. How does the wavelength of a sound affect the way it moves around corners?
3. How does the temperature of a material affect the speed of sound passing through it? Explain why in terms of the particles within the material.
4. What causes the Doppler effect, and in what ways is it used?
5. **Think Critically** Chemists sometimes use ultrasound machines to clean glassware. How could sound be used to remove particles from glass?

Skill Builder Activities

6. **Using an Electronic Spreadsheet** Think about ten different sounds you've heard today. Make a computer spreadsheet that lists each sound, the vibrating object that made the sound, and how the object was vibrating. **For more help, refer to the Technology Skill Handbook.**
7. **Solving One-Step Equations** If sound travels through water at 1,483 m/s, how far will it travel in 5 s? The speed of sound through air at 20° C is about 343 m/s. How far will sound travel through air in the same amount of time? **For more help, refer to the Math Skill Handbook.**

Activity

Observe and Measure Reflection of Sound

Like all waves, sound waves can be reflected. When sound waves strike a surface, in what direction does the reflected sound wave travel? In this activity, you'll focus sound waves using cardboard tubes to help answer this question.

What You'll Investigate

How are the angles made by incoming and reflected sound waves related?

Materials

cardboard tubes, 20- to 30-cm-long (2)
watch that ticks audibly
protractor

Goals

- **Observe** reflection of sound waves.
- **Measure** the angles incoming and reflected sound waves make with a surface.

Safety Precautions

Procedure

1. Work in groups of three. Each person should listen to the watch—first without a tube and then through a tube. The person who hears the watch most easily is the listener.
2. One person should hold one tube at an angle with one end above a table. Hold the watch at the other end of the tube.
3. The listener should hold the second tube at an angle, with one end near his or her ear and the other end near the end of the first tube that is just above the table. The tubes should be in the same vertical plane.

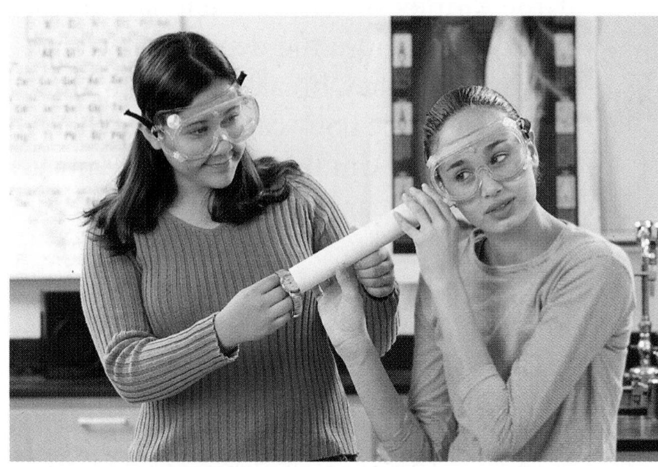

4. Move the first tube until the watch sounds loudest. The listener might need to cover the other ear to block out background noises.
5. With the tubes held steady, the third person should measure the angle that each tube makes with the table.

Conclude and Apply

1. Are the two angles approximately equal or quite different? How does the angle of reflection compare with the angle made by the incoming wave?
2. Predict how your results would change if the waves reflected from a soft surface instead of a hard surface.

Communicating Your Data

Make a scientific illustration to show how the experiment was done. Describe your results using the illustration. **For more help, refer to the** **Science Skill Handbook.**

Music

What is music?

What do you like to listen to—rock 'n' roll, country, blues, jazz, rap, or classical? Music and noise are groups of sounds. Why do humans hear some sounds as music and other sounds as noise?

The answer involves sound patterns. Music is a group of sounds that have been deliberately produced to make a regular pattern. Look at **Figure 12.** The sounds that make up music usually have a regular pattern of pitches, or notes. Some natural sounds, such as the patter of rain on a roof, the sound of ocean waves splashing, or the songs of birds can sound musical. On the other hand, noise is usually a group of sounds with no regular pattern. Sounds you hear as noise are irregular and disorganized, such as the sounds of traffic on a city street or the roar of jet aircraft.

However, the difference between music and noise can vary from person to person. What one person considers to be music, another person might consider noise.

Natural Frequencies Music is created by vibrations. When you sing, your vocal cords vibrate. When you beat a drum, the drumhead vibrates. When you play a guitar, the strings vibrate.

If you tap on a bell with a hard object, the bell produces a sound. When you tap on a bell that is larger or smaller or has a different shape you hear a different sound. The bells sound different because each bell vibrates at different frequencies. A bell vibrates at frequencies that depend on its shape and the material it is made from. Every object will vibrate at certain frequencies called its **natural frequencies.**

As You Read

What You'll Learn

- **Explain** the difference between music and noise.
- **Describe** how different instruments produce music.
- **Explain** how you hear.

Vocabulary

natural frequency
resonance
fundamental frequency
overtone
reverberation
eardrum

Why It's Important

Music is made by people in every part of the world.

Figure 12
Music and noise have different types of sound patterns.

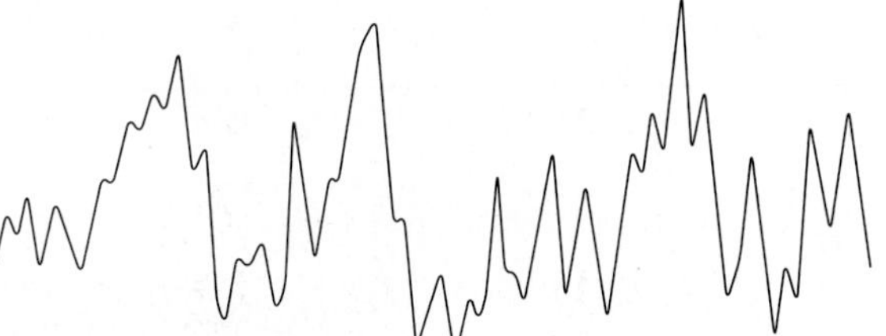

A **Noise has no specific or regular sound wave pattern.**

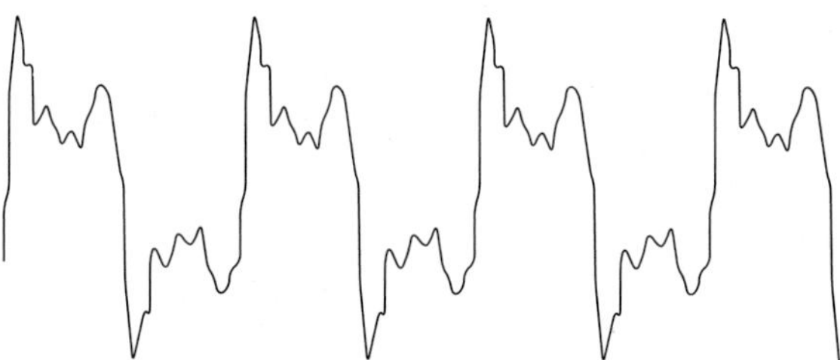

B **Music is organized sound. Music has regular sound wave patterns and structures.**

Musical Instruments and Natural Frequencies Many objects vibrate at one or more natural frequencies when they are struck or disturbed. Like a bell, the natural frequencies of any object depend on the size and shape of the object and the material it is made from. Musical instruments use the natural frequencies of strings, drumheads, or columns of air contained in pipes to produce various musical notes.

What determines the natural frequencies?

Resonance You may have seen the comedy routine in which a loud soprano sings high enough to shatter glass. Sometimes sound waves cause an object to vibrate. When a tuning fork is struck, it vibrates at its natural frequency and produces a sound wave with the same frequency. Suppose you have two tuning forks with the same natural frequency. You strike one tuning fork, and the sound waves it produces strike the other tuning fork. These sound waves would cause the tuning fork that wasn't struck to absorb energy and vibrate. This is an example of resonance. **Resonance** occurs when an object is made to vibrate at its natural frequencies by absorbing energy from a sound wave or another object vibrating at these frequencies.

Musical instruments use resonance to amplify their sounds. Look at **Figure 13.** The vibrating tuning fork might cause the table to vibrate at the same frequency, or resonate. The combined vibrations of the table and the tuning fork increase the loudness of the sound waves produced.

INTEGRATION

Resonance is important in fields outside of music. Earthquake-proof buildings, for example, are designed to resonate at frequencies that are different from those encountered in earthquakes.

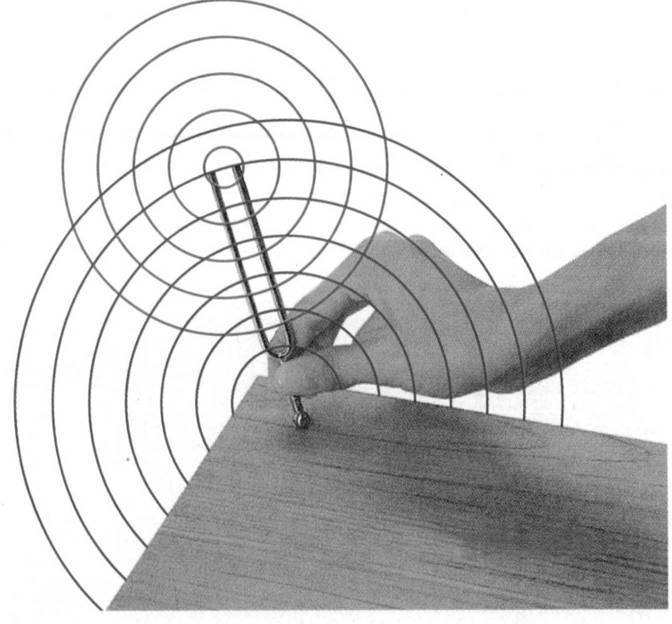

Figure 13
When a vibrating tuning fork is placed against a table, resonance might cause the table to vibrate.

Overtones

Before a concert, all orchestra musicians tune their instruments by playing the same note. Even though the note has the same pitch, it sounds different for each instrument. It also sounds different from a tuning fork that vibrates at the same frequency as the note.

A tuning fork produces a single frequency, called a pure tone. However, the notes produced by musical instruments are not pure tones. Most objects have more than one natural frequency at which they can vibrate. As a result, they produce sound waves of more than one frequency.

If you play a single note on a guitar, the pitch that you hear is the lowest frequency produced by the vibrating string. The lowest frequency produced by a vibrating object is the **fundamental frequency.** The vibrating string also produces higher frequencies. These higher frequencies are **overtones.** Overtones have frequencies that are multiples of the fundamental frequency, as in **Figure 14.** The number and intensity of the overtones produced by each instrument are different and give instruments their distinctive sound quality.

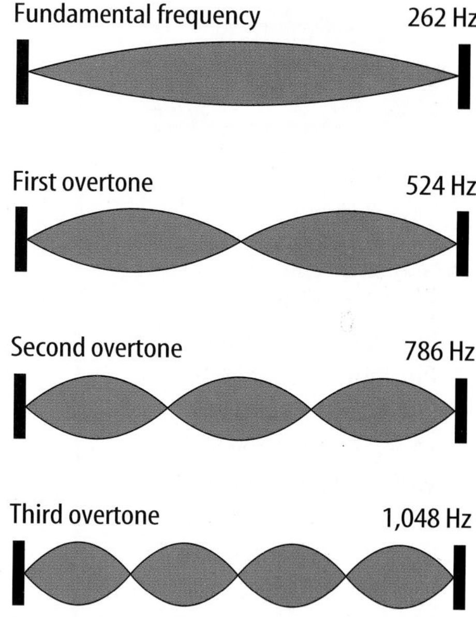

Figure 14
A string vibrates at a fundamental frequency, as well as at overtones. The overtones are multiples of that frequency.

Musical Scales

A musical instrument is a device that produces musical sounds. These sounds are usually part of a musical scale that is a sequence of notes with certain frequencies. For example, **Figure 15** shows the sequence of notes that belong to the musical scale of C. Notice that the frequency produced by the instrument doubles after eight successive notes of the scale are played. Other musical scales consist of a different sequence of frequencies.

How many musical instruments can you name? To find out more about musical instruments, see the **Musical Instruments Field Guide** at the back of the book.

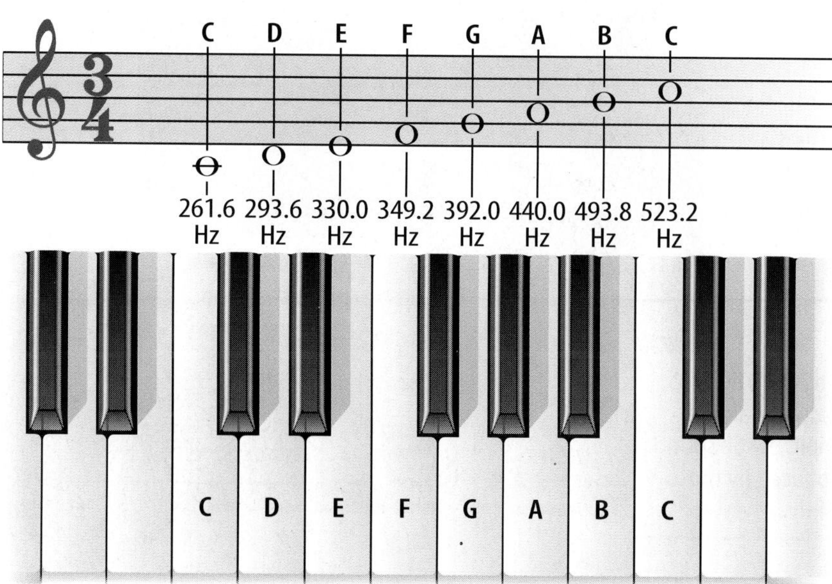

Figure 15
A piano produces a sequence of notes that are a part of a musical scale. *How are the frequencies of the two C notes on this scale related?*

Mini LAB

Modeling a Stringed Instrument

Procedure 

1. Stretch a **rubber band** between your fingers.
2. Pluck the rubber band. Listen to the sound and observe the shape of the vibrating band. Record what you hear and see.
3. Stretch the band farther and repeat step 2.
4. Shorten the length of the band that can vibrate by holding your finger on one point. Repeat step 2.
5. Stretch the rubber band over an open box, such as a **shoe box.** Repeat step 2.

Analysis

1. How did the sound change when you stretched the rubber band? Was this what you expected? Explain.
2. How did the sound change when you stretched the band over the box? Did you expect this? Explain.

Stringed Instruments

Stringed instruments, like the cello shown in **Figure 16,** produce music by making strings vibrate. Different methods are used to make the strings vibrate—guitar strings are plucked, piano strings are struck, and a bow is slid across cello strings. The strings often are made of wire. The pitch of the note depends on the length, diameter, and tension of the string—if the string is shorter, narrower, or tighter, the pitch increases. For example, pressing down on a vibrating guitar string shortens its length and produces a note with a higher pitch. Similarly, the thinner guitar strings produce a higher pitch than the thicker strings.

Amplifying Vibrations The sound produced by a vibrating string is soft. To amplify the sound, stringed instruments usually have a hollow chamber, or box, called a resonator, which contains air. The resonator absorbs energy from the vibrating string and vibrates at its natural frequencies. For example, the body of a guitar is a resonator that amplifies the sound that is produced by the vibrating strings. The vibrating strings cause the guitar's body and the air inside it to resonate. As a result, the vibrating guitar strings sound louder, just as the tuning fork that was placed against the table sounded louder.

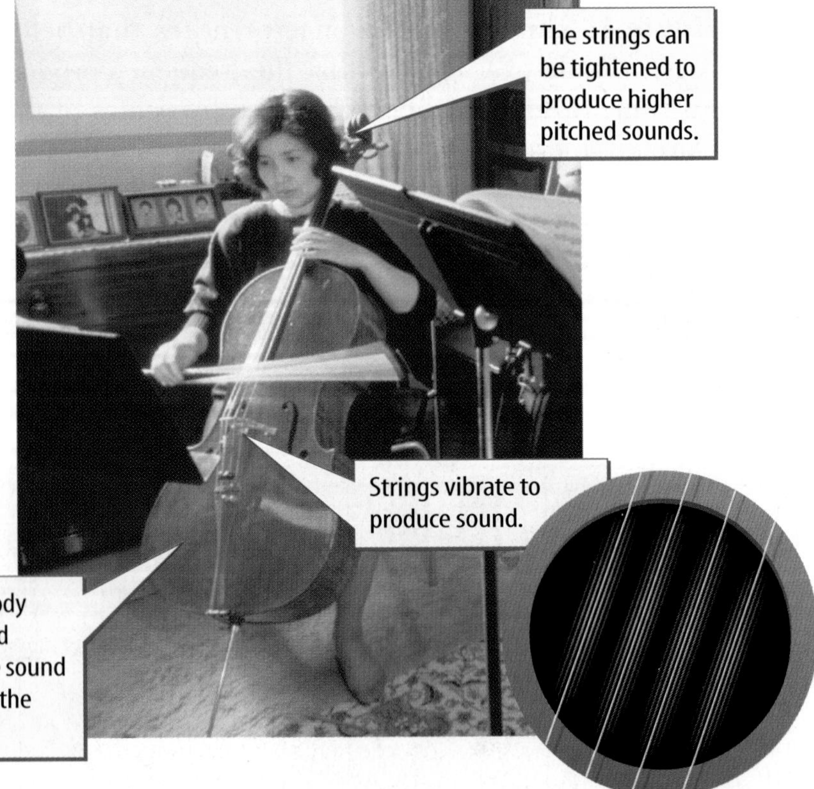
The strings can be tightened to produce higher pitched sounds.
Strings vibrate to produce sound.
The cello's body resonates and amplifies the sound produced by the strings.

Figure 16
A cello is a stringed instrument. When strings vibrate, the natural frequencies of the instrument's body amplify the sound.

Percussion

Percussion instruments, such as the drum shown in **Figure 17A,** are struck to make a sound. Striking the top surface of the drum causes it to vibrate. The vibrating drumhead is attached to a chamber that resonates and amplifies the sound.

Drums and Pitch Some drums have a fixed pitch, but some can be tuned to play different notes. For example, if the drumhead on a kettledrum is tightened, the natural frequency of the drumhead is increased. As a result, the pitches of the sounds that are produced by the kettledrum get higher. A steel drum, shown in **Figure 17B,** plays different notes in the scale when different areas in the drum are struck. In a xylophone, wood or metal bars of different lengths are struck. The longer the bar is, the lower the note that it produces is.

A

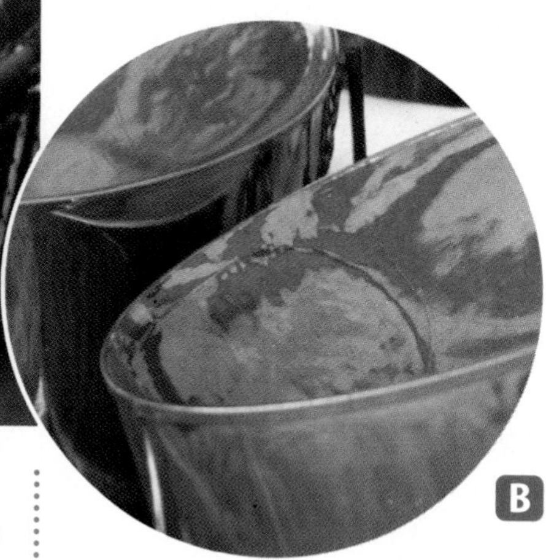

Figure 17
The sounds produced by drums depend on the material that is vibrating. A The vibrating drumhead of this drum is amplified by the resonating air in the body of the drum. B The vibrating steel surface in a steel drum produces loud sounds that don't need to be amplified by an air-filled chamber.

Brass and Woodwinds

Just as the bars of a xylophone have different natural frequencies, so do the air columns in pipes of different lengths. Brass and woodwind instruments, such as those in **Figure 18,** are essentially pipes or tubes of different lengths that sometimes are twisted around to make them easier to hold and carry. To make music from these instruments, the air in the pipes is made to vibrate at various frequencies.

Different methods are used to make the air column vibrate. A musician playing a brass instrument, such as a trumpet, makes the air column vibrate by vibrating the lips and blowing into the mouthpiece. Woodwinds such as clarinets, saxophones, and oboes contain one or two reeds in the mouthpiece that vibrate the air column when the musician blows into the mouthpiece. Flutes also are woodwinds, but a flute player blows across a narrow opening to make the air column vibrate.

Figure 18
Brass and woodwind instruments produce sounds in a vibrating column of air. *What other instruments make sound this way?*

Figure 19
A flute changes pitch as holes are opened and closed.

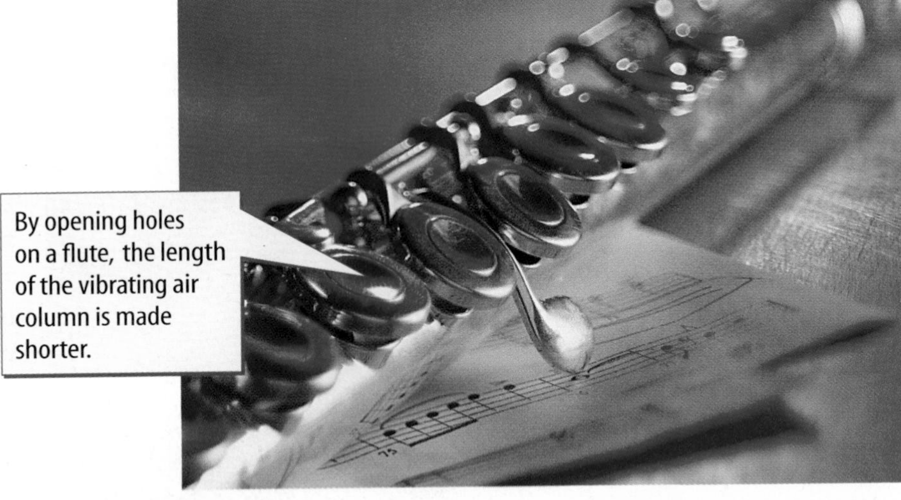

By opening holes on a flute, the length of the vibrating air column is made shorter.

Changing Pitch in Woodwinds To change the note that is being played in a woodwind instrument, a musician changes the length of the resonating column of air. By making the length of the vibrating air column shorter, the pitch of the sound produced is made higher. In a woodwind such as a flute, saxophone, or clarinet, this is done by closing and opening finger holes along the length of the instrument, as shown in **Figure 19.**

Changing Pitch in Brass In brass instruments, musicians vary the pitch in other ways. One is by blowing harder to make the air resonate at a higher natural frequency. Another way is by pressing valves that change the length of the tube.

Beats

When two notes are close in frequency, they interfere in a distinctive way. The two waves combine to form a wave that varies slowly in loudness. This slow variation creates beats. **Figure 20** shows the beats that are produced by the interference of two waves with frequencies of 9 Hz and 12 Hz. The frequency of the beat is the difference in the frequencies—in this case 3 Hz. Listening to two tones at the same time with a frequency difference of 3 Hz, you would hear the sound get louder and softer—a beat—three times each second.

Figure 20
Beats are formed when two frequencies that are nearly the same are played together. The sound wave in A has a frequency of 12 Hz and the sound wave in B has a frequency of 9 Hz. When these two sounds are played together, they interfere and form the wave in C that has a frequency of 3 Hz. You would hear 3 beats each second.

A

B

C

Beats Help Tune Instruments Beats are used to help tune instruments. For example, a piano tuner might hit a tuning fork and then the corresponding key on the piano. Beats are heard when the difference in pitch is small. The piano string is tuned properly when the beats disappear. You might have heard beats while listening to an orchestra tune before a performance. You also can hear beats produced by two engines vibrating at slightly different frequencies.

Reverberation

Sound is reflected by hard surfaces. In an empty gymnasium, the sound of your voice can be reflected back and forth several times by the floor, walls, and ceiling. Repeated echoes of sound are called **reverberation.** In a gym, reverberation makes the sound of your voice linger before it dies out. Some reverberation can make voices or music sound bright and lively. However, reverberation can produce a confusing mess of noise if too many sounds linger for too long. Too little reverberation makes the sound flat and lifeless. Concert halls and theaters, such as the one in **Figure 21,** are designed to produce the appropriate level of reverberation. Acoustical engineers use soft materials to reduce echoes. Special panels that are attached to the walls or suspended from the ceiling are designed to reflect sound toward the audience.

SCIENCE Online

Research Visit the Glencoe Science Web site at **science.glencoe.com** for more information about how concert halls are designed to produce the proper amount of reverberation. Communicate to your class what you learn.

Figure 21
The shape of a concert hall and the materials it contains are designed to control the reflection of sound waves.

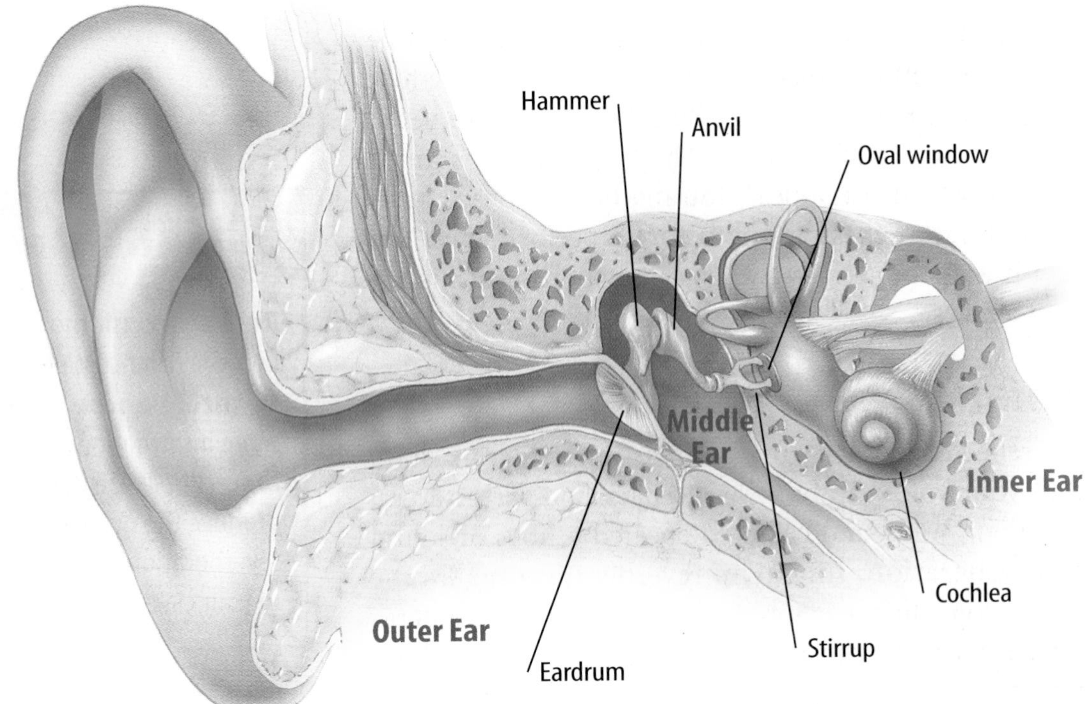

Figure 22
The human ear has three different parts—the outer ear, the middle ear, and the inner ear.

Figure 23
Animals, such as rabbits and owls, have ears that are adapted to their different needs.

The Ear

Sound is all around you. Sounds are as different as the loud buzz of an alarm clock and the quiet hum of a bee. You hear sounds with your ears. The ear is a complex organ that is able to detect a wide range of sounds. The human ear is illustrated in **Figure 22.** It has three parts—the outer ear, the middle ear, and the inner ear.

The Outer Ear—Sound Collector Your outer ear collects sound waves and directs them into the ear canal. Notice that your outer ear is shaped roughly like a funnel. This shape helps collect sound waves.

Animals that rely on hearing to locate predators or prey often have larger, more adjustable ears than humans, as shown in **Figure 23.** A barn owl, which relies on its excellent hearing for hunting at night, does not have outer ears made of flesh. Instead, the arrangement of its facial feathers helps direct sound to its ears. Some sea mammals, on the other hand, have only small holes for outer ears, even though their hearing is good.

The Middle Ear—Sound Amplifier When sound waves reach the middle ear, they vibrate the **eardrum,** which is a membrane that stretches across the ear canal like a drumhead. When the eardrum vibrates, it transmits vibrations to three small connected bones—the hammer, anvil, and stirrup. The bones amplify the vibrations, just as a lever can change a small movement at one end into a larger movement at the other.

The Inner Ear—Sound Interpreter The stirrup vibrates a second membrane called the oval window. This marks the start of the inner ear, which is filled with fluid. Vibrations in the fluid are transmitted to hair-tipped cells lining the cochlea, as shown in **Figure 24.** Different sounds vibrate the cells in different ways. The cells generate signals containing information about the frequency, intensity, and duration of the sound. The nerve impulses travel along the auditory nerve and are transmitted to the part of the brain that is responsible for hearing.

Figure 24
The inner ear contains tiny hair cells that convert vibrations into nerve impulses that travel to the brain.

Reading Check *Where are waves detected and interpreted in the ear?*

Hearing Loss

The ear can be damaged by disease, age, and exposure to loud sounds. For example, constant exposure to loud noise can damage hair cells in the cochlea. If damaged mammalian hair cells die, some loss of hearing results because mammals cannot make new hair cells. Also, some hair cells and nerve fibers in the inner ear degenerate and are lost as people age. It is estimated that about 30 percent of people over 65 have some hearing loss due to aging.

The higher frequencies are usually the first to be lost. The loss of the higher frequencies also distorts sound. The soft consonant sounds, such as those made by the letters *s, f, h, sh,* and *ch,* are hard to hear. People with high-frequency hearing loss have trouble distinguishing these sounds in ordinary conversation.

Section  Assessment

1. How are music and noise different?
2. Two bars on a xylophone are 10 cm and 14 cm long. Which bar will produce a lower pitch when struck? Explain.
3. Why would the sound of a guitar string sound louder when attached to the body of the guitar than when plucked alone?
4. What are the parts of the human ear, and how do they enable you to hear sound?
5. **Think Critically** As the size of stringed instruments increases from violin to viola, cello, and bass, the sound of the instruments becomes lower pitched. Explain.

Skill Builder Activities

6. **Making Models** Illustrate the fundamental and first overtone for a string. **For more help, refer to the Science Skill Handbook.**
7. **Communicating** Imagine that human hearing is much more sensitive than it currently is. Write a story describing a day in the life of your main character. Be sure to describe your setting in detail. For example, does your story take place in a crowded city or a scenic national park? How would life be different? Describe your story in your Science Journal. **For more help, refer to the Science Skill Handbook.**

Activity Design Your Own Experiment

Music

The pitch of a note that is played on an instrument sometimes depends on the length of the string, the air column, or some other vibrating part. Exactly how does sound correspond to the size or length of the vibrating part? Is this true for different instruments?

Recognize the Problem

What causes different instruments to produce different notes?

Form a Hypothesis

Based on your reading and observations, make a hypothesis about what changes in an instrument to produce different notes.

Goals

- **Design** an experiment to compare the changes that are needed in different instruments to produce a variety of different notes.
- **Observe** which changes are made when playing different notes.
- **Measure and record** these changes whenever possible.

Possible Materials

musical instruments
measuring tape
tuning forks

Safety Precautions

Properly clean the mouthpiece of any instrument before it is used by another student.

Test Your Hypothesis

Plan

1. You should do this activity as a class, using as many instruments as possible. You might want to go to the music room or invite friends and relatives who play an instrument to visit the class.
2. As a group, decide how you will measure changes in instruments. For wind instruments, can you measure the length of the vibrating air column? For stringed instruments, can you measure the length and thickness of the vibrating string?
3. Refer to the table of wavelengths and frequencies for notes in the scale. Note that no measurements are given—if you measure C to correspond to a string length of 30 cm, for example, the note G will correspond to two thirds of that length.
4. Decide which musical notes you will compare. Prepare a table to collect your data. List the notes you have selected.

Ratios of Wavelengths and Frequencies of Musical Notes

Note	Wavelength	Frequency
C	1	1
D	8/9	9/8
E	4/5	5/4
F	3/4	4/3
G	2/3	3/2
A	3/5	5/3
B	8/15	15/8
C	1/2	2

Do

1. Make sure your teacher approves your plan before you start.
2. Carry out the experiment as planned.
3. While doing the experiment, record your observations and complete the data table.

Analyze Your Data

1. **Compare** the change in each instrument when the two notes are produced.
2. **Compare and contrast** the changes between instruments.
3. What were the controls in this experiment?
4. What were the variables in this experiment?
5. How did you eliminate bias?

Draw Conclusions

1. How does changing the length of the vibrating column of air in a wind instrument affect the note that is played?
2. **Describe** how you would modify an instrument to increase the pitch of a note that is played.

Demonstrate to another teacher or to family members how the change in the instrument produces a change in sound.

It's a Wrap!

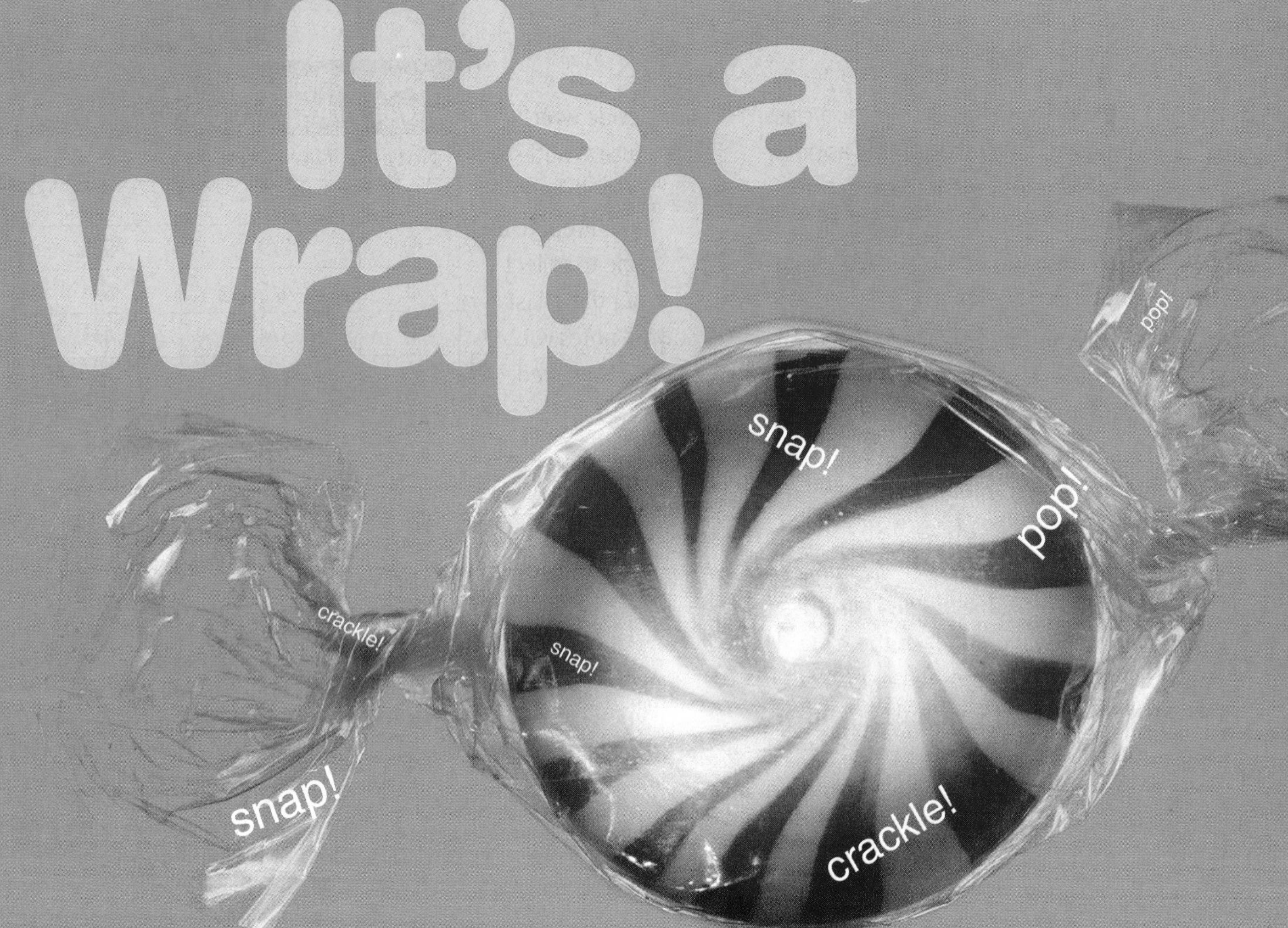

No matter how quickly or slowly you open a candy wrapper, it always will make a noise

You're at the movies, and it's the most exciting part of the film. The audience is silent with their eyes riveted to the screen. At that moment, you decide to unwrap the candy you got at the concession stand—"CRACKLE!" The loud noise isn't from the movie. It's from the candy wrapper. Your friends shush you. So you try to open the wrapper more carefully—"POP!" Now you try opening it more slowly—"SNAP!" No matter how you open the candy wrapper—fast or slow—it makes a lot of annoying noise.

Just about everyone has been in that situation at a movie or a concert. And just about everyone has wondered why you can't unwrap candy without making a racket—no matter how hard you try. But now, finally, thanks to the work of a few curious physicists, we know the answer.

To test the plastic problem, researchers took some crinkly wrappers and put them in a silent room. Then the researchers stretched out the wrappers and recorded the sound they made. Next, the crinkling sound was run through a computer. After analyzing the sound, the research team discovered something very interesting—the wrapper didn't make a nonstop, continuous sound. Instead, it made many little separate popping noises. Each of these sound bursts took only a thousandth of a second.

Pop Goes the Wrapper

The researchers found that the loudness of the pops had nothing to do with how fast the plastic was unwrapped. The pops randomly took place. The reason? Little creases in the plastic suddenly snapped into a new position as the wrapper was stretched.

So, if you unwrap candy more slowly, the time between pops will be longer, but the amount of noise made by the pops will be the same. And whether you open the wrapper fast or slow, you'll always hear pops. "And there's nothing you can do about it," said a member of the research team.

Is there another payoff to the candy wrapper research? One scientist said that by understanding what makes a plastic wrapper "snap" when it changes shape, the information can actually help doctors understand molecules in the human body. These molecules, like plastic, can change shape.

But, in the meantime, what are you supposed to do when you absolutely have to open candy in a silent theater? Be considerate of others in the audience. Open the candy as fast as you can, and just get it over with. You can even wait until a noisy part of the movie to hide the crinkle, or open the candy before the film begins.

The pop chart

SOUND LEVEL OVER TIME

The sound that a candy wrapper makes is emitted as a series of pulses or clicks. So, opening a wrapper slowly only increases the length of time in between clicks, but the amount of noise remains the same.

(TALLER SPIKES SIGNIFY LOUDER CLICKS)

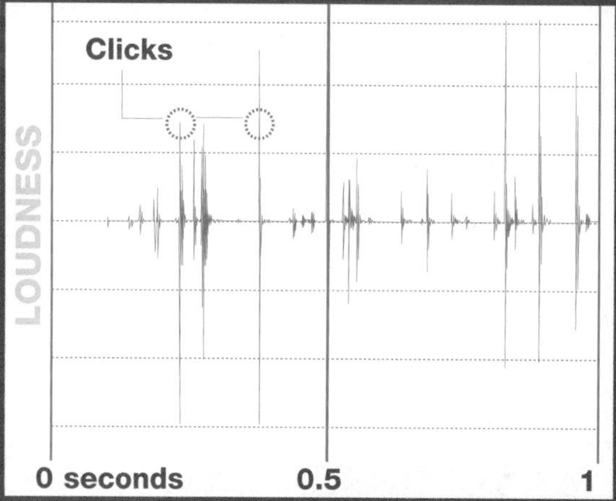

Source: Eric Kramer, Simon's Rock College, 2000

CONNECTIONS Recall and Retell **Have you ever opened a candy wrapper in a quiet place? Did it bother other people? If so, did you try to open it more slowly? What happened?**

SCIENCE *Online*

For more information, visit science.glencoe.com

Chapter 12 Study Guide

Reviewing Main Ideas

Section 1 What is sound?

1. Sound is a compressional wave that travels through matter, such as air. Sound is produced by something that vibrates.
2. The speed of sound is different in different materials. In general, sound travels faster in solids than in liquids, and faster in liquids than in gases. *Will the sound of a train travel faster through the air or through these tracks?*

3. The larger the amplitude of a sound wave, the more energy it carries. The loudness of a sound wave increases as its amplitude increases.
4. The pitch of a sound wave corresponds to its frequency. Sound waves can reflect, or bounce, from objects and diffract, or bend around objects.
5. The Doppler effect occurs when the source of sound and the listener are in motion relative to each other. Sound is shifted up or down in pitch. *What happens to the pitch of the train's horn as it approaches the person?*

Section 2 Music

1. Music is made of sounds that are used in a regular pattern. Noise is made of sounds that are irregular and disorganized.
2. Objects vibrate at their natural frequencies. These depend on the shape of the object and the material it's made of.
3. Resonance occurs when an object is made to vibrate by absorbing energy at one of its natural frequencies.
4. Musical instruments produce notes by vibrating at their natural frequencies. Resonance is used to amplify the sound. *How does resonance make this violin sound louder?*

5. Beats occur when two sounds of nearly the same frequency interfere. The beat frequency is the difference in frequency of the sounds.
6. The ear collects sound waves, amplifies the vibrations, and converts the vibrations to nerve impulses.

FOLDABLES Reading & Study Skills

After You Read

Use the library to find answers to any questions remaining on your Question Study Foldable.

Chapter 12 Study Guide

Visualizing Main Ideas

Complete the following concept map on sound.

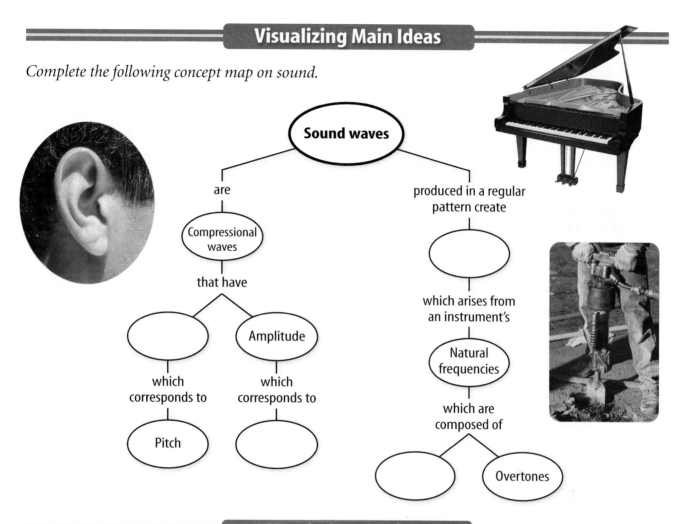

Sound waves

are

Compressional waves

that have

[blank] — which corresponds to — Pitch

Amplitude — which corresponds to — [blank]

produced in a regular pattern create

[blank]

which arises from an instrument's

Natural frequencies

which are composed of

[blank]

Overtones

Vocabulary Review

Vocabulary Words

a. Doppler effect
b. eardrum
c. echo
d. fundamental frequency
e. loudness
f. natural frequency
g. overtone
h. pitch
i. resonance
j. reverberation

Study Tip

Recopy your notes from class. As you do, explain each concept in more detail to make sure that you understand it completely.

Using Vocabulary

Distinguish between the terms in each of the following pairs.

1. overtones, fundamental frequency

2. pitch, sound wave

3. pitch, Doppler effect

4. loudness, resonance

5. fundamental, natural frequency

6. loudness, amplitude

7. natural frequency, overtone

8. reverberation, resonance

Chapter 12 Assessment

Checking Concepts

Choose the word or phrase that best answers the question.

1. A tone that is lower in pitch is lower in what characteristic?
   A) frequency **C)** loudness
   B) wavelength **D)** resonance

2. If frequency increases, what decreases if speed stays the same?
   A) pitch **C)** loudness
   B) wavelength **D)** resonance

3. What part of the ear is damaged most easily by continued exposure to loud noise?
   A) eardrum **C)** oval window
   B) stirrup **D)** hair cells

4. What is an echo?
   A) diffracted sound
   B) resonating sound
   C) reflected sound
   D) Doppler-shifted sound

5. A trumpeter depresses keys to make the column of air resonating in the trumpet shorter. What happens to the note that is being played?
   A) The pitch is higher. **C)** It is quieter.
   B) The pitch is lower. **D)** It is louder.

6. When tuning a violin, a string is tightened. What happens to the note that is being played on that string?
   A) The pitch is higher. **C)** It is quieter.
   B) The pitch is lower. **D)** It is louder.

7. If air becomes warmer, what happens to the speed of sound in air?
   A) It increases. **C)** It doesn't change.
   B) It decreases. **D)** It oscillates.

8. Sound is what type of wave?
   A) slow **C)** compressional
   B) transverse **D)** fast

9. What does the middle ear do?
   A) focuses sound
   B) interprets sound
   C) collects sound
   D) transmits and amplifies sound

10. An ambulance siren speeds away from you. What happens to the pitch you hear?
    A) It increases. **C)** It decreases.
    B) It becomes louder. **D)** Nothing happens.

Thinking Critically

11. Some xylophones have open pipes of different lengths hung under each bar. The longer the bar is, the longer the corresponding pipe is. Explain how these pipes amplify the sound of the xylophone.

12. Why don't you notice the Doppler effect for a slow-moving train?

13. Suppose the movement of the bones in the middle ear were reduced. Which would be more affected—the ability to hear quiet sounds or the ability to hear certain frequencies? Explain your answer.

14. Two flutes are playing at the same time. One flute plays a note with frequency 524 Hz. If two beats are heard per second, what are the possible frequencies the other flute is playing?

15. The triangle is a percussion instrument consisting of an open metal triangle hanging from a string. The triangle is struck by a metal rod, and a chiming sound is heard. If the metal triangle is held in the hand rather than by the string, a quiet, dull sound is made when it is struck. Explain why holding the triangle makes it sound quieter.

Developing Skills

16. **Predicting** If the holes of a flute are all covered while playing, then all uncovered, what happens to the length of the vibrating air column? What happens to the pitch of the note?

17. **Identifying and Manipulating Variables and Controls** Describe an experiment to demonstrate that sound is diffracted.

18. **Making and Using Tables** Make a table to show the first three overtones for a note of G, which has a frequency of 392 Hz.

19. **Interpreting Scientific Illustrations** The picture shows pan pipes. How are different notes produced by blowing on pan pipes?

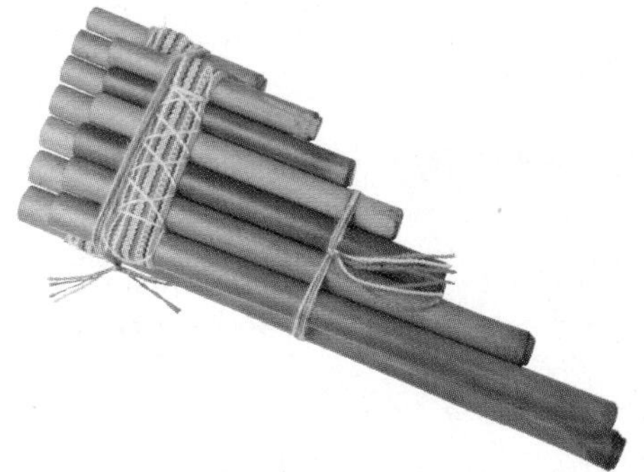

Performance Assessment

20. **Recital** Perform a short musical piece on an instrument. Explain how your actions changed the notes that were produced.

21. **Pamphlet** Create a pamphlet describing how a hearing aid works.

Technology

Go to the Glencoe Science Web site at **science.glencoe.com** or use the **Glencoe Science CD-ROM** for additional chapter assessment.

Test Practice

Sound travels in waves that change as the pitch and loudness of the sound vary. These pictures illustrate four recorded sounds.

Q.

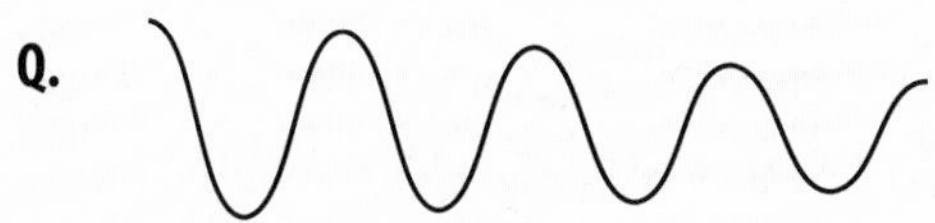

R.

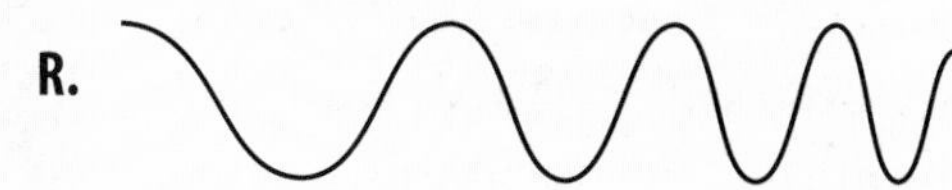

S.

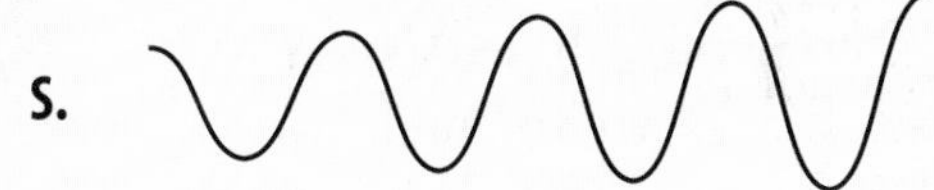

T.

Study the pictures and answer the following questions.

1. Which of the four sounds was getting louder while it was recorded?
   A) Q
   B) R
   C) S
   D) T

2. Which sound had the highest pitch while it was recorded?
   F) Q
   G) R
   H) S
   J) T

CHAPTER

13 Electromagnetic Waves

Wherever you go, you are being bombarded by electromagnetic waves. Some, such as visible light, can be seen. Infrared rays can't be seen but feel warm on your skin. The paint on the tricycle in this picture is being heat cured in an infrared oven. In this chapter, you will learn how electromagnetic waves are formed. You also will learn ways in which electromagnetic waves are used, from cooking to satellite communications.

What do you think?

Science Journal Look at the photograph below with a classmate. Discuss what you think this might be. Here is a hint: *Scientists built this to get a clearer picture.* Write your answer or best guess in your Science Journal.

Light is a type of wave called an electromagnetic wave. You see light every day, but visible light is only one type of electromagnetic wave. Other electromagnetic waves are all around you, but you cannot see them. How can you detect electromagnetic waves that can't be seen with your eyes?

Detecting invisible light

1. Cut a slit 2 cm long and 0.25 cm wide in the center of a sheet of black paper.
2. Cover a window that is in direct sunlight with the paper.
3. Position a glass prism in front of the light coming through the slit so it makes a visible spectrum on the floor or table.
4. Place one thermometer in the spectrum and a second thermometer just beyond the red light.
5. Measure the temperature in each region after 5 min.

Observe

Write a paragraph in your Science Journal comparing the temperatures of the two regions and offer an explanation for the observed temperatures.

Before You Read

Making a Main Ideas Study Fold **Make the following Foldable to help you identify the major topics about electromagnetic waves.**

1. Stack four sheets of paper in front of you so the short sides are at the top.
2. Slide the top sheet up so about 2 cm of the next sheet shows. Slide each sheet up so about 2 cm of the next sheet shows.
3. Fold the sheets top to bottom to form eight tabs. Staple along the top fold.
4. Label the tabs *Electromagnetic Spectrum, Radio Waves, Microwaves, Infrared Rays, Visible Light, Ultraviolet Light, X Rays,* and *Gamma Rays.*
5. As you read the chapter, list the things you learn about these electromagnetic waves under the tabs.

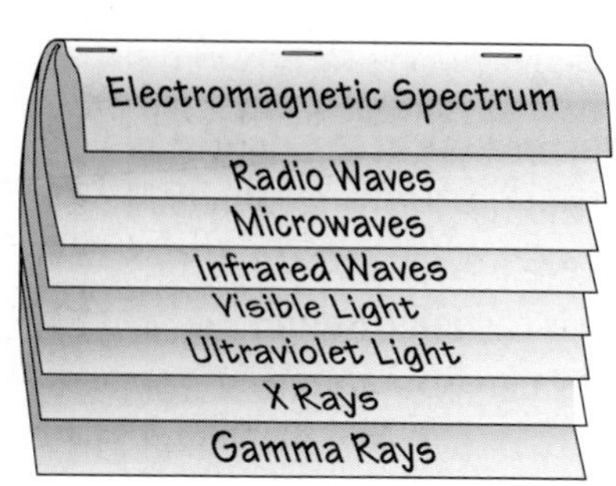

SECTION 1

The Nature of Electromagnetic Waves

As You Read

***What* You'll Learn**

- **Explain** how electromagnetic waves are produced.
- **Describe** the properties of electromagnetic waves.

Vocabulary

electromagnetic wave
radiant energy

***Why* It's Important**

The energy Earth receives from the Sun is carried by electromagnetic waves.

Waves in Space

On a clear day you feel the warmth in the Sun's rays, and you see the brightness of its light. Energy is being transferred from the Sun to your skin and eyes. Who would guess that the way in which this energy is transferred has anything to do with radios, televisions, microwave ovens, or the X-ray pictures that are taken by a doctor or dentist? Yet the Sun and the objects shown in **Figure 1** use the same type of wave to move energy from place to place.

Transferring Energy A wave transfers energy from one place to another without transferring matter. How do waves transfer energy? Waves, such as water waves and sound waves, transfer energy by making particles of matter move. The energy is passed along from particle to particle as they collide with their neighbors. Mechanical waves are the types of waves that use matter to transfer energy.

How can a wave transfer energy from the Sun to Earth? Mechanical waves, for example, can't travel in the space between Earth and the Sun where no matter exists. Instead, this energy is carried by a different type of wave called an electromagnetic wave. An **electromagnetic wave** is a wave that can travel through empty space and is produced by charged particles that are in motion.

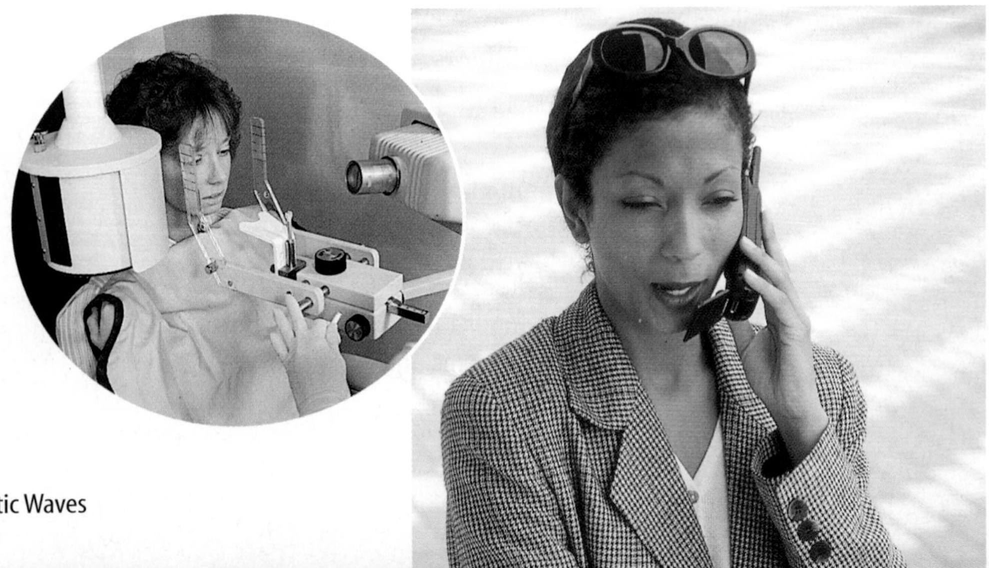

Figure 1
Getting an X ray at the dentist's office and talking on a cell phone are possible because energy is carried through space by electromagnetic waves.

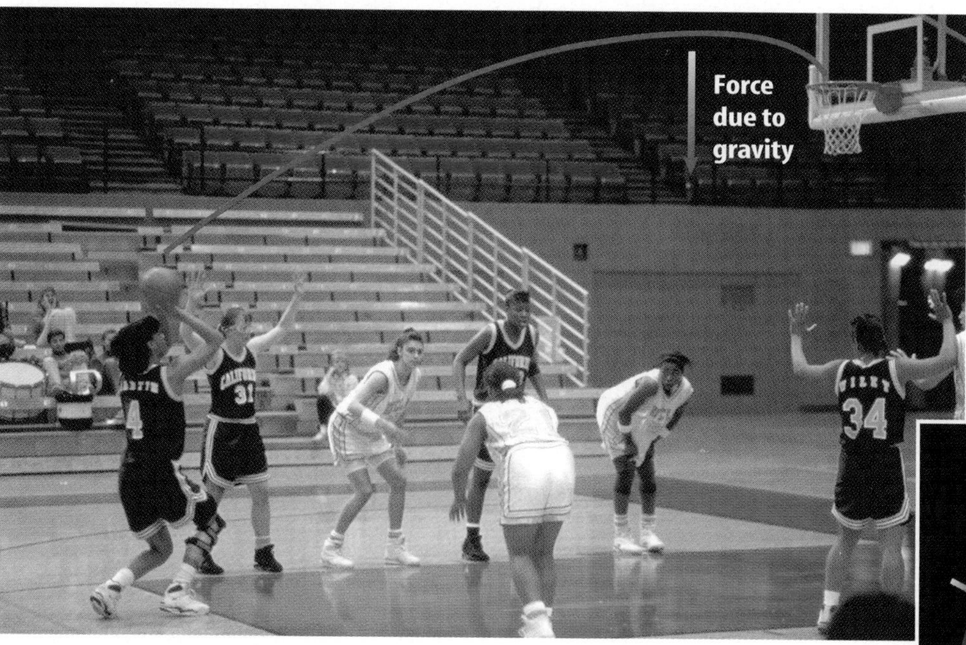

Figure 2
A gravitational field surrounds all objects, such as Earth.

A When a ball is thrown, Earth's gravitational field exerts a downward force on the ball at every point along the ball's path.

B Earth's gravitational field extends out through space, exerting a force on all masses.

Forces and Fields

An electromagnetic wave is made of two parts—an electric field and a magnetic field. These fields are force fields. A force field enables an object to exert forces on other objects, even though they are not touching. Earth produces a force field called the gravitational field. This field exerts the force of gravity on all objects that have mass.

Reading Check *What force field surrounds Earth?*

How does Earth's force field work? If you throw a ball in the air as high as you can, it always falls back to Earth. At every point along the ball's path, the force of gravity pulls down on the ball, as shown in **Figure 2A.** In fact, at every point in space above or at Earth's surface, a ball is acted on by a downward force exerted by Earth's gravitational field. The force exerted by this field on a ball could be represented by a downward arrow at any point in space. **Figure 2B** shows this force field that surrounds Earth and extends out into space. It is Earth's gravitational field that causes the Moon to orbit Earth.

Magnetic Fields You know that magnets repel and attract each other even when they aren't touching. Two magnets exert a force on each other when they are some distance apart because each magnet is surrounded by a force field called a magnetic field. Just as a gravitational field exerts a force on a mass, a magnetic field exerts a force on other magnets and on magnetic materials. Magnetic fields cause other magnets to line up along the direction of the magnetic field.

Research In addition to a gravitational field, Earth also is surrounded by a magnetic field. Visit the Glencoe Science Web site at **science.glencoe.com** for more information about Earth's gravitational and magnetic force fields. Place the information you gather on a poster to share with your class.

Figure 3
Force fields surround all magnets and electric charges.

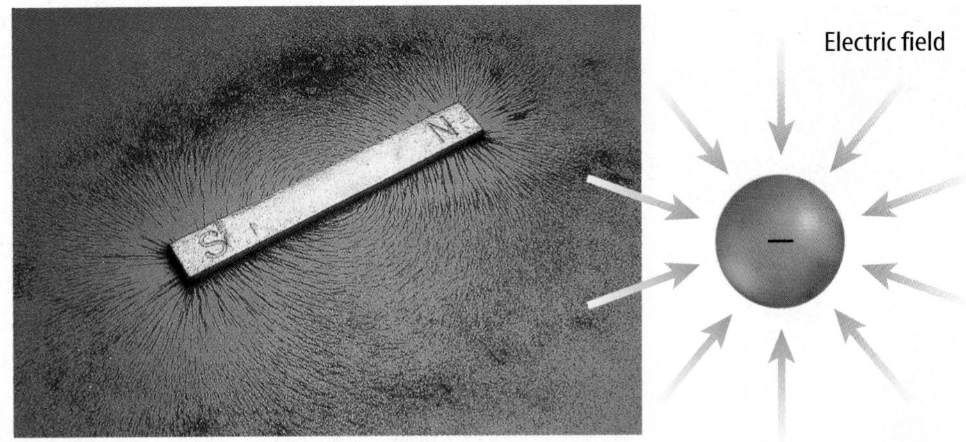

A A magnetic field surrounds all magnets. The magnetic field exerts a force on iron filings, causing them to line up with the field.

B The electric field around an electric charge extends out through space, exerting forces on other charged particles.

Electric Fields Recall that atoms contain protons, neutrons, and electrons. Protons and electrons have a property called electric charge. The two types of electric charge are positive and negative. Protons have positive charge and electrons have negative charge.

Just as a magnet is surrounded by a magnetic field, a particle that has electric charge, such as a proton or an electron, is surrounded by an electric field, as shown in **Figure 3.** The electric field is a force field that exerts a force on all other charged particles that are in the field.

Making Electromagnetic Waves

An electromagnetic wave is made of electric and magnetic fields. How is such a wave produced? Think about a wave on a rope. You can make a wave on a rope by shaking one end of the rope up and down. Electromagnetic waves are produced by making charged particles, such as electrons, move back and forth, or vibrate.

A charged particle always is surrounded by an electric field. But a charged particle that is moving also is surrounded by a magnetic field. For example, when an electric current flows in a wire, electrons are moving in the wire. As a result, the wire is surrounded by a magnetic field, as shown in **Figure 4.** So a moving charged particle is surrounded by an electric field and a magnetic field.

Figure 4
Electrons moving in a wire produce a magnetic field in the surrounding space.

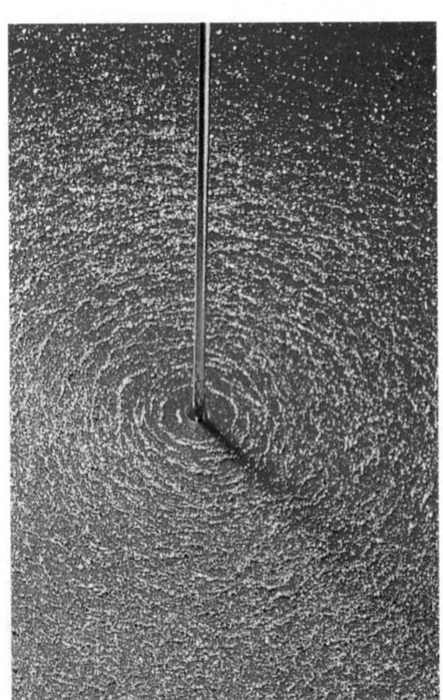

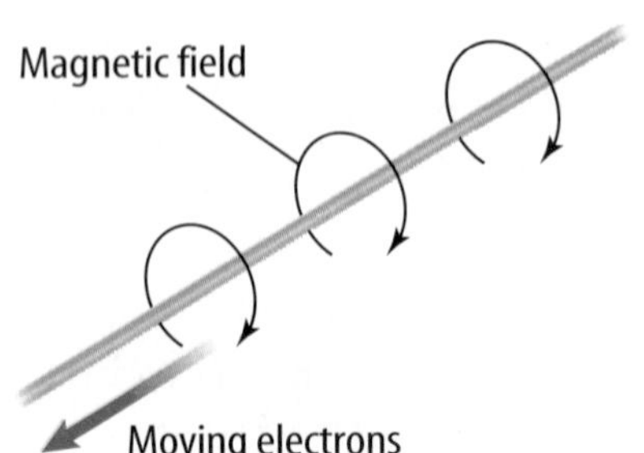

Producing Waves When you shake a rope up and down, you produce a wave that moves away from your hand. As a charged particle vibrates by moving up and down or back and forth, it produces changing electric and magnetic fields that move away from the vibrating charge in many directions. These changing fields traveling in many directions form an electromagnetic wave. **Figure 5A** shows these changing fields along one direction.

Observing Electric Fields

Procedure

1. Rub a **hard, plastic comb** vigorously with a **wool sweater or wool flannel shirt.**
2. Turn on a **water faucet** to create the smallest possible continuous stream of water.
3. Hold the comb near the stream of water and observe.

Analysis

1. What happened to the stream of water when you held the comb near it?
2. Explain why the stream of water behaved this way.

Properties of Electromagnetic Waves

Like all waves, an electromagnetic wave has a frequency and a wavelength. When you create a wave on a rope, you move your hand up and down while holding the rope. Look at **Figure 5B.** Frequency is how many times you move the rope through one complete up and down cycle in 1 s. Wavelength is the distance from one crest to the next or from one trough to the next.

Wavelength and Frequency An electromagnetic wave is produced by a vibrating charged particle. When the charge makes one complete vibration, one wavelength is created, as shown in **Figure 5A.** Like a wave on a rope, the frequency of an electromagnetic wave is the number of wavelengths that pass by a point in 1 s. This is the same as the number of times in 1 s that the charged particle makes one complete vibration.

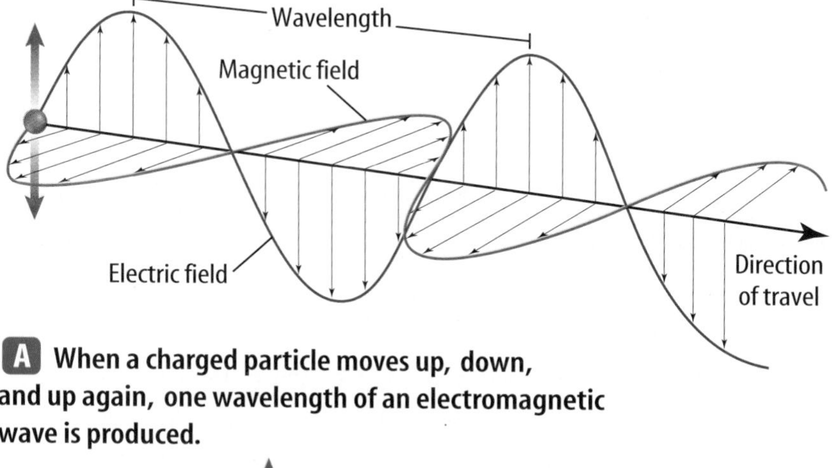

A **When a charged particle moves up, down, and up again, one wavelength of an electromagnetic wave is produced.**

Figure 5
The vibrating motion of an electric charge produces an electromagnetic wave. One complete cycle of vibration produces one wavelength of a wave.

Rest position

One wavelength

B **By shaking the end of a rope down, up, and down again, you make one wavelength.**

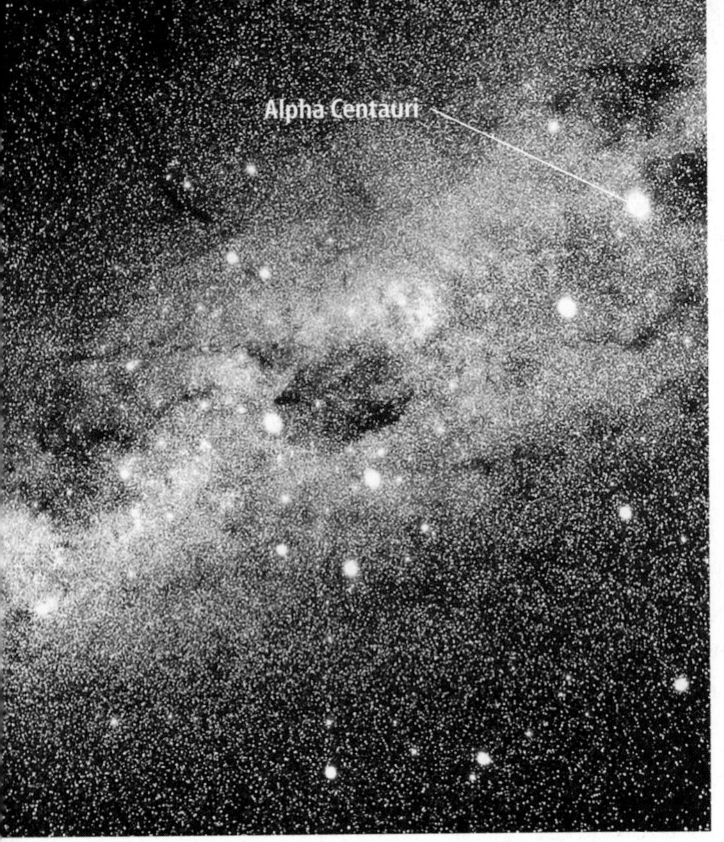

Radiant Energy The energy carried by an electromagnetic wave is called **radiant energy.** What happens if an electromagnetic wave strikes another charged particle? The electric field part of the wave exerts a force on this particle and causes it to move. Some of the radiant energy carried by the wave is transferred into the energy of motion of the particle.

Reading Check *What is radiant energy?*

The amount of energy that an electromagnetic wave carries is determined by the wave's frequency. The higher the frequency of the electromagnetic wave, the more energy it has.

The Speed of Light All electromagnetic waves, such as light, microwaves, and X rays, travel through space at the same speed. This speed has been measured as about 300,000 km/s in space. Because light is an electromagnetic wave, this speed sometimes is called the speed of light. If something could travel at the speed of light, it could travel around the world more than seven times in 1 s. Even though light travels incredibly fast, stars other than the Sun are so far away that it takes years for the light they emit to reach Earth. **Figure 6** shows one of the closest stars to the solar system, Alpha Centauri. This star is more than 40 trillion km from Earth.

Figure 6
The light that reaches Earth today from Alpha Centauri left the star more than four years ago.

Section 1 Assessment

1. What is an electromagnetic wave?
2. How are electromagnetic waves produced?
3. What two fields surround a moving charged particle?
4. How does the amount of energy carried by a low-frequency wave compare to the amount carried by a high-frequency wave?
5. **Think Critically** Unlike sound waves, electromagnetic waves can travel through a vacuum. What observations can you make to support this statement?

Skill Builder Activities

6. **Comparing and Contrasting** How are electromagnetic waves similar to mechanical waves? How are they different? **For more help, refer to the** Science Skill Handbook.
7. **Calculating Ratios** To go from Earth to Mars, light takes 4 min and a spacecraft takes four months. To go to the nearest star, light takes four years. How long would the same spacecraft take to travel to the nearest star? **For more help, refer to the** Math Skill Handbook.

SECTION 2

The Electromagnetic Spectrum

Electromagnetic Waves

The room you are sitting in is bathed in a sea of electromagnetic waves. These electromagnetic waves have a wide range of wavelengths and frequencies. For example, TV and radio stations broadcast electromagnetic waves that pass through walls and windows. These waves have wavelengths from about 1 m to over 500 m. Light waves that you see are electromagnetic waves that have wavelengths more than a million times shorter than the waves broadcast by radio stations.

Classifying Electromagnetic Waves The wide range of electromagnetic waves with different frequencies and wavelengths is called the **electromagnetic spectrum. Figure 7** shows the electromagnetic spectrum. Though many different types of electromagnetic waves exist, they all are produced by electric charges that are moving or vibrating. The faster the charge moves or vibrates, the higher the energy of the resulting electromagnetic waves is. Electromagnetic waves carry radiant energy that increases as the frequency increases. For waves that travel with the same speed, the wavelength increases as frequency decreases. So the energy carried by an electromagnetic wave decreases as the wavelength increases.

As You Read

What You'll Learn

- **Explain** differences among kinds of electromagnetic waves.
- **Identify** uses for different kinds of electromagnetic waves.

Vocabulary

electromagnetic spectrum, radio wave, infrared wave, visible light, ultraviolet radiation, X ray, gamma ray

Why It's Important

Electromagnetic waves are used to cook food, to send and receive information, and to diagnose medical problems.

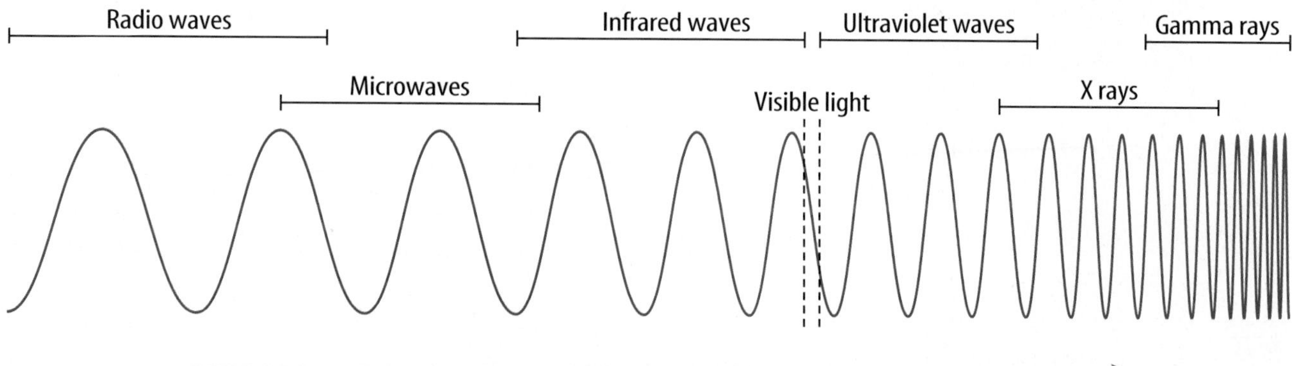

Figure 7
Electromagnetic waves have a spectrum of different frequencies and wavelengths.

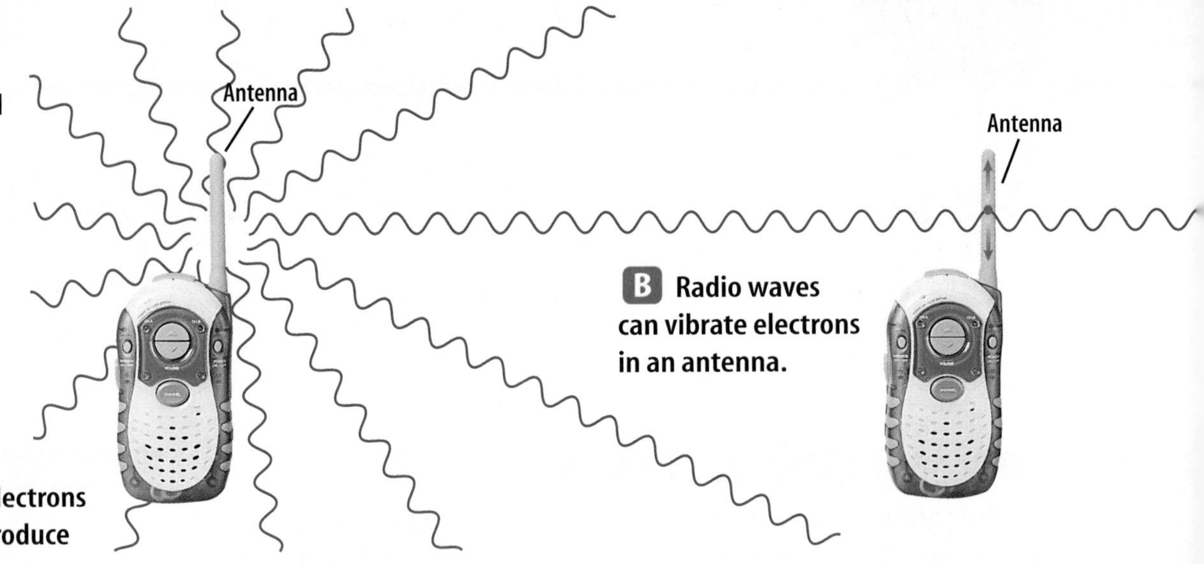

Figure 8
Antennas are useful in generating and detecting radio waves.

Antenna

Antenna

B Radio waves can vibrate electrons in an antenna.

A Vibrating electrons in an antenna produce radio waves.

Radio Waves

Electromagnetic waves with wavelengths longer than about 0.3 m are called radio waves. **Radio waves** have the lowest frequencies of all the electromagnetic waves and carry the least energy. Television signals, as well as AM and FM radio signals, are types of radio waves. Like all electromagnetic waves, radio waves are produced by moving charged particles. One way to make radio waves is to make electrons vibrate in a piece of metal, as shown in **Figure 8A.** This piece of metal is called an antenna. By changing the rate at which the electrons vibrate, radio waves of different frequencies can be produced that travel outward from the antenna.

Detecting Radio Waves These radio waves can cause electrons in another piece of metal, such as another antenna, to vibrate, as shown in **Figure 8B.** As the electrons in the receiving antenna vibrate, they form an alternating current. This alternating current can be used to produce a picture on a TV screen and sound from a loudspeaker. Varying the frequency of the radio waves broadcast by the transmitting antenna changes the alternating current in the receiving antenna. This produces the different pictures you see and sounds you hear on your TV.

Microwaves Radio waves with wavelengths between about 0.3 m and 0.001 m are called microwaves. They have a higher frequency and a shorter wavelength than the waves that are used in your home radio. Microwaves are used to transmit some phone calls, especially from cellular and portable phones. **Figure 9** shows a microwave tower.

Microwave ovens use microwaves to heat food. Microwaves produced inside a microwave oven cause water molecules in your food to vibrate faster, which makes the food warmer.

Figure 9
Towers such as the one shown here are used to send and receive microwaves.

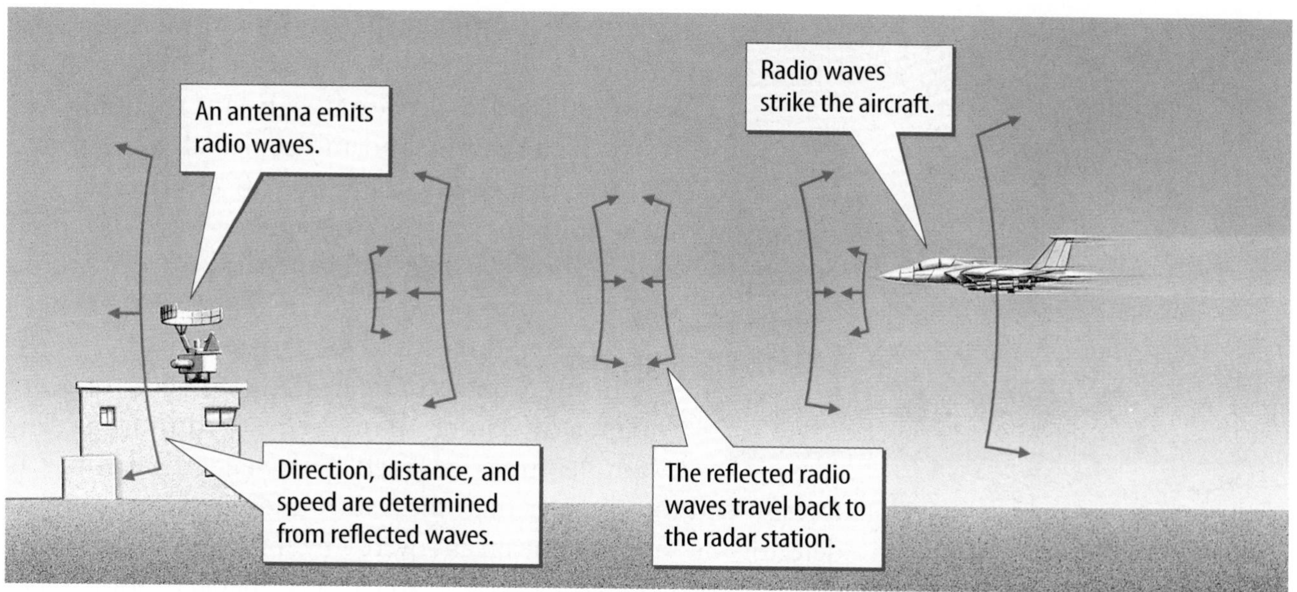
An antenna emits radio waves.
Radio waves strike the aircraft.
Direction, distance, and speed are determined from reflected waves.
The reflected radio waves travel back to the radar station.

Figure 10
Radar stations determine direction, distance, and speed of aircraft.

Radar You might be familiar with echolocation, in which sound waves are reflected off an object to determine its size and location. Some bats and dolphins use echolocation to navigate and hunt. Radar, an acronym for RAdio Detecting And Ranging, uses electromagnetic waves to detect objects in the same way. Radar was first used during World War II to detect and warn of incoming enemy aircraft.

Reading Check *What does radar do?*

A radar station sends out radio waves that bounce off an object such as an airplane. Electronic equipment measures the time it takes for the radio waves to travel to the plane, be reflected, and return. Because the speed of the radio waves is known, the distance to the airplane can be calculated from the following formula.

$$\text{distance} = \text{speed} \times \text{time}$$

An example of radar being used is shown in **Figure 10.** Because electromagnetic waves travel so quickly, the entire process takes only a fraction of a second.

Infrared Waves

You might know from experience that when you stand near the glowing coals of a barbecue or the red embers of a campfire, your skin senses the heat and becomes warm. Your skin may also feel warm near a hot object that is not glowing. The heat you are sensing with your skin is from electromagnetic waves. These electromagnetic waves are called **infrared waves** and have wavelengths between about one thousandth and 0.7 millionths of a meter.

Mini LAB

Observing the Focusing of Infrared Rays

Procedure

1. Place a **concave mirror** 2 m to 3 m away from an **electric heater.** Turn on the heater.
2. Place the palm of your hand in front of the mirror and move it back until you feel heat on your palm. Note the location of the warm area.
3. Move the heater to a new location. How does the warm area move?

Analysis

1. Did you observe the warm area? Where?
2. Compare the location of the warm area to the location of the mirror.

Figure 11
A pit viper hunting in the dark can detect the infrared waves that the warm body of its prey emits.

Detecting Infrared Waves Infrared rays are emitted by almost every object. In any material the atoms and molecules are in constant motion. Electrons in the atoms and molecules also move and vibrate. As a result, they give off electromagnetic waves. Most of the electromagnetic waves given off by an object at room temperature are infrared waves and have a wavelength of about 0.000 01 m, or one hundred thousandth of a meter.

Infrared detectors can detect objects that are warmer or cooler than their surroundings. For example, areas covered with vegetation, such as forests, tend to be cooler than their surroundings. Using infrared detectors on satellites, the areas covered by forests and other vegetation, as well as water, rock, and soil, can be mapped. Some types of night vision devices use infrared detectors that enable objects to be seen in nearly total darkness.

Animals and Infrared Waves Some animals also can detect infrared waves. Snakes called pit vipers, such as the one shown in **Figure 11,** have a pit located between the nostril and the eye that detects infrared waves. Rattlesnakes, copperheads, and water moccasins are pit vipers. These pits help pit vipers hunt at night by detecting the infrared waves their prey emits.

Visible Light

As the temperature of an object increases, the atoms and molecules in the object move faster. The electrons also vibrate faster, and produce electromagnetic waves of higher frequency and shorter wavelength. If the temperature is high enough, the object might glow, as in **Figure 12.** Some of the electromagnetic waves that the hot object is emitting are now detectable with your eyes. Electromagnetic waves you can detect with your eyes are called **visible light.** Visible light has wavelengths between about 0.7 and 0.4 millionths of a meter. What you see as different colors are electromagnetic waves of different wavelengths. Red light has the longest wavelength (lowest frequency), and blue light has the shortest wavelength (highest frequency).

Most objects that you see do not give off visible light. They simply reflect the visible light that is emitted by a source of light, such as the Sun or a lightbulb.

Figure 12
When objects are heated, their electrons vibrate faster. When the temperature is high enough, the vibrating electrons will emit visible light.

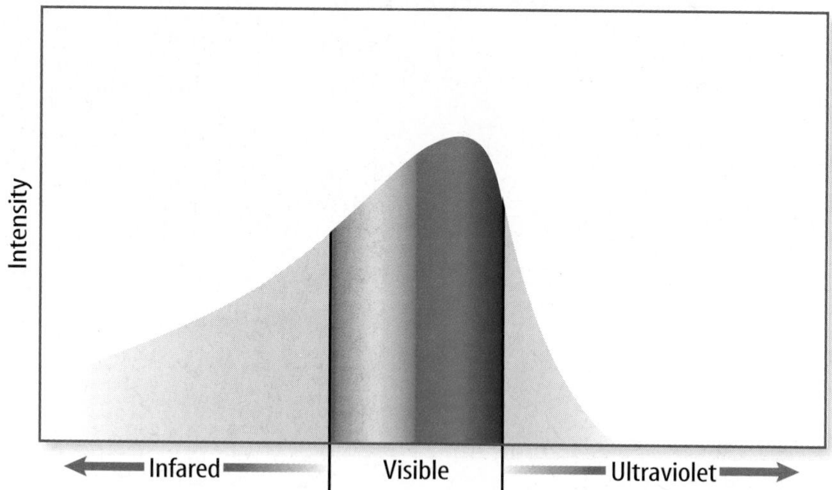

Figure 13
Electromagnetic waves from the Sun have a range of frequencies centered about the visible region. *Which frequencies of light is the Sun brightest in?*

Ultraviolet Radiation

Ultraviolet radiation is higher in frequency than visible light and has even shorter wavelengths—between 0.4 millionths of a meter and about ten billionths of a meter. Ultraviolet radiation has higher frequencies than visible light and carries more energy. The radiant energy carried by an ultraviolet wave can be enough to damage the large, fragile molecules that make up living cells. Too much ultraviolet radiation can damage or kill healthy cells.

Figure 13 shows the electromagnetic waves emitted by the Sun, some of which are in the ultraviolet region. Too much exposure to those ultraviolet waves can cause sunburn. Exposure to these waves over a long period of time can lead to early aging of the skin and possibly skin cancer. You can protect yourself from receiving too much ultraviolet radiation by wearing sunglasses and sunscreen, and staying out of the Sun when it is most intense.

Figure 14
Sterilizing devices, such as this goggle sterilizer, use ultraviolet waves to kill organisms on the equipment.

Beneficial Uses of UV Radiation A few minutes of exposure each day to ultraviolet radiation from the Sun enables your body to produce the vitamin D it needs. Most people receive that amount during normal activity. The body's natural defense against too much ultraviolet radiation is to tan. However, a tan can be a sign that overexposure to ultraviolet radiation has occurred.

Ultraviolet radiation's cell-killing effect has led to its use as a disinfectant for surgical equipment in hospitals. In some high school chemistry labs, ultraviolet rays are used to sterilize goggles, as shown in **Figure 14.**

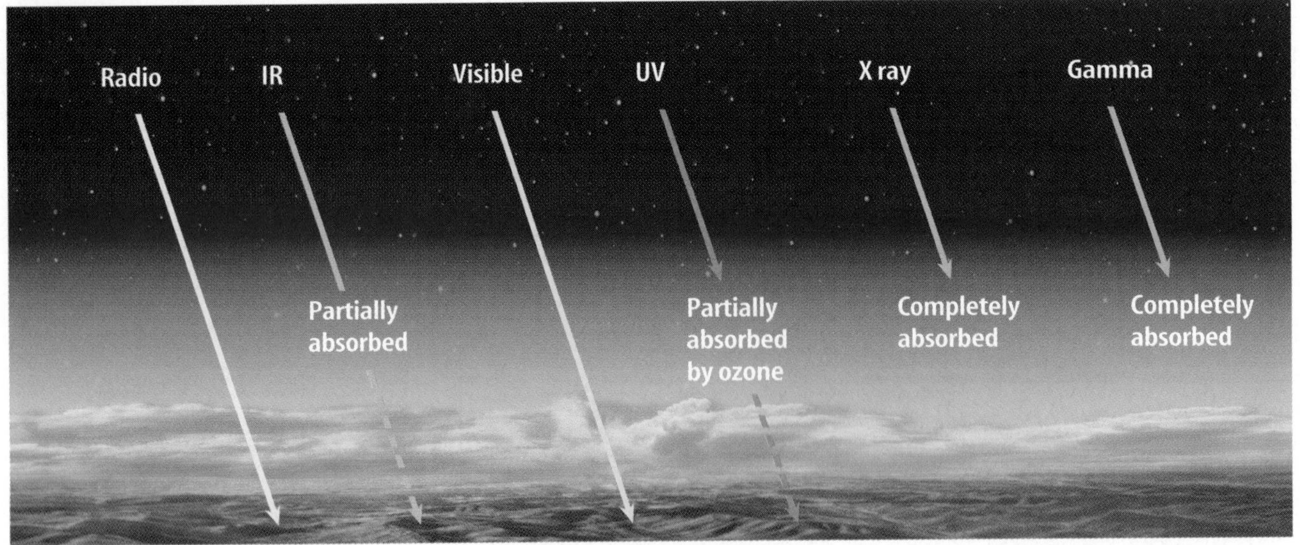

Figure 15
Earth's atmosphere serves as a shield to block certain types of electromagnetic waves from reaching the surface.

The Ozone Layer Much of the ultraviolet radiation arriving at Earth is absorbed in the upper atmosphere by ozone, as shown in **Figure 15.** Ozone is a molecule that has three oxygen atoms and is formed high in Earth's atmosphere.

However, chemical compounds called CFCs, which are used in air conditioners and refrigerators, can react chemically with ozone. This reaction causes ozone to break down and increases the amount of ultraviolet radiation that penetrates the atmosphere. To prevent this, the use of CFCs is being phased out.

Ultraviolet radiation is not the only type of electromagnetic wave absorbed by Earth's atmosphere. Higher energy waves of X rays and gamma rays also are absorbed. The atmosphere is transparent to radio waves and visible light and partially transparent to infrared waves.

Life Science INTEGRATION

Warm-blooded animals, such as mammals, produce their own body heat. Cold-blooded animals, such as reptiles, absorb heat from the environment. Brainstorm the possible advantages of being either warm-blooded or cold-blooded. Which animals would be easier for a pit viper to detect?

X Rays and Gamma Rays

Ultraviolet rays can penetrate the top layer of your skin. **X rays,** with an even higher frequency than ultraviolet rays, have enough energy to go right through skin and muscle. A shield made from a dense metal, such as lead, is required to stop X rays.

Gamma rays have the highest frequency and, therefore, carry the most energy. Gamma rays are the hardest to stop. They are produced by changes in the nuclei of atoms. When protons and neutrons bond together in nuclear fusion or break apart from each other in nuclear fission, enormous quantities of energy are released. Some of this energy is released as gamma rays.

Just as too much ultraviolet radiation can hurt or kill cells, too much X ray or gamma radiation can have the same effect. Because the energy of the waves is so much higher, the exposure that is needed to cause damage is much less.

Using High-Energy Electromagnetic Radiation The fact that X rays can pass through the human body makes them useful for medical diagnosis, as shown in **Figure 16.** X rays pass through the less dense tissues in skin and other organs. These X rays strike a film, creating a shadow image of the denser tissues. X-ray images help doctors detect injuries and diseases, such as broken bones and cancer. A CT scanner uses X rays to produce images of the human body as if it had been sliced like a loaf of bread.

Although the radiation received from getting one medical or dental X ray is not harmful, the cumulative effect of numerous X rays can be dangerous. The operator of the X-ray machine usually stands behind a shield to avoid being exposed to X rays. Lead shields or aprons are used to protect the parts of the patient's body that are not receiving the X rays.

Using Gamma Rays Although gamma rays are dangerous, they also have beneficial uses, just as X rays do. A beam of gamma rays focused on a cancerous tumor can kill the tumor. Gamma radiation also can cleanse food of disease-causing bacteria. More than 1,000 Americans die each year from *Salmonella* bacteria in poultry and *E. coli* bacteria in meat. Although gamma radiation has been used since 1963 to kill bacteria in food, this method is not widely used in the food industry.

Figure 16
Dense tissues such as bone absorb more X rays than softer tissues do. Consequently, dense tissues leave a shadow on film that can be use to diagnose medical and dental conditions.

Astronomy Across the Spectrum

Some astronomical objects produce no visible light and can be detected only through the infrared and radio waves they emit. Some galaxies emit X rays from regions that do not emit visible light. Studying stars and galaxies like these using only visible light would be like looking at only one color in a picture. **Figure 17** shows how different electromagnetic waves can be used to study the universe.

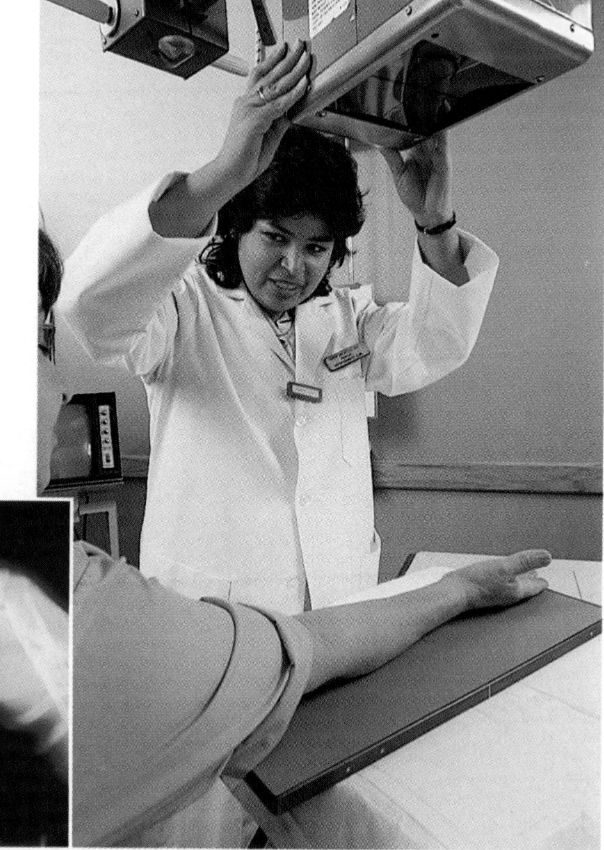

Figure 17

For centuries, astronomers studied the universe using only the visible light coming from planets, moons, and stars. But many objects in space also emit X rays, ultraviolet and infrared radiation, and radio waves. Scientists now use telescopes that can "see" these different types of electromagnetic waves. As these images of the Sun reveal, the new tools are providing remarkable views of objects in the universe.

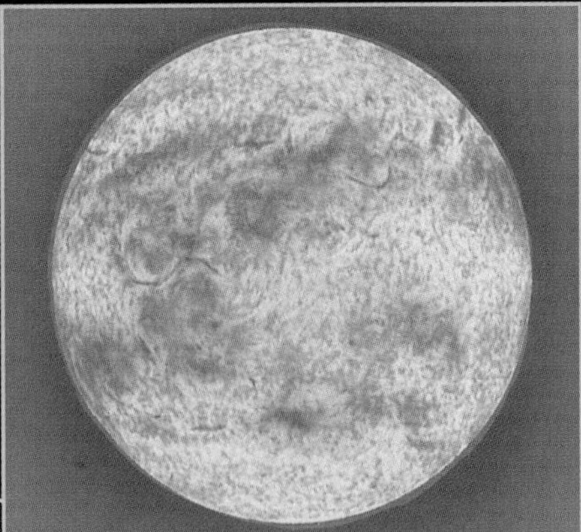

▲ **INFRARED RADIATION** An infrared telescope reveals that the Sun's surface temperature is not uniform. Some areas are hotter than others.

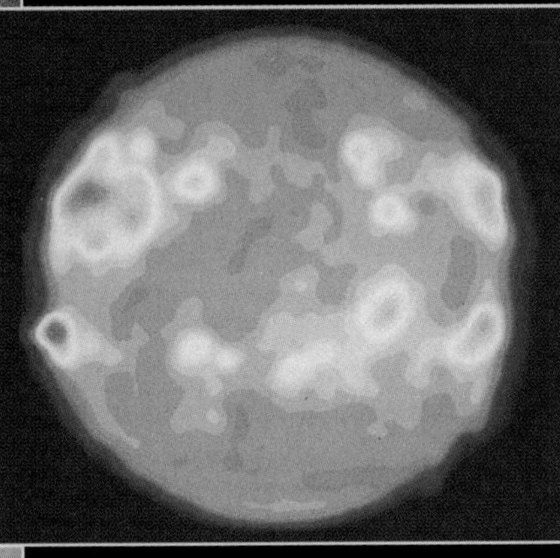

▲ **RADIO WAVES** Radio telescopes detect radio waves given off by the Sun, which have much longer wavelengths than visible light.

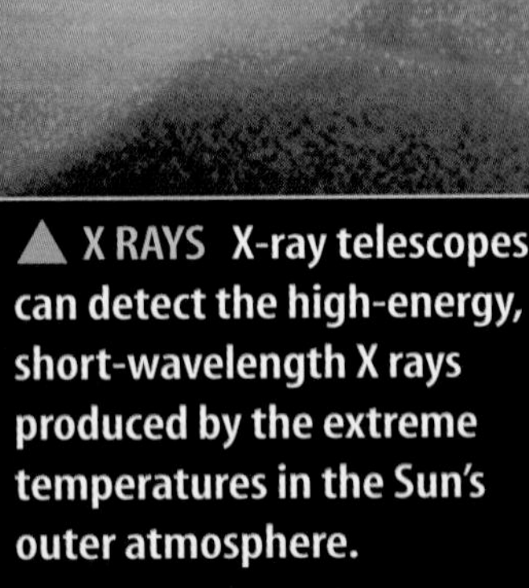

▲ **X RAYS** X-ray telescopes can detect the high-energy, short-wavelength X rays produced by the extreme temperatures in the Sun's outer atmosphere.

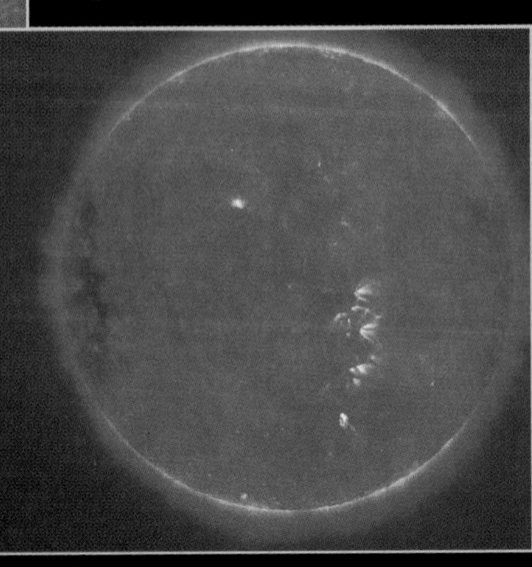

▶ **ULTRAVIOLET RADIATION** Telescopes sensitive to ultraviolet radiation—electromagnetic waves with shorter wavelengths than visible light—can "see" the Sun's outer atmosphere.

Figure 18
Launching satellite observatories above Earth's atmosphere is the only way to see the universe at electromagnetic wavelengths that are absorbed by Earth's atmosphere.

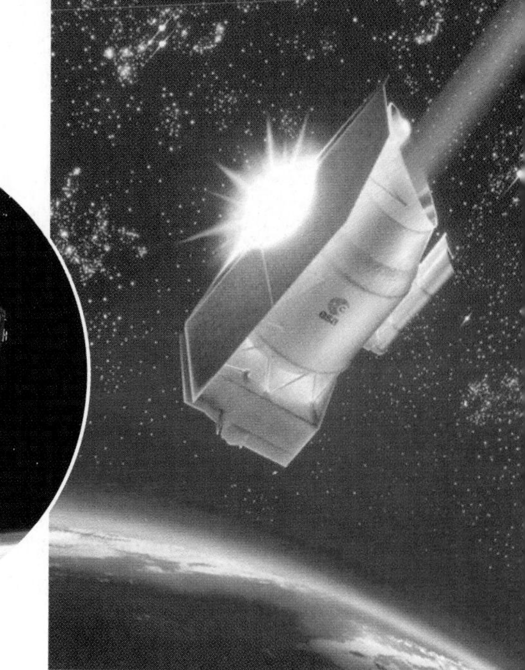

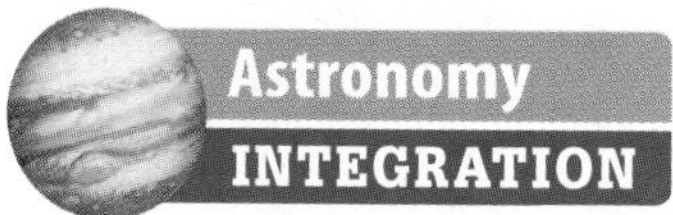
Astronomy INTEGRATION

Satellite Observations Recall from **Figure 15** that Earth's atmosphere blocks some parts of the electromagnetic spectrum. For example, X rays, gamma rays, most ultraviolet rays, and some infrared rays cannot pass through. However, telescopes in orbit above Earth's atmosphere can obtain more information than can be obtained at Earth's surface about stars, galaxies, and other objects in the universe. **Figure 18** shows three such satellites—the Extreme Ultraviolet Explorer, the Chandra X-Ray Observatory, and the Infrared Space Observatory.

Reading Check ***Why are telescopes sent into space on artificial satellites?***

Section  2 Assessment

1. List three types of electromagnetic waves produced by the Sun.
2. Why is ultraviolet light more damaging to cells than infrared light is?
3. Give an application of infrared waves.
4. Describe the difference between X rays and gamma rays.
5. **Think Critically** Why does Earth emit mainly infrared waves and the Sun emit visible light and ultraviolet waves?

Skill Builder Activities

6. **Recognizing Cause and Effect** If visible light is the effect, what is the cause? Do the different colors of light have different causes? **For more help, refer to the** Science Skill Handbook.
7. **Using a Database** What do images of the same object look like if different wavelengths are detected? Use a database to research this topic and present a report to your class. **For more help, refer to the** Technology Skill Handbook.

Activity

Prisms of Light

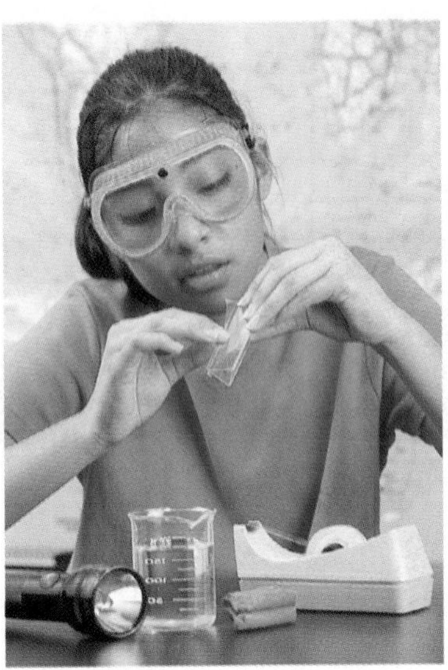

Do you know what light is? Many would answer that light is what you turn on to see at night. However, white light is made of many different frequencies of the electromagnetic spectrum. A prism can separate white light into its different frequencies. You see different frequencies of light as different colors. What colors do you see when light passes through a prism?

What You'll Investigate

What happens to visible light as it passes through a prism?

Goals

- **Construct** a prism and observe the different colors that are produced.
- **Infer** how the bending of light waves depends on their wavelength.

Materials

microscope slides (3)
transparent tape
clay
flashlight
water

Safety Precautions

Procedure

1. Carefully tape the three slides together on their long sides so they form a long prism.
2. Place one end of the prism into a softened piece of clay so the prism is standing upright.
3. Fill the prism with water and put it on a table that is against a dark wall.
4. Shine a flashlight beam through the prism so the light becomes visible on the wall.

Conclude and Apply

1. What was the order of the colors you saw on the wall?
2. How does the position of the colors on the wall change as you change the direction of the flashlight beam?
3. How does the order of colors on the wall change as you change the direction of the flashlight beam?
4. After passing through the water prism, which color light waves have changed direction, or have been bent, the most? Which color has been bent the least?
5. How does the amount of bending of a light wave depend on its wavelength? How does it depend on the frequency?

Compare your conclusions with those of other students in your class. **For more help, refer to the** **Science Skill Handbook.**

Using Electromagnetic Waves

Telecommunications

In the past week, have you spoken on the phone, watched television, done research on the Internet, or listened to the radio? Today you can talk to someone far away or transmit and receive information over long distances almost instantly. Thanks to telecommunications, the world is becoming increasingly connected through the use of electromagnetic waves.

Using Radio Waves

Radio waves usually are used to send and receive information over long distances. Using radio waves to communicate has several advantages. For example, radio waves pass through walls and windows easily. Radio waves do not interact with humans, so they are not harmful to people like ultraviolet rays or X rays are. So most telecommunication devices, such as TVs, radios, and telephones, use radio waves to transmit information such as images and sounds. **Figure 19** shows how radio waves can be used to transmit information—in this case transmitting information that enables sounds to be reproduced at a location far away.

As You Read

***What* You'll Learn**

- **Explain** different methods of electronic communication.
- **Compare and contrast** AM and FM signals.

Vocabulary

Carrier wave
Global Positioning System

***Why* It's Important**

Telecommunication enables people to contact others and collect information worldwide.

Figure 19
Transmitting sounds by radio waves uses conversions among sound, electrical, and radiant energies.

Antenna converts electrical energy into radiant energy
Receiving antenna converts radiant energy into electrical energy
Speaker converts electrical energy into sound energy
Microphone converts sound energy into electrical energy

Figure 20
A signal can be carried by a carrier wave in two ways—amplitude modulation or frequency modulation.

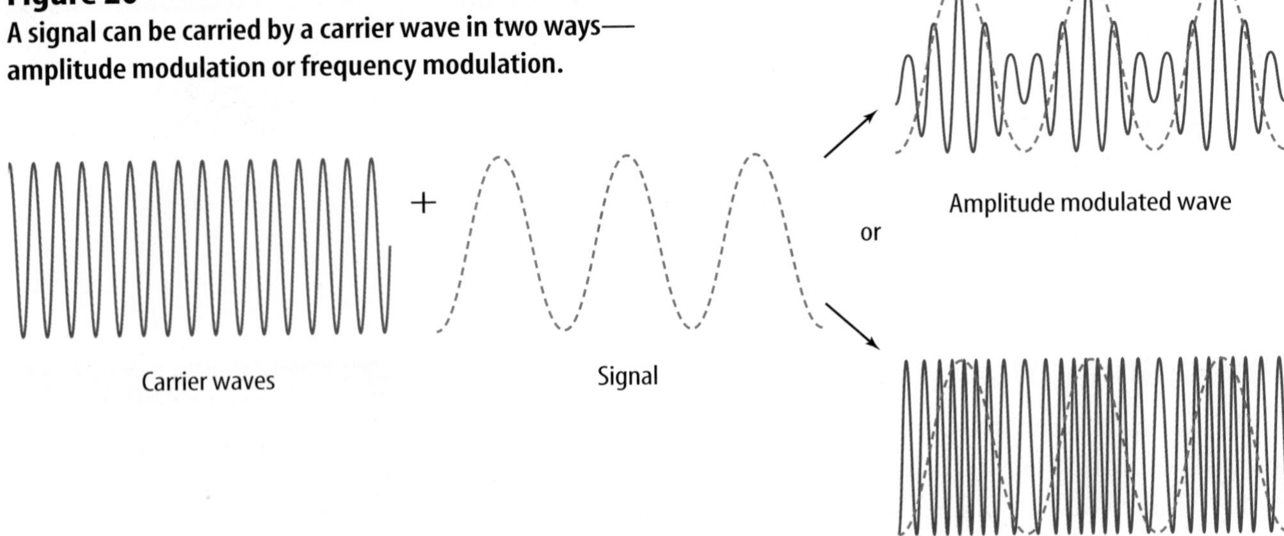

Radio Transmission How is information, such as images or sounds, broadcast by radio waves? Each radio and television station is assigned a particular frequency at which it broadcasts radio waves. The radio waves broadcast by a station at its assigned frequency are the **carrier waves** for that station. To listen to a station you tune your radio or television to the frequency of the station's carrier waves. To carry information on the carrier wave, either the amplitude or the frequency of the carrier wave is changed, or modulated.

Amplitude Modulation The letters *AM* in AM radio stand for amplitude modulation, which means that the amplitude of the carrier wave is changed to transmit information. The original sound is transformed into an electrical signal that is used to vary the amplitude of the carrier wave, as shown in **Figure 20.** Note that the frequency of the carrier wave doesn't change—only the amplitude changes. An AM receiver tunes to the frequency of the carrier wave. In the receiver, the varying amplitude of the carrier waves produces an electric signal. The radio's loudspeaker uses this electric signal to produce the original sound.

Pulsars are astronomical objects that emit periodic bursts of radio waves. The pattern of pulses is regular. Investigate how pulsars originate and communicate to your class what you learn. Why might pulsars have seemed to be signals from intelligent life?

Frequency Modulation FM radio works in much the same way as AM radio, but the frequency instead of the amplitude is modulated, as shown in **Figure 20.** An FM receiver contains electronic components that use the varying frequency of the carrier wave to produce an electric signal. As in an AM radio, this electric signal is converted into sound waves by a loudspeaker.

✔ Reading Check ***What is frequency modulation?***

Telephones

A telephone contains a microphone in the mouthpiece that converts a sound wave into an electric signal. The electric signal is carried through a wire to the telephone-switching system. There, the signal might be sent through other wires or be converted into a radio or microwave signal for transmission through the air. The electric signal also can be converted into a light wave for transmission through fiber-optic cables.

At the receiving end, the signal is converted back to an electric signal. A speaker in the earpiece of the phone changes the electric signal into a sound wave.

✔ Reading Check ***What device converts sound into an electric signal?***

Math Skills Activity

Calculating the Wavelength of Radio Frequencies

Example Problem

You are listening to an FM station with a frequency of 94.9 MHz or 94,900,000 Hz. How long are the wavelengths that strike the antenna? For any wave, the wavelength equals the wave speed divided by the frequency. The speed of radio waves is 300,000,000 m/s. The SI unit of frequency, Hz, is equal to l/s.

Solution

1. *This is what you know:* frequency = 94,900,000 Hz
   wave speed = 300,000,000 m/s
2. *This is what you need to find:* wavelength
3. *This is the equation you need to use:* wavelength = wave speed / frequency
4. *Substitute the known values:* wavelength = (300,000,000 m/s) / (94,900,000 Hz)
   = 3.16 m

Check your answer by multiplying the units. Do you calculate a unit of distance for your answer?

Practice Problems

1. Your friend prefers an AM radio station at 1,520 kHz (1,520 thousand vibrations each second). What is the wavelength of this frequency? Which has a longer wavelength, AM or FM radio waves?
2. An AM radio station operates at 580 kHz (580 thousand vibrations each second). What is the wavelength of this frequency? What is the relationship between frequency and wavelength?

For more help, refer to the Math Skill Handbook.

Figure 21
Electromagnetic waves make using telephones easier.

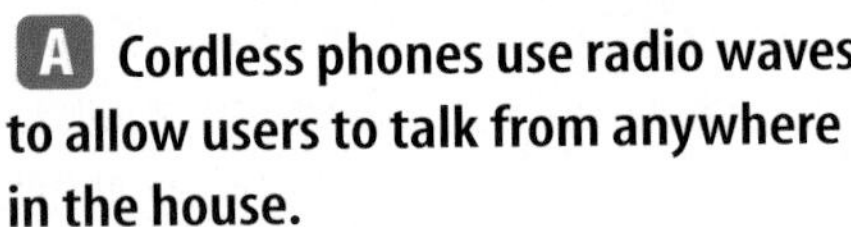

A Cordless phones use radio waves to allow users to talk from anywhere in the house.

B Radio waves enable cell phone users to send or receive calls without using wires.

Remote Phones A telephone does not have to transmit its signal through wires. In a cordless phone, the electrical signal produced by the microphone is transmitted through an antenna in the handset to the base. **Figure 21A** shows how incoming signals are transmitted from the base to the handset. A cellular phone uses an antenna to broadcast and receive information between the phone and a base station, as shown in **Figure 21B.** The base station uses radio waves to communicate with other stations in a network.

Research Visit the Glencoe Science Web site at **science.glencoe.com** for more information about how satellites are used in around-the-world communications. Summarize what you learn in an informational handout.

Pagers The base station also is used in a pager system. When you dial a pager, the signal is sent to a base station. From there, an electromagnetic signal is sent to the pager. The pager beeps or vibrates to indicate that someone has called. With a touch-tone phone, you can transmit numeric information, such as your phone number, which the pager will receive and display.

Communications Satellites

How do you send information to the other side of the world? Radio waves can't be sent directly through Earth. Instead, radio signals are sent to satellites. The satellites can communicate with other satellites or with ground stations. Some communications satellites are in geosynchronous orbit, meaning each satellite remains above the same point on the ground.

The Global Positioning System

Satellites also are used as part of the **Global Positioning System,** or GPS. GPS is used to locate objects on Earth. The system consists of satellites, ground-based stations, and portable units with receivers, as illustrated in **Figure 22.**

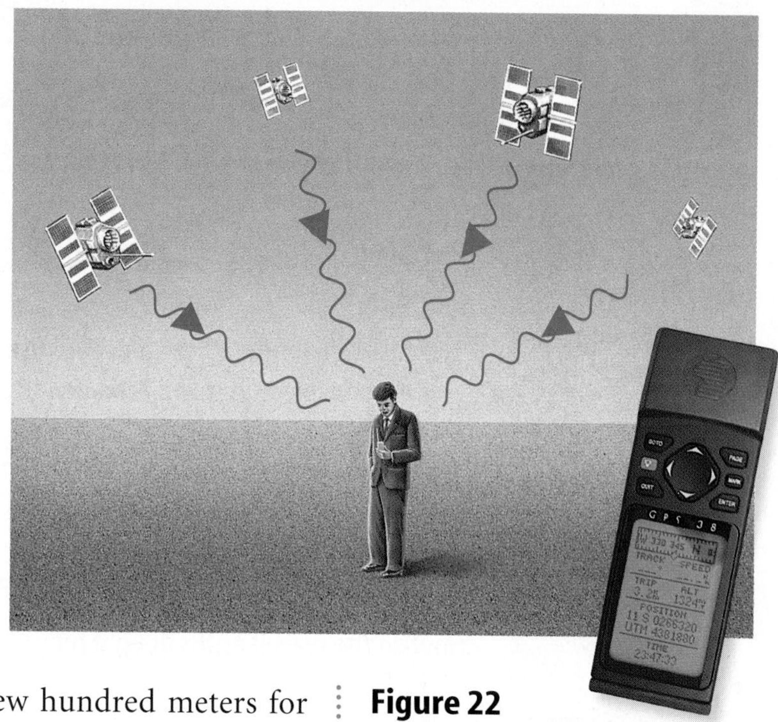

Figure 22
The signals broadcast by GPS satellites enable portable, hand-held receivers to determine the position of an object or person.

A GPS receiver measures the time it takes for radio waves to travel from several satellites to the receiver. This determines the distance to each satellite. The receiver then uses this information to calculate its latitude, longitude, and elevation. The accuracy of GPS receivers ranges from a few hundred meters for hand-held units, to several centimeters for units that are used to measure the movements of Earth's crust.

Reading Check *What is GPS used for?*

Other forms of communication have been developed over the past few decades. For example, an Internet connection transfers images and sound using the telephone network, just as a television signal transfers images and sound using radio waves. What forms of telecommunications do you think you'll be using a few decades from now?

Section  3 Assessment

1. What is a modulated radio signal?
2. What does a microphone do? What does a speaker do?
3. What types of information does a GPS receiver provide for its user?
4. What is a communications satellite?
5. **Think Critically** Make a diagram showing how a communication satellite could be used to relay information from a broadcasting station in New York to a receiving station in London.

Skill Builder Activities

6. **Researching Information** Find out more about a form of telecommunications, such as email or shortwave radio. **For more help, refer to the Science Skill Handbook.**
7. **Communicating** Think of a story you have enjoyed about a time before telecommunications or one in which telecommunication was not possible. How would telecommunications have changed the story? **For more help, refer to the Science Skill Handbook.**

Activity Design Your Own Experiment

Spectrum Inspection

You've heard the term "red-hot" used to describe something that is unusually hot. When a piece of metal is heated it may give off a red glow or even a yellow glow. All objects emit electromagnetic waves. How do the wavelengths of these waves depend on the temperature of the object?

Recognize the Problem

How do the wavelengths of light produced by a lightbulb depend on the temperature of the lightbulb?

Form a Hypothesis

The brightness of a lightbulb increases as its temperature increases. Form a hypothesis describing how the wavelengths emitted by a lightbulb will change as the brightness of a lightbulb changes.

Goals

- **Design** an experiment that determines the relationship between brightness and the wavelengths emitted by a lightbulb.
- **Observe** the wavelengths of light emitted by a lightbulb as its brightness changes.

Safety Precautions

WARNING: Be sure all electrical cords and connections are intact and that you have a dry working area. Do not touch the bulbs as they may be hot.

Possible Materials

diffraction grating
power supply with variable resistor switch
clear, tubular lightbulb and socket
red, yellow, and blue colored pencils

Test Your Hypothesis

Plan

1. **Decide** how you will determine the effect of lightbulb brightness on the colors of light that are emitted.
2. As shown in the photo at the right, you will look toward the light through the diffraction grating to detect the colors of light emitted by the bulb. The color spectrum will appear to the right and to the left of the bulb.
3. **List** the specific steps you will need to take to test your hypothesis. Describe precisely what you will do in each step. Will you first test the bulb at a bright or dim setting? How many settings will you test? (Try at least three.) How will you record your observations in an organized way?
4. **List** the materials you will need for your experiment. Describe exactly how and in which order you will use these materials.
5. **Identify** any constants and variables in your experiment.

Do

1. Make sure your teacher approves your plan before you start.
2. **Perform** your experiment as planned.
3. While doing your experiment, write down any observations you make in your Science Journal.

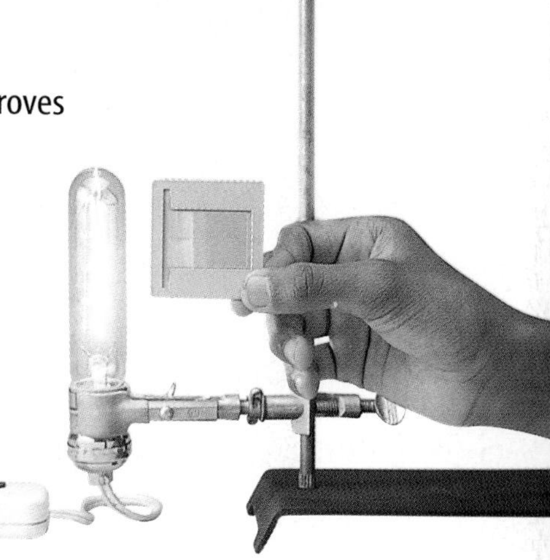

Analyze Your Data

1. Use the colored pencils to draw the color spectrum emitted by the bulb at each brightness.
2. Which colors appeared as the bulb became brighter? Did any colors disappear?
3. How did the wavelengths emitted by the bulb change as the bulb became brighter?
4. Infer how the frequencies emitted by the lightbulb changed as it became hotter.

Draw Conclusions

1. If an object becomes hotter, what happens to the wavelengths it emits?
2. How do the wavelengths that the bulb emits change if it is turned off?
3. From your results, infer whether red stars or yellow stars are hotter.

Compare your results with others in your class. How many different colors were seen?

Hedy Lamarr, actor and inventor

Hopping the

Ringgggg. There it is—that familiar beep! Out come the cellular phones—from purses, pockets, book bags, belt clips, and briefcases. At any given moment, a million wireless signals are flying through the air—and not just cell phone signals. With radio and television signals, Internet data, and even Global Positioning System information coming at us, the air seems like a pretty crowded place. How do all of these signals get to the right place? How does a cellular phone pick out its own signal from among the clutter? The answer lies in a concept developed in 1940 by Hedy Lamarr.

Lamarr was born in Vienna, Austria. In 1937, she left Austria to escape Hitler's invading Nazi army. Lamarr left for another reason, as well. She was determined to pursue a career as an actor. And she became a famous movie star.

In 1940, Lamarr came up with an idea to keep radio signals that guided torpedoes from being jammed. Her idea, called frequency hopping, involved breaking the radio signal that was guiding the torpedo into tiny parts and rapidly changing their frequency. The enemy would not be able to keep up with the frequency changes and thus would not be able to divert the torpedo from its target. Lamarr worked with a partner who helped her figure out how to make the idea work. They were awarded a patent for their idea in 1942.

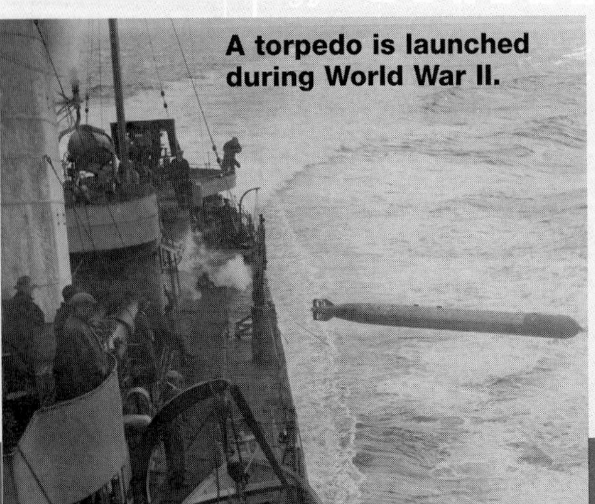
A torpedo is launched during World War II.

Spread Spectrum

Lamarr's idea was ahead of its time. The digital technology that allowed efficient operation of her system wasn't invented until decades later. However, after 1962, frequency hopping was adopted and used in U.S. military communications. It was the development of cellular phones, however, that benefited the most from Lamarr's concept. Cellular phones and other wireless technologies operate by breaking their signals into smaller parts, called packets. The packets are encoded in a certain way for particular receivers and are spread across bands of the electromagnetic spectrum. In this way, millions of users can use the same frequencies at the same time.

Frequencies

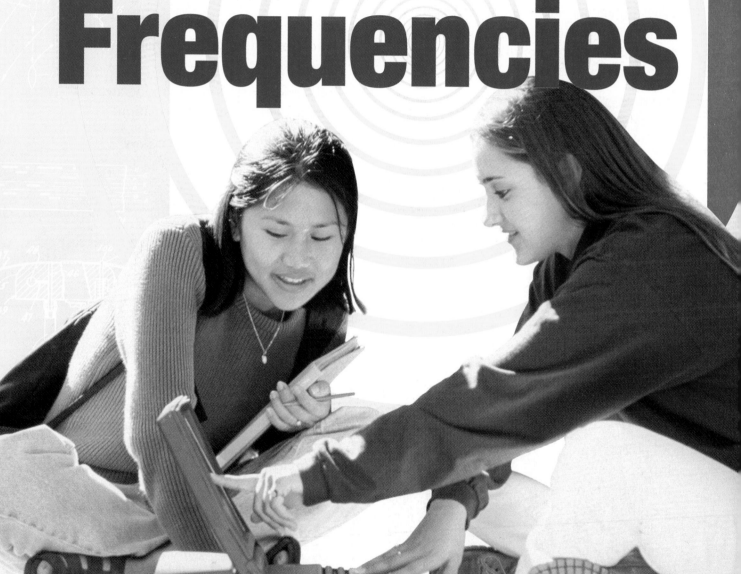

CONNECTIONS Brainstorm **How are you using wireless technology in your life right now? List ways it makes your life easier. Are there drawbacks to some of the uses for wireless technology? What are they?**

SCIENCE *Online*

For more information, visit science.glencoe.com

Chapter 13 Study Guide

Reviewing Main Ideas

Section 1 The Nature of Electromagnetic Waves

1. Vibrating charges generate vibrating electric and magnetic fields. These vibrating fields travel through space and are called electromagnetic waves.
2. Electromagnetic waves, like all waves, have wavelength, frequency, amplitude, and carry energy. *How are ocean waves similar to electromagnetic waves?*

Section 2 The Electromagnetic Spectrum

1. Radio waves have the longest wavelength and lowest energy. Radar uses radio waves to locate objects.
2. All objects emit infrared waves. Most objects you see reflect the visible light emitted by a source of light. *How could a person be seen in total darkness?*

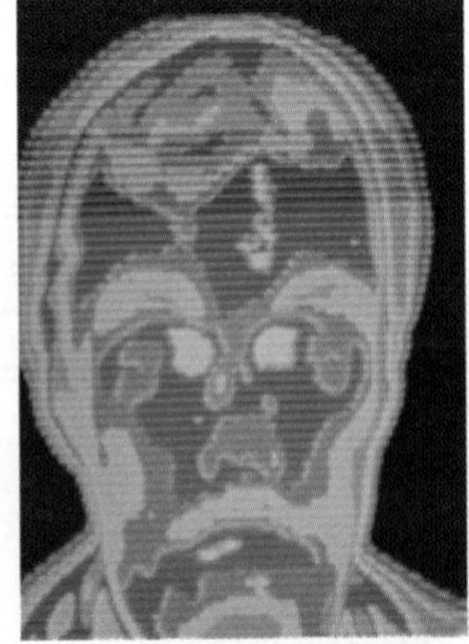

3. Ultraviolet waves have a higher frequency and carry more energy than visible light.
4. X rays and gamma rays are highly penetrating and can be dangerous to living organisms.

Section 3 Using Electromagnetic Waves

1. Communications systems use visible light, radio waves, or electrical signals to transmit information.
2. Radio and TV stations use modulated carrier waves to transmit information.
3. Electromagnetic waves are used in telephone technologies to make communication easier and faster. *What is one way an electromagnetic wave is used in telephone communication?*

4. Communications satellites relay information from different points on Earth so a transmission can go around the globe. The Global Positioning System uses satellites to determine the position of an object on Earth.

FOLDABLES Reading & Study Skills

After You Read

Using the information on your Foldable, compare and contrast visible and invisible waves that form the electromagnetic spectrum.

Visualizing Main Ideas

Complete the following spider map about electromagnetic waves.

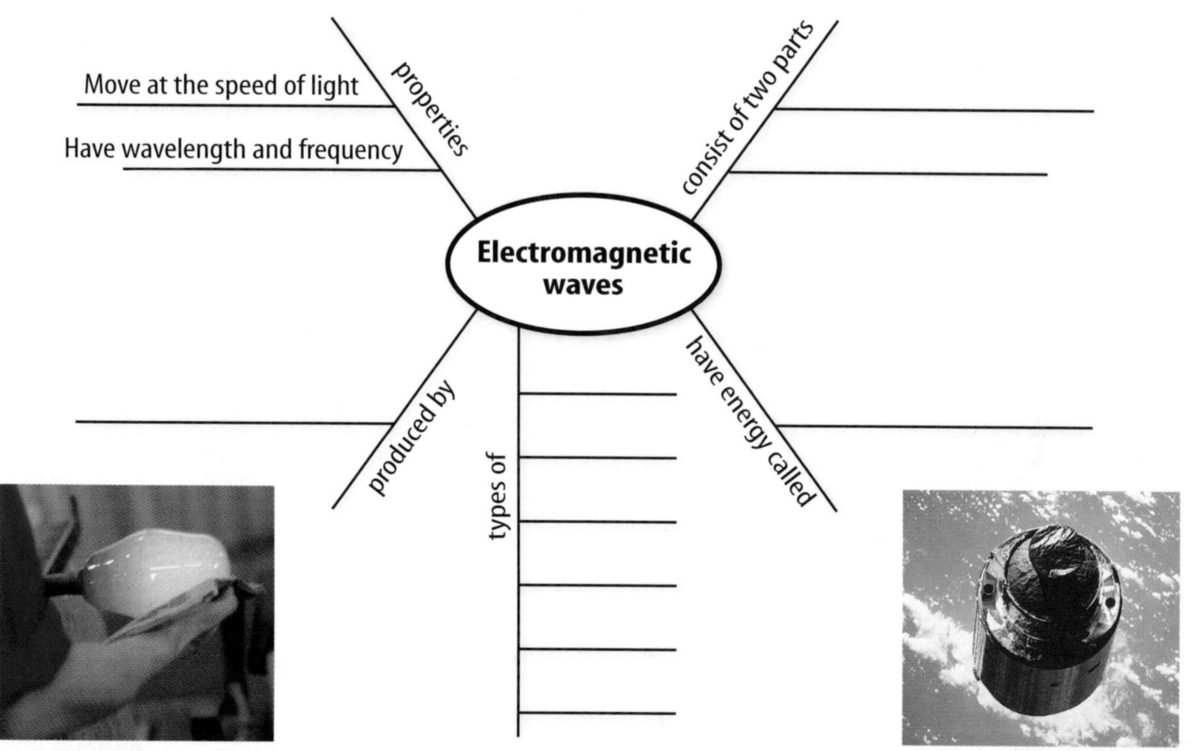

Vocabulary Review

Vocabulary Words

a. carrier wave
b. electromagnetic spectrum
c. electromagnetic wave
d. gamma ray
e. Global Positioning System
f. infrared wave
g. radiant energy
h. radio wave
i. ultraviolet radiation
j. visible light
k. X ray

Study Tip

After you read a chapter, write ten questions that it answers. Wait one day and then try to recall the answers. Look up what you can't remember.

Using Vocabulary

Explain the difference between the terms in each of the following pairs.

1. infrared wave, radio wave
2. radio wave, carrier wave
3. communications satellite, Global Positioning System
4. visible light, ultraviolet radiation
5. X ray, gamma ray
6. electromagnetic wave, radiant energy
7. carrier wave, AM radio signal
8. infrared wave, ultraviolet wave

Chapter 13 Assessment

Checking Concepts

Choose the word or phrase that best answers the question.

1. Which type of force field surrounds a moving electron?
A) electric and magnetic
B) electric
C) magnetic
D) none of these

2. What does a microphone transform?
A) light waves to sound waves
B) radio waves to an electrical signal
C) sound waves to electromagnetic waves
D) sound waves to an electrical signal

3. Which of the following electromagnetic waves have the lowest frequency?
A) visible light
B) infrared waves
C) radio waves
D) X rays

4. What happens to the energy of an electromagnetic wave as its frequency increases?
A) It increases.
B) It decreases.
C) It stays the same.
D) It oscillates up and down.

5. What type of wave can hot objects emit?
A) radio
B) infrared
C) visible
D) ultraviolet

6. What can detect radio waves?
A) film
B) antenna
C) eyes
D) skin

7. Which wave can pass through people?
A) infrared
B) visible
C) ultraviolet
D) gamma

8. Which color has the lowest frequency?
A) green
B) violet
C) yellow
D) red

9. What is the key device that allows cordless phones to function?
A) X ray
B) satellite
C) GPS
D) antenna

10. What does *A* in AM stand for?
A) amplitude
B) antenna
C) astronomical
D) Alpha centauri

Thinking Critically

11. Infrared light was discovered when a scientist placed a thermometer in each band of the light spectrum produced by a prism. Would the area just beyond red have been warmer or cooler than the room? Explain.

12. Astronomers have built telescopes on Earth that have flexible mirrors that can eliminate the distortions due to the atmosphere. What advantages would a space-based telescope have over these?

13. Heated objects often give off visible light of a particular color. Explain why an object that glows bluish-white is hotter than one that glows red.

14. How can an X ray be used to determine the location of a cancerous tumor?

15. Why are many communications systems based on radio waves?

Developing Skills

16. Calculating Ratios How far does light travel in 1 min? How does this compare with the distance to the Moon?

17. Recognizing Cause and Effect As you ride in the car, the radio alternates between two different stations. How can the antenna pick up two stations at once?

18. Classifying List the colors of the visible spectrum in order of increasing frequency.

19. **Comparing and Contrasting** Compare and contrast ultraviolet and infrared light.

20. **Concept Mapping** Electromagnetic waves are grouped according to their frequencies. In the following concept map, write each frequency group and one way humans make use of the electromagnetic waves in that group. For example, in the second set of ovals, you might write "X rays" and "to see inside the body."

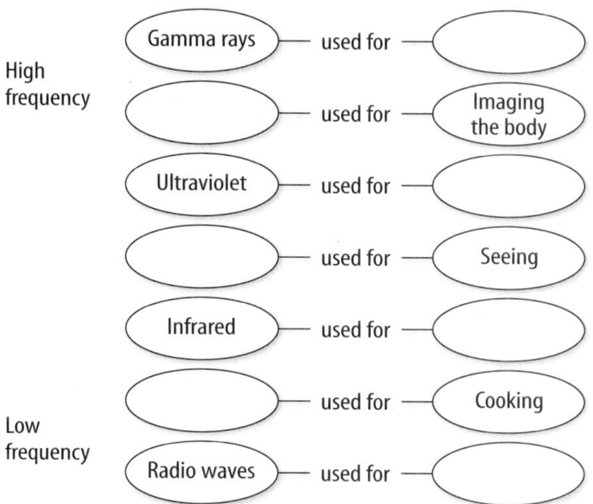

Performance Assessment

21. **Oral Presentation** Explain to the class how a radio signal is generated, transmitted, and received.

22. **Poster** Make a poster showing the parts of the electromagnetic spectrum. Show how frequency, wavelength, and energy change throughout the spectrum. How is each wave generated? What are some uses of each?

Technology

Go to the Glencoe Science Web site at **science.glencoe.com** or use the **Glencoe Science CD-ROM** for additional chapter assessment.

Test Practice

Mr. Rubama's class was studying how radio waves are transmitted. An experimental setup involving radio waves and glass is shown below.

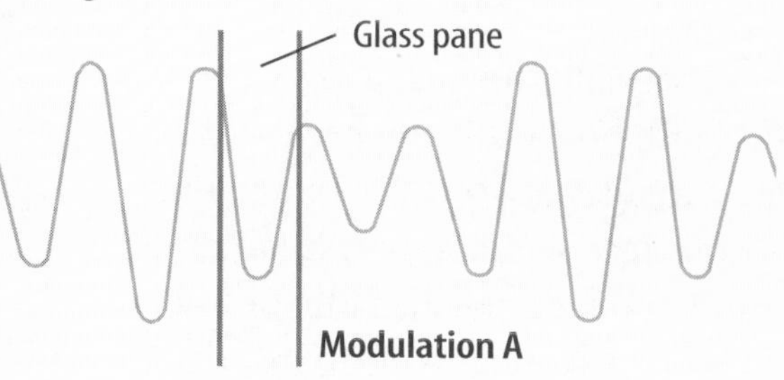

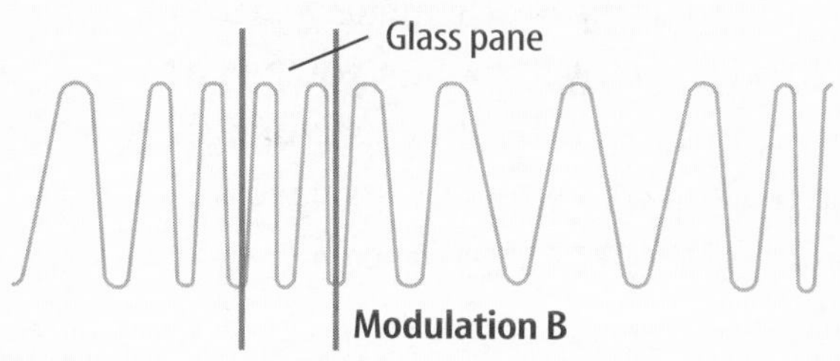

Study the illustrations and answer the following questions.

1. Which of these questions would most likely be answered by this experiment?
   A) How fast do radio waves travel through the air?
   B) Why do some waves travel more quickly than other waves?
   C) Where do radio waves come from?
   D) Can radio waves travel through glass?

2. Which of the following describes how the wave in Modulation A is different from the wave in Modulation B?
   F) It is a radio wave.
   G) It is frequency modulated.
   H) It is amplitude modulated.
   J) It is a carrier wave.

CHAPTER 14

Light, Mirrors, and Lenses

You walk through a door of the fun house and are bombarded by images of yourself. In one mirror, your face seems smashed. You turn around and face another mirror—your chin and neck are gigantic. How do mirrors in a fun house make you look so strange? In this chapter, you'll learn how mirrors and lenses create images. You'll also learn why objects have the colors they have.

What do you think?

Science Journal Look at the picture below with a classmate. Discuss what you think this might be or what is happening. Here's a hint: *It helps you keep in touch.* Write down your answer or your best guess in your Science Journal.

Everything you see results from light waves entering your eyes. These light waves are either given off by objects, such as the Sun and lightbulbs, or reflected by objects, such as trees, books, and people. Lenses and mirrors can cause light to change direction and make objects seem larger or smaller. What happens to light as it passes from one material to another?

Observe the bending of light

1. Place two paper cups next to each other and put a penny in the bottom of each cup.
2. Fill one of the cups with water and observe how the penny looks.
3. Looking straight down at the cups, slide the cup with no water away from you just until you can no longer see the penny.
4. Pour water into this cup and observe what seems to happen to the penny.

Observe

In your Science Journal, record your observations. Did adding water make the cup look deeper or shallower?

Before You Read

Making a Question Study Fold **Asking yourself questions helps you stay focused so you will better understand light, mirrors, and lenses when you are reading the chapter.**

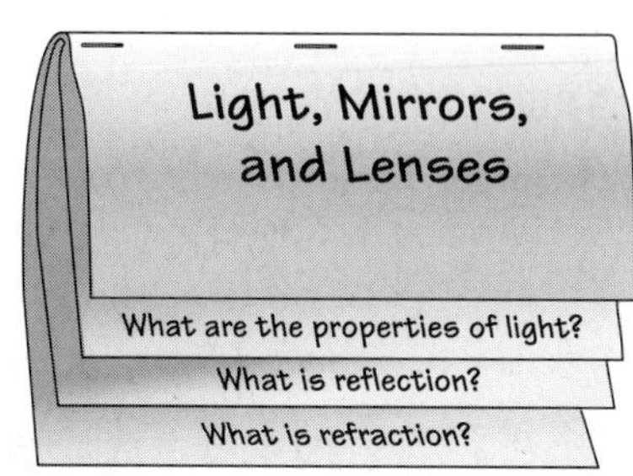

1. Stack two sheets of paper in front of you so the short side of both sheets is at the top.
2. Slide the top sheet up so about 4 cm of the bottom sheet shows.
3. Fold both sheets top to bottom to form four tabs and staple along the fold as shown.
4. Title the Foldable *Light, Mirrors, and Lenses* as shown. Write these questions on the flaps: *What are the properties of light? What is reflection? What is refraction?*
5. Before you read the chapter, try to answer the questions with what you already know. As you read the chapter, add to or correct your answers under the flaps.

SECTION 1

Properties of Light

As You Read

What You'll Learn

- **Describe** the wave nature of light.
- **Explain** how light interacts with materials.
- **Determine** why objects appear to have color.

Vocabulary

light ray
medium
reflection

Why It's Important

Much of what you know about your surroundings comes from information carried by light waves.

Figure 1
Waves carry energy as they travel.

What is light?

Drop a rock on the smooth surface of a pond and you'll see ripples spread outward from the spot where the rock struck. The rock produced a wave much like the one in **Figure 1A.** A wave is a disturbance that carries energy through matter or space. The matter in this case is the water, and the energy originally comes from the impact of the rock. As the ripples spread out, they carry some of that energy.

Light is a type of wave that carries energy. A source of light such as the Sun or a lightbulb gives off light waves into space, just as the rock hitting the pond causes waves to form in the water. But while the water waves spread out only on the surface of the pond, light waves spread out in all directions from the light source. **Figure 1B** shows how light waves travel.

Sometimes, however, it is easier to think of light in a different way. A **light ray** is a narrow beam of light that travels in a straight line. You can think of a source of light as giving off, or emitting, a countless number of light rays that are traveling away from the source in all directions.

A **Ripples on the surface of a pond are produced by an object hitting the water. As the ripples spread out from the point of impact, they carry energy.**

B **A source of light, such as a lightbulb, gives off light rays that travel away from the light source in all directions.**

Light Travels Through Space There is, however, one important difference between light waves and the water wave ripples on a pond. If the pond dried up and had no water, ripples could not form. Waves on a pond need a material—water—in which to travel. The material through which a wave travels is called a **medium.** Light is an electromagnetic wave and doesn't need a medium in which to travel. Electromagnetic waves can travel in a vacuum, as well as through materials such as air, water, and glass.

Light and Matter

What can you see when you are in a closed room with no windows and the lights are out? You can see nothing until you turn on a light or open a door to let in light from outside the room. Most objects around you do not give off light on their own. They can be seen only if light waves from another source bounce off them and into your eyes, as shown in **Figure 2.** The process of light striking an object and bouncing off is called **reflection.** Right now, you can see these words because light emitted by a source of light is reflecting from the page and into your eyes. Not all the light rays reflected from the page strike your eyes. Light rays striking the page are reflected in many directions, and only some of these rays enter your eyes.

Reading Check *What must happen for you to see most objects?*

TRY AT HOME Mini LAB

Observing Colors in the Dark

Procedure

1. Get six pieces of **paper** that are different colors and about 10 cm × 10 cm.
2. Darken a room and wait 10 min for your eyes to adjust to the darkness.
3. Write on each paper what color you think the paper is.
4. Turn on the lights and see if your night vision detected the colors.

Analysis

1. If the room were perfectly dark, what would you see? Explain.
2. Your eyes contain structures called rods and cones. Rods don't detect color, but need only a little light. Cones detect color, but need more light. Which structure was working in the dark room? Explain.

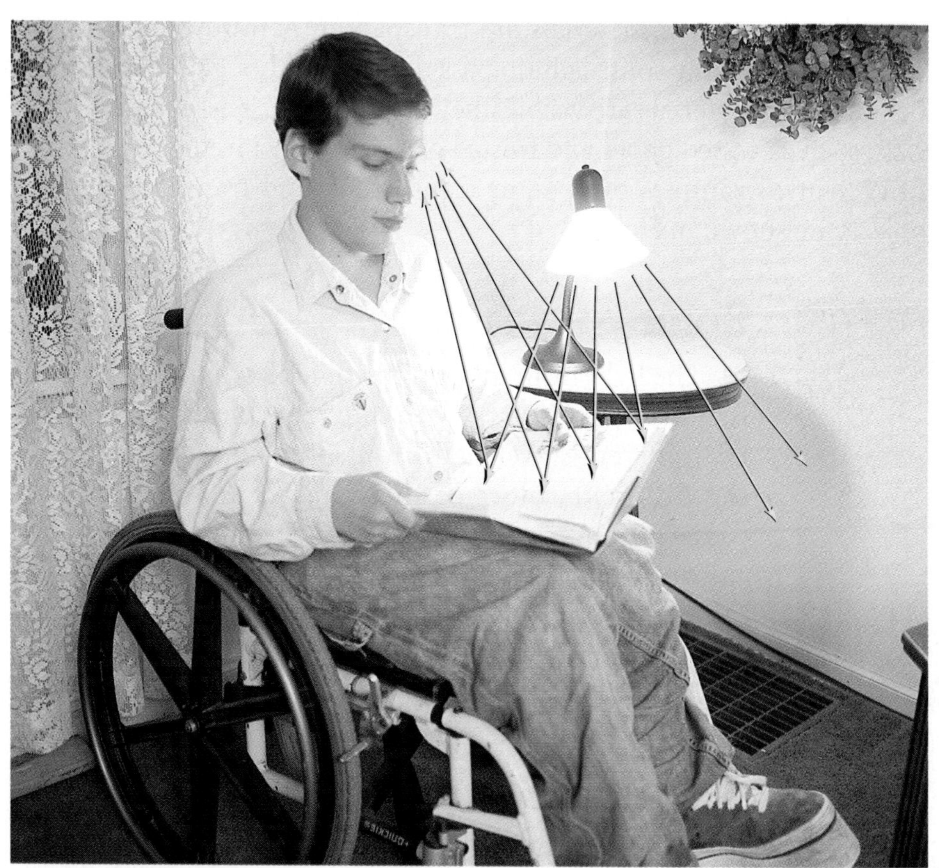

Figure 2
Light waves are given off by the lightbulb. Some of these light waves hit the page and are reflected. The student sees the page when some of these reflected waves enter the student's eyes.

A **An opaque object allows no light to pass through it.**

B **A translucent object allows some light to pass through it.**

C **A transparent object allows almost all light to pass through it.**

Figure 3
Materials are opaque, translucent, or transparent depending on how much light passes through them. *Which type of material reflects the least amount of light?*

Opaque, Translucent, and Transparent When light waves strike an object, some of the waves are absorbed by the object, some of the waves are reflected by it, and some of the light waves might pass through it. What happens to light when it strikes the object depends on the material that the object is made of.

All objects reflect and absorb some light waves. Materials that let no light pass through them are opaque (oh PAYK). You cannot see other objects through opaque materials. On the other hand, you clearly can see other objects through materials such as glass and clear plastic that allow nearly all the light that strikes them to pass through. These materials are transparent. A third type of material allows only some light to pass through. Although objects behind these materials are visible, they are not clear. These materials, such as waxed paper and frosted glass, are translucent (trans LEW sent). Examples of opaque, translucent, and transparent objects are shown in **Figure 3.**

Figure 4
A beam of white light passing through a prism is separated into many colors. *What colors can you see emerging from the prism?*

Color

The light from the Sun might look white, but it is a mixture of colors. Each different color of light is a different wavelength. You sometimes can see the different colors of the Sun's light when it passes through raindrops to make a rainbow. As shown in **Figure 4,** white light is separated into different colors when it passes through a prism. The colors in white light range from red to violet. When light waves from all these colors enter the eye at the same time, the brain interprets the mixture as being white.

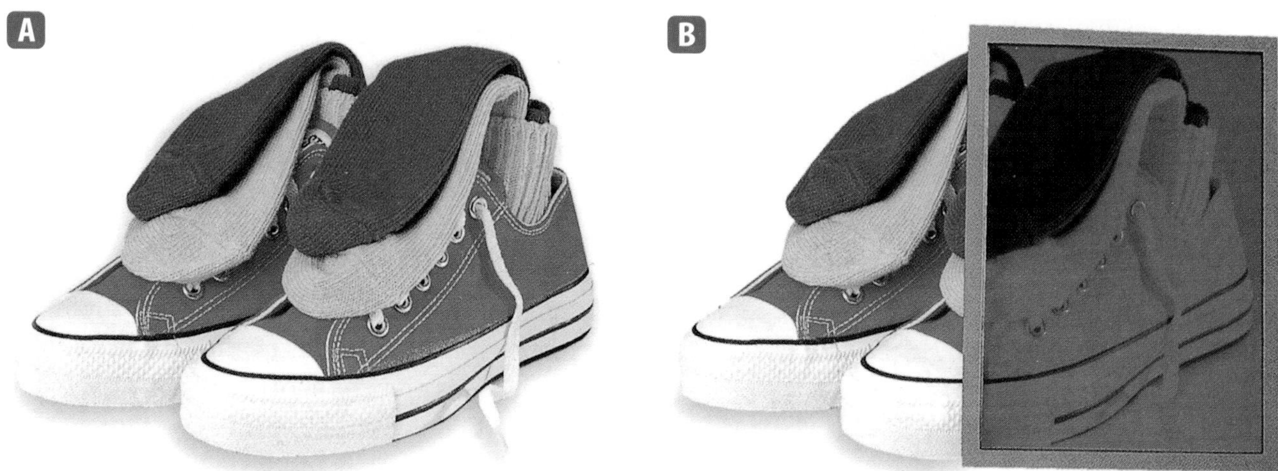

Why do Objects Have Color? Why does grass look green or a rose look red? When a mixture of light waves strikes an object that is not transparent, the object absorbs some of the light waves. Some of the light waves that are not absorbed are reflected. If an object reflects red waves and absorbs all the other waves, it looks red. Similarly, if an object looks blue, it reflects only blue light waves and absorbs all the others. An object that reflects all the light waves that strike it looks white, while one that reflects none of the light waves that strike it looks black. **Figure 5** shows gym shoes and socks as seen under white light and as seen when viewed through a red filter that allows only red light to pass through it.

Figure 5
The color of an object depends on the light waves it reflects.
A Examine the pair of gym shoes and socks as they are seen under white light. *Why do the socks look blue under white light?*
B The same shoes and socks were photographed through a red filter. *Why do the blue socks look black when viewed under red light?*

Primary Light Colors How many colors exist? People often say white light is made up of red, orange, yellow, green, blue, and violet light. This isn't completely true, though. Many more colors than this exist. In reality, most humans can distinguish thousands of colors, including some such as brown, pink, and purple, that are not found among the colors of the rainbow.

Light of almost any color can be made by mixing different amounts of red, green, and blue light. Red, green, and blue are known as the primary colors. Look at **Figure 6.** White light is produced where beams of red, green, and blue light overlap. Yellow light is produced where red and green light overlap. You see the color yellow because of the way your brain interprets the combination of the red and green light striking your eye. This combination of light waves looks the same as yellow light produced by a prism, even though these light waves have only a single wavelength.

Figure 6
By mixing light from the three primary colors—red, blue, and green—almost all of the visible colors can be made.

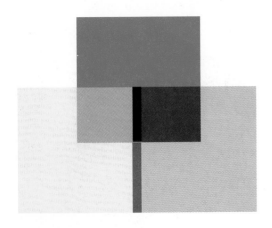

Figure 7
The three primary color pigments—yellow, magenta, and cyan—can form almost all the visible colors when mixed together in various amounts.

Primary Pigment Colors If you like to paint, you might mix two or more different colors to make a new color. Materials like paint that are used to change the color of other objects, such as the walls of a room or an artist's canvas, are called pigments. Mixing pigments together forms colors in a different way than mixing colored lights does.

Like all materials that appear to be colored, pigments absorb some light waves and reflect others. The color of the pigment you see is the color of the light waves that are reflected from it. However, the primary pigment colors are not red, blue, and green—they are yellow, magenta, and cyan. You can make almost any color by mixing different amounts of these primary pigment colors, as shown in **Figure 7.**

 **Reading Check** *What are the primary pigment colors?*

Although primary pigment colors are not the same as the primary light colors, they are related. Each primary pigment color results when a pigment absorbs a primary light color. For example, a yellow pigment absorbs blue light and it reflects red and green light, which you see as yellow. A magenta pigment, on the other hand, absorbs green light and reflects red and blue light, which you see as magenta. Each of the primary pigment colors is the same color as white light with one primary color removed.

Section 1 Assessment

1. At night in your room, you are reading a magazine. Describe the path light takes that enables you to see the page.
2. Do the light rays traveling outward from a light source carry energy? Explain.
3. What colors are reflected by an object that appears black? Explain.
4. What is the difference between primary light colors and primary pigment colors?
5. **Think Critically** When you're in direct sunlight, why do you feel cooler if you're wearing light-colored clothes than if you're wearing darker-colored clothes?

Skill Builder Activities

6. **Drawing Conclusions** A white plastic bowl and a black plastic bowl have been sitting in the sunlight. You observe that the black bowl feels warmer than the white bowl. From this information, conclude which of the bowls absorbs and which reflects more sunlight. **For more help, refer to the** Science Skill Handbook.
7. **Communicating** Read an article about the greenhouse effect and draw a diagram in your Science Journal explaining how the greenhouse effect involves absorption. **For more help, refer to the** Science Skill Handbook.

Reflection and Mirrors

The Law of Reflection

You've probably noticed your image on the surface of a pool or lake. If the surface of the water was smooth, you could see your face clearly. If the surface of the water was wavy, however, your face might have seemed distorted. The image you saw was the result of light reflecting from the surface and traveling to your eyes. How the light was reflected determined the sharpness of the image you saw.

When a light ray strikes a surface and is reflected as in **Figure 8,** the reflected ray obeys the law of reflection. Imagine a line that is drawn perpendicular to the surface where the light ray strikes. This line is called the normal to the surface. The incoming ray and the normal form an angle called the angle of incidence. The reflected light ray forms an angle with the normal called the angle of reflection. According to the **law of reflection,** the angle of incidence is equal to the angle of reflection. This is true for any surface, no matter what material it is made of.

As You Read

***What* You'll Learn**

- **Explain** how light is reflected from rough and smooth surfaces.
- **Determine** how mirrors form an image.
- **Describe** how concave and convex mirrors form an image.

Vocabulary

law of reflection
focal point
focal length

***Why* It's Important**

Mirrors can change the direction of light waves and enable you to see images, such as your own face, that normally would not be in view.

Reflection from Surfaces

Why can you see your reflection in some surfaces and not others? Why does a piece of shiny metal make a good mirror, but a piece of paper does not? The answers have to do with the smoothness of each surface.

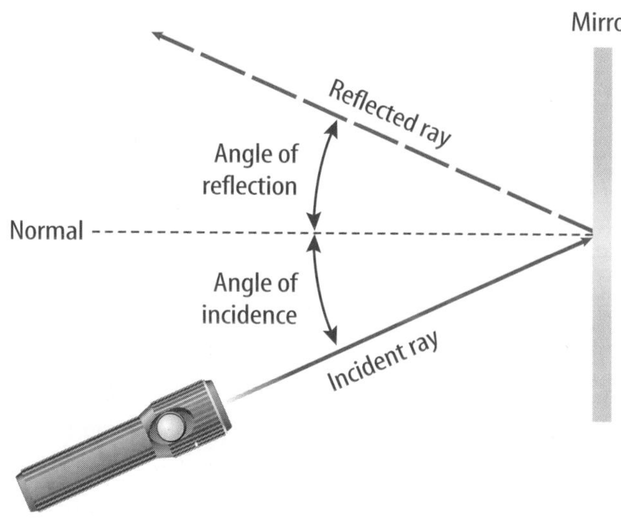

Figure 8
A light ray strikes a surface and is reflected. The angle of incidence is always equal to the angle of reflection. This is the law of reflection.

Figure 9
A highly magnified view of the surface of a paper towel shows that the surface is made of many cellulose wood fibers that make it rough and uneven.

Magnification: 35×

Regular and Diffuse Reflection Even though the surface of the paper might seem smooth, it's not as smooth as the surface of a mirror. **Figure 9** shows how rough the surface of a piece of paper looks when it is viewed under a microscope. The rough surface causes light rays to be reflected from it in many directions, as shown in **Figure 10A.** This uneven reflection of light waves from a rough surface is diffuse reflection. The smoother surfaces of mirrors, as shown in **Figure 10B,** reflect light waves in a much more regular way. For example, parallel rays remain parallel after they are reflected from a mirror. Reflection from mirrors is known as regular reflection. Light waves that are regularly reflected from a surface form the image you see in a mirror or any other smooth surface. Whether a surface is smooth or rough, every light ray that strikes it obeys the law of reflection.

Why does a rough surface cause a diffuse reflection?

Scattering of Light When diffuse reflection occurs, light waves that were traveling in a single direction are reflected, and then travel in many different directions. Scattering occurs when light waves traveling in one direction are made to travel in many different directions. Scattering also can occur when light waves strike small particles, such as dust. You may have seen dust particles floating in a beam of sunlight. When the light waves in the sunbeam strike a dust particle, they are scattered in all directions. You see the dust particle as bright specks of light when some of these scattered light waves enter your eye.

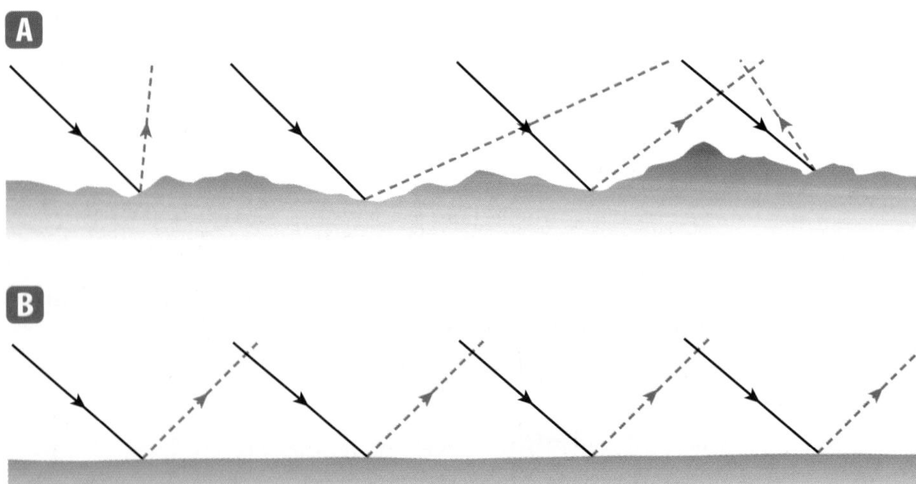

Figure 10
The roughness of a surface determines whether it looks like a mirror. A A rough surface causes parallel light rays to be reflected in many different directions. B A smooth surface causes parallel light rays to be reflected in a single direction. This type of surface looks like a mirror.

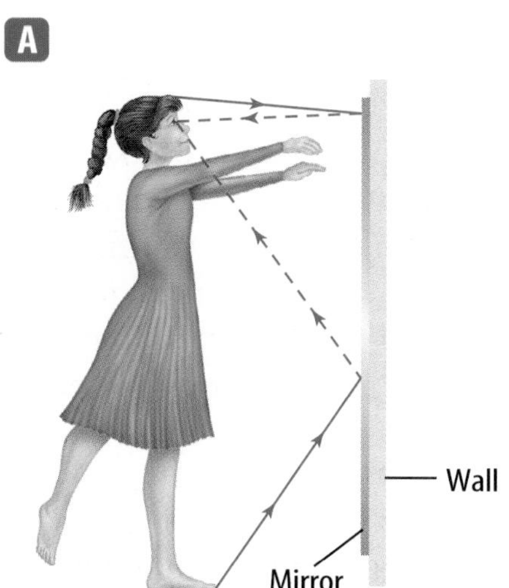

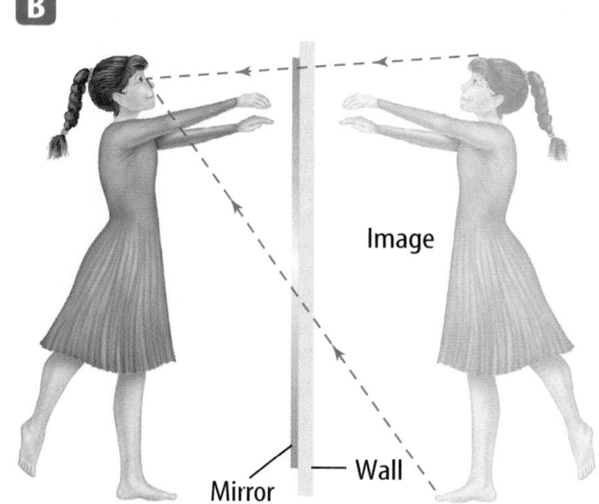

Figure 11
A plane mirror forms an image by changing the direction of light rays. A Light rays that bounce off of a person strike the mirror. Some of these light rays are reflected into the person's eye. B The light rays that are shown entering the person's eye seem to be coming from a person behind the mirror.

Reflection by Plane Mirrors Did you glance in the mirror before leaving for school this morning? If you did, you probably looked at your reflection in a plane mirror. A plane mirror is a mirror with a flat reflecting surface. In a plane mirror, your image looks much the same as it would in a photograph. However, you and your image are facing in opposite directions. This causes your left side and your right side to switch places on your mirror image. Also, your image seems to be coming from behind the mirror. How does a plane mirror form an image?

Reading Check *What is a plane mirror?*

Figure 11 shows a person looking into a plane mirror. Light waves from the Sun or another source of light strike each part of the person. These light rays bounce off of the person according to the law of reflection, and some of them strike the mirror. The rays that strike the mirror also are reflected according to the law of reflection. **Figure 11A** shows the path traveled by a few of the rays that have been reflected off the person and reflected back to the person's eye by the mirror.

The Image in a Plane Mirror Why does the image you see in a plane mirror seem to be behind the mirror? This is a result of how your brain processes the light rays that enter your eyes. Although the light rays bounced off the mirror's surface, your brain interprets them as having followed the path shown by the dashed lines in **Figure 11B.** In other words, your brain always assumes that light rays travel in straight lines without changing direction. This makes the reflected light rays look as if they are coming from behind the mirror, even though no source of light is there. The image also seems to be the same distance behind the mirror as the person is in front of the mirror.

When a particle like a marble or a basketball bounces off a surface, it obeys the law of reflection. Because light also obeys the law of reflection, people once thought that light must be a stream of particles. Today, experiments have shown that light can behave as though it were both a wave and a stream of energy bundles called photons. Read an article about photons and write a description in your Science Journal.

Concave and Convex Mirrors

Some mirrors are not flat. A concave mirror has a surface that is curved inward, like the inside of a spoon. Unlike plane mirrors, concave mirrors cause light rays to come together, or converge. A convex mirror, on the other hand, has a surface that curves outward, like the outside of a spoon. Convex mirrors cause light waves to spread out, or diverge. These two types of mirrors form images that are different from the images that are formed by plane mirrors. Examples of a concave and a convex mirror are shown in **Figure 12.**

Reading Check *What's the difference between a concave and convex mirror?*

Concave Mirrors The way in which a concave mirror forms an image is shown in **Figure 13.** A straight line drawn perpendicular to the center of a concave or convex mirror is called the optical axis. Light rays that travel parallel to the optical axis and strike the mirror are reflected so that they pass through a single point on the optical axis called the **focal point.** The distance along the optical axis from the center of the mirror to the focal point is called the **focal length.**

The image formed by a concave mirror depends on the position of the object relative to its focal point. If the object is farther from the mirror than the focal point, the image appears to be upside down, or inverted. The size of the image decreases as the object is moved farther away from the mirror. If the object is closer to the mirror than one focal length, the image is upright and gets smaller as the object moves closer to the mirror.

A concave mirror can produce a focused beam of light if a source of light is placed at the mirror's focal point, as shown in **Figure 13.** Flashlights and automobile headlights use concave mirrors to produce directed beams of light.

A

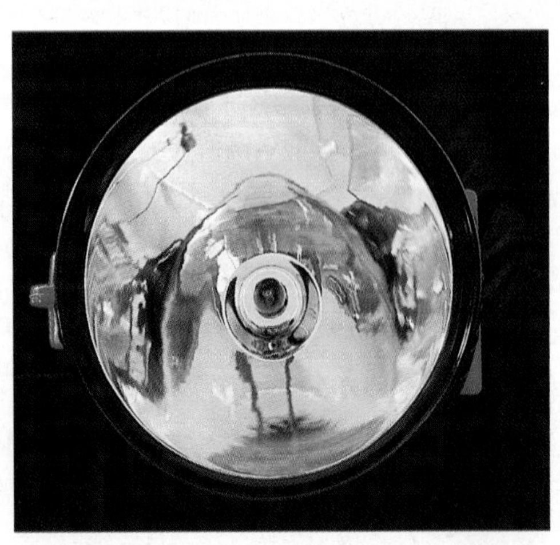

B

Figure 12
Not all mirrors are flat. A A concave mirror has a surface that's curved inward. B A convex mirror has a surface that's curved outward.

NATIONAL GEOGRAPHIC VISUALIZING REFLECTIONS IN CONCAVE MIRRORS

Figure 13

Glance into a flat plane mirror and you'll see an upright image of yourself. But look into a concave mirror, and you might see yourself larger than life, right side up, or upside down—or not at all! This is because the way a concave mirror forms an image depends on the position of an object in front of the mirror, as shown here.

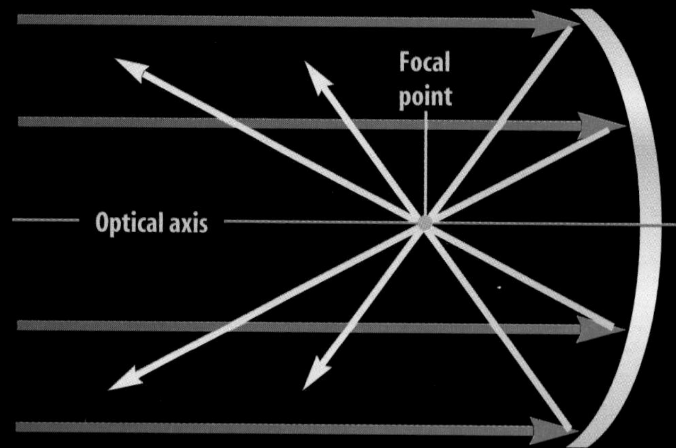

A concave mirror reflects all light rays traveling parallel to the optical axis so that they pass through the focal point.

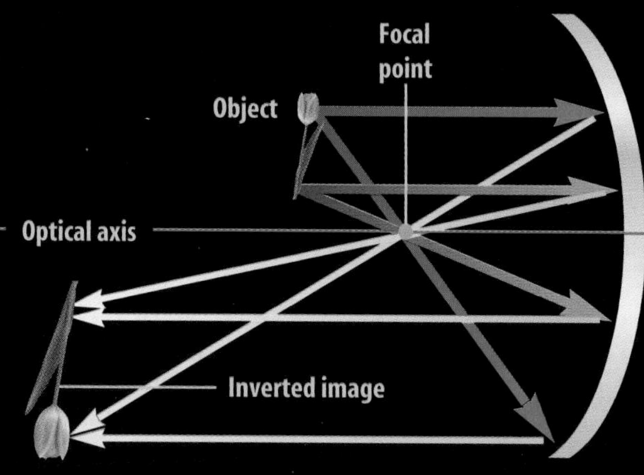

When an object, such as this flower, is placed beyond the focal point, the mirror forms an image that is inverted.

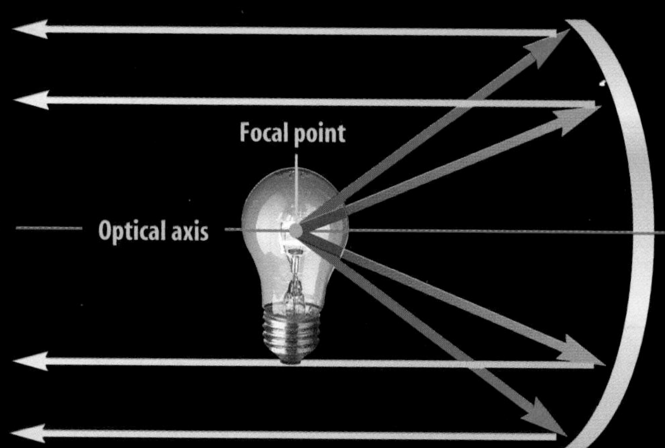

When a source of light is placed at the focal point, a beam of parallel light rays is formed. The concave mirror in a flashlight, for example, creates a beam of parallel light rays.

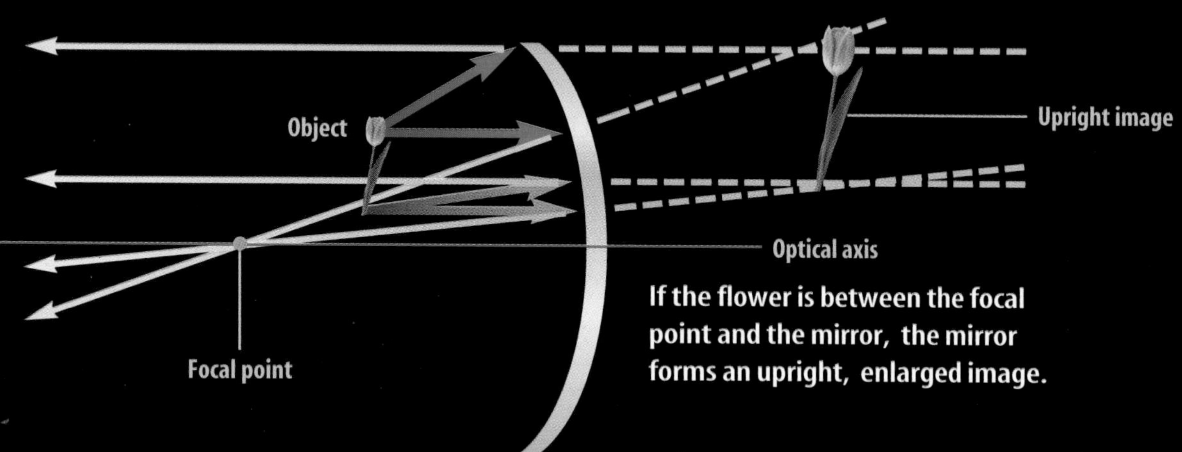

If the flower is between the focal point and the mirror, the mirror forms an upright, enlarged image.

Figure 14
A convex mirror always forms an image that is smaller than the object.

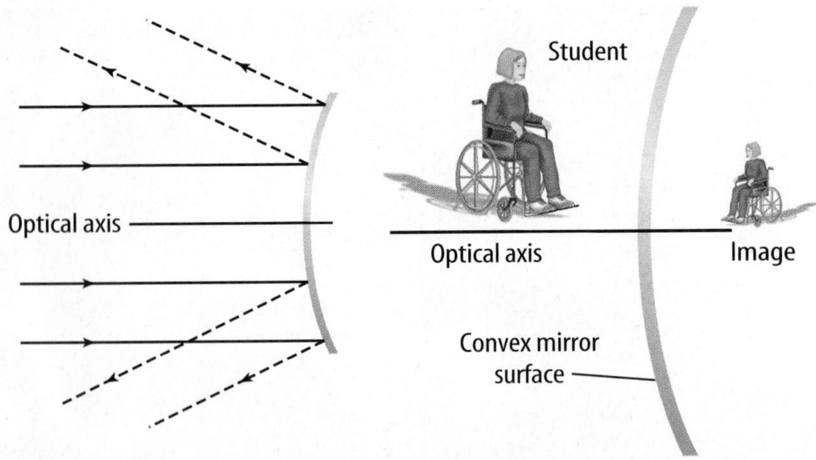

A **A convex mirror causes incoming light rays that are traveling parallel to the optical axis to spread apart after they are reflected.**

B **No matter how far the object is from a convex mirror, the image is always upright and smaller than the object.**

Convex Mirrors A convex mirror has a reflecting surface that curves outward. Because the reflecting surface curves outward, a convex mirror causes light rays to spread apart, or diverge, as shown in **Figure 14A.** Like the image formed by a plane mirror, the image formed by a convex mirror seems to be behind the mirror, as shown in **Figure 14B.** Also like a plane mirror, the image formed by a convex mirror is always upright. Unlike a plane mirror or a concave mirror, however, the image formed by a convex mirror is always smaller than the object.

Convex mirrors are used as security mirrors mounted above the aisles in stores and as outside rearview mirrors on cars, trucks and other vehicles. When used in this way, objects in the mirror seem smaller and farther away than they actually are. As a result, you can see a larger area reflected in a convex mirror. A convex mirror is said to have a larger angle of view than a plane mirror.

Section  Assessment

1. Describe how light reflects from rough and smooth surfaces.
2. Why are concave mirrors used in flashlights and automobile headlights?
3. What happens to the image in a concave mirror when an object is closer to the mirror than one focal length?
4. Why do side mirrors on cars carry the warning that objects are closer than they appear to be?
5. **Think Critically** The surface of a car is covered with dust and looks dull. After the car is washed and waxed, you can see your image reflected in the car's surface. Explain.

Skill Builder Activities

6. **Forming Hypotheses** When you look at a window at night, you sometimes can see two images of yourself reflected from the window. Make a hypothesis to explain why two images are seen. **For more help, refer to the Science Skill Handbook.**
7. **Using an Electronic Spreadsheet** Design a table using spreadsheet software to compare the images formed by plane, concave, and convex mirrors. Include in your table how the images depend on the distance of the object from the mirror. **For more help, refer to the Technology Skill Handbook.**

Activity

Reflection from a Plane Mirror

A light ray strikes the surface of a plane mirror and is reflected. Does a relationship exist between the direction of the incoming light ray and the direction of the reflected light ray?

What You'll Investigate

How does the angle of incidence compare with the angle of reflection for a plane mirror?

Materials

flashlight
protractor
metric ruler
scissors
tape
small plane mirror, at least 10 cm on a side
black construction paper
modeling clay
white unlined paper

Goals

- **Measure** the angle of incidence and the angle of reflection for a light ray reflected from a plane mirror.

Safety Precautions   

Procedure

1. With the scissors, cut a slit in the construction paper and tape it over the flashlight lens.
2. Place the mirror at one end of the unlined paper. Push the mirror into the lump of clay so it stands vertically, and tilt the mirror so it leans slightly toward the table.
3. **Measure** with the ruler to find the center of the bottom edge of the mirror and mark it. Then use the protractor and the ruler to draw a line on the paper perpendicular to the mirror from the mark. Label this line *P*.
4. Using the protractor and the ruler, draw lines on the paper outward from the mark at the center of the mirror at angles of 30°, 45°, and 60° to line *P*.

5. Turn on the flashlight and place it so the beam is along the 60° line. This is the angle of incidence. Locate the reflected beam on the paper, and measure the angle that the reflected beam makes with line *P*. Record this angle in your data table. This is the angle of reflection. If you cannot see the reflected beam, slightly increase the tilt of the mirror.
6. Repeat step 5 for the 30°, 45°, and *P* lines.

Conclude and Apply

1. What happened to the beam of light when it was shined along line *P*?
2. What can you infer about the relationship between the angle of incidence and the angle of reflection?

Communicating Your Data

Make a poster that shows your measured angles of reflection for angles of incidence of 30°, 45°, and 60°. Write the relationship between the angles of incidence and reflection at the bottom.

SECTION 3

Refraction and Lenses

As You Read

What You'll Learn

- **Determine** why light rays refract.
- **Explain** how convex and concave lenses form images.

Vocabulary

refraction
lens
convex lens
concave lens

Why It's Important

Many of the images you see every day in photographs, on TV, and in movies are made using lenses.

Refraction

Objects that are in water can sometimes look strange. A pencil in a glass of water sometimes looks as if it's bent, or as if the part of the pencil in air is shifted compared to the part in water. A penny that can't be seen at the bottom of a cup suddenly appears as you add water to the cup. Illusions such as these are due to the bending of light rays as they pass from one material to another. What causes light rays to change direction?

The Speeds of Light

The speed of light in empty space is about 300 million m/s. Light passing through a material such as air, water, or glass, however, travels more slowly than this. This is because the atoms that make up the material interact with the light waves and slow them down. **Figure 15** compares the speed of light in some different materials.

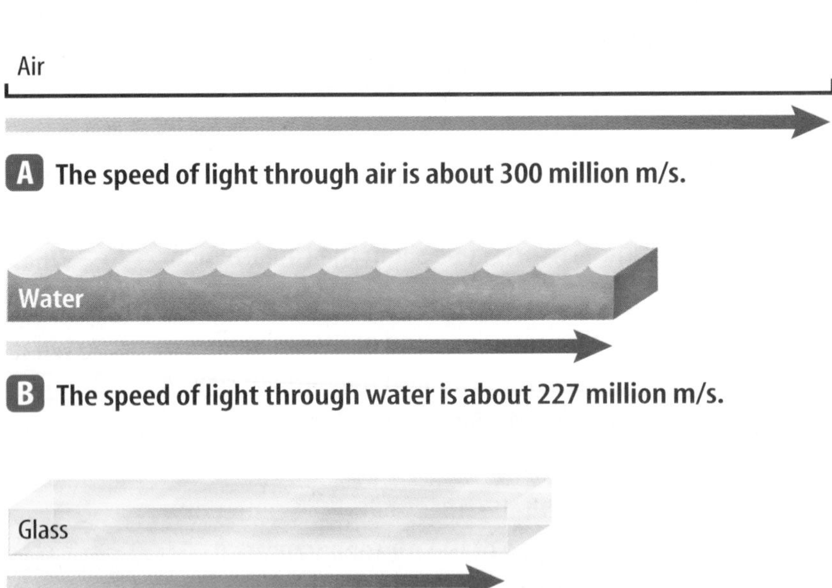

A The speed of light through air is about 300 million m/s.

B The speed of light through water is about 227 million m/s.

C The speed of light through glass is about 197 million m/s.

D The speed of light through diamond is about 125 million m/s.

Figure 15
Light travels at different speeds in different materials.

The Refraction of Light Waves

Light rays from the part of a pencil that is underwater travel through water, glass, and then air before they reach your eye. The speed of light is different in each of these mediums. What happens when a light wave travels from one medium into another in which its speed is different? If the wave is traveling at an angle to the boundary between the two media, it changes direction, or bends. This bending is due to the change in speed the wave undergoes as it moves from one medium into the other. The bending of light waves due to a change in speed is called **refraction.** **Figure 16** shows an example of refraction. The greater the change in speed is, the more the light wave bends, or refracts.

Reading Check *What causes light to bend?*

Figure 16
A light ray is bent as it travels from air into water. *In which medium does light travel more slowly?*

Why does a change in speed cause the light wave to bend? Think about what happens to the wheels of a car as they move from pavement to mud at an angle, as in **Figure 17.** The wheels slip a little in the mud and don't move forward as fast as they do on the pavement. The wheel that enters the mud first gets slowed down a little, but the other wheel on that axle continues at the original speed. The difference in speed between the two wheels then causes the wheel axle to turn, so the car turns a little. Light waves behave in the same way.

Imagine again a light wave traveling at an angle from air into water. The first part of the wave to enter the water is slowed, just as the car wheel that first hit the mud was slowed. The rest of the wave keeps slowing down as it moves from the air into the water. As long as one part of the light wave is moving faster than the rest of the wave, the wave continues to bend.

Figure 17
An axle turns as the wheels cross the boundary between pavement and mud. *How would the axle turn if the wheels were going from mud to pavement?*

Convex and Concave Lenses

Do you like photographing your friends and family? Have you ever watched a bird through binoculars or peered at something tiny through a magnifying glass? All of these activities involve the use of lenses. A **lens** is a transparent object with at least one curved side that causes light to bend. The amount of bending can be controlled by making the sides of the lenses more or less curved. The more curved the sides of a lens are, the more light will be bent after it enters the lens.

Figure 18
A convex lens forms an image that depends on the distance from the object to the lens.

A **Light rays that are parallel to the optical axis are bent so they pass through the focal point.**

B **If the object is more than two focal lengths from the lens, the image formed is smaller than the object and inverted.**

C **If the object is closer to the lens than one focal length, the image formed is enlarged and upright.**

Convex Lenses A lens that is thicker in the center than at the edges is a **convex lens.** In a convex lens, light rays traveling parallel to the optical axis are bent so they meet at the focal point, as shown in **Figure 18A.** The more curved the lens is, the closer the focal point is to the lens, and so the shorter the focal length of the lens is. Because convex lenses cause light waves to meet, they also are called converging lenses.

The image formed by a convex lens is similar to the image formed by a concave mirror. For both, the type of image depends on how far the object is from the mirror or lens. Look at **Figure 18B.** If the object is farther than two focal lengths from the lens, the image seen through the lens is inverted and smaller than the object.

Reading Check *How can a convex lens be used to make objects appear upside down?*

If the object is closer to the lens than one focal length, then the image formed is right-side up and larger than the object, as shown in **Figure 18C.** A magnifying glass forms an image in this way. As long as the magnifying glass is less than one focal length from the object, you can make the image larger by moving the magnifying glass away from the object.

Research Visit the Glencoe Science web site at **science.glencoe.com** for information about the optical devices that use convex lenses. Prepare a poster or other presentation for your class describing some of these devices.

Concave Lenses A lens that is thicker at the edges than in the middle is a **concave lens.** A concave lens also is called a diverging lens. **Figure 19** shows how light rays traveling parallel to the optical axis are bent after passing through a concave lens.

A concave lens causes light rays to diverge, so light rays are not brought to a focus. The type of image that is formed by a concave lens is similar to one that is formed by a convex mirror. The image is upright and smaller than the object.

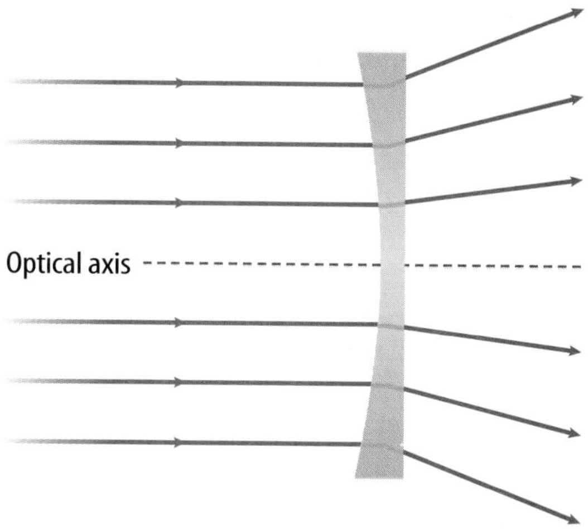

Figure 19
A concave lens causes light rays traveling parallel to the optical axis to diverge.

Total Internal Reflection

When you look at a glass window, you sometimes can see your reflection in the window. You see a reflection because some of the light waves reflected from you are reflected back to your eyes when they strike the window. This is an example of a partial reflection—only some of the light waves striking the window are reflected. However, sometimes all the light waves that strike the boundary between two transparent materials can be reflected. This process is called total internal reflection.

The Critical Angle To see how total internal reflection occurs, look at **Figure 20.** Light travels faster in air than in water, and the refracted beam is bent away from the normal. As the angle between the incident beam and the normal increases, the refracted beam bends closer to the air-water boundary. At the same time, more of the light energy striking the boundary is reflected and less light energy passes into the air.

If a light beam in water strikes the boundary so that the angle with the normal is greater than an angle called the critical angle, total internal reflection occurs. Then all the light waves are reflected at the air-water boundary, just as if a mirror were there. The size of the critical angle depends on the two materials involved. For light passing from water to air the critical angle is about 48 degrees.

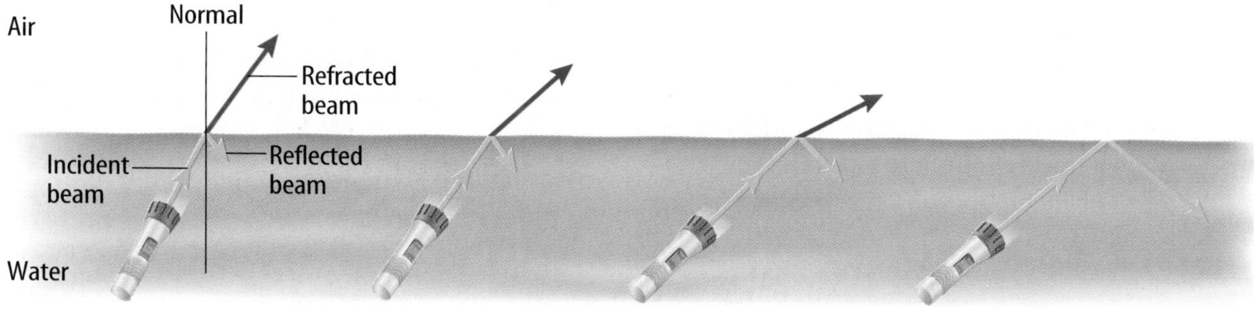

Figure 20
When a light beam passes from one medium to another, some of its energy is reflected (red) and some is refracted (blue). As the incident beam makes a larger angle with the normal, less light energy is refracted, and more is reflected. At the critical angle, all the light is reflected.

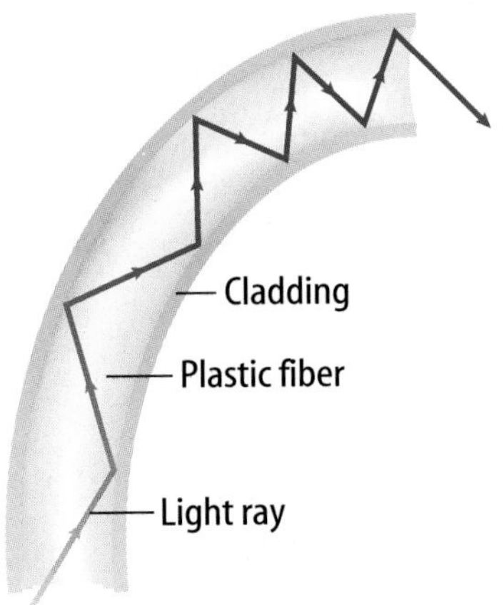

Figure 21
An optical fiber is made of materials that cause total internal reflection to occur. As a result, a light beam can travel for many kilometers through an optical fiber and lose almost no energy.

Optical Fibers

A device called an optical fiber can make a light beam travel in a path that is curved or even twisted. Optical fibers are thin, flexible, transparent fibers. An optical fiber is like a light pipe. Even if the fiber is bent, light that enters one end of the fiber comes out the other end.

Total internal reflection makes light transmission in optical fibers possible. A thin fiber of glass or plastic is covered with another material called cladding in which light travels faster. When light strikes the boundary between the fiber and the cladding, total internal reflection can occur. In this way, the beam bounces along inside the fiber as shown in **Figure 21**.

Using Optical Fibers Optical fibers are used most commonly in communications. For example, television programs and computer information can be coded in light signals. These signals then can be sent from one place to another using optical fibers. Because of total internal reflection, signals can't leak from one fiber to another and interfere with others. As a result, the signal is transmitted clearly. Phone conversations also can be changed into light and sent along optical fibers. One optical fiber the thickness of a human hair can carry thousands of phone conversations.

Section  Assessment

1. How is the image that is formed by a concave lens similar to the image that is formed by a convex mirror?
2. To magnify an object, would you use a convex lens or a concave lens?
3. Describe two ways, using convex and concave lenses, to form an image that is smaller than the object.
4. What are some uses for convex and concave lenses?
5. **Think Critically** A light wave is bent more when it travels from air to glass than when it travels from air to water. Is the speed of light greater in water or glass? Explain.

Skill Builder Activities

6. **Predicting** Air that is cool is more dense than air that is warm. Look at **Figure 15** and predict whether the speed of light is faster in warm air or cool air. **For more help, refer to the Science Skill Handbook.**
7. **Solving One-Step Equations** Earth is about 150 million km from the Sun. Use the formula

$$\text{Distance} = \text{speed} \times \text{time}$$

to calculate how many seconds it takes a beam of light to travel from Earth to the Sun. About how many minutes does it take? About how many hours does it take? **For more help, refer to the Math Skill Handbook.**

Using Mirrors and Lenses

Microscopes

For almost 500 years, lenses have been used to observe objects that are too small to be seen with the unaided eye. The first microscopes were simple and magnified less than 100 times. Today a compound microscope like the one in **Figure 22A** uses a combination of lenses to magnify objects by as much as 2,500 times.

Figure 22B shows how a microscope forms an image. An object, such as an insect or a drop of water from a pond, is placed close to a convex lens called the objective lens. This lens produces an enlarged image inside the microscope tube. The light rays from that image then pass through a second convex lens called the eyepiece lens. This lens further magnifies the image formed by the objective lens. By using two lenses, a much larger image is formed than a single lens can produce.

As You Read

What You'll Learn

- **Explain** how microscopes magnify objects.
- **Explain** how telescopes make distant objects visible.
- **Describe** how a camera works.

Vocabulary

refracting telescope
reflecting telescope

Why It's Important

Microscopes and telescopes are used to view parts of the universe that can't be seen with the unaided eye.

Figure 22
A compound microscope uses lenses to magnify objects.

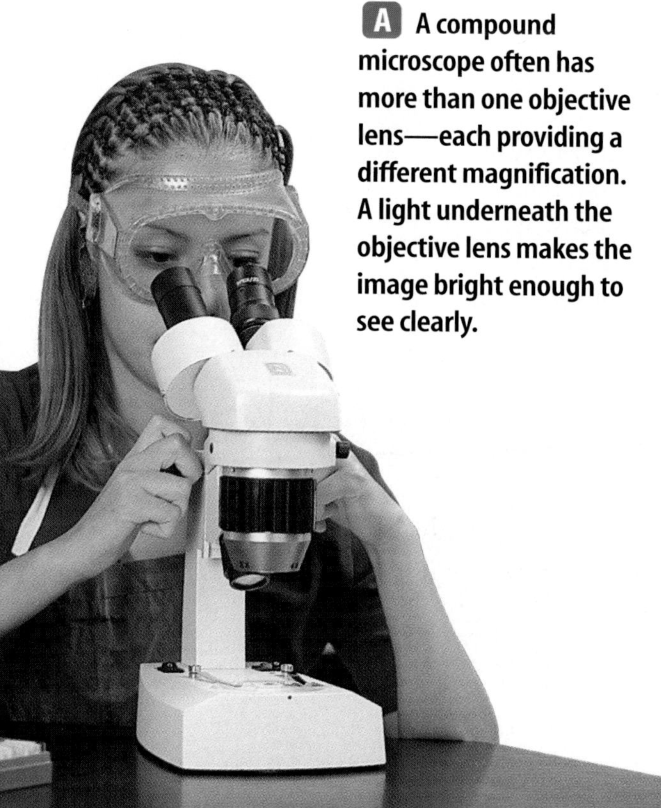

A A compound microscope often has more than one objective lens—each providing a different magnification. A light underneath the objective lens makes the image bright enough to see clearly.

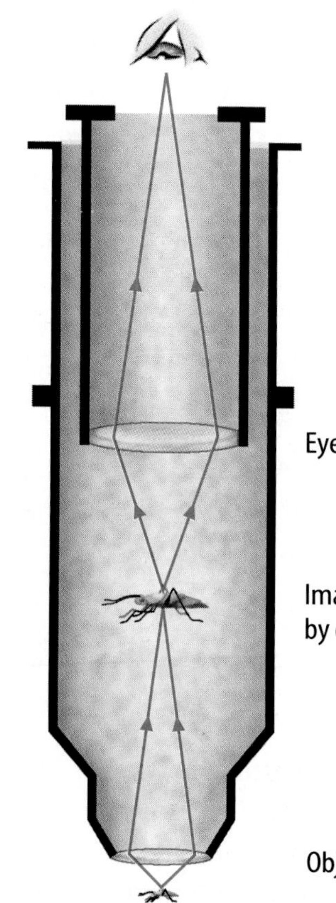

B The objective lens in a compound microscope forms an enlarged image, which is then magnified by the eyepiece lens.

Mini LAB

Forming an Image with a Lens

Procedure

1. Fill a **glass test tube** with **water** and seal it with a **stopper.**
2. Write your name on a **10-cm × 10-cm card.** Lay the test tube on the card and observe the appearance of your name.
3. Hold the test tube about 1 cm above the card and observe the appearance of your name. Record your observations.
4. Observe what happens to your name as you slowly move the test tube away from the card. Record your observations.

Analysis

1. Is the water-filled test tube a concave lens or a convex lens?
2. Compare the image that formed when the test tube was close to the card with the image that formed when the test tube was far from the card.

Telescopes

Just as microscopes are used to magnify very small objects, telescopes are used to examine objects that are very far away. The first telescopes were made at about the same time as the first microscopes. Much of what is known about the Moon, the solar system, and the distant universe has come from images and other information gathered by telescopes.

Refracting Telescopes The simplest **refracting telescopes** use two convex lenses to form an image of a distant object. Just as in a compound microscope, light passes through an objective lens that forms an image. That image is then magnified by an eyepiece, as shown in **Figure 23A.**

An important difference between a telescope and a microscope is the size of the objective lens. The main purpose of a telescope is not to magnify an image. A telescope's main purpose is to gather as much light as possible from distant objects. The larger an objective lens is, the more light that can enter it. This makes images of faraway objects look brighter and more detailed when they are magnified by the eyepiece. With a large enough objective lens, it's possible to see stars and galaxies that are many trillions of kilometers away. **Figure 23B** shows the largest refracting telescope ever made.

Reading Check *How does a telescope's objective lens enable distant objects to be seen?*

Figure 23 Refracting telescopes use a large objective lens to gather light from distant objects.

Objective lens

Eyepiece lens

A A refracting telescope is made from an objective lens and an eyepiece. The objective lens forms an image that is magnified by the eyepiece.

B The refracting telescope at the Yerkes Observatory in Wisconsin has the largest objective lens in the world. It has a diameter of about 1 m.

Figure 24
Reflecting telescopes gather light by using a concave mirror.

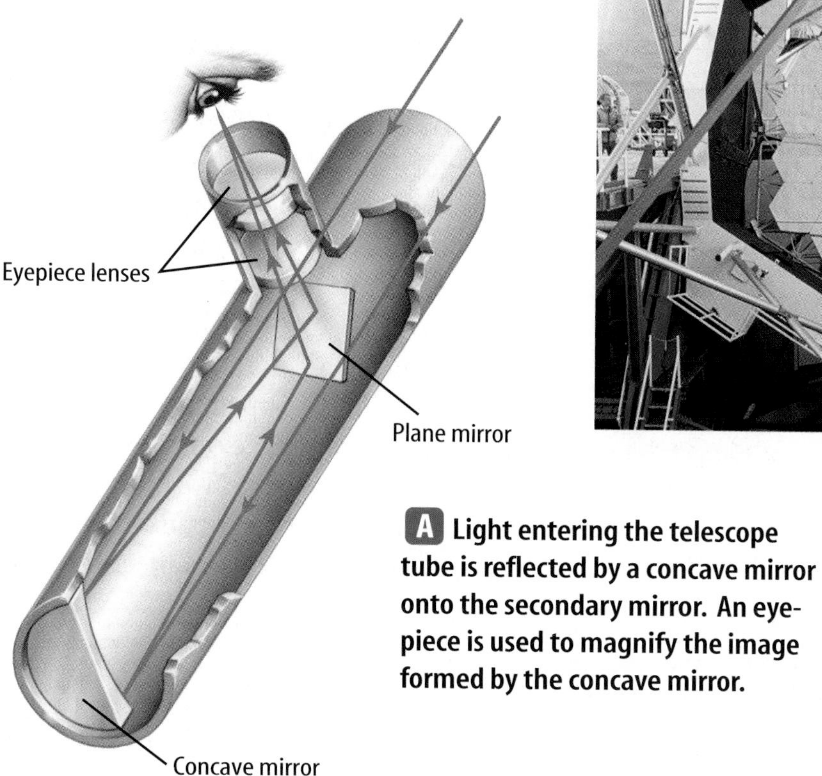

A Light entering the telescope tube is reflected by a concave mirror onto the secondary mirror. An eyepiece is used to magnify the image formed by the concave mirror.

B The Keck telescope in Mauna Kea, Hawaii, is the largest reflecting telescope in the world.

Reflecting Telescopes Refracting telescopes have size limitations. One problem is that the objective lens can be supported only around its edges. If the lens is extremely large, it cannot be supported enough to keep the glass from sagging slightly under its own weight. This causes the image that the lens forms to become distorted.

Reflecting telescopes can be made much larger than refracting telescopes. **Reflecting telescopes** have a concave mirror instead of a concave objective lens to gather the light from distant objects. As shown in **Figure 24A,** the large concave mirror focuses light onto a secondary mirror that directs it to the eyepiece, which magnifies the image.

Because only the one reflecting surface on the mirror needs to be made carefully and kept clean, telescope mirrors are less expensive to make and maintain than lenses of a similar size. Also, mirrors can be supported not only at their edges but also on their back sides. They can be made much larger without sagging under their own weight. The Keck telescope in Hawaii, shown in **Figure 24B,** is the largest reflecting telescope in the world. Its large concave mirror is 10 m in diameter, and is made of 36 six-sided segments. Each segment is 1.8 m in size and the segments are pieced together to form the mirror.

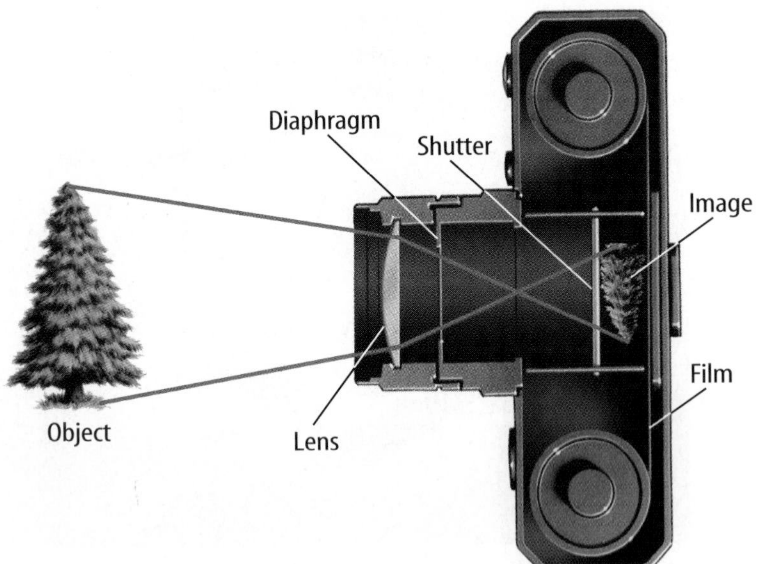

Figure 25
A camera uses a convex lens to form an image on a piece of light-sensitive film. The image formed by a camera lens is smaller than the object and is inverted.

Cameras

You probably see photographs taken by cameras almost every day. A typical camera uses a convex lens to form an image on a section of film, just as your eye's lens focuses an image on your retina. The convex lens has a short focal length so that it forms an image that is smaller than the object and inverted on the film. Look at the camera shown in **Figure 25.** When the shutter is open, the convex lens focuses an image on a piece of film that is sensitive to light. Light-sensitive film contains chemicals that undergo chemical reactions when light hits it. The brighter parts of the image affect the film more than the darker parts do.

Reading Check *What type of lens does a camera use?*

If too much light strikes the film, the image formed on the film is overexposed and looks washed out. On the other hand, if too little light reaches the film, the photograph might be too dark. To control how much light reaches the film, many cameras have a device called a diaphragm. The diaphragm is opened to let more light onto the film and closed to reduce the amount of light that strikes the film.

Lasers

Perhaps you've seen the narrow, intense beams of laser light used in a laser light show. Intense laser beams are also used for different kinds of surgery. Why can laser beams be so intense? One reason is that a laser beam doesn't spread out as much as ordinary light as it travels.

Spreading Light Beams Suppose you shine a flashlight on a wall in a darkened room. The size of the spot of light on the wall depends on the distance between the flashlight and the wall. As the flashlight moves farther from the wall, the spot of light gets larger. This is because the beam of light produced by the flashlight spreads out as it travels. As a result, the energy carried by the light beam is spread over an increasingly larger area as the distance from the flashlight gets larger. As the energy is spread over a larger area, the energy becomes less concentrated and the intensity of the beam decreases.

Figure 26
Laser light is different from the light produced by a lightbulb.

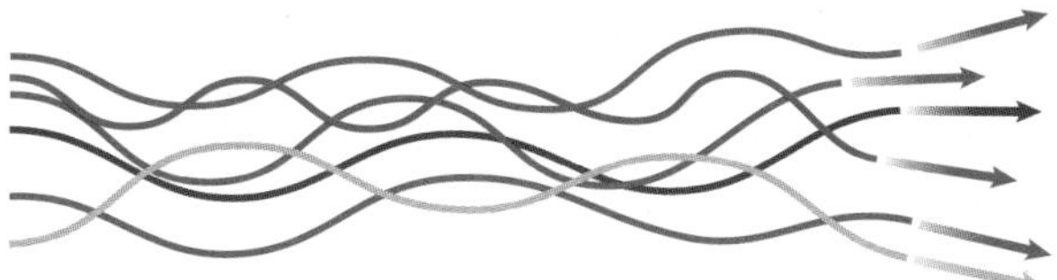

A **The light from a bulb contains waves with many different wavelengths that are out of phase and traveling in different directions.**

B **The light from a laser contains waves with only one wavelength that are in phase and traveling in the same direction.**

Using Laser Light Laser light is different from the light produced by the flashlight in several ways, as shown in **Figure 26.** One difference is that in a beam of laser light, the crests and troughs of the light waves overlap, so the waves are in phase.

Because a laser beam doesn't spread out as much as ordinary light, a large amount of energy can be applied to a very small area. This property enables lasers to be used for cutting and welding materials and as a replacement for scalpels in surgery. Less intense laser light is used for such applications as reading and writing to CDs or in grocery store bar-code readers. Surveyors and builders use lasers to measure distances, angles, and heights. Laser beams also are used to transmit information through space or through optical fibers.

Section  Assessment

1. How is a compound microscope different from a magnifying lens?
2. Compare and contrast reflecting and refracting telescopes. Why aren't refracting telescopes bigger than reflecting telescopes?
3. Why is the objective lens of a refracting telescope bigger than the objective lens of a microscope?
4. Describe how laser light is different from the light produced by a light bulb.
5. **Think Critically** Could a camera with a concave lens instead of a convex lens still take pictures? Explain.

Skill Builder Activities

6. **Communicating** Using words, pictures, or other media, think of a way to explain to a friend how convex and concave lenses work. **For more help, refer to the** Science Skill Handbook.
7. **Solving One-Step Equations** The size of an image is related to the magnification of an optical instrument by the following formula:

   $$\text{Image size} = \text{magnification} \times \text{object size}$$

   A blood cell has a diameter of about 0.001 cm. How large is the image formed by a microscope with a magnification of 1,000? **For more help, refer to the** Math Skill Handbook.

Activity

Image Formation by a Convex Lens

The type of image formed by a convex lens, also called a converging lens, is related to the distance of the object from the lens. This distance is called the object distance. The location of the image also is related to the distance of the object from the lens. The distance from the lens to the image is called the image distance. What happens to the position of the image as the object gets nearer or farther from the lens?

What You'll Investigate

How are the image distance and object distance related for a convex lens?

Materials

convex lens
modeling clay
meterstick
flashlight
masking tape
20-cm square piece of cardboard with a white surface

Goals

- **Measure** the image distance as the object distance changes.
- **Observe** the type of image formed as the object distance changes.

Safety Precautions

Procedure

1. **Design** a data table to record your data. Make three columns in your table—one column for the object distance, another for the image distance, and the third for the type of image.
2. Use the modeling clay to make the lens stand upright on the lab table.
3. Form the letter *F* on the glass surface of the flashlight with masking tape.
4. Turn on the flashlight and place it 1 m from the lens. Position the flashlight so the flashlight beam is shining through the lens.
5. **Record** the distance from the flashlight to the lens in the object distance column in your data table.
6. Hold the cardboard vertically upright on the other side of the lens, and move it back and forth until a sharp image of the letter *F* is obtained.

Convex Lens Data

Object Distance (m)	Image Distance (m)	Image Type

7. **Measure** the distance of the card from the lens using the meterstick, and record this distance in the Image Distance column in your data table.
8. **Record** in the third column of your data table whether the image is upright or inverted, and smaller or larger.
9. Repeat steps 4 through 8 for object distances of 0.50 m and 0.25 m and record your data in your data table.

Conclude and Apply

1. How did the image distance change as the object distance decreased?
2. How did the image change as the object distance decreased?
3. What would happen to the size of the image if the flashlight were much farther away than 1 m?

Demonstrate this activity to a third-grade class and explain how it works. **For more help, refer to the** Science Skill Handbook.

Oops! Accidents in SCIENCE

SOMETIMES GREAT DISCOVERIES HAPPEN BY ACCIDENT!

Eyeglasses

"It is not yet twenty years since the art of making spectacles, one of the most useful arts on Earth, was discovered. I, myself, have seen and conversed with the man who made them first."

This quote from an Italian monk dates back to 1306 and is one of the first historical records to refer to eyeglasses. Unfortunately, the monk, Giordano, never actually named the man he met. Thus, the inventor of eyeglasses—one of the most widely used forms of technology today—remains unknown.

The mystery exists, in part, because different cultures in different places used some type of magnifying tool to improve their vision. These tools eventually merged into what today is recognized as a pair of glasses. For example, a rock-crystal lens, made by early Assyrians who lived 3,500 years ago in what is now Iraq, may have been used to improve vision. About 2,000 years ago, the Roman writer Seneca looked through a glass globe of water to make the letters appear bigger in the books he read. By the tenth century, glasses were invented in China, but they were used to keep away bad luck, not to improve vision. Trade between China and Europe, however, likely led some unknown inventor to come up with an idea. The inventor fused two metal-ringed magnifying lenses together so they could perch on the nose.

In 1456, the printing press was invented. Large numbers of books could now be printed quickly and more cheaply than ever before. In Europe, eyeglasses began to appear in paintings of scholars, clergy, and the upper classes—the only people who knew how to read at the time. Although the ability to read spread fairly quickly, eyeglasses were so expensive that only the rich could afford them. In the early 1700s, for example, glasses cost roughly $200, which is comparable to thousands of dollars today. By the mid-1800s, improvements in manufacturing techniques made eyeglasses much less expensive to make, and thus this important invention became widely available to people of all walks of life.

Cheryl Landry at work with a Bosnian teenage soldier

Inventor Unknown

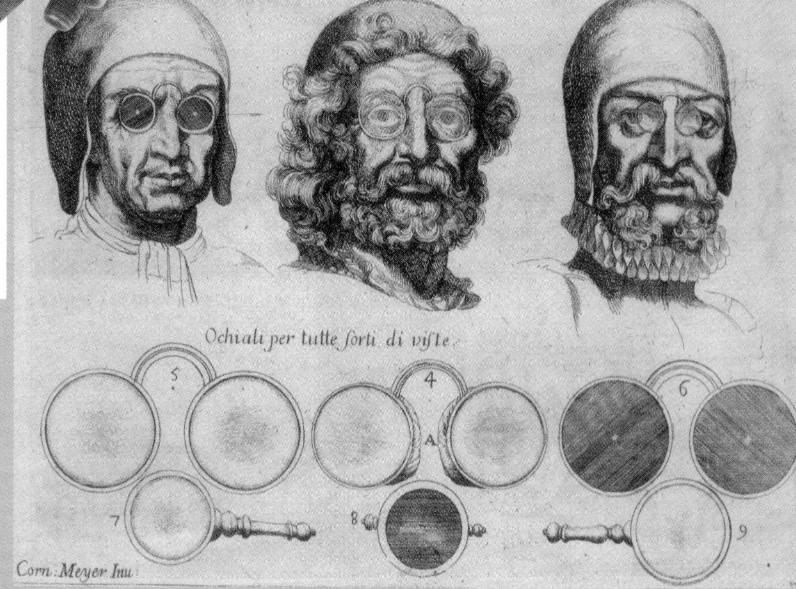

This Italian engraving from the 1600s shows glasses of all strengths.

How Eyeglasses Work

Eyeglasses are used to correct farsightedness and nearsightedness, as well as other vision problems. Farsighted people have difficulty seeing things close up because light rays from nearby objects do not converge enough to form an image on the retina. This problem can be corrected by using convex lenses that cause light rays to converge before they enter the eye. Nearsighted people have problems seeing distant objects because light rays from far-away objects are focused in front of the retina. Concave lenses that cause light rays to diverge are used to correct this vision problem.

CONNECTIONS **Research** In many parts of the world, people have no vision care, and eye diseases and poor vision go untreated. Research the work of groups that bring eye care to people. Start with eye doctor Cheryl Landry, who works with the Bosnian Children's Fund.

SCIENCE *Online*

For more information, visit science.glencoe.com

Chapter 14 Study Guide

Reviewing Main Ideas

Section 1 Properties of Light

1. Light is a wave that can travel through different materials, including a vacuum.
2. When a light wave strikes an object, some of the light wave's energy is reflected, some is absorbed, and some might be transmitted through the object.
3. The color of a light wave depends on its wavelength. The color of an object depends on which wavelengths of light are reflected by the object. *Why does this flower look red?*

4. Almost any color can be made by mixing the primary light colors or the primary pigment colors.

Section 2 Reflection and Mirrors

1. Light reflected from the surface of an object obeys the law of reflection: the angle of incidence equals the angle of reflection.
2. Diffuse reflection occurs when a surface is rough. Regular reflection occurs from very smooth surfaces and produces a clear, mirrorlike image. *Is the image in the photo a diffuse reflection?*

3. Concave mirrors cause light waves to converge, or meet. Convex mirrors cause light waves to diverge, or spread apart.

Section 3 Refraction and Lenses

1. Light waves can change speed when they travel from one medium to another. The waves bend, or refract, at the boundary between the two media.
2. A convex lens causes light waves to converge, and a concave lens causes light waves to diverge. *What would happen to the image of the insect if the magnifying glass in the photo were moved farther away?*

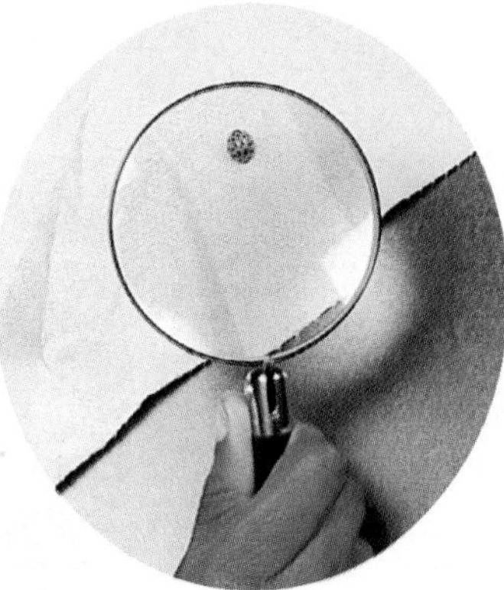

Section 4 Using Mirrors and Lenses

1. A compound microscope is used to enlarge small objects. A convex objective lens forms an enlarged image that is further enlarged by an eyepiece.
2. Most telescopes today are reflecting telescopes, which use a concave mirror to form a real image that is enlarged by an eyepiece.
3. Cameras use a convex lens to form an image on light-sensitive film.

After You Read

FOLDABLES Reading & Study Skills

On the back of the top flap of your Making a Question Study Fold, explain why most telescopes are reflecting telescopes.

Visualizing Main Ideas

Complete the following concept map.

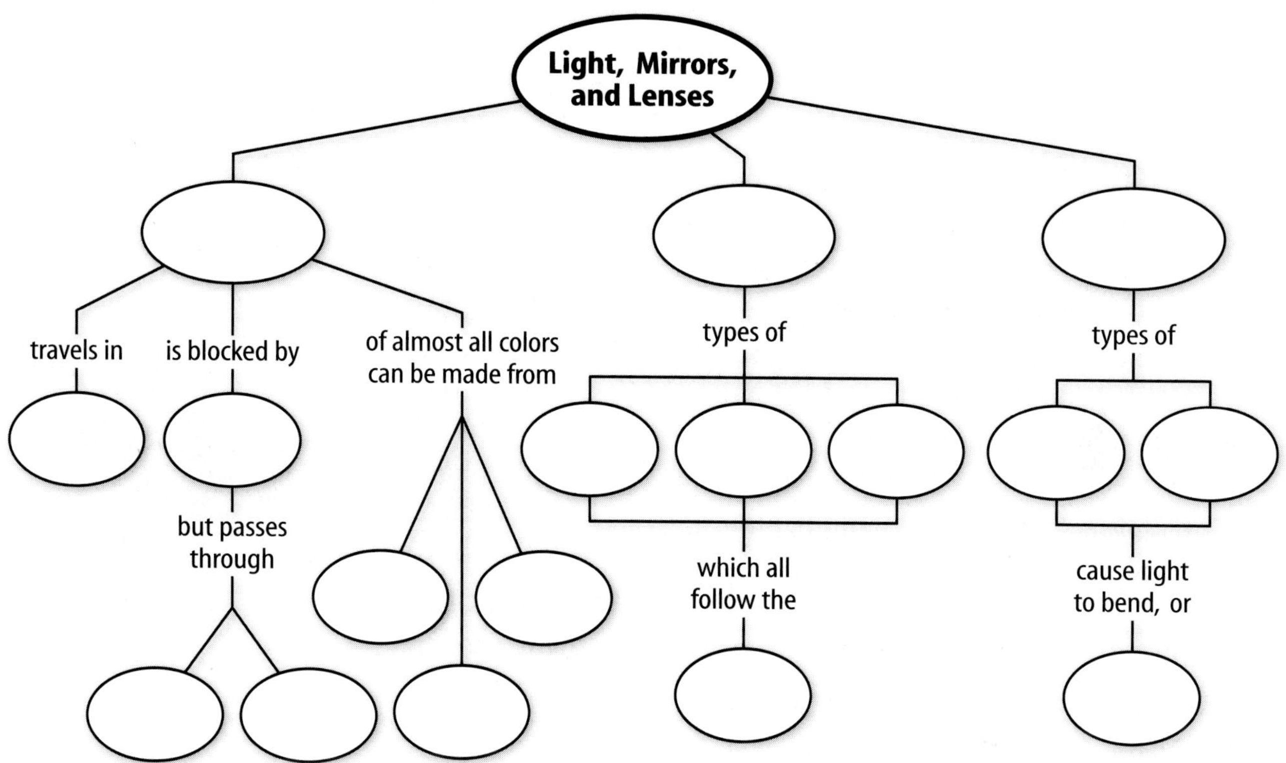

Vocabulary Review

Vocabulary Words

a. concave lens
b. convex lens
c. focal length
d. focal point
e. law of reflection
f. lens
g. light ray
h. medium
i. reflecting telescope
j. reflection
k. refracting telescope
l. refraction

Study Tip

If you're not sure of the relationships between terms in a question, make a concept map of the terms to see how they fit together. Ask your teacher if the relationships you drew are correct.

Using Vocabulary

Explain the differences between the terms in the following sets.

1. reflection, refraction
2. concave lens, convex lens
3. light ray, medium
4. focal length, focal point
5. lens, medium
6. law of reflection, refraction
7. reflecting telescope, refracting telescope
8. focal point, light ray
9. lens, focal length

Chapter 14 Assessment

Checking Concepts

Choose the word or phrase that best answers the question.

1. Light waves travel the fastest through which of the following?
   A) air **C)** water
   B) diamond **D)** a vacuum
2. What determines the color of light?
   A) a prism **C)** its wavelength
   B) its refraction **D)** its incidence
3. If an object reflects red and green light, what color does the object appear to be?
   A) yellow **C)** green
   B) red **D)** purple
4. If an object absorbs all the light that hits it, what color is it?
   A) white **C)** black
   B) blue **D)** green
5. What type of image is formed by a plane mirror?
   A) upright **C)** magnified
   B) inverted **D)** all of the above
6. How is the angle of incidence related to the angle of reflection?
   A) It's greater. **C)** It's the same.
   B) It's smaller. **D)** It's not focused.
7. Which of the following can be used to magnify objects?
   A) a concave lens **C)** a convex mirror
   B) a convex lens **D)** all of the above
8. Which of the following describes the light waves that make up laser light?
   A) same wavelength **C)** in phase
   B) same direction **D)** all of the above
9. What is an object that reflects some light and transmits some light called?
   A) colored **C)** opaque
   B) diffuse **D)** translucent
10. What is the main purpose of the objective lens or concave mirror in a telescope?
   A) invert images **C)** gather light
   B) reduce images **D)** magnify images

Thinking Critically

11. Do all light rays that strike a convex lens pass through the focal point?
12. Does a plane mirror focus light rays? Why or why not?
13. Explain why a rough surface, such as the road in this photo, is a better reflector when it is wet.

14. If the speed of light were the same in all materials, could lenses be used to magnify objects? Why or why not?
15. A singer is wearing a blue outfit. What color spotlights would make the outfit appear to be black? Explain.

Developing Skills

16. **Comparing and Contrasting** Compare and contrast plane and convex mirrors.
17. **Predicting** You see a person's eyes in a mirror. Explain whether he or she can see you.
18. **Testing a Hypothesis** A convex lens supposedly has a focal length of 0.50 m. Design an experiment that would determine whether the focal length of the lens is 0.50 m.
19. **Researching Information** Research the ways laser light is used to correct medical and vision problems. Write a page summarizing your results.

20. Making and Using Graphs The graph below shows how the distance of an image from a convex lens is related to the distance of the object from the lens.

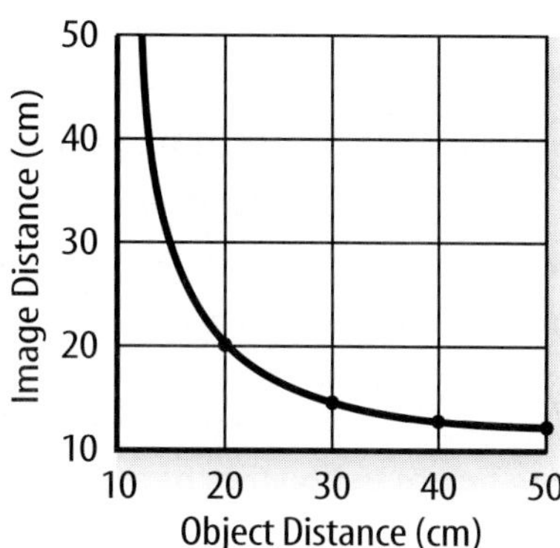

A) How does the image move as the object gets closer to the lens?

B) You can find the magnification of the image with the equation

$$\text{Magnification} = \frac{\text{image distance}}{\text{object distance}}$$

At which object distance is the magnification equal to 2?

Performance Assessment

21. Poster Make a poster describing the difference between the primary colors of light and the primary colors of pigment.

22. Reverse Writing In a plane mirror, images are reversed. With this in mind, write a "backwards" note to a friend and have him or her read it in a mirror.

TECHNOLOGY

Go to the Glencoe Science Web site at **science.glencoe.com** or use the **Glencoe Science CD-ROM** for additional chapter assessment.

Test Practice

Nelson learned that the speed of light is 300,000 km/s. Since he knew that the fastest passenger jet, the SST, flies faster than the speed of sound, he did some research to compare the speeds of sound and light.

The Speed of Sound and Light in Different Media

Medium	Speed of Sound (m/s)	Speed of Light (10^8 m/s)
Glass	5,971	1.6
Water	1,486	2.2
Air	335	3.0
Vacuum	0	3.0

Study the table above and answer the following questions.

1. According to the table, in which medium is the speed of sound the fastest and the speed of light the slowest?

A) glass
B) water
C) air
D) vacuum

2. According to the table, which medium is able to transmit only light?

F) glass
G) water
H) air
J) vacuum

Reading Comprehension

Read the passage. Then read each question that follows the passage. Decide which is the best answer to each question.

The History of the Telescope: An International Story

Roger Bacon, an English scientist, first wrote about the basic ideas behind the operation of a telescope in the 1200s. It was not until the early 1600s, however, that Hans Lippershey, a Dutchman who made spectacles for people with poor vision, made the first telescope. Lippershey noticed that objects appeared closer if he viewed them through a combination of a concave and a convex lens. He placed the lenses in a tube to hold them more easily. This was the world's first refracting telescope.

A few years later, an Italian scientist, Galileo, was the first to point a telescope toward the stars. Galileo learned of the Dutch invention in 1609. At the time, it was mainly used to see objects on Earth, such as distant ships and enemy armies. This is why the telescope was first called a "spyglass." Galileo made his own telescope and began using it to view the sky. Before this, Galileo had not been particularly interested in astronomy. That quickly changed as he recorded observations of the Moon's surface, spots on the Sun, and four moons circling Jupiter.

Another advance in telescope technology occurred in 1663 when James Gregory, a Scottish scientist, designed the first reflecting telescope. Isaac Newton built the first reflecting telescope 25 years later. The earliest, most valuable contribution to astronomy made by Americans was the construction of the Hooker telescope, a reflecting telescope on Mount Wilson. Completed in 1917, its 254 cm reflecting concave mirror allowed astronomers to see other galaxies clearly for the first time.

Since then, scientists have continued to design and build larger and more powerful telescopes. The development of the modern telescope is the result of many years of work by many scientists across the world.

Test-Taking Tip As you read the passage, make a time line of the history of the telescope.

1. The telescope was first called a "spyglass" because it _____.

A) was helpful in observing the Moon and stars
B) was designed by Roger Bacon
C) could be used to watch other people
D) was first made by a Dutchman

2. According to the passage, scientists often _____.

F) build upon one another's work
G) are slow workers
H) aren't interested in many things
J) never read the work of other scientists

3. The earliest, most valuable contribution to astronomy made by Americans was _____.

A) the first refracting telescope built in the 1600s
B) Roger Bacon's basic ideas about the operation of a telescope in the 1200s
C) the construction of the Hooker telescope on Mount Wilson, which allowed astronomers to see other galaxies clearly for the first time
D) using a telescope to view the Moon's surface, spots on the Sun, and four moons circling Jupiter

Standardized Test Practice

Reasoning and Skills

Power of a Lens

Lens	Diopter	Focal length (m)
1	1/4	4
2	1/5	5
3	1/6	6
4	1/7	7
5	1/9	?

1. Diopters are one way to measure the strength of a lens. What is the focal length of lens 5?

A) 5
B) 8
C) 9
D) 10

Test-Taking Tip Study the values for the first four lenses and consider how the diopter value is related to the focal length.

Wavelengths of Electromagnetic Waves

Type of Wave	Wavelength
Radio wave	Greater than 0.3 m
Microwave	0.3 m – 0.001 m
Infrared wave	0.001 m – 0.000 000 7 m
Visible light wave	0.000 000 7 m – 0.000 000 4 m

2. A wave with a wavelength of 0.03 m would be what type of wave?

F) radio wave
G) microwave
H) infrared wave
J) visible light wave

Test-Taking Tip Read the table's column headings carefully and then reread the question.

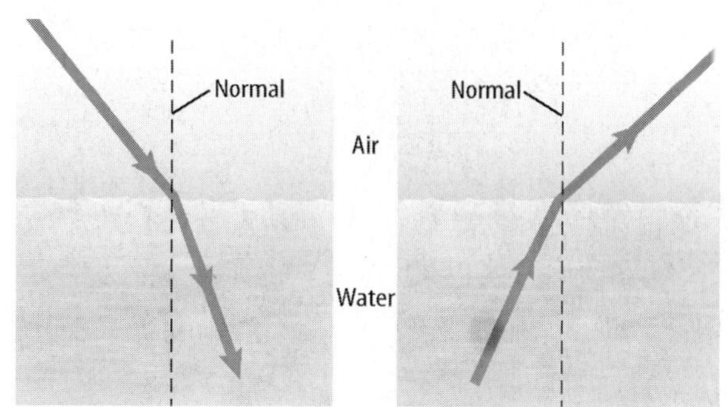

3. What is happening to the wave in this figure?

A) it is being diffracted
B) it is being refracted
C) it is experiencing constructive interference
D) it is experiencing destructive interference

Test-Taking Tip Review the difference between diffraction, refraction, constructive interference, and destructive interference.

4. Explain the relationship between the amplitude of a sound wave and the loudness of a sound. How is the amplitude of the sound wave related to the amount of energy it carries?

Test-Taking Tip Recall the definition of the terms *amplitude* and *loudness*.

How Are Cone-bearing Trees & Static Electricity Connected?

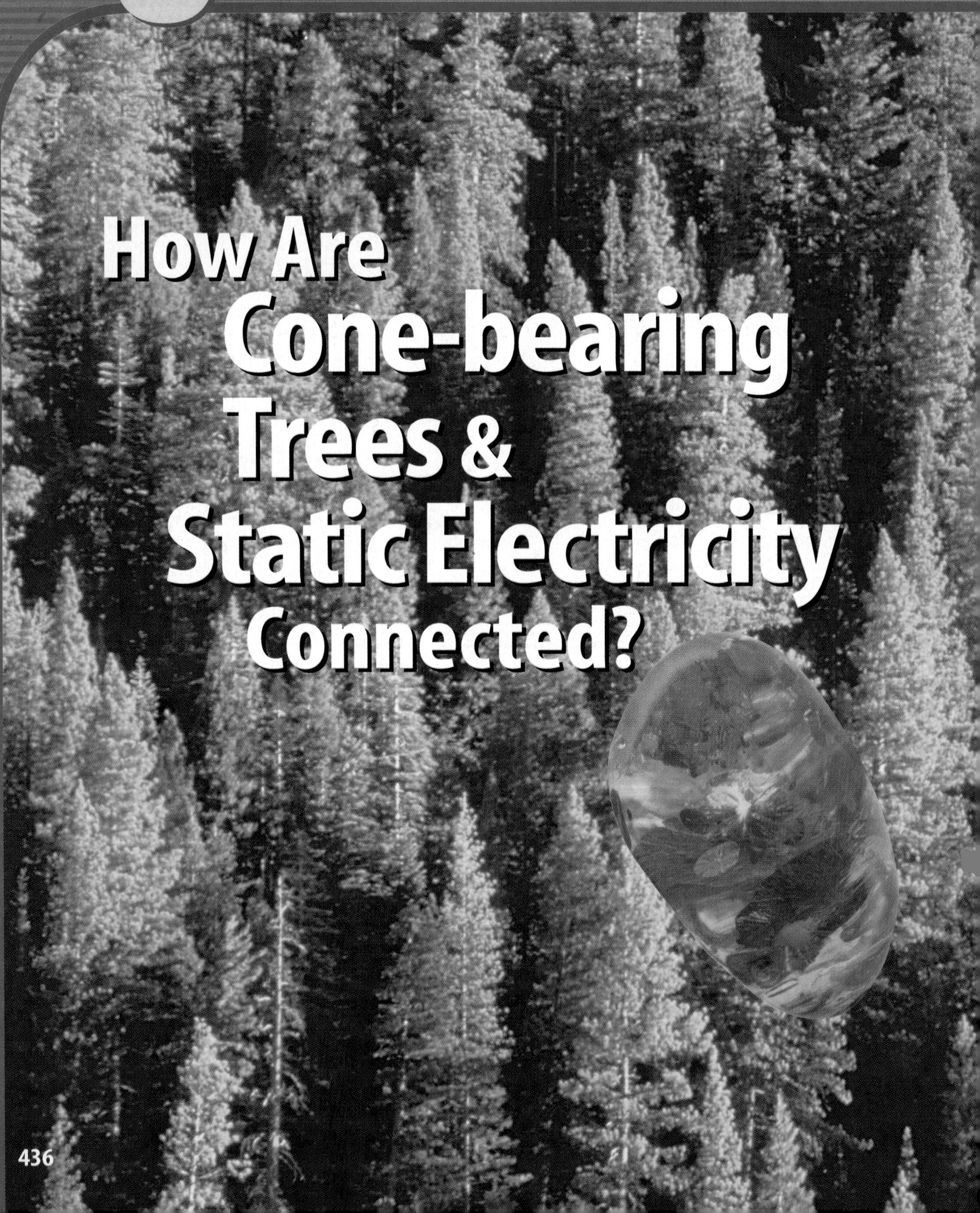

When the bark of a cone-bearing tree is broken it secretes resin, which hardens and seals the tree's wound. The resin of some ancient trees fossilized over time, forming a golden, gemlike substance called amber. The ancient Greeks prized amber highly, not only for its beauty, but also because they believed it had magical qualities. They had noticed that when amber was rubbed with wool or fur, small bits of straw or ash would stick to it. Because of amber's color and its unusual properties, some believed that amber was solidified sunshine. The Greek name for amber was *elektron* which means "substance of the Sun."

By the seventeenth century, the behavior of amber had sparked the curiosity of a number of scientists, and an explanation of amber's behavior finally emerged. When amber is rubbed by wool or fur, static electricity is produced. Today, a device called a Van de Graaff generator, like the one shown below, can produce static electricity involving millions of volts, and has been used to explore the nature of matter in atom-smashing experiments.

SCIENCE CONNECTION

STATIC ELECTRICITY When you dry clothes in a gas or electric dryer, the fabrics often stick together. This "clinging" is due to static electricity. Using the Glencoe Science Web site at **science.glencoe.com** or library resources, find out how clothing becomes charged in a dryer, and how anti-static products work. Write a paragraph in your Science Journal about what you find.

CHAPTER 15

Electricity

This spark generator uses voltages of millions of volts to produce these electric discharges that resemble lightning. Other electric discharges, like those that occur when you walk across a carpeted floor, are not as visible. In your home, electric currents flow through wires, and also power lights, televisions, and other appliances. In this chapter, you will learn about electric charges and the forces they exert on each other. You also will learn how electric charges moving in a circuit can do useful work.

What do you think?

Science Journal Look at the picture below with a classmate. Discuss what this might be. Here's a hint: *Think power—lots of power.* Write your answer or best guess in your Science Journal.

No computers? No CD players? No video games? Can you imagine life without electricity? You depend on it every day, and not just to make life more fun. Electricity heats and cools homes and provides light. It provides energy that can be used to do work. This energy comes from the forces that electric charges exert on each other. What is the nature of these electric forces?

Investigate electric forces

1. Inflate a rubber balloon.
2. Put some small bits of paper on your desktop and bring the balloon close to the bits of paper. Observe what happens.
3. Charge the balloon by holding it by the knot and rubbing the balloon on your hair or on a piece of wool.
4. Bring the balloon close to the bits of paper and observe what happens.
5. Charge two balloons using the procedure in step 3 and bring them close to each other, holding them by their knots.
6. Repeat step 3, then touch the balloon with your hand. Now what happens when you bring the balloon close to the bits of paper?

Observe

Record your observations of electric forces in your Science Journal.

Before You Read

Making a Vocabulary Study Fold **Make the following Foldable to help you better understand the terms *charge, current,* and *circuit.***

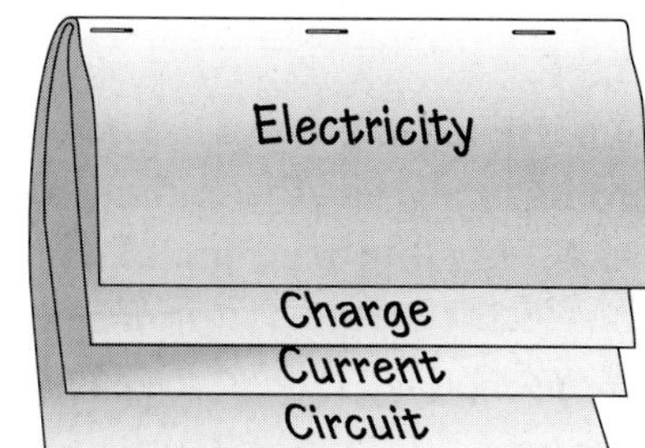

1. Stack two sheets of paper in front of you so the short side of both sheets is at the top.
2. Slide the top sheet up so that about 4 cm of the bottom sheet show.
3. Fold both sheets top to bottom to form four tabs and staple along the fold.
4. Label the tabs *Electricity, Charge, Current,* and *Circuit.*
5. Before you read the chapter, write your definition of charge, current, and circuit under the tabs. As you read the chapter, correct your definition and write more information about each.

Electric Charge

As You Read

What You'll Learn

- **Describe** how objects can become electrically charged.
- **Explain** how electric charges affect other electric charges.
- **Distinguish** between insulators and conductors.
- **Describe** how electric discharges such as lightning occur.

Vocabulary

ion
static charge
electric force
electric field
insulator
conductor
electric discharge

Why It's Important

All electrical phenomena result from the behavior of electric charges.

Electricity

You can't see, smell, or taste electricity, so it might seem mysterious. However, electricity is not so hard to understand when you start by thinking small—very small. All solids, liquids, and gases are made of tiny particles called atoms. Atoms, as shown in **Figure 1,** are made of even smaller particles called protons, neutrons, and electrons. Protons and neutrons are held together tightly in the nucleus at the center of an atom, but electrons swarm around the nucleus in all directions. Protons and electrons possess electric charge, but neutrons have no electric charge.

Positive and Negative Charge Two types of electric charge exist—positive and negative. Protons carry a positive charge, and electrons carry a negative charge. The amount of negative charge on an electron is exactly equal to the amount of positive charge on a proton. Because atoms have equal numbers of protons and electrons, the amount of positive charge on all the protons in the nucleus of an atom is exactly balanced by the negative charge on all the electrons moving around the nucleus. Therefore, atoms are electrically neutral, which means they have no overall electric charge.

Some atoms can become negatively charged if they gain extra electrons. Other atoms can easily lose electrons thereby becoming positively charged. A positively or negatively charged atom is called an **ion** (I ahn).

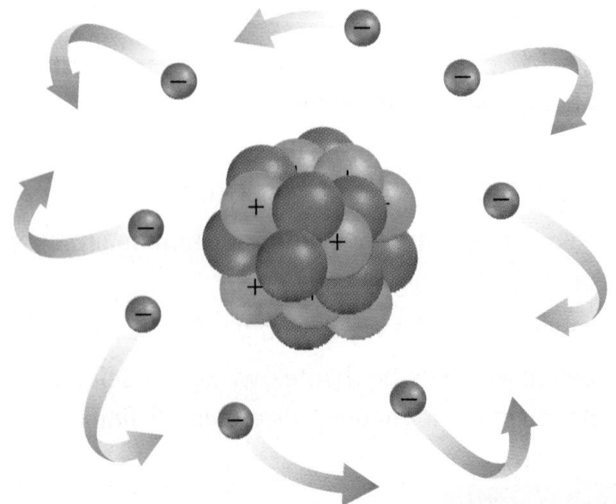

Figure 1
An atom is made of positively charged protons (orange), negatively charged electrons (red), and neutrons (blue) with no electric charge. *Where are the protons and neutrons located in an atom?*

Figure 2
Rubbing can move electrons from one object to another. Because hair holds electrons more loosely than the balloon holds them, electrons are pulled off the hair when the two make contact. *Which object has become positively charged and which has become negatively charged?*

Electrons Move in Solids Electrons can move from atom to atom and from object to object. Rubbing is one way that electrons can be transferred. If you ever have taken clinging clothes from a clothes dryer, you have seen what happens when electrons are transferred from one object to another.

Suppose you rub a balloon on your hair. The atoms in your hair hold their electrons more loosely than the atoms on the balloon hold theirs. As a result, electrons are transferred from the atoms in your hair to the atoms on the surface of the balloon, as shown in **Figure 2.** Because your hair loses electrons, it becomes positively charged. The balloon gains electrons and becomes negatively charged. Your hair and the balloon become attracted to one another and make your hair stand on end. This imbalance of electric charge on an object is called a **static charge.** In solids, static charge is due to the transfer of electrons between objects. Protons cannot be removed easily from the nucleus of an atom and usually do not move from one object to another.

Reading Check *How does an object become electrically charged?*

Ions Move in Solutions Sometimes, a flow of charge can be caused by the movement of ions instead of the movement of electrons. Table salt—sodium chloride—is made of sodium ions and chloride ions that are fixed in place and cannot move through the solid. However, when salt is dissolved in water, the sodium and chloride ions break apart and spread out evenly in the water forming a solution, as shown in **Figure 3.** Now the positive and negative ions are free to move. Solutions containing ions play an important role in enabling different parts of your body to communicate with each other. **Figure 4** shows how a nerve cell uses ions to transmit signals. These signals moving throughout your body enable you to sense, move, and even think.

Figure 3
When table salt (NaCl) dissolves in water, the sodium ions and chloride ions break apart. These ions now are able to carry electric energy.

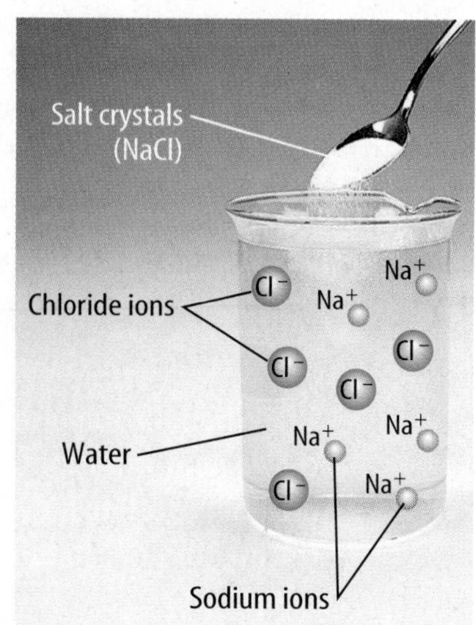

Figure 4

The control and coordination of all your bodily functions involves signals traveling from one part of your body to another through nerve cells. Nerve cells use ions to transmit signals from one nerve cell to another.

A When a nerve cell is not transmitting a signal, it moves positively charged sodium ions (Na^+) outside the membrane of the nerve cell. As a result, the outside of the cell membrane becomes positively charged and the inside becomes negatively charged.

B A chemical released by another nerve cell called a neurotransmitter starts the impulse moving along the cell. At one end of the cell, the neurotransmitter causes sodium ions to move back inside the cell membrane.

C As sodium ions pass through the cell membrane, the inside of the membrane becomes positively charged. This triggers sodium ions next to this area to move back inside the membrane, and an electric impulse begins to move down the nerve cell.

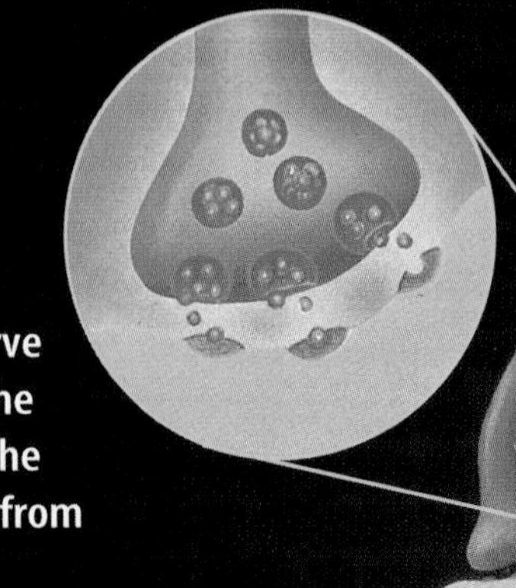

D When the impulse reaches the end of the nerve cell, a neurotransmitter is released that causes the next nerve cell to move sodium ions back inside the cell membrane. In this way, the signal is passed from cell to cell.

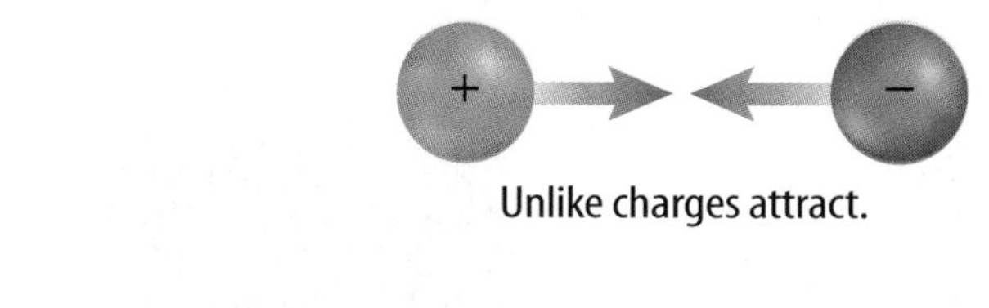
+
−
Unlike charges attract.

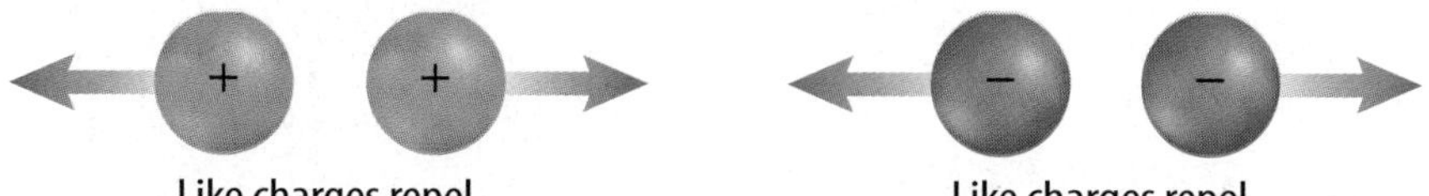
+
+
−
−
Like charges repel.
Like charges repel.

Figure 5
A positive charge and a negative charge attract each other. Two positive charges repel each other, as do two negative charges.

Electric Forces

The electrons in an atom swarm around the nucleus. What keeps these electrons close to the nucleus? The positively-charged protons in the nucleus exert an attractive electric force on the negatively-charged electrons. All charged objects exert an **electric force** on each other. The electric force between two charges can be attractive or repulsive, as shown in **Figure 5.** Objects with the same type of charge repel one another and objects with opposite charges attract one another. This rule is often stated as "like charges repel, and unlike charges attract."

The electric force between two electric charges gets stronger as the distance between them decreases. A positive and a negative charge are attracted to each other more strongly if they are closer together. Two like charges are pushed away more strongly from each other the closer they are. The electric force on two objects that are charged, such as two balloons that have been rubbed on wool, also increases if the amount of charge on the objects increases.

Electric Fields You might have noticed examples of how charged objects don't have to be touching to exert an electric force on each other. For instance, two charged balloons push each other apart even though they are not touching. Also, bits of paper and a charged balloon don't have to be touching for the balloon to attract the paper. How are charged objects able to exert forces on each other without toughing?

Electric charges exert a force on each other at a distance through an **electric field** that exists around every electric charge. **Figure 6** shows the electric field around a positive and a negative charge. An electric field gets stronger as you get closer to a charge, just as the electric force between two charges becomes greater as the charges get closer together.

Figure 6
The lines with arrowheads represent the electric field around charges. The direction of each arrow is the direction a positive charge would move if it were placed in the field.

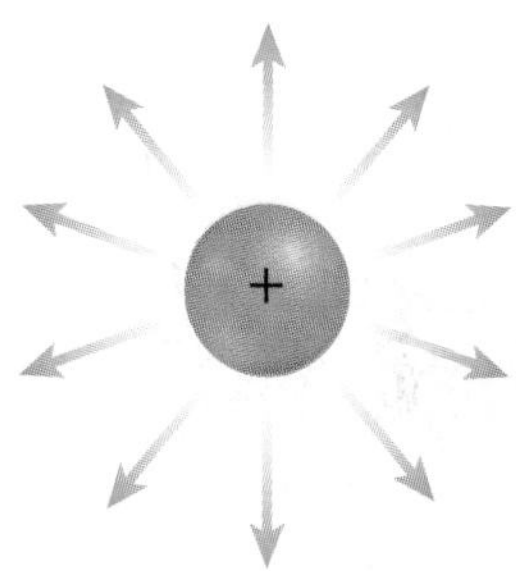
+

A The electric field arrows point away from a positive charge.

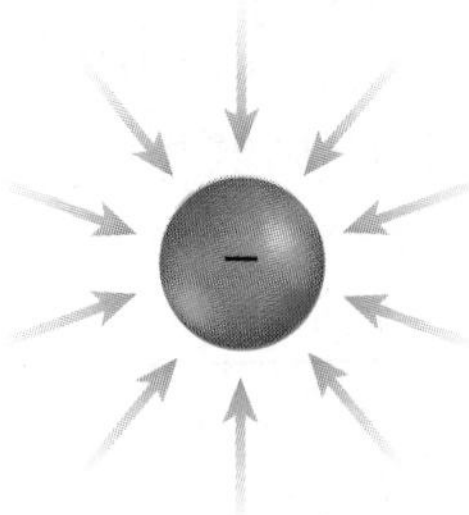
−

B The electric field arrows point toward a negative charge. *Why are these arrows in the opposite direction of the arrows around the positive charge?*

Figure 7
Electric charges move more easily through conductors than through insulators.

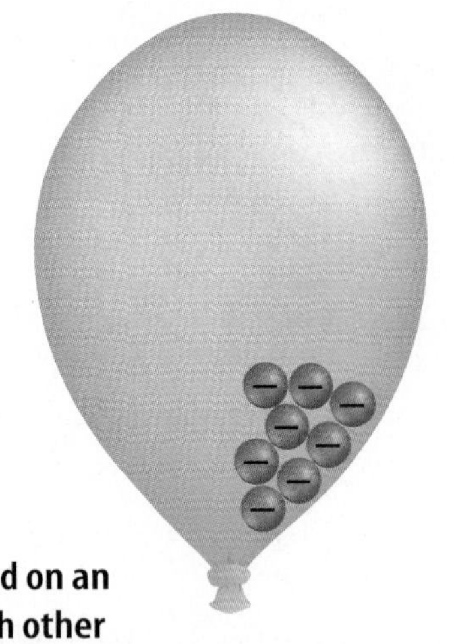

A Charges placed on an insulator repel each other but cannot move easily on the surface of the insulator. As a result, the charges remain in one place.

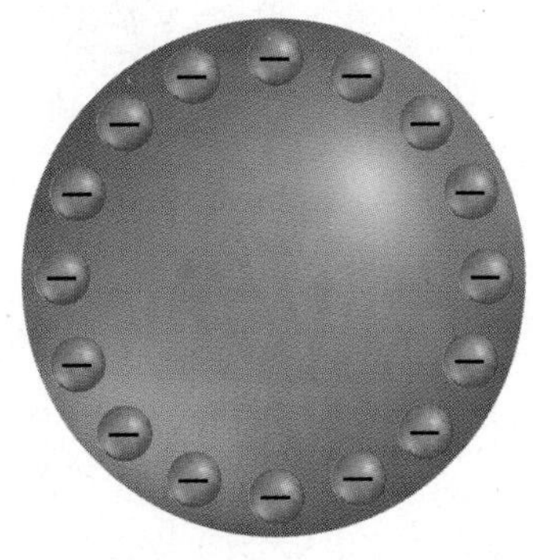

B Charges placed on a conductor repel each other but can move easily on the conductor's surface. Thus, they spread out as far apart as possible.

Insulators and Conductors

Rubbing a balloon on your hair transfers electrons from your hair to the balloon. However, only the part of the balloon that was rubbed on your hair becomes charged because electrons cannot move easily through rubber. As a result, the electrons that were rubbed onto the balloon stay in one place, as shown in **Figure 7A.** A material in which electrons cannot move easily from place to place is called an **insulator.** Examples of insulators are plastic, wood, glass, and rubber.

Materials that are **conductors** contain electrons that can move more easily through the material. Look at **Figure 7B.** Excess electrons on the surface of a conductor spread out over the entire surface.

Research Visit the Glencoe Science Web site at **science.glencoe.com** for news on recent breakthroughs in superconductor research. Communicate to your class what you learn.

Metals as Conductors The best conductors are metals such as copper, gold, and aluminum. In metal atoms, a few electrons are not attracted as strongly to the nucleus as the other electrons, and are loosely held by the atom. When metal atoms form a solid, the metal atoms can move only short distances. However, the electrons that are loosely-held by the atoms can move easily through the solid piece of metal. In an insulator, the electrons are held tightly in the atoms that make up the insulator and therefore cannot move easily.

An electric wire is made from a conductor coated with an insulator such as plastic. Electrons move easily through the copper but do not move easily through the plastic insulation. This prevents electrons from moving through the insulation and causing an electric shock if someone touches the wire.

Induced Charge

Has this ever happened to you? You walk across a carpet and as you reach for a metal doorknob, you feel an electric shock. Maybe you even see a spark jump between your fingertip and the doorknob. To find out what happened, look at **Figure 8.**

As you walk, electrons are rubbed off the rug by your shoes. The electrons then spread over the surface of your skin. As you bring your hand close to the doorknob, the electric field around the excess electrons on your hand repel the electrons in the doorknob. Because the doorknob is a good conductor, its electrons move easily. The part of the doorknob closest to your hand then becomes positively charged. This separation of positive and negative charges due to an electric field is called an induced charge.

If the electric field in the space between your hand and the knob is strong enough, charge can be pulled across that space, as shown in **Figure 8C.** This rapid movement of excess charge from one place to another is an **electric discharge.** Lightning is also an electric discharge. In a storm cloud, air currents cause the bottom of the cloud to become negatively charged. This negative charge induces a positive charge in the ground below the cloud. Lightning occurs when electric charge moves between the cloud and the ground.

Lightning can occur in ways other than from a cloud to the ground. To find out more about lightning, see the **Lightning Field Guide** at the back of the book.

Figure 8
A spark that jumps between your fingers and a metal doorknob starts at your feet.

A As you walk across the floor, you rub electrons from the carpet onto the bottom of your shoes. These electrons then spread out over your skin, including your hands.

B As you bring your hand close to the metal doorknob, electrons on the doorknob move as far away from your hand as possible. The part of the doorknob closest to your hand is left with a positive charge.

C The attractive electric force between the electrons on your hand and the induced positive charge on the doorknob might be strong enough to pull electrons from your hand to the doorknob. You might see this as a spark and feel a mild electric shock.

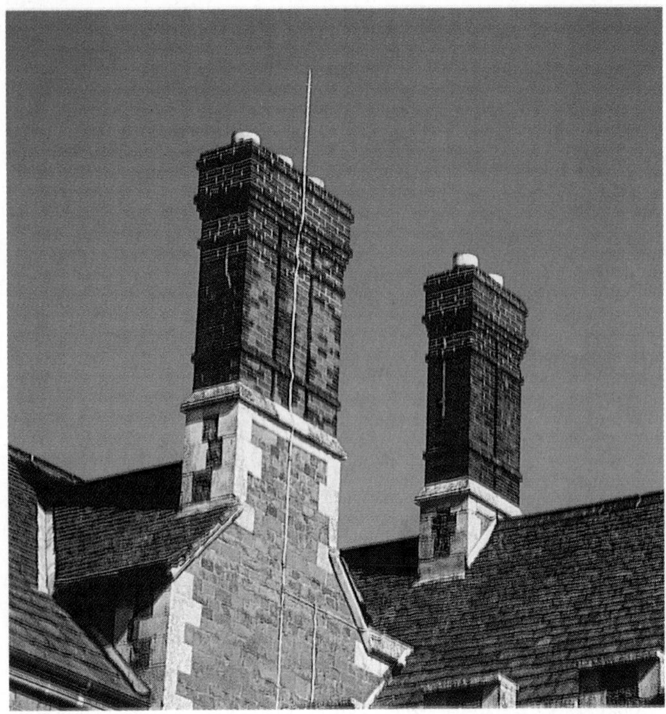

Figure 9
A lightning rod can protect a building from being damaged by a lightning strike. *Should a lightning rod be an insulator or a conductor?*

Grounding

Lightning is an electric discharge that can cause damage and injury because a lightning bolt releases an extremely large amount of electric energy. Even electric discharges that release small amounts of energy can damage delicate circuitry in devices such as computers. One way to avoid the damage caused by electric discharges is to make the excess charges flow harmlessly into Earth's surface. Earth can be a conductor, and because it is so large, it can absorb an enormous quantity of excess charge.

The process of providing a pathway to drain excess charge into Earth is called grounding. The pathway is usually a conductor such as a wire or a pipe. You might have noticed lightning rods at the top of buildings and towers, as shown in **Figure 9.** These rods are made of metal and are connected to metal cables that conduct electric charge into the ground if the rod is struck by lightning.

Reading Check ***How can tall structures be protected against lightning strikes?***

Section 1 Assessment

1. What is the difference between an object that is negatively charged and one that is positively charged?
2. Two electrically charged objects repel each other. What can you say about the type of charge on each object?
3. Contrast insulators and conductors. List three materials that are good insulators and three that are good conductors.
4. Why does an electric discharge occur?
5. **Think Critically** Excess charge placed on the surface of a conductor tends to spread over the entire surface, but excess charge placed on an insulator tends to stay where it was placed originally. Explain.

Skill Builder Activities

6. **Recognizing Cause and Effect** Clothes that are dried on a clothesline outdoors don't stick to each other when they are taken out of the laundry basket. Clothes that are dried in a clothes dryer do tend to stick to each other. What is the reason for this difference? **For more help, refer to the** Science Skill Handbook.
7. **Communicating** You are sitting in a car. You slide out of the car seat, and as you start to touch the metal car door, a spark jumps from your hand to the door. In your Science Journal, describe how the spark was formed. Use at least four vocabulary words in your explanation. **For more help, refer to the** Science Skill Handbook.

Electric Current

Flow of Charge

An electric discharge, such as a lightning bolt, can release a huge amount of energy in an instant. However, electric lights, refrigerators, TVs, and stereos need a steady source of electric energy that can be controlled. This source of electric energy comes from an **electric current,** which is the flow of electric charge. In solids, the flowing charges are electrons. In liquids, the flowing charges are ions, which can be positively or negatively charged. Electric current is measured in units of amperes (A). A model for electric current is flowing water. Water flows downhill because a gravitational force acts on it. Similarly, electrons flow because an electric force acts on them.

A Model for a Simple Circuit How does a flow of water provide energy? If the water is separated from Earth by using a pump, the higher water now has gravitational potential energy, as shown in **Figure 10.** As the water falls and does work on the waterwheel, the water loses potential energy and the waterwheel gains kinetic energy. For the water to flow continuously, it must flow through a closed loop. Electric charges will flow continuously only through a closed conducting loop called a **circuit.**

As You Read

***What* You'll Learn**

- **Relate** voltage to the electric energy carried by an electric current.
- **Describe** a battery and how it produces an electric current.
- **Explain** electrical resistance.

Vocabulary

electric current, circuit, voltage, resistance

***Why* It's Important**

The electric appliances you use rely on electric current.

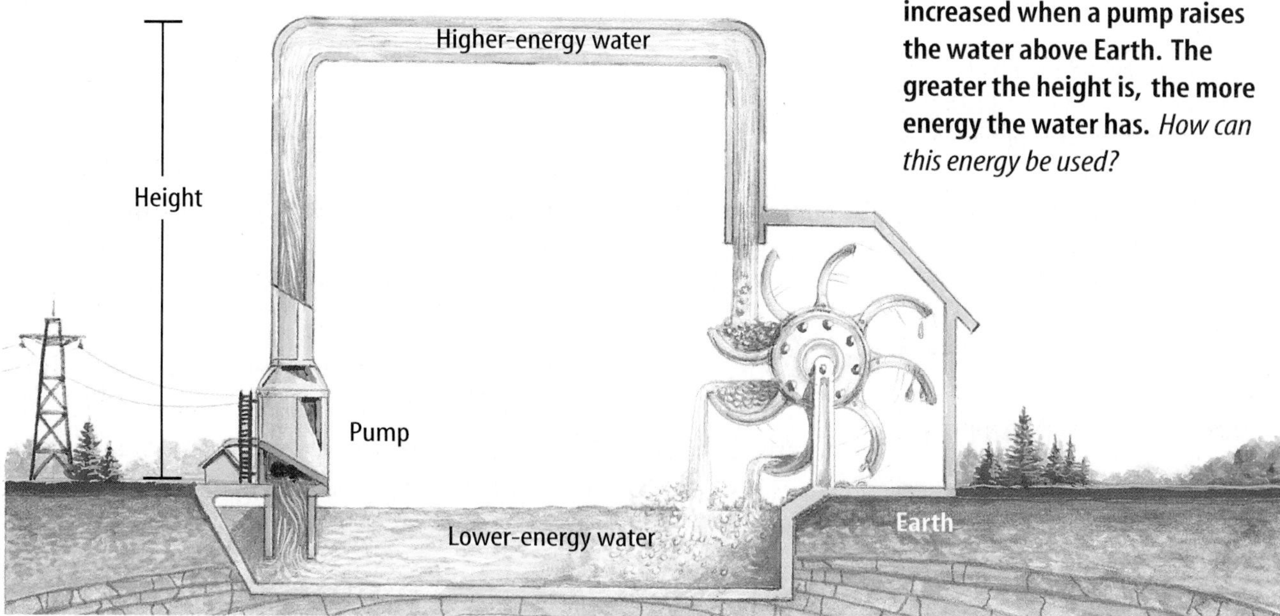

Figure 10
The potential energy of water is increased when a pump raises the water above Earth. The greater the height is, the more energy the water has. *How can this energy be used?*

Figure 11
As long as there is a closed path for electrons to follow, electrons flow in a circuit from the negative battery terminal to the positive terminal.

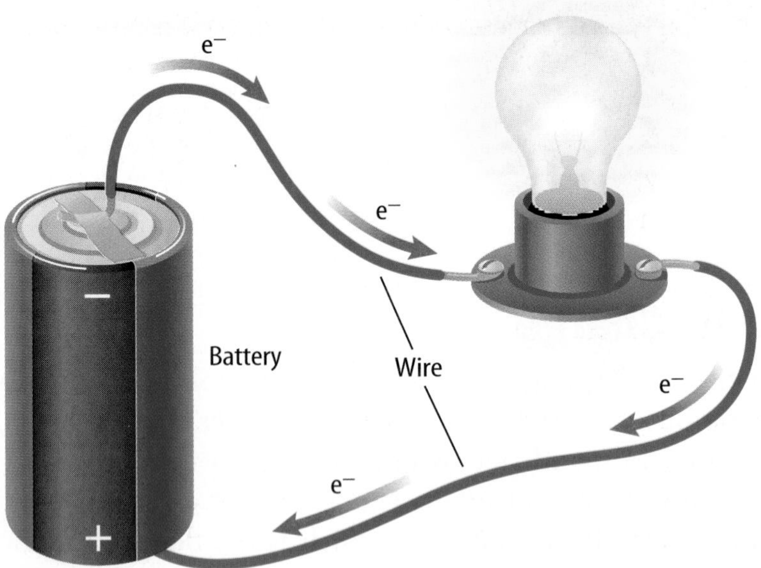

Electric Circuits The simplest electric circuit contains a source of electrical energy, such as a battery, and an electric conductor, such as a wire, connected to the battery. For the simple circuit shown in **Figure 11,** a closed path is formed by wires connected to a lightbulb and to a battery. Electric current flows in the circuit as long as none of the wires, including the glowing filament wire in the lightbulb, is disconnected or broken.

Voltage In a water circuit, a pump increases the gravitational potential energy of the water by raising the water from a lower level to a higher level. In an electric circuit, a battery increases the electric potential energy of electrons. This electric potential energy can be transformed into other forms of energy. The voltage of a battery is a measure of how much electric potential energy each electron can gain. As voltage increases, more electric potential energy is available to be transformed into other forms of energy. Voltage is measured in volts (V).

How a Current Flows You may think that when an electric current flows in a circuit, electrons travel completely around the circuit. Actually, individual electrons move slowly through a wire in an electric circuit. When the ends of the wire are connected to a battery, electrons in the wire begin to move toward the positive battery terminal. As an electron moves it collides with other electric charges in the wire, and is deflected in a different direction. After each collision, the electron again starts moving toward the positive terminal. A single electron may undergo more than ten trillion collisions each second. As a result, it may take several minutes for an electron in the wire to travel one centimeter.

Investigating the Electric Force

Procedure

1. Pour a layer of **salt** on a **plate.**
2. Sparingly sprinkle grains of **pepper** on top of the salt. Do not use too much pepper.
3. Rub a **rubber** or **plastic comb** on an article of **wool clothing.**
4. Slowly drag the comb through the salt and observe.

Analysis

1. How did the salt and pepper react to the comb?
2. Explain why the pepper reacted differently than the salt.

Batteries A battery supplies energy to an electric circuit. When the positive and negative terminals in a battery are connected in a circuit, the electric potential energy of the electrons in the circuit is increased. As these electrons move toward the positive battery terminal, this electric potential energy is transformed into other forms of energy, just as gravitational potential energy is converted into kinetic energy as water falls.

A battery supplies energy to an electric circuit by converting chemical energy to electric potential energy. For the alkaline battery shown in **Figure 12,** the two terminals are separated by a moist paste. Chemical reactions in the moist paste cause electrons to be transferred to the negative terminal from the atoms in the positive terminal. As a result, the negative terminal becomes negatively charged and the positive terminal becomes positively charged. This causes electrons in the circuit to be pushed away from the negative terminal and to be attracted to the positive terminal.

Battery Life Batteries don't supply energy forever. Maybe you know someone whose car wouldn't start after the lights had been left on overnight? Why do batteries run down? Batteries contain only a limited amount of the chemicals that react to produce chemical energy. These reactions go on as the battery is used and the chemicals are changed into other compounds. Once the original chemicals are used up, the chemical reactions stop and the battery is "dead."

Many chemicals are used to make an alkaline battery. Zinc is a source of electrons and positive ions, manganese dioxide is used to collect the electrons at the positive terminal, and water is used to carry ions through the battery. Visit the Glencoe Science Web site at **science.glencoe.com** for information about the chemistry of batteries.

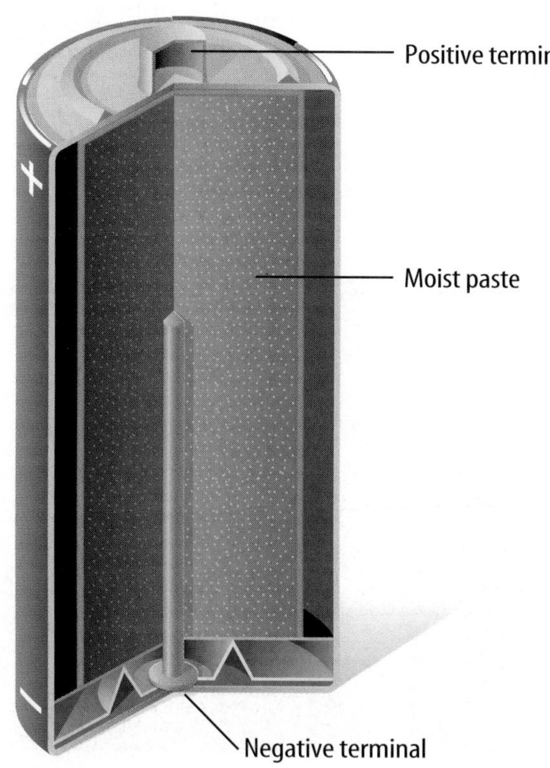

Figure 12
When this alkaline battery is connected in an electric circuit, chemical reactions occur in the moist paste of this alkaline battery that move electrons from the positive terminal to the negative terminal.

Resistance

Electrons can move much more easily through conductors than through insulators, but even conductors interfere somewhat with the flow of electrons. The measure of how difficult it is for electrons to flow through a material is called **resistance.** The unit of resistance is the ohm (Ω). Insulators generally have much higher resistance than conductors.

As electrons flow through a circuit, they collide with the atoms and other electric charges in the materials that make up the circuit. Look at **Figure 13.** These collisions cause some of the electrons' electric energy to be converted into thermal energy—heat—and sometimes into light. The amount of electric energy that is converted into heat and light depends on the resistance of the materials in the circuit.

Wires and Filaments The amount of electric energy that is converted into thermal energy increases as the resistance of the wire increases. Copper, which is one of the best electric conductors, has low resistance. Copper is used in household wiring because little electric energy is lost as electrons flow through copper wires. As a result, not much heat is produced. Because copper wires don't heat up much, the wires don't become hot enough to melt through their insulation, which makes fires less likely to occur. On the other hand, tungsten wire has a higher resistance. As electrons flow through tungsten wire, it becomes extremely hot—so hot, in fact, that it glows with a bright light. The high temperature makes tungsten a poor choice for household wiring, but the light it gives off makes it an excellent choice for the filaments of lightbulbs.

Reading Check *Is having resistance in electrical wires ever beneficial?*

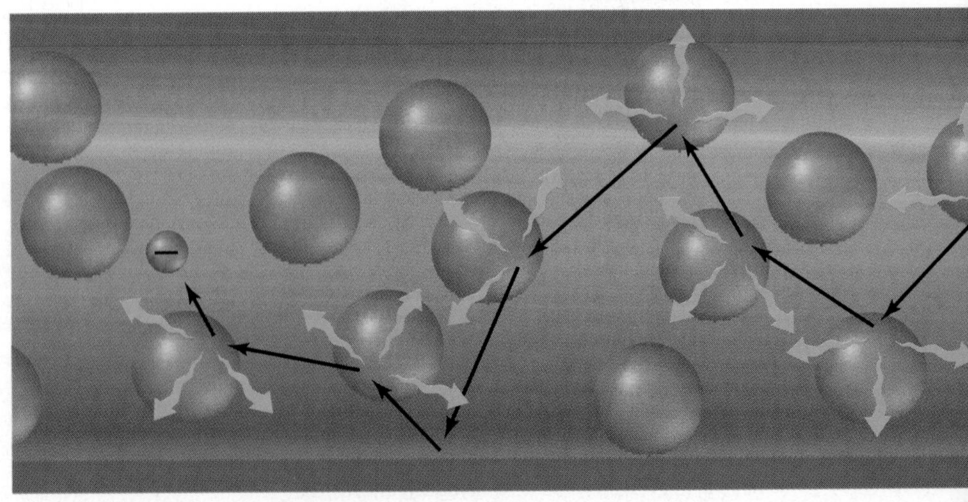

Figure 13
As electrons flow through a wire, they travel in a zigzag path as they collide with atoms and other electrons. These collisions cause the electrons to lose some electric energy. *Where does this electric energy go?*

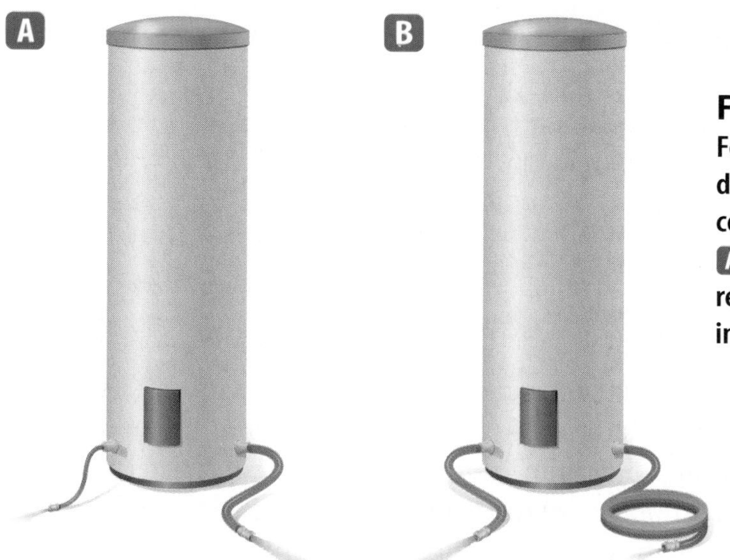

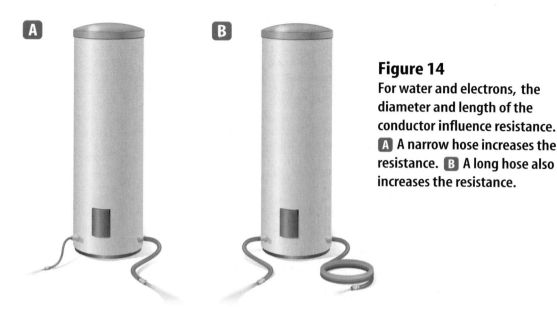

Figure 14
For water and electrons, the diameter and length of the conductor influence resistance. A A narrow hose increases the resistance. B A long hose also increases the resistance.

Slowing the Flow The electric resistance of a wire also depends on the length and thickness of the wire. Imagine water flowing through a hose, as shown in **Figure 14.** As the hose becomes more narrow or longer, the water flow decreases. In a similar way, the length and diameter of a wire affects electron flow. The electric resistance increases as the wire becomes longer or as it becomes narrower.

Section  Assessment

1. How does increasing the voltage in a circuit affect the energy of the electrons flowing in the circuit?
2. How does a battery cause electrons to move in an electric circuit?
3. For the same length, which has more resistance—a garden hose or a fire hose? Which has more resistance—a thin wire or a thick wire?
4. Why is copper often used in household wiring?
5. **Think Critically** Some electrical devices require two batteries, usually placed end to end. How does the voltage of the combination compare with the voltage of a single battery? Try it.

Skill Builder Activities

6. **Drawing Conclusions** Observe the size of various batteries, such as a watch battery, a camera battery, a flashlight battery, and an automobile battery. Conclude whether the voltage produced by a battery is related to its physical size. **For more help, refer to the Science Skill Handbook.**
7. **Communicating** The terms *circuit, current,* and *resistance* are often used in everyday language. In your Science Journal, record several different ways of using the words *circuit, current,* and *resistance.* Compare and contrast the everyday use of the words with their scientific definitions. **For more help, refer to the Science Skill Handbook.**

SECTION 3

Electric Circuits

As You Read

What You'll Learn

- **Explain** how voltage, current, and resistance are related in an electric circuit.
- **Investigate** the difference between series and parallel circuits.
- **Determine** the electric power used in a circuit.
- **Describe** how to avoid dangerous electric shock.

Vocabulary

Ohm's law
series circuit
parallel circuit
electric power

Why It's Important

Electric circuits enable the flow of electric current to be controlled in all electrical devices.

Controlling the Current

When you connect a conductor, such as a wire or a lightbulb, between the positive and negative terminals of a battery, electrons flow in the circuit. The amount of current is determined by the voltage supplied by the battery and the resistance of the conductor. To help understand this relationship, imagine a bucket with a hose at the bottom, as shown in **Figure 15.** If the bucket is raised, water will flow out of the hose faster than before. Increasing the height will increase the current.

Voltage and Resistance Think back to the pump and waterwheel in **Figure 10.** Recall that the raised water has energy that is lost when the water falls. Increasing the height from which the water falls increases the energy of the water. Increasing the height of the water is similar to increasing the voltage of the battery. Just as the water current increases when the height of the water increases, the electric current in a circuit increases as voltage increases.

If the diameter of the tube in **Figure 15** is decreased, resistance is greater and the flow of the water decreases. In the same way, as the resistance in an electric circuit increases, the current in the circuit decreases.

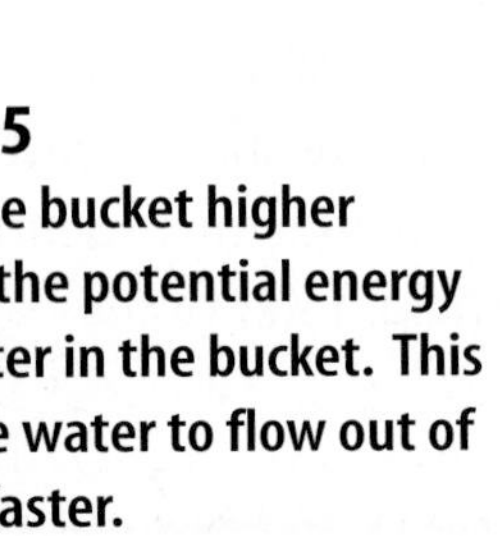

Figure 15
Raising the bucket higher increases the potential energy of the water in the bucket. This causes the water to flow out of the hose faster.

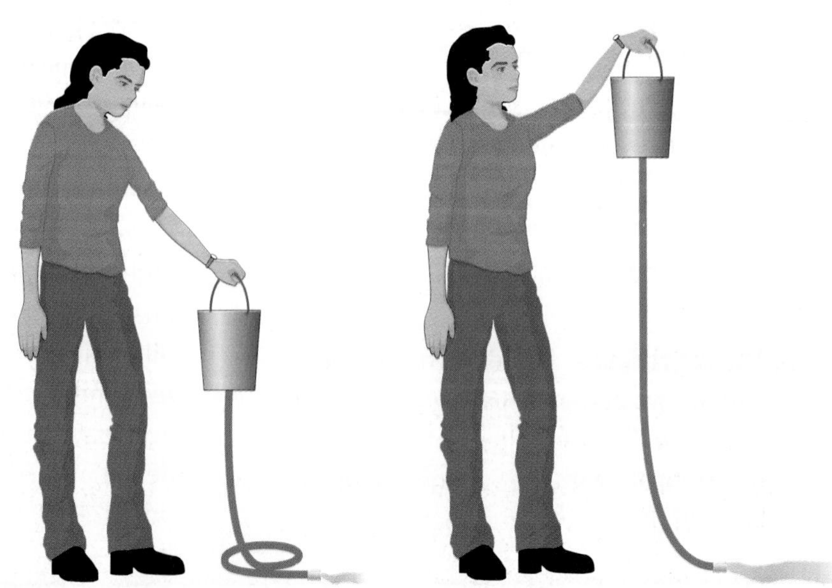

Ohm's Law A nineteenth-century German physicist, Georg Simon Ohm, carried out experiments that measured how changing the voltage and resistance in a circuit affected the current. The relationship he found among voltage, current and resistance is now known as **Ohm's law.** In equation form, Ohm's law is written as follows.

$$\text{current} = \frac{\text{voltage}}{\text{resistance}}$$

$$I\,(\text{A}) = \frac{V\,(\text{V})}{R\,(\Omega)}$$

According to Ohm's law, when the voltage in a circuit increases the current increases, just as water flows faster from a bucket that is raised higher. However, when the resistance is increased, the current in the circuit decreases.

Math Skills Activity

Calculating the Current in a Lightbulb

Example Problem

In homes, the standard electric outlet provides 110 V. What is the current through a lightbulb with a resistance of 220 Ω?

Solution

1. *This is what you know:* voltage: $V = 110$ V; resistance: $R = 220\ \Omega$
2. *This is what you need to find:* current: I
3. *This is the equation you need to use:* $I = V/R$
4. *Substitute the known values:* $I = (110\text{ V})/(220\ \Omega) = 0.5\text{ A}$

Check your answer by multiplying it by the resistance of 220 Ω. Do you calculate the given voltage of 110 V?

Practice Problems

1. What is the resistance of a lightbulb connected to a 110-V outlet that requires a current of 0.2 A?
2. Which draws more current at the same voltage, a lightbulb with higher resistance or a lightbulb with lower resistance? Use a mathematical example to answer this question.

For more help, refer to the Math Skill Handbook.

Mini LAB

Identifying Simple Circuits

Procedure

1. The filament in a lightbulb is a piece of wire. For the bulb to light, an electric current must flow through the filament in a complete circuit. Examine the base of a **flashlight bulb** carefully. Where are the ends of the filament connected to the base?
2. Connect one piece of **wire,** a **battery,** and a flashlight bulb to make the bulb light. (There are four possible ways to do this.)

Analysis

Draw and label a diagram showing the path that is followed by the electrons in your circuit. Explain your diagram.

Series and Parallel Circuits

Circuits control the movement of electric current by providing paths for electrons to follow. For current to flow, the circuit must provide an unbroken path for current to follow. Have you ever been putting up holiday lights and had a string that would not light because a single bulb was missing or had burned out and you couldn't figure out which one it was? Maybe you've noticed that some strings of lights don't go out no matter how many bulbs burn out or are removed. These two strings of holiday lights are examples of the two kinds of basic circuits—series and parallel.

Wired in a Line A **series circuit** is a circuit that has only one path for the electric current to follow, as shown in **Figure 16.** If this path is broken, then the current no longer will flow and all the devices in the circuit stop working. If the entire string of lights went out when only one bulb burned out, then the lights in the string were wired as a series circuit. When the bulb burned out, the filament in the bulb broke and the current path through the entire string was broken.

Reading Check ***How many different paths can electric current follow in a series circuit?***

In a series circuit, electrical devices are connected along the same current path. As a result, the current is the same through every device. However, each new device that is added to the circuit decreases the current throughout the circuit. This is because each device has electrical resistance, and in a series circuit, the total resistance to the flow of electrons increases as each additional device is added to the circuit. By Ohm's law, as the resistance increases, the current decreases.

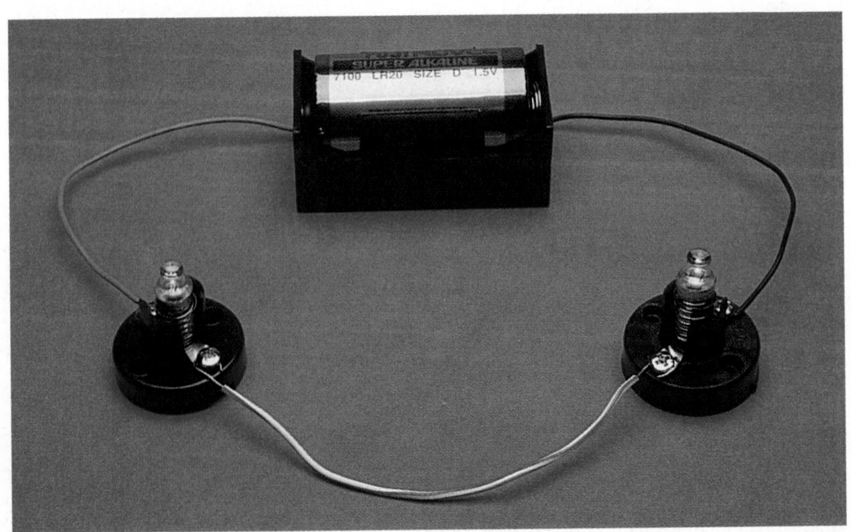

Figure 16
This circuit is an example of a series circuit. A series circuit has only one path for electric current to follow. *What happens to the current in this circuit if any of the connecting wires are removed?*

Branched Wiring What if you wanted to watch TV and had to turn on all the lights, a hair dryer, and every other electrical appliance in the house to do so? That's what it would be like if all the electrical appliances in your house were connected in a series circuit.

Instead, houses, schools, and other buildings are wired using parallel circuits. A **parallel circuit** is a circuit that has more than one path for the electric current to follow, as shown in **Figure 17.** The current branches so that electrons flow through each of the paths. If one path is broken, electrons continue to flow through the other paths. Adding or removing additional devices in one branch does not break the current path in the other branches, so the devices on those branches continue to work normally.

In a parallel circuit, the resistance in each branch can be different, depending on the devices in the branch. The lower the resistance is in a branch, the more current flows in the branch. So the current in each branch of a parallel circuit can be different.

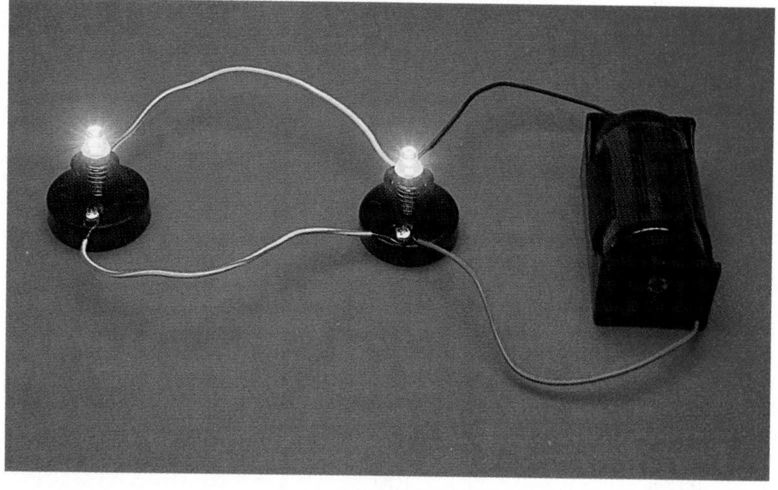

Figure 17
This circuit is an example of a parallel circuit. A parallel circuit has more than one path for electric current to follow. *What happens to the current in the circuit if either of the wires connecting the two lightbulbs is removed?*

Protecting Electric Circuits

In a parallel circuit, the current that flows out of the battery or electric outlet increases as more devices are added to the circuit. As the current through the circuit increases, the wires heat up.

To keep the wire from becoming hot enough to cause a fire, the circuits in houses and other buildings have fuses or circuit breakers like those shown in **Figure 18** that limit the amount of current in the wiring. When the current becomes larger than 15 A or 20 A, a piece of metal in the fuse melts or a switch in the circuit breaker opens, stopping the current. The cause of the overload can then be removed, and the circuit can be used again by replacing the fuse or resetting the circuit breaker.

Figure 18
You might have fuses in your home that prevent electric wires from overheating.

A In some buildings, each circuit is connected to a fuse. The fuses are usually located in a fuse box.

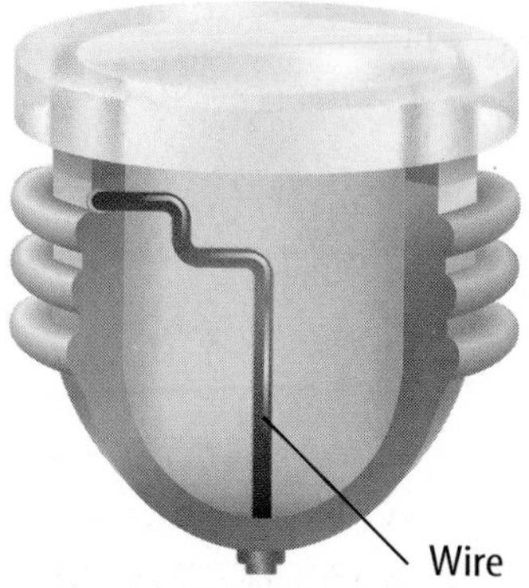

B A fuse contains a piece of wire that melts and breaks when the current flowing through the fuse becomes too large.

Table 1 Power Ratings of Common Appliances

Appliance	Power (W)
Computer	150
Color TV	140
Stereo	60
Refrigerator	350
Toaster	1,100
Microwave	800
Hair dryer	1,200

Electric Power

Electric energy is used in many ways to do useful jobs. Toasters and electric ovens convert electric energy to heat, stereos convert electric energy to sound, and a fan blade rotates as electric energy is converted to mechanical energy. The rate at which an appliance converts electric energy to another form of energy is the **electric power** used by the appliance.

Calculating Power The rate at which energy is used in the circuit is related to the amount of energy carried by the electrons, which increases as the voltage increases. The power that is used also is related to the rate at which electrons flow into the circuit. As a result, the power that is used in a circuit can be determined by multiplying the current by the voltage.

$$\text{Power} = \text{current} \times \text{voltage}$$
$$P\,(\text{W}) = I\,(\text{A}) \times V\,(\text{V})$$

Table 1 lists the power required by several common appliances. The unit of power is the watt, W.

Math Skills Activity

Calculating the Electric Power Used by a Lightbulb

Example Problem

How much power does a lightbulb use if the current is 0.55 A and the voltage is 110 V?

Solution

1. *This is what you know:* voltage: $V = 110$ V; current: $I = 0.55$ A
2. *This is what you need to find:* power: P
3. *This is the equation you need to use:* $P = I \times V$
4. *Substitute the known values:* $P = 0.55\text{ A} \times 110\text{ V} = 60\text{ W}$

Check your answer by dividing it by the current of 0.55 A. Did you calculate the given voltage of 110 V?

Practice Problem

How much current does a 25-W bulb require in a 110-V circuit?

For more help, refer to the Math Skill Handbook.

Cost of Electric Energy Power is the rate at which energy is used, or the amount of energy that is used per second. When you use a hair dryer, the amount of electric energy that is used depends on the power of the hair dryer and the amount of time you use it. If you used it for 5 min yesterday and 10 min today, you used twice as much energy today as yesterday.

Using electric energy costs money. Electric companies generate electric energy and sell it in units of kilowatt-hours to homes, schools, and businesses. One kilowatt-hour, kWh, is an amount of electric energy equal to using 1 kW of power continuously for 1 h. This would be the amount of energy needed to light ten 100-W lightbulbs for 1 h, or one 100-W lightbulb for 10 h.

Figure 19
Electric meters measure the amount of electric energy used in kilowatt-hours. *Find the electric meter that records the electric energy used in your house.*

What does kWh stand for and what does it measure?

An electric company usually charges its customers for the number of kilowatt-hours they use every month. The number of kilowatt-hours used in a building such as a house or a school is measured by an electric meter, which usually is attached to the outside of the building, as shown in **Figure 19.**

Electrical Safety

Have you ever had a mild electric shock? You probably felt only a mild tingling sensation, but electricity can have much more dangerous effects. In 1997, electric shocks killed an estimated 490 people in the United States. **Table 2** lists a few safety tips to help prevent electrical accidents.

Table 2 Situations to Avoid

Situations to Avoid
Never use appliances with frayed or damaged electric cords.
Unplug appliances before working on them, such as when prying toast out of a jammed toaster.
Avoid all water when using plugged-in appliances.
Never touch power lines with anything, including kite string and ladders.
Always respect warning signs and labels.

Data Update Visit the Glencoe Science Web site at **science.glencoe.com** to find the cost of electric energy in various parts of the world. Communicate to your class what you learn.

Life Science INTEGRATION

The scale below shows how the effect of electric current on the human body depends on the amount of current that flows into the body.

Current	Effect
0.0005 A	Tingle
0.001 A	Pain threshold
0.01 A	Inability to let go
0.025 A	
0.05 A	Difficulty breathing
0.10 A	
0.25 A	
0.50 A	Heart failure
1.00 A	

Electric Shock You experience an electric shock when an electric current enters your body. In some ways your body is like a piece of insulated wire. The fluids inside your body are good conductors of current. The electrical resistance of dry skin is much higher. Skin insulates the body like the plastic insulation around a copper wire. Your skin helps keep electric current from entering your body.

A current can enter your body when you accidentally become part of an electric circuit. Whether you receive a deadly shock depends on the amount of current that flows into your body. The current that flows through the wires connected to a 60 W lightbulb is 0.5 A. This amount of current entering your body could be deadly. Even a current as small as 0.001 A can be painful.

Lightning Safety On average, more people are killed every year by lightning in the United States than by hurricanes or tornadoes. Most lightning deaths and injuries occur outdoors. If you are outside and can see lightning or hear thunder, you should take shelter in a large, enclosed building if possible. A metal vehicle such as a car, bus, or van can provide protection if you avoid contact with metal surfaces.

You should avoid high places and open fields, and stay away from isolated high objects such as trees, flagpoles, or light towers. Avoid picnic shelters, baseball dugouts, bleachers, metal fences, and bodies of water. If you are caught outdoors, get in the lightning-safety position—squat low to the ground on the balls of your feet with your hands on your knees.

Section  Assessment

1. As the resistance in a simple circuit increases, what happens to the current?
2. What are the differences between a series circuit and a parallel circuit?
3. You have the stereo on while you're working on the computer. Which appliance is using more power?
4. How is your body like a piece of insulated wire?
5. **Think Critically** What determines whether a 100-W lightbulb costs more to use than a 1,200-W hair dryer does?

Skill Builder Activities

6. **Making and Using Tables** Suppose using 1,000 W for 1 h costs $0.08. Calculate the cost of using each of the appliances in **Table 1** for 24 h. Present your results in a table. **For more help, refer to the Science Skill Handbook.**
7. **Using Proportions** A typical household uses 1,000 kWh of electrical energy every month. If a power company supplies electrical energy to 10,000 households, how much electrical energy must it supply every year? **For more help, refer to the Math Skill Handbook.**

Activity

Current in a Parallel Circuit

In this activity, you will investigate how the current in a circuit changes when two or more lightbulbs are connected in parallel. Because the brightness of a lightbulb increases or decreases as more or less current flows through it, the brightness of the bulbs in the circuits can be used to determine which circuit has more current.

Materials

1.5-V lightbulbs (4)
1.5-V batteries (2)
10-cm-long pieces of insulated wire (8)
battery holders (2)
minibulb sockets (4)

What You'll Investigate

How does connecting devices in parallel affect the electric current in a circuit?

Goal

- **Observe** how the current in a parallel circuit changes as more devices are added.

Safety Precautions   

Procedure

1. Connect one lightbulb to the battery in a complete circuit. After you've made the bulb light, disconnect the bulb from the battery to keep the battery from running down. This circuit will be the brightness tester.

2. Make a parallel circuit by connecting two bulbs as shown in the diagram. Reconnect the bulb in the brightness tester and compare its brightness with the brightness of the two bulbs in the parallel circuit. Record your observations.
3. Add another bulb to the parallel circuit as shown in the figure. How does the brightness of the bulbs change?

4. Disconnect one bulb in the parallel circuit. What happens to the brightness of the remaining bulbs?

Conclude and Apply

1. Compared to the brightness tester, is the current in the parallel circuit more or less?
2. How does adding additional devices affect the current in a parallel circuit?
3. Are the electric circuits in your house wired in series or parallel? How do you know?

Communicating Your Data

Compare your conclusions with those of other students in your class. **For more help, refer to the Science Skill Handbook.**

Activity
A Model for Voltage and Current

The flow of electrons in an electric circuit is something like the flow of water in a hose connected to a water tank. By raising or lowering the height of the tank, you can increase or decrease the potential energy of the water. In this activity you will model the flow of current in a circuit by investigating how the flow of water in a tube depends on the diameter of the tube and the height the water falls.

What You'll Investigate

How is the flow of water through a tube affected by changing the height of a container of water and the diameter of the tube?

Materials

plastic funnel
rubber or plastic tubing of different diameters (1 m each)
meterstick
ring stand with ring
stopwatch
**clock displaying seconds*
hose clamp
**binder clip*
500-mL beakers (2)
**Alternate Materials*

Goal

- **Model** the flow of current in a simple circuit.

Safety Precautions

Flow Rate Data

Trial	Height (cm)	Diameter (mm)	Time (s)	Flow Rate (mL/s)
1				
2				
3				
4				

Procedure

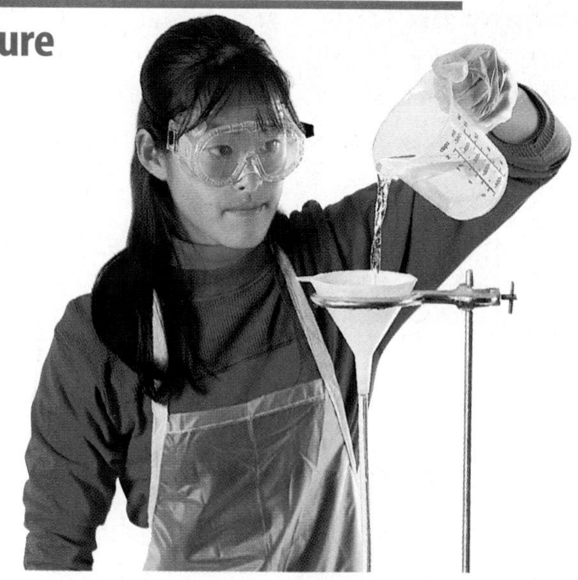

1. **Design** a data table in which to record your data. It should be similar to the table on the previous page.
2. Connect the tubing to the bottom of the funnel and place the funnel in the ring of the ring stand.
3. **Measure** the inside diameter of the rubber tubing. Record your data.
4. Place a 500-mL beaker at the bottom of the ring stand and lower the ring so the open end of the tubing is in the beaker.
5. Use the meterstick to measure the height from the top of the funnel to the bottom of the ring stand.
6. Working with a classmate, pour water into the funnel fast enough to keep the funnel full but not overflowing. Measure and record the time needed for 100 mL of water to flow into the beaker. Use the hose clamp to start and stop the flow of water.
7. Connect tubing with a different diameter to the funnel and repeat steps 2 through 6.
8. Reconnect the original piece of tubing and repeat steps 4 through 6 for several lower positions of the funnel, lowering the height by 10 cm each time.
9. **Calculate** the rate of flow for each trial by dividing 100 mL by the measured time.

Conclude and Apply

1. Make a graph that shows how the rate of flow depends on the funnel height. How does the rate of flow depend on the height of the funnel?
2. How does the rate of flow depend on the diameter of the tubing? Is this what you expected to happen? Explain.
3. Which of the variables that you changed in your trials corresponds to the voltage in a circuit? The resistance?
4. Based on your results, how would the current in a circuit depend on the voltage? How would the current depend on the resistance?

Share your graph with other students in your class. Did other students draw the same conclusions as you? **For more help, refer to the Science Skill Handbook.**

Fire in the Forest

Smokey the Bear is partly correct—most forest fires are started by people either deliberately or accidentally. However, some fires are caused by nature. Though lightning is responsible for only about ten percent of forest fires, it causes about one half of all fire damage. For example, in 2000, fires set by lightning raged in 12 states at the same time, burning nearly 20,000 km^2 of land. That is roughly equal in area to the state of Massachusetts. Fires sparked by lightning often strike in remote, difficult-to-reach areas, such as national parks and range lands.

Burning undetected for days, these fires can spread out of control and are hard to extinguish. Sometimes, firefighters must jump into the heart of these blazing areas to put the fires out. In addition to threatening lives, the fires can destroy millions of dollars worth of homes and property. Air pollution caused by smoke from forest fires also can have harmful effects on people. When wood products and fossil fuels are burned, they release particulate matter into the atmosphere. This can damage the human respiratory system, especially for those with preexisting conditions, such as asthma.

People aren't the only victims of forest fires. The fires kill animals, as well. Those who survive the blaze often perish because their habitats have been destroyed. Monster blazes also cause damage to the environment. They spew carbon dioxide and other gases into the atmosphere. Some of these gases may contribute to the greenhouse effect that warms the planet. In addition, fires give off carbon monoxide, which can cause ozone to form. In the lower atmosphere, ozone can damage vegetation, kill trees, and irritate lung tissue. Moreover, massive forest fires harm the logging industry, cause soil erosion in the ruined land, and are responsible for the loss of water reserves that normally collect in a healthy forest.

Plant life returns after a forest fire in Yellowstone National Park.

But fires caused by lightning also have some positive effects. In old, thick forests, trees often become diseased and insect-ridden. By removing these unhealthy trees, fires allow healthy trees greater access to water and nutrients. Fires also clean away a forest's dead trees, underbrush, and needles. This not only clears out space for new vegetation, it provides new food for them, as well. Dead organic matter returns its nutrients to the ground as it decays, but it can take a century for dead logs to rot completely.

Fires ignited by lightning might not be all bad

A fire completes the decay process almost instantly, allowing nutrients to be recycled a lot faster. The removal of these combustible materials prevents more widespread fires from occurring. It also lets new grasses and trees grow on the burned ground. The new types of vegetation attract new types of animals. This, in turn, creates a healthier and more diverse forest.

CONNECTIONS Research **Find out more about the job of putting out forest fires. What training is needed? What gear do firefighters wear? Why would people risk their lives to save a forest? Use the media center to learn more about forest firefighters and their careers. Report to the class.**

SCIENCE *Online*

For more information, visit science.glencoe.com

Chapter 15 Study Guide

Reviewing Main Ideas

Section 1 Electric Charge

1. The two types of electric charge are positive and negative. Like charges repel and unlike charges attract.
2. An object becomes negatively charged if it gains electrons and positively charged if it loses electrons.
3. Electrically charged objects have an electric field surrounding them and exert electric forces on one another.
4. Electrons can move easily in conductors, but not so easily in insulators. *Why isn't the building shown below harmed when lightning strikes it?*

Section 2 Electric Current

1. Electric current is the flow of charges—usually either electrons or ions.
2. The energy carried by the current in a circuit increases as the voltage in the circuit increases.
3. In a battery, chemical reactions provide the energy that causes electrons to flow in a circuit.
4. As electrons flow in a circuit, some of their electrical energy is lost due to resistance in the circuit. *In a simple circuit, why do electrons stop flowing if the circuit is broken?*

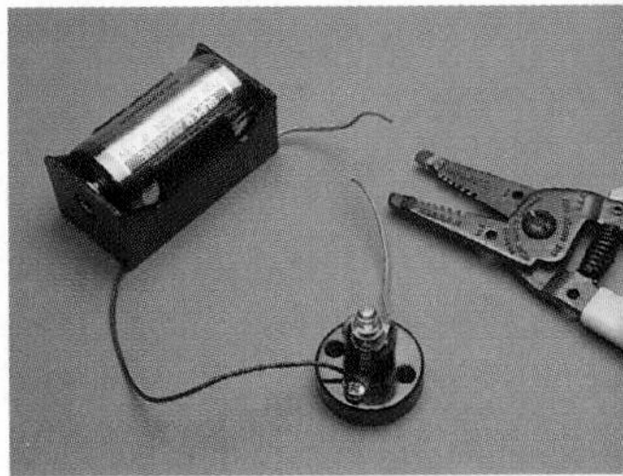

Section 3 Electric Circuits

1. In an electric circuit, the voltage, current, and resistance are related by Ohm's law, expressed as $I = V/R$.
2. The two basic kinds of electric circuits are parallel circuits and series circuits. A series circuit has only one path for the current to follow, but a parallel circuit has more than one path.
3. The rate at which electric devices use electrical energy is the electric power used by the device. Electric companies charge customers for using electrical energy in units of kilowatt-hours.
4. The amount of current flowing through the body determines how much damage occurs. The current from wall outlets can be dangerous. *Hair dryers often come with a reset button. What is the purpose of the button, and how might the reset mechanism work?*

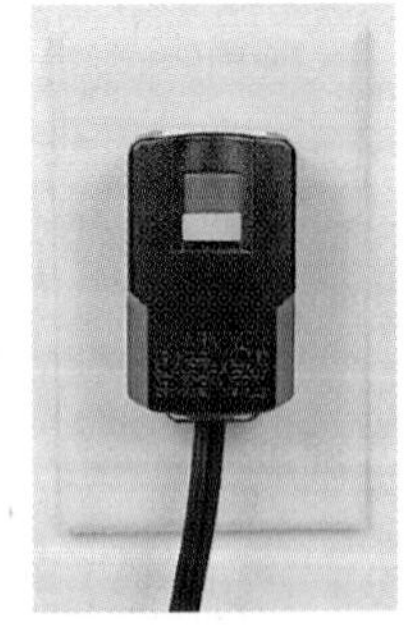

After You Read

Using the information on your Foldable, under the *Electricity* tab, explain the differences between the two types of charges and between the two types of circuits.

Visualizing Main Ideas

Correctly order the following concept map, which illustrates how electric current moves through a simple circuit.

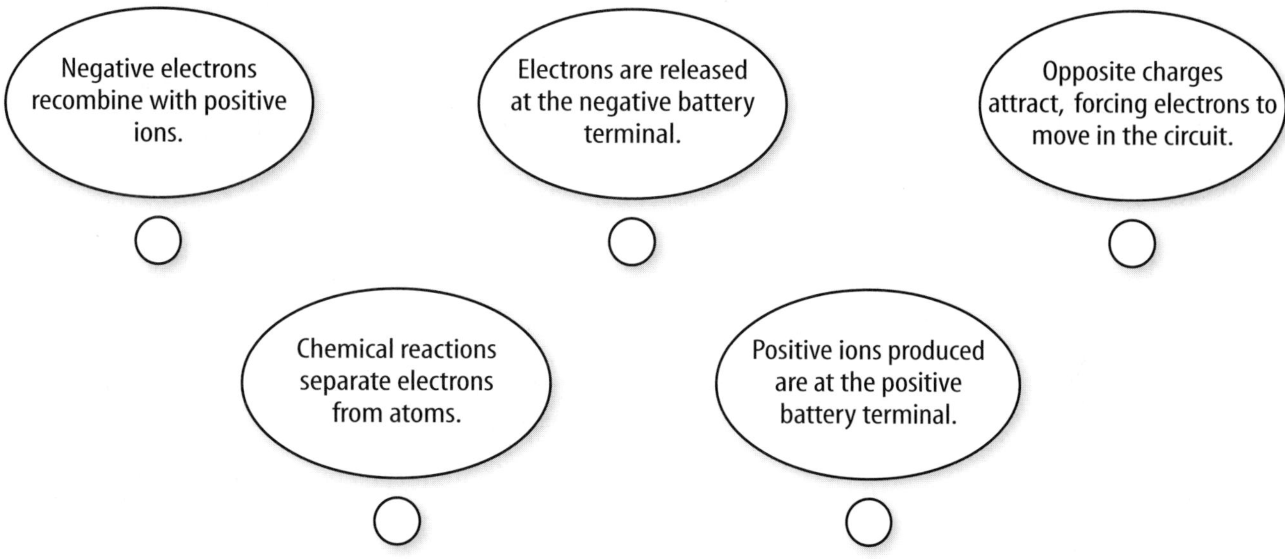

Vocabulary Review

Vocabulary Words

a. circuit
b. conductor
c. electric current
d. electric discharge
e. electric field
f. electric force
g. electric power
h. insulator
i. ion
j. Ohm's law
k. parallel circuit
l. resistance
m. series circuit
n. static charge
o. voltage

Study Tip

Whether or not you've taken a particular type of test or practiced for an exam many times, it's a good idea to start by reading the instructions provided at the beginning of each section. It only takes a moment.

Using Vocabulary

Answer the following questions using complete sentences.

1. What is the term for the flow of charge?
2. What is the relationship among voltage, current, and resistance in a circuit?
3. In which material do electrons move easily?
4. What is the name for the unbroken path that current follows?
5. What is the term for an excess of electric charge in one place?
6. What is an atom that has lost or gained electrons called?
7. Which circuits have more than one path for electrons to follow?
8. What is the rate at which electrical energy is converted to other forms of energy?

Chapter 15 Assessment

Checking Concepts

Choose the word or phrase that best answers the question.

1. An object that is positively charged _____.
   A) has more neutrons than protons
   B) has more protons than electrons
   C) has more electrons than protons
   D) has more electrons than neutrons

2. What is the force between two electrons?
   A) unbalanced **C)** attractive
   B) neutral **D)** repulsive

3. How much power does the average hair dryer use?
   A) 20 W **C)** 750 W
   B) 75 W **D)** 1,200 W

4. What property of a wire increases when it is made thinner?
   A) resistance **C)** current
   B) voltage **D)** charge

5. What property does Earth have that causes grounding to drain static charges?
   A) It is a planet.
   B) It has a high resistance.
   C) It is a conductor.
   D) It is like a battery.

6. Why is a severe electric shock dangerous?
   A) It can stop the heart from beating.
   B) It can cause burns.
   C) It can interfere with breathing.
   D) All of the above are true.

7. Because an air conditioner uses more electric power than a lightbulb in a given amount of time, what also must be true?
   A) It must have a higher resistance.
   B) It must use more energy every second.
   C) It must have its own batteries.
   D) It must be wired in series.

8. What unit of electrical energy is sold by electric companies?
   A) ampere **C)** volt
   B) ohm **D)** kilowatt-hour

9. What surrounds electric charges that causes them to affect each other even though they are not touching?
   A) an induced charge **C)** a conductor
   B) a static discharge **D)** an electric field

10. As more devices are added to a series circuit, what happens to the current?
    A) decreases **C)** stays the same
    B) increases **D)** stops

Thinking Critically

11. Why do materials have electrical resistance?

12. Explain why a balloon that has a static charge will stick to a wall.

13. If you connect two batteries in parallel, will the lightbulb glow brighter than if just one battery is used? Explain, using water as an analogy.

14. If you have two charged objects, how can you tell whether the type of charge on them is the same or different?

15. Explain why the outside cases of electric appliances usually are made of plastic.

Developing Skills

16. **Classifying** Look at several objects around your home. Classify these objects as insulators or conductors.

17. Making and Using Graphs The following data show the current and voltage in a circuit containing a portable CD player and in a circuit containing a portable radio.

a. Make a graph with the horizontal axis as current and the vertical axis as voltage. Plot the data for both appliances.

b. Which line is more horizontal—the plot of the radio data or the CD player data?

c. Use Ohm's law to determine the electrical resistance of each device.

d. For which device is the line more horizontal—the device with the higher or lower resistance?

Portable Radio

Voltage (V)	Current (A)
2.0	1.0
4.0	2.0
6.0	3.0

Portable CD Player

Voltage (V)	Current (A)
2.0	0.5
4.0	1.0
6.0	1.5

18. Collecting Data Determine the total cost of keeping all the lights turned on in your living room for 24 h if the cost of electricity is $0.08 per kilowatt-hour.

Performance Assessment

19. Design a Board Game Design a board game about a series or parallel circuit. The rules of the game could be based on opening or closing the circuit, adding fuses, and/or resetting a circuit breaker.

Technology

Go to the Glencoe Science Web site at **science.glencoe.com** or use the **Glencoe Science CD-ROM** for additional chapter assessment.

Test Practice

A student is interested in setting up and comparing four different circuits. The table below lists her results.

Type of Electric Circuit

Circuit	Number of Resistors	Circuit Type	Battery Voltage
A	2	Series	6 V
B	3	Parallel	12 V
C	4	Series	4 V
D	5	Parallel	8 V

Study the chart above and answer the following questions.

1. The voltage across a resistor in a parallel circuit equals the battery voltage. In a series circuit, the voltage across a resistor is less than the battery voltage. In which circuit is the voltage across an individual resistor the greatest?

A) Circuit A
B) Circuit B
C) Circuit C
D) Circuit D

2. A certain electric motor requires at least 5 volts to run. According to the table, the battery in which circuit could NOT be used to run the motor?

F) Circuit A
G) Circuit B
H) Circuit C
J) Circuit D

CHAPTER

16 Magnetism

This maglev train is designed to travel at speeds up to 500 km/h. However, you won't see any steam or exhaust coming out of its engine. In fact this train is not even touching the track. That's because it is suspended by magnetic forces and propelled by a traveling magnetic field. In this chapter, you will learn why magnets attract certain materials. You will also learn how electricity and magnetism are connected, and how an electric current can create a magnetic field.

What do you think?

Science Journal Look at the picture below with a classmate. Discuss what is happening. Here's a hint: *No glue or tape is involved.* Write your answer or best guess in your Science Journal.

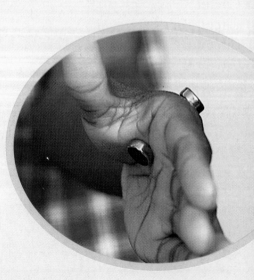

Perhaps you've driven bumper cars with your friends, and remember the jolt you felt when you crashed into another car. Quite a force can be generated from that small car powered by an electric motor. How does the motor produce a force that gets the tires moving? The answer involves magnetism. The following activity will demonstrate how a magnet is able to exert forces.

Observe and measure force between magnets 

1. Place two bar magnets on opposite ends of a sheet of paper.
2. Slowly slide one magnet toward the other until it moves. Measure the distance between the magnets.
3. Turn one magnet around 180°. Repeat the activity. Then turn the other magnet and repeat again.
4. Repeat the activity with one magnet perpendicular to the other, in a T shape.

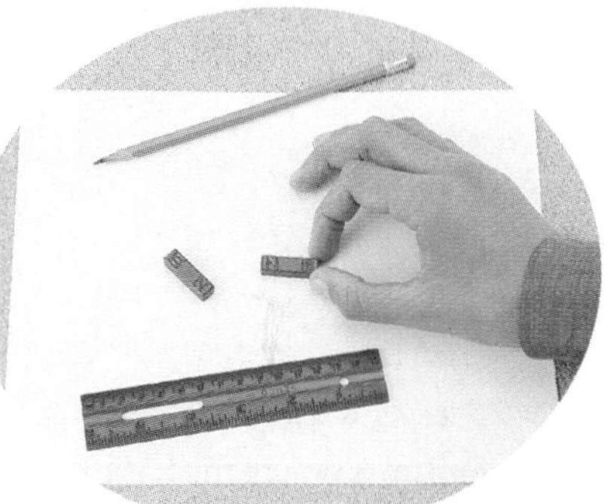

Observe

In your Science Journal, record your results. In each case, how close did the magnets have to be to affect each other? Did the magnets move together or apart? How did the forces exerted by the magnets change as the magnets were moved closer together? Explain.

Before You Read

FOLDABLES
Reading & Study Skills

Making a Compare and Contrast Study Fold **Make the following Foldable to help you see how magnetic forces and magnetic fields are similar and different.**

1. Place a sheet of paper in front of you so the long side is at the top. Fold the paper in half from the left side to the right side. Unfold.
2. Fold each side in to the fold line to divide the paper into fourths.
3. Label the flaps *Magnetic Force* and *Magnetic Field*.
4. As you read the chapter, write information about each topic on the inside of each flap.

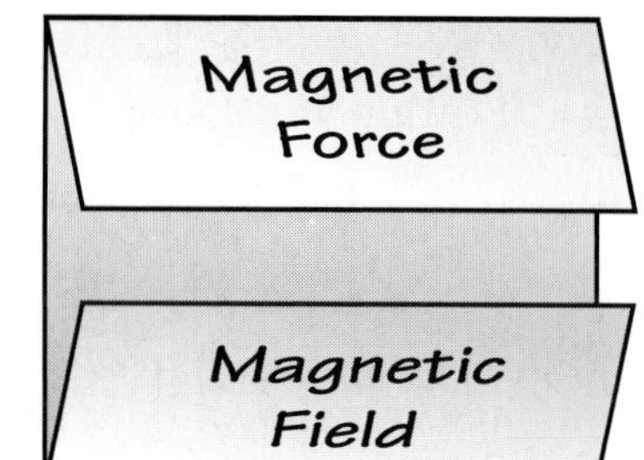

What is magnetism?

As You Read

What You'll Learn

- **Describe** the behavior of magnets.
- **Relate** the behavior of magnets to magnetic fields.
- **Explain** why some materials are magnetic.

Vocabulary

magnetic field
magnetic domain
magnetosphere

Why It's Important

Magnetism is one of the basic forces of nature.

Early Uses

Do you use magnets to attach papers to a metal surface such as a refrigerator? Have you ever wondered why magnets and some metals attract? Thousands of years ago, people noticed that a mineral called magnetite attracted other pieces of magnetite and bits of iron. They discovered that when they rubbed small pieces of iron with magnetite, the iron began to act like magnetite. When these pieces were free to turn, one end pointed north. These might have been the first compasses. The compass was an important development for navigation and exploration, especially at sea. Before compasses, sailors had to depend on the Sun or the stars to know in which direction they were going.

Magnets

A piece of magnetite is a magnet. Magnets attract objects made of iron or steel, such as nails and paper clips. Magnets also can attract or repel other magnets. Every magnet has two ends, or poles. One end is called the north pole and the other is the south pole. As shown in **Figure 1,** a north magnetic pole always repels other north poles and always attracts south poles. Likewise, a south pole always repels other south poles and attracts north poles.

Figure 1
Two north poles or two south poles repel each other. North and south magnetic poles are attracted to each other.

The Magnetic Field You have to handle a pair of magnets for only a short time before you can feel that magnets attract or repel without touching each other. How can a magnet cause an object to move without touching it? Recall that a force is a push or a pull that can cause an object to move. Just like gravitational and electric forces, a magnetic force can be exerted even when objects are not touching. And like these forces, the magnetic force becomes weaker as the magnets get farther apart. This magnetic force is exerted through a **magnetic field.** Magnetic fields surround all magnets. If you sprinkle iron filings near a magnet, the iron filings will outline the magnetic field around the magnet. Take a look at **Figure 2A.** The iron filings form a pattern of curved lines that start on one pole and end on the other. These curved lines are called magnetic field lines. Magnetic field lines help show the direction of the magnetic field.

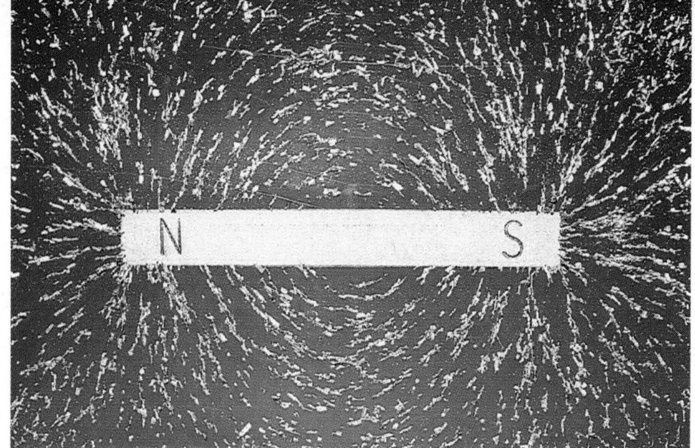

A Iron filings show the magnetic field lines around a bar magnet.

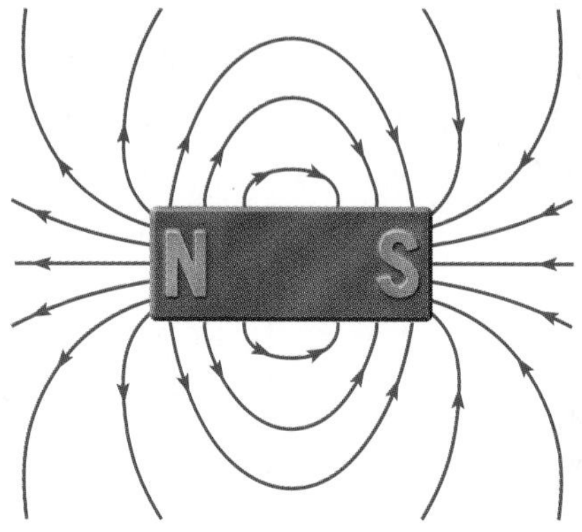

B Magnetic field lines start at the north pole of the magnet and end on the south pole.

Figure 2
A magnetic field surrounds a magnet. Where the magnetic field lines are close together, the field is strong. *For this magnet, where is the field strongest?*

What is the evidence that a magnetic field exists?

Magnetic field lines begin at a magnet's north pole and end on the south pole, as shown in **Figure 2B.** The field lines are close together where the field is strong and get farther apart as the field gets weaker. As you can see in the figures, the magnetic field is strongest close to the magnetic poles and grows weaker farther from the poles.

Field lines that curve toward each other show attraction. Field lines that curve away from each other show repulsion. **Figure 3** illustrates the magnetic field lines between a north and a south pole and the field lines between two north poles.

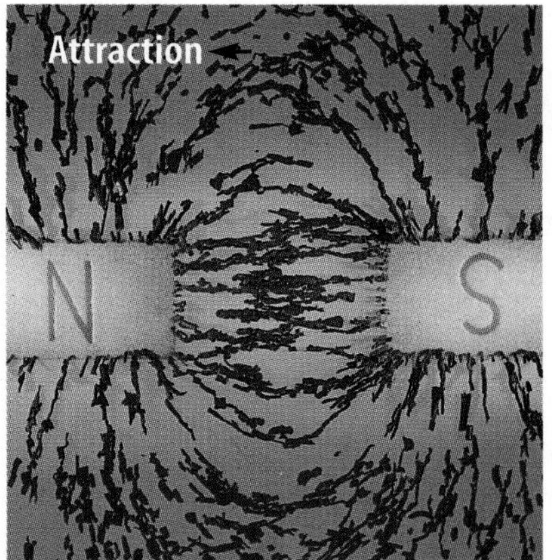

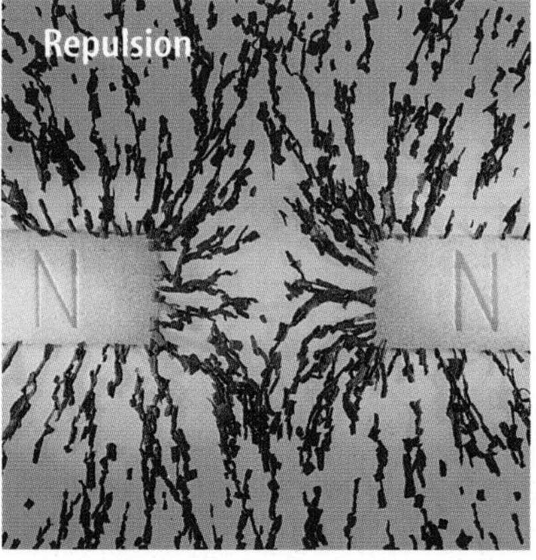

Figure 3
Magnetic field lines show attraction and repulsion. *What would the field between two south poles look like?*

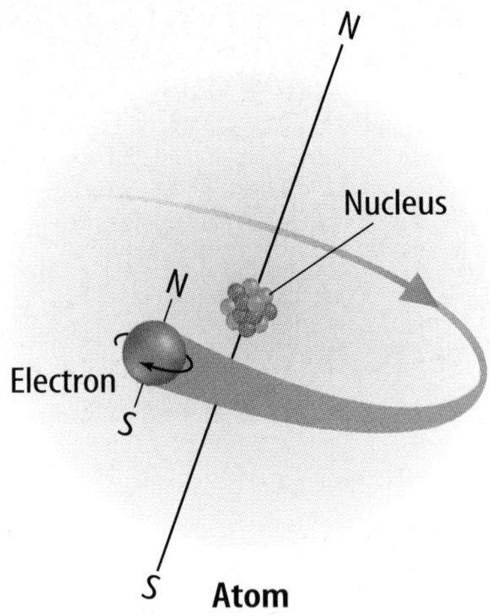

Figure 4
Movement of electrons produces magnetic fields. *What are the two types of motion shown in the illustration?*

Making Magnetic Fields A magnet is surrounded by a magnetic field that enables the magnet to exert a magnetic force. How are magnetic fields made? A moving electric charge creates a magnetic field.

Inside every magnet are moving charges. All atoms contain negatively charged particles called electrons. Not only do these electrons swarm around the nucleus of an atom, they also spin, as shown in **Figure 4.** Because of its movement, each electron produces a magnetic field. The atoms that make up magnets have their electrons arranged so that each atom is like a small magnet. In a material such as iron, a large number of atoms will have their magnetic fields pointing in the same direction. This group of atoms, with their fields pointing in the same direction, is called a **magnetic domain.**

A material that can become magnetized, such as iron or steel, contains many magnetic domains. When the material is not magnetized, these domains are oriented in different directions, as shown in **Figure 5A.** The magnetic fields created by the domains cancel, so the material does not act like a magnet.

A magnet contains a large number of magnetic domains that are lined up and pointing in the same direction. Suppose a strong magnet is held close to a material such as iron or steel. The magnet causes the magnetic field in many magnetic domains to line up with the magnet's field, as shown in **Figure 5B.** As you can see in **Figure 5C** this process magnetizes paper clips.

Figure 5
Some materials can become temporary magnets.

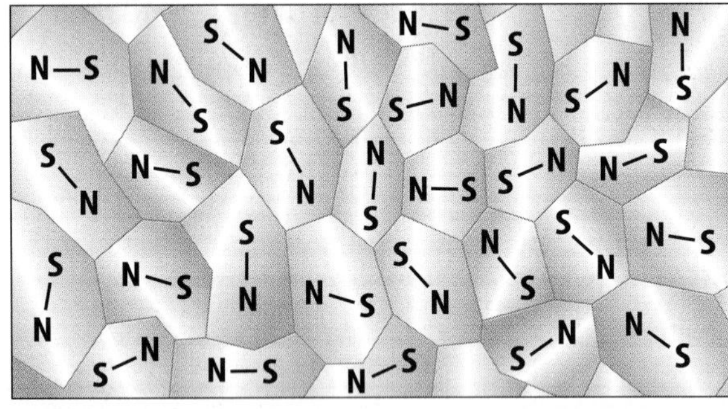

A Microscopic sections of iron and steel act as tiny magnets. Normally, these domains are oriented randomly and their magnetic fields cancel each other.

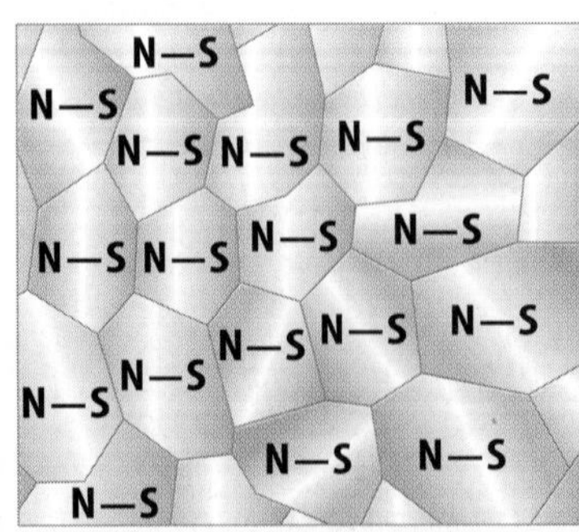
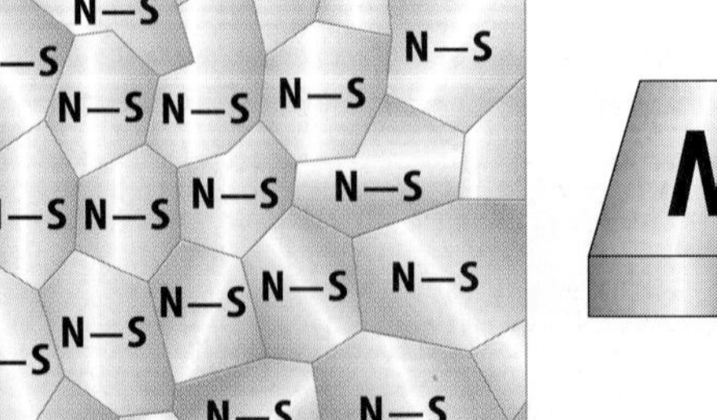

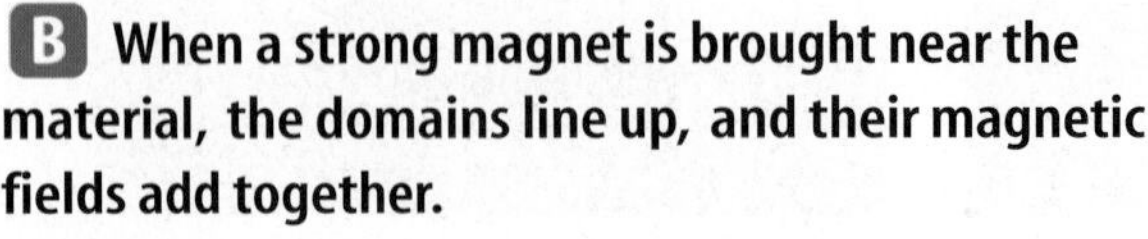

B When a strong magnet is brought near the material, the domains line up, and their magnetic fields add together.

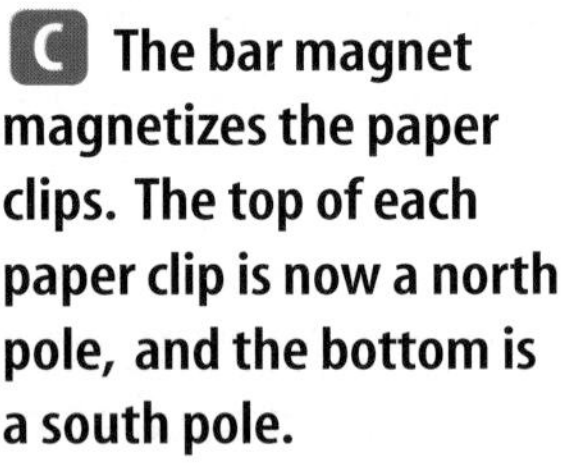

C The bar magnet magnetizes the paper clips. The top of each paper clip is now a north pole, and the bottom is a south pole.

Earth's Magnetic Field

Magnetism isn't limited to bar magnets. Earth has a magnetic field, as shown in **Figure 6.** The region of space affected by Earth's magnetic field is called the **magnetosphere** (mag NEE tuh sfihr). The origin of Earth's magnetic field is thought to be deep within Earth in the outer core layer. One theory is that movement of molten iron in the outer core is responsible for generating Earth's magnetic field. The shape of Earth's magnetic field is similar to that of a huge bar magnet tilted about 11° from Earth's geographic north and south poles.

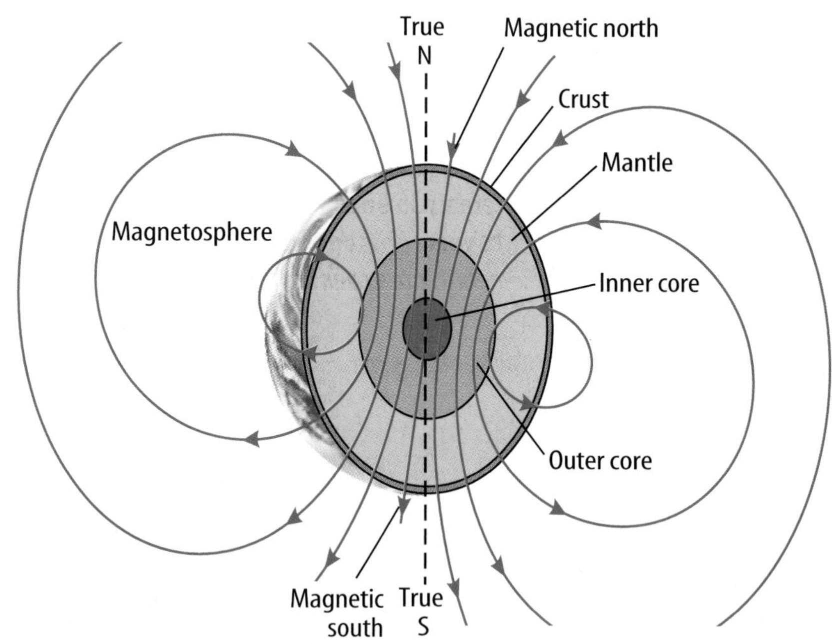

Figure 6
Earth has a magnetic field similar to the field of a bar magnet.

Problem-Solving Activity

Finding the Magnetic Declination

The north pole of a compass points toward the magnetic pole, rather than true north. Imagine drawing a line between your location and the north pole, and a line between your location and the magnetic pole. The angle between these two lines is called the magnetic declination. Sometimes knowing the magnetic declination can be important if you need to know the direction to true north, rather than to the magnetic pole. However, the magnetic declination changes depending on your position.

Identifying the Problem

Suppose your location is at 50° N and 110° W. You wish to head true north. The location of the north pole is at 90° N and 110° W, and the location of the magnetic pole is at about 80° N and 105° W. What is the magnetic declination angle at your location?

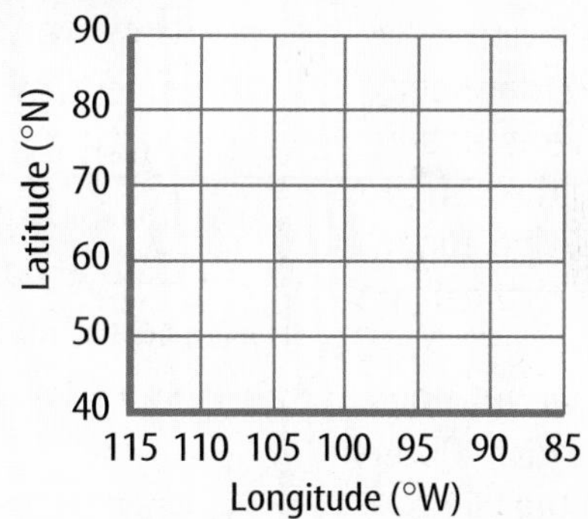

Solving the Problem

1. Label a graph like the one shown above.
2. On the graph, plot your location, the location of the magnetic pole, and the location of the north pole.
3. Draw a line from your location to the north pole, and a line from your location to the magnetic pole.
4. Using a protractor measure the angle between the two lines.

Figure 7
Earth's magnetic pole does not remain in one location from year to year. *How do you think the pole might move over the next few years?*

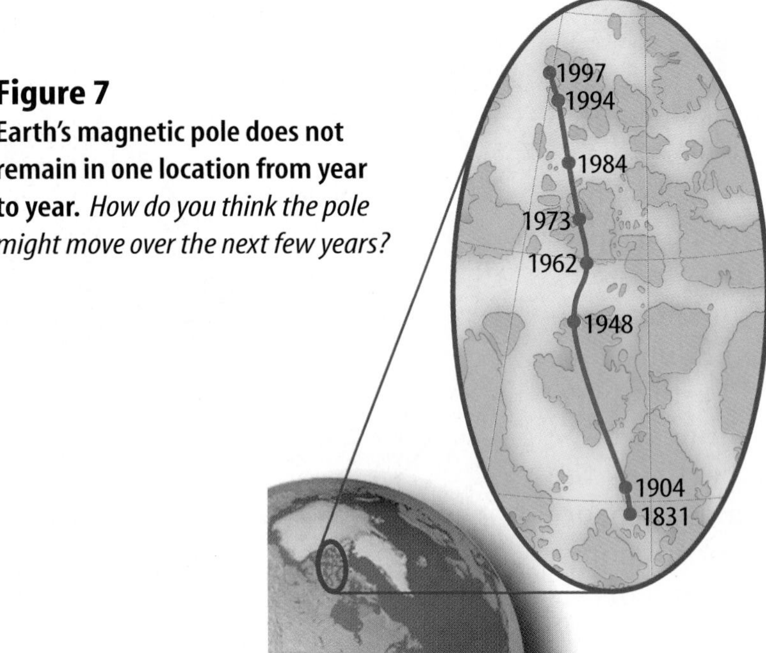

Observing Magnetic Fields

Procedure

1. Place **iron filings** in a **plastic petri dish.** Cover the dish and **tape** it closed.
2. Collect **several magnets.** Place the magnets on the table and hold the dish over each one. Draw a diagram of what happens to the filings in each case.
3. Arrange two or more magnets under the dish. Observe the pattern of the filings.

Analysis

1. What happens to the filings close to the poles? Far from the poles?
2. Compare the fields of the individual magnets. How can you tell which magnet is strongest? Weakest?

Nature's Magnets Honeybees, rainbow trout, and homing pigeons have something in common with sailors and hikers. They take advantage of magnetism to find their way. Instead of using compasses, these animals and others have tiny pieces of magnetite in their bodies. These pieces are so small that they may contain a single magnetic domain. Scientists have shown that some animals use these natural magnets to detect Earth's magnetic field. They appear to use Earth's magnetic field, along with other clues like the position of the Sun or stars, to help them navigate.

Earth's Changing Magnetic Field Earth's magnetic poles do not stay in one place. The magnetic pole in the north today, as shown in **Figure 7,** is in a different place from where it was 20 years ago. In fact, not only does the position of the magnetic poles move, but Earth's magnetic field sometimes reverses direction. For example, 700 thousand years ago, a compass needle that now points north would point south. During the past 20 million years, Earth's magnetic field has reversed direction more than 70 times. The magnetism of ancient rocks contains a record of these magnetic field changes. When some types of molten rock cool, magnetic domains of iron in the rock line up with Earth's magnetic field. After the rock cools, the orientation of these domains is frozen into position. Consequently, these old rocks preserve the orientation of Earth's magnetic field as it was long ago.

Figure 8
The compass needles align with the magnetic field lines around the magnet. *What happens to the compass needles when the bar magnet is removed?*

The Compass How can humans detect and measure Earth's magnetic field? The compass is a useful tool for finding and mapping magnetic fields. A compass has a needle that is free to turn. The needle itself is a small magnet with a north and a south magnetic pole. A magnet placed close to a compass causes the needle to rotate until it is aligned with the magnetic field line that passes through the compass, as shown in **Figure 8.**

Earth's magnetic field also causes a compass needle to rotate. The north pole of the compass needle points toward Earth's magnetic pole that is near the geographic north pole. Unlike poles attract, so this magnetic pole is actually a magnetic south pole. Earth's magnetic field is like that of a bar magnet with the magnet's south pole near Earth's north pole.

Research A compass needle doesn't point directly toward the north. How much the needle is offset from the north varies from place to place. Visit the Glencoe Science Web site at **science.glencoe.com** to find out where the compass points in your location.

Section  Assessment

1. Why do atoms behave like magnets?
2. Explain why magnets attract iron but do not attract paper.
3. How is the behavior of electric charges similar to that of magnetic poles?
4. Around a magnet, where is the field the strongest? Where is it the weakest?
5. **Think Critically** A horseshoe magnet is a bar magnet bent into the shape of the letter U. When would two horseshoe magnets attract each other? Repel? Have little effect?

Skill Builder Activities

6. **Comparing and Contrasting** Compare and contrast the three phenomena of *gravity, electricity,* and *magnetism*. Use the terms *force* and *field* in your comparison. **For more help, refer to the Science Skill Handbook.**
7. **Communicating** Imagine you are an early explorer. In your Science Journal, explain how a compass would change your work. Describe the difficulties of working without a compass. **For more help, refer to the Science Skill Handbook.**

Activity

Make a Compass

A valuable tool for hikers and campers is a compass. Almost 1,000 years ago, Chinese inventors found a way to magnetize pieces of iron. They used this method to manufacture compasses. You can use the same procedure to make a compass.

What You'll Investigate

How do you construct a compass?

Materials

petri dish	tape
**clear bowl*	marker
water	paper
sewing needle	plastic spoon
magnet	**Alternate material*

Goals

- **Observe** induced magnetism.
- **Build** a compass.

Safety

Procedure

1. Reproduce the circular protractor shown. Tape it under the bottom of your dish so it can be seen but not get wet. Add water until the dish is half full.
2. Mark one end of the needle with a marker. Magnetize a needle by placing it on the magnet aligned north and south for 1 min.
3. Float the needle carefully in the dish. Use a plastic spoon to lower the needle onto the water. Turn the dish so the marked part of the needle is above the 0° mark. This is your compass.
4. Bring the magnet near your compass. Observe how the needle reacts. Measure the angle the needle turns.

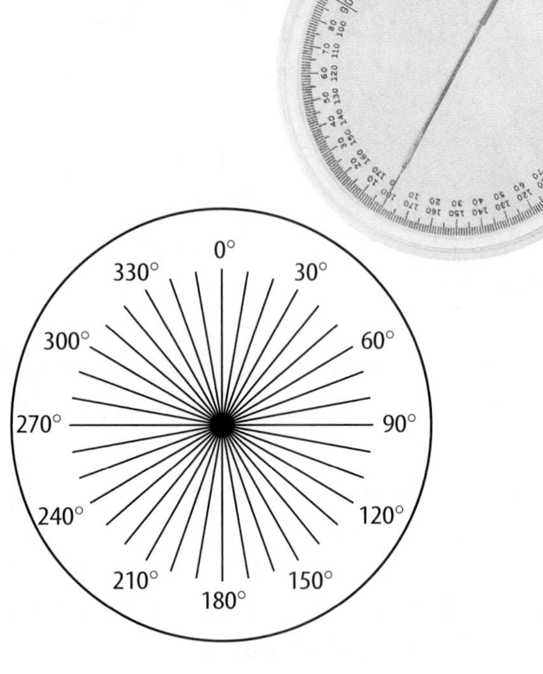

Conclude and Apply

1. **Explain** why the marked end of the needle always pointed the same way in step 3, even though you rotated the dish.
2. **Describe** the behavior of the compass when the magnet was brought close.
3. Does the marked end of your needle point to the north or south pole of the bar magnet? Infer whether the marked end of your needle is a north or a south pole. How do you know?

Communicating Your Data

Make a half-page insert that will go into a wilderness survival guide to describe the procedure for making a compass. Share your half-page insert with your classmates. **For more help, refer to the Science Skill Handbook.**

SECTION 2

Electricity and Magnetism

Current Can Make a Magnet

Magnetic fields are produced by moving electric charges. Electrons moving around the nuclei of atoms produce magnetic fields. The motion of these electrons causes some materials, such as iron, to be magnetic. You cause electric charges to move when you flip a light switch or turn on a portable CD player. When electric current flows in a wire, electric charges move in the wire. As a result, a wire that contains an electric current also is surrounded by a magnetic field. **Figure 9A** shows the magnetic field produced around a wire that carries an electric current.

Electromagnets Look at the magnetic field lines around the coils of wire in **Figure 9B.** The magnetic fields around each coil of wire add together to form a stronger magnetic field inside the coil. When the coils are wrapped around an iron core, the magnetic field of the coils magnetizes the iron. The iron then becomes a magnet, which adds to the strength of the magnetic field inside the coil. A current-carrying wire wrapped around an iron core is called an **electromagnet,** as shown in **Figure 9C.**

As You Read

What You'll Learn

- **Describe** the relationship between electricity and magnetism.
- **Explain** how electricity can produce motion.
- **Explain** how motion can produce electricity.

Vocabulary

electromagnet
generator
motor
alternating current
aurora
transformer

Why It's Important

The electric current that comes from your wall socket is available because of magnetism.

Figure 9
A current-carrying wire produces a magnetic field.

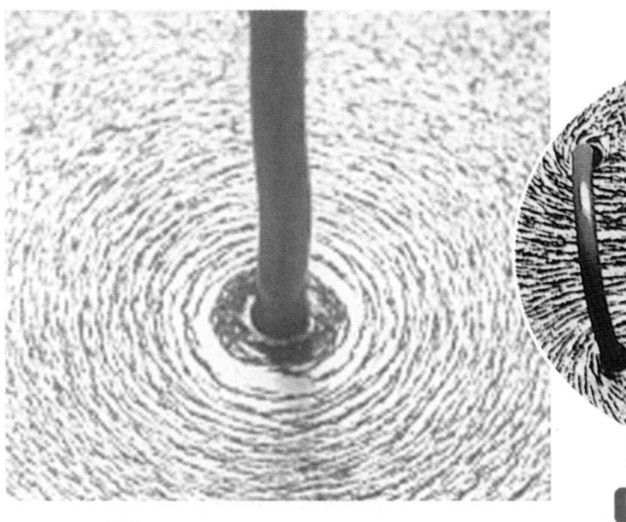

A Iron particles show the magnetic field lines around a current-carrying wire.

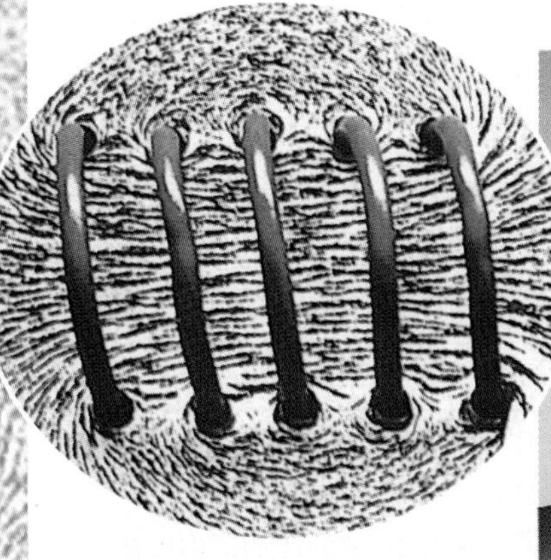

B When a wire is wrapped in a coil, the field inside the coil is made stronger.

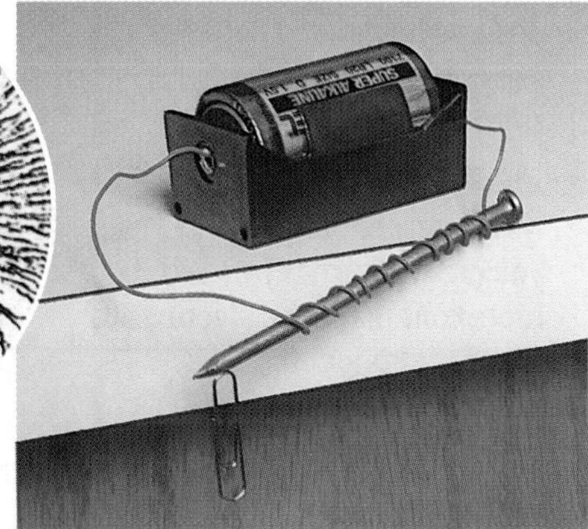

C An iron core inside the coils increases the magnetic field because the core becomes magnetized.

Figure 10
An electric doorbell uses an electromagnet. Each time the electromagnet is turned on, the hammer strikes the bell. *How is the electromagnet turned off?*

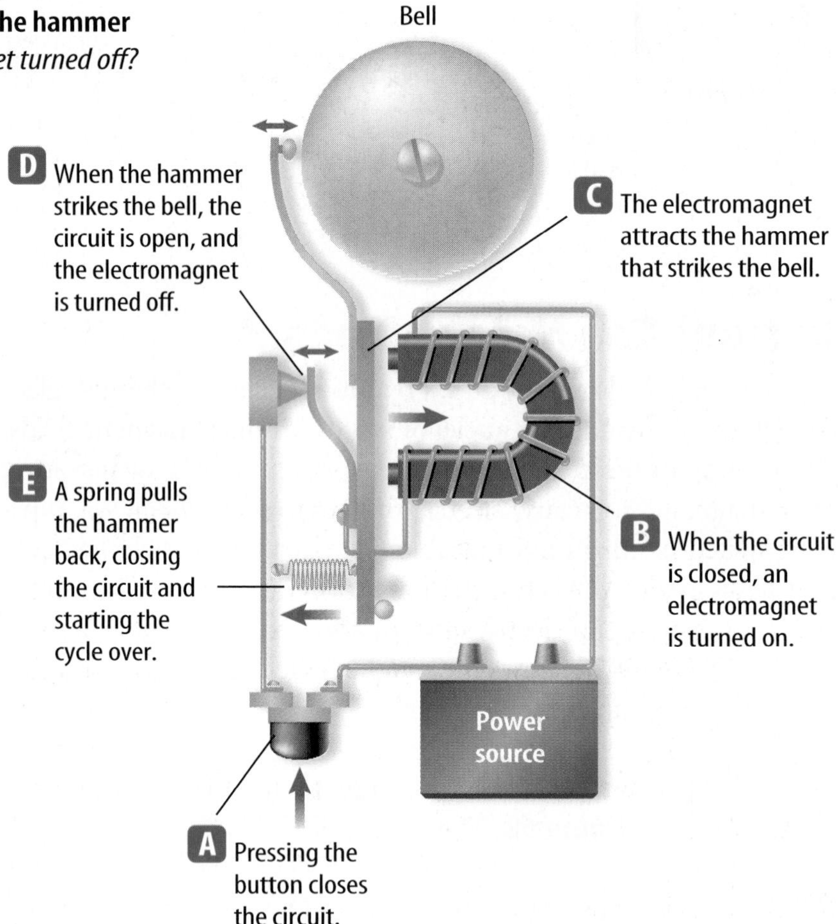

Bell
D When the hammer strikes the bell, the circuit is open, and the electromagnet is turned off.
C The electromagnet attracts the hammer that strikes the bell.
E A spring pulls the hammer back, closing the circuit and starting the cycle over.
B When the circuit is closed, an electromagnet is turned on.
Power source
A Pressing the button closes the circuit.

TRY AT HOME Mini LAB

Assembling an Electromagnet

Procedure

1. Wrap a **wire** around a **16-penny steel nail** ten times. Connect one end of the wire to a **D-cell battery,** as shown in **Figure 9C.** Leave the other end loose until you use the electromagnet. **WARNING:** *When current is flowing in the wire, it can become hot over time.*
2. Connect the wire. Observe how many **paper clips** you can pick up with the magnet.
3. Disconnect the wire and rewrap the nail with 20 coils. Connect the wire and observe how many paper clips you can pick up. Disconnect the wire again.

Analysis

1. How many paper clips did you pick up each time? Did more coils make the electromagnet stronger or weaker?
2. Graph the number of coils versus number of paper clips attracted. Predict how many paper clips would be picked up with five coils of wire. Check your prediction.

Using Electromagnets The magnetic field of an electromagnet is turned on or off when the electric current is turned on or off. By changing the current, the strength and direction of the magnetic field of an electromagnet can be changed. This has led to a number of practical uses for electromagnets. A doorbell, as shown in **Figure 10,** is a familiar use of an electromagnet. When you press the button by the door, you close a switch in a circuit that includes an electromagnet. The magnet attracts an iron bar attached to a hammer. The hammer strikes the bell. When the hammer strikes the bell, the hammer has moved far enough to open the circuit again. The electromagnet loses its magnetic field, and a spring pulls the iron bar and hammer back into place. This movement closes the circuit, and the cycle is repeated as long as the button is pushed.

Some gauges, such as the gas gauge in a car, use a galvanometer to move the gauge pointer. **Figure 11** shows how a galvanometer makes a pointer move. Ammeters and voltmeters used to measure current and voltage in electric circuits also use galvanometers, as shown in **Figure 11.**

VISUALIZING VOLTMETERS AND AMMETERS

Figure 11

The gas gauge in a car uses a device called a galvanometer to make the needle of the gauge move. Galvanometers are also used in other measuring devices. A voltmeter uses a galvanometer to measure the voltage in a electric circuit. An ammeter uses a galvanometer to measure electric current. Multimeters can be used as an ammeter or voltmeter by turning a switch.

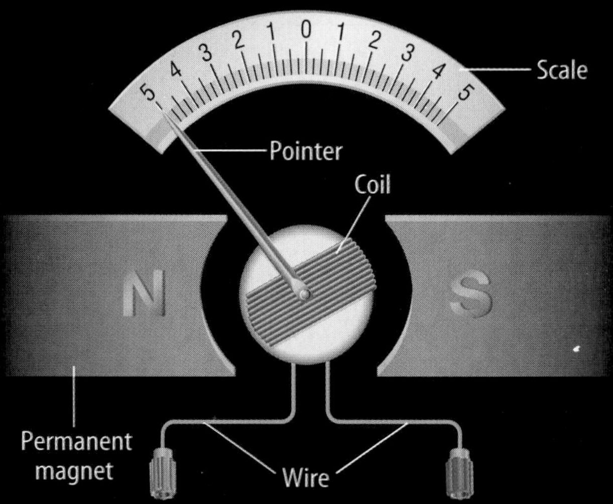

A galvanometer has a pointer attached to a coil that can rotate between the poles of a permanent magnet. When a current flows through the coil, it becomes an electromagnet. Attraction and repulsion between the magnetic poles of the electromagnet and the poles of the permanent magnet makes the coil rotate. The amount of rotation depends on the amount of current in the coil.

To measure the current in a circuit an ammeter is used. An ammeter contains a galvanometer and has low resistance. To measure current, an ammeter is connected in series in the circuit, so all the current in the circuit flows through it. The greater the current in the circuit, the more the needle moves.

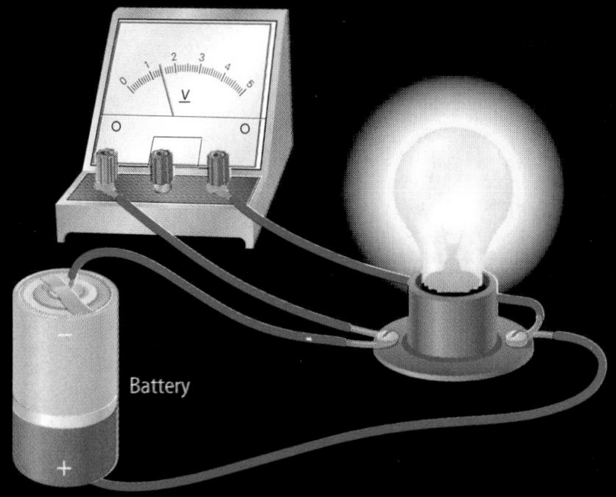

To measure the voltage in a circuit a voltmeter is used. A voltmeter also contains a galvanometer and has high resistance. To measure voltage, a voltmeter is connected in parallel in the circuit, so almost no current flows through it. The higher the voltage in the circuit, the more the needle moves.

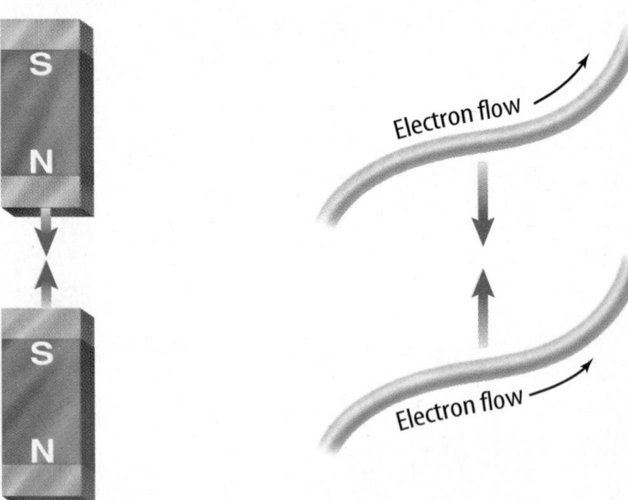

Magnets Push and Pull Currents

Look around for electric appliances that produce motion, such as a fan. How does the electric energy entering the fan become transformed into the kinetic energy of the moving fan blades? Recall that current-carrying wires produce a magnetic field. This magnetic field behaves the same way as the magnetic field that a magnet produces. Two current-carrying wires can attract each other as if they were two magnets, as shown in **Figure 12.**

Figure 12
Two wires carrying current in the same direction attract each other, just as unlike magnetic poles do.

Electric Motor Just as two magnets exert a force on each other, a magnet and a current-carrying wire exert forces on each other. The magnetic field around a current-carrying wire will cause it to be pushed or pulled by a magnet, depending on the direction the current is flowing in the wire. As a result, some of the electric energy carried by the current is converted into kinetic energy of the moving wire, as shown in **Figure 13A.** Any device that converts electric energy into kinetic energy is a **motor.** To keep a motor running, the current-carrying wire is formed into a loop so the magnetic field can force the wire to spin continually, as shown in **Figure 13B.**

Figure 13
In an electric motor, the force a magnet exerts on a current-carrying wire transforms electric energy into kinetic energy.

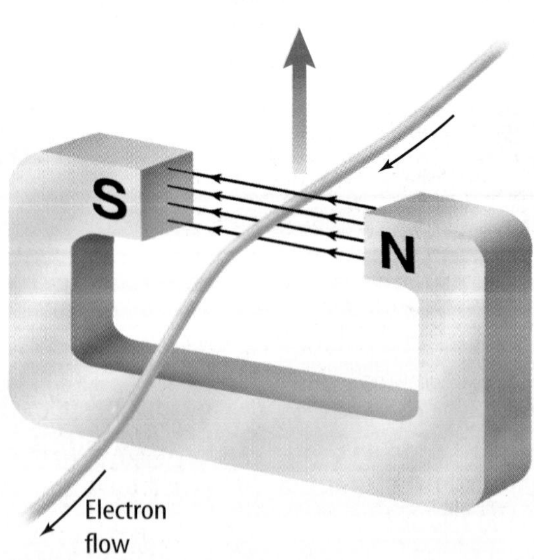

A **A magnetic field like the one shown will push a current-carrying wire upward.**

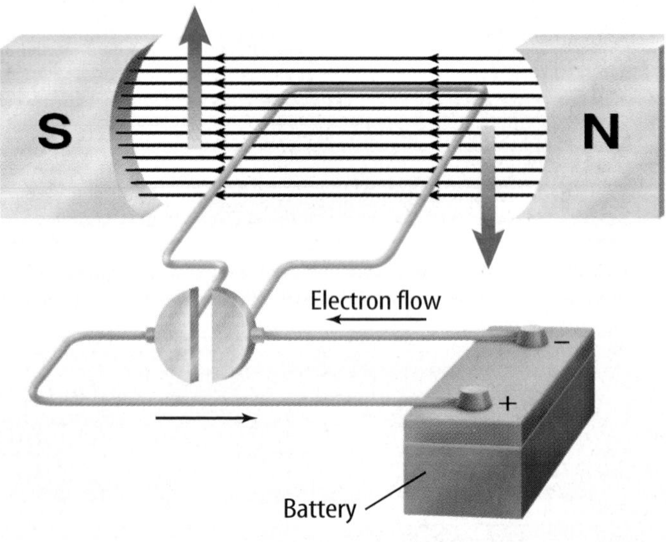

B **The magnetic field exerts a force on the wire loop, causing it to spin as long as current flows in the loop.**

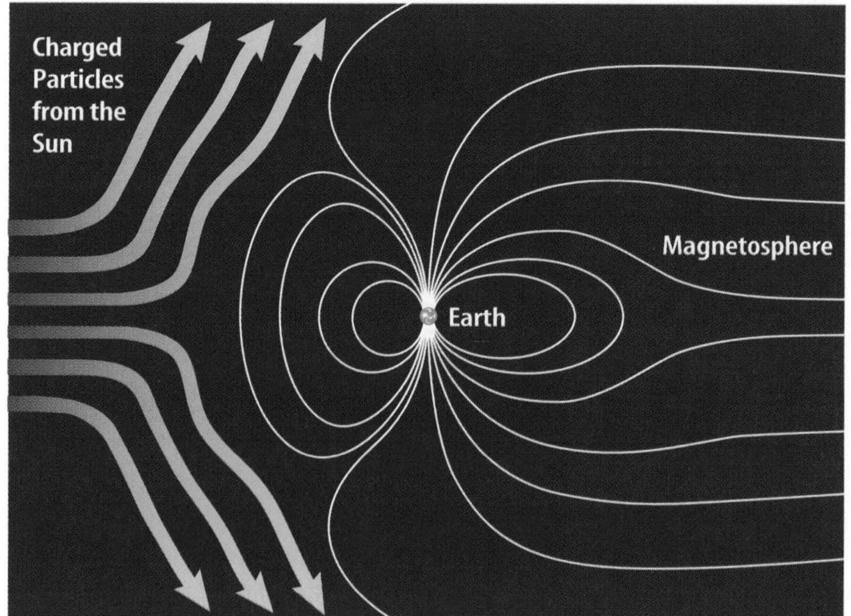

Figure 14
Earth's magnetosphere deflects most of the charged particles streaming from the Sun. *Why is the magnetosphere stretched away from the Sun?*

Earth's Magnetosphere The Sun emits charged particles that stream through the solar system like an enormous electric current. Just like a current-carrying wire is pushed or pulled by a magnetic field, Earth's magnetic field pushes and pulls on the electric current generated by the Sun. This causes most of the charged particles in this current to be deflected so they never strike Earth, as shown in **Figure 14.** As a result, living things on Earth are protected from damage that might be caused by these charged particles. At the same time, the solar current pushes on Earth's magnetosphere so it is stretched away from the Sun.

The Aurora Sometimes the Sun ejects a large number of charged particles all at once. Most of these charged particles are deflected by Earth's magnetosphere. However, some of the ejected particles from the Sun produce other charged particles in Earth's outer atmosphere. These charged particles spiral along Earth's magnetic field lines toward Earth's magnetic poles. There they collide with atoms in the atmosphere. These collisions cause the atoms to emit light. The light emitted causes a display known as the **aurora** (uh ROR uh), as shown in **Figure 15.** In northern latitudes, the aurora sometimes is called the northern lights.

Figure 15
An aurora is a natural light show that occurs in the southern and northern skies.

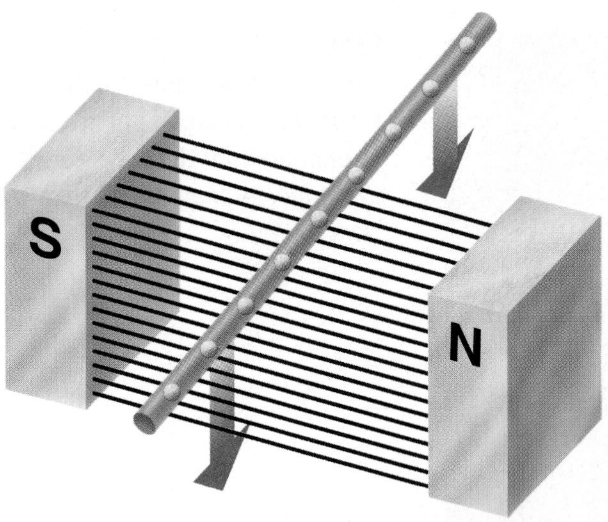

A If a wire is pulled through a magnetic field, the electrons in the wire also move downward.

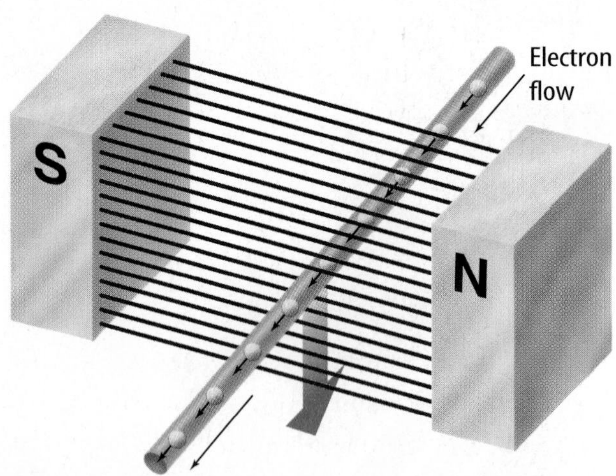

B The magnetic field then exerts a force on the moving electrons, causing them to move along the wire.

Figure 16
When a wire is made to move through a magnetic field, an electric current can be produced in the wire.

Figure 17
In a generator, a power source spins a wire loop in a magnetic field. Every half turn, the current will reverse direction. This type of generator supplies alternating current to the lightbulb.

Using Magnets to Create Current

In an electric motor, a magnetic field turns electricity into motion. A device called a **generator** uses a magnetic field to turn motion into electricity. Electric motors and electric generators both involve conversions between electric energy and kinetic energy. In a motor, electric energy is changed into kinetic energy. In a generator, kinetic energy is changed into electric energy. **Figure 16** shows how a current can be produced in a wire that moves in a magnetic field. As the wire moves, the electrons in the wire also move in the same direction, as shown in **Figure 16A.** The magnetic field exerts a force on the moving electrons that pushes them along the wire, as shown in **Figure 16B,** creating an electric current.

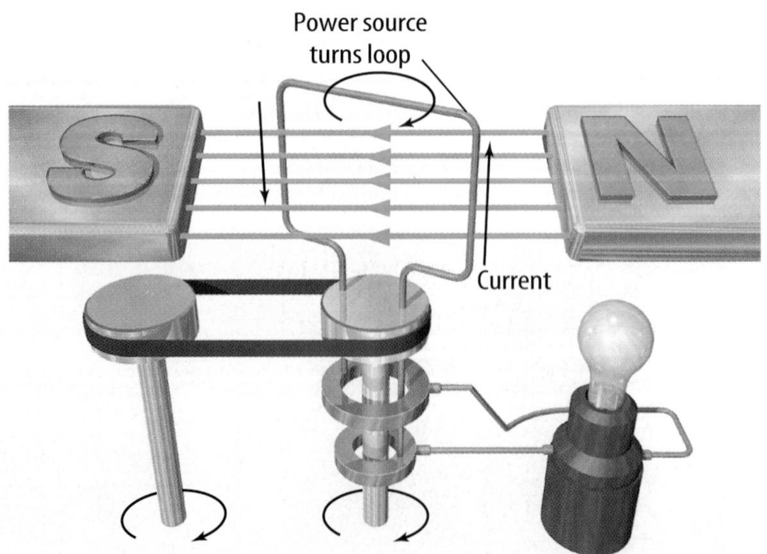

Electric Generators To produce electric current, the wire is fashioned into a loop, as in **Figure 17.** A power source provides the kinetic energy to spin the wire loop. With each half turn, the current in the loop changes direction. This causes the current to alternate from positive to negative. Such a current is called an **alternating current** (AC). In the United States, electric currents change from positive to negative to positive 60 times each second.

Types of Current A battery produces direct current instead of alternating current. In a direct current (DC) electrons flow in one direction. In an alternating current, electrons change their direction of movement many times each second. Some generators are built to produce direct current instead of alternating current.

Reading Check *What type of currents can be produced by a generator?*

Power Plants Electric generators produce almost all of the electric energy used all over the world. Small generators can produce energy for one household, and large generators in electric power plants can provide electric energy for thousands of homes. Different energy sources such as gas, coal, and water are used to provide the kinetic energy to rotate coils of wire in a magnetic field. Coal-burning power plants, like the one pictured in **Figure 18,** are the most common. More than half of the electric energy generated by power plants in the United States comes from burning coal.

Research Visit the Glencoe Science Web site at **science.glencoe.com** for more information about the different types of power plants used in your region of the country. Communicate to your class what you learn.

Voltage The electric energy produced at a power plant is carried to your home in wires. Recall that voltage is a measure of how much energy the electric charges in a current are carrying. The electric transmission lines from electric power plants transmit electric energy at a high voltage of about 700,000 V. Transmitting electric energy at a low voltage is less efficient because more electric energy is converted into heat in the wires. However, high voltage is not safe for use in homes and businesses. A device is needed to reduce the voltage.

Figure 18
Coal-burning power plants supply much of the electric energy for the world.

Figure 19
Electricity travels from a generator to your home.

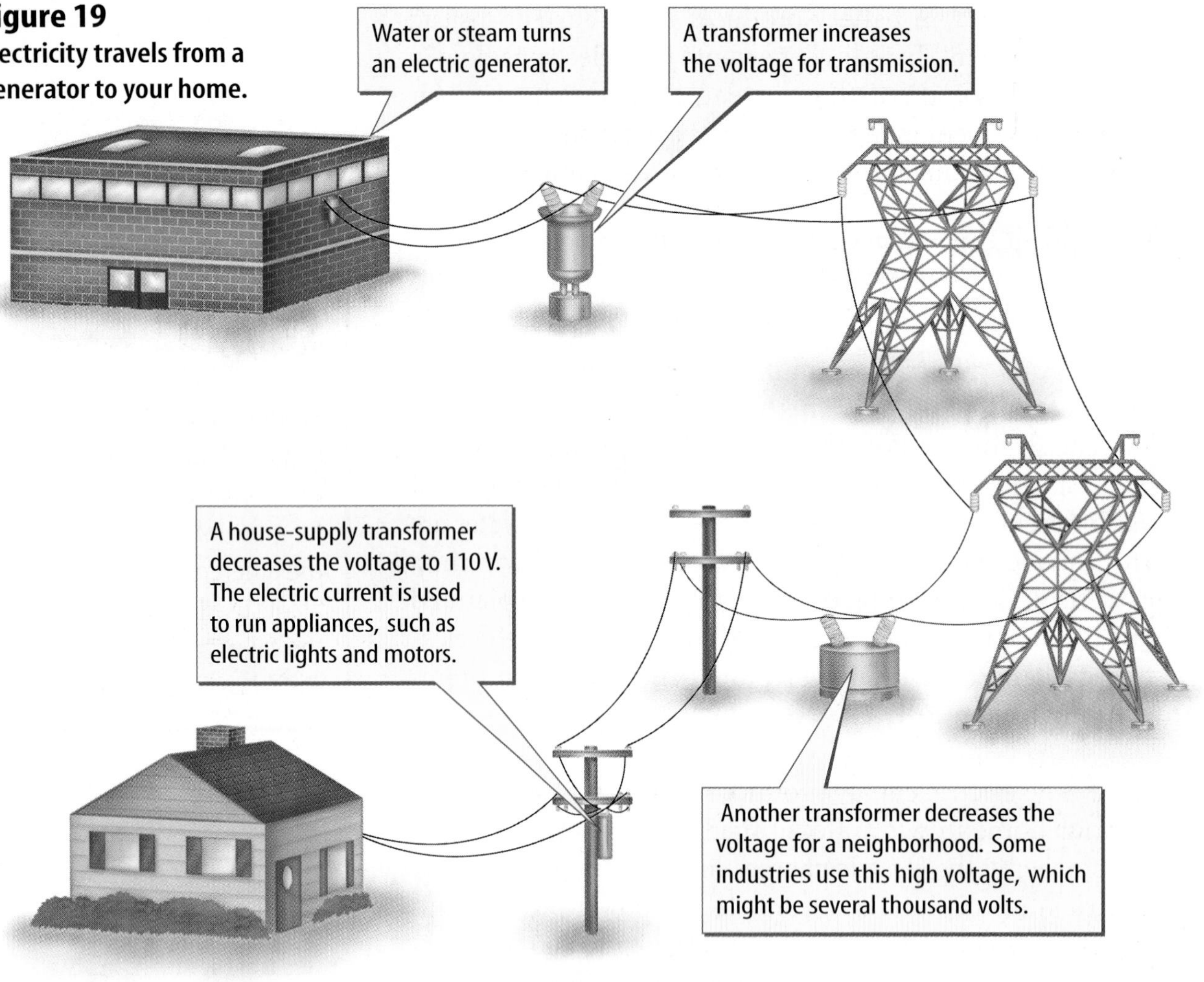

Water or steam turns an electric generator.

A transformer increases the voltage for transmission.

A house-supply transformer decreases the voltage to 110 V. The electric current is used to run appliances, such as electric lights and motors.

Another transformer decreases the voltage for a neighborhood. Some industries use this high voltage, which might be several thousand volts.

Changing Voltage

A **transformer** is a device that changes the voltage of an alternating current with little loss of energy. Transformers are used to increase the voltage before transmitting an electric current through the power lines. Other transformers are used to decrease the voltage to the level needed for home or industrial use. Such a power system is shown in **Figure 19.** Transformers also are used in power adaptors. For battery-operated devices, a power adaptor must change the 110 V from the wall outlet to the same voltage produced by the device's batteries.

Reading Check *What does a transformer do?*

A transformer usually has two coils of wire wrapped around an iron core, as shown in **Figure 20.** One coil is connected to an alternating current source. The current creates a magnetic field in the iron core, just like in an electromagnet. Because the current is alternating, the magnetic field it produces also switches direction. This alternating magnetic field in the core then causes an alternating current in the other wire coil.

Figure 20
A transformer can increase or decrease voltage. The ratio of input coils to output coils equals the ratio of input voltage to output voltage. *If the input voltage here is 60 V, what is the output voltage?*

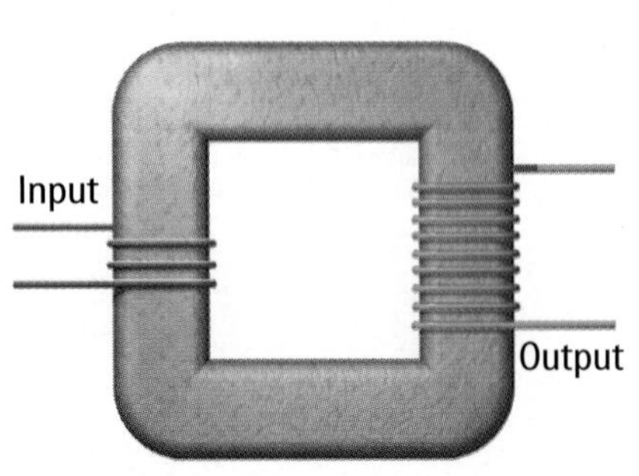

The Transformer Ratio Whether a transformer increases or decreases the input voltage depends on the number of coils on each side of the transformer. The ratio of the number of coils on the input side to the number of coils on the output side is the same as the ratio of the input voltage to the output voltage. For the transformer in **Figure 20** the ratio of the number of coils on the input side to the number of coils on the output side is three to nine, or one to three. If the input voltage is 60 V, the output voltage will be 180 V.

In a transformer the voltage is greater on the side with more coils. If the number of coils on the input side is greater than the number of coils on the output side, the voltage is decreased. If the number of coils on the input side is less than the number on the output side, the voltage is increased.

Superconductors

Electric current can flow easily through materials, such as metals, that are electrical conductors. However, even in conductors, there is some resistance to this flow and heat is produced as electrons collide with atoms in the material.

Unlike an electrical conductor, a material known as a superconductor has no resistance to the flow of electrons. Superconductors are formed when certain materials are cooled to low temperatures. For example, aluminum becomes a superconductor at about −272°C. When an electric current flows through a superconductor, no heat is produced and no electric energy is converted into heat.

Superconductors and Magnets Superconductors also have other unusual properties. For example, a magnet is repelled by a superconductor. As the magnet gets close to the superconductor, the superconductor creates a magnetic field that is opposite to the field of the magnet. The field created by the superconductor can cause the magnet to float above it, as shown in **Figure 21.**

Figure 21
A small magnet floats above a superconductor. The magnet causes the superconductor to produce a magnetic field that repels the magnet.

Figure 22
The particle accelerator at Fermi National Accelerator Laboratory near Batavia, Illinois, accelerates atomic particles to nearly the speed of light. The particles travel in a beam only a few millimeters in diameter. Magnets made of superconductors keep the beam moving in a circular path about 2 km in diameter.

Using Superconductors Large electric currents can flow through electromagnets made from superconducting wire and can produce extremely strong magnetic fields. The particle accelerator shown in **Figure 22** uses more than 1,000 superconducting electromagnets to help accelerate subatomic particles to nearly the speed of light.

Other uses for superconductors are being developed. Transmission lines made from a superconductor could transmit electric power over long distances without having any electric energy converted to heat. It also may be possible to construct extremely fast computers using microchips made from superconductor materials.

Figure 23
A patient is being placed inside an MRI machine. The strong magnetic field inside the machine enables images of tissues inside the patient's body to be made.

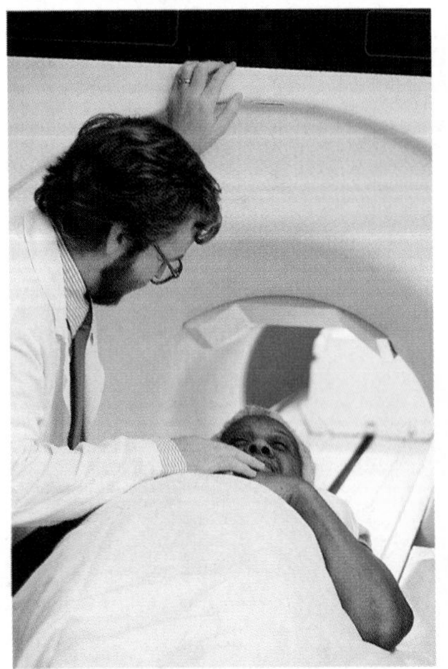

Magnetic Resonance Imaging

A method called magnetic resonance imaging, or MRI, uses magnetic fields to create images of the inside of a human body. MRI images can show if tissue is damaged or diseased, and can detect the presence of tumors.

Unlike X-ray imaging, which uses X-ray radiation that can damage tissue, MRI uses a strong magnetic field and radio waves. The patient is placed inside a machine like the one shown in **Figure 23.** Inside the machine an electromagnet made from superconductor materials produces a magnetic field more than 20,000 times stronger than Earth's magnetic field.

Producing MRI Images About 63 percent of all the atoms in your body are hydrogen atoms. The nucleus of a hydrogen atom is a proton, which behaves like a tiny magnet. The strong magnetic field inside the MRI tube causes these protons to line up along the direction of the field. Radio waves are then applied to the part of the body being examined. The protons absorb some of the energy in the radio waves, and change the direction of their alignment.

When the radio waves are turned off, the protons realign themselves with the magnetic field and emit the energy they absorbed. The amount of energy emitted depends on the type of tissue in the body. This energy emitted is detected and a computer uses this information to form an image, like the one shown in **Figure 24.**

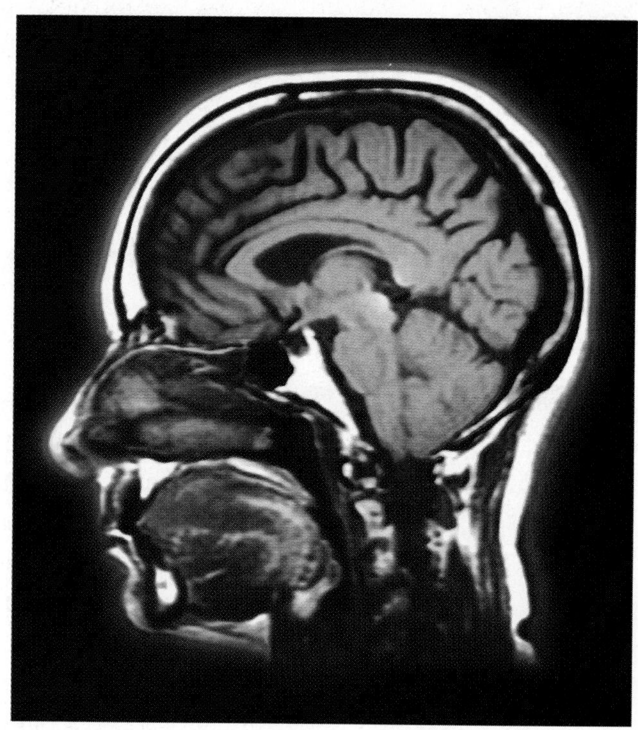

Figure 24
This MRI image shows a side view of the brain. An MRI scan can produce images from several angles, as well as cross-sections.

Connecting Electricity and Magnetism Electric forces and magnetic forces are similar in some ways. Both forces can repel or attract. Like electric charges repel each other, and like magnetic poles repel each other. Positive and negative electric charges attract, and north and south magnetic poles attract.

Electric charges and magnets are connected in another important way. Moving electric charges produce magnetic fields, and magnetic fields exert forces on moving electric charges. It is this connection enables electric motors and generators to operate.

Section  Assessment

1. What is an electromagnet? How can you make one in the classroom?
2. How does a transformer work?
3. How does a magnetic field affect a current-carrying wire?
4. How does a generator turn motion into electrical energy?
5. **Think Critically** How is an electric motor similar to an aurora? Use the terms current, field, and kinetic energy in your answer.

Skill Builder Activities

6. **Researching Information** Research the types of power plants in your state. Make a poster showing the fuels that are used. **For more help, refer to the Science Skill Handbook.**
7. **Calculating Ratios** A transformer has ten turns of wire on the input side and 50 turns of wire on the output side. If the input voltage is 120 V, what will the output voltage be? **For more help, refer to the Math Skill Handbook.**

Activity

How does an electric motor work?

Electric motors are used in many appliances. For example, a computer contains a cooling fan and motors to spin the hard drive. A CD player contains electric motors to spin the CD. Some cars contain electric motors that move windows up and down, change the position of the seats, and blow warm or cold air into the car's interior. All these electric motors consist of an electromagnet and a permanent magnet. In this activity you will build a simple electric motor that will work for you.

What You'll Investigate

How can you change electric energy into motion?

Goals

- **Assemble** a small electric motor.
- **Observe** how the motor works.

Safety Precautions

Hold only the insulated part of each wire when they are attached to the battery. Use care when hammering the nails. After cutting the wire, the ends will be sharp.

Materials

22-gauge enameled wire (4 m)
steel knitting needle
**steel rod*
nails (4)
hammer
ceramic magnets (2)
18-gauge insulated wire (60 cm)
masking tape
fine sandpaper
approximately 15-cm wooden board
wooden blocks (2)
6-V battery
**1.5-V batteries connected in a series* (4)
wire cutters
**scissors*
**Alternate materials*

Procedure

1. Use sandpaper to strip the enamel from about 4 cm of each end of the 22-gauge wire.
2. Leaving the stripped ends free, make this wire into a tight coil of at least 30 turns. A D-cell battery or a film canister will help in forming the coil. Tape the coil so it doesn't unravel.
3. Insert the knitting needle through the coil. Center the coil on the needle. Pull the wire's two ends to one end of the needle.
4. Near the ends of the wire, wrap masking tape around the needle to act as insulation. Then tape one bare wire to each side of the needle at the spot where the masking tape is.
5. Tape a ceramic magnet to each block so that a north pole extends from one and a south pole from the other.
6. Make the motor. Tap the nails into the wood block as shown in the figure. Try to cross the nails at the same height as the magnets so the coil will be suspended between them.

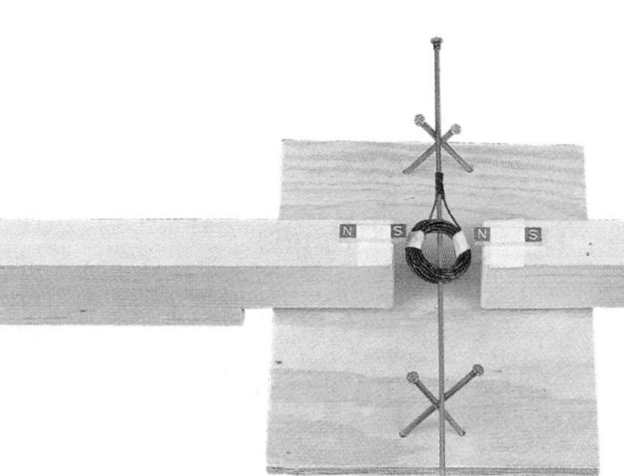

7. Place the needle on the nails. Use bits of wood or folded paper to adjust the positions of the magnets until the coil is directly between the magnets. The magnets should be as close to the coil as possible without touching it.
8. Cut two 30-cm lengths of 18-gauge wire. Use sandpaper to strip the ends of both wires. Attach one wire to each terminal of the battery. Holding only the insulated part of each wire, place one wire against each of the bare wires taped to the needle to close the circuit. Observe what happens.

Conclude and Apply

1. **Describe** what happens when you close the circuit by connecting the wires. Were the results expected?
2. **Describe** what happens when you open the circuit.
3. **Predict** what would happen if you used twice as many coils of wire.

Compare your conclusions with other students in your class. **For more help, refer to the** Science Skill Handbook.

Chapter 16 Study Guide

Reviewing Main Ideas

Section 1 What is magnetism?

1. All magnets have two poles—north and south. Like poles repel each other and unlike poles attract.
2. Electrons act like tiny magnets. Groups of atoms can align to form magnetic domains. If domains align, then a magnet is formed. *Why do magnets stick to some objects, such as refrigerators, but not others?*

3. A magnetic force acts through a magnetic field. Magnetic fields extend through space and point from a north pole to a south pole.
4. Earth has a magnetic field that can be detected using a compass. *What might be the cause for these green and red lights above Earth in the photo taken from the space shuttle in orbit?*

Section 2 Electricity and Magnetism

1. Electric current creates a magnetic field. Electromagnets are made from a coil of wire that carries a current, wrapped around an iron core. *How is this crane able to lift the scrap iron particles?*

2. A magnetic field exerts a force on a moving charge or a current-carrying wire.
3. Motors transform electric energy into kinetic energy. Generators transform kinetic energy into electric energy.
4. Transformers are used to increase and decrease voltage in AC circuits. *In this step-down transformer, which has more turns, the input coil or the output coil?*

After You Read

Using the information on your Foldable, compare and contrast the terms *magnetic force* and *magnetic field.* Write your observations under the flaps in your Foldable.

Chapter 16 Study Guide

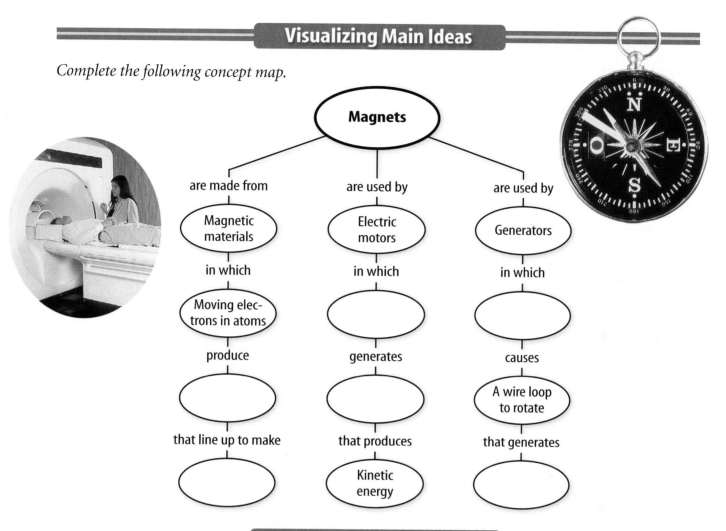

Visualizing Main Ideas

Complete the following concept map.

Magnets

- are made from → Magnetic materials → in which → Moving electrons in atoms → produce → ( ) → that line up to make → ( )
- are used by → Electric motors → in which → ( ) → generates → ( ) → that produces → Kinetic energy
- are used by → Generators → in which → ( ) → causes → A wire loop to rotate → that generates → ( )

Vocabulary Review

Vocabulary Words

a. alternating current
b. aurora
c. electromagnet
d. generator
e. magnetic domain
f. magnetic field
g. magnetosphere
h. motor
i. transformer

Study Tip

Look for examples in your home of what you are studying in science class. For instance, where can you find electric motors in your home?

Using Vocabulary

Explain the relationship that exists between each set of vocabulary words below.

1. generator, transformer
2. magnetic force, magnetic field
3. alternating current, direct current
4. current, electromagnet
5. motor, generator
6. electron, magnetism
7. magnetosphere, aurora
8. magnet, magnetic domain

Chapter 16 Assessment

Checking Concepts

Choose the word or phrase that best answers the question.

1. What can iron filings be used to show?
   - **A)** magnetic field
   - **B)** electric field
   - **C)** gravitational field
   - **D)** none of these
2. Why does the needle of a compass point to magnetic north?
   - **A)** Earth's north pole is strongest.
   - **B)** Earth's north pole is closest.
   - **C)** Only the north pole attracts compasses.
   - **D)** The compass needle aligns itself with Earth's magnetic field.
3. What will the north poles of two bar magnets do when brought together?
   - **A)** attract
   - **B)** create an electric current
   - **C)** repel
   - **D)** not interact
4. How many poles do all magnets have?
   - **A)** one
   - **B)** two
   - **C)** three
   - **D)** one or two
5. When a current-carrying wire is wrapped around an iron core, what can it create?
   - **A)** an aurora
   - **B)** a magnet
   - **C)** a generator
   - **D)** a motor
6. What does a transformer between utility wires and your house do?
   - **A)** increases voltage
   - **B)** decreases voltage
   - **C)** leaves voltage the same
   - **D)** changes DC to AC
7. Which energy transformation occurs in an electric motor?
   - **A)** electrical to kinetic
   - **B)** electrical to thermal
   - **C)** potential to kinetic
   - **D)** kinetic to electrical
8. What prevents most charged particles from the Sun from hitting Earth?
   - **A)** the aurora
   - **B)** Earth's magnetic field
   - **C)** high-altitude electric fields
   - **D)** Earth's atmosphere
9. Which of these objects do magnetic fields NOT interact with?
   - **A)** magnets
   - **B)** steel
   - **C)** current
   - **D)** paper
10. Which energy transformation occurs in an electric generator?
    - **A)** electrical to kinetic
    - **B)** electrical to thermal
    - **C)** potential to kinetic
    - **D)** kinetic to electrical

Thinking Critically

11. Why don't ordinary bar magnets line themselves up with Earth's magnetic field when you set them on a table?
12. If you were given a magnet with unmarked poles, how could you determine which pole was which?
13. A nail is magnetized by holding the south pole of a magnet against the head of the nail. Is the point of the nail a north or a south pole? Sketch your explanation.

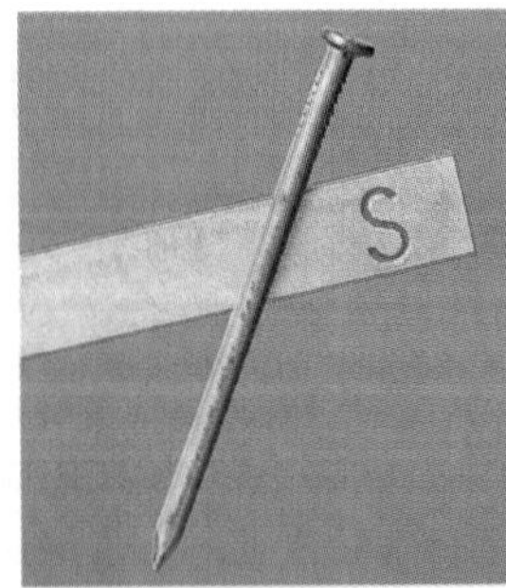

14. If you add more coils to an electromagnet, does the magnet get stronger or weaker? Why? What happens if the current increases?
15. What are the sources of magnetic fields? How can you demonstrate this?

Developing Skills

16. **Identifying and Manipulating Variables and Controls** How could you test and compare the strength of two different magnets?
17. **Forming Operational Definitions** Give an operational definition of an electromagnet.
18. **Concept Mapping** Explain how a doorbell uses an electromagnet by placing the following phrases in the cycle concept map: *circuit open, circuit closed, electromagnet turned on, electromagnet turned off, hammer attracted to magnet and strikes bell,* and *hammer pulled back by a spring.*

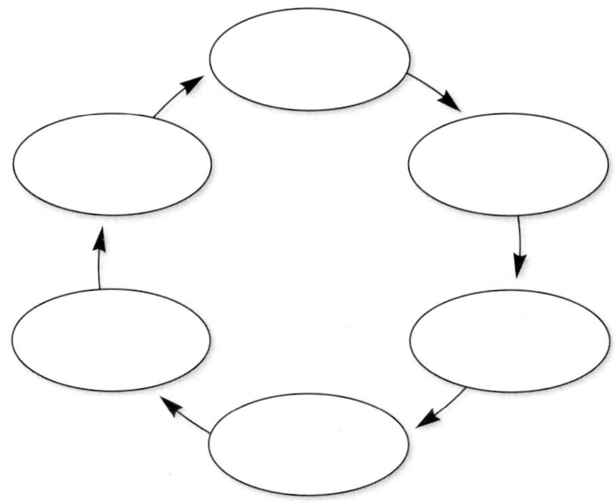

Performance Assessment

19. **Multimedia Presentation** Prepare a multimedia presentation to inform your classmates on the future uses of magnets and magnetism.

Technology

Go to the Glencoe Science Web site at **science.glencoe.com** or use the **Glencoe Science CD-ROM** for additional chapter assessment.

Test Practice

Magnetism affects all aspects of modern life. The table below lists some examples of processes involving magnetic fields.

Processes Involving Magnetic Fields

Example	Process	Result
Motor	Converts electrical energy into kinetic	Used in elecric fans
Generator	Converts mechanical energy into electrical	Produce light
Charged particles from Sun	Charged particles trapped in Earth's magnetosphere	Aurora
Transformer	Change voltage through power lines	Deliver current to homes

Study the table and answer the following questions.

1. According to this information, which process most likely occurs naturally?
   A) conversion of electrical energy into kinetic
   B) conversion of mechanical energy into electric energy
   C) trapped charged particles in Earth's magnetosphere
   D) voltage changes through power lines
2. Hydroelectric power plants use the gravitational potential energy of water to turn generators, which then produce electricity. According to the table above, which process is this an example of?
   F) motor
   G) generator
   H) charged particles
   J) transformer

Standardized Test Practice

Reading Comprehension

Read the passage. Then read each question that follows the passage. Decide which is the best answer to each question.

Magnetic Levitation Train

One of the first things people learn about magnets is that like magnetic poles repel each other. This is the basic principle behind the Magnetic Levitation Train, or Maglev.

Maglev is a high-speed train. It uses high-strength magnets to lift and propel the train to incredible speeds as it hovers only a few centimeters above the track. This helps the train to reach higher speeds than conventional trains. A full-size Maglev in Japan achieved a speed of over 500 km/h! Its electromagnetic motor can be precisely controlled to provide smooth acceleration and braking between stops. The magnetic field prevents the train from drifting away from the center of the guideway.

Because there is no friction between wheels and rails, Maglevs eliminate the principal limitation of conventional trains, which is the high cost of maintaining the tracks to avoid excessive vibration and wear that can cause dangerous derailments. Critics point out that Maglevs require enormous amounts of energy. However, studies have shown that Maglevs use 30 percent less energy than other high-speed trains traveling at the same speed. Others worry about the dangers from magnetic fields; however, measurements show that humans are exposed to magnetic fields no stronger than those from toasters or hair dryers.

This year in Japan a series of Maglevs will be tested on a 43-km demonstration line. Perhaps someday Maglevs will carry commuters to and from work and school in the United States.

Test-Taking Tip After you read the passage, write a one-sentence summary of the main idea for each paragraph.

This is a Maglev test train in Japan.

1. Which of the following statements best summarizes this passage?
- **A)** Maglev transportation is currently in use in Germany and Japan.
- **B)** Maglev might be a high-speed transport system of the future.
- **C)** Maglevs use more energy than conventional high-speed trains.
- **D)** Maglevs expose passengers to strong magnetic fields.

2. In this passage, the word conventional means _____.
- **F)** customary
- **G)** innovative
- **H)** political
- **J)** unusual

Standardized Test Practice

Reasoning and Skills

Read each question and choose the best answer.

1. Voltage increases when the output coil in a transformer has more turns of wire than the input coil. Which of the following increases voltage the most?

A)

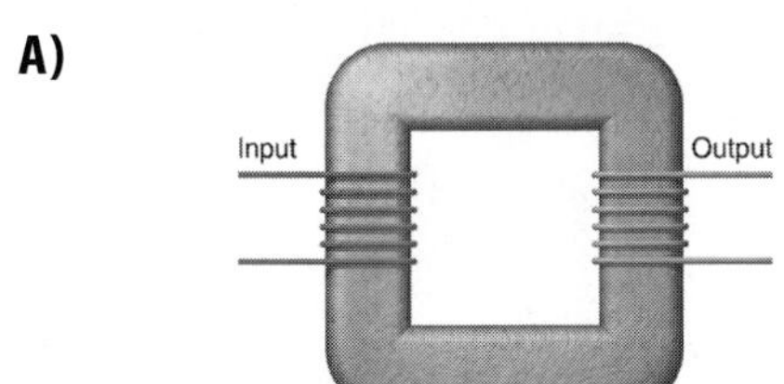

B)

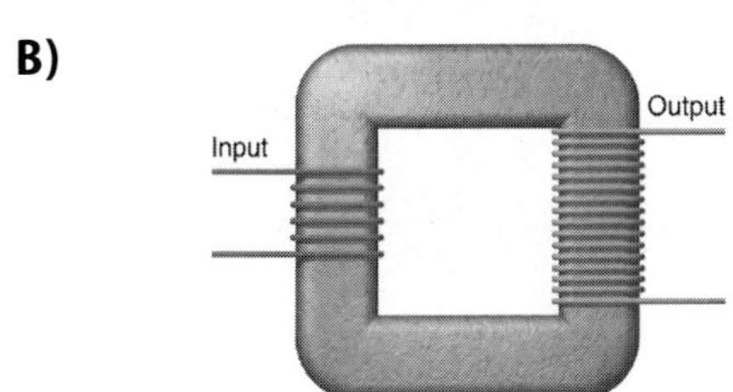

C)

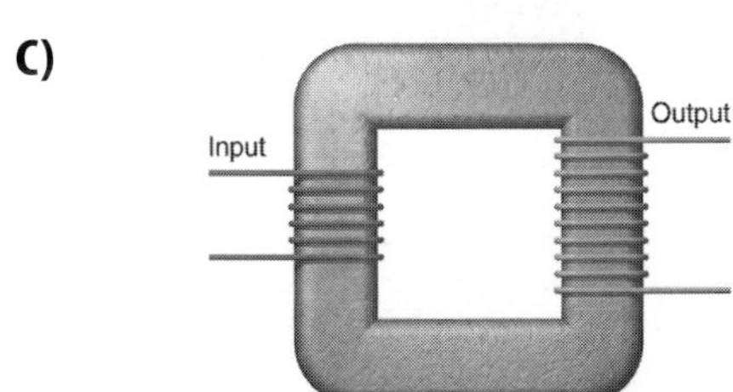

D)

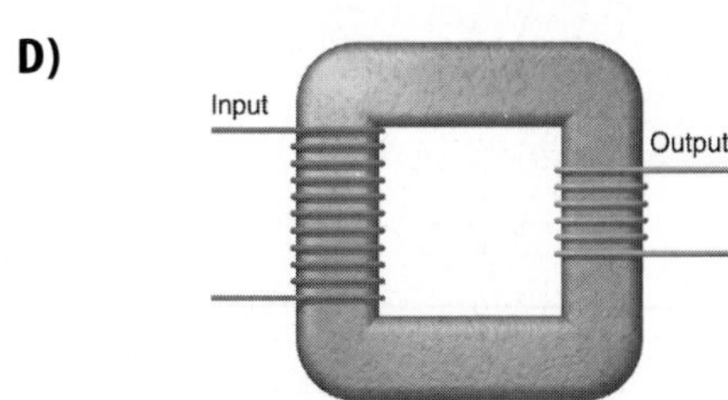

Test-Taking Tip Use the information provided in the question to closely consider each answer choice.

2. Which of the following materials would make a good conductor?
   F) plastic
   G) wood
   H) glass
   J) copper

Test-Taking Tip Remember that electrons move easily through conductors.

3. Shahid wanted to pick up pieces of metal with a magnet. Which of the following statements describes a situation in which the magnet would NOT pick up the pieces of metal?
   A) The metal pieces were too close to the magnet.
   B) The magnet was brand new.
   C) The metal pieces were made out of aluminum foil.
   D) The metal pieces and the magnet have the same magnetic poles.

Test-Taking Tip Review what you have learned about magnetic materials.

Consider this question carefully before writing your answer on a separate sheet of paper.

4. Recall what you know about the production of electric current. Explain the similarities and differences between direct current (DC) and alternating current (AC).

Test-Taking Tip Use the clues *direct* and *alternating* to guide your answer.

Student Resources

CONTENTS

It's early morning in the kitchen, and, whether you know it or not, chemistry is occurring all around you. Breakfast—with its wake-up sights and smells—is almost ready. Butter, syrup, freshly squeezed orange juice, hot tea, and yogurt with strawberries wait on the counter. Eggs and pancakes sizzle on the griddle. Slices of bread are toasting. Some foods are liquids. Others are solids. Most are mixtures. Some of these are undergoing changes while you watch. Using this field guide, you can identify the different types of mixtures you drink and eat, and the chemical and physical changes that occur as foods are prepared.

How are mixtures classified?

Mixtures contain two or more substances that have not combined to form a new substance. The proportions of the substances that make up a mixture can vary. Mixtures are classified as homogeneous or heterogeneous.

You cannot see the separate substances in a homogeneous mixture no matter how closely you look. Cranberry juice is a homogeneous mixture. You can easily identify the separate substances that are in a heterogeneous mixture. Breakfast cereals are heterogeneous mixtures.

Kitchen Chemistry

Homogeneous Mixtures

Homogeneous mixtures can be solids, liquids, or gases. Stainless steel, for example, is a solid mixture of iron, carbon, and chromium. You might have cookware, containers, and utensils made of stainless steel. Also found in abundance in your kitchen is a familiar mixture of gases, primarily nitrogen, oxygen, and argon. This mixture is the air you breathe. Much of the chemistry in your kitchen occurs in solutions. Solutions are homogeneous mixtures, therefore you cannot see their different parts. Tea and syrup are solutions of solids that are dissolved in liquids.

Tea and syrup

Stainless steel is a homogeneous mixture.

Field Activity

Use this field guide to help identify the mixtures and changes in your kitchen. Observe the preparation of a few meals. In your Science Journal, record the meal being prepared and a description of the types of mixtures, chemical changes, and physical changes you observe.

Heterogeneous Mixtures

You can see the different parts of a heterogeneous mixture. Familiar heterogeneous mixtures tend to be solids or solids and liquids. For example, the strawberries are visible in the bowl of yogurt and so are the blueberries in the muffin.

If you have left butter or cooking oil heating too long in a frying pan, you know that the smoke that rises from the pan is visible in the air. This mistake created a heterogeneous mixture.

Blueberry muffins and yogurt with strawberries are heterogeneous mixtures.

How are changes classified?

A change to a substance can be classified as chemical or physical. During a chemical change, one or more new substances are formed. When a physical change occurs, the identity of the substance remains the same.

Chemical Changes in the Kitchen

You can recognize a chemical change if one or more of the following occurs: the substance changes color, the substance produces a new odor, the substance absorbs or releases heat or light; or the substance releases a gas.

Grilled hamburgers and vegetables are examples of chemical changes.

Browning

Browning is a chemical change that occurs when sugars and proteins in foods form new flavors and smells. It produces the barbecue flavors of foods that are cooked on a grill and the caramelized flavor of a roasted marshmallow.

A marshmallow is browning on a skewer.

Protein Denaturation

A protein in its natural state is a long chain of chemical units. After it has formed, this chain folds into a specific shape determined by attractions, or weak bonds, between chemical units in that protein. Denaturation involves breaking the weak bonds in a protein and changing its shape.

The proteins in a raw egg are folded into balls, sheets, and coils. Heating the egg breaks some of the weak bonds that hold the proteins in these tight shapes. As cooking continues, the proteins unravel and begin forming weak bonds with other proteins. This causes the egg to solidify.

Eggs that are cooked sunny side up are an example of protein denaturation.

Bubbling pancake batter shows gas production.

Gas Production

The new substances that are produced during a chemical change are sometimes gases. Gas production occurs in the preparation of some foods.

The bubbles you see in pancake batter as it cooks are caused by a chemical change in the batter. Baking powder is a mixture of baking soda, $NaHCO_3$ (sodium bicarbonate), and an acidic substance. When water is added to baking powder, the acidic solution that forms reacts with baking soda to make carbon dioxide gas. As a pancake cooks, the bubbles of carbon dioxide rise through the batter, leaving spaces that fluff out the pancake making it light in texture.

Physical Changes in the Kitchen

You can recognize a physical change when the substance changes shape, size, or state. For example, water can become ice, or a chocolate bar can melt.

Melting

Melting is the physical change in which a solid becomes a liquid. The pat of butter is changing from a solid to a liquid. Melting occurs because heat from the warm toast weakens the attractions between the molecules of butter. The cheese in a grilled-cheese sandwich is another good example.

Melting butter is an example of a solid becoming a liquid.

Freezing

Making ice cream demonstrates how a liquid becomes a solid.

Freezing is the physical change in which a liquid becomes a solid. Chemical substances have a freezing point—the temperature at which this change occurs. Most of the water in a liquid ice-cream mixture freezes into small ice crystals, and air bubbles give the solid mixture its smooth, creamy texture. Water frozen in the form of ice cubes is used to chill beverages. Freezing also is used to preserve a wide variety of foods.

Boiling

Boiling is the physical change in which a liquid becomes a gas. Popcorn kernels contain 11 percent to 14 percent water. When it is heated, that water changes to steam. Because steam takes up many times the volume of liquid water, it creates enough pressure to burst the kernels. Some cereals, vegetables, and other foods can be cooked in boiling water or in the steam that is produced when water boils.

Popcorn is produced by boiling.

Amusement Park Rides

If you like smooth, gentle rides, don't expect to get one at an amusement park. Amusement park rides are designed to provide thrills—plummeting down hills at 160 km/h, whizzing around curves so fast you think you'll fall out of your seat, zooming upside down, plunging over waterfalls, dropping so fast and far that you feel weightless. It's all part of the fun.

May the Force Be with You

What you might not realize as you're screaming with delight is that amusement park rides are lessons in physics. You can apply Newton's laws of motion to everything from the water slide and the bumper cars to the roller coasters. Amusement park ride designers know how to use the laws of motion to jolt, bump, and jostle you enough to make you scream, while still keeping you safe from harm. They don't just plan how the laws of motion cause these rides to move, they also plan how you will move when you are on the rides. These designers also use Newton's law of motion when they design and build the rides to make the structures safe and lasting. Look at the forces at work on some popular amusement park rides.

Free-fall ride

Free Fall

Slowly you rise up, up, up. Gravity is pulling you downward, but your seat exerts an upward force on you. Then, in an instant, you're plummeting toward the ground at speeds of more than 100 km/h. When you fall, your seat falls at the same rate and no longer exerts a force on you. Because you don't feel your seat pushing upward, you have the feeling of being weightless—at least for a few seconds.

Field Activity

The next time you're at an amusement park, watch the rides. When you return home, make drawings of the rides using arrows to show how they move. Group the rides according to their movements. Compare your drawings and observations to the information in this field guide.

Roller Coaster: Design

The biggest coasters—some as tall as a 40-story building—are made of steel. Steel roller coasters are stronger and sway less than wooden roller coasters. This allows for more looping, more hills, and faster speeds.

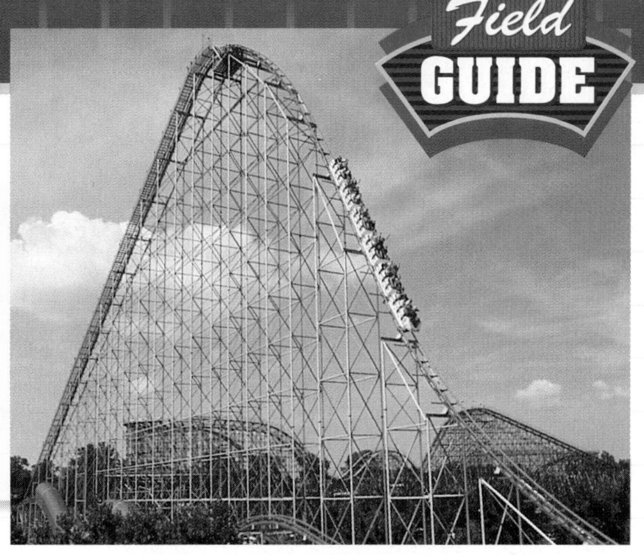

Roller coaster

Roller Coaster: The Coaster's Motion

Roller coasters are gravity-powered trains. Some coasters have motor-driven chains that move the cars to the top of the first hill. Then, gravity keeps it going.

The first hill is the highest point on the track. As the coaster rolls down the first hill, it converts potential energy to kinetic energy that sends it up the next hill. With each hill it climbs, it loses a little energy due to friction. That is why each hill is generally lower than the one before it.

Roller Coaster: Your Ride

Inertia is at work when you sweep around curves on a roller coaster. Inertia is the tendency for a body that's moving in a certain direction to keep moving in the same direction. For example, when the coaster swings right, inertia tries to keep you going in a straight line at a constant speed. As a result, you are pushed to the left side of your car.

Inertia tends to keep bodies moving in a straight line.

Bumper Cars: The Car's Motion

You control your bumper car's acceleration with the accelerator pedal. When the car you're in bumps head-on into another car, your car comes to an abrupt stop. The big rubber bumper around the bottom of the car diffuses the force of the collision by prolonging the impact.

Bumper Cars: Your Ride

When you first accelerate in a bumper car, you feel as though you are being pushed back in your seat. This sensation and the jolt you feel when you hit another car are due to inertia. On impact, your car stops, but your inertia makes you continue to move forward. It's the same jolt you feel in a car when someone slams on the brakes.

In a bumper-car collision, inertia keeps each rider moving forward.

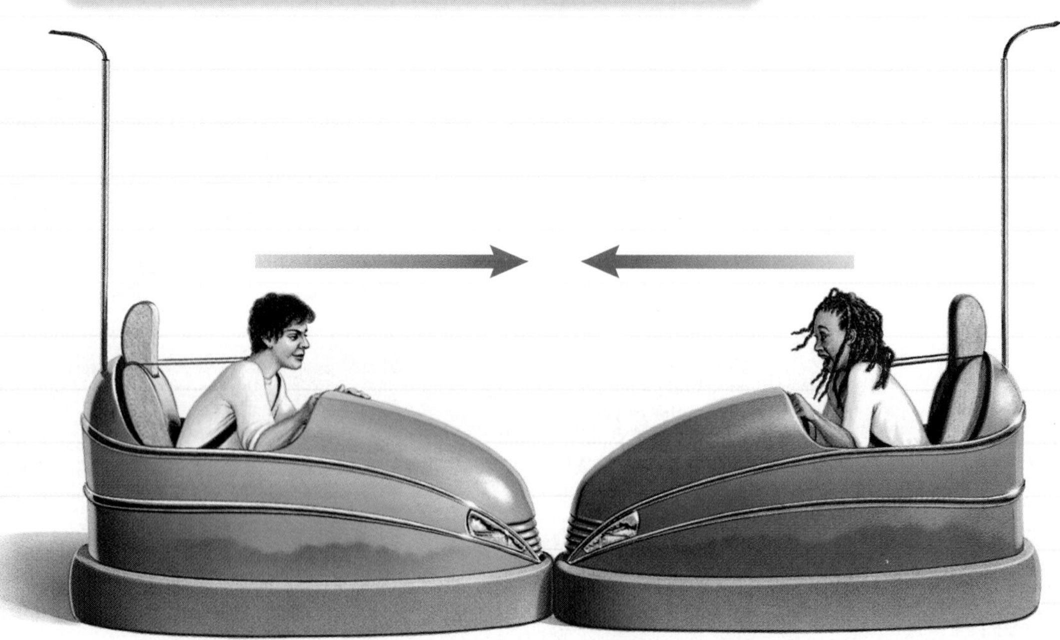

Swing Ride: Design

Some of the more powerful swing rides make about eight revolutions around the central pole each minute. These swing rides are capable of moving their riders at speeds of close to 50 km/h.

Swing Ride: Forces

As the swings rotate, your inertia wants to fling you outward, but the chain that connects your seat to the ride's central pole prevents you from being flung into the air. You can see the changes in force as the swing ride changes speeds. As the ride speeds up and the forces exerted on the chain increase, your swing rises, moves outward, and travels almost parallel to the ground. As the ride slows, these forces on the chains decrease, returning the swings slowly to their original position.

The arrows show the forces at work in a swing ride.

Some people have defined music as "patterns of tones." A tone is a sound with a specific pitch. In music, a tone might also be called a note. Pitch describes how high or low the tone is. Like all sounds, musical tones are produced when an object vibrates. Higher pitches are produced by more vibrations per second, and therefore have a higher frequency.

Most musical instruments use resonance to amplify sounds. To amplify a sound means to increase its volume. Resonance occurs when one object causes another object to vibrate at the same frequency—or pitch.

How Resonance Works

A vibrating object produces sound waves. These waves can affect other objects and cause them to vibrate. As more matter vibrates, a louder sound is produced. For example, resonance is at work in a guitar. When a guitar's strings are plucked or strummed, the strings vibrate. The strings' vibrations make the thin soundboard—in this case, the front of the guitar—vibrate. The soundboard's vibrations make the air inside the guitar's hollow body vibrate. The vibrating air amplifies the sounds that were first produced by the strings.

Musical Instruments

Mandolin

Stringed Instruments

Tones are produced in stringed instruments by making stretched strings vibrate. Each string is tuned to a different pitch. When playing stringed instruments such as the harp, each string produces only one pitch. The player creates different pitches by plucking different strings.

When playing stringed instruments such as the guitar and violin, the player can change the pitch of each string by pressing down on one end and making it shorter. Stringed instruments may be strummed, plucked, or played with a bow.

Harp

Field Activity

Watch an orchestra or band perform in a live concert or on television. In your Science Journal, name all of the different instruments you recognize. Then use this field guide to identify the category in which each instrument is classified.

Wind Instruments—Woodwinds

Woodwind instruments include the clarinet, the saxophone, and the recorder. These instruments are played by blowing into a mouthpiece or across a hole. Some woodwinds, such as clarinets, have a thin flexible reed in the mouthpiece that vibrates. The reed causes the air in the tube to vibrate. As the air vibrates inside the woodwind's hollow tube, tones are produced. Musicians change this instrument's pitch by covering holes with their fingers or by pressing keys that cover holes. Covering a hole changes the length of the column of air inside the tube.

Wind Instruments—Brass

Brass instruments include the trumpet, the trombone, and the tuba. Their mouthpieces are larger than woodwinds' mouthpieces. Brass instruments are played by pressing the lips against a mouthpiece and blowing so the lips vibrate. Musicians change brass instruments' pitches by tensing or relaxing their lips. With most brass instruments, the pitch also can be changed by pressing valves, which changes the length of the vibrating column of air inside the instrument.

Percussion Instruments—Idiophones

Idiophones vibrate to produce tones. Musicians play them by hitting, shaking, scraping, or plucking them. Idiophones such as cymbals, bells, gongs, music boxes, and xylophone keys play only one pitch. Triangles, clappers, rattles, and cymbals have indefinite pitches—their pitches depend on how they are played and how they are constructed.

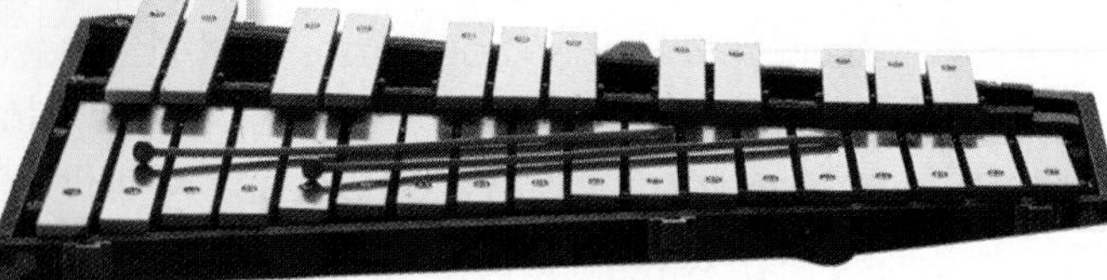

Xylophone

Percussion Instruments—Membranophones

Membranophones produce sound when their membranes—the stretched tops of drums or the tiny membranes within kazoos—vibrate. Drums are usually struck with hands, with beaters such as drumsticks, or with knotted cords to produce tones.

Bongo

Electric Instruments

Electric instruments such as the electric guitar and electric violin are played like regular instruments. However, rather than using resonance to amplify their sound, their vibrations are converted to electrical signals that are amplified electronically. The amplified electric signal is then converted to sound by a loudspeaker.

Guitar and Amplifier

Piano

Keyboard Instruments—Piano

Each piano key is attached to a small hammer. When the player presses a key, the hammer hits a string and makes it vibrate. The strings are different lengths and each string produces a different pitch. The piano's body amplifies the tones.

Pipe Organ

Keyboards—Pipe Organ

Pressing a pipe organ's key opens a pipe to let air vibrate inside it. The pipes are different lengths, and each produces a different pitch.

Synthesizer

Electronic Instruments

Unlike all other types of musical instruments, electronic instruments do not rely on vibrations to produce sounds. Instead, these instruments produce electrical signals that a computer then converts to sounds. Even though a synthesizer has a keyboard, it is classified as an electronic instrument because it produces sounds electronically. Today, it is the most widely used electronic instrument.

Lightning

When storm clouds form, the particles in clouds collide with one another, removing electrons from some and adding them to others. Positive charges accumulate at the top of the cloud, leaving the negative ones at the bottom. These negative charges repel electrons in the ground below. As a result, the ground beneath the cloud becomes positively charged. The negative charges in the cloud are attracted toward the positively charged ground. They move downward in a zigzag path called a stepped leader. As the leader approaches the ground, a streamer of positive charges rises to meet it. When they meet, a return stroke—an electric spark called lightning—blasts up to the cloud.

The cycle of leader and return strokes can repeat many times in less than a second to comprise a single flash of lightning that you see.

Common Types of Lightning

The most common type of lightning strikes from one part of a cloud to another part of the same cloud. This type of lightning can occur ten times more often than lightning from a cloud to the ground. Other forms include strikes from one cloud to a different cloud, and from a cloud to the surrounding air.

Cloud-to-Ground Lightning

This type of lightning is characterized by a single streak of light connecting the cloud and the ground or a streak with one or more forks in it. Occasionally, a tall object on Earth will initiate the leader strike, causing what is known as ground-to-cloud lightning.

Cloud-to-ground lightning

Field Activity

During a thunderstorm, observe lightning from a safe location in your home or school. Using this field guide, identify and record in your Science Journal the types of lightning you saw. Also, note the date and time of the thunderstorm in your Science Journal.

Cloud-to-Cloud Lightning

Cloud-to-cloud lightning is the most common type of lightning. It can occur between clouds (intercloud lightning) or within a cloud (intracloud lightning). The lightning is often hidden by the clouds, such that the clouds themselves seem to be glowing flashes of light.

Cloud-to-Air Lightning

When a lightning stroke ends in midair above a cloud or forks off the main stroke of cloud-to-ground lightning, it causes what is known as cloud-to-air lightning. This type of lightning is usually not as powerful or as bright as cloud-to-ground lightning.

Cloud-to-air lightning

Some forms of lightning differ in appearance from the forked flashes commonly considered to be lightning. However, the discharge in the cloud occurs for the same reason—to neutralize the accumulation of charge.

Sheet lightning

Sheet Lightning

Sheet lightning appears to fill a large section of the sky. Its appearance is caused by light reflecting off the water droplets in the clouds. The actual strokes of lightning are far away or hidden by the clouds. When the lightning is so far away that no thunder is heard, it is often called heat lightning and usually can be seen during summer nights.

Ribbon Lightning

Ribbon lightning is a thicker flash than ordinary cloud-to-ground lightning. In this case, wind blows the channel that is created by the return stroke sideways. Because each return stroke follows this channel, each is moved slightly to the side of the last stroke, making each return stroke of the flash visible, and thus a wider, ribbonlike band of light is produced.

Ribbon lightning

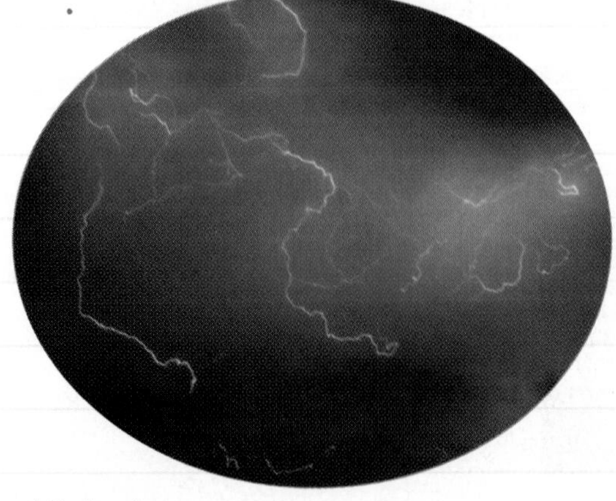

Bead lightning

Chain Lightning

Chain lightning, also called bead lightning, is distinguished by a dotted line of light as it fades. The cause is still uncertain, but it might be due to the observer's position relative to lightning or to parts of the flash being hidden by clouds or rain.

Some forms of lightning are rare or poorly understood and have different appearances than the previously described forms.

Sprites

Sprites are red or blue flashes of light that are sometimes cone shaped and occur high above a thundercloud, 60 to 100 km above Earth. The flashes are associated with thunderstorms that cover a vast area. Sprites are estimated to occur in about 1 percent of all lightning strokes.

Sprites

Ball Lightning

There have been numerous eyewitness accounts of the existence of ball lightning, which appears as a sphere of red, yellow, orange or white light, usually between 1 cm to 1 m in size. Ball lightning seems to occur during thunderstorms, and appears within a few meters of the ground. The ball may move horizontally at a speed of a few meters per second, or may float in the air. Ball lightning usually lasts for several seconds and may vanish either quietly or explosively. Unlike other forms of lightning which can be seen by many observers at large distances, the small size of ball lightning and its random occurrence make it difficult to study. As a result, the causes of ball lightning still are not known, and even its existence is disputed.

St. Elmo's Fire

St. Elmo's Fire is a bluish-green glowing light that sometimes appears during thunderstorms around tall, pointed objects like the masts of ships and lightning rods. It also occurs around the wings and propellers of airplanes flying through thunderstorms. A sizzling or crackling noise often accompanies the glow. St. Elmo's Fire is caused by the strong electric field between the bottom of a thundercloud and the ground. This electric field is strongest around pointed objects. If this field is strong enough, it can pull electrons from atoms in the air. The glow is produced when these electrons collide with other atoms and molecules in the air.

Living in Space

Early astronauts were crammed into tiny space capsules where they could barely move in their seats. Food was a tasteless paste squeezed from a tube or a hard, bite-sized cube. Today, space shuttle astronauts have a two-level cabin with sleeping bunks, a galley for preparing food, and exercise equipment. Living in space isn't what it used to be.

Living in Orbit

Although conditions on a spacecraft are better now than in the past, the problems astronauts face are the same. They still go about their daily life, but space has no air, food, or water. This makes it hard to prepare meals and wash dishes afterward. It complicates how you drink beverages out of a glass. Due to these challenges, space shuttle crews must carry everything they need with them to survive in space.

By far the biggest challenges for astronauts come from the effects of weightlessness. Imagine eating a meal as part of it floats away, or sleeping in a bed that drifts into walls. NASA scientists have found ways to overcome such problems. This field guide offers a look at some of them.

Life-Support System

People need oxygen to breathe. The shuttle carries canisters of super-cold liquid oxygen and pressurized nitrogen to create an atmosphere in the crew compartment that is similar to Earth's—79 percent nitrogen and 21 percent oxygen. The shuttle also circulates air through canisters of lithium hydroxide and activated charcoal, removing carbon dioxide and odors from it. Crew members must change one of the two canisters every 12 h.

Field Activity

Read a science-fiction description of people living and working in space. In your Science Journal, describe how people performed daily tasks such as eating, sleeping, and getting around. Go to the Glencoe Science Web site at **science.glencoe.com** and click on the NASA link to find out more about living and working in space. Compare what you wrote with what you learn in this field guide.

Electricity

Fuel cells generate electricity by chemically combining hydrogen and oxygen. As a by-product, they produce 3 kg of water each hour—some of which is used to prepare food.

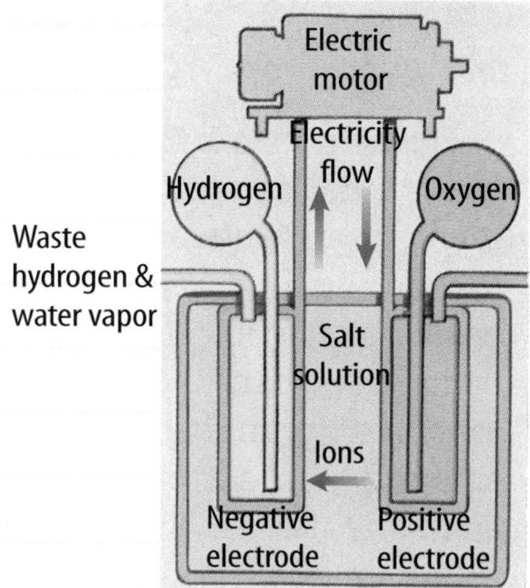

The Shuttle Café

BREAKFAST
DRIED APRICOTS · BREAKFAST ROLL
GRANOLA w/BLUEBERRIES · VANILLA INSTANT BREAKFAST · GRAPEFRUIT DRINK

LUNCH
GROUND BEEF · PICKLE SAUCE · NOODLES AND CHICKEN · STEWED TOMATOES · PEARS · ALMONDS
STRAWBERRY DRINK

DINNER
TUNA · MACARONI AND CHEESE · PEAS w/BUTTER-SAUCE · PEACH AMBROSIA · LEMONADE
CHOCOLATE PUDDING

CONDIMENTS
PEPPER · SALT · BARBECUE-SAUCE · CATSUP · HOT PEPPER SAUCE
MAYONNAISE
MUSTARD

A Typical Menu

Astronauts eat three meals per day, chosen for them from a list of 70 foods and 20 beverages. They eat foods such as sausage, eggs, bread, fruits, vegetables, rice, and even turkey with gravy.

Food Preservation

Foods are not refrigerated. Some foods are freeze-dried, so water is added before they are eaten. Some foods are heated to kill bacteria and sealed in airtight foil packets. Irradiated food, such as bread and some meat, has been exposed to radiation to kill bacteria.

Food Preparation

Astronauts prepare and eat their food in the galley. A different person serves each meal, which takes about 20 min to prepare. The astronaut injects water into dried or powdered foods that need it, and puts hot dishes into the oven to warm them. Some foods can be eaten right out of the pouches.

These astronauts are enjoying a meal together.

Working Out

To help prevent bone and muscle deterioration due to space's weightless environment, astronauts exercise for 15 min each day on 7-day to 14-day missions. They work out for 30 min daily on 30-day missions. They can use a treadmill, a rowing machine, or an exercise bike. Even with this exercise, astronauts can lose more than one percent of their bone density for each month they are in space.

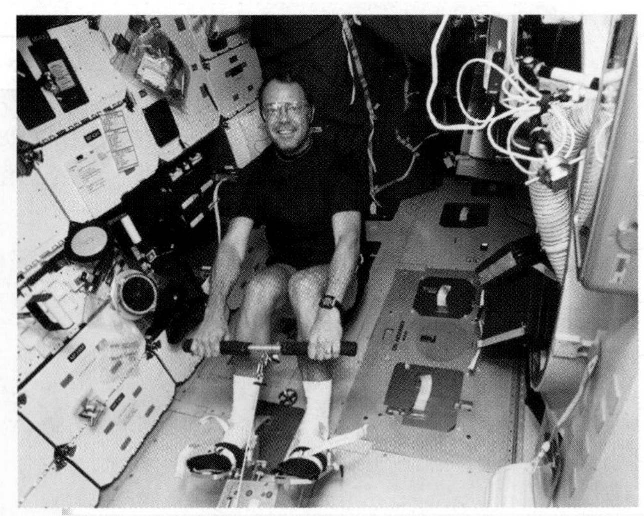

Using a rowing machine

Using a treadmill

Exercise Equipment

The base of the treadmill hooks into the floor or walls. An astronaut can stand on the treadmill with rubber bungee cords attached to a belt and shoulder harness. The cord is tightened to increase resistance.

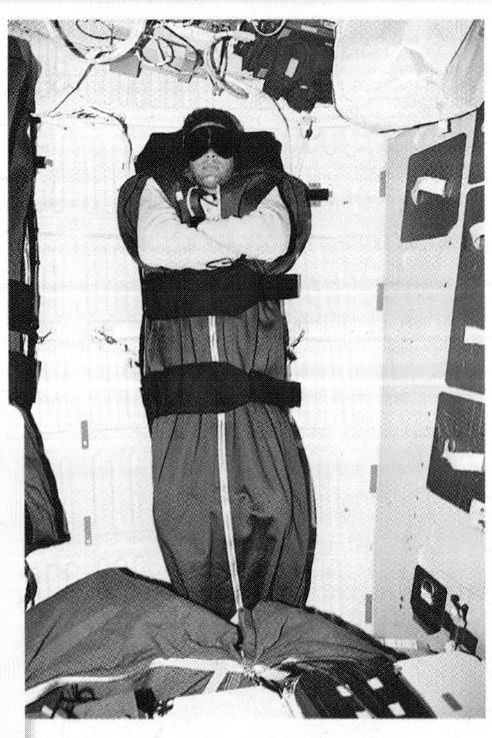

Sleeping compartments

Getting Some Sleep

The condition of weightlessness enables astronauts to sleep in unusual places. Each astronaut's sleep station contains a bed made up of a padded board with a fireproof sleeping bag attached. Two astronauts sleep on bunks facing up. One sleeps on the underside of the lower bunk, facing the floor. The fourth sleeps vertically against the wall.

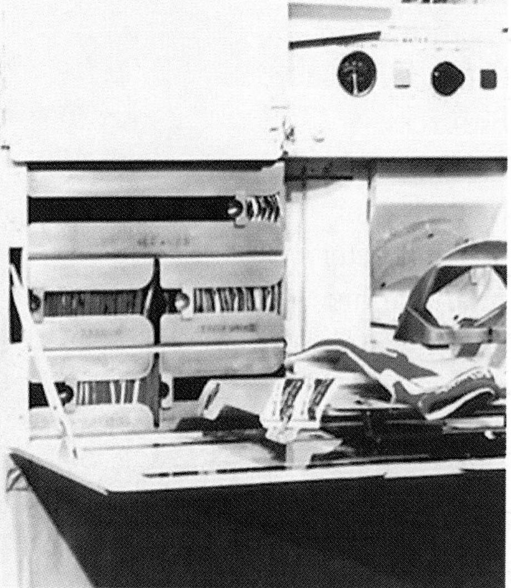

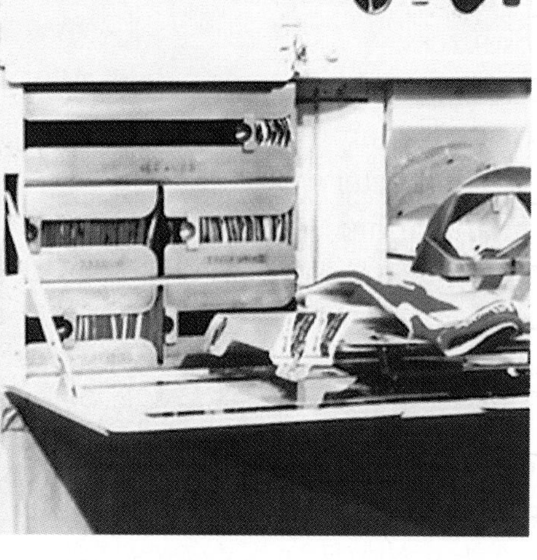

This is their hand-washing station.

This astronaut uses a wet cloth to keep clean.

Cleaning Up

After 8 h of sleep, astronauts have 45 min for morning hygiene. There aren't any showers or baths in space. To keep clean, astronauts just wipe themselves (and their hair) off with a wet cloth. They also can wash their hands at the hand-washing station. Water is air-blasted at their hands and then immediately sucked up.

Waste Management

Astronauts have a special toilet they use in space. It utilizes air instead of water to remove bodily wastes. The waste is then held in a tank until the spacecraft returns to Earth.

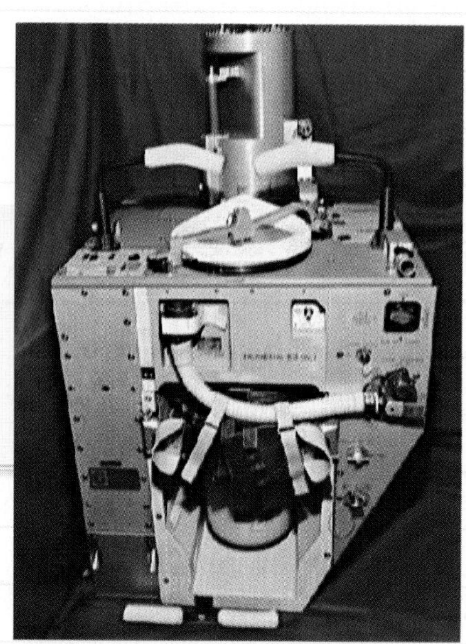

Here is a space shuttle toilet.

Organizing Information

As you study science, you will make many observations and conduct investigations and experiments. You will also research information that is available from many sources. These activities will involve organizing and recording data. The quality of the data you collect and the way you organize it will determine how well others can understand and use it. In **Figure 1,** the student is obtaining and recording information using a thermometer.

Putting your observations in writing is an important way of communicating to others the information you have found and the results of your investigations and experiments.

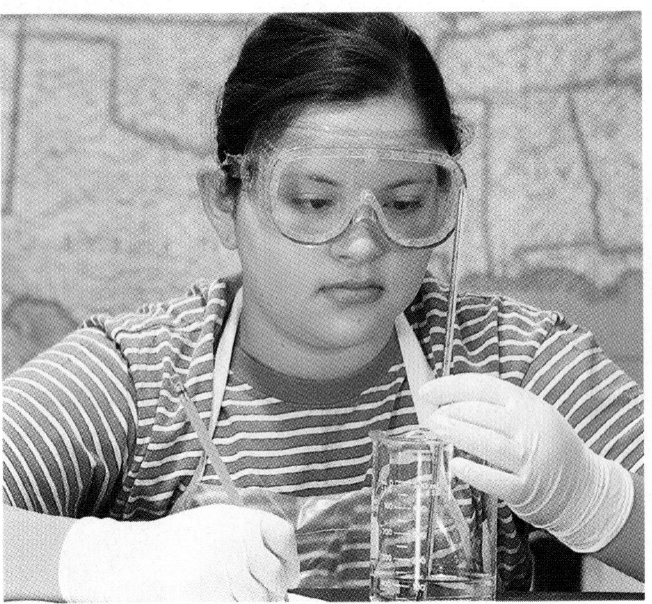

Figure 1
Making an observation is one way to gather information directly.

Researching Information

Scientists work to build on and add to human knowledge of the world. Before moving in a new direction, it is important to gather the information that already is known about a subject. You will look for such information in various reference sources. Follow these steps to research information on a scientific subject:

Step 1 Determine exactly what you need to know about the subject. For instance, you might want to find out about one of the elements in the periodic table.

Step 2 Make a list of questions, such as: Who discovered the element? When was it discovered? What makes the element useful or interesting?

Step 3 Use multiple sources such as textbooks, encyclopedias, government documents, professional journals, science magazines, and the Internet.

Step 4 List where you found the sources. Make sure the sources you use are reliable and the most current available.

Evaluating Print and Nonprint Sources

Not all sources of information are reliable. Evaluate the sources you use for information, and use only those you know to be dependable. For example, suppose you want to find ways to make your home more energy efficient. You might find two Web sites on how to save energy in your home. One Web site contains "Energy-Saving Tips" written by a company that sells a new type of weatherproofing material you put around your door frames. The other is a Web page on "Conserving Energy in Your Home" written by the U.S. Department of Energy. You would choose the second Web site as the more reliable source of information.

In science, information can change rapidly. Always consult the most current sources. A 1985 source about saving energy would not reflect the most recent research and findings.

Interpreting Scientific Illustrations

As you research a science topic, you will see drawings, diagrams, and photographs. Illustrations help you understand what you read. Some illustrations are included to help you understand an idea that you can't see easily by yourself. For instance, you can't see the tiny particles in an atom, but you can look at a diagram of an atom as labeled in **Figure 2** that helps you understand something about it. Visualizing a drawing helps many people remember details more easily. Illustrations also provide examples that clarify difficult concepts or give additional information about the topic you are studying.

Most illustrations have a label or caption. A label or caption identifies the illustration or provides additional information to better explain it. Can you find the caption or labels in **Figure 2?**

Figure 2
This drawing shows an atom of carbon with its six protons, six neutrons, and six electrons.

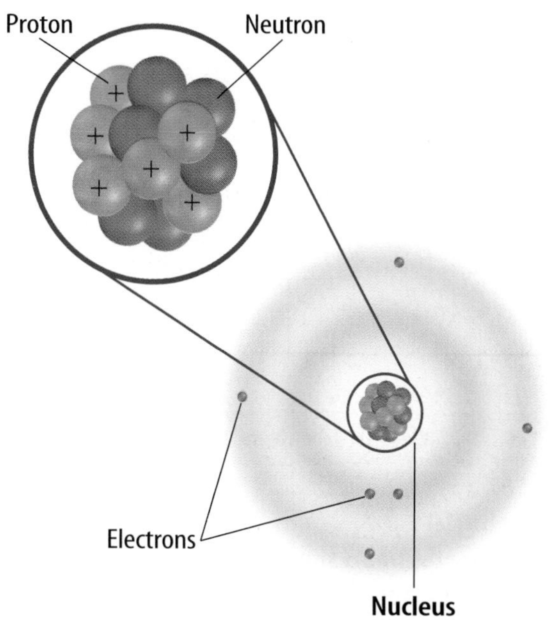

Venn Diagram

A Venn diagram illustrates how two subjects compare and contrast. In other words, you can see the characteristics that the subjects have in common and those that they do not.

The Venn diagram in **Figure 3** shows the relationship between two different substances made from the element carbon. However, due to the way their atoms are arranged, one substance is the gemstone diamond, and the other is the graphite found in pencils.

Concept Mapping

If you were taking a car trip, you might take some sort of road map. By using a map, you begin to learn where you are in relation to other places on the map.

A concept map is similar to a road map, but a concept map shows relationships among ideas (or concepts) rather than places. It is a diagram that visually shows how concepts are related. Because a concept map shows relationships among ideas, it can make the meanings of ideas and terms clear and help you understand what you are studying.

Overall, concept maps are useful for breaking large concepts down into smaller parts, making learning easier.

Figure 3
A Venn diagram shows how objects or concepts are alike and how they are different.

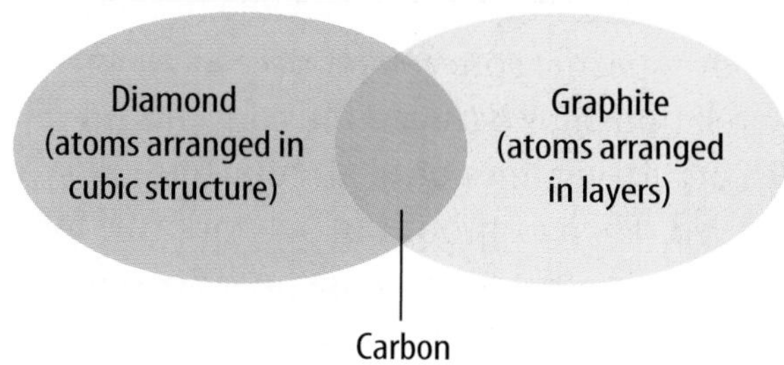

Skill Handbooks

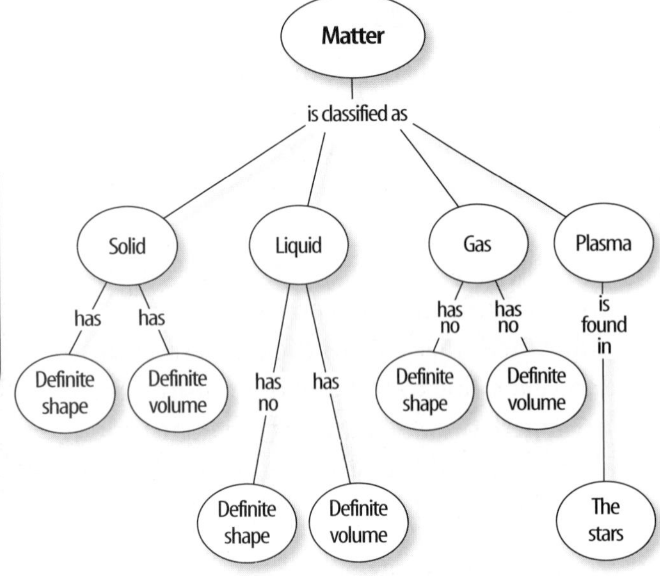

Figure 4
A network tree shows how concepts or objects are related.

Network Tree Look at the network tree in **Figure 4,** that describes the different types of matter. A network tree is a type of concept map. Notice how some words are in ovals while others are written across connecting lines. The words inside the ovals are science terms or concepts. The words written on the connecting lines describe the relationships between the concepts.

When constructing a network tree, write the topic on a note card or piece of paper. Write the major concepts related to that topic on separate note cards or pieces of paper. Then arrange them in order from general to specific. Branch the related concepts from the major concept and describe the relationships on the connecting lines. Continue branching to more specific concepts. If necessary, write the relationships between the concepts on the connecting lines until all concepts are mapped. Then examine the network tree for relationships that cross branches and add them to the network tree.

Events Chain An events chain is another type of concept map. It models the order, or sequence, of items. In science, an events chain can be used to describe a sequence of events, the steps in a procedure, or the stages of a process.

When making an events chain, first find the one event that starts the chain. This event is called the initiating event. Then, find the next event in the chain and continue until you reach an outcome. Suppose you are asked to describe why and how a sound might make an echo. You might draw an events chain such as the one in **Figure 5.** Notice that connecting words are not necessary in an events chain.

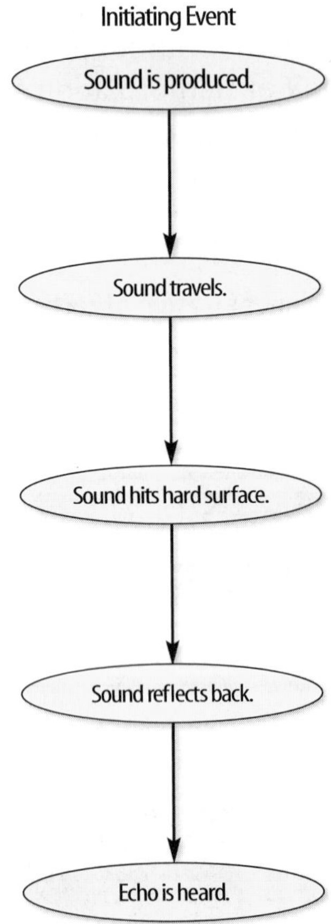

Figure 5
Events chains show the order of steps in a process or event.

Cycle Map A cycle concept map is a specific type of events chain map. In a cycle concept map, the series of events does not produce a final outcome. Instead, the last event in the chain relates back to the beginning event.

You first decide what event will be used as the beginning event. Once that is decided, you list events in order that occur after it. Words are written between events that describe what happens from one event to the next. The last event in a cycle concept map relates back to the beginning event. The number of events in a cycle concept varies but is usually three or more. Look at the cycle map shown in **Figure 6.**

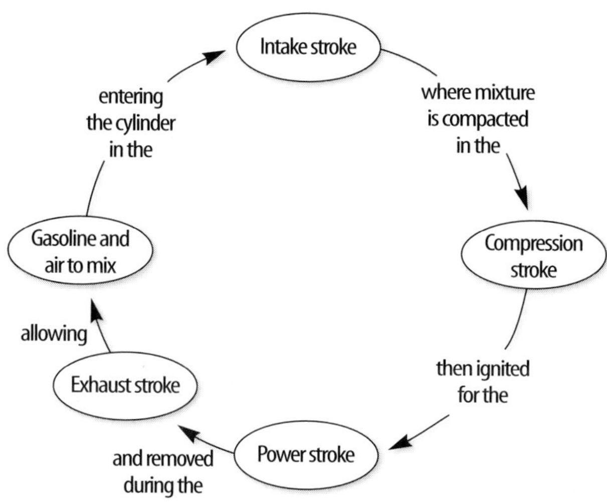

Figure 6
A cycle map shows events that occur in a cycle.

Spider Map A type of concept map that you can use for brainstorming is the spider map. When you have a central idea, you might find you have a jumble of ideas that relate to it but are not necessarily clearly related to each other. The spider map on sound in **Figure 7** shows that if you write these ideas outside the main concept, then you can begin to separate and group unrelated terms so they become more useful.

Figure 7
A spider map allows you to list ideas that relate to a central topic but not necessarily to one another.

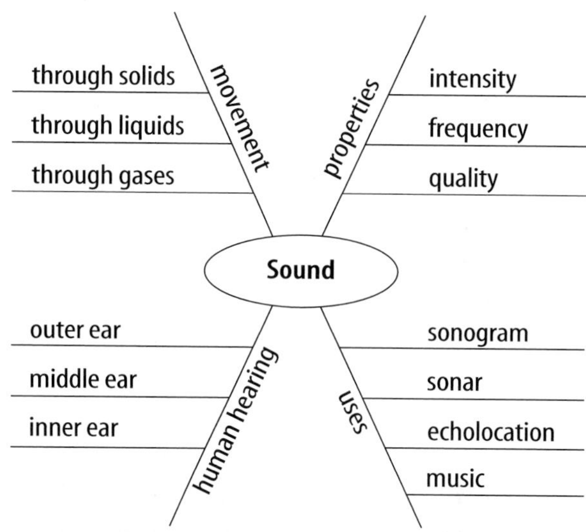

Writing a Paper

You will write papers often when researching science topics or reporting the results of investigations or experiments. Scientists frequently write papers to share their data and conclusions with other scientists and the public. When writing a paper, use these steps.

Step 1 Assemble your data by using graphs, tables, or a concept map. Create an outline.

Step 2 Start with an introduction that contains a clear statement of purpose and what you intend to discuss or prove.

Step 3 Organize the body into paragraphs. Each paragraph should start with a topic sentence, and the remaining sentences in that paragraph should support your point.

Step 4 Position data to help support your points.

Step 5 Summarize the main points and finish with a conclusion statement.

Step 6 Use tables, graphs, charts, and illustrations whenever possible.

Investigating and Experimenting

You might say the work of a scientist is to solve problems. When you decide to find out why your neighbor's hydrangeas produce blue flowers while yours are pink, you are problem solving, too. You might also observe that your neighbor's azaleas are healthier than yours are and decide to see whether differences in the soil explain the differences in these plants.

Scientists use orderly approaches to solve problems. The methods scientists use include identifying a question, making observations, forming a hypothesis, testing a hypothesis, analyzing results, and drawing conclusions.

Scientific investigations involve careful observation under controlled conditions. Such observation of an object or a process can suggest new and interesting questions about it. These questions sometimes lead to the formation of a hypothesis. Scientific investigations are designed to test a hypothesis.

Identifying a Question

The first step in a scientific investigation or experiment is to identify a question to be answered or a problem to be solved. You might be interested in knowing how beams of laser light like the ones in **Figure 8** look the way they do.

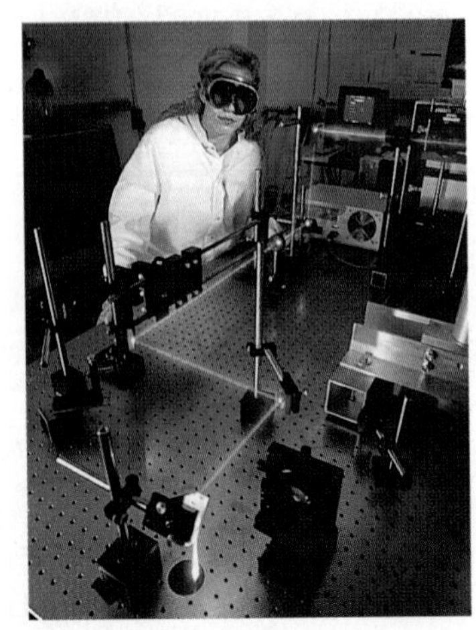

Figure 8
When you see lasers being used for scientific research, you might ask yourself, "Are these lasers different from those that are used for surgery?"

Forming Hypotheses

Hypotheses are based on observations that have been made. A hypothesis is a possible explanation based on previous knowledge and observations.

Perhaps a scientist has observed that certain substances dissolve faster in warm water than in cold. Based on these observations, the scientist can make a statement that he or she can test. The statement is a hypothesis. The hypothesis could be: *A substance dissolves in warm water faster.* A hypothesis has to be something you can test by using an investigation. A testable hypothesis is a valid hypothesis.

Predicting

When you apply a hypothesis to a specific situation, you predict something about that situation. First, you must identify which hypothesis fits the situation you are considering. People use predictions to make everyday decisions. Based on previous observations and experiences, you might form a prediction that if substances dissolve in warm water faster, then heating the water will shorten mixing time for powdered fruit drinks. Someone could use this prediction to save time in preparing a fruit punch for a party.

Testing a Hypothesis

To test a hypothesis, you need a procedure. A procedure is the plan you follow in your experiment. A procedure tells you what materials to use, as well as how and in what order to use them. When you follow a procedure, data are generated that support or do not support the original hypothesis statement.

For example, premium gasoline costs more than regular gasoline. Does premium gasoline increase the efficiency or fuel mileage of your family car? You decide to test the hypothesis: "If premium gasoline is more efficient, then it should increase the fuel mileage of my family's car." Then you write the procedure shown in **Figure 9** for your experiment and generate the data presented in the table below.

Figure 9
A procedure tells you what to do step by step.

Procedure

1. Use regular gasoline for two weeks.
2. Record the number of kilometers between fill-ups and the amount of gasoline used.
3. Switch to premium gasoline for two weeks.
4. Record the number of kilometers between fill-ups and the amount of gasoline used.

Gasoline Data

Type of Gasoline	Kilometers Traveled	Liters Used	Liters per Kilometer
Regular	762	45.34	0.059
Premium	661	42.30	0.064

These data show that premium gasoline is less efficient than regular gasoline in one particular car. It took more gasoline to travel 1 km (0.064) using premium gasoline than it did to travel 1 km using regular gasoline (0.059). This conclusion does not support the hypothesis.

Are all investigations alike? Keep in mind as you perform investigations in science that a hypothesis can be tested in many ways. Not every investigation makes use of all the ways that are described on these pages, and not all hypotheses are tested by investigations. Scientists encounter many variations in the methods that are used when they perform experiments. The skills in this handbook are here for you to use and practice.

Identifying and Manipulating Variables and Controls

In any experiment, it is important to keep everything the same except for the item you are testing. The one factor you change is called the independent variable. The factor that changes as a result of the independent variable is called the dependent variable. Always make sure you have only one independent variable. If you allow more than one, you will not know what causes the changes you observe in the dependent variable. Many experiments also have controls—individual instances or experimental subjects for which the independent variable is not changed. You can then compare the test results to the control results.

For example, in the fuel-mileage experiment, you made everything the same except the type of gasoline that was used. The driver, the type of automobile, and the type of driving were the same throughout. In this way, you could be sure that any mileage differences were caused by the type of fuel—the independent variable. The fuel mileage was the dependent variable.

If you could repeat the experiment using several automobiles of the same type on a standard driving track with the same driver, you could make one automobile a control by using regular gasoline over the four-week period.

Collecting Data

Whether you are carrying out an investigation or a short observational experiment, you will collect data, or information. Scientists collect data accurately as numbers and descriptions and organize it in specific ways.

Observing Scientists observe items and events, then record what they see. When they use only words to describe an observation, it is called qualitative data. For example, a scientist might describe the color, texture, or odor of a substance produced in a chemical reaction. Scientists' observations also can describe how much there is of something. These observations use numbers, as well as words, in the description and are called quantitative data. For example, if a sample of the element gold is described as being "shiny and very dense," the data are clearly qualitative. Quantitative data on this sample of gold might include "a mass of 30 g and a density of 19.3 g/cm^3." Quantitative data often are organized into tables. Then, from information in the table, a graph can be drawn. Graphs can reveal relationships that exist in experimental data.

When you make observations in science, you should examine the entire object or situation first, then look carefully for details. If you're looking at an element sample, for instance, check the general color and pattern of the sample before using a hand lens to examine its surface for any smaller details or characteristics. Remember to record accurately everything you see.

Scientists try to make careful and accurate observations. When possible, they use instruments such as microscopes, metric rulers, graduated cylinders, thermometers, and balances. Measurements provide numerical data that can be repeated and checked.

Sampling When working with large numbers of objects or a large population, scientists usually cannot observe or study every one of them. Instead, they use a sample or a portion of the total number. To *sample* is to take a small, representative portion of the objects or organisms of a population for research. By making careful observations or manipulating variables within a portion of a group, information is discovered and conclusions are drawn that might apply to the whole population.

Estimating Scientific work also involves estimating. To estimate is to make a judgment about the size or the number of something without measuring or counting every object or member of a population. Scientists first measure or count the amount or number in a small sample. A geologist, for example, might remove a 10-g sample from a large rock that is rich in copper ore, as in **Figure 10.** Then a chemist would determine the percentage of copper by mass and multiply that percentage by the total mass of the rock to estimate the total mass of copper in the large rock.

Figure 10
Determining the percentage of copper by mass that is present in a small piece of a large rock, which is rich in copper ore, can help estimate the total mass of copper ore that is present in the rock.

Measuring in SI

The metric system of measurement was developed in 1795. A modern form of the metric system, called the International System, or SI, was adopted in 1960. SI provides standard measurements that all scientists around the world can understand.

The metric system is convenient because unit sizes vary by multiples of 10. When changing from smaller units to larger units, divide by a multiple of 10. When changing from larger units to smaller, multiply by a multiple of 10. To convert millimeters to centimeters, divide the millimeters by 10. To convert 30 mm to centimeters, divide 30 by 10 (30 mm equal 3 cm).

Prefixes are used to name units. Look at the table below for some common metric prefixes and their meanings. Do you see how the prefix *kilo-* attached to the unit *gram* is *kilogram*, or 1,000 g?

Metric Prefixes

Prefix	Symbol	Meaning	
kilo-	k	1,000	thousand
hecto-	h	100	hundred
deka-	da	10	ten
deci-	d	0.1	tenth
centi-	c	0.01	hundredth
milli-	m	0.001	thousandth

Now look at the metric ruler shown in **Figure 11.** The centimeter lines are the long, numbered lines, and the shorter lines are millimeter lines.

When using a metric ruler, line up the 0-cm mark with the end of the object being measured, and read the number of the unit where the object ends. In this instance, it would be 4.50 cm.

Figure 11
This metric ruler has centimeter and millimeter divisions.

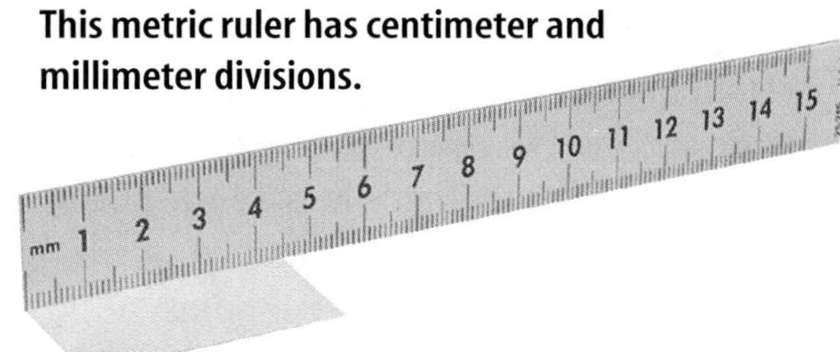

Liquid Volume The unit that is used to measure liquids is the liter. A liter has the volume of 1,000 cm^3. The prefix *milli-* means "thousandth (0.001)." A milliliter is one thousandth of 1 L, and 1 L has the volume of 1,000 mL. One milliliter of liquid completely fills a cube measuring 1 cm on each side. Therefore, 1 mL equals 1 cm^3.

Beakers and graduated cylinders are used to measure liquid volume. The surface of liquids is always curved when viewed in a glass cylinder. This curved surface is the *meniscus.* A meniscus must be looked at along a horizontal line of sight as in **Figure 12.** A graduated cylinder is marked from bottom to top in milliliters. This one contains 79 mL of a liquid.

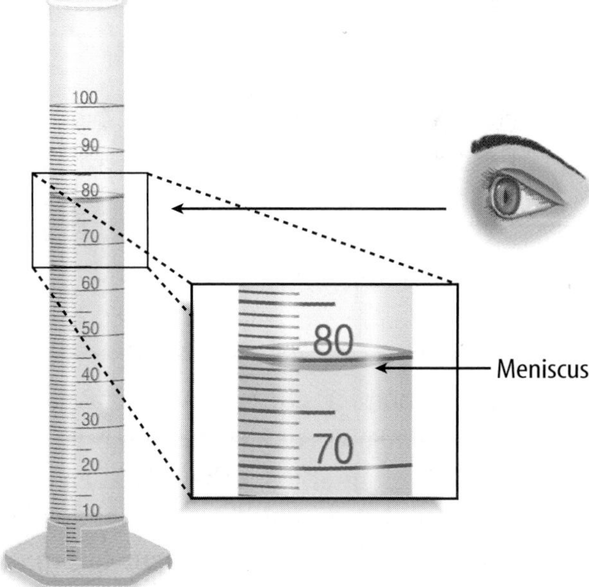

Figure 12
Graduated cylinders measure liquid volume.

Skill Handbooks

Mass Scientists measure mass in grams. You might use a beam balance similar to the one shown in **Figure 13.** The balance has a pan on one side and a set of beams on the other side. Each beam has a rider that slides on the beam.

Before you find the mass of an object, slide all the riders back to the zero point. Check the pointer on the right to make sure it swings an equal distance above and below the zero point. If the swing is unequal, find and turn the adjusting screw until you have an equal swing.

Place an object on the pan. Slide the largest rider along its beam until the pointer drops below zero. Then move it back one notch. Repeat the process on each beam until the pointer swings an equal distance above and below the zero point. Sum the masses on each beam to find the mass of the object. Move all riders back to zero when finished.

Figure 13
A triple beam balance is used to determine the mass of an object.

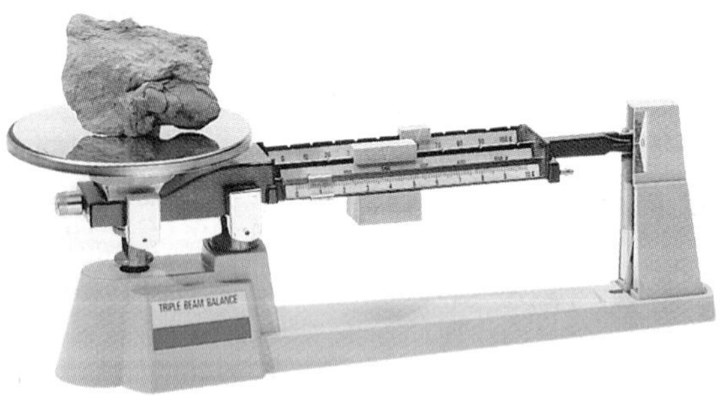

You should never place a hot object on the pan or pour chemicals directly onto the pan. Instead, find the mass of a clean container. Remove the container from the pan, then place the chemicals in the container. Find the mass of the container with the chemicals in it. To find the mass of the chemicals, subtract the mass of the empty container from the mass of the filled container.

Making and Using Tables

Browse through your textbook and you will see tables in the text and in the activities. In a table, data, or information, are arranged so that they are easier to understand. Activity tables help organize the data you collect during an activity so results can be interpreted.

Making Tables To make a table, list the items to be compared in the first column and the characteristics to be compared in the first row. The title should clearly indicate the content of the table, and the column or row heads should tell the reader what information is found in there. The table below lists materials collected for recycling on three weekly pick-up days. The inclusion of kilograms in parentheses also identifies for the reader that the figures are mass units.

Recyclable Materials Collected During Week

Day of Week	Paper (kg)	Aluminum (kg)	Glass (kg)
Monday	5.0	4.0	12.0
Wednesday	4.0	1.0	10.0
Friday	2.5	2.0	10.0

Using Tables How much paper, in kilograms, is being recycled on Wednesday? Locate the column labeled "Paper (kg)" and the row "Wednesday." The information in the box where the column and row intersect is the answer. Did you answer "4.0"? How much aluminum, in kilograms, is being recycled on Friday? If you answered "2.0," you understand how to read the table. How much glass is collected for recycling each week? Locate the column labeled "Glass (kg)" and add the figures for all three rows. If you answered "32.0," then you know how to locate and use the data provided in the table.

Recording Data

To be useful, the data you collect must be recorded carefully. Accuracy is key. A well-thought-out experiment includes a way to record procedures, observations, and results accurately. Data tables are one way to organize and record results. Set up the tables you will need ahead of time so you can record the data right away.

Record information properly and neatly. Never put unidentified data on scraps of paper. Instead, data should be written in a notebook like the one in **Figure 14.** Write in pencil so information isn't lost if your data get wet. At each point in the experiment, record your information and label it. That way, your data will be accurate and you will not have to determine what the figures mean when you look at your notes later.

Figure 14
Record data neatly and clearly so they are easy to understand.

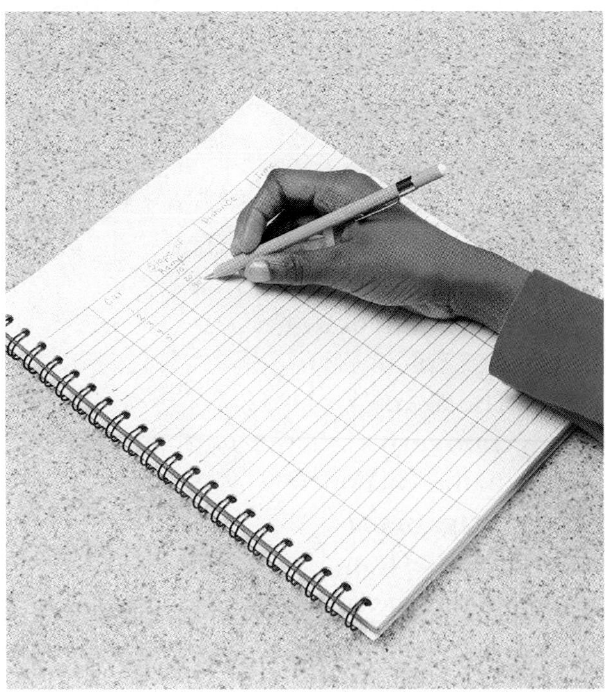

Recording Observations

It is important to record observations accurately and completely. That is why you always should record observations in your notes immediately as you make them. It is easy to miss details or make mistakes when recording results from memory. Do not include your personal thoughts when you record your data. Record only what you observe to eliminate bias. For example, when you record the time required for five students to climb the same set of stairs, you would note which student took the longest time. However, you would not refer to that student's time as "the worst time of all the students in the group."

Making Models

You can organize the observations and other data you collect and record in many ways. Making models is one way to help you better understand the parts of a structure you have been observing or the way a process for which you have been taking various measurements works.

Models often show things that are too large or too small for normal viewing. For example, you normally won't see the inside of an atom. However, you can understand the structure of the atom better by making a three-dimensional model of an atom. The relative sizes, the positions, and the movements of protons, neutrons, and electrons can be explained in words. An atomic model made of a plastic-ball nucleus and pipe-cleaner electron shells can help you visualize how the parts of the atom relate to each other.

Other models can be devised on a computer. Some models, such as those that illustrate the chemical combinations of different elements, are mathematical and are represented by equations.

Making and Using Graphs

After scientists organize data in tables, they might display the data in a graph that shows the relationship of one variable to another. A graph makes interpretation and analysis of data easier. Three types of graphs are the line graph, the bar graph, and the circle graph.

Line Graphs A line graph like in **Figure 15** is used to show the relationship between two variables. The variables being compared go on two axes of the graph. For data from an experiment, the independent variable always goes on the horizontal axis, called the *x*-axis. The dependent variable always goes on the vertical axis, called the *y*-axis. After drawing your axes, label each with a scale. Next, plot the data points.

A data point is the intersection of the recorded value of the dependent variable for each tested value of the independent variable. After all the points are plotted, connect them.

Distance v. Time

Distance (km)

Time (hr)

Figure 15
This line graph shows the relationship between distance and time during a bicycle ride lasting several hours.

Bar Graphs Bar graphs compare data that do not change continuously. Vertical bars show the relationships among data.

To make a bar graph, set up the *y*-axis as you did for the line graph. Draw vertical bars of equal size from the *x*-axis up to the point on the *y*-axis that represents value of *x*.

Figure 16
The amount of aluminum collected for recycling during one week can be shown as a bar graph or circle graph.

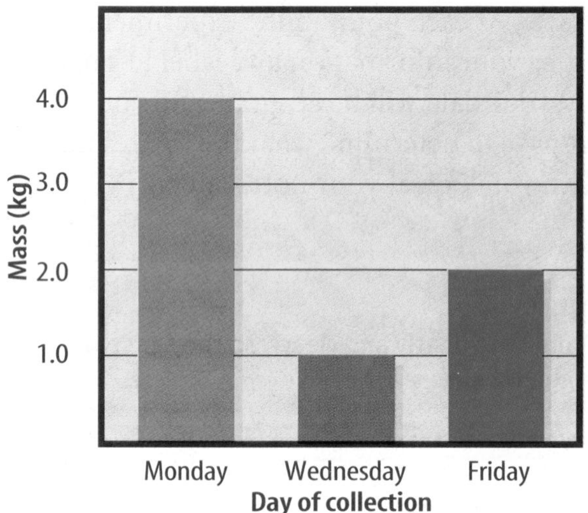

Circle Graphs A circle graph uses a circle divided into sections to display data as parts (fractions or percentages) of a whole. The size of each section corresponds to the fraction or percentage of the data that the section represents. So, the entire circle represents 100 percent, one-half represents 50 percent, one-fifth represents 20 percent, and so on.

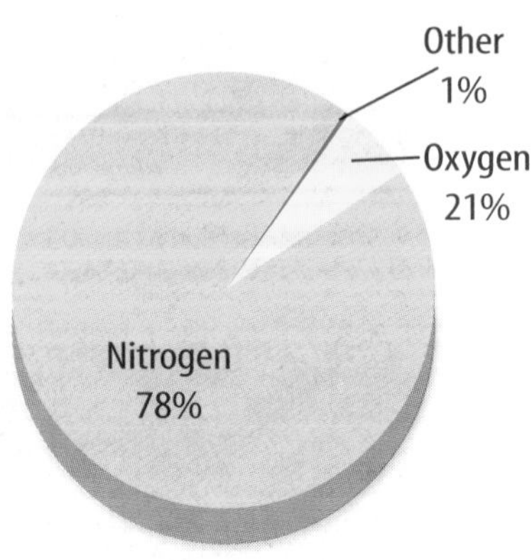

Analyzing Results

To determine the meaning of your observations and investigation results, you will need to look for patterns in the data. You can organize your information in several of the ways that are discussed in this handbook. Then you must think critically to determine what the data mean. Scientists use several approaches when they analyze the data they have collected and recorded. Each approach is useful for identifying specific patterns in the data.

Forming Operational Definitions

An operational definition defines an object by showing how it functions, works, or behaves. Such definitions are written in terms of how an object works or how it can be used; that is, they describe its job or purpose.

For example, a ruler can be defined as a tool that measures the length of an object (how it can be used). A ruler also can be defined as something that contains a series of marks that can be used as a standard when measuring (how it works).

Classifying

Classifying is the process of sorting objects or events into groups based on common features. When classifying, first observe the objects or events to be classified. Then select one feature that is shared by some members in the group but not by all. Place those members that share that feature into a subgroup. You can classify members into smaller and smaller subgroups based on characteristics.

How might you classify a group of chemicals? You might first classify them by state of matter, putting solids, liquids, and gases into separate groups. Within each group, you could then look for another common feature by which to further classify members of the group, such as color or how reactive they are.

Remember that when you classify, you are grouping objects or events for a purpose. For example, classifying chemicals can be the first step in organizing them for storage. Both at home and at school, poisonous or highly reactive chemicals should all be stored in a safe location where they are not easily accessible to small children or animals. Solids, liquids, and gases each have specific storage requirements that may include waterproof, airtight, or pressurized containers. Are the dangerous chemicals in your home stored in the right place? Keep your purpose in mind as you select the features to form groups and subgroups.

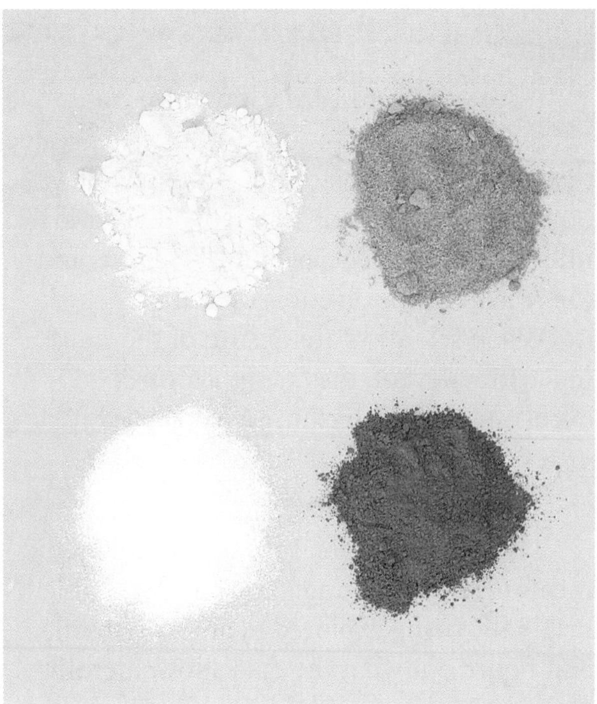

Figure 17
Color is one of many characteristics that are used to classify chemicals.

Comparing and Contrasting

Observations can be analyzed by noting the similarities and differences between two or more objects or events that you observe. When you look at objects or events to see how they are similar, you are comparing them. Contrasting is looking for differences in objects or events. The table below compares and contrasts the characteristics of two elements.

Elemental Characteristics		
Element	Aluminum	Gold
Color	silver	gold
Classification	metal	metal
Density (g/cm^3)	2.7	19.3
Melting Point (°C)	660	1064

Recognizing Cause and Effect

Have you ever heard a loud pop right before the power went out and then suggested that an electric transformer probably blew out? If so, you have observed an effect and inferred a cause. The event is the effect, and the reason for the event is the cause.

When scientists are unsure of the cause of a certain event, they design controlled experiments to determine what caused it.

Interpreting Data

The word *interpret* means "to explain the meaning of something." Look at the problem originally being explored in an experiment and figure out what the data show. Identify the control group and the test group so you can see whether or not changes in the independent variable have had an effect. Look for differences in the dependent variable between the control and test groups.

These differences you observe can be qualitative or quantitative. You would be able to describe a qualitative difference using only words, whereas you would measure a quantitative difference and describe it using numbers. If there are differences, the independent variable that is being tested could have had an effect. If no differences are found between the control and test groups, the variable that is being tested apparently had no effect.

For example, suppose that three beakers each contain 100 mL of water. The beakers are placed on hot plates, and two of the hot plates are turned on, but the third is left off for a period of 5 min. Suppose you are then asked to describe any differences in the water in the three beakers. A qualitative difference might be the appearance of bubbles rising to the top in the water that is being heated but no rising bubbles in the unheated water. A quantitative difference might be a difference in the amount of water that is present in the beakers.

Inferring Scientists often make inferences based on their observations. An inference is an attempt to explain, or interpret, observations or to indicate what caused what you observed. An inference is a type of conclusion.

When making an inference, be certain to use accurate data and accurately described observations. Analyze all of the data that you've collected. Then, based on everything you know, explain or interpret what you've observed.

Drawing Conclusions

When scientists have analyzed the data they collected, they proceed to draw conclusions about what the data mean. These conclusions are sometimes stated using words similar to those found in the hypothesis formed earlier in the process.

Conclusions To analyze your data, you must review all of the observations and measurements that you made and recorded. Recheck all data for accuracy. After your data are rechecked and organized, you are almost ready to draw a conclusion such as "salt water boils at a higher temperature than freshwater."

Before you can draw a conclusion, however, you must determine whether the data allow you to come to a conclusion that supports a hypothesis. Sometimes that will be the case, other times it will not.

If your data do not support a hypothesis, it does not mean that the hypothesis is wrong. It means only that the results of the investigation did not support the hypothesis. Maybe the experiment needs to be redesigned, but very likely, some of the initial observations on which the hypothesis was based were incomplete or biased. Perhaps more observation or research is needed to refine the hypothesis.

Avoiding Bias Sometimes drawing a conclusion involves making judgments. When you make a judgment, you form an opinion about what your data mean. It is important to be honest and to avoid reaching a conclusion if there were no supporting evidence for it or if it were based on a small sample. It also is important not to allow any expectations of results to bias your judgments. If possible, it is a good idea to collect additional data. Scientists do this all the time.

For example, the *Hubble Space Telescope* was sent into space in April, 1990, to provide scientists with clearer views of the universe. The *Hubble* is the size of a school bus and has a 2.4-m-diameter mirror. The *Hubble* helped scientists answer questions about the planet Pluto.

For many years, scientists had only been able to hypothesize about the surface of the planet Pluto. The *Hubble* has now provided pictures of Pluto's surface that show a rough texture with light and dark regions on it. This might be the best information about Pluto scientists will have until they are able to send a space probe to it.

Evaluating Others' Data and Conclusions

Sometimes scientists have to use data that they did not collect themselves, or they have to rely on observations and conclusions drawn by other researchers. In cases such as these, the data must be evaluated carefully.

How were the data obtained? How was the investigation done? Was it carried out properly? Has it been duplicated by other researchers? Were they able to follow the exact procedure? Did they come up with the same results? Look at the conclusion, as well. Would you reach the same conclusion from these results? Only when you have confidence in the data of others can you believe it is true and feel comfortable using it.

Communicating

The communication of ideas is an important part of the work of scientists. A discovery that is not reported will not advance the scientific community's understanding or knowledge. Communication among scientists also is important as a way of improving their investigations.

Scientists communicate in many ways, from writing articles in journals and magazines that explain their investigations and experiments, to announcing important discoveries on television and radio, to sharing ideas with colleagues on the Internet or presenting them as lectures.

People who study science rely on computers to record and store data and to analyze results from investigations. Whether you work in a laboratory or just need to write a lab report with tables, good computer skills are a necessity.

Using a Word Processor

Suppose your teacher has assigned a written report. After you've completed your research and decided how you want to write the information, you need to put all that information on paper. The easiest way to do this is with a word processing application on a computer.

A computer application that allows you to type your information, change it as many times as you need to, and then print it out so that it looks neat and clean is called a word processing application. You also can use this type of application to create tables and columns, add bullets or cartoon art to your page, include page numbers, and check your spelling.

Helpful Hints

- If you aren't sure how to do something using your word processing program, look in the help menu. You will find a list of topics there to click on for help. After you locate the help topic you need, just follow the step-by-step instructions you see on your screen.
- Just because you've spell checked your report doesn't mean that the spelling is perfect. The spell check feature can't catch misspelled words that look like other words. If you've accidentally typed *cold* instead of *gold*, the spell checker won't know the difference. Always reread your report to make sure you didn't miss any mistakes.

Figure 18
You can use computer programs to make graphs and tables.

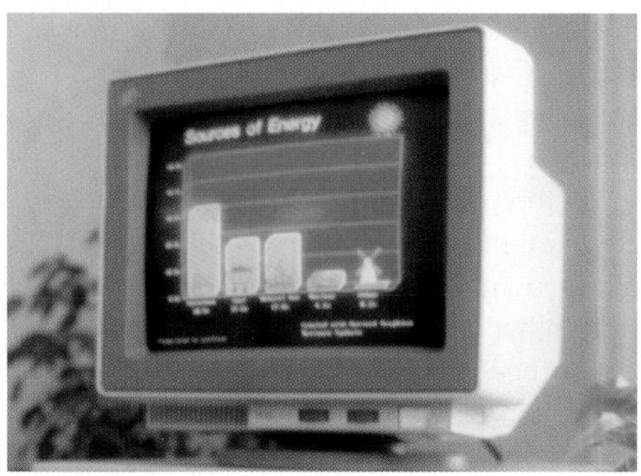

Using a Database

Imagine you're in the middle of a research project, busily gathering facts and information. You soon realize that it's becoming more difficult to organize and keep track of all the information. The tool to use to solve information overload is a database. Just as a file cabinet organizes paper records, a database organizes computer records. However, a database is more powerful than a simple file cabinet because at the click of a mouse, the contents can be reshuffled and reorganized. At computer-quick speeds, databases can sort information by any characteristics and filter data into multiple categories.

Helpful Hints

- Before setting up a database, take some time to learn the features of your database software by practicing with established database software.
- Periodically save your database as you enter data. That way, if something happens such as your computer malfunctions or the power goes off, you won't lose all of your work.

Doing a Database Search

When searching for information in a database, use the following search strategies to get the best results. These are the same search methods used for searching internet databases.

- Place the word *and* between two words in your search if you want the database to look for any entries that have both the words. For example, "gold *and* silver" would give you information that mentions both gold and silver.
- Place the word *or* between two words if you want the database to show entries that have at least one of the words. For example "gold *or* silver" would show you information that mentions either gold or silver.
- Place the word *not* between two words if you want the database to look for entries that have the first word but do not have the second word. For example, "gold *not* jewelry" would show you information that mentions gold but does not mention jewelry.

In summary, databases can be used to store large amounts of information about a particular subject. Databases allow biologists, Earth scientists, and physical scientists to search for information quickly and accurately.

Using an Electronic Spreadsheet

Your science fair experiment has produced lots of numbers. How do you keep track of all the data, and how can you easily work out all the calculations needed? You can use a computer program called a spreadsheet to record data that involve numbers. A spreadsheet is an electronic mathematical worksheet.

Type your data in rows and columns, just as they would look in a data table on a sheet of paper. A spreadsheet uses simple math to do data calculations. For example, you could add, subtract, divide, or multiply any of the values in the spreadsheet by another number. You also could set up a series of math steps you want to apply to the data. If you want to add 12 to all the numbers and then multiply all the numbers by 10, the computer does all the calculations for you in the spreadsheet. Below is an example of a spreadsheet that records test car data.

Helpful Hints

- Before you set up the spreadsheet, identify how you want to organize the data. Include any formulas you will need to use.
- Make sure you have entered the correct data into the correct rows and columns.
- You also can display your results in a graph. Pick the style of graph that best represents the data with which you are working.

Figure 19
A spreadsheet allows you to display large amounts of data and do calculations automatically.

EM-016C-MSS02.excl

	A	B	C	D	E
1	Test Runs	Time	Distance	Speed	
2	Car 1	5 mins	5 miles	60 mph	
3	Car 2	10 mins	4 miles	24 mph	
4	Car 3	6 mins	3 miles	30 mph	

Skill Handbooks

Using a Computerized Card Catalog

When you have a report or paper to research, you probably go to the library. To find the information you need in the library, you might have to use a computerized card catalog. This type of card catalog allows you to search for information by subject, by title, or by author. The computer then will display all the holdings the library has on the subject, title, or author requested.

A library's holdings can include books, magazines, databases, videos, and audio materials. When you have chosen something from this list, the computer will show whether an item is available and where in the library to find it.

Helpful Hints

- Remember that you can use the computer to search by subject, author, or title. If you know a book's author but not the title, you can search for all the books the library has by that author.
- When searching by subject, it's often most helpful to narrow your search by using specific search terms, such as *and, or,* and *not.* If you don't find enough sources this way, you can broaden your search.
- Pay attention to the type of materials found in your search. If you need a book, you can eliminate any videos or other resources that come up in your search.
- Knowing how your library is arranged can save you a lot of time. If you need help, the librarian will show you where certain types of materials are kept and how to find specific holdings.

Using Graphics Software

Are you having trouble finding that exact piece of art you're looking for? Do you have a picture in your mind of what you want but can't seem to find the right graphic to represent your ideas? To solve these problems, you can use graphics software. Graphics software allows you to create and change images and diagrams in almost unlimited ways. Typical uses for graphics software include arranging clip art, changing scanned images, and constructing pictures from scratch. Most graphics software applications work in similar ways. They use the same basic tools and functions. Once you master one graphics application, you can use other graphics applications.

Figure 20
Graphics software can use your data to draw bar graphs.

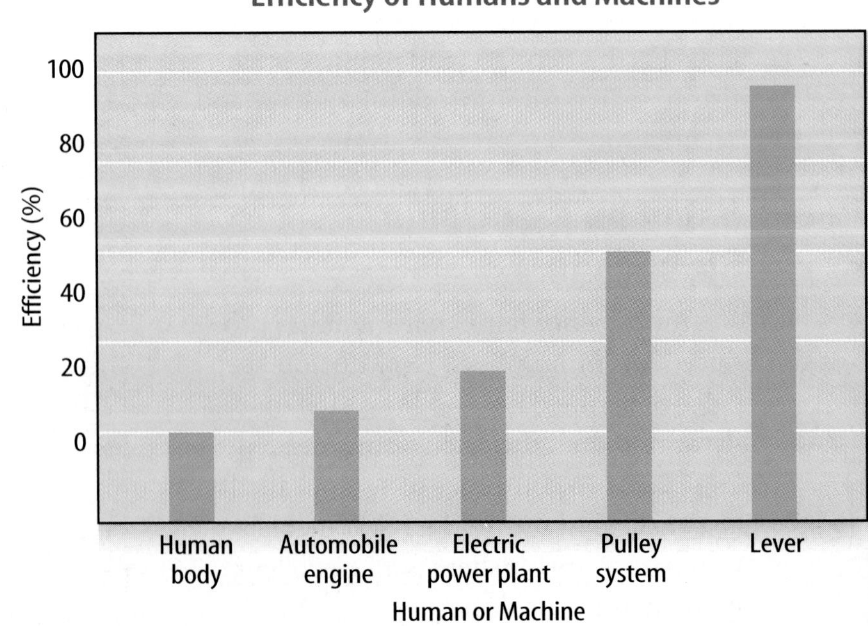

Figure 21
Graphics software can use your data to draw circle graphs.

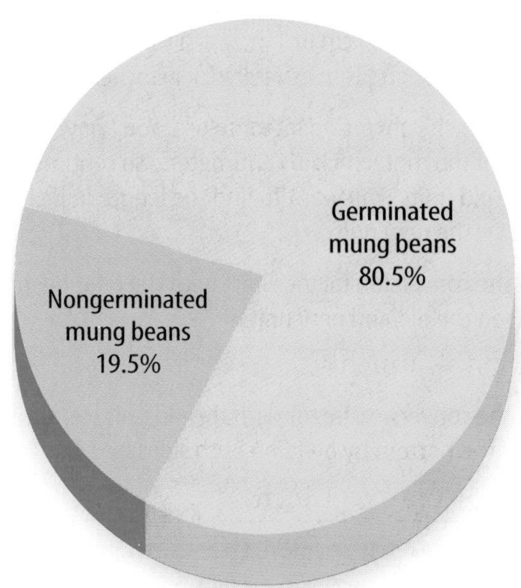

Helpful Hints

- As with any method of drawing, the more you practice using the graphics software, the better your results will be.
- Start by using the software to manipulate existing drawings. Once you master this, making your own illustrations will be easier.
- Clip art is available on CD-ROMs and the Internet. With these resources, finding a piece of clip art to suit your purposes is simple.
- As you work on a drawing, save it often.

Developing Multimedia Presentations

It's your turn—you have to present your science report to the entire class. How do you do it? You can use many different sources of information to get the class excited about your presentation. Posters, videos, photographs, sound, computers, and the Internet can help show your ideas.

First, determine what important points you want to make in your presentation. Then, write an outline of what materials and types of media would best illustrate those points. Maybe you could start with an outline on an overhead projector, then show a video, followed by something from the Internet or a slide show accompanied by music or recorded voices. You might choose to use a presentation builder computer application that can combine all these elements into one presentation. Make sure the presentation is well constructed to make the most impact on the audience.

Figure 22
Multimedia presentations use many types of print and electronic materials.

Helpful Hints

- Carefully consider what media will best communicate the point you are trying to make.
- Make sure you know how to use any equipment you will be using in your presentation.
- Practice the presentation several times.
- If possible, set up all of the equipment ahead of time. Make sure everything is working correctly.

Use this Math Skill Handbook to help solve problems you are given in this text. You might find it useful to review topics in this Math Skill Handbook first.

Converting Units

In science, quantities such as length, mass, and time sometimes are measured using different units. Suppose you want to know how many miles are in 12.7 km.

Conversion factors are used to change from one unit of measure to another. A conversion factor is a ratio that is equal to one. For example, there are 1,000 mL in 1 L, so 1,000 mL equals 1 L, or:

$$1{,}000 \text{ mL} = 1 \text{ L}$$

If both sides are divided by 1 L, this equation becomes:

$$\frac{1{,}000 \text{ mL}}{1 \text{ L}} = 1$$

The **ratio** on the left side of this equation is equal to 1 and is a conversion factor. You can make another conversion factor by dividing both sides of the top equation by 1,000 mL:

$$1 = \frac{1 \text{ L}}{1{,}000 \text{ mL}}$$

To **convert units,** you multiply by the appropriate conversion factor. For example, how many milliliters are in 1.255 L? To convert 1.255 L to milliliters, multiply 1.255 L by a conversion factor.

Use the **conversion factor** with new units (mL) in the numerator and the old units (L) in the denominator.

$$1.255 \cancel{\text{L}} \times \frac{1{,}000 \text{ mL}}{1 \cancel{\text{L}}} = 1{,}255 \text{ mL}$$

The unit L divides in this equation, just as if it were a number.

Example 1 There are 2.54 cm in 1 inch. If a meterstick has a length of 100 cm, how long is the meterstick in inches?

Step 1 Decide which conversion factor to use. You know the length of the meterstick in centimeters, so centimeters are the old units. You want to find the length in inches, so inch is the new unit.

Step 2 Form the conversion factor. Start with the relationship between the old and new units.

$$2.54 \text{ cm} = 1 \text{ inch}$$

Step 3 Form the conversion factor with the old unit (centimeter) on the bottom by dividing both sides by 2.54 cm.

$$1 = \frac{2.54 \text{ cm}}{2.54 \text{ cm}} = \frac{1 \text{ inch}}{2.54 \text{ cm}}$$

Step 4 Multiply the old measurement by the conversion factor.

$$100 \cancel{\text{cm}} \times \frac{1 \text{ inch}}{2.54 \cancel{\text{cm}}} = 39.37 \text{ inches}$$

The meterstick is 39.37 inches long.

Example 2 There are 365 days in one year. If a person is 14 years old, what is his or her age in days? (Ignore leap years).

Step 1 Decide which conversion factor to use. You want to convert years to days.

Step 2 Form the conversion factor. Start with the relation between the old and new units.

$$1 \text{ year} = 365 \text{ days}$$

Step 3 Form the conversion factor with the old unit (year) on the bottom by dividing both sides by 1 year.

$$1 = \frac{1 \text{ year}}{1 \text{ year}} = \frac{365 \text{ days}}{1 \text{ year}}$$

Step 4 Multiply the old measurement by the conversion factor:

$$14 \cancel{\text{years}} \times \frac{365 \text{ days}}{1 \cancel{\text{year}}} = 5{,}110 \text{ days}$$

The person's age is 5,110 days.

Practice Problem A book has a mass of 2.31 kg. If there are 1,000 g in 1 kg, what is the mass of the book in grams?

Using Fractions

A **fraction** is a number that compares a part to the whole. For example, in the fraction $\frac{2}{3}$, the 2 represents the part and the 3 represents the whole. In the fraction $\frac{2}{3}$, the top number, 2, is called the numerator. The bottom number, 3, is called the denominator.

Sometimes fractions are not written in their simplest form. To determine a fraction's **simplest form,** you must find the greatest common factor (GCF) of the numerator and denominator. The greatest common factor is the largest factor that is common to the numerator and denominator.

For example, because the number 3 divides into 12 and 30 evenly, it is a common factor of 12 and 30. However, because the number 6 is the largest number that evenly divides into 12 and 30, it is the **greatest common factor.**

After you find the greatest common factor, you can write a fraction in its simplest form. Divide both the numerator and the denominator by the greatest common factor. The number that results is the fraction in its **simplest form.**

Example Twelve of the 20 chemicals used in the science lab are in powder form. What fraction of the chemicals used in the lab are in powder form?

Step 1 Write the fraction.

$$\frac{\text{part}}{\text{whole}} = \frac{12}{20}$$

Step 2 To find the GCF of the numerator and denominator, list all of the factors of each number.

Factors of 12: 1, 2, 3, 4, 6, 12 (the numbers that divide evenly into 12)

Factors of 20: 1, 2, 4, 5, 10, 20 (the numbers that divide evenly into 20)

Step 3 List the common factors.

1, 2, 4.

Step 4 Choose the greatest factor in the list of common factors.

The GCF of 12 and 20 is 4.

Step 5 Divide the numerator and denominator by the GCF.

$$\frac{12 \div 4}{20 \div 4} = \frac{3}{5}$$

In the lab, $\frac{3}{5}$ of the chemicals are in powder form.

Practice Problem There are 90 rides at an amusement park. Of those rides, 66 have a height restriction. What fraction of the rides has a height restriction? Write the fraction in simplest form.

Calculating Ratios

A **ratio** is a comparison of two numbers by division.

Ratios can be written 3 to 5 or 3:5. Ratios also can be written as fractions, such as $\frac{3}{5}$. Ratios, like fractions, can be written in simplest form. Recall that a fraction is in **simplest form** when the greatest common factor (GCF) of the numerator and denominator is 1.

Example A chemical solution contains 40 g of salt and 64 g of baking soda. What is the ratio of salt to baking soda as a fraction in simplest form?

Step 1 Write the ratio as a fraction. $\frac{\text{salt}}{\text{baking soda}} = \frac{40}{64}$

Step 2 Express the fraction in simplest form. The GCF of 40 and 64 is 8.

$$\frac{40}{64} = \frac{40 \div 8}{64 \div 8} = \frac{5}{8}$$

The ratio of salt to baking soda in the solution is $\frac{5}{8}$.

Practice Problem Two metal rods measure 100 cm and 144 cm in length. What is the ratio of their lengths in simplest fraction form?

Using Decimals

A **decimal** is a fraction with a denominator of 10, 100, 1,000, or another power of 10. For example, 0.854 is the same as the fraction $\frac{854}{1,000}$.

In a decimal, the decimal point separates the ones place and the tenths place. For example, 0.27 means twenty-seven hundredths, or $\frac{27}{100}$, where 27 is the **number of units** out of 100 units. Any fraction can be written as a decimal using division.

Example Write $\frac{5}{8}$ as a decimal.

Step 1 Write a division problem with the numerator, 5, as the dividend and the denominator, 8, as the divisor. Write 5 as 5.000.

Step 2 Solve the problem.

```
   0.625
8)5.000
  48
   20
   16
    40
    40
     0
```

Therefore, $\frac{5}{8} = 0.625$.

Practice Problem Write $\frac{19}{25}$ as a decimal.

Using Percentages

The word *percent* means "out of one hundred." A **percent** is a ratio that compares a number to 100. Suppose you read that 77 percent of Earth's surface is covered by water. That is the same as reading that the fraction of Earth's surface covered by water is $\frac{77}{100}$. To express a fraction as a percent, first find an equivalent decimal for the fraction. Then, multiply the decimal by 100 and add the percent symbol. For example, $\frac{1}{2} = 1 \div 2 = 0.5$. Then $0.5 \times 100 = 50 = 50\%$.

Example Express $\frac{13}{20}$ as a percent.

Step 1 Find the equivalent decimal for the fraction.

$$\begin{array}{r} 0.65 \\ 20\overline{)13.00} \\ \underline{120} \\ 100 \\ \underline{100} \\ 0 \end{array}$$

Step 2 Rewrite the fraction $\frac{13}{20}$ as 0.65.

Step 3 Multiply 0.65 by 100 and add the % sign.

$$0.65 \cdot 100 = 65 = 65\%$$

So, $\frac{13}{20} = 65\%$.

Practice Problem In one year, 73 of 365 days were rainy in one city. What percent of the days in that city were rainy?

Using Precision and Significant Digits

When you make a **measurement,** the value you record depends on the precision of the measuring instrument. When adding or subtracting numbers with different precision, the answer is rounded to the smallest number of decimal places of any number in the sum or difference. When multiplying or dividing, the answer is rounded to the smallest number of significant figures of any number being multiplied or divided. When counting the number of **significant figures,** all digits are counted except zeros at the end of a number with no decimal such as 2,500, and zeros at the beginning of a decimal such as 0.03020.

Example The lengths 5.28 and 5.2 are measured in meters. Find the sum of these lengths and report the sum using the least precise measurement.

Step 1 Find the sum.

$$\begin{array}{rl} 5.28\text{ m} & \text{2 digits after the decimal} \\ +\ 5.2\ \ \text{m} & \text{1 digit after the decimal} \\ \hline 10.48\text{ m} & \end{array}$$

Step 2 Round to one digit after the decimal because the least number of digits after the decimal of the numbers being added is 1.

The sum is 10.5 m.

Practice Problem Multiply the numbers in the example using the rule for multiplying and dividing. Report the answer with the correct number of significant figures.

Solving One-Step Equations

An **equation** is a statement that two things are equal. For example, $A = B$ is an equation that states that A is equal to B.

Sometimes one side of the equation will contain a **variable** whose value is not known. In the equation $3x = 12$, the variable is x.

The equation is solved when the variable is replaced with a value that makes both sides of the equation equal to each other. For example, the solution of the equation $3x = 12$ is $x = 4$. If the x is replaced with 4, then the equation becomes $3 \cdot 4 = 12$, or $12 = 12$.

To solve an equation such as $8x = 40$, divide both sides of the equation by the number that multiplies the variable.

$$8x = 40$$
$$\frac{8x}{8} = \frac{40}{8}$$
$$x = 5$$

You can check your answer by replacing the variable with your solution and seeing if both sides of the equation are the same.

$$8x = 8 \cdot 5 = 40$$

The left and right sides of the equation are the same, so $x = 5$ is the solution.

Sometimes an equation is written in this way: $a = bc$. This also is called a **formula.** The letters can be replaced by numbers, but the numbers must still make both sides of the equation the same.

Example 1 Solve the equation $10x = 35$.

Step 1 Find the solution by dividing each side of the equation by 10.

$$10x = 35 \qquad \frac{10x}{10} = \frac{35}{10} \qquad x = 3.5$$

Step 2 Check the solution.

$$10x = 35 \qquad 10 \times 3.5 = 35 \qquad 35 = 35$$

Both sides of the equation are equal, so $x = 3.5$ is the solution to the equation.

Example 2 In the formula $a = bc$, find the value of c if $a = 20$ and $b = 2$.

Step 1 Rearrange the formula so the unknown value is by itself on one side of the equation by dividing both sides by b.

$$a = bc$$
$$\frac{a}{b} = \frac{bc}{b}$$
$$\frac{a}{b} = c$$

Step 2 Replace the variables a and b with the values that are given.

$$\frac{a}{b} = c$$
$$\frac{20}{2} = c$$
$$10 = c$$

Step 3 Check the solution.

$$a = bc$$
$$20 = 2 \times 10$$
$$20 = 20$$

Both sides of the equation are equal, so $c = 10$ is the solution when $a = 20$ and $b = 2$.

Practice Problem In the formula $h = gd$, find the value of d if $g = 12.3$ and $h = 17.4$.

Using Proportions

A **proportion** is an equation that shows that two ratios are equivalent. The ratios $\frac{2}{4}$ and $\frac{5}{10}$ are equivalent, so they can be written as $\frac{2}{4} = \frac{5}{10}$. This equation is an example of a proportion.

When two ratios form a proportion, the **cross products** are equal. To find the cross products in the proportion $\frac{2}{4} = \frac{5}{10}$, multiply the 2 and the 10, and the 4 and the 5. Therefore **$2 \cdot 10 = 4 \cdot 5$, or $20 = 20$.**

Because you know that both proportions are equal, you can use cross products to find a missing term in a proportion. This is known as **solving the proportion.** Solving a proportion is similar to solving an equation.

Example The heights of a tree and a pole are proportional to the lengths of their shadows. The tree casts a shadow of 24 m at the same time that a 6-m pole casts a shadow of 4 m. What is the height of the tree?

Step 1 Write a proportion.

$$\frac{\text{height of tree}}{\text{height of pole}} = \frac{\text{length of tree's shadow}}{\text{length of pole's shadow}}$$

Step 2 Substitute the known values into the proportion. Let *h* represent the unknown value, the height of the tree.

$$\frac{h}{6} = \frac{24}{4}$$

Step 3 Find the cross products.

$$h \cdot 4 = 6 \cdot 24$$

Step 4 Simplify the equation.

$$4h = 144$$

Step 5 Divide each side by 4.

$$\frac{4h}{4} = \frac{144}{4}$$

$$h = 36$$

The height of the tree is 36 m.

Practice Problem The ratios of the weights of two objects on the Moon and on Earth are in proportion. A rock weighing 3 N on the Moon weighs 18 N on Earth. How much would a rock that weighs 5 N on the Moon weigh on Earth?

Using Statistics

Statistics is the branch of mathematics that deals with collecting, analyzing, and presenting data. In statistics, there are three common ways to summarize the data with a single number—the mean, the median, and the mode.

The **mean** of a set of data is the arithmetic average. It is found by adding the numbers in the data set and dividing by the number of items in the set.

The **median** is the middle number in a set of data when the data are arranged in numerical order. If there were an even number of data points, the median would be the mean of the two middle numbers.

The **mode** of a set of data is the number or item that appears most often.

Another number that often is used to describe a set of data is the range. The **range** is the difference between the largest number and the smallest number in a set of data.

A **frequency table** shows how many times each piece of data occurs, usually in a survey. The frequency table below shows the results of a student survey on favorite color.

Color	Tally	Frequency
red	||||	4
blue	~~||||~~	5
black	||	2
green	|||	3
purple	~~||||~~ ||	7
yellow	~~||||~~ |	6

Based on the frequency table data, which color is the favorite?

Example The speeds (in m/s) for a race car during five different time trials are 39, 37, 44, 36, and 44.

To find the mean:

Step 1 Find the sum of the numbers.

$$39 + 37 + 44 + 36 + 44 = 200$$

Step 2 Divide the sum by the number of items, which is 5.

$$200 \div 5 = 40$$

The mean measure is 40 m/s.

To find the median:

Step 1 Arrange the measures from least to greatest.

$$36,\ 37,\ \underline{39},\ 44,\ 44$$

Step 2 Determine the middle measure.

The median measure is 39 m/s.

To find the mode:

Step 1 Group the numbers that are the same together.

44, 44, 36, 37, 39

Step 2 Determine the number that occurs most in the set.

$\underline{44, 44}$, 36, 37, 39

The mode measure is 44 m/s.

To find the range:

Step 1 Arrange the measures from largest to smallest.

44, 44, 39, 37, 36

Step 2 Determine the largest and smallest measures in the set.

$\underline{44}$, 44, 39, 37, $\underline{36}$

Step 3 Find the difference between the largest and smallest measures.

$$44 - 36 = 8$$

The range is 8 m/s.

Practice Problem Find the mean, median, mode, and range for the data set 8, 4, 12, 8, 11, 14, 16.

Safety in the Science Classroom

1. Always obtain your teacher's permission to begin an investigation.
2. Study the procedure. If you have questions, ask your teacher. Be sure you understand any safety symbols shown on the page.
3. Use the safety equipment provided for you. Goggles and a safety apron should be worn during most investigations.
4. Always slant test tubes away from yourself and others when heating them or adding substances to them.
5. Never eat or drink in the lab, and never use lab glassware as food or drink containers. Never inhale chemicals. Do not taste any substances or draw any material into a tube with your mouth.
6. Report any spill, accident, or injury, no matter how small, immediately to your teacher, then follow his or her instructions.
7. Know the location and proper use of the fire extinguisher, safety shower, fire blanket, first aid kit, and fire alarm.
8. Keep all materials away from open flames. Tie back long hair and tie down loose clothing.
9. If your clothing should catch fire, smother it with the fire blanket, or get under a safety shower. NEVER RUN.
10. If a fire should occur, turn off the gas; then leave the room according to established procedures.

Follow these procedures as you clean up your work area

1. Turn off the water and gas. Disconnect electrical devices.
2. Clean all pieces of equipment and return all materials to their proper places.
3. Dispose of chemicals and other materials as directed by your teacher. Place broken glass and solid substances in the proper containers. Make sure never to discard materials in the sink.
4. Clean your work area. Wash your hands thoroughly after working in the laboratory.

First Aid

Injury	Safe Response ALWAYS NOTIFY YOUR TEACHER IMMEDIATELY
Burns	Apply cold water.
Cuts and Bruises	Stop any bleeding by applying direct pressure. Cover cuts with a clean dressing. Apply ice packs or cold compresses to bruises.
Fainting	Leave the person lying down. Loosen any tight clothing and keep crowds away.
Foreign Matter in Eye	Flush with plenty of water. Use eyewash bottle or fountain.
Poisoning	Note the suspected poisoning agent.
Any Spills on Skin	Flush with large amounts of water or use safety shower.

PERIODIC TABLE OF THE ELEMENTS

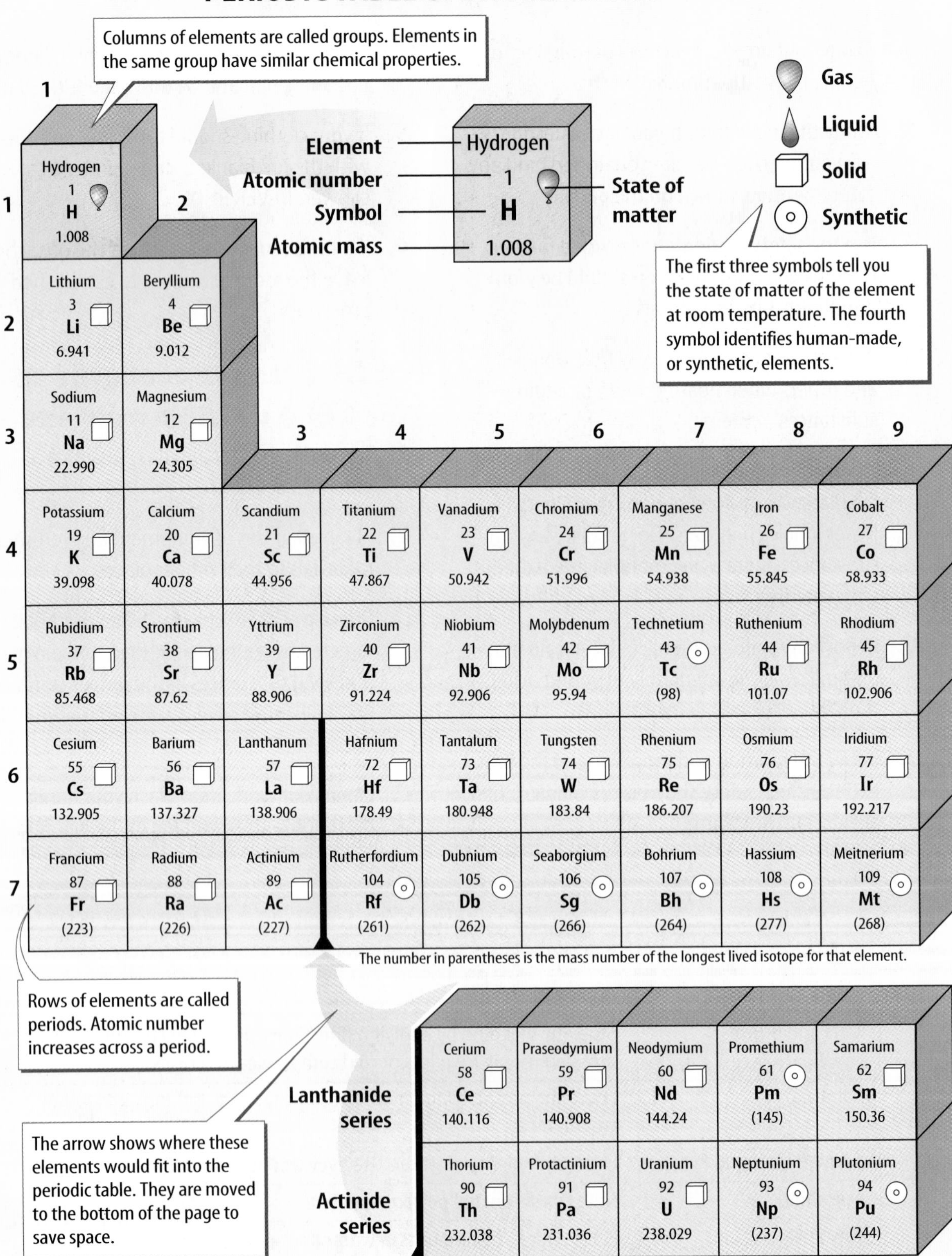

Period	1	2	3	4	5	6	7	8	9
1	Hydrogen 1 H 1.008 (Gas)								
2	Lithium 3 Li 6.941 (Solid)	Beryllium 4 Be 9.012 (Solid)							
3	Sodium 11 Na 22.990 (Solid)	Magnesium 12 Mg 24.305 (Solid)							
4	Potassium 19 K 39.098 (Solid)	Calcium 20 Ca 40.078 (Solid)	Scandium 21 Sc 44.956 (Solid)	Titanium 22 Ti 47.867 (Solid)	Vanadium 23 V 50.942 (Solid)	Chromium 24 Cr 51.996 (Solid)	Manganese 25 Mn 54.938 (Solid)	Iron 26 Fe 55.845 (Solid)	Cobalt 27 Co 58.933 (Solid)
5	Rubidium 37 Rb 85.468 (Solid)	Strontium 38 Sr 87.62 (Solid)	Yttrium 39 Y 88.906 (Solid)	Zirconium 40 Zr 91.224 (Solid)	Niobium 41 Nb 92.906 (Solid)	Molybdenum 42 Mo 95.94 (Solid)	Technetium 43 Tc (98) (Synthetic)	Ruthenium 44 Ru 101.07 (Solid)	Rhodium 45 Rh 102.906 (Solid)
6	Cesium 55 Cs 132.905 (Solid)	Barium 56 Ba 137.327 (Solid)	Lanthanum 57 La 138.906 (Solid)	Hafnium 72 Hf 178.49 (Solid)	Tantalum 73 Ta 180.948 (Solid)	Tungsten 74 W 183.84 (Solid)	Rhenium 75 Re 186.207 (Solid)	Osmium 76 Os 190.23 (Solid)	Iridium 77 Ir 192.217 (Solid)
7	Francium 87 Fr (223) (Solid)	Radium 88 Ra (226) (Solid)	Actinium 89 Ac (227) (Solid)	Rutherfordium 104 Rf (261) (Synthetic)	Dubnium 105 Db (262) (Synthetic)	Seaborgium 106 Sg (266) (Synthetic)	Bohrium 107 Bh (264) (Synthetic)	Hassium 108 Hs (277) (Synthetic)	Meitnerium 109 Mt (268) (Synthetic)

The number in parentheses is the mass number of the longest lived isotope for that element.

Series					
Lanthanide series	Cerium 58 Ce 140.116 (Solid)	Praseodymium 59 Pr 140.908 (Solid)	Neodymium 60 Nd 144.24 (Solid)	Promethium 61 Pm (145) (Synthetic)	Samarium 62 Sm 150.36 (Solid)
Actinide series	Thorium 90 Th 232.038 (Solid)	Protactinium 91 Pa 231.036 (Solid)	Uranium 92 U 238.029 (Solid)	Neptunium 93 Np (237) (Synthetic)	Plutonium 94 Pu (244) (Synthetic)

Metal

Metalloid

Nonmetal

Recently discovered

The color of an element's block tells you if the element is a metal, nonmetal, metalloid, or has been discovered so recently that more study is needed.

SCIENCE *Online*
Visit the Glencoe Science Web site at **science.glencoe.com** for updates to the periodic table.

10	11	12	13	14	15	16	17	18
								Helium 2 **He** 4.003
			Boron 5 **B** 10.811	Carbon 6 **C** 12.011	Nitrogen 7 **N** 14.007	Oxygen 8 **O** 15.999	Fluorine 9 **F** 18.998	Neon 10 **Ne** 20.180
			Aluminum 13 **Al** 26.982	Silicon 14 **Si** 28.086	Phosphorus 15 **P** 30.974	Sulfur 16 **S** 32.065	Chlorine 17 **Cl** 35.453	Argon 18 **Ar** 39.948
Nickel 28 **Ni** 58.693	Copper 29 **Cu** 63.546	Zinc 30 **Zn** 65.39	Gallium 31 **Ga** 69.723	Germanium 32 **Ge** 72.64	Arsenic 33 **As** 74.922	Selenium 34 **Se** 78.96	Bromine 35 **Br** 79.904	Krypton 36 **Kr** 83.80
Palladium 46 **Pd** 106.42	Silver 47 **Ag** 107.868	Cadmium 48 **Cd** 112.411	Indium 49 **In** 114.818	Tin 50 **Sn** 118.710	Antimony 51 **Sb** 121.760	Tellurium 52 **Te** 127.60	Iodine 53 **I** 126.904	Xenon 54 **Xe** 131.293
Platinum 78 **Pt** 195.078	Gold 79 **Au** 196.967	Mercury 80 **Hg** 200.59	Thallium 81 **Tl** 204.383	Lead 82 **Pb** 207.2	Bismuth 83 **Bi** 208.980	Polonium 84 **Po** (209)	Astatine 85 **At** (210)	Radon 86 **Rn** (222)
Ununnilium * 110 **Uun** (281)	Unununium * 111 **Uuu** (272)	Ununbium * 112 **Uub** (285)		Ununquadium * 114 **Uuq** (289)		Ununhexium * 116 **Uuh** (289)		Ununoctium * 118 **Uuo** (293)

* Names not officially assigned. Discovery of elements 114, 116, and 118 recently reported. Further information not yet available.

Europium 63 **Eu** 151.964	Gadolinium 64 **Gd** 157.25	Terbium 65 **Tb** 158.925	Dysprosium 66 **Dy** 162.50	Holmium 67 **Ho** 164.930	Erbium 68 **Er** 167.259	Thulium 69 **Tm** 168.934	Ytterbium 70 **Yb** 173.04	Lutetium 71 **Lu** 174.967
Americium 95 **Am** (243)	Curium 96 **Cm** (247)	Berkelium 97 **Bk** (247)	Californium 98 **Cf** (251)	Einsteinium 99 **Es** (252)	Fermium 100 **Fm** (257)	Mendelevium 101 **Md** (258)	Nobelium 102 **No** (259)	Lawrencium 103 **Lr** (262)

REFERENCE HANDBOOK C

SI—Metric/English, English/Metric Conversions	When you want to convert:	To:	Multiply by:
Length	inches	centimeters	2.54
	centimeters	inches	0.39
	yards	meters	0.91
	meters	yards	1.09
	miles	kilometers	1.61
	kilometers	miles	0.62
Mass and Weight*	ounces	grams	28.35
	grams	ounces	0.04
	pounds	kilograms	0.45
	kilograms	pounds	2.2
	tons (short)	tonnes (metric tons)	0.91
	tonnes (metric tons)	tons (short)	1.10
	pounds	newtons	4.45
	newtons	pounds	0.22
Volume	cubic inches	cubic centimeters	16.39
	cubic centimeters	cubic inches	0.06
	liters	quarts	1.06
	quarts	liters	0.95
	gallons	liters	3.78
Area	square inches	square centimeters	6.45
	square centimeters	square inches	0.16
	square yards	square meters	0.83
	square meters	square yards	1.19
	square miles	square kilometers	2.59
	square kilometers	square miles	0.39
	hectares	acres	2.47
	acres	hectares	0.40
Temperature	To convert °Celsius to °Fahrenheit		$°C \times 9/5 + 32$
	To convert °Fahrenheit to °Celsius		$5/9\ (°F - 32)$

*Weight is measured in standard Earth gravity.

This glossary defines each key term that appears in bold type in the text. It also shows the chapter, section, and page number where you can find the words used.

A

acceleration: rate of change of velocity; can cause an object to speed up, slow down, or turn, and can be calculated by dividing the change in speed by the given time. (Chap. 6, Sec. 2, p. 172)

accuracy: compares a measurement to the true value. (Chap. 2, Sec. 1, p. 45)

alternating current (AC): electric current that changes its direction many times each second. (Chap. 16, Sec. 2, p. 482)

alternative resources: any renewable and inexhaustible sources of energy to generate electricity, including solar energy, wind, and geothermal energy. (Chap. 8, Sec. 3, p. 245)

amplitude: distance a wave rises above or falls below its normal level, which is related to the energy that the wave carries; in a transverse wave, is one half the distance between a crest and a trough. (Chap. 11, Sec. 2, p. 321)

Archimedes' (ar kuh MEE deez) **principle:** states that the buoyant force on an object is equal to the weight of the fluid displaced by the object. (Chap. 4, Sec. 3, p. 123)

atom: a very small particle that makes up most kinds of matter and consists of smaller parts called protons, neutrons, and electrons. (Chap. 3, Sec. 1, p. 75)

atomic mass: average mass of an atom of an element; its unit of measure is the atomic mass unit (u), which is 1/12 the mass of a carbon-12 atom. (Chap. 3, Sec. 2, p. 86)

atomic number: number of protons in the nucleus of each atom of a given element; is the top number in the periodic table. (Chap. 3, Sec. 2, p. 85)

aurora: southern and northern lights that appear when charged particles trapped in the magnetosphere collide with Earth's atmosphere above the poles. (Chap. 16, Sec. 2, p. 481)

B

balanced forces: two or more equal forces whose effects cancel each other out and do not change the motion of an object. (Chap. 7, Sec. 1, p. 195)

bar graph: a type of graph that uses bars of varying sizes to show relationships between variables. (Chap. 2, Sec. 3, p. 58)

buoyant force: upward force exerted on an object immersed in a fluid. (Chap. 4, Sec. 3, p. 122)

C

carrier wave: particular transmission frequency assigned to a radio station. (Chap. 13, Sec. 3, p. 390)

chemical change: any change of a material into a new material with different properties. (Chap. 5, Sec. 3, p. 147)

chemical energy: energy that is stored in chemicals. (Chap. 8, Sec. 1, p. 231)

chemical property: characteristic of something that permits its change to something new. (Chap. 5, Sec. 2, p. 141)

circle graph: a type of graph that shows the parts of a whole; sometimes called a pie graph, each piece of which represents a percentage of the total. (Chap. 2, Sec. 3, p. 58)

circuit: closed conducting loop through which electric current can flow. (Chap. 15, Sec. 2, p. 447)

compound: a substance produced when elements combine and whose properties are different from each of the elements in it. (Chap. 3, Sec. 3, p. 89)

compound machine: device made up of a combination of two or more simple machines. (Chap. 9, Sec. 3, p. 269)

compressional wave: a type of mechanical wave in which matter in the medium moves forward and backward in the same direction the wave travels. (Chap. 11, Sec. 1, p. 319)

concave lens: lens that is thicker at its edges than in the middle and causes light rays traveling parallel to the optical axis to diverge. (Chap. 14, Sec. 3, p. 419)

condensation: change of matter from a gas to a liquid state. (Chap. 4, Sec. 2, p. 115)

conduction: transfer of heat by direct contact; occurs when particles of one substance collide with particles of another substance, transferring kinetic energy. (Chap. 10, Sec. 2, p. 291)

conductor: material, such as copper or silver, through which electrons can move easily or any material that transfers heat easily. (Chap. 10, Sec. 2, p. 293) (Chap. 15, Sec. 1, p. 444)

constant: variable that is not changed in an experiment. (Chap. 1, Sec. 2, p. 18)

controlled experiment: involves observing the effect of one thing while keeping all other things constant. (Chap. 1, Sec. 2, p. 18)

convection: transfer of thermal energy by the movement of heated molecules from one place to another in a gas or liquid. (Chap. 10, Sec. 2, p. 292)

convex lens: converging lens that is thicker in the middle than at its edges. (Chap. 14, Sec. 3, p. 418)

critical thinking: involves using knowledge and thinking skills to evaluate evidence and explanations. (Chap. 1, Sec. 4, p. 27)

D

density: physical property of matter that can be found by dividing the matter's mass by its volume. (Chap. 4, Sec. 3, p. 123) (Chap. 5, Sec. 1, p. 136)

diffraction: bending of waves around a barrier. (Chap. 11, Sec. 3, p. 329)

Doppler effect: change in the frequency or pitch of a sound that occurs when the sound source and the listener are in motion relative to each other. (Chap. 12, Sec. 1, p. 350)

E

eardrum: membrane stretching across the ear canal that vibrates when sound waves reach the middle ear. (Chap. 12, Sec. 2, p. 362)

Earth science: study of Earth systems and systems in space, including weather and climate systems and the study of nonliving things such as rocks, oceans, and planets. (Chap. 1, Sec. 1, p. 10)

echo: a reflected sound wave. (Chap. 12, Sec. 1, p. 349)

efficiency: ability of a machine to convert input work to output work. (Chap. 9, Sec. 2, p. 267)

electrical energy: energy carried by electric current that comes out of batteries and wall sockets, is generated at large power plants, and is readily transformed into other types of energy. (Chap. 8, Sec. 1, p. 232)

electric current: flow of charge—either flowing electrons or flowing ions—through a conductor. (Chap. 15, Sec. 2, p. 447)

electric discharge: rapid movement of excess charge from one place to another. (Chap. 15, Sec. 1, p. 445)

electric field: field through which electric charges exert a force on each other. (Chap. 15, Sec. 1, p. 443)

electric force: attractive or repulsive force exerted by all charged objects on each other. (Chap. 15, Sec. 1, p. 443)

electric power: rate at which an electric appliance converts electrical energy into another form of energy; usage is measured by electric meters in kilowatt-hours. (Chap. 15, Sec. 3, p. 456)

electromagnet: magnet created by wrapping a current-carrying wire around an iron core. (Chap. 16, Sec. 2, p. 477)

electromagnetic spectrum: range of electromagnetic waves, including radio waves, visible light, and X rays, with different frequencies and wavelengths. (Chap. 13, Sec. 2, p. 379)

electromagnetic waves: transverse waves that can travel through matter or space, are produced by the motion of electrically charged particles, and include X rays, ultraviolet waves, and visible light. (Chap. 11, Sec. 1, p. 320) (Chap. 13, Sec. 1, p. 374)

electron: invisible, negatively charged particle located in a cloudlike formation that surrounds the nucleus of an atom. (Chap. 3, Sec. 1, p. 78)

element: natural or synthetic material that cannot be broken down into simpler materials by ordinary means; has unique properties and is generally classified as a metal, metalloid, or nonmetal. (Chap. 3, Sec. 2, p. 82)

energy: the ability to cause change. (Chap. 8, Sec. 1, p. 228)

engine: device that converts thermal energy into mechanical energy. (Chap. 10, Sec. 3, p. 297)

estimation: method of making an educated guess at a measurement. (Chap. 2, Sec. 1, p. 43)

F

focal length: distance along the optical axis from the center of a concave mirror to the focal point. (Chap. 14, Sec. 2, p. 412)

focal point: single point on the optical axis of a concave mirror where reflected light rays pass through. (Chap. 14, Sec. 2, p. 412)

force: a push or a pull. (Chap. 7, Sec. 1, p. 194)

freezing: change of matter from a liquid state to a solid state. (Chap. 4, Sec. 2, p. 113)

frequency: number of wavelengths that pass a given point in one second, measured in hertz (Hz). (Chap. 11, Sec. 2, p. 323)

friction: rubbing force that acts against the motion between two touching surfaces and always slows an object down. (Chap. 7, Sec. 1, p. 196)

fundamental frequency: lowest natural frequency that is produced by a vibrating string or vibrating column of air. (Chap. 12, Sec. 2, p. 357)

G

gamma ray: highest-frequency, most penetrating electromagnetic wave. (Chap. 13, Sec. 2, p. 384)

gas: matter that does not have a definite shape or volume; has particles that move at high speeds in all directions. (Chap. 4, Sec. 1, p. 108)

generator: device that uses a magnetic field to turn kinetic energy into electrical energy and can produce direct current and alternating current. (Chap. 8, Sec. 2, p. 238) (Chap. 16, Sec. 2, p. 482)

Global Positioning System (GPS): uses satellites, ground-based stations, and portable units with receivers to locate objects on Earth. (Chap. 13, Sec. 3, p. 393)

graph: used to collect, organize, and summarize data in a visual way, making it easy to use and understand. (Chap. 2, Sec. 3, p. 57)

H

heat: movement of thermal energy from a substance at a higher temperature to a substance at a lower temperature. (Chap. 4, Sec. 2, p. 110) (Chap. 10, Sec. 2, p. 290)

hypothesis: reasonable guess that can be tested and is based on what is known and what is observed. (Chap. 1, Sec. 2, p. 14)

I

inclined plane: simple machine with a flat, sloped surface, or ramp, that makes it easier to lift a heavy load by using less force over a greater distance. (Chap. 9, Sec. 3, p. 269)

inertia: tendency of an object to resist a change in its motion. (Chap. 6, Sec. 3, p. 177)

infer: to draw a conclusion based on observation. (Chap. 1, Sec. 2, p. 16)

infrared wave: electromagnetic wave that is sensed as heat and is emitted by almost every object. (Chap. 13, Sec. 2, p. 381)

input force: force exerted on a machine; also called effort force. (Chap. 9, Sec. 2, p. 264)

instantaneous speed: the speed of an object at one instant of time. (Chap. 6, Sec. 1, p. 169)

insulator: material, such as wood or glass, through which electrons cannot move easily. (Chap. 15, Sec. 1, p. 444)

interference: ability of two or more waves to combine and form a new wave when they overlap. (Chap. 11, Sec. 3, p. 331)

internal combustion engine: engine in which fuel is burned in a combustion chamber inside the engine. (Chap. 10, Sec. 3, p. 298)

ion: a positively or negatively charged atom. (Chap. 15, Sec. 1, p. 440)

isotopes (I suh tohps): two or more atoms of the same element that have different numbers of neutrons in their nuclei. (Chap. 3, Sec. 2, p. 85)

K

kelvin (K): SI unit for temperature. (Chap. 2, Sec. 2, p. 54)

kilogram (kg): SI unit for mass. (Chap. 2, Sec. 2, p. 53)

kinetic energy: energy an object has due to its motion. (Chap. 8, Sec. 1, p. 229)

L

law of conservation of energy: states that energy can change its form but it is never created or destroyed. (Chap. 8, Sec. 2, p. 234)

law of conservation of matter: states that matter is not created or destroyed but only changes its form. (Chap. 3, Sec. 1, p. 76)

law of conservation of momentum: states that the total momentum of objects that collide with each other doesn't change. (Chap. 6, Sec. 3, p. 179)

law of reflection: states that the angle of incidence is equal to the angle of reflection. (Chap. 14, Sec. 2, p. 409)

lens: transparent object that has at least one curved surface that causes light to bend. (Chap. 14, Sec. 3, p. 417)

lever: simple machine consisting of a rigid rod or plank that pivots or rotates about a fulcrum. (Chap. 9, Sec. 3, p. 272)

life science: study of living systems and how they interact. (Chap. 1, Sec. 1, p. 9)

light ray: narrow beam of light traveling in a straight line. (Chap. 14, Sec. 1, p. 404)

line graph: a type of graph used to show the relationship between two variables that are numbers on an *x*-axis and a *y*-axis. (Chap. 2, Sec. 3, p. 57)

liquid: matter with a definite volume but no definite shape that can flow from one place to another. (Chap. 4, Sec. 1, p. 106)

loudness: the human perception of how much energy a sound wave carries. (Chap. 12, Sec. 1, p. 346)

M

magnetic domain: group of atoms whose fields point in the same direction. (Chap. 16, Sec. 1, p. 472)
magnetic field: area surrounding a magnet through which magnetic force is exerted and that extends between a magnet's north and south poles. (Chap. 16, Sec. 1, p. 471)
magnetosphere: magnetic field surrounding Earth that deflects most of the charged particles flowing from the Sun. (Chap. 16, Sec. 1, p. 473)
mass: amount of matter in an object. (Chap. 2, Sec. 2, p. 53)(Chap. 6, Sec. 3, p. 177)
mass number: sum of the number of protons and neutrons in the nucleus of an atom. (Chap. 3, Sec. 2, p. 85)
matter: anything that takes up space and has mass. (Chap. 3, Sec. 1, p. 74) (Chap. 4, Sec. 1, p. 104)
measurement: way to describe objects and events with numbers—for example, length, volume, mass, weight, and temperature. (Chap. 2, Sec. 1, p. 42)
mechanical advantage: number of times the input force is multiplied by a machine; can be calculated by dividing the output force by the input force. (Chap. 9, Sec. 2, p. 265)
mechanical wave: a type of wave that can travel only through matter. (Chap. 11, Sec. 1, p. 317)
medium: material through which a wave can travel. (Chap. 14, Sec. 1, p. 405)
melting: change of matter from a solid state to a liquid state. (Chap. 4, Sec. 2, p. 111)
metal: element that is malleable, ductile, a good conductor of electricity, and generally has a shiny or metallic luster. (Chap. 3, Sec. 2, p. 86)
metalloid: element that has characteristics of both metals and nonmetals and is a solid at room temperature. (Chap. 3, Sec. 2, p. 87)
meter (m): SI unit for length. (Chap. 2, Sec. 2, p. 51)
mixture: a combination of compounds and elements that has not formed a new substance and whose proportions can be changed without changing the mixture's identity. (Chap. 3, Sec. 3, p. 91)
model: any representation of an object or an event that is used as a tool for understanding the natural world; can communicate observations and ideas, test predictions, and save time, money, and lives. (Chap. 1, Sec. 3, p. 21)
momentum: a measure of how difficult it is to stop a moving object; a product of mass and velocity. (Chap. 6, Sec. 3, p. 178)
motor: device that transforms electrical energy into kinetic energy. (Chap. 16, Sec. 2, p. 480)

N

natural frequency: frequency at which a musical instrument or other object vibrates when it is struck or disturbed; relative to its size, shape, and the material it is made from. (Chap. 12, Sec. 2, p. 355)
net force: combination of all forces acting on an object. (Chap. 7, Sec. 1, p. 195)
neutron: an uncharged particle located in the nucleus of an atom. (Chap. 3, Sec. 1, p. 80)
Newton's first law of motion: states that objects at rest will remain at rest or move with a constant velocity unless a force is applied. (Chap. 7, Sec. 1, p. 196)
Newton's second law of motion: states that an object acted upon by a net force will accelerate in the direction of the force. (Chap. 7, Sec. 2, p. 200)
Newton's third law of motion: states that forces always act in equal but opposite pairs. (Chap. 7, Sec. 3, p. 207)
nonmetals: elements that are usually gases or brittle solids and poor conductors of electricity and heat; are the basis of the chemicals of life. (Chap. 3, Sec. 2, p. 87)

nonrenewable resources: any energy sources that eventually will run out, such as coal and oil. (Chap. 8, Sec. 3, p. 242)
nuclear energy: energy stored in atomic nuclei that can be transformed into other forms of energy by complex power plants. (Chap. 8, Sec. 1, p. 232)
nucleus (NEW klee us): positively charged, central part of an atom. (Chap. 3, Sec. 1, p. 79)

O

Ohm's law: relationship among voltage, current, and resistance in a circuit. (Chap. 15, Sec. 3, p. 453)
output force: force exerted by a machine to overcome some resistance; also called resistance force. (Chap. 9, Sec. 2, p. 264)
overtones: multiples of the fundamental frequency. (Chap. 12, Sec. 2, p. 357)

P

parallel circuit: circuit that has more than one path for electric current to follow. (Chap. 15, Sec. 3, p. 455)
Pascal's principle: states that when a force is applied to a confined fluid, an increase in pressure is transmitted equally to all parts of the fluid. (Chap. 4, Sec. 3, p. 124)
photovoltaic: device that transforms radiant energy directly into electrical energy. (Chap. 8, Sec. 3, p. 246)
physical change: any change in the size, shape, form, or state of matter in which the matter's identity remains the same. (Chap. 5, Sec. 3, p. 145)
physical property: any characteristic of matter—such as color, shape, and taste—that can be detected by the senses without changing the identity of the matter. (Chap. 5, Sec. 1, p. 136)
physical science: study of matter, which is anything that takes up space and has mass, and the study of energy, which is the ability to cause change. (Chap. 1, Sec. 1, p. 10)
pitch: how high or low a sound is. (Chap. 12, Sec. 1, p. 348)
potential energy: energy stored in an object due to its position. (Chap. 8, Sec. 1, p. 230)
power: rate at which work is done. (Chap. 9, Sec. 1, p. 261)
precision: describes how closely measurements agree with each other and how carefully measurements were made. (Chap. 2, Sec. 1, p. 44)
pressure: force exerted on a surface divided by the total area over which the force is exerted. (Chap. 4, Sec. 3, p. 118)
proton: positively charged particle located in the nucleus of an atom; counted to identify the atomic number. (Chap. 3, Sec. 1, p. 79)
pulley: simple machine made from a grooved wheel with a rope or chain wrapped around the groove. (Chap. 9, Sec. 3, p. 274)

R

radiant energy: energy carried by an electromagnetic wave. (Chap. 8, Sec. 1, p. 231) (Chap. 13, Sec. 1, p. 378)
radiation: transfer of thermal energy by electromagnetic waves. (Chap. 10, Sec. 2, p. 291)
radio waves: lowest-frequency electromagnetic waves that carry the least amount of energy and are used in most forms of telecommunications technology—such as TVs, telephones, and radios. (Chap. 13, Sec. 2, p. 380)
rate: a ratio of two different kinds of measurements. (Chap. 2, Sec. 2, p. 54)
reactivity: describes how easily something reacts with something else. (Chap. 5, Sec. 2, p. 142)
reflecting telescope: uses a concave mirror to gather light from distant objects. (Chap. 14, Sec. 4, p. 423)
reflection: occurs when a wave strikes an object or surface and bounces off. (Chap. 11, Sec. 3, p. 327) (Chap. 14, Sec. 1, p. 405)

refracting telescope: uses two convex lenses to gather light and form an image of a distant object. (Chap. 14, Sec. 4, p. 422)

refraction: bending of a wave as it moves from one medium into another medium. (Chap. 11, Sec. 3, p. 328) (Chap. 14, Sec. 3, p. 417)

renewable resources: any energy sources that are replenished continually. (Chap. 8, Sec. 3, p. 244)

resistance: a measure of how difficult it is for electrons to flow through a material; unit is the ohm (Ω). (Chap. 15, Sec. 2, p. 450)

resonance: sound amplification that occurs when an object is vibrated at its natural frequency by absorbing energy from a sound wave or other object vibrating at this frequency. (Chap. 12, Sec. 2, p. 356)

reverberation: repeated echoes of sounds. (Chap. 12, Sec. 2, p. 361)

S

salts: compounds made of a metal and a nonmetal that are formed along with water when acids and bases react with each other. (Chap. 5, Sec. 2, p. 144)

science: way of learning more about the natural world that provides possible explanations to questions and involves using a collection of skills. (Chap. 1, Sec. 1, p. 6)

scientific law: a rule that describes a pattern in nature but does not try to explain why something happens. (Chap. 1, Sec. 1, p. 7)

scientific theory: a possible explanation for repeatedly observed patterns in nature. (Chap. 1, Sec. 1, p. 7)

screw: simple machine made from an inclined plane wrapped around a cylinder. (Chap. 9, Sec. 3, p. 271)

series circuit: circuit that has only one path for electric current to follow. (Chap. 15, Sec. 3, p. 454)

SI: International System of Units, related by multiples of ten, that allows quantities to be measured in the exact same way throughout the world. (Chap. 2, Sec. 2, p. 50)

simple machine: device that has only one movement; an inclined plane, lever, wheel and axle, and pulley. (Chap. 9, Sec. 3, p. 269)

solid: matter with a definite shape and volume; has tightly packed particles that move mainly by vibrating. (Chap. 4, Sec. 1, p. 105)

specific heat: amount of energy necessary to raise the temperature of 1 kg of a substance by 1°C. (Chap. 10, Sec. 2, p. 294)

speed: rate of change of position, which can be calculated by dividing the distance traveled by the time it takes to travel that distance. (Chap. 6, Sec. 1, p. 168)

state of matter: physical property that describes a substance as a solid, liquid, or gas. (Chap. 5, Sec. 1, p. 138)

static charge: buildup of electric charge on an object. (Chap. 15, Sec. 1, p. 441)

substance: matter that has the same composition and properties throughout. (Chap. 3, Sec. 3, p. 89)

system: collection of structures, cycles, and processes that relate to and interact with each other. (Chap. 1, Sec. 1, p. 8)

T

table: presents information in rows and columns, making it easier to read and understand. (Chap. 2, Sec. 3, p. 57)

technology: use of science to help people in some way. (Chap. 1, Sec. 1, p. 11)

temperature: measure of average value of the kinetic energy of the particles in a substance; can be measured using Fahrenheit, Celsius, and Kelvin scales. (Chap. 4, Sec. 2, p. 110) (Chap 10, Sec. 1, p. 286)

thermal energy: total value of the kinetic and potential energy of a group of molecules. (Chap. 8, Sec. 1, p. 230)(Chap. 10, Sec. 1, p. 289)

thermal pollution: an increase in the temperature of a body of water caused by adding warmer water. (Chap. 10, Sec. 2, p. 295)

transformer: device used to increase or decrease the voltage of an alternating current with little loss of energy. (Chap. 16, Sec. 2, p. 484)

transverse wave: a type of mechanical wave in which the wave energy causes matter in the medium to move up and down or back and forth at right angles to the direction the wave travels. (Chap. 11, Sec. 1, p. 318)

turbine: set of steam-powered fan blades that spins a generator at a power plant. (Chap. 8, Sec. 2, p. 238)

U

ultraviolet radiation: electromagnetic waves with higher frequencies and shorter wavelengths than visible light. (Chap. 13, Sec. 2, p. 383)

unbalanced forces: two or more unequal forces acting on an object, causing the object to accelerate. (Chap. 7, Sec. 1, p. 195)

V

vaporization: change of matter from a liquid state to a gas. (Chap. 4, Sec. 2, p. 114)

variable: factor that can be changed in an experiment. (Chap. 1, Sec. 2, p. 18)

velocity: speed and direction of a moving object. (Chap. 6, Sec. 1, p. 171)

visible light: electromagnetic waves with wavelengths between 0.4 and 0.7 millionths of a meter that can be seen with your eyes. (Chap. 13, Sec. 2, p. 382)

voltage: a measure of how much electrical energy each electron of a battery has; measured in volts (V). (Chap. 15, Sec. 2, p. 448)

W

wave: rhythmic disturbance that carries energy but not matter. (Chap. 11, Sec. 1, p. 316)

wavelength: in transverse waves, the distance between the tops of two adjacent crests or the bottoms of two adjacent troughs; in compressional waves, the distance from the centers of adjacent rarefactions. (Chap. 11, Sec. 2, p. 322)

wedge: simple machine consisting of an inclined plane that moves; can have one or two sloping sides. (Chap. 9, Sec. 3, p. 270)

weight: the gravitational force between you and Earth. (Chap. 7, Sec. 2, p. 201)

wheel and axle: simple machine made from two different-sized, circular objects that are attached and rotate together. (Chap. 9, Sec. 3, p. 272)

work: is done when a force exerted on an object causes that object to move some distance; is equal to force times distance. (Chap. 9, Sec. 1, p. 258)

X

X ray: high-energy electromagnetic wave that is highly penetrating and can be used for medical diagnosis. (Chap. 13, Sec. 2, p. 384)

Este glosario define cada término clave que aparece en negrillas en el texto. También muestra el capítulo, la sección y el número de página en donde se usa dicho término.

A

acceleration / aceleración: tasa de cambio en la velocidad; gracias a ella, un objeto puede acelerar, decelerar o girar; se puede calcular dividiendo el cambio en rapidez entre el tiempo dado. (Cap. 6, Sec. 2, pág. 172)

accuracy / exactitud: compara una medida con el verdadero valor. (Cap. 2, Sec. 1, pág. 45)

alternating current (AC) / corriente alterna (CA): corriente eléctrica que cambia de dirección muchas veces cada segundo. (Cap. 16, Sec. 2, pág. 482)

alternative resources / recursos alternos: toda fuente de energía, tanto renovable como inagotable, que se utiliza para generar electricidad; incluye la energía solar, la energía eólica y la energía geotérmica. (Cap. 8, Sec. 3, pág. 245)

amplitude / amplitud: distancia a la cual una onda sube o baja de su nivel normal, la cual se relaciona con la energía que transporta la onda; en una onda transversal, es la mitad de la distancia entre una cresta y un seno. (Cap. 11, Sec. 2, pág. 321)

Archimedes' principle / principio de Arquímides: establece que la fuerza de flotación de un cuerpo equivale al peso del líquido que ese cuerpo desplaza. (Cap. 4, Sec. 3, pág. 123)

atom / átomo: partícula diminuta que forma la mayoría de la materia y que está a su vez formada por partículas más pequeñas llamadas protones, neutrones y electrones. (Cap. 3, Sec. 1, pág. 75)

atomic mass / masa atómica: masa promedio del átomo de un elemento; su unidad de medida es la unidad de masa atómica (u), que equivale a 1/12 de la masa de un átomo de carbono 12. (Cap. 3, Sec. 2, pág. 86)

atomic number / número atómico: número de protones en el núcleo de cada átomo de un elemento determinado; es el número en la parte superior de cada casilla en la tabla periódica. (Cap. 3, Sec. 2, pág. 85)

aurora / aurora: luces boreales y australes que parecen cambiar cuando las partículas atrapadas en la magnetosfera chocan con la atmósfera de la Tierra por encima de los polos. (Cap. 16, Sec. 2, pág. 481)

B

balanced forces / fuerzas equilibradas: dos o más fuerzas iguales cuyos efectos se anulan entre sí y no cambian el movimiento de un objeto. (Cap. 7, Sec. 1, pág. 195)

bar graph / gráfica de barras: tipo de gráfica que usa barras de distintos tamaños para mostrar relaciones entre variables. (Cap. 2, Sec. 3, pág. 58)

buoyant force / fuerza de flotabilidad: fuerza ascendente que se ejerce sobre un cuerpo sumergido en un líquido. (Cap. 4, Sec. 3, pág. 122)

C

carrier wave / onda portadora: frecuencia de transmisión particular asignada a una estación radial. (Cap. 13, Sec. 3, pág. 390)

chemical change /cambio químico: cualquier cambio de un material a otro material nuevo con distintas propiedades. (Cap. 5, Sec. 3, pág. 147)

chemical energy / energía química: energía almacenada en sustancias químicas. (Cap. 8, Sec. 1, pág. 231)

chemical property / propiedad química: Característica de algo en la naturaleza que le permite convertirse en algo nuevo. (Cap. 5, Sec. 2, pág. 141)

circle graph / gráfica circular: tipo de gráfica que muestra partes de un todo; cada parte de la gráfica es un sector que representa un porcentaje del total. (Cap. 2, Sec. 3, pág. 58)

circuit / circuito: bucle conductor cerrado por donde puede fluir la corriente eléctrica. (Cap. 15, Sec. 2, pág. 447)

compound / compuesto: sustancia formada por la combinación de elementos y cuyas propiedades son diferentes a las de los elementos que la forman. (Cap. 3, Sec. 3, pág. 89)

compound machine / máquina compuesta: dispositivo hecho de una combinación de máquinas simples. (Cap. 9, Sec. 3, pág. 269)

compressional wave / onda de compresión: tipo de onda mecánica en la cual la materia del medio oscila en la misma dirección en que viaja la onda. (Cap. 11, Sec. 1, pág. 319)

concave lens / lente cóncavo: lente que es más gruesa en los bordes que en el medio y que desvía los rayos luminosos que viajan paralelos al eje óptico. (Cap. 14, Sec. 3, pág. 419)

condensation / condensación: cambio de la materia del estado gaseoso al líquido. (Cap. 4, Sec. 2, pág. 115)

conduction / conducción: transferencia de energía por contacto directo; ocurre cuando las partículas de una sustancia chocan contra las partículas de otra sustancia y transfieren energía cinética. (Cap. 10, Sec. 2, pág. 291)

conductor / conductor: material, como el cobre o la plata, a través del cual los electrones se pueden desplazar fácilmente o cualquier material que transfiere energía fácilmente. (Cap. 10, Sec. 2, pág. 293; Cap. 15, Sec. 1, pág. 444)

constant / constante: variable que no se cambia en un experimento. (Cap. 1, Sec. 2, pág. 18)

controlled experiment / experimento controlado: implica la observación del efecto que produce una cosa mientras se mantienen constantes las demás cosas. (Cap. 1, Sec. 2, pág. 18)

convection / convección: transferencia de energía térmica de un lugar a otro en un gas o un líquido debido al movimiento de moléculas calentadas. (Cap. 10, Sec. 2, pág. 292)

convex lens / lente convexo: lente convergente que es más gruesa en el medio que en los bordes. (Cap. 14, Sec. 3, pág. 418)

critical thinking / pensamiento crítico: implica el uso del conocimiento y las destrezas del pensamiento para evaluar pruebas y explicaciones. (Cap. 1, Sec. 4, pág. 27)

D

density / densidad: propiedad física de la materia que se puede calcular dividiendo la masa de la materia entre su volumen. (Cap. 4, Sec. 3, pág. 123; Cap. 5, Sec. 1, pág. 136)

diffraction / difracción: desviación de las ondas alrededor de un obstáculo. (Cap. 11, Sec. 3, pág. 329)

Doppler effect / efecto Doppler: cambio en la frecuencia o el tono de un sonido, el cual ocurre cuando la fuente sonora y el oyente están en movimiento relativo uno del otro. (Cap. 12, Sec. 1, pág. 350)

E

eardrum / tímpano: membrana que se extiende a través del canal auditivo y la cual vibra cuando las ondas sonoras llegan al oído medio. (Cap. 12, Sec. 2, pág. 362)

Earth science / ciencias terrestres: estudio de los sistemas terrestres y los espaciales, entre ellos, los sistemas del tiempo y del clima, y el estudio de las cosas sin vida como las rocas, los océanos y los planetas. (Cap. 1, Sec. 1, pág. 10)

echo / eco: onda sonora reflejada. (Cap. 12, Sec. 1, pág. 349)

efficiency / eficiencia: capacidad de una máquina de convertir el trabajo de entrada en trabajo de salida. (Cap. 9, Sec. 2, pág. 267)

electrical energy / energía eléctrica: energía transportada por la corriente eléctrica que sale de las pilas y de los enchufes de pared, se genera en centrales eléctricas grandes y se transforma fácilmente en otros tipos de energía. (Cap. 8, Sec. 1, pág. 232)

electric current / corriente eléctrica: flujo de corriente, ya sea un flujo de electrones o de iones, a través de un conductor. (Cap. 15, Sec. 2, pág. 447)

electric discharge / descarga eléctrica: movimiento rápido del exceso de carga de un lugar a otro. (Cap. 15, Sec. 1, pág. 445)

electric field / campo eléctrico: campo a través del cual las cargas eléctricas ejercen una fuerza mutua. (Cap. 15, Sec. 1, pág. 443)

electric force / fuerza eléctrica: fuerza de atracción o de repulsión que ejercen todos los objetos con carga. (Cap. 15, Sec. 1, pág. 443)

electric power / potencia eléctrica: tasa a la cual un artefacto eléctrico convierte la energía eléctrica en otra forma de energía; su uso se mide en kilovatios-hora con contadores de electricidad. (Cap. 15, Sec. 3, pág. 456)

electromagnet / electroimán: imán que se crea al enrollar un alambre que conduce corriente alrededor de un núcleo de hierro. (Cap. 16, Sec. 2, pág. 477)

electromagnetic spectrum / espectro electromagnético: rango de ondas electromagnéticas, que incluyen las ondas radiales, la luz visible y los rayos X, las cuales poseen distintas frecuencias y longitudes de onda. (Cap. 13, Sec. 2, pág. 379)

electromagnetic waves / ondas electromagnéticas: ondas transversales que pueden viajar a través de la materia o el espacio, se producen debido al movimiento de partículas cargadas eléctricamente e incluyen los rayos X, las ondas ultravioletas y la luz visible. (Cap. 11, Sec. 1, pág. 320; Cap. 13, Sec. 1, pág. 374)

electron / electrón: partícula invisible y de carga negativa localizada en una región en forma de nube que rodea el núcleo de un átomo. (Cap. 3, Sec. 1, pág. 78)

element / elemento: material natural o sintético que no puede romperse en materiales más simples mediante métodos ordinarios; tiene propiedades e speciales y generalmente se clasifica como metal, metaloide o no metal. (Cap. 3, Sec. 2, pág. 82)
energy / energía: la capacidad de causar cambios. (Cap. 8, Sec. 1, pág. 228)
engine /motor: dispositivo que convierte la energía térmica en energía mecánica. (Cap. 10, Sec. 3, pág. 297)
estimation / estimación: método de hacer una conjetura razonada de una medida. (Cap. 2, Sec. 1, pág. 43)

F

focal length / longitud focal: distancia a lo largo del eje óptico desde el centro de un espejo cóncavo al punto focal. (Cap. 14, Sec. 2, pág. 412)
focal point / punto focal: punto único en el eje óptico de un espejo cóncavo a través del cual pasan los rayos luminosos reflejados. (Cap. 14, Sec. 2, pág. 412)
force / fuerza: un empuje o un jalón. (Cap. 7, Sec. 1, pág. 194)
freezing / congelación: cambio de la materia del estado líquido al sólido. (Cap. 4, Sec. 2, pág. 113)
frequency / frecuencia: número de longitudes de onda que pasan por un punto dado en un segundo; se miden en hertz (Hz). (Cap. 11, Sec. 2, pág. 323)
friction / fricción: fuerza frotadora que actúa contra el movimiento entre dos superficies en contacto y que siempre aminora la velocidad de un objeto. (Cap. 7, Sec. 1, pág. 196)
fundamental frequency / frecuencia fundamental: frecuencia natural más baja que produce una cuerda o una columna de aire que vibra. (Cap. 12, Sec. 2, pág. 357)

G

gamma ray / rayo gama: la onda electromagnética más penetrante y de alta frecuencia. (Cap. 13, Sec. 2, pág. 384)
gas / gas: materia que no posee una forma o un volumen definido; posee partículas que se mueven a gran velocidad en todas direcciones. (Cap. 4, Sec. 1, pág. 108)
generator / generador: dispositivo que utiliza un campo magnético para convertir la energía cinética en energía eléctrica y el cual puede producir corriente directa y corriente alterna. (Cap. 8, Sec. 2, pág. 238; Cap. 16, Sec. 2, pág. 482)
Global Positioning System (GPS) / Sistema de Posición Global (SPG): usa satélites, estaciones terrestres y equipo portátil con receptores para ubicar objetos sobre la Tierra. (Cap. 13, Sec. 3, pág. 393)
graph / gráfica: se usa para recopilar, organizar y resumir datos de una manera visual, facilitando de esta manera su uso y comprensión. (Cap. 2, Sec. 3, pág. 57)

H

heat / calor: movimiento de la energía térmica de una sustancia con mayor temperatura a una sustancia con menor temperatura. (Cap. 4, Sec. 2, pág. 110; Cap. 10, Sec. 2, pág. 290)
hypothesis / hipótesis: conjetura razonable que se puede poner a prueba y que se basa en lo que se sabe y lo observable. (Cap. 1, Sec. 2, pág. 14)

I

inclined plane / plano inclinado: máquina simple con una superficie plana e inclinada, o rampa, que facilitar levantar cargas pesadas requiriendo menos fuerza a lo largo de una distancia mayor. (Cap. 9, Sec. 3, pág. 269)

inertia / inercia: tendencia que muestra un objeto de resistir cambios en su movimiento. (Cap. 6, Sec. 3, pág. 177)

infer / inferir: sacar una conclusión basándose en una observación. (Cap. 1, Sec. 2, pág. 16)

infrared wave / onda infrarroja: onda electromagnética que se siente como calor y la cual emiten casi todos los objetos. (Cap. 13, Sec. 2, pág. 381)

input force / fuerza de entrada: fuerza que se ejerce sobre una máquina, también se conoce como fuerza de esfuerzo. (Cap. 9, Sec. 2, pág. 264)

instantaneous speed / rapidez instantánea: rapidez de un cuerpo en un momento dado de tiempo. (Cap. 6, Sec. 1, pág. 169)

insulator / aislador: material a través del cual no pueden fluir los electrones fácilmente; por ejemplo, la madera o el vidrio. (Cap. 15, Sec. 1, pág. 444)

interference / interferencia: capacidad de dos o más ondas de combinarse y formar una nueva onda cuando se traslapan. (Cap. 11, Sec. 3, pág. 331)

internal combustion engine / motor de combustión interna: motor en que el combustible se quema en una cámara de combustión dentro del motor. (Cap. 10, Sec. 3, pág. 298)

ion / ion: átomo con carga positiva o negativa. (Cap. 15, Sec. 1, pág. 440)

isotopes / isótopos: dos o más átomos del mismo elemento que tienen números diferentes de neutrones en su núcleo. (Cap. 3, Sec. 2, pág. 85)

K

kelvin (K) / kelvin (K): unidad de temperatura del SI. (Cap. 2, Sec. 2, pág. 54)

kilogram (kg) / kilogramo (kg): unidad de masa del SI. (Cap. 2, Sec. 2, pág. 53)

kinetic energy / energía cinética: energía que tiene un cuerpo debido a su movimiento. (Cap. 8, Sec. 1, pág. 229)

L

law of conservation of energy / ley de conservación de la energía: establece que la energía puede transformarse pero nunca se crea ni se destruye. (Cap. 8, Sec. 2, pág. 234)

law of conservation of matter / ley de la conservación de la materia: enuncia que la materia no se puede crear ni destruir, sino que sólo cambia de forma. (Cap. 3, Sec. 1, pág. 76)

law of conservation of momentum / ley de conservación del momento: establece que el momento total de los cuerpos que chocan entre sí no cambia. (Cap. 6, Sec. 3, pág. 179)

law of reflection / ley de la reflexión: establece que el ángulo de incidencia es igual al ángulo de reflexión. (Cap. 14, Sec. 2, pág. 409)

lens / lente: objeto transparente que tiene por lo menos una superficie que hace que la luz se doble. (Cap. 14, Sec. 3, pág. 417)

lever / palanca: maquina simple que consta de una barra o tablón que gira alrededor de un fulcro. (Cap. 9, Sec. 3, pág. 272)

life science / ciencias biológicas: estudio de los sistemas vivos y sus interacciones. (Cap. 1, Sec. 1, pág. 9)

light ray / rayo luminoso: rayo angosto de luz que viaja en línea recta. (Cap. 14, Sec. 1, pág. 404)

line graph / gráfica lineal: tipo de gráfica que se utiliza para mostrar la relación entre dos variables, en forma de números, en un eje *x* y un eje *y*. (Cap. 2, Sec. 3, pág. 57)

liquid / líquido: materia que posee un volumen definido pero no una forma definida y que puede fluir de un lugar a otro. (Cap. 4, Sec. 1, pág. 106)

loudness / volumen: el grado de fortaleza de un sonido; se mide según la amplitud (grado de compresión) de una onda sonora y se puede describir según la escala de decibeles. (Cap. 12, Sec. 1, pág. 346)

M

magnetic domain / dominio magnético: grupo de átomos cuyos campos magnéticos apuntan en la misma dirección. (Cap. 16, Sec. 1, pág. 472)

magnetic field / campo magnético: área que rodea un imán a través de la cual se ejerce la fuerza magnética y que se extiende entre el polo norte del imán y el polo sur. (Cap. 16, Sec. 1, pág. 471)

magnetosphere / magnetosfera: campo magnético que rodea la Tierra y el cual desvía la mayor parte de las partículas cargadas provenientes del Sol. (Cap. 16, Sec. 1, pág. 473)

mass / masa: cantidad de materia que posee un cuerpo. (Cap. 2, Sec. 2, pág. 53; Cap. 6, Sec. 3, pág. 177)

mass number / número de masa: suma del número de protones y neutrones en el núcleo de un átomo. (Cap. 3, Sec. 2, pág. 85)

matter / materia: todo lo que ocupa espacio y posee masa. (Cap. 3, Sec. 1, pág. 74; Cap. 4, Sec. 1, pág. 104)

measurement / medida: manera de describir objetos y eventos con números; por ejemplo: longitud, volumen, masa, peso y temperatura. (Cap. 2, Sec. 1, pág. 42)

mechanical advantage / ventaja mecánica: número de veces que una máquina multiplica una fuerza de entrada; se puede calcular dividiendo la fuerza de salida entre la fuerza de entrada. (Cap. 9, Sec. 2, pág. 265)

mechanical wave / onda mecánica: tipo de onda que sólo puede viajar a través de la materia. (Cap. 11, Sec. 1, pág. 317)

medium / medio: material a través del cual puede viajar una onda. (Cap. 14, Sec. 1, pág. 405)

melting / fusión: cambio de la materia del estado sólido al líquido. (Cap. 4, Sec. 2, pág. 111)

metal / metal: elemento maleable, dúctil, buen conductor de electricidad y que generalmente tiene lustre metálico o brillante. (Cap. 3, Sec. 2, pág. 86)

metalloid / metaloide: elemento que tiene tanto características de metales como de no metales y que es sólido a temperatura ambiente. (Cap. 3, Sec. 2, pág. 87)

meter (m) / metro (m): unidad de longitud del SI. (Cap. 2, Sec. 2, pág. 51)

mixture / mezcla: una combinación de compuestos y elementos que no ha formado una nueva sustancia y cuyas proporciones pueden variarse al cambiar la identidad de la mezcla. (Cap. 3, Sec. 3, pág. 91)

model / modelo: cualquier representación de un objeto o un fenómeno que se utiliza como instrumento para comprender el mundo natural; puede comunicar observaciones e ideas. probar predicciones y ahorrar tiempo, dinero y vidas. (Cap. 1, Sec. 3, pág. 21)

momentum / momento: medida del grado de dificultad que existe para detener un cuerpo en movimiento; el producto de la masa por la velocidad. (Cap. 6, Sec. 3, pág. 178)
motor / motor: dispositivo que puede transformar la energía eléctrica en energía cinética. (Cap. 16, Sec. 2, pág. 480)

N

natural frequency / frecuencia natural: frecuencia a la cual vibra un instrumento musical u otro objeto cuando se puntea o se perturba, con relación a su tamaño, forma y el material del cual está hecho. (Cap. 12, Sec. 2, pág. 355)
net force / fuerza neta: combinación de todas las fuerzas que actúan sobre un objeto. (Cap. 7, Sec. 1, pág. 195)
neutron / neutrón: partícula sin carga ubicada en el núcleo de un átomo. (Cap. 3, Sec. 1, pág. 80)
Newton's first law of motion / primera ley del movimiento de Newton: establece que los objetos en reposo permanecerán en reposo o se moverán a una velocidad constante, a menos que se les aplique una fuerza. (Cap. 7, Sec. 1, pág. 196)
Newton's second law of motion / segun–-da ley del movimiento de Newton: establece que un objeto, al cual se le ha aplicado una fuerza neta, acelerará en la dirección de tal fuerza. (Cap. 7, Sec. 2, pág. 200)
Newton's third law of motion / tercera ley del movimiento de Newton: establece que las fuerzas siempre actúan en pares iguales pero opuestos. (Cap. 7, Sec. 3, pág. 207)
nonmetals / no metales: elementos que por lo general son gases o sólidos quebradizos y malos conductores de electricidad y calor; son las bases de las sustancias químicas de la vida. (Cap. 3, Sec. 2, pág. 87)
nonrenewable resources / recursos no renovables: toda fuente de energía que se agota a la larga, como por ejemplo, el carbón y el petróleo. (Cap. 8, Sec. 3, pág. 242)
nuclear energy / energía nuclear: energía almacenada en los núcleos atómicos que se puede transformar en otras formas de energía en centrales eléctricas muy complejas. (Cap. 8, Sec. 1, pág. 232)
nucleus / núcleo: parte central de un átomo; tiene carga positiva. (Cap. 3, Sec. 1, pág. 79)

O

Ohm's law / ley de Ohm: relación entre el voltaje, la corriente y la resistencia en un circuito. (Cap. 15, Sec. 3, pág. 453)
output force / fuerza de salida: fuerza ejercida por una máquina para sobreponer alguna resistencia; conocida también como fuerza de resistencia. (Cap. 9, Sec. 2, pág. 264)
overtones / sobretonos: múltiplos de la frecuencia fundamental. (Cap. 12, Sec. 2, pág. 357)

P

parallel circuit / circuito paralelo: circuito que tiene más de una trayectoria para el flujo de la corriente eléctrica. (Cap. 15, Sec. 3, pág. 455)

Pascal's principle / principio de Pascal: establece que cuando se le aplica una fuerza a un líquido confinado, un aumento en la presión se transmite de manera uniforme a todas las partes del líquido. (Cap. 4, Sec. 3, pág. 124)

photovoltaic / célula fotovoltaica: dispositivo que transforma la energía radiante directamente en energía eléctrica. (Cap. 8, Sec. 3, pág. 246)

physical change / cambio físico: cualquier cambio en tamaño, aspecto o estado de la materia en que la identidad de una muestra de materia permanece igual. (Cap. 5, Sec. 3, pág. 145)

physical property / propiedad física: cualquier característica de la materia, como color, forma y sabor, que pueden detectar los sentidos sin cambiar la identidad de la materia. (Cap. 5, Sec. 1, pág. 136)

physical science / ciencias físicas: estudio de la materia, que es todo lo que ocupa espacio y posee masa, y el estudio de la energía, la cual es la capacidad de producir cambios. (Cap. 1, Sec. 1, pág. 10)

pitch / tono: el grado de agudeza o gravedad de un sonido. (Cap. 12, Sec. 1, pág. 348)

potential energy / energía potencial: energía almacenada en un cuerpo debido a su posición. (Cap. 8, Sec. 1, pág. 230)

power / potencia: tasa a la cual se realiza trabajo. (Cap. 9, Sec. 1, pág. 261)

precision / precisión: describe el grado de aproximación de las medidas entre sí y el grado de exactitud con que se tomaron tales medidas. (Cap. 2, Sec. 1, pág. 44)

pressure / presión: fuerza ejercida sobre una superficie dividida entre el área total sobre la cual se ejerce la fuerza. (Cap. 4, Sec. 3, pág. 118)

proton / protón: partícula con carga positiva ubicada en el núcleo de un átomo y la cual se cuenta para identificar el número atómico. (Cap. 3, Sec. 1, pág. 79)

pulley / polea: máquina simple compuesta de una rueda acanalada con una cuerda o cadena enrollada alrededor de la parte acanalada. (Cap. 9, Sec. 3, pág. 274)

R

radiant energy / energía radiante: energía que transportan las ondas electromagnéticas. (Cap. 8, Sec. 1, pág. 231; Cap. 13, Sec. 1, pág. 378)

radiation / radiación: transferencia de energía térmica por las ondas magnéticas. (Cap. 10, Sec. 2, pág. 291)

radio waves / ondas radiales: ondas electromagnéticas de la más baja frecuencia que transportan la menor cantidad de energía y las cuales se utilizan en casi todas las formas de telecomunicaciones, por ejemplo, los televisores, los telfonos y los radios. (Cap. 13, Sec. 2, pág. 380)

rate / tasa: razón de dos clases distintas de medidas. (Cap. 2, Sec. 2, pág. 54)

reactivity / reactividad: describe el grado de facilidad de una sustancia. (Cap. 5, Sec. 2, pág. 142)

reflecting telescope / telescopio reflector: usa un espejo cóncavo para recoger la luz de objetos distantes. (Cap. 14, Sec. 4, pág. 423)

reflection / reflexión: ocurre cuando una onda choca contra un cuerpo o una superficie y rebota. (Cap. 11, Sec. 3, pág. 327; Cap. 14, Sec. 1, pág. 405)

refracting telescope / telescopio refractor: usa dos lentes convexas para recoger la luz y formar una imagen de un objeto distante. (Cap. 14, Sec. 4, pág. 422)

refraction / refracción: desviación de una onda a medida que se mueve de un medio a otro. (Cap. 11, Sec. 3, pág. 328; Cap. 14, Sec. 3, pág. 417)

renewable resources / recursos renovables: toda fuente de energía que se regenera continuamente. (Cap. 8, Sec. 3, pág. 244)

resistance / resistencia: una medida del grado de dificultad con que los electrones pueden fluir a través de un material; la unidad de medida es el omnio (Ω). (Cap. 15, Sec. 2, pág. 450)

resonance / resonancia: amplificación sonora que ocurre cuando un objeto vibra a su frecuencia natural al absorber energía de una onda sonora u otro objeto que vibra a esa misma frecuencia. (Cap. 12, Sec. 2, pág. 356)

reverberation / reverberación: ecos de sonidos repetidos. (Cap. 12, Sec. 2, pág. 361)

S

salts / sales: compuestos hechos de metales y no metales que se forman junto con el agua cuando los ácidos y las bases reaccionan entre sí. (Cap. 5, Sec. 2, pág. 144)

science / ciencia: manera de aprender más acerca de la naturaleza que ofrece posibles explicaciones a preguntas e implica el uso de un número de destrezas. (Cap. 1, Sec. 1, pág. 6)

scientific law / ley científica: una regla que describe un patrón en la naturaleza pero que no intenta explicar por qué suceden las cosas. (Cap. 1, Sec. 1, pág. 7)

scientific theory / teoría científica: una posible explicación para los patrones que se observan repetidamente en la naturaleza. (Cap. 1, Sec. 1, pág. 7)

screw / tornillo: máquina simple hecha de un plano inclinado enrollado alrededor de un silingro. (Cap. 9, Sec. 3, pág. 271)

series circuit / circuito en serie: circuito con una sola trayectoria a través de la cual puede fluir la corriente eléctrica. (Cap. 15, Sec. 3, pág. 454)

SI / SI: Sistema internacional de unidades, relacionado por múltiplos de diez, que permite que las cantidades se midan de la misma manera exacta en todo el mundo. (Cap. 2, Sec. 2, pág. 50)

simple machine / máquina simple: dispositivo que sólo tiene un movimiento; plano inclinado, rueda y eje y polea. (Cap. 9, Sec. 3, pág. 269)

solid / sólido: materia con forma y volumen definidos; tiene partículas muy apretadas que se mueven principalmente por vibración. (Cap. 4, Sec. 1, pág. 105)

specific heat / calor específico: cantidad de energía necesaria para elevar 1°C la temperatura de un kg de una sustancia. (Cap. 10, Sec. 2, pág. 294)

speed / rapidez: tasa de cambio de posición, la cual se puede calcular dividiendo la distancia viajada entre el tiempo que se toma viajar tal distancia. (Cap. 6, Sec. 1, pág. 168)

state of matter / estado de la materia: propiedad física que describe una sustancia como un sólido, un líquido o un gas. (Cap. 5, Sec. 1, pág. 138)

static charge / carga estática: acumulación de cargas eléctricas en un objeto. (Cap. 15, Sec. 1, pág. 441)

substance / sustancia: materia que tiene la misma composición y propiedades a lo largo de toda su extensión. (Cap. 3, Sec. 3, pág. 89)

system / sistema: conjunto de estructuras, ciclos y procesos que se relacionan e interactúan entre sí. (Cap. 1, Sec. 1, pág. 8)

Spanish Glossary

T

table / tabla: despliega información en hileras y columnas facilitando la lectura y comprensión de los datos. (Cap. 2, Sec. 3, pág. 57)

technology / tecnología: uso de la ciencia para ayudar a las personas de alguna manera. (Cap. 1, Sec. 1, pág. 11)

temperature / temperatura: medida de la energía cinética promedio de las partículas de una sustancia; puede medirse usando las escalas Fahrenheit, Celsius o Kelvin. (Cap. 4, Sec. 2, pág. 110; Cap. 10, Sec. 1, pág. 286)

thermal energy / energía térmica: valor total de la energía cinética y la potencial de un grupo de moléculas. (Cap. 8, Sec. 1, pág. 230; Cap. 10, Sec. 1, pág. 289)

thermal pollution / contaminación térmica: aumento en la temperatura de una masa de agua, el cual ocurre cuando se añade agua más caliente en la masa de agua. (Cap. 10, Sec. 2, pág. 295)

transformer / transformador: dispositivo que se usa para aumentar o rebajar el voltaje de una corriente alterna y el cual produce poca pérdida de energía. (Cap. 16, Sec. 2, pág. 484)

transverse wave / onda transversal: tipo de onda mecánica en la cual la energía de la onda hace que la materia del medio suba o baje u oscile formando ángulos rectos con la dirección en que viaja la onda. (Cap. 11, Sec. 1, pág. 318)

turbine / turbina: conjunto de álabes accionados a vapor que hace girar un generador en una central eléctrica. (Cap. 8, Sec. 2, pág. 238)

U

ultraviolet radiation / radiación ultravioleta: ondas electromagnéticas con frecuencias más altas y longitudes de onda más cortas que la luz visible. (Cap. 13, Sec. 2, pág. 383)

unbalanced forces / fuerzas desequilibradas: dos o más fuerzas desiguales que actúan sobre un objeto, haciendo que éste acelere. (Cap. 7, Sec. 1, pág. 195)

V

vaporization / vaporización: cambio de la materia del estado líquido al gaseoso. (Cap. 4, Sec. 2, pág. 114)

variable / variable: factor que se puede cambiar en un experimento. (Cap. 1, Sec. 2, pág. 18)

velocity / velocidad: rapidez y dirección de un cuerpo en movimiento. (Cap. 6, Sec. 1, pág. 171)

visible light / luz visible: ondas electromagnéticas con longitudes de onda entre 0.4 y 0.7 millonésimas de metro y las cuales se pueden ver a simple vista. (Cap. 13, Sec. 2, pág. 382)

voltage / voltaje: una medida de la cantidad de energía eléctrica que tiene cada electrón en una batería; se mide en voltios (V). (Cap. 15, Sec. 2, pág. 448)

W

wave / onda: perturbación rítmica que transporta energía pero no materia. (Cap. 11, Sec. 1, pág. 316)

wavelength / longitud de onda: en las ondas transversales, es la distancia entre la parte superior de dos crestas adyacentes o la parte inferior de dos senos adyacentes; en las ondas de compresión, es la distancia desde los centros de rarefacciones adyacentes. (Cap. 11, Sec. 2, pág. 322)

wedge / cuña: máquina simple que consta de un plano inclinado que se mueve; puede tener un o dos lados inclinados. (Cap. 9, Sec. 3, pág. 270)

weight / peso: fuerza gravitatoria entre cualquier cuerpo y la Tierra. (Cap. 7, Sec. 2, pág. 201)

wheel and axle / rueda y eje: máquina simple compuesta de dos objetos circulares de distinto tamaño que están unidos y que giran juntos. (Cap. 9, Sec. 3, pág. 272)

work / trabajo: se hace trabajo cuando una fuerza ejercida sobre un objeto hace que el objeto se mueve cierta distancia; es igual a fuerza por distancia. (Cap. 9, Sec. 1, pág. 258)

X

X ray / rayo X: onda electromagnética de alta frecuencia que es muy penetrante y la cual se usa en el diagnóstico médico. (Cap. 13, Sec. 2, pág. 384)

Index

The index for *Introduction to Physical Science* will help you locate major topics in the book quickly and easily. Each entry in the index is followed by the number of the pages on which the entry is discussed. A page number given in **boldfaced** type indicates the page on which that entry is defined. A page number given in *italic* type indicates a page on which the entry is used in an illustration or photograph. The abbreviation *act.* indicates a page on which the entry is used in an activity.

A

B

C

Index

E

Index

N

O

T

Art Credits

Glencoe would like to acknowledge the artists and agencies who participated in illustrating this program: Absolute Science Illustration; Andrew Evansen; Argosy; Articulate Graphics; Craig Attebery represented by Frank & Jeff Lavaty; CHK America; Gagliano Graphics; Pedro Julio Gonzalez represented by Melissa Turk & The Artist Network; Robert Hynes represented by Mendola Ltd.; Morgan Cain & Associates; JTH Illustration; Laurie O'Keefe; Matthew Pippin represented by Beranbaum Artist's Representative; Precision Graphics; Publisher's Art; Rolin Graphics, Inc.; Wendy Smith represented by Melissa Turk & The Artist Network; Kevin Torline represented by Berendsen and Associates, Inc.; WILDlife ART; Phil Wilson represented by Cliff Knecht Artist Representative; Zoo Botanica.

Photo Credits

Abbreviation key: AA=Animals Animals; AH=Aaron Haupt; AMP=Amanita Pictures; BC=Bruce Coleman, Inc.; CB=CORBIS; DM=Doug Martin; DRK=DRK Photo; ES=Earth Scenes; FP=Fundamental Photographs; GH=Grant Heilman Photography; IC=Icon Images; KS=KS Studios; LA=Liaison Agency; MB=Mark Burnett; MM=Matt Meadows; PE=PhotoEdit; PD=PhotoDisc; PQ=PictureQuest; PR=Photo Researchers; SB=Stock Boston; TSA=Tom Stack & Associates; TSM=The Stock Market; VU=Visuals Unlimited.

Cover Paul Ruben

vii Tom Prettyman/PE; **ix** NASA; **x** Siegfried Layda/Stone; **xi** Doug Cheeseman/Peter Arnold, Inc.; **xii** VCG/FPG; **xiii** Lester Lefkowitz/TSM; **xiv** Roger Ressmeyer/CB; **xv** file photo; **xvi** Ken Frick; **xvii** D. Boone/CB; **xviii** Ernst Haas/Stone; xix MB; **1** Bob Daemmrich; **2** file photo; **2-3** Wolfgang Kaehler; **3** file photo; **4** National Marine Mammal Lab; **4-5 14** Richard Hutchings; **15** MM; **16** IC; **17** Richard Hutchings/PE/PQ; **18** Rudi VonBriel; **19** Bob Daemmrich; **20** Glasheen Graphics/Index Stock; **21** (t)David Young-Wolff/PE, (c)John Bavosi/Science Photo Library/PR, (bl)A. Ramey/PE, (br)Donald C. Johnson/TSM; **22** CB/PQ; **23** Todd Gipstein/CB; **24** (tl)Betty Pat Gatliff, (tr)Richard Nowitz/Words & Pictures/PQ, (c)Betty Pat Gatliff, (bl)Michael O'Brian/Mud Island, Inc., (br)Betty Pat Gatliff; **25** (tl)CB, (tr)Tom Wurl/SB/PQ, (b)Jim Sugar Photography/CB; **26** (l)Stock Montage, (r)North Wind Picture Archives; **27** Digital Art/CB; **28** SuperStock; **29** (t)Lester V. Bergman/CB, (b)Bob Handelman/Stone; **31** John Evans; **32** (t)AH, (b)MM; **34** Benainous-Deville/LA; **35** (t)UPI/Bettmann/CB, (b)Reuters/CB; **36** Robert Glusic/PD; **38** Tim Courlas; **39** Charles D. Winters/PR; **40** First Image; **40-41** Brent Jones/SB; **41** MM; **42** Paul Almasy/CB; **43** AFP/CB; **44** David Young-Wolff/PE; **45** (tl)Lowell D. Franga, (tr)The Purcell Team/CB, (b)Len Delessio/Index Stock; **46** Photos by Richard T. Nowitz, imaging by Janet Dell Russell Johnson; **47** MM; **49** First Image; **51** Tom Prettyman/PE; **53** (t)Michael Dalton/FP, (cl)David Young-Wolff/PE, (cr)Dennis Potokar/PR, (b)MM; **55** Michael Newman/PE; **57** John Cancalosi/SB; **60 61** Richard Hutchings; **62** (t)Fletcher & Baylis/PR, (b)Owen Franken/CB; **63** CMCD/PD; **64** Fred Bavendam/Stone; **65** First Image; **69** MM; **70** CB/PQ; **70-71** Stephen Frisch/SB/PQ; **72** AMP; **72-73** Jack Affleck/Index Stock; **73** Morrison Photography; **74** (l)Gary C. Will/VU, (c)MB/SB, (r)CB; **76** MB; **77** (l)MB, (r)NASA; **78** Van Bucher/PR; **82** Fermi National Accelerator Laboratory/Science Photo Library/PR; **83** Tom Stewart/TSM; **84** (t cl cr)Bettmann/CB, (b)New York Public Library, General Research Division, Astor, Lenox, and Tilden Foundations; **86** Emmanuel Scorcelletti/LA; **88** DM; **89** NASA; **90** MB; **91** Klaus Guldbrandsen/Science Photo Library/PR; **92** (tl)Mark Thayer, (tr)CB, (bl)Kenneth Mengay/LA, (bc)Arthur Hill/VU, (br)RMIP/Richard Hayes; **92-93** KS; **94** IC; **95** Michael Newman/PE; **96** (tl)Stone, (tr)John Eastcott & Yva Momatiuk/DRK, (c)Robert Essel/TSM, (bl)Ame Hodalic/CB, (br)Norman Owen Tomalin/BC; **98** (tl)Skip Comer, (tr)DM, (b)AMP; **102** Jim Cummins/FPG; **102-103** Roger Ressmeyer/CB; **103** First Image; **104** Layne Kennedy/CB; **105** (t)Telegraph Colour Library/FPG, (b)Paul Silverman/FP; **106** Bill Aron/PE; **107** (l)John Serrao/PR, (r)H. Richard Johnston/FPG; **108** Tom Tracy/Photo Network/PQ; **109** Annie Griffiths Belt/CB; **110** AMP; **111** (t)David Weintraub/SB, (b)James L. Amos/Peter Arnold, Inc.; **112** Dave King/DK Images; **113** Joseph Sohm/ChromoSohm/CB; **114** Michael Dalton/FP; **115** Swarthout & Associates/TSM; **116** Tony Freeman/PE; **118** David Young-Wolff/PE; **119** (tl tr)Joshua Ets-Hokin/PD, (b)Richard Hutchings; **120** Robbie Jack/CB; **121** Dominic Oldershaw; **122** A. Ramey/SB; **123** First Image; **124** (l)Tony Freeman/PE, (r)Stephen Simpson/FPG; **126** (l)Lester Lefkowitz/TSM, (r)Bob Daemmrich; **127** Bob Daemmrich; **128 129** Daniel Belknap; **130** (t bl)KS, (br)Jeff Smith/Fotosmith; **131** (l)Andrew Ward/Life File/PD, (r)NASA/TRACE; **134** Bruce Dale/National Geographic; **134-135** Frank Lane Picture Agency/CB; **135** MM; **136** Steven R. Krous/SB/PQ;

137 Ryan McVay/PD; **138** David W. Hamilton/Image Bank; **139** (t)Morrison Photography, (b)Jose Azel/Aurora/PQ; **140** Morrison Photography; **141** (l)AH, (r)Arthur S. Aubry/PD; **142** (t c)Morrison Photography, (b)Bob Daemmrich/SB; **143** Morrison Photography; **144** AH; **145** AFP/CB; **146** (tl)Morrison Photography, (tr)Art Montes de Oca/FPG, (bl)Anthony Ise/PD, (br)Novastock/Index Stock; **147** (l)John Maher/SB/PQ, (c)MM, (r)AP Photo/Jim McKnight; **148** Morrison Photography; **149** (l)Brenda Tharp/PR, (r)Charles Benes/FPG; **150** Gerry Ellis/ENP Images; **151 152 153** Morrison Photography; **154** (l)Will & Deni McIntyre/PR, (r)Robert Nickelsberg/Time Magazine; **154-155** Morton Beebe, SF/CB; **156** (t)AH, (c)AMP, (b)MM; **157** (l)file photo, (r)courtesy Diamond International; **159** (tr)Michael Nelson/FPG, (others)Morrison Photography; **162-163** John Terence Turner/FPG; **163** (t)Artville, (b)Charles L. Perrin; **164** Jeremy Woodhouse/PD; **164-165** Peter Griffith/Masterfile; **165** MB; **166** Telegraph Colour Library/FPG; **167** Geoff Butler; **170** Richard Hutchings; **173** Runk/Schoenberger from Grant Heilman; **175** Mark Doolittle/Outside Images/PQ; **176** Rick Graves/Stone; **177** (l)TSM, (r)Will Hart/PE; **179** (t)Richard Megna/FP, (bl)Jodi Jacobson/Peter Arnold, Inc., (br)Jules Frazier/PD; **180** MB; **181** Slim Films; **182** Robert Brenner/PE; **183** Laura Sifferlin; **184** (t)Richard Olivier/CB, (b)IC; **185** IC; **187** Alexis Duclos/LA; **188** Tom & DeeAnn McCarthy/TSM; **189** (t)Rudi Von Briel/PE, (bl)AFP/CB, (br)PD; **192** Russell D. Curtis/PR; **192-193** Fujifotos/The Image Works; **193** Richard Hutchings; **194** (l)Globus Brothers Studios, NYC, (r)SB; **195** Bob Daemmrich; **196** (t)Beth Wald/Adventure Photo, (b)David Madison; **197** Rhoda Sidney/SB/PQ; **199** (l)Myrleen Cate/PE, (r)David Young-Wolff/PE; **200** Bob Daemmrich; **202** (t)Stone, (b)Myrleen Cate/PE; **204** David Madison; **206** (t)Tom Sanders/Adventure Photo, (b)Richard Fuller/David Madison Sports Images; **207** Mary M. Steinbacher/PE; **208** (t)Betty Sederquist/VU, (b)Jim Cummins/FPG; **209** (tl)Denis Boulanger/Allsport, (tr)Donald Miralle/Allsport, (b)Tony Freeman/PE/PQ; **210** (t)David Madison, (b)NASA; **212** NASA; **213** Richard Hutchings; **214 215** First Image; **216** Didier Charre/Image Bank; **217** Tom Wright/CB; **218** (t)William R. Sallaz/Duomo, (c)Bob Daemmrich, (b)First Image; **219** (t)Philip Bailey/TSM, (c)Romilly Lockyer/Image Bank, (b)Tony Freeman/PE; **222** Tony Freeman/PE; **224-225** Douglas Peebles/CB; **225** Henry Ford Museum & Greenfield Village; **226** Charles Krebs/Stone; **226-227** Roger Ressmeyer/CB; **227** MM; **228** (l)file photo, (c)file photo, (r)MB; **229** (t)Bob Daemmrich, (c)Al Tielemans/Duomo, (b)Bob Daemmrich; **230** KS; **231** (tl tr) Bob Daemmrich, (b)Andrew McClenaghan/ Science Photo Library/PR; **232** MB/PR; **233** Lori Adamski Peek/Stone; **234** Richard Hutchings; **235** Ron Kimball/Ron Kimball Photography; **236** (tl)Judy Lutz, (tc tr bl)Stephen R. Wagner, (br)Lennart Nilsson; **238 240** KS; **246** (t)Dr. Jeremy Burgess/Science Photo Library/PR, (b)John Keating/PR; **247** Geothermal Education Office; **248** Carsand-Mosher; **249** Billy Hustace/Stone; **250** SuperStock; **251** Roger Ressmeyer/ CB; **252** (t)James Blank/FPG, (c)Robert Torres/Stone, (bl br)SuperStock; **253** (l)Lowell Georgia/CB, (r)Mark Richards/PE; **254** Reuters NewMedia Inc./CB; **256** (t)Sandia National Laboratories, (b)Tony Page/Stone; **256-257** Dan Habib/Impact Visuals/PQ; **257** MB; **258** Mary Kate Denny; **259** (t)Tony Freeman/PE, (b)Richard Hutchings; **266** (l)Frank Siteman/SB, (r)David Young-Woolf/PE; **269** Duomo; **270** Robert Brenner/PE; **271** (t)Tom McHugh/PR, (b)AMP; **272** AMP; **273** (t)Dorling Kindersley, (bl br)Bob Daemmrich; **274** (l)Siegfried Layda/Stone, (r)Wernher Krutein/LA; **276** Tony Freeman/PE; **277** AH; **278** (l)Ed Kashi/CB, (r)Secci-Lecaque/Roussel-USCLAF/CNRI-Science Photo Library/PR; **279** (t)Keri Pickett, (b)James Balog/Contact; **280** (tl)Gabe Palmer/TSM, (tr)Ken Frick, (b)StudiOhio; **281** (l)Inc. Janeart/The Image Bank, (r)Ryan McVay/PD; **284** Archive Photos; **284-285** Dave Jacobs/Stone; **285** AH; **286** John Evans; **287** (t)Nancy P. Alexander/VU, (b)Morton & White; **289** Tom Stack; **290** DM; **291** MM; **292** Jeremy Hoare/PD; **293** Donnie Kamin/PE; **294** SuperStock; **295** Colin Raw/Stone; **296** AH; **298** (l)Barbara Stitzer/PE, (c)Doug Menuez/PD, (r)Addison Geary/SB; **299** Slim Films; **300** C. Squared Studios/PD; **302 303** Morton & White; **304-305** Chip Simons/FPG; **305** Joseph Sohm/CB; **306** (l)James Holmes/Science Photo Library/PR, (r)Jenny Hager/The Image Works; **307** SuperStock; **312-313** Matthew Borkoski/SB/PQ; **313** L. Fritz/H. Armstrong Roberts; **314** Jerome Wexler/PR; **314-315** Douglas Peebles/CB; **315** Spencer Grant/PE; **316** (l)file photo, (r)David Young-Wolff/PE; **317** David Young-Wolff/PE; **318** Mark Thayer; **321** Steven Starr/SB; **327** Ken Frick; **328** MB; **329** Ernst Haas/Stone; **330** Peter Beattie/LA; **332** (t)D. Boone/CB, (b)Stephen R. Wagner; **333** Seth Resnick/SB; **334** (t)Reuters NewMedia, Inc./CB, (b)Timothy Fuller; **336** (t)John Evans, (b)SuperStock; **337** Roger Ressmeyer/CB; **338** Mark Thayer; **342** Paul Silverman/FP; **342-343** Roger Ressmeyer/CB; **343** Timothy Fuller; **347** (t)Joe Towers/TSM, (c)Bob Daemmrich/SB/PQ, (b)Jean-Paul Thomas/Jacana Scientific Control/PR; **349** Stephen Dalton/PR; **350** NOAA; **351** Slim Films; **352** Spencer Grant/PE; **354** Timothy Fuller; **356** Mark Thayer;

358 Dilip Mehta/Contact Press Images/PQ; **359** (tl)CB, (tr)Paul Seheult/Eye Ubiquitous/CB, (b)IC; **360** William Whitehurst/TSM; **361** SuperStock; **362** (t)Geostock/PD, (b)SuperStock; **363** Fred E. Hossler/VU; **364** (t)Ryan McVay/PD, (b)Oliver Benn/Stone; **366** Douglas Whyte/TSM; **367** (t)Steve Labadessa/Time Inc., (c)courtesy 3M, (b)Bernard Roussel/The Image Bank; **368** (t)Edmond Van Hoorick/PD, (c)Will McIntyre/PR, (b)Kim Steele/PD; **369** (tl)The Photo Works/PR, (tr)PD, (cl)Artville, (cr)PD, (b)Gary Braasch/Stone; **370** (t)PhotoSpin/Artville/PQ, (b)C. Squared Studios/PD; **372** Stephanie Maze/CB; **372-373** Roger Ressmeyer/CB; **373** IC; **374** (l)Bob Abraham/TSM, (r)Jeff Greenberg/VU; **375** (l)David Young-Wolff/PE, (r)NRSC, Ltd./Science Photo Library/PR; **376** (t)Grantpix/PR, (b)Richard Megna/FP; **378** Luke Dodd/Science Photo Library/PR; **380** (t)MM, (b)Jean Miele/TSM; **382** (t)Gregory G. Dimijian/PR, (b)Charlie Westerman/Liaison; **383** AH; **385** (l)MM, (r)Bob Daemmrich/The Image Works; **386** (t) NASA, (cl), Yohkoh Data Archive Centr'e; (cr)Max Planck Institute for Radio Astronomy/Science Photo Library/PR, (b)ESA/Science Photo Library/PR; **387** (l)NASA/Science Photo Library/PR, (c)Harvard-Smithsonian Center for Astrophysics, (r)ESA; **388** Timothy Fuller; **391** MM; **393** Ken M. Johns/PR; **394** Michael Thomas/Stock South/PQ; **395** Dominic Oldershaw; **396** (t)Culver Pictures, (b)Hulton Getty Library/LA; **397** Aurthur Tilley/FPG; **398** (t)G. Brad Lewis/LA, (c)George B. Diebold/TSM, (b)Yoav Levy/Phototake/PQ; **399** (l)Macduff Everton/CB, (r)NASA/Mark Marten/PR; **400** Michael Thomas/Stock South/PQ; **402** Novastock/PE; **402-403** Cary Wolinsky/SB/PQ; **403** MM; **404** Dick Thomas/VU; **405** John Evans; **406** (t)Bob Woodward/TSM, (cl)Ping Amranand/Pictor, (cr)SuperStock, (b)Runk/Schoenberger from Grant Heilman; **407** (l)Mark Thayer, (r)Dr. Dennis Kunkel/PhotoTake NYC; **410** David Toase/PD; **412** (l)Bill Aron/PE, (r)Paul Silverman/FP; **413** (l)Digital Stock, (r)Joseph Pamieri/Pictor; **415** Geoff Butler; **417** Richard Megna/FP; **420** David M. Dennis; **421** David Young-Wolff/PE; **422 423** Roger Ressmeyer/CB; **425** Charles O'Rear/CB; **426** (t)MM, (b)Geoff Butler; **427** Geoff Butler; **428-429** Ed Welche's Antiques/Winslow, ME; **429** (t)courtesy Cheryl Landry, (b)The Stapleton Collection/Bridgeman Art Library; **430** (t)file photo, (c)MB, (b)Jeremy Horner/Stone; **432** Carol Christensen/Stock South/PQ; **436** Layne Kennedy/CB; **436-437** Richard Pasley/SB/PQ; **437** MB; **438** H. David Seawall/CB; **438-439** Peter Menzel/SB/PQ; **439** Geoff Butler; **441** (t)Richard Hutchings, (b)KS; **442** Stephen R. Wagner; **446** J. Tinning/PR; **454** DM; **455** (t)DM, (b)Geoff Butler; **457** Bonnie Freer/PR; **459** MM; **460 461** Richard Hutchings; **462-463** Tom & Pat Leeson/PR; **463** William Munoz/PR; **464** (t)DM, (c)AP Photo/Matt York, (b)IC; **466** DM; **468** John Evans; **468-469** Argus Fotoarchiv/Peter Arnold, Inc.; **469** MM; **471** Richard Megna/FP; **472** AMP; **474** PD; **475** John Evans; **477** (l)Kodansha, (c)Manfred Kage/ Peter Arnold, Inc., (r)DM; **481** Bjorn Backe Papilio/ CB; **483** Norbert Schafer/TSM; **485** AT&T Bell Labs/ Science Photo Library/PR; **486** (tl)Science Photo Library/PR, (tr)Fermilab/Science Photo Library/PR, (b)SuperStock; **487** PD; **488** (t)file photo, (b)AH; **489** AH; **490** (tl)IC, (tr)Digital Vision/PQ, (bl)StockTrek/PD, (br)Spencer Grant/PE; **491** (l)SIU/Peter Arnold, Inc., (r)Latent Image; **492** file photo; **496-497** PD; **498** (t)KS, (b)Bill Aron/PR; **499** (t)IC, (bl br)KS; **500** (t)Don Tremain/PD, (b)AH; **501** KS; **502** file photo; **503** (t)Dan Feicht, (b)VU; **504** Jose Carrillo/PE; **505** (t)AH, (b)Michael J. Howell/Rainbow/PQ; **506** (t)CB, (b)Artville; **507** (tl tr c)PD, (b)Artville; **508** (t c)Artville, (b)StudiOhio; **509** (t)PD, (c)Wolfgang Kaehler/CB, (b)CB; **510** CB; **511** (t)Bill Vaine/CB, (b)John Dudak/PhotoTake NYC/PQ; **512** (t)NOAA Photo Library/Central Library, OAR/ERL/National Severe Storms Laboratory (NSSL), (c)Richard Hamilton Smith/CB, (b)Jeffry W. Myers/CB; **513** AP Photo/Geophysical Institute, University of Alaska Fairbanks via RE/MAX; **514** NASA; **515** (l)NASA, (r)Roger Ressmeyer/CB; **516** (t)NASA/Roger Ressmeyer/CB, (c b)NASA; **517** NASA; **518** Timothy Fuller; **522** Roger Ball/TSM; **524** (l)Geoff Butler, (r)Coco McCoy/Rainbow/PQ; **525** Dominic Oldershaw; **526** StudiOhio; **527** First Image; **529** MM; **532** Paul Barton/TSM; **535** Davis Barber/PE.

PERIODIC TABLE OF THE ELEMENTS

Columns of elements are called groups. Elements in the same group have similar chemical properties.

Element	Hydrogen
Atomic number	1
Symbol	H
Atomic mass	1.008

State of matter

Gas

Liquid

Solid

Synthetic

The first three symbols tell you the state of matter of the element at room temperature. The fourth symbol identifies human-made, or synthetic, elements.

Period	1	2	3	4	5	6	7	8	9
1	Hydrogen 1 **H** 1.008								
2	Lithium 3 **Li** 6.941	Beryllium 4 **Be** 9.012							
3	Sodium 11 **Na** 22.990	Magnesium 12 **Mg** 24.305							
4	Potassium 19 **K** 39.098	Calcium 20 **Ca** 40.078	Scandium 21 **Sc** 44.956	Titanium 22 **Ti** 47.867	Vanadium 23 **V** 50.942	Chromium 24 **Cr** 51.996	Manganese 25 **Mn** 54.938	Iron 26 **Fe** 55.845	Cobalt 27 **Co** 58.933
5	Rubidium 37 **Rb** 85.468	Strontium 38 **Sr** 87.62	Yttrium 39 **Y** 88.906	Zirconium 40 **Zr** 91.224	Niobium 41 **Nb** 92.906	Molybdenum 42 **Mo** 95.94	Technetium 43 **Tc** (98)	Ruthenium 44 **Ru** 101.07	Rhodium 45 **Rh** 102.906
6	Cesium 55 **Cs** 132.905	Barium 56 **Ba** 137.327	Lanthanum 57 **La** 138.906	Hafnium 72 **Hf** 178.49	Tantalum 73 **Ta** 180.948	Tungsten 74 **W** 183.84	Rhenium 75 **Re** 186.207	Osmium 76 **Os** 190.23	Iridium 77 **Ir** 192.217
7	Francium 87 **Fr** (223)	Radium 88 **Ra** (226)	Actinium 89 **Ac** (227)	Rutherfordium 104 **Rf** (261)	Dubnium 105 **Db** (262)	Seaborgium 106 **Sg** (266)	Bohrium 107 **Bh** (264)	Hassium 108 **Hs** (277)	Meitnerium 109 **Mt** (268)

The number in parentheses is the mass number of the longest lived isotope for that element.

Rows of elements are called periods. Atomic number increases across a period.

The arrow shows where these elements would fit into the periodic table. They are moved to the bottom of the page to save space.

Lanthanide series	Cerium 58 **Ce** 140.116	Praseodymium 59 **Pr** 140.908	Neodymium 60 **Nd** 144.24	Promethium 61 **Pm** (145)	Samarium 62 **Sm** 150.36
Actinide series	Thorium 90 **Th** 232.038	Protactinium 91 **Pa** 231.036	Uranium 92 **U** 238.029	Neptunium 93 **Np** (237)	Plutonium 94 **Pu** (244)